Dictionary

of

FILM FINANCE

and

DISTRIBUTION

OTHER BOOKS OF INTEREST FROM MARQUETTE BOOKS

John Wheeler, *Last Man Out: Memoirs of the Last American Reporter Castro Kicked Out of Cuba in the 1960s* (forthcoming 2008). ISBN: 978-0-922993-84-0

Norma Sawyers, *50 Ways to Cope with Your Child's Death: A Guide for Grieving Parents* (2008). ISBN: 978-0-922993-24-6

Steve Hallock, *War Stories from Great American Journalists of the Late 20th Century* (forthcoming 2008). ISBN: 978-0-922993-85-7

Eric G. Stephan and R. Wayne Pace, *The Seven Secrets of Successful, Happy People* (2008). ISBN: 978-0-922993-75-8

Dan Robison, *Death Chant: Kimo's Battle with the Shamanic Forces* (2006). ISBN: 0-922993-52-1

Phillip J. Tichenor, *Athena's Forum: A Historical Novel* (2005).ISBN: 0-922993-27-0

Melvin DeFleur, *A Return to Innocence: A Novel* (2005). ISBN: 0-922993-50-5

Dan Robison, *Wind Seer: The Story of One Native American Boy's Contribution to the Anasazi Culture* (2005).ISBN: 0-922993-27-0

Ray Edwards, *Justice Never Sleeps: A Novel of Murder and Revenge in Spokane* (2005). ISBN: 0-922993-26-2

John M. Burke, *From Prairie to Palace: The Lost Biography of Buffalo Bill* (2005). ISBN: 0-922993-21-1

Dan Robison, *Kimo's Escape: The Story of a Hawaiian Boy Who Learns to Believe in Himself* (2005). ISBN: 0-922993-28-9

Tonya Holmes Shook, *The Drifters: A Christian Historical Novel about the Melungeon Shantyboat People* (2005). ISBN: 0-922993-19-X

David Demers, *China Girl: One Man's Adoption Story* (2004). ISBN: 0-922993-08-4

Dictionary

of

FILM FINANCE

and

DISTRIBUTION

A Guide for Independent Filmmakers

JOHN W. CONES

MARQUETTE BOOKS LLC
SPOKANE, WASHINGTON

475349

Copyright © 2008 by Marquette Books LLC

This publication is designed to provide accurate and authoritative information about the concepts
defined herein. It is sold with the understanding that the author is not engaged in rendering legal,
accounting or other professional services. If legal advice or other expert assistance is required, the
services of a professional person should be engaged.
All opinions expressed herein are those of the author.

Printed in the United States of America

Library of Congress Cataloging-in-Publication Data

Cones, John W.
    Dictionary of film finance and distribution : a guide for independent filmmakers / John W. Cones.
        p. cm.
    Includes bibliographical references.
    ISBN 978-0-922993-93-2 (hardcover : alk. paper) -- ISBN 978-0-922993-94-9 (pbk. : alk. paper)
    1. Motion picture industry--Finance--Dictionaries. 2. Motion pictures--Distribution--Dictionaries.
I. Title.
PN1993.5.A1C642 2008
384'.8303--dc22

                                                                        2007036685

MARQUETTE BOOKS LLC
3107 East 62nd Avenue
Spokane, Washington 99223
books@marquettebooks.com
www.MarquetteBooks.com

To my son,
J. Christopher Cones

CONTENTS

ACKNOWLEDGMENTS

Many of the entries in this book contain information drawn from as many as six or seven sources, lecture notes, books on the industry, conversations with people who work in the industry, trade press articles, magazine articles, etc. Thus, I gratefully acknowledge the many sources listed in the bibliography.

I also wish to express my special thanks to Los Angeles copyright attorney Greg Victoroff, screenwriter Gail McNamara, film/law school graduate Jeff Foy, feature film technical consultant James Kelly Durgin, director of photography Levie Isaacks, producer Tony Anselmo, New York entertainment attorney Wilder Knight and writer/attorney Thomas M. Sipos for their assistance in editing the first edition of this book.

It is also appropriate for me to acknowledge here—without suggesting that such persons are in any way directly responsible for the information or opinions expressed in this book—all of the lecturers and panelists presenting film finance and distribution related topics that I have listened to and learned from during the past several years:

At IFP/West-sponsored events: Zanne Devine (Director of Acquisitions, Universal Pictures), George Jackson (Producer "New Jack City"), Neal Jimenez (Screenwriter "River's Edge"), Bobby Newmyer (Producer "sex, lies and videotape"), John Singleton (Director and Screenwriter "Boyz N The Hood"), Courtenay Valenti (Production Executive, Warner Bros. Studios), Tom Garvin (Producer's Representative and Partner, Ervin, Cohen & Jessup), Christopher Murray (Partner in the Entertainment Department of the law firm of O'Melveny & Myers), Barbara Boyle (President of Sovereign Pictures), Douglas T. McHenry (Partner and Producer/Director with the Jackson McHenry Company at Warner Bros.), Irene Romero (Executive Vice President, Mercantile National Bank), Charles Kolstad (West Coast Entertainment Industry Tax Partner for Coopers & Lybrand), Robert Manning (Head of the Entertainment/ Leisure Time Group at Oppenheimer & Co.) and Stephen Bannon (Partner at Bannon & Co., a Beverly Hills-based merchant bank).

At the 1992 UCLA Law Symposium: Peter Dekom (Partner, Bloom, Dekom & Hergott), Carrie J. Menkel-Meadow (Professor, UCLA School of Law), Ellen Peck (Judge of the State Bar of California Disciplinary Court), Dennis Perluss (Partner, Hufstedler, Miller, Kaus & Beardsley), Martin Singer (Partner, Lavely & Singer), Kenneth Ziffren (Partner, Ziffren, Brittenham & Branca), Leigh Brecheen (Partner, Bloom, Dekom & Hergott), Thomas Hansen (Partner, Hansen, Jacobson & Teller), Edward Masket (Executive Vice President-Administration, MCA Television Group), Sanford Wernick (Vice President, The Brillstein Company), Laurie Younger (Senior Vice President-Business Affairs, Walt Disney Television), Harold Vogel (First Vice President, Merrill Lynch & Co.), Stuart Glickman (Vice Chairman and Chief Executive Officer, The Carsey-Werner Company), Leonard Hill

(Chairman of the Board, Allied Communications), Robert Jacquemin (President, Buena Vista Television), Art Stolnitz (Executive Vice President-Business Affairs & Finance, Lorimar Television), Ron Sunderland (Executive Vice President-Business Affairs & Contracts, Capital Cities/ABC), Valerie Cavanaugh (Executive Vice President, Gracie Films), Gary Barber (President, Morgan Creek), John Ptak (Agent, Creative Artists Agency), Strauss Zelnick (President, Chief Operating Officer, 20th Century Fox), Keith Fleer (Of Counsel, Sinclair Tenenbaum & Co.), Martin Bauer (President, United Talent Agency), Leon Brachman (Business Executive), Bertram Fields (Partner, Greenberg, Glusker, Fields, Claman & Machtinger), Barry Hirsch (Partner, Armstrong & Hirsch), Peter Hoffman (President & Chief Executive Officer, Carolco Pictures) and E. Barry Haldeman (Partner, Greenberg, Glusker, Fields, Claman & Machtinger).

At the 1992 Third Decade Council Annual Conference (not already mentioned): Peter Benedek (United Talent Agency), Preston Beckman (Vice President, Program Planning & Scheduling at NBC Entertainment), James L. Brooks (Writer/Director/Co-Producer of "Terms of Endearment"), Stephen J. Cannell (Writer/Producer), Mark Canton (Chairman of Columbia Pictures), Caldecot Chubb (Producer "Cherry 2000"), Carlton Cuse (Boam/Cuse Productions), Sean Daniel (President of Sean Daniel Company), Diane English (Creator/Writer/Executive Producer of "Murphy Brown"), Marc Ezralow (Producer of "Memorial Day Massacre"), Neil Alan Friedman (Executive Vice President of the Edward R. Pressman Film Corporation), Robert G. Friedman (President of Warner Bros. Worldwide Theatrical Advertising & Publicity), Tom Hansen (Hansen, Jacobson & Teller), Ted Harbert (Executive Vice President, Prime Time, ABC Entertainment), Peter Hoffman (Carolco Pictures), Jerry Katzman (President William Morris Agency), Jamie Kellner (President and CEO of Fox Broadcasting Company), Kerry McCluggage (President of Universal Television), Michael Nathanson (President, Worldwide Production at Columbia Pictures), David Nicksay (President and Head of Production of Morgan Creek Productions), John Ptak (Creative Artists Agency), Steven Roffer (The Steven Roffer Company), Tom Schulman (Writer "Dead Poet's Society"), Tom Sherak (Executive Vice President of Twentieth Century Fox), Joel Silver (Producer the "Lethal Weapon" series), Nigel Sinclair (Managing Partner Sinclair Tenenbaum & Co.), Gary Ross (Co-Author for "BIG"), Robert Stein (United Talent Agency), Rosalie Swedlin (Longview Entertainment), Jonathan Taplin (Producer "Mean Streets"), Straus Zelnick (President and COO of 20th Century Fox) and Laura Ziskin (Producer "Pretty Woman").

At the 1991 and 1992 UCLA Extension Class "Contractual Aspects of Producing, Financing and Distributing Film" and other UCLA Extension sponsored seminars of the author: profit participation auditor Stephen Sills (Partner, Sills and Adelman), Deborah Dubelman (Director of Legal and Business Affairs, Republic Pictures Corporation), Mark Resnick (Senior Vice President, Legal Affairs, Columbia Pictures), Greg Victoroff (copyright attorney), Teri Williams (Entertainment Attorney), Gary Watson (formerly a Legal Affairs Attorney at Universal, now with the law firm of Greenberg, Glusker, Fields, Claman & Machtinger), Irene Speiser (Vice President, Entertainment Industries Division, Mercantile National Bank), Lionel Sobel (Professor, Loyola Law School), Steve Cardone (International Film Guarantors), Glenn Harvey (DAIWA Bank), Anna Bagdasarian (Bank of California), Susan Schaefer (Entertainment Attorney), Madelyn Adams (20th Century Fox Marketing), Doc Littlefield (Profit Participation Auditing Section at Deloitte-Touche) and Jonathan Dana (Triton Pictures).

At the 1991 Paul Kagan Seminar on Motion Picture Finance: Don Harris (AMC Film Marketing), Anna Bagdasarian (Bank of California), Michael Mendelsohn (Banque Paribas), Mitchell Julis (Canyon Partners), John Davis (Davis Entertainment), David Friendly (Imagine Films Entertainment), Joseph Cohen (Largo Entertainment & Inter Media Group), Lynda Obst (Lynda Obst Productions), Ken Badish (Moviestore Entertainment), Robert Shaye (New Line Cinema), Brandon Tartikoff (Paramount Pictures), William Shields (Trans Atlantic Pictures), Barry Reardon (Warner Bros. Distribution), Brian Maki (Yasuda Trust & Banking), Ken Ziffren (Ziffren, Brittenham & Branca) and Paul Kagan (Kagan Seminars).

At the AFI Producers on Producing Series (1991): Renny Harlin ("Rambling Rose"), Debra Hill & Lynda Obst ("The Fisher King"), Don Phillips ("The Indian Runner") and Ron Ronholtz ("Homicide").

At other AFI seminars: Gary Prebula (Moderator, Writer/Director), and fellow panel members Irene Speiser (Mercantile National Bank), Bill Nestel (Rastar Productions), J. David Williams (Willsfield Productions), Robert Vince (President of Motion Picture Bond Co.), Lewis Horwitz (The Lewis Horwitz Organization), Tekla Morgan (President, International Film Guarantors), Leroy Bobbitt (Partner, Loeb & Loeb, Entertainment Division), Sam Grogg (Chief Executive Officer and Executive Producer of Apogee Productions and it's subsidiary, Magic Pictures), Jerry Leider (Chairman of the Caucus for Producers, Writers and Director and Producer of "The Jazz Singer"), Jason Zelin (Vice President, New Business Development Liaison for The Completion Bond Company), Mitchell Cannold (Principal LillyAnna Productions and Co-Executive Producer for "Dirty Dancing"), Steve

Monas (Senior Vice President for Business Affairs at Vision International), Harold Messing (Entertainment Attorney, Los Angeles and New York) and Michael Wiese (Moderator, Producer/Director).

At Cinetex '90 my fellow panel members: Michael Sherman (Jeffer, Mangels, Butler & Marmaro), John Sansone (President, Entertainment Business Services International) and Joel Koenig (Partner in Charge, Century City office of Deloitte & Touche).

At the American Academy of Independent Film Producers seminar in 1986 (with titles as of that year): Lawrence Garret (Director of Sales and Acquisitions for Arista Films), Dov S-S Simens (The Film Doctor), Lance Hool (Producer "Missing In Action"), Hank McCann (Casting Director for "Pennies From Heaven"), Dom Spinosa (Head of MGM's Payroll Department), Susan Strasberg (Actress), Eric Epstein (Attorney), Ezra Doner (Vice President, Business Affairs, Cinema Group), Randy Gaiber (Bank of California), Wilbur Hobbs (Wells Farbo Bank), Mary Savarese (Cohen Insurance), David Rudich (Music Rights Attorney) and Roger Corman (Producer). I also thank the members of the 1992 Winter Quarter UCLA Extension class "Contractual Aspects of Producing, Financing and Distributing Film," who saw earlier drafts of this book.

Although I have learned a great deal from my brief exposure to the above named persons, none of these individuals or entities is responsible for the definitions, usage examples or commentary contained in this book. I alone take full responsibility for whatever deficiencies are contained herein.

John Cones, Entertainment and Film Attorney
Los Angeles, Fall 2007

INTRODUCTION

Like many industries, the U.S. film industry has developed its own unique vocabulary to describe its activities and operations. Many books, articles and agreements include a small glossary to help people understand this lexicon. Several major film dictionaries also are available (see Bibliography). These books do a good job in defining concepts associated with the technical, production or marketing aspects of the film business. However, they typically have very little content about the financing and distribution aspects of filmmaking — i.e., the business side of the movie-making business.

I wrote this dictionary to help fill this void. More specifically, my goal was to help level the playing field a bit when it comes to negotiating financing and distribution of films. The large film studios and theater chains employ attorneys and others who are experts in negotiating film contracts. In contrast, most independent filmmakers and producers have limited knowledge of the law, in part because the schools and universities that educated them stress the technical, creative or production side of filmmaking, not the business side. One consequence of this disparity is that independent filmmakers and producers are usually at a disadvantage when it comes to negotiating the financing and distribution of a film.

The information in this book should prove valuable to a wide range of people seeking to independently produce a film, including attorneys, distributors, executive producers, producers, associate producers, studio executives, screen writers, directors, exhibitors, broker/dealers, money finders, accountants, auditors, investors, profit participants, federal and state government officials and film students.

The terms and phrases defined and discussed in this dictionary are those of feature film finance and distribution, which includes film production, marketing, accounting, insurance, securities, legal structures (e.g., corporate, limited partnership and limited liability company financing vehicles), and general financial arenas. All of the principal forms of feature film finance are covered, including studio/distributors, production companies, lending institutions, co-financing, pre-sales, grants, foreign and passive investor financing. Some additional terms and phrases are included, not because they commonly appear in film finance or movie distribution agreements but because they are essential to a well-rounded understanding of the industry and environment in which such film finance and distribution agreements are negotiated (see "Contract of Adhesion"). Still other terms were selected and included because they may help readers understand some of the terms in this dictionary. In many instances, the definitions also show how the term or phrase is specifically used in the film industry.

PERSPECTIVE OF THIS BOOK

As mentioned above, this book was written to help independent filmmakers and producers negotiate successfully with big studios and film distributors. For some terms and concepts, this book provides more than a descriptive definition—it seeks to more fully explore the film industry by analyzing some of the reasons why this business is dominated by the major studio/distributors and why independent feature film producers as a group have so little clout in the industry (see "Inferior Bargaining Position").

Many of the ideas expressed in this book came from experts who spoke at industry seminars listed in the "Acknowledgments" section, or from the books and articles listed in the bibliography and the conversations I have had with several hundred independent producers during the past five years. Many attended one or more of the several hundred seminar lectures on film finance and distribution that I have given in Los Angeles, New York, San Francisco, Las Vegas, Dallas, Houston, and elsewhere. I am a practicing film attorney. I also have worked as an association executive, a lobbyist and a radio/television news reporter. All of these roles have helped shaped the content of this book.

WHY FOCUS ON DISTRIBUTION?

Some readers may be wondering why a book on film finance would also discuss distribution. The reason is that film finance cannot be adequately explained if no provision is made for how invested money may or may not return to financiers and/or investors (i.e., the financial side of distribution). The feature film industry has a history of anti-competitive practices, and distribution is often at the center of these problems. My hope is that the emphasis on antitrust issues may help aspiring filmmakers to recognize that there are certain significant barriers to entry (see the entries on "Barriers to Entry," "Insider's Game" and "Relationship Driven Business")—so significant that many will find it impossible for them to get a fair hearing for their talents or ideas. The editorial emphasis on antitrust law issues also may help aspiring filmmakers avoid violating the law (see "Business Practices," "Conduct Restrictions" and "Predatory Practices"). Finally, for readers who have little knowledge of the legal proscriptions against such conduct, this book may help keep them out of trouble as well as uncover and report abuses to the U.S. Justice Department and/or their own friendly antitrust law litigator in the event a civil remedy is appropriate (see "Remedy" and "RICO").

HOW TO USE THIS BOOK

Like other dictionaries, this book may be used as a reference source to determine the meaning of a specific term as used in a given context. But because all of the terms included herein relate to the rather broad field of film finance and distribution, it can also be used as a textbook to gain a fairly comprehensive understanding of the business.

For classroom use or independent study, readers may also take certain broad subject areas, such as those listed on the so-called "Motion Picture Production Chart" (i.e., Acquisition, Development, Packaging, Production Financing, Pre-Production, Principal Photography, Post-Production and Delivery—see next section for details), and use the extensive cross-referencing of terms in that chart or within the definitions of the terms themselves. My updated list of "337

Business Practices of the Major Studio/Distributors" (see page 7) also can also be used in this way. An entire reading assignment for a class can be organized around these groupings of terms.

For readers who are relatively new to the field of film finance and distribution, I have also included a section called "Overview of the Motion Picture Industry," which helps place the terms defined in this dictionary into a general context.

All entries in this book are alphabetized by letter rather than by word (i.e., multiple words are treated as single words). Also, certain abbreviations or acronyms appear as entries in the main text but generally refer to the corresponding full term as it would appear elsewhere in the text. Terms and phrases mentioned within other defined terms and phrases are not capitalized or italicized because that can be distracting. Instead, terms are cross-referenced at the end of each defined term.

TERMS ASSOCIATED WITH MOTION PICTURE PRODUCTION

The development and production of a motion picture can be broken down into stages or steps, beginning with "Acquisition" and ending with "Delivery." These stages are also known as the "Producer's Task List." Here are some of the key terms associated with each stage that are defined in this dictionary.

1. ACQUISITION

Acquisition Agreement
Book
Certificate of Authorship
Chain of Title
Copyright
Fair Use

Fixed Work
License
Literary Work
Magazine Article
Option Agreement
Original Screenplay
Plagiarism

Play
Public Domain
Submission Release
Underlying Property
Work Made for Hire

2. DEVELOPMENT

Basic Story Outline
Copyright Registration
Development Financing
Final Screenplay
First Draft

Idea/Concept
One-Line Description
Polish
Rewrite

Screenplay
Synopsis
Treatment
WGA Registration

3. PACKAGING

1st Draft Script Breakdown
Casting
Completion Bond
Director Commitment
Director Deferments
Distribution Agreements
Lab Deferments

Packaging Attorney
Packaging Service
Packaging Agent
Partial Financing
Pre-Sales, if any
Producer Deferments
Producer/Director Undertakings

Production Budget
Production Board
Script and Breakdown
Star Commitments
Star Deferments
Tentative Budget
Tentative Shooting Schedule

4. PRODUCTION FINANCING

Blocked Funds	Grants	P-F/D
Co-Productions	Joint Venture	Pre-Sales Agreements
Corporate Financing	Limited Partnership	Studio
Currency Deals	Limited Liability Company	Subsidies
Debt Capitalization	Loans	Tax Shelters
Facilities Deals	Negative Pickup Agreement	

5. PRE-PRODUCTION

Annotated Script	Equipment Rental Agreements	Producer's Agreement
Chain of Title Documents	Film/Sound Lab Agreements	Script Clearance
Crew/Performer Agreements	Location & Stage Agreements	Shooting Script
Deal Memos	Music Agreements	Written Releases
Director Agreement	Producer's Liability Insurance	

6. PHOTOGRAPHY

Cast/Extras	Film Stock/Sound Stock	Second Units
Dailies (Rushes)	Insurance	Set Design
Director	Lab Film Processing Letter	Staff
Director's Cast List	Location List	Studio Rental
Editing	Post-Production Schedule	Transportation
Equipment Rentals	Producer	
Fees and Taxes	Publicity	

7. POST PRODUCTION

Dialogue Replacement	Music	Pre-Mix Session
Dirty Dupes	Negative	Sound Effects
Editing	Optical Effects	Special Effects
Foley Stage Recording	Pick-up Photography	Titles

8. DELIVERY

Action Continuity	Final Screenplay	Photographs
Certificate of Insurance	Inter-Positive	Publicity Material
Composite Optical Soundtrack	Internegatives	Residual Information
Credit Statement	Laboratory Letter	Screen Credits
Delivery Schedule	Laboratory Access Letter	Shooting Script
Dialogue	Main and End Titles	Sound Album Materials
Dialogue and Sound Items	MPAA Certificate	Television Cover Shots
Film Credits	Original Picture Negative	Title and Copyright Reports
Film and Soundtrack Materials	Out-takes (Cutouts)	Work Print
Final Answer Print		

337 BUSINESS PRACTICES OF THE MAJOR STUDIO/DISTRIBUTORS

T he following terms are associated with the business practices of the major studio/distributors and were collected from reports in trade papers, books about the industry, magazine articles, lawsuits and law journal articles. These terms and others are defined in this dictionary.

Account Number
Actual Breakeven
Adhesion Contract/Contract of Adhesion
Adjusted Gross
Adjustment
Admission Price Discrimination
Advertising Overhead
Advertising Costs
Allocations
Allowances
Ancillary Rights
Anti-Competitive Practices
Anticipated Expenses
Antitrust Law Violations
Apportioned Expense
Approved Elements
Arbitration
Article Twenty
Artificial Breakeven
Artificial Pickup
Assignment
Association Antitrust Policies
Attendance Checking
Audit
Average Negative Cost
Bad Debt
Bad Faith Denial of Contract
Bankruptcy

Bargaining Power
Barriers to Entry
Below-the-Line Fringes
Best Efforts Clause
Bidding War
Blacklisting
Blind Bidding
Block Booking
Blocked Currencies
Blurbs
Boilerplate
Breach of Contract
Breakeven
Buchwald Case
Buying A Gross
Cartel
Cash Breakeven
Censorable Material
Checking and Collection Costs
Closed Bidding
Co-Feature
Collective Bargaining Agreements
Combination in Restraint of Trade
Combination Ad
Commercial Bribery
Commingling of Funds
Commonly Understood
Completion Bonds

Concentrated Ownership
Conduct Provisions
Confidence Game
Conflicting Dates
Conflicts of Interest
Conscious Parallelism
Conspiracy
Consultation
Continuous Supply of Product
Contractual Overhead
Contractual Breakeven
Contractually Defined Profits
Controlled Availability
Controlled Theatre
Cooperative Advertising
Corporate Opportunity
Covenant of Good Faith and Fair Dealing
Creative Accounting
Creative Control
Cross-Collateralization
Customarily Kept by the Distributor
Customary
Day and Date
De Facto Cross-Collateralization
Deal Memo
Deem
Default Disaster
Deferments or Deferrals

Delivery Date Acceleration
Delivery Requirements
Delivery
Development Hell
Development Deal
Direct Distribution Expense
Discounts
Discretion
Discretionary Cross-Collateralization
Discrimination
Distribution Commitment
Distributor Credit
Distributor Commercials
Dividend
Dominant Media Conglomerates
Double Add-Back
Double Distribution Fees
Double Feature
Dues and Assessments
Duress
Economic Abuses
Economic Reprisal
Entire Agreement Clause
Errors and Omissions Insurance
Exclusions
Exploitation Film
Extortion
Facilities Allocations
Feature Film Limited Partnership
Fiduciary
Film Rentals
Film Schools
Final Judgment
Final Marketing Outlet
Final Cut
Financial Management
First Position Gross
First-Run Zoning
Five O'Clock Look
Floor
Foreign Receipts
Foreign Tax Credits
Formula Deal
Franchise Agreements
Fraud
Free Enterprise System
Frequency of Payments
Front End Load
Generally Accepted Accounting Principles
Glamour Industry
Good Faith

Grant of Rights
Graylisting
Greed
Gross Floor
Gross Participants
Gross Points
Gross Receipts
Hard to Audit Expenses
Hidden Agendas
Holdback Periods
Home Video Royalty
Homogenous Films
Horizontal Price Fixing
House Nut
Idea
Illegal Trade Practice
Illegal Combination
Illusory Promise
Improperly Claimed Expenses
Incestuous Share Dealing
Independent Audit Rights
Independent Checking Company
Independent Feature Project (IFP)
Industry Assessments
Inferior Bargaining Position
Initial Actual Breakeven
Insider's Game
Interest
Laziness
Level Playing Field
Leverage
Liability Limitation
Licensing Process
Lie, Cheat and Steal Syndrome
Limits on Dividends
Litigation Disclaimer
Litigation Budget
Loan Sharking
Lobbying
Long Form Agreement
Mafia
Major Exhibition Chains
Management
Manipulation
Market Power
Market Share
Marketplace of Ideas
Merger Guidelines
Minimum Admission Prices
Minimum Rating
Mod-Controlled Distribution Company

Model Agreement
Money Laundering
Monopoly
Most Favored Nations Clause
Motion Picture Association of America
Movies With A Message
MPAA Cartel
MPAA Rating and Certificate
Multi-Cultural Society
Name-Dropping
NC-17
Negative Costs
Negotiated Contractual Definitions
Negotiated Deal
Nepotism
Net Profit Participation
Number of Screens
Objective Delivery Requirements
Off-the-Bottom Expenses
Off-the-Top Expenses
Offset Rights
Oligopoly
Ongoing Costs
Oral Representations
Ordinary Interest
Ordinary Course of Business
Outright Sales
Outstandings
Over-Budget Penalty
Over-Reported Travel
Overhead or Overhead Costs
Overreaching
Package Sales
Parallel Business Behavior
Paramount Consent Decree of 1948
Per Se Violations
Perpetuity
Polarization
Political Influence
Power
Predatory Practices
Prejudice
Price Fixing
Price Discrimination
Print Costs
Problem Producer
Producer's Share
Producers Guild of America (PGA)
Production Overhead
Production Costs
Profit Participations

Overview of the Motion Picture Industry

The theatrical motion picture industry in the United States has changed substantially over the last three decades and continues to evolve rapidly. Historically, the "major studios" financed, produced and distributed the vast majority of American-made motion pictures seen by most U.S. moviegoers. However, during the most recent decade, many of the motion pictures released have been produced by so-called independent producers, even though some of the production financing for such pictures and distribution funds have been provided by the major studio/distributors. Other independent films are distributed by independent distributors who are not affiliated with the major studios.

What follows is a simplified overview of the complex process of producing and distributing motion pictures and is intended to help investors understand the motion picture business. This overview does not describe what will necessarily occur in the case of any particular motion picture.

Production of Motion Pictures

During the film-making process, which generally takes 12 to 24 months, a film normally progresses through several stages. The four general stages of motion picture production are development, pre-production, principal photography and post-production. A brief summary of each of the four stages follows.

Development

In the development stage, literary material for a motion picture project is acquired, either outright, through an option to acquire such rights, or by hiring a writer to create original literary material. If the literary material is not in script form, a writer must create a script. The script must be sufficiently detailed to provide the production company and others participating in the financing of a motion picture enough information to estimate the cost of producing the motion picture. Projects in development often do not become completed motion pictures.

Pre-Production

During the pre-production stage, the production company usually selects a director, actors and actresses, prepares a budget and secures the necessary financing. In cases involving unique or desired talent, commitments must be made to keep performers available for the picture. Some pre-production activities may occur during development.

Principal Photography

Principal photography is the process of filming a motion picture and is the most costly stage of the production of a motion picture. Principal photography may take 12 weeks or more to complete. Bad weather at locations, the illness of a cast or crew member, disputes with local authorities or labor unions, a director's or producer's decision to re-shoot scenes for artistic reasons and other often unpredictable events can seriously delay the scheduled completion of principal photography and substantially increase its costs. Once a motion picture reaches the principal photography stage, it usually will be completed.

Post-Production

During the post-production stage, the editing of the raw footage and the scoring and mixing of dialogue, music and sound effects tracks take place, and master printing elements are prepared.

Distribution of Films

Motion picture revenue is derived from the worldwide licensing of a motion picture in some or all of the following media: (a) theatrical exhibition; (b) non-theatrical exhibition (viewing in airplanes, hotels, military bases and other facilities); (c) pay television systems for delivery to television receivers by means of cable, over-the-air and satellite delivery systems; (d) commercial television networks; (e) local commercial television stations,

(f) reproduction on video cassettes, DVDs (and video discs) for home video use, and (g) the Internet and other new technologies such as Video on Demand (VOD) and Near Video On Demand (NVOD). Revenue may also be derived from licensing "ancillary rights" to a motion picture for the creation of books, published music, soundtrack albums and merchandise. A picture is not always sold in all of these markets or media.

The timing of revenues received from the various sources varies from film to film (see release sequence chart below). Typically, 90 percent of theatrical receipts from distribution in the United States are received in the first 12 months after a film is first exhibited. In the rest of the world, 40 percent is typically received in the first year, 50 percent in the second year and 10 percent in the third and remaining years.

Most home video royalties also come during the first year (80%). Pay and cable license fees are typically received 65 percent in the third year, 25 percent in the fourth year and 10 percent in the fifth year following theatrical release.

The majority of syndicated domestic television receipts are typically received in the fourth, fifth and sixth years after theatrical release if there are no network television licenses and the sixth, seventh and eighth years if there are network licenses.

The markets for film products have been undergoing rapid changes because of technological and other innovations. As a consequence, the sources of revenues available have been changing rapidly and the relative importance of the various markets as well as the timing of such revenues has also changed and can be expected to continue to change.

SAMPLE FEATURE FILM RELEASE SEQUENCE

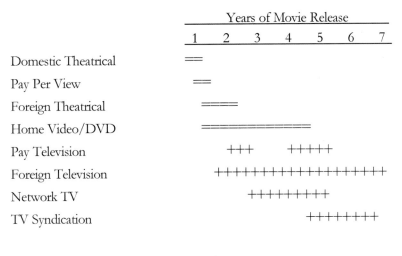

	Years of Movie Release						
	1	2	3	4	5	6	7
Domestic Theatrical	==						
Pay Per View	==						
Foreign Theatrical	====						
Home Video/DVD	=============						
Pay Television		+++	+++++				
Foreign Television		++++++++++++++++++++++++					
Network TV		+++++++++					
TV Syndication			++++++++				

== Windows with open-ended time periods

++ Windows with exclusive runs

Sources: LINK Resources, *Off-Hollywood & Entertainment Industry Economics*, 2nd ed.

SOURCES OF REVENUE

Movie release sequences are a function of the marketplace and to some extent the prerogative of individual distributors. Thus, release sequences change from time to time, as new delivery technology is introduced and may vary with specific films. As a result of the different time periods during which movies are exhibited and/or viewed in various markets and media, the revenue stream generated by a given movie may typically continue for seven years or more.

In the sample release sequence provided above, all but home video, network television, the presentation of classic pictures on pay television and television syndication are completed by the end of year two; thus, the great percentage of the revenue generated by movies comes during and immediately after the earlier windows, assuming payments are made promptly. Also, the percentages of revenue generated by each market vary from year to year (e.g., foreign has been growing in recent years relative to domestic theatrical). The release sequence chart does not consider the potential revenue from a movie sound track album, merchandising possibilities or its value as part of a film library.

The following is a brief summary of each of the sources of revenue of motion pictures and the distribution/licensing process associated with such sources.

U.S. Theatrical Distribution

In recent years, United States theatrical exhibition has generated a declining percentage of the total income earned by most pictures, largely because of the increasing importance of cable and pay television, home video and other ancillary markets. Nevertheless, the total revenues generated in the U.S. theatrical market are still substantial and are still likely to account for a large percentage of revenues for a particular film. In addition, performance in the U.S. theatrical market generally also has a profound effect on the value of the picture in other media and markets.

Motion pictures may be distributed to theatrical markets through branch offices. Theatrical distribution requires the commitment of substantial funds in addition to a motion picture's negative cost. The distributor must arrange financing and personnel to (a) create the motion picture's advertising campaign and distribution plan, (b) disseminate advertising, publicity and promotional material by means of magazines, newspapers, trailers ("coming attractions") and television, (c) duplicate and distribute prints of the motion picture, (d) "book" the motion picture in theaters and (e) collect from exhibitors the distributor's share of the box office receipts from the motion picture. A distributor must carefully monitor the theaters to which it licenses its picture to ensure that the exhibitor keeps only the amounts to which it is entitled by contract and promptly pays all amounts due to the distributor. Distributors will sometimes reach negotiated settlements with exhibitors as to the amounts to be paid, and such settlements may relate to amounts due for several pictures.

For a picture's initial theatrical release, a U.S. exhibitor will usually pay to a distributor a percentage of box office receipts which is negotiated based on the expected appeal of the motion picture and the stature of the distributor. The negotiated percentage of box office receipts remitted to the distributor is generally known as "film rentals" and is typically characterized in distribution agreements as a portion of the distributor's "gross receipts." Such rentals customarily diminish during the course of a picture's theatrical run. Typically, the distributor's share of total box office receipts over the entire initial theatrical release period will average between 25 to 60 percent depending on numerous factors; the exhibitor will retain the remaining 75 to 40 percent (See John W. Cones, *The Feature Film Distribution Deal* [Carbondale, IL: Southern Illinois University Press, 1997]). The exhibitor will also retain all receipts from the sale of food and drinks at the theater (concessions). Occasionally, an exhibitor will pay to the distributor a flat fee or percentage of box office receipts against a guaranteed amount. Pay television and new home entertainment equipment (such as video games, computers and video cassette players) offer a more general competitive alternative to motion picture theatrical exhibition of feature films.

Major film distributors are often granted the right to license exhibition of a film in perpetuity, and normally have the responsibility for advertising and supplying prints and other materials to the exhibitors. Under some arrangements, the distributor retains a distribution fee from the gross receipts, which averages about 33 percent of the film's gross receipts (see *The Feature Film Distribution Deal*) and recoups the costs incurred in distributing the film. The principal costs incurred are the cost of duplicating the digital master into prints for actual exhibition and advertising of the motion picture. The distribution deal usually stipulates that the parties providing the financing are entitled to recover the cost of producing the film. However, bank-financed productions will typically require that the bank be paid back its principal, interest and fees before the film is actually released (i.e., upon delivery to the distributor).

Expenses incurred in distributing a motion picture are substantial and vary depending on many factors. These factors include the initial response by the public to the motion picture, the nature of its advertising campaign, the pattern of its release (e.g., the number of theaters booked and the length of time that a motion picture is in release). The amount film distributors spend on prints and advertising is generally left to the discretion of the distributor. In some instances, however, the producer may negotiate minimum expenditures or ceilings on such items.

Foreign Theatrical Distribution

While the value of the foreign theatrical market varies due to currency exchange rate fluctuations and the political conditions in the world or specific territories, it continues to provide a significant source of revenue for theatrical distribution. In recent years foreign theatrical revenues have often been accountable for more than 50 percent of a domestically produced U.S. film's gross theatrical revenue. Because this market is comprised of a multiplicity of countries and, in some cases, requires the making of foreign language versions, the distribution pattern stretches over a longer period of time than does exploitation of a film in the United States theatrical market. Major studio/distributors usually distribute motion pictures in foreign countries through local entities. These local entities generally will be either wholly owned by the distributor (a joint venture between the distributor and another motion picture company) or an independent agent (or sub-distributor). Such local entities may also distribute

motion pictures of other producers, including other major studios.

Film rental agreements with foreign exhibitors take a number of different forms, but they typically provide for payment to a distributor of a fixed percentage of box office receipts or a flat amount. Risks associated with foreign distribution include fluctuations in currency values and government restrictions or quotas on the percentage of receipts that may be paid to the distributor, the remittance of funds to the United States and the importation of motion pictures into a foreign country.

New Technologies

High-tech movie megaplexes are changing the very landscape of the domestic and foreign distribution marketplace, especially in France, Italy, Eastern Europe and Russia. In the U.S. market, which started the trend, giant cineplexes or megaplexes with 10 to 12 screens per complex, have replaced single- or three-screen theaters. The 35mm negative is not dead, but its days may be numbered. A report by SRI Consulting recently stated that "movies encoded as digital files, either recorded on optical disc and physically shipped or broadcast via satellite or land line, will increasingly replace film prints as the preferred method for distributing movies to theaters ... ."

Home Video Rights

Since its inception, the home video market in the United States has experienced substantial growth in the last decade. Certain foreign territories, particularly Europe, have seen an increased utilization of home video units because of the relative lack of diversified television programming, although those circumstances have been changing also. Consequently, sales of video cassettes have increased in such markets in recent years. Although growth in this area may be reduced because of an increase in television programming in such foreign territories, receipts from home video or DVD in these markets can be expected to continue to be significant.

Films are generally released on home video six to nine months after initial domestic theatrical release of the picture, but before the exhibition of the picture on cable/pay or network television.

Domestic TV Distribution

Television rights in the United States are generally licensed first to pay television for an exhibition period following home video release, thereafter to network television for an exhibition period, then to pay television again, and finally syndicated to independent stations. Therefore, the owner of a film may receive payments resulting from television licenses over a period of six years or more.

Domestic Cable and Pay TV

Pay television rights include rights granted to cable, direct broadcast satellite, microwave, pay per view and other services paid for by subscribers. Cable and pay television networks usually license pictures for initial exhibition commencing six to 12 months after initial domestic theatrical release, as well as for subsequent showings. Pay television services such as Home Box Office, Inc. ("HBO") and Showtime/The Movie Channel, Inc. ("Showtime") have entered into output contracts with one or more major production companies on an exclusive or non-exclusive basis to assure themselves a continuous supply of motion picture programming. Some pay television services have required exclusivity as a precondition to such contracts.

The pay television market is characterized by a large number of sellers and few buyers. However, the number of motion pictures utilized by these buyers is significantly large and a great majority of motion pictures that receive theatrical exhibition in the United States are, in fact, shown on pay television.

Domestic Network TV

In the United States, broadcast network rights are granted to ABC, CBS, NBC or other entities formed to distribute programming to a large group of stations. The commercial television networks in the United States license motion pictures for a limited number of exhibitions during a period that usually commences two to three years after a motion picture's initial theatrical release. During recent years, only a small percentage of motion pictures have been licensed to network television, and the fees paid for such motion pictures have declined. This decline is generally attributed to the growth of the pay television and home video markets, and the ability of commercial television networks to produce and acquire made-for-television motion pictures at a lower cost than license fees previously paid for theatrical motion pictures.

Domestic TV Syndication

Distributors also license the right to broadcast a motion picture on local, commercial television stations in the United States, usually for a period of five years after initial theatrical release of the motion picture, but earlier if the producer has not entered into a commercial television network license. This activity, known as "syndication," has become an important source of revenues as the number of, and competition for, programming among local television stations has increased.

Foreign TV Syndication

Motion pictures are now being licensed in the foreign television market in a manner similar to that in the United States. The number of foreign television stations as well as the modes of transmission (i.e., pay, cable, network, satellite, etc.), have been expanding rapidly, and the value of such markets has been increasing and should continue to expand.

Producers may license motion pictures to foreign television stations during the same period they license such motion pictures to television stations in the United States; however, governmental restrictions and the timing of the initial foreign theatrical release of the motion pictures in the territory may delay the exhibition of such motion pictures in such territory.

Non-Theatrical Distribution

In addition to the markets and media discussed above, the owner of a film may also be able to license the rights for non-theatrical uses to specialized distributors who, in turn, make the film available to airlines, hotels, schools, off-shore oil rigs, public libraries, prisons, community groups, the armed forces and ships at sea.

Internet and Broadband

Recent technological advances, such as digital satellite transmission, cable modems and DSL, all geared to high-speed broadband Internet access, provide another potential revenue source for feature films. In the near future, there may be several "Net-casters" with the ability to release and distribute a theatrical quality, full-length motion picture over the Internet on a global basis, essentially by-passing the high costs and fee structure of traditional distributors.

Relicensing

The collective retained rights in a group of previously produced motion pictures is often a key asset, because such pictures may be relicensed in the pay and commercial television, home video and non-theatrical markets, and occasionally may be re-released for theatrical exhibition.

Although no one can be certain of the value of these rights, certain older films retain considerable popularity, and may be relicensed for theatrical or television exhibition. New technologies brought about by the continuing improvements in electronics may also give rise to new forms of exhibition which will develop value in the future.

Other Ancillary Markets

A distributor may earn revenues from other ancillary sources, unless the necessary exploitation rights in the underlying literary property have been retained by writers, talent, composers or other third parties. The right to use the images of characters in a motion picture may be licensed for merchandising items such as toys, T-shirts and posters.

Motion picture rights may also be licensed for novelizations of the screenplay, comic book versions of the screenplay and books about the making of the motion picture. The soundtrack of a motion picture may be separately licensed for soundtrack records and may generate revenue in the form of mechanical performance royalties, public performance royalties and sheet music publication royalties.

Dictionary of Terms

abandonment provision — A clause in a production-financing distribution agreement that sets out under what circumstances the studio financier may be permitted to stop production and further financing of a motion picture (see "production-financing distribution agreement").

abbreviated force majeure clause — A provision in contracts that is intended to excuse a party from performance of its obligations in the event that such performance is prevented by forces outside the control of such party and that does not specify the events or acts that excuse performance (see "force majeure clause").

above-the-line — The portion of a film's budget that covers major creative elements and personnel (i.e., those creatively unique and individually identifiable elements). These are primarily story acquisition, screenplay rights, script development, writer, executive producer, producer, director and principal members of the cast. The phrase "above-the-line" refers to the location on the film budget of the specific expense item/person (see "acquisition agreement," "below-the-line," "development" and "principal players").

above-the-line costs — Film production-period costs relating to acquiring the story rights,
property rights associated with the screenplay, script development and signing the producer, director and principal members of the cast (see "above-the-line" and "below-the-line costs").

above-the-line deferrals — The postponement of payment for some or all of the salary or other remuneration due to be paid to above-the-line personnel. Such deferrals are often negotiated in low-budget motion picture projects and sometimes are required in lender financed pictures (see "deferments" and "negative pickups").

above-the-line employment agreements — Employment contracts for persons whose line-item film budget entries appear "above-the-line" in the film's budget (i.e., above the line that separates those persons whose services are considered creatively unique and individually identifiable from those that are not). Above-the-line employment agreements are individually negotiated (see "below-the-line" and "employment agreements").

above the regular title — (same as "above the title").

above the title — A reference to the position of front credits that appear before the main title on the motion picture screen. Occasionally, the position of front credits may be a negotiating issue for certain participants in a film (see "director," "producer," "star" and "studio").

absorption — (see "absorption arrangement").

absorption arrangement — With respect to feature film sub-distribution arrangements, either when an independent distributor uses a major studio/distributor for actual distribution or where the independent distributor uses other independent sub-distributors, a situation in which the independent distributor absorbs the fee of the actual distributor within its own distribution fee in order to avoid double charging the revenue stream of the film for distribution fees ("double distribution fees," "pass through," "override" and "sub-distribution").

absorption formula — (see "absorption arrangement").

abridgement — A shortened form of a literary work retaining the general sense and unity of the original (see "underlying property").

abusive tax shelter — An investment transaction, often structured as a limited partnership or other flow-through vehicle, that is devoid of any economic purpose other than the generation of tax benefits or whose claimed tax benefits are questionable (see "tax shelter").

Academy Awards — Film industry honors (along with statuettes called Oscars) presented each Spring since the late 1920's by the Academy of Motion Picture Arts and Sciences for excellence in a variety of categories. In recent years, the fact that a motion picture wins an Academy Award has added as much as 10 million dollars to the

film's gross box office receipts during the film's continuing or subsequent runs. Thus, the ability of a distributor to influence the votes of the Academy members on such issues is extremely valuable and to that end, many distributors have conducted expensive promotional campaigns to Academy members in search of those votes (see "Academy of Motion Pictures Arts & Sciences," "distribution expenses" and "Oscar").

Academy of Motion Picture Arts & Sciences (AMPAS) — A professional honorary organization created in 1927 and now composed of more than 4,000 motion picture crafts-persons. The Academy was formed for the general purpose of providing incentives for higher levels of technical and professional achievement among all branches of filmmaking. Its stated specific purposes are to advance the arts and sciences of motion pictures; foster cooperation among creative leaders for cultural, educational and technological progress; recognize outstanding achievements; cooperate on technical research and improvement of methods and equipment; provide a common forum and meeting ground for various branches and crafts; represent the viewpoint of actual creators of the motion picture; and foster educational activities between the professional community and the public-at-large. The Academy states that it does not get involved in economic, labor or political issues. The Academy awards the Oscars, maintains a film library and sponsors student film awards and speaker programs. Membership is by invitation of the Board of Governors and is limited to those who have achieved distinction in the arts and sciences of motion pictures. Some of the criteria for admittance are: film credits of a caliber that reflect the high standards of the Academy, nomination for an Academy Award, achievement of unique distinction, earning special merit or making an outstanding contribution to film (see "insider's game," "members of the club" and "Oscars").

Academy Players Directory — A multiple volume publication of the Academy of Motion Picture Arts and Sciences that contains a photographic listing of actors and actresses (see "Academy of Motion Picture Arts and Sciences").

accelerated cost recovery — IRS approved methods used in depreciating (i.e., recovering the cost through tax deductions) of fixed (qualifying) assets within a shorter period than the expected useful (economic) lives of the assets (i.e., a faster recovery of such cost). Such methods of depreciation thus provide earlier tax benefits than traditional straight-line depreciation. The income forecast method of depreciation sometimes used for films is a form of accelerated cost recovery (see "depreciation," "income forecast method" and "straight-line depreciation").

accelerated rate — Occurring more often during the same period or at an increased frequency (e.g., a gross participation may be paid at an accelerated rate depending on how certain the distributor is of its ability to obtain revenues that make up the distributor gross receipts out of which such participations are to be paid; see "gross participations," "gross profit participant," "gross receipts" and "participant").

acceleration — The declaration by the federal Securities and Exchange Commission (SEC) that a registration statement for a public offering of securities is effective, which in turn means that the registered securities can be sold. Acceleration usually occurs the day the underwriting agreement (in an underwritten

offering) is signed or after the SEC comments are complied with, and the registration statement is filed in final form. Securities are sometimes sold to raise money from investors for film projects (see "effective" and "waiting period").

accountable gross — A contractually defined term used in some film distribution agreements to mean something akin to distributor's gross receipts minus specified off-the-top deductions (see "adjusted gross," "exclusions," "film rentals," "off-the-top" and "producer's share").

accountant — One who is trained and skilled in the system of recording and summarizing business and financial transactions and analyzing, verifying and reporting the results, but who is not necessarily certified by a state accountancy certification agency (see "certified public accountant" and "public accountant").

accountant's opinion — Statement signed by an independent public accountant describing the scope of the examination of the books and records or an individual or organization. Since financial reporting involves considerable discretion, the accountant's opinion may be an important consideration for a lender or investor (also called "certificate of accounts," "auditor's certificate," "limited review" and "qualified opinion").

account executive — A brokerage firm employee with the legal powers of an agent who advises and executes orders for investor clients of the firm (see "broker/dealer" and "registered representative").

accounting method — The method by which a business (corporation, partnership or sole proprietorship) keeps its books and records for purposes of computing income and deductions and determining taxable income. Generally, the method of accounting affects the timing of an item of income or deduction. The two major methods of accounting are accrual and cash (see "accrual method of accounting," "cash method of accounting," "FASB" and "GAAP").

accounting period — A chronological division for recording and summarizing business and financial transactions; typically, either monthly, quarterly, semi-annually or annually (see "accounting method").

accounting principles and practices — The rules, regulations and guides relating to a specific industry. With respect to the film industry, such principles and practices generally fall into three broad categories: cost capitalization, cost amortization and revenue recognition and reporting (see "amortization," "capitalization," "FASB Statement No. 53," "GAAP," "revenue recognition and reporting" and "videocassette revenue reporting").

accounting records — Written or otherwise recorded information relating to the business and financial transactions of an entity (see "accounting principles and practices").

accounting release date — The date on which amortization of a film begins. For television, it is the date on which the film is first telecast (see "release date").

account number — A studio accounting number assigned to a given film production at the studio and that is generally all that is required of someone to charge expenses for goods or services to the film's account at the studio. In a studio financing context, producers must carefully monitor and review studio charges to

make certain they are all authorized (see "audit," "creative accounting," "over-budget" and "over-budget penalty").

accounts receivable — Money owed to a business for merchandise or services sold on open account ("bad debt").

accredited investor — A wealthy investor as specifically defined by the SEC's Regulation D [i.e., any person or entity who comes within any of eight categories of persons or entities described in Rule 501 of the SEC's Regulation D that are excluded from the Regulation D limitation on the number of investors that may purchase a security exempted pursuant to Regulation D. Accredited investors include: (1) a bank, insurance company, registered investment company, business development company, or small business investment company; (2) an employee benefit plan, within the meaning of the Employee Retirement Income Security Act, if a bank, insurance company, or registered investment adviser makes the investment decisions, or if the plan has total assets in excess of $5 million; (3) a charitable organization, corporation or partnership with assets exceeding $5 million; (4) a director, executive officer, or general partner of the company selling the securities; (5) a business in which all the equity owners are accredited investors; (6) a natural person with a net worth of at least $1 million; (7) a natural person with income exceeding $200,000 in each of the two most recent years or joint income with a spouse exceeding $300,000 for those years and a reasonable expectation of the same income level in the current year; or (8) a trust with assets of at least $5 million, not formed to acquire the securities offered, and whose purchases are directed by a sophisticated person.] (see "investor numerical limitation," "investor sophistication requirements," "investor suitability," "private placement" and "Regulation D").

accredited investor exemption — A federal statutory exemption from the securities registration requirements provided by Section 4(6) of the 1933 Securities Act that specifically exempts from registration offers and sales of securities to accredited investors when the total offering price is less than $5 million. The definition of accredited investors is the same as that used in Regulation D. Like the exemptions in Rule 505 and 506, this exemption does not permit any form of advertising or public solicitation. There are no document delivery requirements, however, all transactions are subject to the anti-fraud provisions of the securities laws (see "accredited investor," "anti-fraud rule" and "Regulation D").

accrual method of accounting — An accounting method under which (1) income is subject to tax after all events fixing the right to receive such income have occurred, and (2) deductions are allowed when the obligation to pay similarly becomes fixed, regardless of when the income is actually received or when the obligation is actually paid or met. The accrual method must be utilized by any business taxpayer that has inventory (see "accounting method" and "cash method of accounting").

accruals — The periodic accumulation of payments that are due (see "accounts receivable" and "settlement transaction").

accrue or accrued — To accumulate, to happen, to come into fact or existence; payments are said to have accrued when they have become a legally enforceable claim (see "uncollectible indebtedness").

A.C.E. — (see "American Cinema Editors").

ACE-NET (Angel Capital Electronic Network) — An Internet site established by the Office of Advocacy of the Small Business Administration ("SBA") where small companies may list their Regulation A and Regulation D 504/SCOR stock offerings for sale to high net worth investors (accredited investors). In addition, ACE-Net anticipates providing mentoring and educational services for small companies needing business planning and securities information. Additional information on the ACE-Net Internet site can be found at http://www.sba.gov/ADVO/ or http://www.ace-net.org. ACE-Net is a cooperative effort between the SBA and nine universities, state-based entities and other non-profit organizations (see "accredited investor," "Regulation A" and "SCOR").

acknowledge — To admit knowledge of; recognize the rights, authority or status of; take notice of; state that a document has been received; or recognize a document as genuine or valid (see "certify").

acknowledgment — A declaration or avowal of one's act or of a fact to give it legal validity; the thing done or given in recognition of something received. For example, an acknowledgment is used with a production/financing distribution agreement to ensure that the financier/distributor will obtain the services of a particular individual producer (see "production-financing/distribution agreement").

A.C. Nielsen Company — (see "Nielsen Media Research").

"A" Counties — The Nielsen Media Research designation for counties that are in the twenty-five largest metropolitan areas in the U.S. in terms of population. The largest cities and consolidated urban areas are found in these counties. Such designations are used by movie distributors in marketing their films (see "ADI Market," "B-County," "C-County," "D-County," "Key" and "Nielsen Media Research").

ACPB — (see "Audited Cash Production Budget").

acquisition agreement — The film industry agreement through which a producer or production company acquires the right to use another's literary work or other property in producing a motion picture. This term may also be used to describe the agreement used by a film distributor to acquire the rights to distribute a film (see "development," "option" or "option contract," "option purchase agreement" and "property").

acquisition deal — An agreement between a film distributor and a producer or production company in which the distributor agrees to acquire the rights to distribute a completed film in specified markets or media for a stated sum, possibly including an advance and an ongoing profit participation (see "advance," "production-financing/distribution agreement" and "rent-a-distributor").

acquisition/distribution agreement— The written contract between a film's producer and the distribution company that sets out the terms and conditions under which the distributor will distribute the film. The acquisition/distribution agreement differs from the production-financing/distribution agreement in that no production financing is provided by the distributor in the former. The primary difference between the acquisition/distribution agreement

and the negative pickup distribution agreement is that the negative pickup commitment is negotiated and made prior to completion of the motion picture (see "in-house production," "production-financing/distribution agreement," "negative pickup distribution agreement," "rent-a-distributor" and "theatrical distribution contract").

acquisition of story rights — The first major stage in the production of a movie and with respect to the categorization of production costs. Acquisition activities (and their corresponding costs) include acquiring the rights to a concept or a license to a copyrighted literary property, such as a book and/or original screenplay (see "acquisition agreement" and "production costs").

acquisitions — Films that have been independently financed and produced by independent producers for which distributors have contractually acquired the right to distribute. Technically, the term should be applied to films acquired through the acquisition distribution agreement, but it is sometimes mistakenly used in a broader sense to include the negative pickup arrangement (see "acquisition distribution agreement," "in-house product," "negative pickup" and "pickups").

act — One of the principal divisions of a screenplay. Generally, screenplays have three acts with some thirty to sixty scenes in each act (see "screenplay").

action — In a film sense, the term action refers to movement in front of the camera. On the set of a motion picture during principal photography, the word "action" is called out by the director after the cameras have started rolling to signify the start of movement and dialogue for the scene being shot. In a legal sense, the term "action" refers to a lawsuit or other judicial proceeding whereby one party pursues a remedy against another for a wrong done, for protection of a right or for prevention of a wrong (see "action-at-law," "equitable remedy," "injunction," "remedy" or "remedies" and "suit").

action-adventure — A film genre in which the story revolves around or emphasizes danger and unknown risks and in which physical activity predominates. As a genre, such films appear to have broad international appeal (i.e., seem to travel better than other genre such as character shows; also the casting of a name star may not be as critical to its success; see "genre").

action-at-law — A judicial proceeding that may only be brought before a court at law as opposed to a court of equity (contrast with "equitable remedy" and "injunction").

action continuity — (see "continuity").

action product — (same as "action-adventure"; see "product").

action still — A photograph of an actual scene in a movie enlarged from a single frame of the motion picture film (see "production still").

action track — The exposed film depicting scenes for a movie, but without any dialogue or effects tracks (see "sound tracks").

active investors — Persons who invest in trade or business activities in which the investors materially participate on a regular basis. Not only must active investors help in making the business' important decisions on a regular basis, but such investors must be capable of participating in such a meaningful way (i.e., have the necessary training, background and experience). Investors in general partnerships, joint ventures and member-managed LLCs are typically active investors, although too many investors coming together in such investment vehicles may preclude all of them from being truly active (see "passive investors," "investor financing," "investor financing agreement" and "securities").

act of God — The result of the direct, immediate and exclusive operation of the forces of nature, uncontrolled and uninfluenced by human force or power, which is of such character that it could not have been prevented or avoided by foresight or prudence. Examples of so-called "acts of God" include natural floods, earthquakes, lightening, etc. (see "force majeure clause").

actor — Specifically in film, a male performing a role in any dramatic production, but more generally, any person, animal or product appearing in front of the camera as the subject, or one of the subjects, of the scene or shot. The term, in the generic sense, may also include the female actress (see "actress" and "player").

actor controls — Provisions in film production and employment agreements with actors or actresses that enable such persons to exercise authority over certain specified decisions (e.g., script approval, going into production without signing the long form agreement and in rare instances final cut authority; see "approvals," "final cut" and "long form agreement").

actress — The traditional term applied to female actors (see "actor").

actual breakeven — The point at which revenue generated by exploitation of a motion picture equals the costs incurred in the production and/or distribution of such motion picture for the applicable entity (e.g., the film's distributor; see "artificial breakeven," "breakeven," "cash breakeven" and "first breakeven").

actual competitors — Genuine or real rivals in an economic context. The concept is important for antitrust analysis purposes and forms one of the six tests making up the U.S. Department of Justice's 1984 Merger Guidelines for analyzing the competitive effects of a vertical merger (see "antitrust laws," "merger guidelines," "Paramount Consent Decree of 1948," "TriStar Case" and "vertical merger").

actual interest rate — The real interest percentage charged for the use of funds (e.g., a film production loan, as opposed to the prime interest rate; see "interest" and "prime rate").

actual production costs — The amount of money actually expended in the production of a feature film as opposed to the amount projected by the film's budget (see "audited cash production budget" and "negative costs").

ad agency — A business engaged in the creation of paid promotional messages and the purchase of media exposure. In some situations involving negotiations with a distributor, independent producers may want to seek certain controls or approvals over the selection of the ad agency in addition to controls and approvals relating to the creation of the film's ad campaign (see "advertising" and "rent-a-distributor").

adaptation — A movie script that modifies a story that first appeared in another medium. Screenplays are sometimes adapted from novels, short stories and magazine articles (see "novel" and "screenplay").

ad art — The original creative art used in a film's print advertising. Ad art is combined and reproduced with title art, credits, copy and other items to create an ad to be used in the print media, typically newspapers or magazines (see "advertising campaign").

ad campaign — (see "advertising campaign").

added scene — A scene that is inserted into a script that has already been assigned scene numbers. Such scene insertions may have significant financial implications, depending on the length and complexity of the added scene (see "budget," "continuity" and "production costs").

addendum — Something added (see "rider").

additional compensation — A contractual category of remuneration paid to actors, directors and sometimes writers, over and above their basic salaries. Thus, the term would include profit participations (see "contingent compensation" and "deferrals").

additional credit — A listing on the motion picture screen in recognition of the contribution of the party listed, in the development, production or distribution of a film, aside from another credit provided to the same person (e.g., a writer who is actively involved with the production of a film may also receive an associate producer credit as an additional credit; see "credits" and "Producers Guild of America."

additional insureds — Persons or entities other than the primary person or entity whose interests are protected by an insurance policy (see "insurance" and "errors and omissions insurance").

a deal — The transaction and documentation associated with a major motion picture (i.e., involving the highest levels of talent and major studio/distributors; see "a title").

adhesion contract — A contract so heavily restrictive of one party, while so non-restrictive of another, that doubts arise as to its validity as a voluntary and uncoerced agreement; implies a grave inequality of bargaining power. The concept often arises in the context of so-called "standard form" printed contracts prepared by one party and submitted to the other on a "take it or leave it" basis. Courts have recognized there is often no true equality of bargaining power in such contracts and have accommodated that reality in interpreting such contracts (see "contract," "distribution agreement," "negotiate," "overreaching," "standard contract," "submissions release" and "unconscionable contract").

ADI market — Area of dominant influence. An Arbitron audience-market classification designating a certain market area in which local television stations have partial or complete signal dominance over stations from other market areas. Commonly referred to as a television broadcast area. Similar to Nielsen DMA (designated market area). Some independent distributors use the ADI market for sub-distribution purposes as opposed to the more traditional sub-distribution areas designated by the exchanges (see "Arbitron Ratings Company," "exchanges" and "sub-distribution").

adjudicate — To hear a case, lawsuit or issue and determine such matter judicially (see "arbitration" and "litigation").

adjusted basis — Tax terminology referring to the base price from which to judge capital gains or losses upon the sale of an asset. During the time that a taxpayer holds an asset, such as a motion picture, certain events require that the taxpayer adjust (either up or down) his, her or its original basis to reflect the effects of such events. The original basis adjusted by such events constitutes the adjusted basis (see "basis").

adjusted capital account balance — A technical accounting term used with limited partnerships and manager-managed LLCs meaning the balance in any investor's capital account increased by an amount equal to the investor's post-payout sharing ratio multiplied by the minimum gain (see "post-payout sharing ratio" and "minimum gain").

adjusted gross — A negotiated and defined term in a movie distribution deal, typically gross receipts minus certain specified deductions, that may be the basis of negotiated percentage participations in that fund (i.e., that pool of money referred to as "adjusted gross"). Such deductions from gross receipts may include prints and advertising costs, taxes, residuals, advances and other specified items from first position gross. If deductions for enough different items are demanded by the distributor and accepted by the prospective adjusted gross participant, the resulting adjusted gross participation may not have any greater value than a net profit participation. Sometimes, the cost of prints and advertising alone may diminish the value of adjusted gross participation to the point that no money will ever be paid to persons or entities with rights to receive such funds (see "accountable gross," "first position gross," "exclusions," "net profits," "off-the-top deductions" and "talent participations").

adjusted gross income — The income on which a business or individual calculates his, her or its federal income tax. For a business, adjusted gross income is determined by subtracting from gross income any unreimbursed business expenses and other deductions (see "income tax").

adjusted rate of return (ARR) — A method of calculating the anticipated rate of return on an investment that is useful in evaluating all of the economic benefits of an investment and in comparing investments. ARR is the rate that equates the total future value of the economic benefits to the present value of the investment (see "after-tax real rate of return," "discounted cash flow," "internal rate of return" and "opportunity cost").

adjustment — The reduction of film rentals owed by an exhibitor to a distributor pursuant to a license agreement, that occurs following a poorer than expected performance at the box office. Such adjustments may be allowed by a distributor in contravention of its obligations to maximize the exploitation of a given film on behalf of net profit participants (see "selling subject to review" and "settlement transactions").

administrative overhead charge — (see "overhead").

admission date — In the context of a limited partnership, limited liability company or other securities offering, the date an investor (unit holder) is admitted as an investor in the investment vehicle (see "limited partners," "limited liability company" and "unit holder" or "unit purchaser").

admission price — The amount charged at a theater's box office for admission to see a movie (see "house nut").

admission price discrimination — An exhibitor business practice in which an exhibitor would charge a different amount at the box office for theater admissions depending on which distributor provided the movie being shown. Such price differentials have at times been contractually or otherwise imposed on the exhibitors by the major studio/distributors (see "antitrust laws," "price fixing" and "Paramount Consent Decree of 1948").

admissions — From the perspective of motion picture analysts, either the number of ticket buying patrons or the gross box office for a given film, group of films or during a specific period of time (see "box office gross" and "concession sales").

ADR — (see "automatic dialogue replacement" and "dialogue replacement").

advance or advances — Money obtained up front in anticipation of profits (e.g., monies paid by a distributor to a producer prior to release of the producer's film). Such advances may be paid upon signing of the distribution agreement and/or upon delivery of the picture. Advances are generally recoupable and distributor advances are generally recouped by the distributor out of the distributor's gross receipts. Advances may be paid in relation to pre-sales, production-financing/distribution agreements, negative pickups, network production agreements, payments to talent, the sale of profit interests or an amount the exhibitor will pay the distributor prior to the film's release. Producers are paid advances on signing of the production agreement or more commonly upon delivery of materials. Arrangements for advances are negotiated and theoretically controlled by the agreements between such parties, although it is not uncommon for parties to film industry agreements to ignore some provisions. Unfortunately, advance payments are generally taxable upon receipt (see "deferral structures," "distribution guarantee," "guarantees," "non-returnable advance," "release commitment," "recoupment," "remedy" and "sue us").

advance licensing — (same as "blind bidding").

advance payments — (see "advance" or "advances" above).

advance teaser campaign — An advertising campaign directed to the movie-going public, consisting of a series of ads and/or commercials, begun well in advance of a film's opening and intended to stimulate the interest and curiosity of potential audiences regarding the upcoming film (see "advertising campaign").

advantage — A benefit resulting from a specific course of action. Contrary to what some in the industry often suggest, there is no across the board "best way to finance a feature film," each form of film finance is associated with certain advantages and disadvantages. In each case, the most appropriate choice may depend not only on the nature of the proposed movie, its anticipated budget level and the attached elements, but also on the special abilities and resources the producer brings to the table (see "availability analysis," "disadvantage" and "pro and con analysis").

advertisement — Any form of selling or promotional communication regarding a motion picture. Such ads may be placed in any of the various media and are generally paid for by either the film's distributor, although sometimes in combination with the exhibitor, or even by the producer, depending on how the film is being distributed (see "co-operative advertising," "four-wall," "publicity" and "self-distribution").

advertising — All forms of paid media exposure (i.e., the creation and dissemination of promotional materials and the conduct of promotional activities including co-operative advertising, institutional advertising, national advertising and trade advertising in whatever form or media). The IRS defines advertising as the announcement or description of property or services in some mass communication medium (such as radio, television, newspaper, trade journals, direct mail or bill-boards) and directed at all or part of the general population of actual or potential customers to induce them to buy or rent the property or service. Advertising need not be directed to the general public, but may be focused toward any group of actual or potential customers. In film, advertising is responsible for the creative ad-look in the paid television and radio spots, the theater trailers, the movie posters and other promotional materials (see "credit," "marketing," "national ad campaign," "positive print," "promotional activities" and "publicity").

advertising appropriation — An allocation of funds from a film's total marketing budget that is used to pay for a film's advertising campaign for a stated time period. Such allocations may be made by the film's producer or distributor depending on how the film is being distributed (see "direct distribution expenses," "four-wall" or "four walling" and "four wall advertising").

advertising campaign — A planned and related series of promotional activities designed to bring about a particular result (i.e., awareness regarding a movie or motivation to go to a movie; see "blurbs" and "primary advertising").

Advertising Code Administration — An industry organization to which all advertising for rated motion pictures must be submitted for approval prior to release of the film to the public. Such advertising includes but is not limited to print ads, radio and tv spots, pressbooks and theatrical trailers (see "Classification and Ratings Administration," "MPAA" and "Ratings Board").

advertising copy — The text of an ad (see "advertising").

advertising costs — The direct expenses incurred in preparing and producing advertising for motion pictures. Advertising costs for opening an "A-level" motion picture in the current marketplace may be in the $30 to $40 million dollar range at a minimum (see "direct distribution expenses").

advertising materials — All of the physical items utilized in the promotion of a film (see "advertising").

advertising overhead — A charge imposed by all of the major studio/distributors and some independents to cover a share of the costs of operating their internal advertising, publicity and other departments. Generally, the charge equals 10 percent of the negative cost of the movie. Net profit participants may have a reasonable basis to question this charge on the grounds that the 10 percent percentage has no relation to actual costs since certain pictures bear a disproportionate share of such expenses and in many instances this overhead charge will exceed the actual costs of the services provided for a given motion picture. In lieu of eliminating or

limiting the amount of the advertising overhead charge, net profit participants may choose to seek to impose a ceiling on the amount that can be charged by the studio or distributor for this item (see "Buchwald Case" and "media buys").

advertising tie-ins — (see "promotional tie-ins" and "product placement").

advocacy — The act or process of advocating or supporting a cause or proposal (see "advocacy group," "advocate," "advocate auditing," "industry groups," "lobbying" and "Net Profit Participant Association").

advocacy group — A professional or trade association that, among other things, speaks for and/or represents the interests of its members in various forums including federal and state legislatures, governmental administrative agencies, government executives, court and the general public (see "industry groups," "lobbying" and "professional association").

advocacy journalism — The act of going beyond the traditional activities of journalism (i.e., the collecting and editing of news for presentation to the public through the media) and presenting a point of view in support of a cause or proposal.

advocate — One who expresses support for a cause or proposal (see "advocacy group," "advocate auditing," "association projects," "IFP," "industry groups," "lobbying" and "lobbyists").

advocate auditing — In the context of the motion picture business, a net profit participation auditor who not only studies a film distributor's accounting practices with respect to a given motion picture and reports to his or her net profit participation clients, but also actively negotiates with the distributor on behalf of those clients (see "auditor" and "net profit participant association").

affiliate — A person or entity that directly, or indirectly through one or more intermediaries, controls or is controlled by, or is under common control with, another specified person or entity; a company that owns less than a majority of the voting interests of another company. Also, two companies that are both subsidiaries of a third company (see "parent corporation" and "subsidiaries").

affiliated person — An individual who is in a position to exert direct influence on the actions of a business entity, including owners of 10 percent or more of its equity securities, corporate directors, senior elected officers and any person in a position to exert influence through them, such as members of their immediate family and other close associates; sometimes called a control person (see "affiliate").

affiliate of an issuer — A person controlling, controlled by or under common control with the issuer of securities. An individual who controls an issuer is also an affiliate of such issuer (see "control person" and "issuer").

affirmative obligation — A duty or responsibility to do a certain thing (e.g., a contractually negotiated duty on the part of a distributor to use its best efforts to maximize the distribution of a motion picture). Producers may want to include such an affirmative obligation in their distribution agreements (see "allocation issues," "conflicts of interest" and "settlement transaction").

AFI — (see "American Film Institute").

AFM — (see "American Film Market").

AFMA — (see "American Film Marketing Association").

after-market — In the film industry, another term for ancillary markets (i.e., the markets in which a film may be exploited following its primary market, that is usually theatrical exhibition; see "ancillary markets").

after-tax real rate of return — The amount of money expressed as a percentage of the investment that an investor can keep, out of the income and capital gains earned from investments and adjusted for inflation (see "adjusted rate of return" and "internal rate of return").

agency — The fiduciary relationship created when one person, the agent, acts on behalf of another with the authority of the latter, the principal. The authority of an agent make take various forms (i.e., real, apparent, express, implied, limited, unlimited, etc., depending on the particular facts and circumstances). Individuals utilizing the services of agents should clearly set out in writing the authority of their agents. The term is also used to refer to a firm of talent agents (see "adhesion contract," "fiduciary" and "power of attorney").

agency packaging — (see "packaging").

agent — Generally, one who, by mutual consent, acts for the benefit of another or represents the interests of another (e.g., in negotiating contracts on their behalf). In the film business, talent agents are licensed and their activities regulated by the state. Actors commonly utilize the services of agents in procuring work and screen writers often utilize the services of agents in selling their scripts to studios, producers or production companies. In film distribution, sales agents may represent producers or distributors in selling or licensing a film in certain markets (see "conflicts of interest" and "packaging").

agent fees — The monetary compensation paid to agents for their services, usually calculated as a percentage of some level of revenue generated by the activities of the agent's principal. The standard talent agent fee is 10 percent (see "sales agent fees").

agent for service of process — An individual named on behalf of a corporation or other entity (e.g., limited partnership or limited liability company) who, as a condition of such entity's doing business or selling securities in a given state, is designated to receive notices of lawsuits or court summons filed in such state against the entity represented (see "consent to service of process").

aggregate advances — The total amount of all advances paid in conjunction with the distribution of a motion picture (i.e., both domestic and foreign advances). Ideally, the aggregate of such advances will equal or exceed the negative cost of the picture involved (see "advance" and "pre-sales").

aggregate offering price — The sum of all cash, services, property, notes, cancellation of debt, or other consideration received by an issuer for issuance of its securities (see "consideration and securities").

agreement — A manifestation of mutual assent between two or more legally competent persons that ordinarily leads to a contract. In common usage, the word "agreement" is a broader term than contract, bargain or promise, since it includes executed sales, gifts and other transfers of property, as well as promises without legal obligation (see "contract").

agreement among underwriters (AAU) — Contract between participating members of an investment banking syndicate (i.e., an agreement signed by members of the underwriting syndicate empowering the managing underwriter to sign the underwriting agreement with the issuer and dividing the compensation and responsibilities among the syndicate members; contrast with "underwriting agreement").

agreement for acquisition of literary material — (see "acquisition agreement").

agreement for below-the-line personnel — (see "below-the-line employment agreements").

AICPA — Acronym for American Institute of Certified Public Accountants.

album — One or more phonograph records, tape recordings or compact discs carrying a major musical work or a group of related selections (see "sound track rights").

album cover — The container with envelopes for phonograph records, tape recordings and compact discs (see "jacket").

"A" level motion picture — (see "'A' title").

alien corporation — Corporation organized under the laws of a foreign country (contrast with "domestic corporation" and "foreign corporation").

allied rights — The power and authority to exploit products associated with a specific motion picture (e.g., merchandising, novelization, sound track recording and music publishing; see "ancillary markets" and "non-theatrical").

Alliance of Motion Picture and Television Producers (AMPTP) — A film industry trade organization that provides services to its member companies relating to all aspects of employment within the television and theatrical motion picture industry and other issues that affect the industry as a whole. The AMPTP acts as the bargaining agent for its member companies in industry-wide bargaining with the industry's unions and guilds and provides its members with advice regarding the administration of their industry-wide agreements. In other words, its most important issues relate to employee/employer relations and this association represents the interests of the major studio/production company employers along with a limited number of other independent production companies. This association is also a sister-association to the MPAA (see "MPAA").

all-media distribution agreement — A contract between a film's producer and a distributor in which the producer grants the distributor the exclusive right to distribute the film in all media and in all languages and versions, usually in the entire world (see "world-wide rights").

allocation — In a film distribution context, the assignment to particular accounts or apportionment among films or entities of the revenues generated by the exploitation of a film or the costs associated with its distribution (e.g., the costs of advertising several films may be allocated by the distributor among such films). Allocation issues also arise in the licensing of films in a package for television, whether for network or syndication. In foreign distribution,

such issues sometimes arise with respect to the allocation of a portion of film rentals to shorts and trailers. In a limited partnership or limited liability company context, the term allocation refers to distributions of partner or member shares of entity income or loss in a manner other than in accordance with such investor's actual percentage ownership interest (see "creative accounting," "special allocations" and "syndicated films").

allocation issues — Concerns, questions or problems relating to the apportionment of a film's gross receipts or other stage of the film's revenue stream. Numerous allocation issues arise in the context of film distribution accounting, partly because distributors have traditionally relied on their superior bargaining strength to permit themselves considerable discretionary authority to make such apportionment decisions (see "adhesion contract," "allocation" and "percentage allocated").

all or none — One of three arrangements under which investment banking and brokerage firms, called underwriters may undertake to sell a stock or securities issue. In an all or none offering the entire issue must be sold or the money is returned to investors and the deal canceled (i.e., the issuer has the right to cancel the whole issue if the underwriting is not fully subscribed; see "best efforts offering," "firm commitment" and "underwriter").

allowances — A share or portion allotted or granted or a sum granted as a reimbursement for expenses. Often a film's distributor will grant certain allowances to the exhibitor for advertising and exploitation of the film. Profit participants must be sure that such allowances are not excessive in what amounts to a disguised attempt to cross-collateralize one movie's revenue with others the distributor is distributing or will distribute (see "cross collateralization" and "de facto cross collateralization").

all territories — Throughout the universe (see "territory" and "world-wide rights").

alter ego doctrine — Legal doctrine under which the law disregards the limited personal liability one enjoys when he or she acts in a corporate capacity and attributes personal liability to such persons for their acts. To invoke the doctrine, it must be shown that the corporation is a mere conduit for the transaction of private business and that no separate identities of the individual and the corporation really exist (see "corporation" and "piercing the corporate veil").

alternate campaign — A film advertising and promotional program that differs from the primary campaign and is used to create new interest and a fresh look for the film. The alternate campaign will often be designed to appeal to a different audience than that of the primary campaign (see "advertising campaign" and "primary campaign").

alternate distributor — A film distribution company selected by a film's producer to take the place of the original distributor pursuant to a specific provision in the distribution agreement that may permit such substitution (see "substitution clause or agreement").

alternative minimum tax (AMT) — A federal tax aimed at ensuring that wealthy individuals and corporations pay at least some income tax (see "income tax").

alternative production financing — The funding of the costs associated with producing a movie through means other than studio financing (see "financing").

alternative scenes — (same as "cover shot").

American Academy of Independent Film Producers (AAIFP) — An organization that was briefly active in the late 1980's and that sponsored a seminar for independent producers covering such topics as distribution, literary rights, payroll accounting, producing, casting, financing and ultra-low budget production, but that has since not been very active. Requests for information on the organization go unanswered (see "FIND," "IFP" and "Producers Guild of America").

American Cinema Editors (A.C.E.) — The honorary professional society of film editors whose professional designation is A.C.E. Membership in the society is by invitation only (see "editor").

American Film Institute (AFI) — An independent, non-profit organization founded in 1967 by the National Endowment for the Arts primarily for the purpose of increasing recognition of the moving image as an art form, to assure the preservation of the art form and to develop and encourage new talent (see "industry groups").

American Film Market (AFM) — A motion picture marketplace devoted exclusively to the international licensing of independently produced movies in the English language. The AFM is sponsored by the International Film and Television Association (formerly the American Film Marketing Association). The market was traditionally held in Santa Monica, in February on an annual basis but in recent years the dates for the event have been changed to late October and early November (see "Cannes Film Festival" and "MIFED").

American Film Marketing Association (AFMA) — (see "International Film and Television Association").

American Motion Picture Labor Cooperative (AMPLC) — A North Hollywood-based organization formed during the 1988 Writers Guild strike for the purpose of representing non-union workers and trying to gain benefits, such as a health plan and access to a credit union (i.e., benefits not available to freelancers) for those workers (see "guild").

American product — Motion pictures produced by U.S. based producers and/or production companies and distributed by U.S. distributors (see "product").

American Society of Association Executives (ASAE) — A national association of association executives based in Washington, D.C. that provides a wide variety of knowledge resources, learning experiences and other tools and resources to help its member association executives grow and maximize their performance. The ASAE also serves as the voice of the association profession and advocates on its behalf. The ASAE also publishes numerous books on association management including the *Association Law Handbook* a useful guide for all professional and trade association executives (see "industry groups").

American Stock Exchange — The second largest United States market maintained for the purpose of buying and selling securities (i.e., second after the New York Stock Exchange; see "stock exchange").

amortization — The liquidation on an installment basis of a financial obligation relating to an intangible asset. Also, recovery of cost or value over a period of time (i.e., the IRS defines amortization as the ratable deduction allowed for loss in value of intangible property due to the passage of time). It is a method of allocating the cost of an intangible asset over time for purposes of offsetting (deducting) such cost from revenues the asset helps to produce. Amortization as permitted by the IRS code illustrates the concept of capital recovery which provides that income does not result until revenues exceed the capital expended to produce such revenues. If property is entitled only to amortization, the recovery of the cost or basis of the item may be limited to a proportionate (i.e., straight-line) deduction over the amortization period (same as "cost amortization"; contrast with "depreciation"; see "capitalization" and "FASB Statement No. 53").

amortization of negative cost — The accounting procedure by which a film's negative cost is charged against the film's revenue (see "amortization," "cost recovery," "income forecast method" and "negative costs").

amortization schedule — A written presentation in tabular form showing the amounts of principal and interest due on a loan at regular intervals and the unpaid balance of the loan after each payment is made (see "amortization").

amortize overhead — The practice of gradually reducing or recovering the cost of an entity's indirect expenses incurred in the production and/or distribution of a film. Major studio/distributors sometimes offer their distribution facilities on a rent-a-distributor basis in order to amortize their overhead without incurring any additional financial risk on such motion pictures (see "rent-a-distributor" and "release slots").

"A" movie — (see "'A' title").

AMPAS — (see "Academy of Motion Picture Arts and Sciences").

AMPLC — (see "American Motion Picture Labor Cooperative").

analyst — In the securities field, a person in a brokerage house who studies a number of companies and makes buy or sell recommendations on the securities of particular companies and industry groups. Most of such analysts specialize in a particular industry (e.g., the entertainment industry, and focus on corporate entities with publicly traded stock; see "communications industry" and "entertainment industry").

ancillaries — (see "ancillary markets").

ancillary agreements — Agreements that are subordinate, subsidiary, supplementary or auxiliary to a primary, preceding or original agreement. If the issue of subsequently negotiated gross participations is not negotiated and provided for in the original agreements relating to the services of a film's creative team, such ancillary agreements may alter their deal with a producer who gives away too many gross participations (see "gross floor" and "gross participants").

ancillary end users — Those entities that exploit films in the ancillary markets (e.g., video companies; see "ancillary markets").

ancillary market rights — (see "ancillary rights").

ancillary markets — Geographical or technological areas of demand for film product that are auxiliary or supplemental to the theatrical market. The ancillary markets include foreign, network and syndicated television, pay cable and home video (see "markets," "non-theatrical" and "theatrical market").

ancillary rights — The additional powers or privileges that a film's producer or distributor or other person or entity is justly entitled to exercise with respect to the original literary property and the feature film that the producer may own (i.e., additional to theatrical exhibition). Such rights may include the right to produce a remake, sequel, television series, stage play and/or soundtrack recording. The issue of whether such sources of revenue are included in the distributor's gross receipts (or treated as a separate revenue stream) may be negotiated in some instances. If the distributor does not include ancillary revenue in gross receipts, it may use an approach similar to that used with regard to videocassette revenues, in which the rights will be exploited by a third party, that is sometimes affiliated with the studio and only a royalty is paid to the distributor, thus significantly reducing the amounts paid to subsequent profit participants. In that situation, net profit participants may want to negotiate for a separate participation in such ancillary revenues (see "ancillary rights," "ancillary markets," "isolated ancillary rights," "outside the pot," "retroactive basis" and "videocassette revenue reporting").

Angel Capital Electronic Network (ACE-NET) — (see "ACE-NET").

angel investor — A financial backer who provides early support for a business venture. The initial incorporation stage for a company and startups of other varieties (e.g., LLCs) creates an opportunity to seek out so-called "angels" to provide "angel financing." The term "angel financing" is typically associated with early stage financing provided by individual wealthy investors, as opposed to that provided by the groups of individuals or companies organized as venture capital firms (see "Venture Capital"). Further, it is not necessary to form a corporation to bring in angel capital, the term may also apply to any form of active investor financing using any of the active investor financing options. As a practical matter, however, the term is most often associated with early stage corporate finance (see "ACE-NET," "corporate financing," "limited liability company" and "venture capital").

"A" negative — The parts of a film negative that are used to print the film that is ultimately employed in the edited and completed motion picture (see "'B' negative").

animal mortality insurance — Insurance against the death or destruction of any animal specifically covered, when used in a film production. A veterinarian's certificate is usually required for this type of coverage (see "insurance").

animation — A filmmaking process in which drawings or three-dimensional objects (e.g., models) are photographed frame by frame so that when the assembled film is projected at normal speeds, the drawings or objects appear to move (see "genre" and "markets").

annotated script — A screenplay, sometimes requested by the errors and omissions insurance carrier, with notes included thereon, indicating which of the various component parts of the script are based on some existing underlying work (e.g., books, stage plays, newspaper articles and/or magazine articles) and citing such works. These notes will help the E&O carrier's attorney evaluate the risk of possible lawsuits based on the screenplay (see "clearance" and "errors and omissions insurance").

announcements in the trades — Ads run in *Variety*, *The Hollywood Reporter*, *Village Voice* or other industry publication announcing some event relating to a film, such as the completion of principal photography. Such ads are considered useful in creating presumed value in a film (see "*Variety*," "*The Hollywood Reporter*" and "trades").

annual basis — An accounting technique in which figures relating to a period of less than one year are extended to cover a twelve month period. The procedure is called annualizing and it must take into account seasonal fluctuations, if any, in order to be accurate (see "accounting method").

annual meeting — The once-a-year meeting at which the officers and managers of a corporation report to its stockholders on the year's results and some or all of the members of the board of directors are elected for a subsequent term (see "corporation").

annual percentage rate (APR) — The cost of credit that consumers pay, expressed as a simple annual percentage (see "interest").

annual report — A formal corporate financial statement issued yearly. The annual report of publicly owned corporations must comply with SEC reporting requirements which include balance sheet, income statement and cash flow reports audited by an independent certified public accountant. These annual reports are filed with the SEC on Form 10K (see "certified public accountant," "Form 10K" and "SEC").

answer print — The first positive composite print (made from the original negative) from the lab with sound, music, color (if in color), title and fades, dissolves and optical effects (i.e., color- and sound-balanced). It "answers" the question affirmatively that a viable working negative exists from which prints can be made for commercial presentation. In brief, a print potentially ready for release to its target audience. However, there are nearly always visual corrections to be made and sometimes changes in sound so that the first answer print is generally a guide to fine-tuning the prints to follow. The answer print, thus usually precedes the first release print (see "release print").

anticipated expenses — A concept often found in film distribution agreements that permits the distributor to deduct from gross receipts an amount adequate to cover future estimated distribution expenses. Such provisions often stipulate that the distributor may in good faith retain sums necessary to pay for costs reasonably anticipated to arise in connection with the picture being distributed (see "creative accounting," "discretion" and "good faith").

anticipated rating — The producer's advance judgment as to what MPAA rating will be assigned to his or her film (see "MPAA rating" and "publicity").

anticipatory breach of contract — In contract law, a breach committed before the arrival of the actual time of required performance. It occurs when one party by declaration repudiates his or her contractual obligation before it is due. The repudiation required is a positive statement indicating that the promisor will not or cannot substantially perform the promised contractual duties (see "breach of contract" and "contract").

anti-blind bidding statutes — State statutes that prohibit the film distribution practice of requiring competing exhibitors to bid on films without an opportunity to first see the film (blind bidding). Generally speaking, the industry organizations that favor blind bidding are the major studio/distributors as represented by the MPAA. Ordinarily, it might be expected that the exhibitor trade group, NATO would be opposed to the practice of blind bidding, but the existence or vigor of that opposition may depend on how many of the NATO members are owned or controlled by the major studio/distributors (see "blind bidding," "lobbying," "MPAA," "NATO," "non-regulatory state," "product splitting," "state legislatures" and "vertical integration").

anti-competitive — Acting in opposition to a free market (i.e., opposed to the effort of two or more parties acting independently to secure the business of a third by offering the most favorable terms, products and/or services; see "anti-competitive business practices").

anti-competitive business practices — A broad term referring to all sorts of activities that tend to reduce free competition in the marketplace. This term would include some business practices that are not actionable under antitrust laws (e.g., even though the MPAA rating system might not be actionable pursuant to a given federal antitrust regulation, independent producers or distributors whose films are rated in a discriminatory manner by this MPAA sponsored organization may well view this MPAA activity as anti-competitive; see "antitrust laws," "block booking," "blind bidding," "conduct restrictions," "predatory practices" and "reciprocal preferences").

anti-fraud rule — State and federal securities law provisions that require the written disclosure of all material aspects of certain securities transactions in advance to prospective investors, prohibit the omission of any material information and prohibit any untrue or misleading representations. Non-compliance may result in a charge of securities fraud (see "disclosure document" and "fraud").

anti-Semitic sword — The use of a false accusation of anti-Semitism in a debate or discussion as a means of distracting the attention of listeners, readers or viewers from the truth of the statements actually being made. In the alternative, even if the accusation of anti-Semitism may be true, the accusation made and/or repeated without supportive and convincing evidence is no more than an irresponsible whispering campaign. Throughout the history of Hollywood, the anti-Semitic sword has been an effective tactic used by Hollywood insiders to squelch criticism (see "anti-Semitism," "discrimination," "reverse discrimination," "prejudice" and "whispering campaign").

anti-Semitism — Open hostility or hatred directed toward Jews generally or toward one or more Jews solely because they are Jewish. Criticism of unfair, unethical, unconscionable, anti-competitive, predatory and/or illegal business practices of business persons who happen to be Jewish does not rise to the level of anti-Semitism, rather is merely criticism of alleged wrongful behavior (see "anti-Semitic sword").

antitrust laws — Federal and state statutes aimed at promoting free competition in the marketplace (i.e., to prevent monopolies and restraint of trade). Any agreement or cooperative effort or intent by two or more entities that affects or restrains, or is likely to affect or restrain their competitors is illegal under these statutes. The two major federal antitrust laws are the Sherman Act and the Clayton Act. The Sherman Act protects the right of individuals to be free to compete and makes illegal any contract, combination or conspiracy in restraint of trade or commerce. The Sherman Act also makes illegal monopolies and attempts, combinations or conspiracies to monopolize. The Clayton Act regulates price discrimination, tying and exclusive-dealing contracts, stock acquisitions which tend to monopolize and certain interlocking directorates (see "blind bidding," "block booking," "Clayton Act," "industry pool," "marketplace of ideas," "monopoly," "price discrimination," "pooling arrangements," "price fixing," "reciprocal preferences," "Sherman Antitrust Act," "tracks" and "tying arrangement").

antitrust law violations — Violations of federal and state statutes aimed at promoting free competition in the marketplace (i.e., to prevent monopolies and restraint of trade). Any agreement or cooperative effort or intent by two or more entities that affects or restrains, or is likely to affect or restrain their competitors, is illegal under these statutes. The relaxation of the federal enforcement of antitrust laws in the years during and since the Reagan presidency may have resulted in numerous film industry activities or business practices that may otherwise be actionable under the antitrust laws, if such laws were being more vigorously enforced. Movie profit participants and even exhibitors must be more aware of such activities and be willing to lobby or litigate when appropriate in order to stem any potential trend toward more anti-competitive business practices (see "antitrust laws," "marketplace of ideas," "Paramount Consent Decree of 1948," "political influence," "remedy," "sue us" and "TriStar Case").

appeal — The primary theme underlying a motion picture advertisement in its effort to elicit a favorable response from a movie's prospective audience (i.e., motivate them to see the picture; see "demand" and "primary audience").

Application for Registration of a Tax Shelter — IRS Form 8264 which is to be used by the organizers of certain tax shelters in registering the tax shelter with the IRS (see "tax shelter registration").

apportion — To divide fairly or according to the parties' respective interests; proportionately, but not necessarily equally (see "allocation," "discretion" and "good faith").

apportioned expense — Costs that are divided according to the parties' interests (i.e., proportionately). Many distribution agreements allow the distributor to have the discretion to apportion numerous distribution expenses relating to advertising, facilities, employees, etc. among films which are marketed in a package. A profit participant cannot make an informed judgment as to whether such apportionments are fair without having access to the information upon which such apportionments are based. Such participants should make sure the audit rights of the producer and/or profit participants include access to such documentation (i.e., try to prevent the distributor from limiting access to documents that relate to the amount of money to be received; see "audit," "contract of adhesion" and "discretion").

appraise — To estimate the value; to put in writing the worth of property (see "catalog").

appraisal — An estimate or opinion of value; a conclusion resulting from the analysis of relevant facts (see "catalog").

approval of the limited partners — In a limited partnership context, most state limited partnership acts authorize the limited partners to vote on certain specified partnership decisions without losing their limited liability. The partnership agreement may also establish the percentage of limited partner votes required for such approval (see "limited partnership agreement").

approvals — The power to review certain feature film elements and exclude such elements from being part of a particular film project. For example, depending on the stature of a production company which is receiving the benefit of a production-financing/distribution agreement from a studio/distributor or a negative pickup distribution deal, the studio/distributor will typically insist on approving such elements as the budget, screenplay, director and principal cast and such approval rights will be set out in the distribution agreement (see "creative control" and "controls").

approved elements — Significant aspects of a film that have been reviewed and approved by the production financing source or distributor that has committed to distribute the film once it is produced (e.g., script, budget, director and lead actors). In a negative pickup arrangement, if the film as produced does not contain the elements approved in advance of production by the distributor or significantly departs from some of those elements, the distributor may be able to avoid its obligation to distribute the film. Producers and directors must not forget about those approvals as the film is produced, because if the distributor does not like the film, the distributor is not likely to forget about its approval rights. The question of what is significant provides an opportunity to disagree. Some effort ought to be made in negotiating the distribution agreement to further define what departures will be allowed and to provide for some mechanism to obtain distributor approvals on changes along the way, if any (see "approved negative cost," "approved script" and "basic elements").

approved negative cost — A film budget that has been reviewed and approved by a film distributor that has committed to distribute the film and provide production financing (see "approved elements" and "approved script").

approved production budget — The amount of money itemized by spending category anticipated to be required to produce a film and that has been approved by the film's financier or financiers (e.g., a studio/distributor; see "production budget" and "production-financing/distribution agreement").

approved production schedule — A timetable and plan for conducting the principal photography of a motion picture that has been approved by the financier (e.g., the studio/distributor pursuant to a production-financing/distribution agreement). Costs resulting from changes to the approved production schedule requested in writing by the distributor may be excluded from any over-budget penalty or other provisions (see "over-budget penalty").

approved screenplay — (same as "approved script").

approved script — A film screenplay approved by a distributor that has committed to distribute the film with such commitment being provided prior to production of the film. If the film as produced significantly departs from the approved script, the distributor may avoid its obligation to distribute the film (see "approved elements").

"A" product — (see "'A' title").

arbitration — The submission of a controversy, by agreement of the parties, to persons chosen by the parties for resolution. An informal, non-judicial method for resolving disputes that generally takes less time and is less expensive than litigation. Film industry agreements sometimes provide for arbitration to resolve any disputes that arise between the parties. For example, motion picture lenders often require that disputes between a film's distributor and its producer relating to whether the film has been properly completed and delivered pursuant to the terms of the distribution agreement be submitted to arbitration to ensure a more rapid and inexpensive resolution of the dispute. In a situation where a producer signs a production-financing distribution agreement with a studio/distributor, the producer may also want to seek an arbitration clause for the same reasons, particularly since the studio will be charging interest on the production costs of the film (see "arbitration clause," "expedited arbitration" and "litigation").

arbitration clause — A clause in a contract providing for arbitration of disputes arising under the contract as opposed to litigating the dispute in court. Before agreeing to such a clause, it is advisable to think through the implications of arbitration. For example, arbitration might be helpful with strictly technical issues, but law courts are generally more sophisticated at handling expert witness type evidence (see "arbitration" and "expedited arbitration").

Arbitron Ratings Company — A national media research and ratings service that uses a quarterly audience survey period to publish audience viewing and listening habits for television, cable and radio at local and national levels, showing market share for the time period covered and statistical analysis using such characteristics as sex and age of the audience (see "ADI Market" and "Nielsen Media Research").

Area of Dominant Influence — (see "ADI Market").

arm's length — The bargaining position of two parties that are unrelated to one another and whose mutual dealings are influenced only by the independent interest of each. The term is used to describe a standard of dealing that reflects no motivation other than that normally to be expected on the part of two unconnected parties transacting in good faith in the ordinary course of business (see "adhesion contract," "conflicts of interest," "negotiate" and "videocassette revenue reporting").

arm's length basis — The manner in which negotiations are objectively and fairly conducted (see "arm's length" and "videocassette revenue reporting").

arrangement — The development of an existing musical composition by scoring for voices or instruments, usually for those other than the voices and instruments for which the music was originally written and including the transposition of keys and elaboration of chord structures. An arrangement must reflect substantial new matter to qualify for copyright protection, although arrangements of any work in the public domain may be freely copyrighted. Arrangements of works protected by copyright may be copyrighted, but only by the copyright owner or with such copyright owner's consent (see "arranger" and "copyright").

arranger — A person who prepares and adapts previously written music for presentation in some form other than its original form (see "arrangement" and "orchestrator").

arrogance — A feeling of superiority manifested in an overbearing manner or presumptuous claims (see "Code of Professional Responsibility," "ethics" and "market power").

art director — The film production person who works with the production designer and is responsible for planning and executing the design of the sets, including the production of all illustrations, continuity sketches, perspectives, scenery, scale models, props, surface coloration and texture, drawings and elevations. The art director also gives approval on sets, properties, set dressing and scenery, and finds and recommends, for the approval of the director and producer, locations that are visually suitable for the production (see "production designer").

art film — A motion picture that stresses artistic qualities as opposed to more commercial elements and thus is expected to appeal to a more narrow and specialized audience (see "art house," "commercial," "key art showcase cities" and "special handling").

art house — (same as "art theater").

articles of incorporation — The document or instrument that is required to be filed with a state's secretary of state, as part of the process of creating a corporation and pursuant to the general corporation laws of that state. The articles may set out certain basic attributes of the corporation such as the type of corporation, the amount of authorized stock and the agent for service of process. Other action needed to complete the incorporation process includes a shareholders meeting, selection of members of the board of directors, a meeting of the board of directors, preparation of minutes for both meetings, approval of bylaws and corporate seal, election of officers, issuance of shares and recording of shares in the stock transfer log (see "articles of organization," "certificate of incorporation," "charter" and "ultra vires activities").

articles of organization — The document or instrument that is required to be filed with the state's secretary of state as the first step in the creation of a limited partnership or limited liability company. To finalize the process of entity formation of a limited partnership, a partnership agreement also needs to be drafted and approved by the limited partners, and for a limited liability company, an operating agreement needs to be drafted and approved by the LLC's members (see "articles of incorporation," "limited liability company" and "limited partnership").

Article Twenty — A controversial article of the IATSE contract that allows major studios to fully finance non-union movies and television shows so long as the studios declare they have no creative control and give the union thirty days notice before production starts. Many union supporters contend Article Twenty has helped to increase non-union movie production (see "artificial pickup," "IATSE" and "industry groups").

artificial break-even — A contractually defined multiple of a film's negative cost (e.g., when gross receipts equal three times the negative cost of the motion picture) that is sometimes treated as actual break-even (see "actual breakeven," "breakeven," "cash breakeven," "creative accounting," "first breakeven" and "rolling breakeven").

artificial pickup — A film project originally controlled and developed by a studio/distributor but that is farmed out pursuant to a negative pickup or anticipated acquisition distribution deal to an outside (but friendly) production company, partly to avoid the higher costs of the below-the-line union crews which the studio would have to pay if the project was produced as an in-house production at the studio (see "acquisition distribution agreement," "Article Twenty," "negative pickup" and "signatories").

artist — A broad term referring to any person skilled in one of the fine arts; one who professes and practices an art in which conception and execution are governed by imagination and taste. In a film, artists may include the screenwriter, actors, actresses, director, cinematographer, art director and others who contribute to the creative process (see "actor" and "artistic control").

artistic control — The power to make decisions relating to the appearance and content of the final feature film product (see "creative differences" and "final cut").

artistic differences — (see "creative differences").

artist's advance — Payment made to an actor, director or writer prior to the performance of their contractual duties either upon the signing of the employment agreement or at other specified times (see "advance").

artist's fee — The amount of compensation provided for in the film's budget to be paid to the actor, writer or director excluding any bonus or contingent compensation (see "artist," "contingent compensation," "deferments" and "salary").

art theater — An exhibitor that specializes in presenting art films, generally in exclusive engagements, rather than in showing the mass marketed and more commercial films typically released by the major studio/distributors (see "art film").

artwork — Graphic, creative or otherwise aesthetic representations relating to a specific film that are used in advertising and promoting the film (see "advertising").

artwork title — The name or credit to be attributed to an aesthetic representation. A distributor may seek in its distribution agreement to limit its obligations to provide credit for artwork (see "credit").

aspect ratio — The ratio of the horizontal to the vertical dimensions (i.e., width-to-height) of a motion picture frame or television screen. Most feature films are shot with 35mm negative film, using an aspect ratio of 1.85 to 1 (also written 1.85:1 or 1.85 x 1). A 1.85 to 1 aspect ratio means that the projected image is 1.85 times wider than it is high. Other 35mm formats include 1.33 to 1, 1.66 to 1 and 2.35 to 1. A 2.35 to 1 aspect ratio produces a very wide image and is most appropriate for pictures requiring many outdoor panoramic scenes (wide-screen). Before wide-screen, the original 35mm movie screen had an aspect ratio of 1 x 1:33, a ratio reflected approximately in TV screen images. The format for a film is generally selected by the producer, director and director of photography (see "format" and "pan and scan").

assembly — The first, rough arrangement of dailies in script order (see "dailies").

assessable security — A security on which a charge or assessment for the obligations of the issuing company may be made (see "securities").

asset — Anything owned by a business, institution or individual that has monetary or exchange value (see "liquid asset").

asset financing — The funding of a business venture by converting particular assets into working cash in exchange for a security interest in those assets (e.g., loans against accounts receivable and inventory loans; see "collateral" and "secured debt").

asset management — The control and direction of a particular individual or entity's investments by a brokerage house, bank, savings institution or other qualified financial advisor. If the assets under management by the asset manager are sufficiently large enough, a certain percentage of the assets may be available for high risk investments such as motion pictures (see "discretionary funds" and "scam").

asset value — The worth of a company's collective assets; a term often used to described the worth of a motion picture company's film library [see "catalog (library)"].

assign — To transfer one's interest in property, a contract or other rights to another. Although often used interchangeably with pledge and hypothecate, the term assign implies transfer of ownership (or of the right to transfer ownership at a later date). Film distribution deals often limit the rights of either or both the producer and distributor to assign their respective rights and obligations (see "distribution agreement," "grant of rights," "hypothecate," "license," "pledge" and "secured debt").

assignee — The person to whom an assignment is made (see "assign").

assignment for the benefit of creditors — The transfer of interests to those to whom money is owed by a debtor (see "assign").

assignment — A written agreement that is used to transfer some or all of an owner's right, title and interest in a specific property to a purchaser. Important provisions of such an assignment include the description of the rights being transferred and the consideration to be paid. Other terms typically include owner warranties and an indemnification provision in favor of the purchaser if one of the owner warranties is breached. Distribution agreements routinely include a form of assignment as an exhibit to the distribution agreement and provide that the producer or production company agrees to sign such assignment along with any UCC-1 financing statements and a laboratory pledgeholder agreement (see "copyright assignment," "laboratory pledgeholder agreement" and "UCC-1 financing statement").

assignor — An individual or entity that assigns or makes an assignment (see "assign").

assigns — Those who take from or under the assignor, whether by conveyance, devise, descent or operation of law (see "personal representative" and "successor").

assistant director (AD) — The film production staff person who helps the film's director. An AD may serve as the director's liaison with governmental authorities and suppliers of services, may also be responsible for insuring that actors are present at the right time and place and otherwise is expected to perform whatever other useful tasks are assigned by the director (see "director" and "Directors Guild of America").

assistant editor — A person who is directly assigned to assist a film editor and whose duties may include synchronizing dailies, taking notes at screenings, obtaining cutting room facilities, breaking down daily takes, pulling out and assembling selected takes, making trims, ordering optical and other preparatory work in film editing rooms (see "editing room assistant").

assistant producer — An aide to the film's producer (see "associate producer," "co-producer credit," "creative producer," "executive producer" and "line producer").

associate producer — A title and film credit given to a film producer's second-in-command who shares business and creative responsibilities. The associate producer is generally involved in pre-production, production and post-production as a supporting producer. The credit is sometimes given to a production manager or first assistant director for contributions that greatly exceed their routine duties. Also it is sometimes awarded to a significant financial backer or an individual who may have brought the literary property or screenplay to the producer (see "credit issues," "producer" and "Producers Guild of America").

association— An organization of persons who have a common interest and have joined together for a certain purposes (e.g., sponsoring educational seminars, conducting annual conferences, collecting, analyzing and disseminating industry information among the association's members and/or representing the association's interests before federal and/or state legislatures; see "AFMA," "association projects," "IFP," "IFP/West," "IFTA," "industry groups," "MPAA," "MPEAA," "NATO," "professional association" and "trade association").

association antitrust policies — The adopted practices of professional and trade associations that relate to governmental regulations and laws on competition. The U.S. antitrust laws apply to the membership policies of trade and professional associations such as the MPAA, MPEAA, AMPTP, FIND, IFTA and NATO. Restrictions on which companies may become a member have particular antitrust implications, since denial of membership, with its attendant benefits, may be held to place the applicant at an economic disadvantage. Generally speaking, trade associations must allow membership to all those in the trade if excluding them would significantly limit their opportunities to compete effectively, thereby creating a restraint on competition. Two other areas of potential concern with respect to the application of the antitrust laws to professional and trade association policy, are (1) agreements among association members that have the effect of fixing or stabilizing prices for particular services and (2) boycotting or refusing to deal with companies that take action which is opposed by the association members (see "anti-competitive

business practices," "antitrust laws," "blacklist," "blind bidding," "block booking," "insider's game," "member of the club," "predatory practices," "price fixing" and "reciprocal preferences").

Association of Net Profit Participants — (see "association projects" and "Net Profit Participant Association").

association projects— The activities a professional and/or trade association undertakes on behalf of its members. Examples of major areas of association activities may include projects of an educational nature (seminars, books, association magazines, etc.) or projects that relate to the representation of the group's interests in a legislative forum, in a court of law or before an executive branch of governments at any level. Specific projects an association of independent feature film producers may choose to undertake might include the following: (1) develop and maintain a reference library specifically to meet the special needs of independent film producers; (2) subscribe to and maintain back issues of various trade publications of interest to independent producers; (3) set up a producer antitrust task force to study possible anti-competitive business practices (i.e., discrimination, vertical integration, block booking, blacklisting, agency packaging, film censoring, etc.), that may be occurring in the film industry and report on their impact on independents; (4) specifically work to eliminate studio or other production company or distributor ownership or control of theaters; (5) lobby on behalf of the association's independent producer members with the U.S. Justice Department and the Federal Trade Commission relating to the vigorous enforcement of federal antitrust laws in the entertainment industry; (6) study and make member producers aware of how antitrust laws also apply to the activities of professional associations; (7) represent the interests of independent producers with respect to matters before state legislatures, Congress and the Federal Communications Commission (e.g., financial interest and syndication rules); (8) speak on behalf of the association's membership with respect to eliminating the conflicts of interest inherent in the MPAA motion picture rating program; (9) organize and maintain film distributor research files for the use of independent producer members of the association; (10) conduct seminars on matters of importance to independent producers, including the distribution deal, the status of the independent producer, performance report cards on distributors, alternative film finance methods, etc. (11) research and make available industry statistics as such statistics specifically relate to independent producers and their films; (12) maintain current referral lists of the entertainment related professionals such as entertainment attorneys, auditing firms, antitrust and entertainment litigating attorneys, and production accountants or payroll services; (17) monitor antitrust litigation relating to the entertainment industry and report on developments to independent producer members (also develop a checklist of anti-competitive business practices to monitor); (18) calculate/publicize the number of theatre screens that are available or used for the exhibition of independently produced and/or independently distributed feature films on a weekly basis; (19) calculate/publicize revenue market share of independent producers vs. MPAA companies; (20) publicize instances of and work to eliminate arbitrary and unfair "blacklisting" in the industry; (21) create a producer's investment club or some similar investment vehicle to pool independent producer investments and to selectively invest in publicly held motion picture studios, production companies, distributors and exhibitors. Such investments would permit the producer investors to participate in the economic benefits of equity ownership in entertainment entities, if any and provide better access to information regarding the activities of such entities; (22) develop authoritative figures to substantiate and publicize among the general public and at film schools specifically, the huge disparity between the number of films that are produced each year and the films that are distributed each year, as well as the number of producers, directors, screenwriters, actors, actresses and others who are competing for positions with the limited number of films produced and the resulting bargaining disadvantage for such groups or individuals produced by such disparity; (23) create and maintain a file describing so-called "creative accounting" practices of studios and/or distributors; (24) organize an extensive "for-credit" student intern program in cooperation with various film schools to help the association meet its person-power needs and to provide unique learning opportunities for film students interested in producing; (25) research questions relating to establishing a professional certification program for independent feature film producers; (26) publish a newsletter and magazine with articles relating to some or all of the above topics and other matters of special interest to independent producers; and (27) develop and make available a model feature film distribution agreement that provides a more balanced approach to issues as between distributors and producers (see "AIVF," "AMPTP," "choosing a distributor," "FIND," "IFP," "lobbying," "MPAA," "MPEAA," "NATO," "political influence" and "professional associations").

assumption agreement— A clause or provision negotiated as between the independent producer and the distributor and inserted into the distribution agreement providing that the distributor assumes responsibility for directly paying some or all contingent compensation commitments made by the producer to talent and/or other profit participants (see "distributor's assumption agreement," "most favored nations clause" and "parri passu").

assumptions — Circumstances that are assumed to be factual for purposes of projecting the hypothetical results of an investment, such as in an investor-financed film offering structured as a limited partnership or manager-managed limited liability company (see "financial projections").

asynchronous sound — Sound on motion picture film that is not in synch or synchronous with the image on the film (see "in synch" and "synchronous sound").

"A" Title — A somewhat subjective term describing a major motion picture with a director, stars and/or other elements that presumably create significant box office appeal (i.e., motion pictures with significant recognizable actors/actresses and established directors that are released by major studio/distributors in the U.S. in a wide manner). Sometimes "A" title films are defined as major studio product that has been released with significant print and advertising commitments or independent product that has performed well in the marketplace or had the equivalent of a major studio release (see "'B' movie" and "commercial").

atmosphere — The extras in a movie as a group (also see "background cast" and "extras").

at risk — Exposed to the danger of loss. Investors in direct participation programs (such as limited partnerships or manager-managed limited liability company offerings) can claim tax deductions only if they can show that their investment was at risk (i.e., that there was a chance of never realizing any profit on the investment and a chance of losing their investment as well). The IRS may be able to disallow such claimed deductions if the investors are not exposed to economic risk (e.g., an offering where the general partner or a film distributor guaranteed the return of all capital to the investors even if the business venture lost money; see "at risk loss limits").

at risk limitation — Tax losses of certain taxpayers are limited to the amount the taxpayer has invested and which is at risk of loss. Such amounts generally include investments of cash or other property and recourse debt (see "recourse debt").

at risk loss limits — Special federal tax rules that apply to most activities, including the activities of a partnership, that are engaged in as a trade or business or for the production of income. These rules limit the amount of loss a partner may deduct to the amounts for which that partner is considered at risk in the activity. A partner is considered at risk to the extent of the amount of cash and the adjusted basis of property contributed to the activity, income retained by the partnership and amounts borrowed by the partnership for use in the activity. A partner is not considered at risk for amounts borrowed by the partner or the partnership unless that partner is personally liable for the repayment or the amounts borrowed are secured by the partner's property other than property used in the activity. Also a partner is not considered at risk for amounts that are protected against loss through guarantees, stop-loss agreements or other similar arrangements (see "at risk" and "basis").

attached to the project — Committed to play a specific role or perform certain duties in relation to a given motion picture. Such commitments may be contingent and may take the form of oral expressions of interest, letters of interest, letters of intent or contractual commitments. On the other hand, it may be unfair to claim that someone is attached to a certain movie unless a firm and fully enforceable commitment supported by consideration is involved (see "letter of intent," "packaging," "pay or play" and "pay and play").

attachment — A proceeding in law by which one's property is seized, that is, a proceeding to take a defendant's property into legal custody to satisfy a plaintiff's demand. A distribution deal may provide for certain specified remedies in the event the producer's property which is the subject of the distribution agreement (i.e., the film or any portion thereof, is attached or levied upon; see "levy").

attendance checking — Activities undertaken on behalf of a producer or distributor designed to verify the actual number of paid moviegoers in attendance at a showing or showings of a film. Such activities may include the hiring of checkers to go to the theater and count those in attendance or to purchase the first and last ticket of the day at a given theater to then compare the ticket numbers with the exhibitor's attendance reports. There are organizations that provide such checking services for producers and distributors. However, in a rent-a-distributor situation a producer may want to hire its own checking service to conduct random checks of attendance at theaters where the producer's film

is being exhibited (see "checker" and "rent-a-distributor").

attorney (attorney-at-law) — A person who has been admitted by a state's highest court or a federal court to practice law in that jurisdiction. In order to be licensed to practice, attorneys generally must pass a course of study at an accredited law school and pass an exam administered by the state bar association. Some states also now require that practicing attorneys participate in a required minimum number of hours of continuing professional education activities (see "Code of Professional Responsibility," "conflicts of interest" and "ethics").

attorney-in-fact — One who is an agent or representative of another and given authority to act in that person's place and name. The document giving the attorney-in-fact authority is called a power of attorney (see "power of attorney").

"A" type vehicle — (same as "'A' title").

auction — The sale of a property to the highest bidder (see "bidding war" and "spec script").

audience — The group of people who see a film or to whom a film is generally directed (see "primary audience" and "secondary audience")

audience demographics — (see "demographics").

audience fractionalization — The dividing up of movie goers and television viewers among numerous and various entertainment alternatives, thus theoretically decreasing the size of the potential audience for any given offering. The trend has caused problems for motion picture production companies and network television which had previously designed movies and programming to appeal to a mass audience (see "homogenous films").

audio cassette — (see "cassette").

audit — An inspection of the accounting records and procedures of a business, government unit or other reporting entity by a trained accountant, for the purpose of verifying the accuracy and completeness of the records. It may be conducted by a member of the organization (internal audit) or by an outsider (independent audit). An IRS audit consists of the verification of the information on the tax return. It is not likely that an audit on behalf of motion picture profit participants will rise to the level of a complete audit which is so thoroughly executed that the auditor's only reservations have to do with unobtainable facts. In a complete audit, the auditor examines the system of internal control and the details of the books of account, including subsidiary records and supporting documents, while reviewing legality, mathematical accuracy, accountability and the application of accepted accounting principles. This is a technical accounting term establishing audit standards (same as unqualified audit). Producers can raise the question of a complete or unqualified audit in negotiations for audit rights although such audits are not likely to be permitted by distributors. Experienced entertainment attorneys recommend that profit participants do audit any motion picture that has any likelihood of going into net profits. An audit of studio books for a domestic theatrical release may cost $30,000 or more, but few if any of such audits, do not pay for themselves. Audits of major studios have uncovered millions of dollars in errors, most of which seem to be in the studio's favor (see "audit rights," "broad auditing

rights," "limited review," "sub-distributor" and "underreported rentals").

audited cash production budget — An audited film budget prepared after completion of the film that excludes deferments (see "audit").

audit fees — The compensation paid to an auditor (e.g., a motion picture net profit participation auditor for his or her services relating to a review of the books and records of a business such as a motion picture distributor). The fees for a film distributor audit relating to a give film may be in the twenty-five to thirty-five thousand dollar range, but for a "successful film" such audits will generally recover ten times that amount for net profit participants (see "audit" and "auditor").

audition — A trial performance to appraise an actor or actresses' suitability for a specific role in a motion picture (see "screen test").

auditor — An accountant (and sometimes attorneys) who are authorized to examine and report on a business' books of account (see "advocate auditing," "audit," "audit rights" and "profit participation auditor").

auditor's certificate — (same as "accountant's opinion").

audit rights — The power and authority to conduct an inspection of the accounting records and procedures of an entity. Such rights present an important issue with respect to the negotiation of feature film distribution agreements, since the calculations relating to gross receipts and net profits are typically very complex and rely on so many contractually defined terms, while the provisions of such agreements also very often leave a great deal of discretion in the hands of the distributor. Unfortunately, experienced motion picture profit participation auditors have reported that even on occasions where an audit has uncovered an inadvertent mistake or actual wrongdoing the results of which tend to financially favor the distributor as opposed to any other participants, some distributors merely shrugged their shoulders and say "oh well" which is the equivalent of saying the producer's only remedy is to sue (see "audit," "blacklist," "broad audit rights," "contract of adhesion," "discretion," "problem producer," "remedy" and "sue us").

audit trail — The step-by-step record by which accounting information can be traced to its source; the physical evidence of an entity's expenditures which are reviewed in an audit (see "audit").

auteur — A French concept holding that the director of a film is the true creator or author of the film, who brings together the script, actors, cinematographer and editor and molds all such contributions into a work of cinematic art with a cohesive vision (see "collaborative process" and "creative control").

author — One who writes or composes a book or other literary work (see "certificate of authorship").

authority — The permission or power held by or delegated to another (see "contract of adhesion," "discretion" and "power").

authorized shares — The maximum number of corporate shares of any class that a corporation may legally create under the terms of its articles of incorporation (see "corporation").

automatic dialogue replacement — The recording and synchronization of non-production, studio-recorded dialogue tracks with corresponding film images. The replacement voice may be that of an actor other than the one shown on the screen and replacement dialogue may be in a language other than that spoken during the original production (also known as "dubbing" and "looping"; see "dialogue replacement").

availability — The date a motion picture can be shown commercially in a market in accordance with the offer by the distributor to the exhibitor (see "true availability").

availability analysis — An objective determination as to whether a specific form of film production financing may be obtained by a producer for a given film project. As a pre-condition to the so-called "pro and con analysis" (i.e., the analysis relating to advantages and disadvantages of the various forms of film finance), the producer must first make a realistic appraisal of what forms of film finance are actually available to him or her for the subject film project. For example, many producers know at the outset that their proposed film is not of interest to the major/studio distributors, that it is not adequately packaged to attract a negative pickup distribution deal, that they do not want to give up creative control or that they do not have access to prospective investors. Thus, several important traditional sources of feature film financing may be eliminated right away by using this initial level of analysis and the producer does not even have to bother with the pro and con analysis for forms of film finance that are not realistically available for a specific project (see "advantage," "disadvantage," "financing" and "pro and con analysis").

average gross per screen — The gross box office receipts per movie screen for a given motion picture per week, unless another period is stated (see "gross per screen").

average major studio margins — A statistical median representing the ratio of the gross profits to net sales for the major studio/distributors. Average major studio margins are closely watched by financial analysts and have reportedly been in decline in recent years (i.e., less than 10 percent). Such margins during most of the 1980s were greater than 10 percent, but were never higher than 17 percent, even during the so-called "product shortage" years of the late 1970s. Some analysts assume that since the major studio/distributors are consistently profitable, their management must of be competent. Alternatively, in light of the fact that studio films generate incredible sums of money, the studio margins are kept arbitrarily low by paying such high salaries and other forms of compensation to top executives, talent, attorneys and agents, most of whom are Hollywood insiders (see "Hollywood insiders," "supply and demand" and "profitability").

average negative cost — An industry statistic usually calculated by the MPAA for films produced by member companies and presented as a statistical median for a given year. The average negative cost for an MPAA movie in 2005 was reportedly in the neighborhood of 60 million dollars. Studio executives and their representatives are fond of pointing to escalating advertising expenses, high labor costs and the demands of gross profit participants as the primary culprits in the escalation of negative costs while spokespersons for "A" level talent counter that if the studios would quit playing games with their books (thus making net profits virtually obsolete) there would be little need to demand gross participations. In addition, studio executive compensation, passed on to each film as part of the overhead charge, adds to the cost (see "creative accounting," "gross participants," "profit participants" and "videocassette revenue reporting").

aviation insurance — Insurance protecting against the risk of loss due to the use of an airplane in the production of a movie (see "insurance").

award advertising — Promotional materials and activities used in conjunction with events designed to honor films or certain film elements (see "advertising").

B

back end — A film's revenues generated from exploitation of the film in all or specified markets. Percentage participations in such revenues are negotiable but are usually not paid until after distribution and/or production costs have been recouped (see "back end deal," "contingent compensation," "gross participant," "net profits," "percentage participation" and "points").

back end deal — A contractual arrangement providing for contingent compensation to be paid to a designated recipient at a defined stage of a film's revenue stream. Such compensation may take several forms including gross participations, net profit participations, bonuses paid upon achieving gross receipts equal to specified multiples of the film's negative costs, escalations of percentage participations triggered by similar revenue levels, retroactive payments and even reductions in such compensation if certain revenue levels are not achieved (see "back end," "contingent compensation" and "percentage participation").

back end negotiations — The discussions relating to who will be paid monies out of a movie's revenue stream, at what point and at what level or percentage (see "back end deal" and "back end participations").

back end participations — Percentage participations in a film's revenue stream generated by the exhibition of a movie (see "percentage participation," "points," "revenue stream" and "up front salary").

background cast — The people, objects, set pieces and scenery that form the setting against which the foreground players and action are placed. An extra is also referred to as a background player (see "atmosphere" and "extra").

backlist — [same as "catalog (library)"].

back lot — That portion of a motion picture studio that is used for exterior filming (see "exterior" and "location").

backstage.com — An online website that provides news and casting information for actors. The service started as Back Stage in New York in1960. Back Stage West in Los Angeles was added in 1994 and then after the Internet came into existence, BackStage.com came online in 1997. The service provides a place where actors can connect with the nationwide performance community. Back Stage is owned by Netherlands-based VNU Inc., whose other entertainment and media publications includes

The Hollywood Reporter, Billboard, Adweek, Mediaweek and *Ross Reports*. VNU also owns measurement company Nielsen Media Research (see "Nielsen Media Research").

bad boy rules — (same as "disqualifiers").

bad debt — An open account balance or loan receivable that has proven uncollectible and is written off; amounts earned by a specific film and owed to the distributor of the film but which the distributor will not be able to collect because the debtor is insolvent. Distributors will generally deduct such amounts before making payments to the producer. Profit participants may want to seek to limit distributor discretion to claim amounts that are uncollectible and establish some objective criteria in the distribution agreement for which "bad debts" may be written off (see "creative accounting" and "uncollectible indebtedness").

bad faith — A willful failure to respond to plain, well-understood statutory or contractual obligations; the absence of good faith (see "covenant of good faith and fair dealing" and "good faith").

bad faith denial of contract — A relatively new tort recovery based on a defendant's bad faith conduct in asserting a stonewall ("see you in court") defense to an ordinary commercial contract. Recent cases have held that the elements of the cause of action are (1) an underlying contract, (2) which is breached by the defendant, (3) who then denies liability by asserting that the contract does not exist, (4) in bad faith and (5) without probable cause (see "bad faith," "probable cause," "sue us" and "tort").

bad title — Ownership rights that are legally insufficient to convey property to a purchaser (see "marketable title").

bad weather insurance — Insurance that provides reimbursement to a film's producer, up to the limit of insurance, for each scheduled filming day canceled due to any type of bad weather (i.e., rain, high winds, storms, clouds, etc.). This coverage can be adapted to include automatic coverage for rescheduled shooting days (see "insurance").

balanced print — A copy of a motion picture that has been color corrected or graded (see "color corrected").

balance sheet — A financial statement that gives an accounting picture of property owned by a company and of claims against the property on a specific date. Generally, a summation of assets is listed on one side and liabilities are listed on the other side. Both sides are always in balance (contrast with "income statement").

balloon payment — Final debt payment that is substantially larger than the preceding payments. Loans with a balloon payment are sometimes referred to as partially amortized loans (see "moratorium").

ballpark figure — An estimate (see "projections").

bank — Federally or state regulated financial institutions, some of which have entertainment divisions that lend funds for film production. Usually such banks will only lend against so-called "bankable" guarantees provided by pre-sale or distribution agreements and most such banks will only lend to established producers with guarantees that in the aggregate exceed the production budget. In addition, such banks will invariably require that a completion bond be in place on the film. Banks do not generally invest in films (i.e, they do not share in the financial risk). Banks make money off the interest charged and, in some instances, on certain fees (see "bank legal fees," "completion bond," "investment bank" or "investment banker," "merchant bank" and "negative pickup").

bankable — A descriptive adjective used in the film business to describe someone or something (e.g., actors, directors, producers, projects, distributors, etc.) whose commitments supposedly can be taken to a bank and on which the bank will lend money for film production purposes, partly because of the prior successful performances of such individuals, entities or projects. Actually, the term, when used in that sense is a misnomer since the banks will still generally require some form of collateral or guarantees in lieu of collateral and that usually means the distribution agreement and guarantee of a credit-worthy distributor (see "bank loan," "bondable" and "collateral").

bankable actors — Actors or actresses whose box office appeal will favorably influence entertainment lenders to be more inclined to lend monies for use in producing a given film if such actors or actresses are committed to playing a role in the film. On the other hand, the phrase is somewhat misleading in the sense that the banks do not actually base their decision to make a production loan on the presence or absence of actors, but instead on the existence of a distribution agreement and guarantee from a credit-worthy distributor (see "bankable").

bankable distribution contract — A film distribution agreement, executed in advance of a film's production which will influence

entertainment lenders to be more inclined to lend money for production of the film. Most entertainment lenders will only be favorably influenced by such distribution contracts with major studio/distributors or a small number of other established independent distributors and agreements that provide a distributor guarantee (see "negative pickup," "pre-sale financing" and "split rights deal").

bankable pre-sale commitments — Contractual commitments to distribute a film in a specific territory or medium made prior to completion of the film by a bank-approved distribution company and/or ancillary market entity for cable, home video, foreign markets, etc. that represent an acceptable credit-risk for the bank to lend production monies to the film's producer while contractually creating an obligation on such committing entities to repay the bank's loan (see "guaranty," "pre-sale financing" and "secured creditor").

bankable stars — (see "bankable actors").

bank borrowings — Loans from banks (see "lender financing" and "lender risk elimination").

bank discounting — (see "discounting").

bank financing — The funding of a film or film projects with bank loans. Banks generally make no value judgment on the quality of a film's script or the potential draw at the box office; rather its officers will look to the contracts the producer has secured from its domestic and foreign theatrical distributor(s), video, DVD, television stations, etc. The bank discounts such contracts to their present value and charges a competitive business rate of interest. Banks will also ask the distributor to agree to repay the bank loan plus interest upon delivery of the completed film (see "bank loan" and "discounting").

banking community — For purposes of the film industry, the entertainment banks as a group (see "bank financing").

bank lines — (see "line of credit").

bank legal fees — The professional fees paid to attorneys representing the interests of the bank or lender in a negative pickup or other lender financed transaction. Such fees are generally paid by the producer/borrower out of the borrowed funds, thus in addition to the legal fees, the bank will receive interest on such fees. The producer may want to seek a cap on bank legal fees (see "conflicts of interest" and "negative pickup").

bank loan — A film production loan provided by a bank. One advantage of this form of film finance is that the producer only has to repay the loan with interest and fees (i.e., the bank usually does not take an equity ownership interest in the project). However, such loans are rarely made to producers without a track record and a bankable distribution commitment, and such loans always require a completion bond (see "completion bond," "financing," "loan" and "negative pickup").

bank required documents — The documents generally required by a bank (or other lending entity) in order to provide a film production loan including proof of the producer's right to film the literary property under consideration, a copy of the distribution guarantee (or guarantees), a copy of the distribution agreement, copy of the completion guarantee, detailed budget, complete financial statement of any other investors involved, security agreement that puts the bank in a first lien position with

respect to the film, the literary property upon which the film will be based and the producer's share of receipts from all sources (i.e., the bank has the first legal claim to these assets), an agreement between the bank and the distributor in which the distributor agrees to pay the producer's share of receipts directly to the bank until the loan, fees and interest are repaid, and in which the distributor agrees to pay any unpaid balance on the loan at the time of maturity or forfeit distribution rights (see "completion bond," "inter-party agreement" and "negative pickup").

bankrupt — A person or entity that has engaged in any of the acts that by law entitle such person or entity's creditors to have his, her or its estate administered for the creditors' benefit (see "bankruptcy").

bankruptcy — A state of insolvency of an individual or an organization; an inability to pay debts when they come due. The taking or acquiescing in the taking of any action seeking relief under, or advantage of, any applicable debtor relief, liquidation, receivership, conservatorship, bankruptcy, moratorium, rearrangement, insolvency, reorganization or similar law affecting the rights or remedies of creditors generally. Bankruptcy is a legal process under federal law intended not only to insure fairness and equality among creditors of a bankrupt but also to help debtors by enabling them to start anew with property they are allowed to retain as exempt from liabilities, unhampered by creditor pressure and the discouragement of pre-existing debts. Feature film profit participants may want to make some effort to determine the financial stability of a distributor before choosing to utilize the services of such a distributor. A profit participant's share will generally not be forthcoming from a bankrupt distributor (see "liquidation," "mob controlled distribution company," "moratorium statutes," "receivership" and "reorganization").

bankruptcy clause — A provision in an agreement that provides certain rights in the event that one or the other of the parties to the contract goes into bankruptcy. In the case of a film distribution deal, the producer may seek to include a bankruptcy clause providing that in the event the distributor becomes insolvent or bankrupt, the rights to distribute the motion picture revert back to the producer (see "bankruptcy").

bargaining position — The various circumstances that add or detract from the strength or weakness of each of the parties involved in negotiating a transaction (e.g., distributors used to make the rather disingenuous argument that the practice of blind bidding tended to equalize the bargaining positions as between distributors and exhibitors; see "blind bidding," "leverage" and "negotiate").

bargaining power — The relative ability to control or favorably influence negotiations between parties. Often in negotiations between film distributors and producers, the relative bargaining power of the parties plays a significant role in determining whether numerous negotiated issues are resolved in favor of one or the other. Distributors typically have the stronger position, partly because the law of supply and demand is in their favor (i.e., there are many more motion pictures produced each year than there are distributors who are willing and able to distribute). In order to improve his or her position, the producer, on the other hand, must first assemble an attractive package and/or produce a quality picture, then seek to interest more than one distributor in its distribution. To the extent that a producer has more than one distributor interested in distributing the producer's film, the producer will theoretically increase his or her bargaining power — all other things being equal (see "inferior bargaining position").

bargaining strength — (see "bargaining position" and "bargaining power").

barred — Prevented or forbidden from beginning or continuing an activity. At one time, the major studio/distributors were barred from holding ownership interests in exhibition chains (see "conduct provisions").

barriers to entry — The impediments that must ordinarily be overcome in order to enter a particular kind of business or industry. For example, the barriers to entry into the distribution of major motion pictures are extremely high since substantial amounts of capital, significant expertise relating to the market place and relationships with talent and exhibitors are required. The concept of barriers to entry and whether such barriers are natural or artificial plays a role in antitrust law analysis relating to competition (see "antitrust laws," "merger guidelines," "Paramount Consent Decree of 1948," "relationship driven business," "reciprocal preferences," "rising production costs," "significant barriers" and "vertical integration").

basic agreement — (see "WGA agreement").

basic cable — The initial cable-television service that usually consists of twelve to twenty channels available off-the-air or via satellite and that is supported by advertising. Basic cable residuals are based on a percentage of the revenues as opposed to the flat dollar payment mandated by the guilds for the network syndication market, thus in recent years much of the off-network programming airs on cable instead of free television (see "cable television" and "free television").

basic elements — The essential components of a motion picture project that are often specified in the "picture specifications" section of a distribution agreement. Such elements are generally considered to include the underlying material or screenplay, director, producer, principal cast and the approved production budget (see "elements").

basic formula — A phrase sometimes used to describe the method employed in calculating net profits. The basic formula is thus commonly stated as: distributor's gross receipts minus distribution fees, minus distribution expenses equals producer's gross, and producer's gross minus the production costs of the motion picture minus interest, if any, leaves net profits, if any. Another shortened version would read: distributor's gross receipts less fees, expenses and costs equal net profits (see "contractually defined terms," "creative accounting," "gross receipts" and "net profits").

basic pay cable — (same as "basic cable").

basic story outline — A brief summary of a proposed motion picture screenplay that is sometimes used by experienced screenwriters or producers to submit a concept to studios or other production companies for development funding (see "one-line description," "logline," "outline," "synopsis" and "treatment").

baseline — A computerized subscriber entertainment industry information service providing information regarding above- and below-the-line film credits, box office grosses, celebrity and company contacts, information on film and TV projects in production and development, audience response and demographic data, industry news and analysis, the official Academy Awards database and pre-publication announcements of new literary properties (see "Entertainment Data, Inc.").

basis — IRS terminology for the capital invested in property; an amount that usually represents the taxpayer's cost in acquiring an asset, such as a motion picture. It is used for computing gain or loss on the sale or exchange of the asset and in calculating the depreciation deduction with respect to the asset. The taxpayer's tax basis in an asset is subject to adjustment due to depreciation and other transactions in which a taxpayer may engage (see "adjusted basis" and "return of capital").

"B" counties — The A.C. Nielsen Company designation for counties in the U.S. that have populations of more than 150,000 people, but are not "A" Counties (see "'A'-counties" and "Nielsen Media Research").

below-the-line — Film budget items relating to the technical expenses and labor (other than above-the-line) involved in producing a film (i.e., relating to mechanical, crew, extras, art, sets, camera, electrical, wardrobe, transportation, raw-film stock, printing and post-production). Below-the-line personnel include the production manager, cinematographer, set designer, special effects persons, wardrobe person and makeup artist. The phrase "below-the-line" refers to the location of the specific expense item/person on the film budget (see "above-the-line costs," "above-the-line employment agreements" and "below-the-line employment agreements").

below-the-line-costs — A major category of costs, charges and expenses incurred during the production of a motion picture other than the above-the-line costs and a third category often referred to as "Other." Below-the-line costs may include such items as mechanical charges, crew labor, overhead, extras, art and set costs, camera, electrical, wardrobe, transportation, raw-film stock and post-production. "Other" costs may include legal, insurance, completion bond, miscellaneous and a contingency (see "above-the-line" and "overhead").

below-the-line employment agreements — The written contract between a feature film production company and production employees who for film budget purposes are not classified as above-the-line (see "above-the-line").

below-the-line fringes — Compensation paid to or for the benefit of a film's crew in addition to their salaries. When such individuals are members of a guild or union, these benefits may include vacation pay and health, welfare and pension contributions. Also, such payments may be made directly to the guild or union by the film's distributor. Some distributors have reportedly overstated the cost of such benefits in determining the negative cost of a movie thus reducing the amount of money that might flow through to the producer group and others in the form of net profits. A producer must determine exactly what the below-the-line fringes are and how much they cost (see "creative accounting" and "unfair business practices").

beneficial exchange rate — A currency exchange rate that favors a particular currency relative to the value of the currency of other countries (i.e., that is more favorable currently than previously; see "exchange rate").

beneficial results — Any helpful, advantageous or useful consequences. The question of whether any beneficial results would flow from a proposed merger resulting in vertical integration is part of the U.S. Justice Department's antitrust law analysis relating to such mergers (see "antitrust laws," "merger guidelines," "Paramount Consent Decree of 1948," "TriStar Case" and "U.S. Justice Department").

beneficiary — The party in whose favor an insurance policy or letter of credit is issued (see "insurance policy" and "letter of credit").

best efforts — A standard of conduct in which the party performing an activity is required to put forth his, her or its maximum effort (see "best efforts clause," "conflicts of interest," "fiduciary" and "reasonable efforts clause").

best efforts clause — A provision in film distribution contracts that obligates the distributor to put forth its best efforts in distributing the film. In the event that a dispute arises between the producer and the distributor relating to the distributor's efforts in distributing the film, this clause would serve as a standard by which a court would determine if the distributor had met certain obligations under the agreement. Best efforts is a higher standard than reasonable efforts, so producers negotiating with distributors would be better advised to use the "best efforts" language in such drafting situations. If other more objective standards of conduct are available, it might be even more effective to use the more specific language in place of the rather generalized best efforts clause (see "affirmative obligation" and "reasonable efforts clause").

best efforts offering — A securities offering in which the underwriter or broker/dealer commits to use its best efforts to sell the issue but without any purchase guaranty (i.e., an underwriting agreement in which the underwriters do not assume the risk of resale and agree to sell the issue acting only as agents of the issuing company; see "all or none," "firm commitment," "managing broker/dealer" and "underwriter").

bias — A partiality toward someone or something (see "discrimination," "favorable portrayal," "marketplace of ideas," "nepotism," "patterns of bias," "prejudice," "reciprocal preferences" and "unfavorable portrayal").

bicycling print — The exhibition of one print at two nearby theaters in staggered showings. The term originated with the transporting by bicycle of consecutive reels of film from one theater to another (see "print").

bid — A written or oral proposal (notification) from a theater-exhibition company in response to a bid solicitation from a film distribution company to bid or negotiate the terms for exhibiting a film and stating the terms under which the exhibitor will agree to exhibit such motion picture. This, supposedly competitive, bid is the exhibitor's offer for the right to license a motion picture for showing in a given market beginning on or about a specific date. The bid usually includes commitments for minimum playing time, if applicable, the holdover figure, clearances, guarantees, an advance paid by the exhibitor to the distributor, if any, film-rental terms and advertising terms (see "anti-blind bidding statutes," "blind bidding" and "negotiated deal").

bid and ask — The quoted prices, generally by market makers, for a stock trading in the over-the-counter market (see "market makers").

bidding — The practice of renting, selling or licensing motion pictures through the use of bids (see "blind bidding").

bidding war — A vigorous competitive auction of a property or property rights. For example, screenwriters and/or their agents occasionally succeed in instigating such competitive bidding for desirable spec scripts. Independent producers also attempt to initiate such bidding contests among distributors for the distribution rights to a completed motion picture. The result in some instances is that the price paid is higher than would have been paid under other circumstances, thus bidding wars sometimes favor the sellers as opposed to the buyers. However, from time to time, a round of such high prices paid for spec scripts will halt rather suddenly, fueling speculation that the major studio/distributors conspired to stop such activities or were at least guilty of conscious parallelism (see "antitrust laws," "conscious parallelism," "conspiracy," "reciprocal preferences" and "spec script").

bid request — A written notification from a distributor to all motion-picture exhibitors who own or operate theaters in a market area, notifying them that a specific motion picture is available for showing in that area on or about a certain date and inviting them to submit an offer (a bid) to license that picture. This request may contain terms such as length of playing time, guarantees, advances, film-rental terms, advertising terms and deadlines for submission. Such a bid request usually specifies that bid offers must be received by a certain time and date, usually no later than ten days subsequent to its issuance (see "blind bidding").

bid request letter — (see "bid request").

big-budget films — Motion pictures with high production costs which may range from $50 million to $100 million or so (see "low-budget films" and "medium-budget films").

Big Eight — An outdated reference to the largest eight U.S. accounting firms as measured by revenue. Due to mergers, acquisitions, criminal indictments and bankruptcies, the big eight has been reduced to the Big Five (see "Big Five").

Big Five — The five largest U.S. accounting firms as measured by revenue. The big five accounting firms are Arthur Andersen, Deloitte & Touche, Ernst & Young, KPMG and PW Coopers (see "Big Eight").

billing — The sequence, position and size of a performer, crew member, staff person or others' credits on the screen and in movie advertisements. Billing issues may be significant negotiating points in the respective agreements of such persons. The term is also used to refer to the actual list of contractually-required credits of persons involved in the production of a film (see "credits," "order of appearance," "order of credits," "prominence" and "top billing").

billing statement — (see "credit statement").

billings basis — With respect to the distributor prepared earnings statements provided to the producer, statements calculated on the basis of what the distributor has billed as opposed to what has actually been collected by the distributor (see "collection basis").

bit player — An actor who has a small speaking part, usually no more than two or three lines (see "extras").

blackball — To ostracize, boycott or exclude; originally the term was based on the use of a small black ball as a negative vote in deciding whether to admit someone for membership in an organization. In August of 2006, some members of the Hollywood community openly called for actor/director Mel Gibson to be blackballed for his alleged anti-Semitism (see "anti-Semitic sword" and "anti-Semitism").

blacklist — A list of persons with whom business is not to be conducted or who are not to be hired. The concept received a great deal of publicity in the '40s and '50s when the fear of communism allegedly prompted many studios to blacklist persons who were suspected of un-American activities. Some in the industry today still fear being openly critical of the status quo within the film industry (i.e., the dominance of the major studio/distributors) for fear of being blacklisted. Obviously, it is not necessary for a physical list actually to exist for those in Hollywood control positions to effectively "blacklist" certain persons considered undesirable for any arbitrary reason. A history of blacklisting in Hollywood existed prior to the so-called Communist blacklisting of the late '40s and early '50s and continues through today (see "anti-Semitism," "bias," "discrimination," "prejudice," "problem producer" and "sue us").

blacklisting — The listing of persons who are not to be hired. Some profit participants who are film industry professionals that hope to continue to work in the film industry, suggest that one of the main reasons why most persons who feel they have legal grounds to bring a cause of action against a major studio/distributor or other distributor is this fear of being blacklisted. Further, it is suggested that one of the main reasons the lawsuits that are initiated are ultimately settled is this same fear (see "anti-

Semitism," "bias," "blackball," "blacklist," "Buchwald Case," "prejudice" and "sue us"; also see "Blacklisting — A Way of Life in Hollywood" in *Hollywood Wars*).

black track print— An answer print that has no sound, just the picture (see "answer print").

blanket network buys — Purchases of national television advertising on the major networks (e.g., by film distributors who are opening a film in wide release; see "media mix").

blind bidding — A film distributor practice through which film-distribution companies (principally the major studio/distributors), send a bid request letter to exhibitors and without having previously screened the film for exhibitors that are invited to bid on exhibition of the film, request that interested exhibition companies submit bids to license a motion picture for showing in a given market. Blind bidding has alternatively been defined as the bidding, negotiating, offering of terms, acceptance of a bid or agreeing to terms for the purpose of entering into a license agreement prior to a trade screening of the motion picture that is the subject of the agreement. Laws that prohibit completion of exhibition contracts before exhibitors have the opportunity to view the movies on which they are bidding have been passed in a number of states. Independent distributors rarely require blind bidding and independent exhibitors consider it unethical at minimum. They ask the question, "How can any retailer in any business be expected to sell a product sight unseen?" Blind bidding provides the large theater chains with a significant competitive advantage over their smaller independent competitors. The larger chains have greater financial resources, thus they can accept the risks inherent in blind bidding (i.e., that they

will contract to exhibit a film that would have been unacceptable if it had been viewed in advance and which results in a poor performance at the box office for the theater). The independent exhibitors are generally out-bid anyway by their larger competitors for a "can't miss" film like a sequel to a prior blockbuster, but with respect to marginal films, the smaller independent exhibitor does not possess the financial resources to take a chance on the film's success. Thus, the blind bidding process effectively leaves the independent exhibitor with the leftovers which for many, results in financial doom. With the re-entry of the major studio/distributors into exhibition and the presumed accompanying participation in the policy decisions of the National Association of Theater Owners, the major studio/distributors have also placed themselves in a position to oppose NATO's support for anti-blind bidding legislation at the state level and NATO may have been the only national association which might have advocated the passage of such laws on behalf of independent exhibitors (see "antitrust laws," "anti-blind bidding statutes," "blind selling," "closed bidding," "five o'clock look," "lobbying," "major exhibition chains," "major studio/distributors," "market share," "negotiated deal," "non-regulatory states," "number of screens," "predatory practices" and "trade screening").

blind check — The covert monitoring of the activities of a theater's box office personnel by a checker who is posing as a regular patron and observing such activity (see "checker" and "open check").

blind pool — A limited partnership or manager-managed limited liability company offering that has not committed its resources or offering proceeds to a specific property or project at the time of capital contributions by the investors (i.e., an investment vehicle that does not specify the properties the management plans to acquire). Investors in a blind pool must more carefully evaluate and rely on the track record or prior performance of the investment vehicle's upper level management as opposed to a specific property. State regulations may impose limits on such offerings (e.g., the percentage of offering proceeds that may be used to acquire such unspecified properties in certain offerings; see "pool investments" and "track record").

blind pool agreements — Motion picture distribution deals that are executed before the specified films to be distributed are identified (see "output deal").

blind selling — A practice whereby a distributor licenses a feature before the exhibitor is afforded an opportunity to view it (the other side of the transaction described as "blind bidding").

block booking — The film distribution practice of tying together one or more motion pictures for licensing within a market (i.e., a distributor will accept a theater's bid on a desirable film or films contingent on the exhibitor's promise that it will also exhibit one or more less desirable films). This practice is considered to be a violation of the federal antitrust laws and was addressed by the Paramount consent decree of 1948 in which the major distributors at that time were forbidden to employ the practice. The basic thrust of this decree was to seek to prohibit block booking (i.e., to ensure that motion pictures must be licensed picture by picture, theater by theater, so as to give all exhibitors equal opportunities to show a given film). In a case involving the film "The Graduate" a U.S. District Court in the Central District of

California held that the studio's practice of block booking violated the Sherman Antitrust Act (see "antitrust laws," "packaging," "Paramount Consent Decree of 1948," "tracks" and "tying arrangement").

blockbuster — A subjective term used to describe a movie whose box office performance far surpasses the box office grosses of the average motion picture released in recent times (see "hit," "successful film" and "tentpole film").

blockbuster strategy — A plan or scheme regularly implemented by executives of the major studio/distributors to use their so-called tentpole films (i.e., their hoped-for blockbusters) as leverage with exhibitors to get the exhibitors to exhibit the distributor's other less appealing movies during the balance of the year). The executives also hope that these so-called "tentpole" or "blockbuster" films will make enough profit to recoup the costs of their other films that do not make enough money to cover their production and releasing costs. The contracts between the major studio/distributors and exhibitors are drafted so that the exhibitors are able to retain a higher percentage of box office revenues the longer a film stays in the theater. For this reason, the exhibitors compete aggressively for the anticipated blockbusters. This gives the distributors leverage in their negotiations with exhibitors and allows the distributors to effectively block book (i.e., tie together as a package) several of their mediocre films with a hoped-for blockbuster; see "anti-competitive business practices," "block booking" and "tentpole film").

blocked currencies — Generally, monies earned by banks or corporations in a foreign country that cannot be removed from that country except under limited circumstances and thus, generally have to be spent within its borders. In the film industry, blocked currencies may be foreign film rentals and producers may want to negotiate a provision in the distribution deal that requires a certain portion of such funds be deposited in an account in such foreign country for the benefit of the producer (see "blocked funds deals" and "restricted currencies").

blocked funds — (same as "blocked currencies").

blocked funds deals — A variant method of motion picture financing that may be able to provide some below-the-line savings and in which a producer purchases blocked funds or currency at a discounted rate from banks or corporations doing business in a specific country. It would be even more advantageous to the producer if instead of having to come up with the monies to purchase such blocked funds, even at the discount rate, the producer could convince the owner of the blocked funds to convert its contribution of blocked funds into an equity position in the picture (see "blocked funds").

blocking — The coordination and setting of movements by actors in a movie scene (under the supervision of the director). Blocking utilizes floor marks and other spotting devices to aid the actor or actress in being at the right place at the right time (see "staging").

blowout — The rapid sale of all of the securities in a new offering (see "offering").

blow-up — An optical process for enlarging a film, usually in the case of feature films from 16mm to 35mm (see "reduction negative").

blue sky fees — The charges imposed by state securities regulatory authorities on public or private offerings of securities in their states (see "notice filing fee"; contrast with "registration fee").

Blue Sky Law Reporter — Five volume set of law books published by Commerce Clearing House, Inc. (CCH) that contains the texts of each state's blue sky laws (see "blue sky laws," "conditions and limitations" and "notice filing requirement").

blue sky laws — Popular name given to state statutes and regulations governing the offer and sale of securities in the various states. The term signifies state securities law compliance matters as opposed to federal securities law. The phrase originated in a state court decision involving securities in which the judge reportedly justified the need for securities laws and regulations as a means of discouraging unscrupulous promoters from coming into their state and selling their good citizens so many feet of "blue sky," meaning worthless property (see "blue sky fees," "conditions and limitations," "consent to service of process" and "securities acts").

blue sky memorandum — A document, usually prepared by securities counsel for the underwriters or securities issuers, that describes the conditions and limitations on the offer and sale of the securities in the states in which such offers and sales are contemplated in an offering. The memorandum is provided to the offering's issuer, the managing broker/dealer and other brokerage firms invited to join the underwriting syndicate or selling group (see "conditions and limitations," "issuer" and "managing broker/dealer").

blurbs — Short, highly commendatory public notices. In feature film advertising, it is common for the publicity staff of a motion picture distributor to use a few positive words or phrases from an otherwise negative review to promote a movie, but in some cases they actually will ask movie critics to manufacture a blurb for the distributor's use in advertising a picture. Some critics reportedly will even send out a series of favorable quotes on a newly released movie hoping one will show up in the movie's ad and result in more name recognition for the critic. Even worse, a SONY employee apparently created a fake (i.e., non-existent) film critic that sent out blurbs on which some moviegoers based their decision to go see certain movies. SONY was sued for the practice (see "advertising," "conflicts of interest," "press kit," "promotional quotes," "puffery" and "unethical business practices").

"B" movie — A genre of motion pictures shot on a low budget, with a short production schedule and without major stars. Most exploitation fare and art film product are considered "B" movies (also called "'B' pictures," "'B' product" and "'B' titles"; see "'A' titles").

"B" negative — The part of a film negative that is not used in the finished cut negative. Sometimes portions of the "B" negative may be used in the preparation of a film trailer. Also some films are re-released with scenes not used in the original theatrical release (see "'A' negative" and "trailer").

BO — (see "box office").

board of directors — A group elected by a corporation's shareholders to set company policy and appoint the chief executives and operating officers (see "corporation").

body copy — The principal text of a motion picture advertisement that conveys the theme of the film (see "copy," "headline," "tag line" and "title treatment").

boilerplate — Language found almost universally in legal documents of a given type, often in small print. In any dynamic industry such as the film industry, there is seldom any such thing as "standard" language in contracts. A producer should not be intimidated or mislead into accepting such language if it does not meet the needs of the specific parties and transaction. In addition, it is prudent to insist on comprehensible documents. They can be complex, but they must be understood by the parties involved (see "contracts" and "contracts of adhesion").

boiler room (or shop) — A place devoted to high-pressure sales by telephone of all sorts of securities, commodities or products, some of which have questionable value. Extensive fraud is usually involved, but successful prosecution is often difficult since the operation may disband before effective legal action may be taken (see "fraud" and "telemarketers").

bomb — A film that fares poorly at the box office (see "blockbuster" and "hit").

bona fide — In good faith; without fraud or deceit (see "good faith").

bond — A long-term note issued under formal legal procedure and secured by some form of collateral (see "corporate bond," "debt financing" and "sinking fund"). Also, a written instrument with sureties, guaranteeing faithful performance of acts or duties contemplated (see "completion bond," "principal" and "surety").

bondable — A descriptive adjective used in the film business to describe someone or something (e.g., producer, production company, director, actors, line producer, etc.) which when attached to a film project will enhance the ability of the producer to obtain a completion bond for the film. The assessment by the completion guarantor will be partly based on the success of such individuals or entities in bringing prior film projects in under budget and on time (see "completion guarantor").

bonus — Something given in addition to what is usual or strictly due. In the case of production-financing/distribution agreements, a bonus is sometimes provided as a form of contingent compensation for the producer who brings the film in under budget and on time. Bonuses may also be awarded to producers, directors, actors and/or writers when revenues generated by the exploitation of a motion picture exceed certain specified levels (see "contingent compensation" and "percentage participations").

book — As a noun the term in its broadest sense refers to a set of written or printed sheets bound together into a volume. Books sometimes serve as the underlying material for a motion picture screenplay (see "novel," "play" and "underlying property"). As a verb in the film industry, the term refers to the activity of scheduling motion picture engagements for theatrical exhibition (see "booker").

booker — The person (usually a film distribution company employee) responsible for all aspects of monitoring and trafficking the actual motion-picture prints throughout the markets over which the booker's branch office, or other unit of distributor organization, has jurisdiction (see "booking" and "booking agent").

booking — The activities related to the scheduling of a motion picture for exhibition in a theatre on a given date (see "booker," "booking agent," "bookings" and "engagement").

booking agent — Any person or business entity, designated by an exhibitor to act on the exhibitor's behalf, who acts as the exhibitor's agent in the renting, selling or licensing of motion pictures for exhibition. A booking agent may (and usually does) represent more than one exhibitor so long as such exhibitors' theaters do not compete (see "booker").

bookings — The contractual arrangements relating to the scheduling and exhibition of a film in a given theater (see "booker").

books and records — The volumes of business journals, accounts and chronicles of any of various kinds; the written evidence of a series of business transactions. In the case of a distribution deal the books and records that relate to the distribution of a film and which are of vital importance to the producer and other net profit participants (see "audit," "creative accounting" and "profit participant").

books of account — The financial records of a business (see "books and records").

book value — In reference to corporations, the net worth of the corporation (i.e., the worth of the assets minus the cost of the liabilities). The various methods of computing book value vary significantly and there is no standard method for ascertaining book value (see "corporation").

bootleg — The unauthorized and therefore illegal reproduction of a film, videocassette or DVD for commercial sale (see "piracy").

borrow — To receive something with the implied or expressed intention of returning the same or an equivalent (see "lender financing").

borrowing agreement — The written contract used by a feature film production company to employ the services of an individual director, artist, performer or crew member who utilizes a loan-out company. Borrowing agreement is the same as lending agreement except expressed from the perspective of the borrowing production company (see "lending agreement," "straight employment agreement" and "three-party agreement").

borrowing base formula — A banking formula used in calculating the amount of funds a bank will lend to a borrower. In film, the formula will include considerations such as the production company's assets and its distribution commitments (see "bank financing" and "loan").

bottom line — The ultimate financial result of a transaction or the operation of a business (see "profit margin").

boutique — A small, specialized business firm that deals with a limited clientele and offers a limited line of products (e.g., a boutique broker/dealer firm or boutique feature film production company; see "financial supermarket").

boutique studio — A film production company operated under the umbrella of a major studio (see "housekeeping deal" and "output deal").

box — (see "jacket").

box office — A movie theater's ticket booth, where moviegoers pay money for the tickets that are presented at the door for admission into the theater and to see a specific movie (see "box office gross" and "checker").

box office appeal — The ability of an actor or actress to attract an audience into a theater that is exhibiting a movie in which such actor or actress stars (see "marquee value").

box office comparables — A comparison of the box office or other performance of films of similar genre and budget that have already been produced and exhibited for the purpose of estimating a reasonable projected performance for a similar film being considered for production and/or financing. Such comparisons are typically presented in tabular form and utilize the gross box office figures or reported distributor rentals for similar films that are made available through the trades or other industry publications. Box office comparables are not part of financial projections but may form the basis for certain assumptions associated with the financial projections (see "financial projections," "grossing potential," "past performance" and "similar pictures").

box office domination — The stronger performance at the theatrical box office of a specific film, genre of films or films distributed by a specific segment of the industry. For example, statistics originally developed by industry analyst Art Murphy and reported in *Variety*, then subsequently included in the Harold Vogel book *Entertainment Industry Economics* (second edition), indicated that approximately 50 percent of the U.S. motion picture screens generated about 67 percent of the box office gross, while about 75 percent of the screens generated approximately 90 percent of the box office gross (see "number of screens").

box office gross — The total amount of money that has been paid by the public to an exhibitor for admission tickets to see a specific motion picture before any expenses or exhibitor percentages are deducted (i.e., the actual dollar amount taken in at the box office). Also the accumulated totals of box office gross for a single film in a market or territory or all markets or territories (see "checker," "concession sales," "house nut," "gross," "gross per screen," "film rentals" and "skimming").

Box Office Magazine — A motion picture trade publication that is published monthly out of Hollywood and which editorially focuses on information relating to the business side of the motion picture industry. The magazine also provides a guide to currently released and upcoming theatrical films, along with reviews (see "trades").

box office receipts — The actual amount taken in at the movie box office (see "box office gross" and "rentals").

box office risk — The possibility that not enough moviegoers will purchase tickets to see a given movie to justify the financial risk involved in producing the motion picture. A lender will generally not assume any of this risk and thus will require that a distributor guarantee a production loan. Thus the only risk the lender assumes is that relating to the credit-worthiness of the distributor (see "distributor credit-worthiness," "lender risk elimination" and "risk").

boycott — A concerted effort to refrain from commercial dealing with a specific business; also a refusal to work for, purchase from or handle the products of a specific business. Although a boycott is not always illegal, a conspiracy to injure a business through intimidation or coercion may violate the Sherman Antitrust Act. Specific interest groups have from time to time resorted to attempts at boycotting a given film based on the perception that the interest group is unfavorably portrayed in the film. Such boycotts directed toward individual films have not been effective over the long run since patterns of bias have continued in the content of motion pictures for many years (see "antitrust laws," "hidden agenda," "favorable portrayal," "marketplace of ideas," "patterns of bias," "Sherman Antitrust Act" and "unfavorable portrayal").

"B" picture — (see "'B' movie").

"B" product — (see "'B' movie").

branch — The office located in a given city (usually major urban areas), staffed by employees of a film-distribution company, responsible for bidding out (licensing) the film company's motion pictures and other products, if any, servicing prints to customers and collecting film rentals that are due. Business is generally conducted with exhibitors within certain geographic regional boundaries or relative proximity to the branch office. The major distribution companies have generally maintained individual branches in twenty-five to thirty major U.S. cities. Branch staffs typically include a branch manager, sales-persons, bookers, cashiers and clerical personnel (see "exchange" and "settlement transaction").

branch manager — The employee of a film distribution company that is responsible for supervising the activities of a given motion picture distribution branch office (see "branch").

breach of contract — A party's failure to perform some contracted-for or agreed-upon act.

In drafting a film distribution agreement vague and subjective terms or phrases should be eliminated, particularly with respect to the film's specifications or delivery requirements. Otherwise, the distributor may seek to use such vague or subjective terms or phrases as an excuse to allege breach of contract by the producer and as grounds for not performing its distributor duties pursuant to the terms of the distribution agreement (i.e., not distributing the film as promised; see "cure" and "default").

break — (noun) A distinct stage in the release of a film within a market (i.e., the calendar date on which a film first becomes available for exhibition within a geographical area). A film's national break may not be the same as that film's break for a more limited geographical area such as major keys, ordinary keys or sub-keys. A break, whether first run break, second-run break, etc. consists of a specific combination of theaters playing a motion picture in a given availability. As a verb, to open a film in several theaters simultaneously (see "availability," "major key," "ordinary key," "play date," "run" and "sub-key").

breakage — The action of breaking a contractual promise (e.g., in the context of a production-financing/distribution agreement, the studio would take the position that a budget overage would constitute breakage of the producer's undertaking not to exceed the approved production budget). Breakage might trigger certain contractual over-budget penalty provisions (see "bonus," "breach of contract" and "over-budget penalty").

break down — (see "production breakdown").

breakeven — The point at which sales equal costs. In film, the specific point at which an exhibited motion picture neither makes nor loses money (i.e., receipts cover all costs attributed to the picture by the individual or entity calculating breakeven). After this point, a film begins to show a profit, before it, a loss. In other words, breakeven is the point in a movie's revenue stream at which the income to the exhibitor, distributor or producing entity is said to equal such entity's cost of producing and/or distributing the movie. Breakeven, thus, will be different for each of the different individuals or entities involved with a film, although the most commonly referred to "breakeven" is the distributor's breakeven. Generally, this is the point at which deferred compensation on a studio financed film is paid. In some cases, the costs of distribution continue to escalate ahead of the pace at which receipts are generated. Reportedly fewer than 5 percent of motion pictures released in recent years and using the major studio/distributor net profits definition have earned a profit (i.e., achieved breakeven; see "actual breakeven," "artificial breakeven," "cash breakeven," "creative accounting," "first breakeven," "gross floor," "profit," "recoupment" and "rolling break-even").

breakeven for distributor — That point in a motion picture's revenue stream after the distributor has deducted its distribution fees, at which the distributor is able to recoup its distribution expenses and advances to the producer, if any, out of the distributor's gross receipts (see "actual breakeven," "artificial breakeven," "cash breakeven" and "creative accounting").

breakeven point — (see "breakeven").

breakout — A significant expansion of a film's bookings after an initial period of an exclusive or limited engagement (e.g., a film that is a surprise hit; see "crossover film").

breakout picture — (same as "breakout").

breakout potential — The prospects that the performance of a motion picture at the box office will be so favorable that its bookings will be significantly increased (see "breakout").

bribery — The voluntary giving or receiving of a gift or something of value in an unlawful attempt to corruptly influence the performance of an official duty (see "commercial bribery," "discount," "kickback" and "rebate").

bridge financing — A short-term loan made in anticipation of intermediate-term or long-term financing (similar to "interim credit facility").

bridge loans — Loans made to corporations during periods of transition (see "corporation").

British territory — A foreign market for film distribution purposes that may be defined in the distribution agreement, typically, as the United Kingdom of Great Britain and Northern Ireland, the Republic of Ireland, the Isle of Man, the Channel Islands, Malta, Gibraltar, and ships and aircraft flying the British flag and camps wherever situated and where British forces are stationed (see "foreign territories").

broad auditing rights — A film producer's negotiated authority to audit the books and records of a distributor with few restrictions. Distributors typically want to limit audit rights by restricting when the audit may be started and conducted, limiting the purpose of the audit, restricting who may conduct the audit, requiring that copies of all reports made by the producer's accountant be delivered to the distributor at the

same time as the producer, placing limits on the amount of time an audit may take, allowing only one audit each year, only permitting individual records to be audited once, limiting the period during which objections may be made, providing that all statements by the distributor are binding unless objected to in writing within a certain period of time, forever barring the producer from instituting any lawsuit unless timely objection is made and only permitting review of the books of the subject picture (even when the picture is marketed with other pictures as a package). Distributors will also insert language that permits them to keep records in their own unique way (see "audit," "audit rights" and "good distributor").

broadcast — The act of transmitting sound or images by radio or television through the airwaves. Commercial broadcasters sell broadcast time that is used for the dissemination of information, entertainment and advertising messages (see "radio" and "television").

broadcast television (TV) — Advertising supported television including networks, independent stations and public broadcasting stations; the industry that transmits visual images and sound through the airwaves via the very-high-frequency (VHF) or ultra-high-frequency (UHF) channels (see "broadcast," "cable," "free television," "pay," "pay-per-view TV" and "television").

broker — Any person or entity engaged in the business of effecting securities transactions for the account of others, but not including a bank; a person who acts as an intermediary between a securities buyer and seller, usually charging a commission. Sometimes a broker purchases securities on behalf of his or her customers, for which he or she is compensated solely by commissions. When a broker buys, he or she buys not for himself or herself, but for his or her customers. The activities of brokers are regulated by the Securities and Exchange Commission and the National Association of Securities Dealers pursuant to the Securities and Exchange Act of 1934 as well as by the state securities regulatory agencies in each state in the U.S. Registered representatives (sometimes called account executives) work for and are supervised by broker/dealer firms (see "broker/dealer," "dealer," "finder," "investment adviser" and "registered representative").

brokerage house — A firm or company of SEC/NASD securities broker/dealers (see "broker," "broker/dealer," "finder," "private securities transaction" and "registered representative").

broker/dealer — A commonly used term including both brokers and dealers since most persons or entities who are either brokers or dealers typically perform or are licensed to perform the activities of both. Such persons or entities must be registered with the Securities and Exchange Commission ("SEC"), the National Association of Securities Dealers ("NASD") and with the appropriate regulatory agency in each state in which such individuals or entities may seek to offer or sell securities including units of film limited partnerships or manager-managed limited liability companies (see "broker," "dealer," "investment adviser" and "registered representative").

broker/dealer sales — One of three methods for marketing securities, in this case, through broker/dealers who are paid commissions for such sales (see "broker/dealer," "finder sales" and "issuer sales").

broker/dealer selling agreement — An agreement between a securities broker/dealer firm and the issuer in a securities offering setting out the terms under which the broker/dealer will sell the securities offered by the issuer (see "managing broker/dealer" and "selling broker/dealer").

"B" title — (see "'B' movie").

Buchwald Case — A breach-of-contract lawsuit filed by humorist Art Buchwald and motion picture producer Alain Bernheim against Paramount Pictures relating to the Eddie Murphy film *Coming to America*. The trial judge first ruled in January of 1990 that Paramount breached its option on Buchwald's treatment and that *Coming to America* was substantially based on Buchwald's treatment. He later ruled that the net-profit formula used by Paramount was unconscionable. The judge characterized the profit-participation formula used by Paramount (which is similar to the net-profit formulas used by all of the major studio/distributors in the film business) as "...an insidious device used by the studios to perpetuate their control...and to create an economic caste system in Hollywood...." Paramount testified during the trial that the movie had grossed more than $300 million worldwide but had not yet reached net profits. Some legal experts suggest that the case will not serve to encourage other plaintiffs who may want to sue the major studio/distributors since an equivalent of some $2 million in attorneys fees and costs were incurred on the plaintiff's side during the trial phase of the litigation. These same experts further suggest that only rarely will anyone hoping to continue to do business in the industry seek a court fight with the major studio/distributors for fear of being blacklisted, whereas in Buchwald's case, he did not have that same concern since he did not ordinarily rely on the motion picture business for his livelihood (see "contract of adhesion," "creative accounting," "gross receipts," "Hollywood outsider," "inferior bargaining position," "market power," "net profits," "profit participation litigation," "sue us," "treatment" and "unconscionable contract").

budget — Generally, a statement of the amount of money that is required for a particular purpose (i.e., an estimate of the anticipated expenditures for a specified period). In film, a listing of all probable expenses anticipated to be involved in the production of a motion picture (see "budget overruns," "hidden contingency" and "litigation budget").

budget administrator — The person responsible for managing a film's budget during the film's production and for seeing that actual expenditures in the various budget categories do not exceed the budgeted amounts (see "budget," "completion bond," "over-budget penalty" and "production accountant").

budget forms — Pre-printed forms setting out typical film production expense categories with spaces for entering the dollar amounts (see "budget").

budget overages — (same as "budget overruns" and "penalty free cushion").

budget overruns — The dollar amounts by which a film budget category is exceeded (see "penalty-free cushion").

burden of persuasion — The obligation of a person in a debate or discussion to present affirmative evidence that tends to demonstrate the truth of statements or allegations made. As an example, if someone in the film industry alleges that someone else is anti-Semitic (not an uncommon allegation in Hollywood and more often than not directed by a Hollywood insider or Hollywood apologist toward a Hollywood outsider) the person making the allegation has the burden of persuasion and without the presentation of persuasive evidence in support of the allegation such allegations are at minimum reckless and irresponsible and should be disregarded (see "burden of proof").

burden of proof — The duty of a party to substantiate an allegation or issue in litigation either to avoid the dismissal of that issue early in the trial or in order to convince the trier of fact as to the truth of that claim and hence to prevail in a civil suit. The term is also used in a less formal sense in business negotiations or discussions to indicate that a party making a statement has the obligation to provide some form of persuasive evidence that the statement is true before the statement need be relied on in such negotiations or discussions (see "burden of persuasion" and "burden of proof file").

burden of proof file — A collection of the written evidence that tends to show compliance with the conditions and limitations imposed on the use of a given exemption from the securities registration requirements (e.g., in a film limited partnership or manager-managed limited liability company offering). Such evidence is compiled by the issuer (e.g., producer/general partner/manager) of such securities and used to demonstrate compliance with the securities law requirements in the event that investors or regulators should question such compliance (see "burden of proof" and "private offering").

burnout — The point in time when a tax shelter's tax benefits are exhausted and when an investor starts to receive income from the investment (see "tax shelter").

Burstyn v. Wilson — The U.S. Supreme Court case first applying the protection of the First Amendment to the medium of feature films. The court also stated in the decision that "It cannot be doubted that motion pictures are a significant medium for the communication of ideas. Their importance as an organ of public opinion is not diminished by the fact that they are designed to entertain as well as to inform." Burstyn v. Wilson (343 U.S. 495, 1952) In this case, the film industry was asking the court to protect film as free speech. The studio position in the Burstyn v. Wilson case, of course, conflicts with the rather disingenuous arguments made so often in more contemporary times whenever a controversial film is criticized and the studio or MPAA executives resort to the "Well, movies are merely entertainment" defense." (see "idea," "MPAA" and "propaganda").

business affairs department — A major administrative unit of the typical motion picture studio/distributor that is primarily responsible for conducting the initial negotiations relating to the more important deal points in the studio's agreements with producers, directors, talent and writers or their respective agents. In contrast, the legal department is primarily responsible for negotiating the details of such agreements and reducing the agreements to long form contracts (see "creative affairs department," "deal memo," "legal department," "long form agreement," "production department" and "studio").

business affairs executive — A studio employee who holds a position of administrative or managerial responsibility in the business affairs

department of the studio (see "business affairs department").

business manager — An individual, usually a CPA, who handles the financial and business aspects of an entertainment client's career. Actors, performers, directors and some producers may have business managers in the entertainment business. A fee of five percent of the artist's gross receipts is commonly charged by the business manager for his or her services. The business manager's functions can range from simple accounting services to paying the client's bills, advising on investments, running tours and other extremely complicated functions. A business manager has strong fiduciary obligations to the client (see "agent" and "fiduciary").

business plan — A written outline and description of a proposed commercial activity or business, often used for planning purposes but also sometimes used in obtaining start-up financing from non-securities venture capital sources or other investors (i.e., active investors). Some elements commonly found in business plans are also similar to a specifically mandated and major section within the much broader securities offering disclosure documents often referred to as the "description of business." To the extent that a business plan is being used to actually raise money, it must be combined with a suitable investment vehicle (see "disclosure document," "offering memorandum," "plan of business," "producer's package" and "prospectus").

business practices — The customary procedures and activities engaged in by commercial enterprises (same as "trade practices"; see "antitrust laws," "anti-competitive business practices," "agency packaging," "blind bidding," "block booking," "conduct restrictions," "creative accounting," "franchise agreements," "predatory practices," "price fixing," "product splitting," "reciprocal preferences" and "tying arrangement").

buyer's market — A market situation in which there are more sellers than buyers; the opposite of a seller's market. Generally speaking, the film distribution arena is a buyer's market (see "law of supply and demand," "leverage" and "seller's market").

buying a gross — A huge advertising and promotional campaign for a film that loses money in the domestic theatrical market but helps not only to generate some level of gross receipts for the film, but creates added value for the film in other markets and media. Producers may want to request some sort of cap or ceiling on the distributor's expenses for a given movie (see "direct distribution expenses").

buy/sell agreement — A contract or contractual provision that provides in the event of the death, retirement or withdrawal of a corporate shareholder the surviving shareholders have the right to purchase the stock of the deceased, retiring or withdrawing shareholder. Such agreements are sometimes referred to as cross-purchase agreements (see "corporation" and "shareholders").

buzz — The talk on the street regarding a film in progress. This early awareness of a film's initial and hopefully favorable "buzz" is considered critical to its subsequent box office performance. Creating this favorable "buzz" is so important that publicists are hired for certain movies primarily to generate such positive preliminary impressions (see "blurbs," "hype," "publicist" and "publicity").

bylaws — Rules adopted by the board of directors of a corporation for the regulation of the conduct of the corporation's affairs and that are subordinate to the provisions of the corporation's articles of incorporation and applicable statutory provisions (see "articles of incorporation" and "charter").

C

cable — (see "cable television").

cable television — Transmission of a television signal (picture and sound) for home viewing by wire (coaxial cable), as opposed to airwave broadcast. Cable systems generally cost extra to install and a fee or monthly subscription charge is assessed for subscription to their specific multi-channel service. Many cable systems offer subscribers an opportunity to see movies, sporting events, and other special programming not available on free TV (see "network," "pay cable," "pay-per-view," "pay TV," "television" and "subscription television").

calendar house— A motion picture theater that exhibits previously released films on a pre-scheduled basis, usually for only a few days, and that provides its patrons with a calendar of scheduled films (see "art house" and "house").

California Limited Offering Exemption — A state law [Section 25102(f) of the California Corporations Code] promulgated by the California legislature that provides an exemption from the state's securities registration requirements for offers or sales of any security in a transaction (other than an offer or sale to a pension or profit-sharing trust of the issuer) that meets certain criteria including a numerical limitation on the number of investors, that

purchasers either have a preexisting personal or business relationship with the issuer's upper level management, no advertising, purchases not be made for resale and a notice filing requirement. Most other states have similar transactional exemptions (see "notice filing requirement").

California Public/Private Exemption — A state law [Section 25102(n) of the California Corporations Code] promulgated by the California legislature that provides an exemption from the state's securities registration requirements and more specifically exempting offerings for amounts up to $5 million made by California companies to "qualified purchasers" whose characteristics are similar to, but not the same as, accredited investors under Regulation D. The exemption allows some methods of general solicitation prior to sales (see "model accredited investor exemption" and "Rule 1001").

call — A demand to repay a secured loan, usually made by a bank when the borrower fails to meet certain contractual obligations such as the timely payment of interest. When the loan is called, the entire principal amount becomes due immediately (see "lender financing").

cameo — A small vivid theatrical role often limited to a single scene. A cameo appearance often involves a name actor or actress (see "bit player").

camera operator — The film production person responsible for operating the camera at all times and maintaining the composition established by the director or, in some cases, by the director of photography (see "director of photography").

campaign — (see "advertising campaign").

campaign concept — The basic underlying theme around which a motion picture's advertising and promotional program is developed and implemented (see "advertising").

campaign package — All aspects of a film advertising and promotional program. The basic film campaign package includes the press kit (which in turn typically contains ad mats, film synopsis, cast list, running time for the film and suggested publicity articles for adaptation by the local media), a one sheet, the trailer (usually under three minutes), television ads, radio spots and black and white (8 x 10) still photos (see "press kit" and "one sheet").

can — The round metal container in which film is stored. A completed film or scene is said to be "in the can" (see "acquisition distribution agreement").

Cannes Film Festival — A major international film festival and market held annually in May at Cannes, France. Films compete for awards and rights to distribute films in various territories and media are bought and sold at Cannes (see "American Film Market," "film festivals," "film market" and "MIFED").

cap — A ceiling, upper limit or maximum (e.g., a film's distributor may seek to negotiate an extension to the term of a distribution agreement if the distributor has not recouped its advances during the stated term, but the producer may want to impose a reasonable limit or a cap on such extension). Also, a producer may want to negotiate a cap on the legal fees a lending bank pays its attorneys in a production loan transaction since such fees are paid out of the producer's loan and the producer thus must pay interest on such legal fees (see "ceiling," "inflation indexed cap" and "override").

capital — Broadly speaking, all the money and other property of a corporation or other enterprise used in transacting its business. The money invested in a business venture (for which a security may be issued) may be referred to as risk capital (see "capital contribution," "capital investment," "return of capital" and "risk capital").

capital accounts — That part of a business's accounting records where capital assets and expenditures, and the liabilities incurred to acquire such assets and make such expenditures, are taken into account. In the context of a limited partnership or manager-managed LLC, the accounts required by the IRS to be established for each investor when special allocations are utilized. The amount of the capital interest of each investor in such investment vehicles consists of that investor's original contributions, as (1) increased by any additional contributions and by that investor's share of the entity's profits and (2) decreased by any distribution to that investor and by that investor's share of the entity's losses. Detailed IRS rules regulate the creation and maintenance of capital accounts and an accountant should be consulted. Capital accounts do not bear interest (see "limited liability company" and limited partnership").

capital assets — Long-term assets that are not bought or sold in the normal course of operating a business (e.g., land, buildings, equipment, fixtures and furniture; see "capital," "capital gain" and "capitalize").

capital contribution — Generally, any capital contributed to a business enterprise. In a limited partnership or manager-managed LLC context, any contribution to the capital of the investment vehicle made by a unit purchaser, general partner or LLC manager (i.e., the amount contributed by an investor to such a direct participation program to purchase an interest). Such contributions generally include cash or other property, although they may include services (contrast with "capital" and "capital investment").

capital expenditure — The costs associated with acquiring or repairing property when such property or improvement has a useful life extending substantially beyond the taxable year (a capital asset). Such costs are not deductible for income tax purposes, but may be depreciated (see "depreciation" and "expenses").

capital gain — The difference between a capital asset's purchase price and selling price, when the difference is positive (see "capital gains rate" and "capital loss"). Almost everything owned and used for personal purposes, pleasure or investment is a capital asset. When a business or individual sells a capital asset, the difference between the amount it is sold for and the asset's basis, which is usually what was paid for it, is a capital gain or a capital loss. While all capital gains must be reported, the business or individual may deduct only capital losses on investment property, not personal property. Capital gains and losses are classified as long-term or short-term, depending on how long the property is held before being sold. If held more than one year, the capital gain or loss is long-term. If held for one year or less, the capital gain or loss is short-term (see "capital assets" and "net capital gain").

capital gains rate — The tax rate required to be paid by taxpayers on capital gains. Prior to 1988, the capital gains rate was lower than the tax rate on ordinary income (see "capital gains tax" and "net capital gain").

capital gains tax — Federal tax on profits from the sale of capital assets. Tax law previously specified a minimum holding period after which a capital gain was taxed at a more favorable rate than ordinary income. The Tax Reform Act of 1986, however, provided that capital gains be taxed at ordinary income rates starting in 1988, although there is considerable interest in Congress for reverting to a lower capital gains rate in the future (see "capital gain").

capital-intensive business — A business that requires large investments in capital assets; sometimes used to mean a high proportion of fixed assets relative to labor costs (see "labor-intensive" and "money laundering").

capital investment — Monies paid by an investor for an interest in a business as in the purchase of stock or other security (e.g., an interest in a film limited partnership or units in a manager-managed LLC). Also, money paid by a business entity for acquisition of a capital asset, or something for permanent use or value in a business (contrast with "capital," "capital contribution" and "risk capital").

capitalization — For accounting purposes, the allocation of an item of expense to the capital account because of the relatively long life of the asset acquired by the expense (see "amortization," "expense" and "FASB Statement No.53").

capitalize — To supply capital for. Also to compute the present value of anticipated income over a period of time or to record capital outlays as additions to asset accounts, not as expenses (see "capitalization" and "expenses"). For accounting purposes, to record capital outlays (business expenditures relating to the purchase or creation of fixed assets) as additions to asset accounts as opposed to expenses (see "capital," "expense" and "FASB Statement No. 34").

capital loss— The amount by which the proceeds from the sale of a capital asset are less than the cost of acquiring it (see "capital gain" and "loss").

capital markets— A general financial term referring to all markets where capital funds (debt or equity) are traded or may be raised, and including private placement sources in addition to the organized markets and exchanges. As profit margins are reduced, industry analysts report capital markets for the motion picture industry are drying up (see "industry profit margins" and "rising production costs").

capital requirements — The permanent financing needed for the normal operation of a business, that is, the long-term and working capital (see "capital").

capital stock — All shares representing ownership of a corporation, including preferred stock and common stock. The number and value of issued shares are normally shown, together with the number of shares authorized, in the capital accounts section of the corporation's balance sheet. Such figures may be viewed with some skepticism since subjective considerations may be involved in the determination of such values (see "corporation").

capital structure — A corporation's financial framework, including long-term debt, preferred stock and net worth. Capital structure differs from a corporation's financial structure which includes additional sources of capital such as short-term debt, accounts payable and other liabilities (see "capital").

capital surplus — A corporation's equity or net worth, not otherwise classifiable as capital stock or retained earnings (see "corporation" and "equity").

capital transaction — Any sale of portions of the property of a limited partnership, manager-managed LLC or interest therein (not including the sale of all or substantially all of the entity's property) and other similar transactions which in accordance with generally accepted accounting practices are attributable to capital (see "capital").

cap on return — In investments, a deal may sometimes be structured so as to limit the upside potential, (i.e., place a ceiling or cap on any prospective return on such investment), for investors in exchange for some downside protection. On the other hand, the fact that an investment provides no cap on the investor's return is likely to be considered desirable from an investor's point of view (see "ceiling," "downside protection," "pre-sales" and "upside potential").

captain — Teamsters union terminology for the person who is in charge of a film production company's transportation requirements. The teamster captain organizes and coordinates the transportation and driving operations of the project. The captain also arranges for the hiring of equipment (see "teamsters").

captions clause — A contractual provision usually found near the end of a written agreement (in the miscellaneous provisions section) which provides that the captions or paragraph headings in such agreement have been inserted for reference and convenience only and that such captions or paragraph headings in no way define, limit or describe the scope of the agreement or intent of any provision in such agreement (see "contract").

CARA — (see "Classification and Rating Administration," "MPAA" and "ratings").

carded preview — The showing of a film before its scheduled release date where the audience is asked to answer questions about their reactions to the movie on a card. This information is then used by the producer, director and distributor to make final modifications to the movie, if any, based on the audience reaction (see "preview" and "test marketing").

carryover — (same as "holdover").

carryover clause — (same as "holdover clause").

carryover figure — (same as "holdover figure").

cartel — A group of independent industrial corporations, usually on an international scale, that agree to restrict trade to their mutual benefit; a group of businesses or nations that agree to influence prices by regulating production and marketing of a product. Although more prevalent outside the U.S., such groups are generally found to violate federal antitrust laws.

A number of countries including the United States have laws specifically prohibiting cartels. A cartel, however, has less control over an industry than a monopoly. Trust is sometimes used as a synonym for cartel (see "antitrust laws," "conscious parallelism," "internationally competitive," "market power," "market share," "monopoly," "MPAA cartel," "oligopoly," "transnational cartelization" and "trust").

cartoon — An animated film short primarily designed to provide comedic entertainment. In some distributor/exhibitor deals a percentage deduction from box office receipts is taken by the exhibitor for showing the cartoon (see "pre-feature entertainment").

cartridge — A cylindrical shipping tube used by distributors in shipping film related materials. The costs associated with cartridges are generally considered distribution expenses (see "direct distribution expenses").

cash — The asset account on a balance sheet that represents paper currency and coins, negotiable money orders and checks, and bank balances (see "currency").

cash basis — The accounting method that recognizes revenues when cash is received and recognizes expenses when cash is paid out (see "accounting method," "accrual method of accounting" and "cash method of accounting").

cash basis items — IRS terminology used in direct participation programs (e.g., limited partnerships and manager-managed LLCs) and meaning items of entity deduction resulting from payments for interest, taxes, services or the use of property (see "direct participation program," "limited liability company" and "limited partnership").

cash breakeven — A concept that may be defined in several ways, but which in its most favorable form for a gross participant is defined as that point in a film's revenue stream at which gross receipts equal the film's negative cost, plus interest and distribution expenses excluding production and advertising overhead. A more favorable definition from the studio/distributor's point of view also takes into consideration some distribution fees, although lower than normal (e.g., 17.5 percent, to reimburse the studio for its internal costs of distribution, plus some level of production overhead). The concept of cash breakeven is sometimes used by the studio/distributors to make sure they have recouped their real costs (as opposed to their real costs plus some profit factor) before the payment of a gross participation obligations is triggered. For example, if gross participations are to escalate at different levels of breakeven, cash breakeven is usually considered the first breakeven (see "actual breakeven," "artificial breakeven," "breakeven," "first breakeven," "reduced distribution fee approach" and "rolling breakeven").

cash distributions — Amounts paid by direct participation programs to their investors in accordance with the terms of the partnership or operating agreement. These distributions initially represent a return of investment and therefore are non-taxable to the recipient. When their cumulative total exceeds an investor's tax basis in the entity (investment vehicle), however, the excess normally will be taxable (also sometimes called "distributable cash" or "partnership net receipts"; see "tax basis").

cash dividend — A cash payment by a corporation to its shareholders, distributed from the corporation's current earnings or accumulated profits and taxable to the shareholder as income (see "double taxation" and "stock dividend").

cash flow — Generally in business, an analysis of all the changes that affect the cash account of a business during an accounting period. In investments, cash flow is the same as cash earnings (i.e., net income plus depreciation and other non-cash charges). In the film business, the term is also used to describe how a movie's revenue stream flows from its source (i.e., the box office or other retail sales to the investors and other net profit participants who are generally last in line, showing what deductions are taken out along the way and by whom (see "cash distributions," "cash flow chart," "distributor's fee," "negative cash flow," "positive cash flow," "pro forma cash flow statement," "revenue stream" and "when the money's paid").

cash flow chart — A graphic illustration of how the money earned by a motion picture travels from the box office to investors including what deductions are made along the way. The structure of such cash flow charts will vary depending on the deals between the distributor and the producer, in addition to whether the production financing involved studio financing, lender financing or investor financing (see "cash flow").

cash flow crunch — A reduction either in the amount of funds returning to the financier's of motion pictures or in the rate at which invested funds return to such financiers. In the film industry today, cash comes back much more slowly than in the past, when domestic theatrical was the dominant market for the exploitation of films. Today, with ancillary markets such as home video/DVD and cable providing the bulk of film revenues, the industry and outside investors actually have to wait much longer to receive invested cash (see "cash flow cycle").

cash flow cycle — Both the route and amount of time involved for invested funds to move through the cycle of development, production, distribution, exhibition and exploitation in the ancillary markets then to return to the financiers of motion pictures (see "cash flow" and "cash flow crunch").

cash flow margins — The leeway between the amount of money coming into a business and that going out (see "cash flow crunch").

cash flow schedule — A projection of the manner in which and the time period during which funds invested will return to the investor or financier. In the context of a production-financing/distribution agreement a mutually approved cash flow schedule is used to establish the amount of production funds required each week in order to produce the movie and it is used to determine the amount of installment payments to be made by the studio/distributor/financier to the production company (see "pro forma cash flow schedule").

cash method of accounting — An accounting method under which income is subject to tax when actually or constructively received and deductions are allowed when actually paid (see "accrual method of accounting").

cash-strapped firm — A business entity that has so little paper currency and coins, negotiable money orders and checks and bank balances that the company's freedom of action is restricted (see "cash-flow crunch").

cassette — A cartridge that houses and protects video or audio tape. Audio cassettes have two channels going in one direction and two in the other, allowing two stereo programs on one cartridge. Tape lengths may vary (e.g., thirty minutes per side and forty-five minutes per side; see "DVD" and "videocassettes").

cast — The performers who play the roles in a film, including stars, feature players, bit and/or day players (see "crew," "day player," "extras," "feature player," "production staff" and "staff").

cast and crew insurance — Insurance that promises to reimburse the production company or producer (i.e., the insured) for any extra expense necessary to complete principal photography of an insured production due to the death, injury, or sickness of any insured performer or director or crew member (see "insurance" and "insurance coverages").

cast/crew agreement — (see "employment agreement").

casting — The activity involved in interviewing, negotiating contracts with and hiring the actors for a film. Usually commitments from some or all of the principal cast are obtained by the producer or director before the balance of the casting is conducted (see "package").

casting director — The film production person who specializes in knowing about their availability, finding and recommending the most appropriate actors and actresses for each speaking role in a film (see "casting").

cast list — A written compilation of the actors and actresses in a given film. In addition to the names of the actors and actresses, a cast list usually includes their corresponding character name, along with their address, phone number and agent contact. A cast list submitted to the

Screen Actors Guild on union films will also include salary information (see "residuals" and "SAG").

casualty insurance — Insurance that protects a policyholder against property loss, damage and related liability (see "insurance" and "liability").

casualty loss — Financial loss caused by damage, destruction or loss of property as the result of an identifiable event that is sudden, unexpected or unusual (see "insurance").

catalog (library) — A collection of copyrighted material or recorded masters embodying performances derived from exclusive and distinctive compositions producing a unique product. Film libraries and music catalogs are often bought and sold. A film library may eventually become a valuable asset for a production or distribution company, thus the ownership rights to a film may be considered an important negotiating point in transactions between a producer and distributor (see "asset value" and "backlist").

catalog promotions — Advertising and publicity used for the purpose of creating demand for packages of film or video titles. Video companies commonly engage in catalog promotions to market packages of previously released titles at reduced prices. In addition to stimulating secondary sales to retailers and providing them with the opportunity to replenish rental inventories, promotions (along with reduced prices) are intended to create demand for certain titles in the consumer purchase or sell-through market (see "backlist," "catalog" and "sell-through market").

cause of action — A claim in law and fact sufficient to demand judicial attention (see "litigation").

caveat emptor — A Latin phrase meaning, "let the buyer beware" and expressing the outdated principal of law that a purchaser buys at his or her own risk (see "warranty").

"C" corporation — A corporation that is not an "S" corporation for that year (same as "regular corporation"; also see "corporation" and "S Corp").

"C" counties — The A.C. Nielsen Company market designation for U.S. counties with a population of more than forty thousand people but that are not "A" or "B" counties (see "'A' counties," "ADI Market," "'B' counties" and "Nielsen Media Research").

cease and desist order — An order of a court or other body having judicial authority prohibiting the person or entity to which it is directed from undertaking or continuing a particular activity or course of conduct (see "injunction").

ceiling — An upper, usually prescribed limit (e.g., in negotiating with a bank for a loan, a producer may seek to establish a ceiling on the interest rate to be paid). Also, with respect to studio administrative and advertising overhead, profit participants or their representatives may want to ask that such overhead be subject to a ceiling if the overhead charges cannot be eliminated altogether or their percentages reduced (see "cap," "floor," "administrative overhead," "advertising overhead" and "offering ceiling").

celebrity — A person who has received a significant amount of public acclaim such as a movie star. Celebrities are often used to promote various products, services and even political ideas, although some segments of the population resent their involvement since their views appear to be simply for hire (see "actor" and "star").

censor — To examine in order to suppress or delete anything considered objectionable to the censoring individual or agency. Government censorship is not the only form of censorship, nor even the most common. Private agencies, institutions and/or individuals can also censor objectionable material. As an example, the Hollywood-based major studio/distributors have a long history of censoring material considered to be objectionable to the broader Jewish community in the U.S. As long as there is little diversity at the top in Hollywood (i.e., not all interest groups have the same power to censor) such censoring activities tend to convert the powerful communications medium of film into an instrument of propaganda.

censorable material — Part of an audio or visual presentation in a film that may be considered objectionable to an individual, agency or in a given jurisdiction. A definition similar to this actually appears in some film distribution agreements as a producer warranty (i.e., the producer promises not to include any "censorable material" in the film). An effort should be made to find more suitable (i.e., less vague) language to express this producer warranty, language that does not have such a chilling effect on the first amendment freedoms of producers, directors and screenwriters (see "obscene material," "pornography" and "ratings").

censorship — The act of applying guidelines as to what can or cannot be said or shown in the performing media arts. Such criteria may differ widely among various artistic media, within the medium itself and among various communities and countries. (see "obscene material," "pornography" and "ratings").

certificate — A formal declaration that can be used to document a fact (see "certify").

certificate of authorship — A document signed by the purported author of a screenplay or other literary work, which attests as to the identity of the original creator of the work, identifies the number of pages, date of completion, title and date of delivery (if applicable) and certifies to the fact that such person wrote such literary work and that he or she owns all right, title and interest in such work throughout the world. The certificate of authorship is generally the first document in a film's chain of title and allows the purchaser to record the copyright in its own name (see "chain of title").

certificate of code rating — (same as "MPAA certificate").

certificate of incorporation — The formal document issued by the secretary of state in the state in which a corporation is incorporated attesting to the fact of incorporation (contrast with "articles of organization"; see "articles of incorporation" and "charter").

certificate of insurance — A document provided by an insurance company that serves as evidence that a specific policy of insurance (e.g., an errors and omissions policy), is currently in effect and the premium has been paid for a specified term (see "insurance").

certificate of limited partnership — The form that is required to be executed and filed with the secretary of state in the state in which a limited partnership is being created as part of the process of forming a limited partnership. Upon approval by the secretary of state, the certificate is date stamped and certified as of the filing date (see "partnership certificate").

certified check — A check for which a bank guarantees payment. It legally becomes an obligation of the bank and the funds to cover it are immediately withdrawn from the depositor's account (see "bank").

certified financial planner (CFP) — A person who has passed exams given by the Institute of Certified Financial Planners, testing the person's knowledge of and ability to coordinate a client's banking, estate, insurance, investment and tax affairs. Financial planners may be compensated on a fee only basis, making no money on the implementation of their recommended plans or by means of a smaller fee while collecting a commission on each financial product or service their clients purchase (see "broker/dealer" and "investment advisor").

certified public accountant (CPA) — A person who meets the educational, training, exam and licensing requirements of the state in which he or she practices the profession of accounting. Accounting involves the recording and summarizing of business and financial transactions along with analyzing, verifying and reporting the results of such transactions. CPA's must take and pass the Uniform Certified Public Exam, which is offered in most states pursuant to the state's accountancy regulatory laws (see "Big Five" and "public accountant").

certify — To attest authoritatively (e.g., a corporate officer may certify as to the authenticity of a document; see "acknowledgment").

chain of title — The successive conveyances of a certain property commencing with the original source, each being (or purporting to be) a complete conveyance of the title down to and including the conveyance to the present holder (see "certificate of authorship," "chain of title documents," "clear title," "title" and "title search").

chain of title documents — The series of written instruments that demonstrate the successive conveyances of a certain property down to and including the conveyance to the present owner (i.e., documentary evidence supporting the producer's claim to the title of and right to film a literary property). Such documents may include a certificate of authorship, option and/or acquisition agreements, assignments, a title search report and opinion, WGA registration of the screenplay and copyright registration certificate. Motion picture financiers, production lenders, completion guarantors, distributors and errors and omissions insurance carriers will generally insist on obtaining copies of these documents prior to providing their respective services on behalf of a given motion picture (see "chain of title").

chairman of the board — A member of a corporation's board of directors who presides over its meetings and who is the highest ranking officer in the corporation, although the chairman may or may not have the most actual executive authority in a firm (see "chief executive officer" and "chief operating officer").

character — The personality or part that an actor re-creates (see "actor").

character actor — A performer who plays supporting roles and is known for playing a particular style or type of role (see "bit player" and "extras").

charter — After the secretary of state approves a corporation's articles of incorporation, the state issues a certificate of incorporation and these two documents together become the charter that gives the corporation its legal existence (see "articles of incorporation," "certificate of incorporation" and "ultra vires activities").

chasing a dream — Pursuit of a goal. Generally, people in the United States with its free enterprise system would not deny anyone the opportunity to pursue an important goal in life, but if that goal is more akin to a mirage, an illusion or a fantasy, then anyone who cares about an individual has an obligation to help the "dreamer" understand how unrealistic the goal is. There is probably no other industry that attracts so many people from all corners of the world to pursue the most unrealistic of dreams as the motion picture business, which is undoubtedly headquartered in Los Angeles, California. For the very few successes, there are thousands of shattered dreams and wasted lives. If this book can help add some balance and a modicum of reality to the perception of opportunity in the motion picture industry it will have provided a valuable service (see "free enterprise system," "law of supply and demand," "level playing field," "numbers game" and "pied piper").

checker — A person hired by producers or distributors or by checking services on behalf of producers or distributors to verify the number of paid ticket purchasing moviegoers in attendance at showings of a given movie (see "attendance checking," "checking and collection costs" and "skimming").

checking and collections costs — Distributor expenses incurred in monitoring the activities of exhibitors to ensure that reported film attendance and receipts are accurate and in investigating the unauthorized usage of motion pictures. These are important activities that can benefit the producer too, but participants may want to audit for documentation of such costs and consider double checking the checking services. Profit participants may also want to seek a cap on such costs (e.g., deductions of such costs shall not exceed 1 percent of the gross receipts for the picture; see "cap," "ceiling," "kickbacks" and "relationship driven business").

checklists — A list of things to be checked or done. In the context of entertainment industry agreements, the important points that need to be negotiated and/or provided for. Examples of entertainment industry agreements include option agreements, literary purchase agreements, screenwriter agreements, actor agreements, loan-out agreements, director's agreements, distribution agreements, etc. Most entertainment attorneys utilize such checklists to help ensure that no important provisions of such agreements are inadvertently overlooked (see "employment agreements" and "entertainment attorneys").

check print — A composite print sent by the laboratory to the producer for approval before release prints are prepared (see "answer print").

chief executive officer (CEO) — A corporation's executive officer principally responsible for the activities of the firm. A corporation's CEO may also be the chairman of the board, the president or an executive vice president (see "chief operating officer").

chief financial officer (CFO) — A corporate executive officer who is responsible for handling funds, signing checks, keeping financial records and financial planning for the corporation (see "chief executive officer").

chief operating officer (COO) — The officer of a firm, usually the president or an executive vice president, who is responsible for day-to-day management (see "chief executive officer").

choice of entity — A common question or issue confronting startup and growing businesses relating to which of the available forms of doing business would best serve the business' current and future needs. The choices generally include the sole proprietorship, general partnership, joint venture, member-managed LLC, manager-managed LLC, limited partnership, regular "C" corporation, "S" corp or non-profit corporation (see "fictitious name").

choosing a distributor — The method used by a producer in selecting the entity that will distribute the producer's film. The following describes an organized approach for identifying feature film distributors, a system that does not rely on the "who do you know" or "who do they know" method, but does require an organization such as a professional association of independent feature film producers to help underwrite the costs associated with research and maintaining the distributor files. [1] First the producer group must identify the available distributors by obtaining a current list of all feature film distributors in the U.S. (East and West Coast). This list should have the addresses, phone numbers, names and titles of key personnel (such lists are commercially available). [2] The producer should eliminate the distributors he or she already knows will not be interested in the movie because (a) they are too big or too little, (b) the producer prefers working with a West Coast or East Coast distributor and/or (c) the producer knows the distributor only handles certain types of movies and not the producer's type. [3] Then the producer should select five to ten distributors that he or she thinks are the best bets based on the producer's general knowledge of film distributors and [4] The producer should conduct a more detailed research and analysis of this limited group [i.e., determine who they are and what their track record is: (a) develop a list of the number and titles of all the movies they have distributed in the last ten years, (b) categorize each movie by genre, (c) obtain a synopsis of each movie, (d) obtain one or more reviews of each movie, (e) get the credits for each movie, (f) rent or purchase videos of some of these movies and view them, (g) evaluate the marketing and publicity campaign for the movies reviewed, (h) obtain and review press clippings for these distributors, (i) determine the box office performance of each such movie and (j) make a judgment as to whether this track record would appear to give the distributor much leverage with exhibitors]. [5] Prepare a producer's package for presentation to distributors (see "Producer's Package" herein). [6] In early meetings with distributors: (a) present and discuss the producer's package, (b) discuss some or all of the issues listed in #4 above with the distributor representative and determine if their history is indicative of the direction they want to go in the future, (c) determine what capabilities the distributor has for distributing your movie worldwide (i.e., do they have well-established organizations with branches in many countries or do they utilize the services of sub-distributors in certain territories), (d) determine whether the distributor is in a position to contribute substantial sums of money toward prints and advertising expenditures, (e) ask about other films the distributor is currently handling (the number and what they are about) so as to determine whether they are already committed to distribute other films which may detract from your film, and (f) discuss with and make suggestions to the distributor as to a marketing strategy for your film; placement, demographics of target markets, grassroots promotions, film festivals, etc. [8] Personal chemistry — Is this somebody you want to work with for a significant period of time on a project that is important to you and others who are relying on you? Again, this system cannot, as a practical matter, be implemented without the support of an effective association of independent producers (see "association projects," "FIND," IFP," "IFP/West," "industry groups," "Mob-Controlled Distribution Company" and "relationship driven business").

choreographer — A performer who creates and/or stages dance numbers (see "actor" and "director").

Christmas season — The second most important playing time of the year (after summer) for motion pictures (see "prime play dates" and "summer season").

churning — Excessive trading in a stock investment account in order to generate commissions for a broker with relatively little concern for the welfare or financial interests of the customer (see "broker/dealer" and "investment advisor").

cinema — A motion picture theater where feature films are exhibited; sometimes used to describe the motion picture industry (see "cinema data").

cinema data — Facts, figures, information and statistics relating to the motion picture industry (see "cinema" and "industry analysts").

cinematographer — A person with skills relating to the art and science of motion picture photography and who serves as cameraman and photographer for a film (see "director of photography").

circuit — A theater chain (same as "exhibitor circuit" and "exhibitor chain"; see "blind bidding," "block booking," "blockbuster mentality," "master agreement," "national circuit," "product splitting" and "tentpole film").

civil action — A legal action maintained to protect a private, civil right, or to compel a civil remedy, as distinguished from a criminal prosecution (see "litigation").

civil liability — The vulnerability of a person or entity to a lawsuit for damages as opposed to criminal charges (i.e, liability to court actions seeking private remedies or the enforcement of personal rights, based on contract, tort, etc.). In a civil action alleging securities fraud, for example, one of the civil remedies that may be available to the plaintiff is the right of rescission (see "rescission"). In such an action involving a private placement, the plaintiff's burden is merely to show that a security was involved, that the plaintiff invested money and that the security was not registered with appropriate securities regulatory authorities. Then the burden of proof shifts to the defendant who must show that although the security was not registered, the defendant complied with all of the conditions and limitations imposed on the use of available exemptions from the registration requirement (see "burden of proof," "burden of proof file," "conditions and limitations" and "private placement").

claim or claims — The assertion of a right to money or property (see "litigation").

claims made policy — An insurance policy that limits the insurance company's liability to only those claims that are made against the insured and reported to the underwriters during the policy period (see "named perils insurance policy").

class — In financial terms, a category of securities. Securities having similar features, but may also be subdivided into classes such as stocks, bonds, common and preferred stock, or Class A and Class B common stock. The different classes in a company's capitalization are itemized on its balance sheet (see "corporate stock" and "securities").

classic films — Feature films that are considered works of enduring excellence or which are noteworthy because of special literary or historical innovations or depictions. Broadly defined, the term may also include foreign films (also see "art film" and "foreign films").

classics department — A department of a major studio or production company that is responsible for the preservation and exploitation of the company's classic films (see "classic films").

Classification and Rating Administration (CARA) — The MPAA agency responsible for rating movies (see "MPAA" and "ratings board").

classified stock — Corporate common stock divided into two or more classes (e.g., a corporation may issue Class A stock to raise the bulk of equity capital while vesting voting rights in Class B stock, which is retained by management and/or the corporation's founders). Such a practice is usually confined to promotional ventures and relatively few publicly held companies have classified stock as part of their capitalization (see "corporation").

Clayton Act — A federal statutory amendment to the Sherman Antitrust Act that prohibits certain types of price and other discrimination, now covered by the Robinson-Patman Act. The Clayton Act also prohibits certain tying, exclusive dealing, total requirements agreements, mergers or acquisitions tending substantially to lessen competition in any line of commerce, along with interlocking directorates (see "agency packaging," "antitrust laws," "block booking," "combination in restraint of trade," "Robinson-Patman Act" and "Sherman Antitrust Act").

clear (banking) — The collection of funds on which a check is drawn and payment of those funds to the holder of the check (see "bank" and "certified check").

clearance — In exhibition, the exclusivity of a film's run within a competitive theater area for a time certain (i.e., the period of time, usually stipulated in license contracts, that must elapse between runs of the same feature within a particular area or in specified theaters); or the relative exclusivity a theater (exhibitor) specifies as a condition to licensing a motion picture within a market. A theater may request an exclusive run within an entire market or may request exclusivity for exhibition of a motion picture only over those theaters that are in geographic proximity and may be considered competitive. In film production, clearance also refers to the permission needed to utilize registered and/or copyrighted material in a film or television program (e.g., music, film clips and long quotations, and to use a location). Clearance in this sense means approving, taking care of or "clearing" all legal matters or questions relating to ownership rights to a film or underlying property, obtaining individual or location releases, making contractual arrangements, etc. In studio film finance, the term clearance refers to the projected profit and loss statement for a film that is continually updated (i.e., before a studio releases a film, it develops a "clearance" based on its best estimate of all revenues and costs; see "clearance procedures," "exclusive engagement," "errors and omissions insurance," "licensing terms," "music clearance," "Paramount Consent Decree of 1948," "personal release," "financial projections," "release," "right of privacy" and "runs").

clearance procedures — The steps to be taken (i.e., matters or questions to be investigated) by the producer's entertainment attorney or the insurer's attorney prior to final cut or first exhibition or broadcast of a film, before such film can be insured. Among other things, the following tasks are usually included: review of the script to eliminate matter that may be defamatory, invades privacy or is otherwise potentially actionable; copyright report; title report; written releases for people and locations; synchronization and performance licenses; along with written agreements between the producer and all creators, authors, writers, performers and any other persons providing material (see "errors and omissions insurance").

clear title — Title free from any encumbrance, obstruction, burden or limitation that presents a doubtful or even a reasonable question of law or fact (see "chain of title," "just title," "title" and "marketable title").

clip — A short portion of filmed material, sometimes used for promotional purposes or in another motion picture. Examples of film clips commonly used in other motion pictures include a movie playing in the background at a drive-in or a television program or commercial playing within a scene in another movie (see "film clip license" and "release").

close corporation — A corporation that meets statutory requirements in some states relating to limits on the number of shareholders and the shares of stock being sold privately. The close corporation election is typically made in the articles of incorporation and a shareholder's agreement modifies the usual powers of the board of directors (see "closely held corporation," "public corporation" and "S Corp").

closed bidding — A distributor practice wherein exhibitor bids on a film about to be released are opened by the distributor privately so that the exhibitors who did not win the bid for exhibition of such picture do not know the particulars of the bids submitted by their competitors. Distributors favor the practice, but exhibitors consider it unethical, since as a result, losing exhibitors are unable to determine how to change their bids so that they might be successful in the future or whether the best bid was actually chosen (see "bid," "blind bidding," "five o'clock look," "product splitting" and "unethical business practices").

closed corporation — A corporation owned by a few people, usually management or family members, whose shares have no public market; also called private corporation or privately held corporation (see "closely held corporation," "public corporation" and "S Corp").

closed town — Film exhibition terminology for a geographical area within which only one exhibitor operates theaters (see "competitive theater area").

closely held corporation — A corporation most of whose voting stock is held by a few shareholders but with enough stock publicly held to provide a basis for trading even though the shares held by the controlling group are not considered likely to be available for purchase (see "close corporation," "closed corporation," "public corporation" and "S Corp").

close-up — A film shot taken at short-range or through a telephoto lens, showing considerable detail of the subject (see "director of photography").

closing or closing date — The date on which the units offered in a limited partnership or other securities offering (or at least the minimum number of units offered) are fully subscribed for and accepted by management and the capital contributions made pursuant to the offering are released from the escrow or other bank account to the entity. In a fully underwritten initial public offering (IPO) of a corporation's stock, the closing generally occurs one week after effectiveness of the securities being registered and in that situation "closing" refers to the formal exchange of the issuer's securities for the proceeds of the offering (see "initial public offering").

clout — With respect to film industry negotiations leading up to striking a bargain (achieving a deal) the word clout refers to the influence, power, pull or leverage that a party to such negotiations has (i.e., the ability of such party to obtain, in the context of such negotiations, the results desired). Knowing what language would favor the interests of the producer in negotiating with a distributor is not the same as having the power to get such language into the distribution agreement (see "contract of adhesion" and "leverage").

code — The Internal Revenue Code of 1954, as amended (see "Internal Revenue Service").

Code of Professional Responsibility — The American Bar Association rules governing the ethical conduct of attorneys. The California State Bar has promulgated its own set of rules of professional conduct which vary somewhat from the ABA ethical standards. In either case, the 1992 UCLA Entertainment Symposium presented a panel discussion relating to attorney ethics in the motion picture and television industries only to discover that some of the entertainment attorneys on the panel and many in the audience appeared to express the belief that the entertainment business is significantly different from most other businesses and that bar association ethical standards cannot be applied in these industries as elsewhere (see "arrogance" and "conflicts of interest" and "ethical malaise).

co-feature — A film that is licensed for theatrical exhibition along with another film, as a package. Such films are typically licensed on a flat rental basis for a week's engagement, thus the distributor will not know and therefore must estimate how much of the film rentals received for the two films is to be allocated to each film in accounting for the revenues of a given film. Distributors will often seek to negotiate a provision in the distribution agreement that allows such allocations to be made in their sole discretion and without allowing the producer of the film to review the percentage allocations made to other films (same as "double feature"; see "creative accounting" and "discretion").

co-insurance — An insurance provision through which the insurer provides indemnity for only a certain percentage of the insured's loss. It reflects a relative division of the risk between the insurer and the insured, dependent upon the relative amount of the policy and the actual value of the property insured thereby (see "insurance").

cold call — A telephone call directed to a person who the caller does not know and the call is made for the purpose of trying to sell some product or service, take a survey or solicit an investment. In the context of a securities offering, a type of general solicitation involving direct contact, usually by telephone, with a prospective investor with whom the issuer has no pre-existing relationship. Cold calling is not permitted in conjunction with private placements (see "conditions and limitations," "general solicitation" and "limitations on manner of offering").

cold reading — An audition situation in which an actor or actress is required to read material he or she has never seen before (see "audition" and "screen test").

collaborative process — A series of actions or operations that proceed toward a particular result and in which people work jointly with others, especially in an intellectual endeavor. Both the financing and production of a motion picture area collaborative processes (see "auteur").

collateral — Assets pledged to a lender until a loan is repaid; property, including accounts, contract rights and chattel paper that have been sold, but are subject to a security interest. In most instances, in order to obtain a bank loan, it is necessary to offer some collateral (i.e., to place within the legal control of the lender some property that may in the event of a default be sold and applied to the amount owed). Collateral for a film production money loan might include the physical film elements that are created during production, the underlying literary property (e.g., screenplay, treatment and/or novel), the copyright in the screenplay or film, the rights to exhibit and exploit the motion picture and the rights to receive payments from various contracts for the exhibition and exploitation of the motion picture (also called "collateral security"; see "secured creditor" and "security agreement" and "studio security agreement").

collateralize — The pledging of an asset to a lender until a loan is repaid (see "assign," "hypothecate" and "pledge").

collection — The converting of accounts receivable into cash. Collecting revenues generated by the exploitation of a motion picture in all markets and media is an important function of a film distributor (see "collections").

collection basis — With respect to the distributor prepared earnings statements provided to the producer, a statement calculated on the basis of monies actually collected or received by the distributor as opposed to billings (see "billings basis").

collection ratio — The ratio of a company's accounts receivable to its average daily sales (see "collections").

collections — Costs incurred in connection with the collection of a film's gross receipts, including attorney and auditor fees and costs and any liability incurred by the distributor in connection therewith; a distributor expense item (see "direct distribution expense").

collection suit — A proceeding in a court of justice by which an individual seeks to obtain payment of monies owed or alleged to be owed (see "litigation").

collective bargaining — In labor law, the negotiation of employment matters between employers and employees through the use of a bargaining agent designated by an uncoerced majority of the employees within the bargaining unit. It is an unfair labor practice for employers to interfere with their employees' right to bargain collectively. Employers have an obligation to bargain with their employees in good faith, that is to meet with the representative at reasonable hours and negotiate about working conditions, hours and wages (see "good faith" and "guild").

collective bargaining agreements — Compacts relating to employment matters between employers and employees negotiated through bargaining agents designated by an uncoerced majority of the employees within the bargaining unit. The major studio/distributors are signatories to collective bargaining agreements between the studios and the various motion picture industry guilds. Recent complaints by studio spokespersons regarding the high costs of motion picture production lay part of the blame on union residual structures and the cost of below-the-line labor both of which are issues determined through collective bargaining. However, it is difficult to expect labor rollbacks on such items in view of the high levels of compensation paid to many studio executives, the gross participations granted to certain artists and studio accounting practices. Also, allegations have surfaced from time to time that the major

studio/distributors have succeeded in improperly influencing union and guild executives with respect to agreement provisions that turn out to be less than favorable for the union or guild membership (see "creative accounting," "gross participations," "guild agreements," residuals" and "signatories").

color corrected — Having conformed the chroma, hue, shade, tint and tinge of the visual images on film to a conventional or approved standard (e.g., the distribution deal delivery schedule may call for the delivery of a color corrected inter-positive). The specific color values of images on a film can be altered during shooting through the use of filters or during processing at the lab (see "balanced print").

column items — Brief written articles suitable for presentation to the print media and designed to elicit publicity for a movie (see "publicity material").

combination ad — One print advertisement in which two or more films are advertised. If combination ads are used, the distributor has to allocate its costs for such ad among the applicable films. In order to determine whether such allocations are fairly made as between the two films, profit participants must be able to review both sides of this transaction (see "allocation," "creative accounting," "double feature," "good faith," "discretion" and "negotiation").

combination in restraint of trade — An alliance of individuals or entities united to achieve an economic end, in this instance, interfering with free competition in business and commercial transactions, where such interference tends to restrict production, affect prices or otherwise control the market to the detriment of purchasers or consumers of goods and services. The MPAA and its member companies may be acting as a combination in restraint of trade as against the commercial interests of independent producers and distributors (see "idea," "concept," "marketplace of ideas" and "restraint of trade").

combined financial statement — A financial statement that brings together the assets, liabilities, net worth and operating figures of two or more affiliated companies (see "financial statement").

combo engagement — (see "double feature").

comfort letter — An independent auditor's letter required in certain securities underwriting agreements to assure that information in the registration statement and prospectus is correctly prepared and that no material changes have occurred since its preparation. Also a letter from one to another of the parties to a legal agreement stating that certain actions not clearly covered in the agreement will or will not be taken (see "prospectus," "registration" and "securities").

coming attractions — (see "trailer").

comment letter — A letter from the SEC describing deficiencies alleged and changes proposed by the SEC's staff in its review of a securities registration statement for a public offering of securities (see "pricing amendment," "public offering," "registration" and "securities").

commercial — When used as an adjective, a descriptive word or concept, applied to ideas, screenplays, completed movies and in some instances television programming, indicating the power of the project to draw paying customers to view it (i.e., the sales power of the project; see "hit").

commercial bribery — A statutory expansion of the crime of bribery that includes breach of a duty by an employee who accepts undisclosed compensation from others in exchange for exercising some discretion relating to the employee's work and granted to such employee by his or her employer (see "bribery," "discount," "kickback" and "rebate").

commercial distribution — Film distribution aimed at a mass audience with a large number of theaters playing the same film simultaneously in a given area or nationally, backed by extensive advertising expenditures, usually with emphasis on television advertising (see "wide release").

commercial loan — A short-term (typically ninety-day) renewable loan to finance the seasonal working capital needs of a business. Interest is typically based on the prime rate (contrast "bridge financing").

commercial paper — A form of debt (i.e., short-term obligations) with maturities ranging from two to two hundred and seventy days issued by banks, corporations and other borrowers to investors with temporarily idle cash. Such instruments are unsecured and usually discounted, although some are interest-bearing (see "interim credit facility").

commercial potential — A prospective judgment about how well a proposed movie will do at the box office (i.e., film financiers must speculate as to whether a sufficient number of moviegoers will pay for theater admission tickets to justify producing a given movie; see "commercial" and "good film").

commercial public exhibition — The showing of a feature film to a general audience made up of paying customers (see "public exhibition").

commercially acceptable — Suitable for commerce (i.e., of a quality that would enable the rights owner to license the film for a fee in the markets for which it was created (see "commercial distribution").

commercials — Generally, paid radio or television advertising broadcasts during breaks in programming (also called "spots" or "spot announcements"). In a feature film context, however, any paid appearance before or during the film of a product, commodity or service. The latter is sometimes referred to as product placement (see "distributor commercials" and "product placement").

commingling of funds — The acts of a fiduciary or trustee who mixes his, her or its own funds with those belonging to a client or customer; generally prohibited unless the fiduciary maintains an exact accounting of the client's funds and how they have been used. A distribution deal may contractually prohibit the co-mingling of the distributor's and producer's funds even though no fiduciary or trust relationship is established. It may be even more desirable from the film producer's perspective to require that the producer group's money be separated and deposited into a special trust account in its name. This requirement would be particularly helpful if the distributor declares bankruptcy (see "creative accounting," "fiduciary" and "trustee").

commission — In contracts, a form of payment for services performed based on a percentage of an amount collected, received or agreed to be paid for results accomplished, as distinguished

from salary (see "salary"). In securities, a fee paid to a broker/dealer for executing a trade or effecting a sale and based on the number of shares traded or the dollar amount of the sale. Also amounts paid to syndicators for underwriting and directing the sale of interests in a direct participation program. Commission expense for a securities offering is considered to be a syndication expense for tax purposes and must be capitalized rather than deducted unless the taxpayer makes the election pursuant to Section 181 of the IRS Code to deduct 100 percent of the film's production costs. (see "offering expenses," "royalties," "Section 181 of the IRS Code" and "syndicated expenses").

commissioned work — A category for "works made for hire" under U.S. copyright law including works specially ordered or commissioned for use as part of a motion picture, where the copyright is owned by the employer (see "work made for hire").

commission restrictions — Securities law limitations on the amount of transaction-related remuneration that can be paid for the sale of securities. Most state exemptions from securities registration, for example, provide that no form of transaction-related remuneration may be paid, directly or indirectly, to persons not licensed as broker/dealers. NASD guidelines on commissions also apply to public offerings (see "blue sky laws," "conditions and limitations" and "NASD").

commitment — An agreement or pledge to do something in the future. In film, producers of independent movies may seek and acquire commitments from major studios to acquire their films once completed. They may also seek pre-sale commitments from other markets (see "discounting," "negative pickups" and "presales").

commitment fee — A lender's charge for contracting to hold credit available. The commitment fee may be replaced by interest when the money is actually borrowed or both fees and interest may be charged (see "bank" and "lender financing").

commodity — An article of commerce; an economic good (see "idea," "intangible," "marketplace of ideas" and "product").

common law — Case made law (i.e., the system of jurisprudence that originated in England and was later adopted in the United States, Canada and other former English colonies). It is based on judicial precedent rather than statutory laws or legislative enactments (see "state legislatures" and "statutes").

commonly understood — Customarily and routinely agreed upon in the business. Many motion picture industry agreements provide that certain terms not otherwise defined within the agreement are to be defined as commonly understood in the industry. Such provisions merely provide a mechanism for determining the meaning of a term that comes into question, thus in the context of arbitration or litigation the fact finder will have to entertain testimony from persons with expertise in the industry to determine whether there actually is a commonly understood meaning for such a term. Unfortunately, many terms are not commonly understood in the industry and it is likely that experts with equal authority may be produced to define such terms to favor both sides of a dispute, leaving the fact finder to have to decide between differing interpretations of the same term. The better practice would be to negotiate

a definition of the term for the purposes of the agreement and include the definition in that original agreement, otherwise the party implementing the agreement has a certain amount of discretion in its conduct until challenged by the other party. Again unfortunately, the bargaining power of contracting parties in the motion picture industry is often vastly unequal, thus the party with the most power tends to get the definitions it wants (see "bargaining power," "contract of adhesion" and "discretion").

common stock — Units of ownership of a corporation; the ordinary stock of a corporation that is generally the voting stock of the corporation (see "preferred stock" and "share").

common stock equivalent — Preferred stocks or bonds that are convertible into common stock or a warrant to purchase common stock at a specified price or discount from the market price (see "corporation").

communication — The process through which information is transmitted; a technique used in the effective expression of ideas. In addition to hopefully being a form of entertainment, the motion picture is a form of communication and clearly one of the most effective, if not the most effective form of communication yet devised by human beings. As stated by the U.S. Supreme Court the motion picture is a significant medium for the communication of ideas (see "entertainment," "idea," "movies with a message" and "propaganda").

communications industry — A group of business enterprises engaged primarily in the dissemination of information (e.g., radio, free television, motion pictures, home video, cable television, newspapers and magazines; see "entertainment," "entertainment industry," "idea," "movies with a message" and "propaganda").

compact disc (CD) — A music industry sound reproduction and record format (i.e., an audio recording and playback device that is covered by a reflective plastic coating and uses a low power laser beam to read the audio information encoded in a series of closely packed spiral recording grooves). The compact disc emerged in the 1980's (following cassette tapes) and replaced the cassette tapes to became the dominant configuration formats for the record industry (see "laser disc").

company — An organization engaged in business as a proprietorship, partnership, corporation or other form of enterprise (see "corporation," "general partnership," "fictitious name company," "joint venture," "limited partnership," "limited liability company" and "sole proprietorship").

comparable films — Motion pictures that are similar in genre and production budget. It is important to producers and distributors to be able to make reasonable estimates of a proposed film's initial and long-term performance potential in all markets and such estimates or projections are generally based on assumptions drawn from information about the performance of similar projects that have been released in recent years (see "box office comparables," "financial projections," "project audience" and "profit projections").

compensation— Pay for work done or services performed. Compensation is generally an important issue to be negotiated in motion picture industry employment agreements and may take the form of salaries or contingent compensation including deferrals and/or profit participations (same as "remuneration"; see "bonus," "contingent compensation," "deferments or deferrals," "gross participants" and "net profit participation").

compensation arrangements — The various methods used to provide remuneration or pay for work done or service performed (see "advance," "compensation," "contingent compensation" and "up front salary").

compensation schedules — Statements of the minimum compensation levels for signatories to the Writer's Guild of America Theatrical and Television Film Basic Agreement as set out in such agreement (see "minimum wage scales" and "WGA Agreement").

competing pictures — Movies that are being exhibited in the same theater or in theaters in the same area close enough in time to cause moviegoers to choose between them. Also, movies produced and distributed or merely distributed by a film distributor that is simultaneously distributing a movie by a producer that may vie for a portion of the same potential audience (see "clout" and "leverage").

competition — The effort of two or more parties to secure the business of a third party by the offer of a better product and/or on the most favorable terms (see "antitrust laws" and "competitor").

competitive theater area — A geographical area, relatively well defined by the historical practice of distributors and exhibitors and by playoff records, within which theaters compete for an audience and within which an exhibitor normally would demand an exclusive run; since a major key may have more than one competitive theater area, the number of theaters simultaneously exhibiting a film's first run within a major key normally is equal to the number of competitive theater areas within that major key (see "key," "playoff record," "run" and "zone").

competitor — A business or individual selling or buying goods or services in the same market as another (see "antitrust laws" and "competition").

complete audit — An audit that is so thoroughly executed that the auditor's only reservations have to do with unobtainable facts. In a complete audit, the auditor examines the system of internal control and the details of the books of account, including subsidiary records and supporting documents, while reviewing legality, mathematical accuracy, accountability and the application of accepted accounting principles (same as "unqualified audit"; see "qualified opinion").

complete liquidation — The operation of winding up the corporation's affairs by settling its debts, realizing upon and distributing its assets. A status of liquidation exists when the corporation ceases to be a going concern and its activities are merely for the purpose of winding up its affairs, paying its debts and distributing any remaining balance to its shareholders. The decisive elements are an intent to liquidate coupled with acts done to carry out that purpose (see "dissolution," "liquidation" and "winding up").

completed motion picture — A finished feature film that is ready for release (except to the extent that a distributor may require certain changes). It is axiomatic in the motion picture industry that a producer who approaches a distributor with a completed motion picture, the production funding of which was not provided by the distributor, is likely to be able to negotiate more favorable terms in the distribution agreement than a producer who has either relied on at least partial funding by the distributor or has obtained a negative pickup agreement from the distributor prior to completion of the film, assuming of course that the quality of the film is the same in either event. Even more favorable terms are presumably available to the producer who approaches the distributor with prints and ads financing available (see "acquisition distribution agreement," "in the can," "negative pickup," "production-financing distribution agreement" and "rent-a-distributor") .

completion and delivery risk — The possibility of loss relating to the failure of a producer to complete and deliver a motion picture to the distributor for distribution in accordance with the delivery schedule. A lender will insist that the producer obtain a completion bond so as to shift the burden of assuming this specific risk from the bank to the completion guarantor (see "lender risk elimination" and "risk").

completion bond — A contractual guarantee assuring that a film will be completed and delivered pursuant to specific requirements, that is, on schedule, within the budget and without substantial deviations from the approved script. The completion bond provides protection against over budget costs and is supplied by a third party guarantor. It is written in the form of a surety instrument and usually authorizes the guarantor to take control over the production of the motion picture if the terms of the agreement are not met. In negotiations with the completion guarantor and the distributor, the producer may want to prevent the distributor from changing the producer's compensation, credit or continuing creative involvement in the event of takeover, particularly when the takeover is prompted by factors beyond the control of the producer. A completion bond is not a form of insurance, rather a surety or guarantee. Some studio produced films may require a completion bond. Nearly all lender financed films will require a completion bond. Independent films financed by investors from outside the industry rarely require such a bond (see "completion bond documentation," "cut-through endorsement," "guaranty," "surety" and "takeover rights").

completion bond documentation — Generally, before issuing a completion bond, a completion guarantor may want to review and approve of the final shooting script, production budget with detail, shooting schedule (production boards), preliminary application for completion guarantee, resumes of key personnel and principal cast, chain of title and supporting agreements regarding the script, producer's agreement with the production entity, director's agreement with the production entity, agreements with key members of the crew, production/finance agreement, evidence of insurance coverage which includes the completion bond company as an additional loss payee, principal artist contracts, post-production schedule (not later than two weeks prior to end of principal photography), music agreements, film and sound laboratory agreements and distribution agreements (if any), in addition to signed undertakings by the producer(s) and director to cast to budget and limit expenses, by the director that the budget, shooting schedule and post-production schedule are achievable and that the allocation of film stock in the budget is sufficient, and by the producer that music and all relevant clearances thereof will be obtained within the budgeted categories, that any delivery requirements pursuant to any distribution agreements and any publicity costs that are in excess of the approved budget will be considered to be distribution costs and expenses and will not be chargeable to the production budget and that legal fees charged to the production budget will be limited to the amounts budgeted therein (see "completion guarantor").

completion bond fee — The consideration paid to a completion guarantor in exchange for the completion guarantee. The fees traditionally range up to 6 percent of a film's budget, including interest, if any, and the 10 percent contingency, but excluding the completion guarantor's fee itself. Completion guarantors have sometimes utilized various means of modifying the fee to attract customers (e.g., requiring only payment of 3 percent up front and the other half only if the guarantor is called upon to advance funds or by providing a bonus or rebate of a portion of its fee) if the production is completed without any claims on the guarantor. Rebates above 10 percent have been typically reserved for the more experienced producers who have previously brought in films without calling upon the guarantee. At times, some fees have fallen to as low as 1.5 percent on the larger budgeted pictures or in instances where a producer can assure a guarantor the opportunity to bond multiple pictures. Such low fees may be dangerous to the bond companies in the long term. Low budget producers must be aware that the guarantor's fee is an added cost of the film's production although the service provided may be worth the expense. Under some circumstances, the completion guarantor may also ask for an equity position in the film (e.g., a specified percentage of net profits for every $10,000 advanced by the completion guarantor toward completion of the film; see "completion guarantor").

completion bond guarantee — (see "completion bond").

completion bond guarantor — A third-party, usually a bonding company, that agrees to advance funds necessary above the final approved budget of a motion picture so that the producer will be able to guarantee delivery of a finished, commercial quality motion picture conforming to the final approved shooting script of such picture, notwithstanding the fact that the final negative cost of the picture may exceed its final approved budget. The fee for such bond will typically range from approximately 3 to 6 percent of the film's production budget (see "surety").

completion fund — A sum of money raised by or set aside by a film industry organization or governmental entity specifically for the purpose of helping to finance the completion of motion pictures. Generally, such funds are used to pay for post-production expenses on selected projects (same as "finishing fund"; see "blind pool").

completion services — (see "post-production services").

component parts — Any of the elements of a film; the constituent portions or ingredients that make up a completed film (see "elements").

composer — The person who writes the music for a film. In the reservation of rights section of production-financing/distribution agreements (and certain other agreements) the parties may acknowledge that there may be certain composers who will wish to retain certain publishing rights in connection with the original compositions they create for use in or in connection with a motion picture (contrast with "music director").

composer's original score — The initial written arrangement of music as prepared by the person who wrote the music for a specific film (see "score" and "scoring").

composite — A single piece of film on which the corresponding sound and picture images appear in synch, either for editorial, camera or projection purposes (see "composite print," "in synch" and "synchronism").

composite dupe negative — A complete duplicate film with synchronized sound and picture images and with the light and dark parts in approximately inverse order to those of the original photographed scenes. A composite negative which, after exposure and processing, produces a duplicate negative picture and sound track image (see "negative").

composite master positive — A complete fine grain film print made solely for the purpose of producing composite or picture and sound dupe negatives that are in turn used for printing release prints (see "print").

composite negative — A complete film that has the light and dark parts in approximately inverse order to those of the original photographed scenes and is exposed and processed to produce both sound track and picture negative images on the same film (see "negative").

composite print — A processed positive film with both the visual images and sound track on the same film (see "composite," "in synch," "print" and "synchronism").

composite spliceless check print — A complete print of a film without editorial splices sent by the lab for approval to check the dupe negative. If okayed, release prints will be struck (see "print").

compound interest — Interest earned on principal plus interest that was earned earlier. Interest can be compounded on a daily, quarterly, half-yearly or annual basis (contrast with "simple interest").

comprehensive liability insurance — An insurance policy that protects the production company against claims for bodily injury or property damage liability arising out of filming a motion picture. The coverage usually includes use of all non-owned vehicles (both on and off camera), including physical damage to such vehicles. It is generally required prior to filming on any city or state roadway or at any locations requiring filming permits (see "worker's compensation insurance").

compromise — To settle by mutual concession (see "adhesion contract," "negotiate" and "leverage").

computer model — A simulated computer-based financial forecast used by some film production and distribution companies in an effort to obtain a clear prospective view of anticipated financial results of the company's proposed plans and strategies. With a computer model the company's executives and owners can adjust their picture mix and change the financing and distribution strategies to hopefully produce more favorable results (see "mental modeling" and "picture mix").

concentrated ownership — A situation in which the means of production in a given industry are controlled by only a few companies (e.g., in the film industry, more than 95 percent of the domestic theatrical box office gross is typically generated by films distributed by the major studio/distributors and their subsidiary/affiliates; see "market power," "major exhibition companies," "MPAA" and "oligopoly").

concentration of economic power — A convergence of financial and productive strength under the control of a few individuals or entities. The question as to whether the particular market is conducive to a concentration of economic power is one of the Justice Department's six tests used in analyzing proposed vertical mergers (see "antitrust laws," "merger guidelines" and "vertical integration").

concept — An abstract idea generalized from particular instances; the central theme of a movie. In the creative process the idea precedes the concept but the concept is considered the first element of a film, as in the joke: "I have an idea for a film and if I had just a little more money I could develop it into a concept." (see "development," "elements," "hook," "idea," "promotional concept" and "theme").

concession revenue — Gross receipts from the sale of food and drinks at a motion picture theater (see "concession sales").

concessions — (see "concession sales").

concession sales — Either the volume or revenue generated by the sales of popcorn, candies, drinks, etc. at a movie theater, 100 percent of which is generally retained by the exhibitor (i.e., not shared with the film's distributor or others; see "house nut").

concurrency — The near-simultaneous release of a U.S. film stateside and in one or more foreign territories. Concurrency is used to take advantage of a film's U.S. promotional campaigns and to help reduce the incentive for piracy (see "foreign territories").

conditions and limitations — Securities law concepts referring to the rules required to be complied with by issuers in offering or selling securities pursuant to federal or state exemptions from the securities registration requirements. Such conditions and limitations typically include numerical limitations on the number of investors, a ceiling on the amount of money to be raised, investor qualifications, commissions that may be paid and to whom, limitations on the manner of conducting the offering, limitations on resales of the securities, issuer qualifications, notice of sale requirements, information disclosure requirements, required legends, the payment of notice filing fees, notice filing requirements including a consent to service of process and purchaser representation requirements (see "limited offering exemption," "limitations on resale," "limitations on manner of offering," "Regulation D" and "blue sky laws").

conducting — In music, the direction of an orchestra or chorus by a leader (conductor) who employs motions of the hand and the body in order to bring about the coordination of all the players and singers (see "arrangement" and "instrumentation").

conduct provisions — In antitrust law, elements of court rulings or consent decrees that prohibit certain specified trade practices. For example, the Paramount Consent decrees, in addition to requiring the then five major vertically integrated motion picture companies (Paramount, Loew's, RKO, Warners and Fox) to divorce production/distribution from exhibition, also required these companies, plus three others that did not own theaters at that time (Columbia, Universal and United Artists) to abstain from fixing admission prices and making franchise agreements (see "antitrust laws," "franchise agreements," "Paramount Consent Decree of 1948," "price fixing" and "vertical integration").

conduct restrictions — (see "conduct provisions").

confidence game — Any scheme whereby a swindler wins the confidence of his or her victim and then cheats the victim out of money by taking advantage of the confidence reposed in the swindler. The elements of the crime of a confidence game are (1) an intentional false representation to the victim as to some present fact, (2) knowing it to be false, (3) with the intent that the victim rely on the representation and (4) the representation being made to obtain the victim's confidence and thereafter his or her money and property (see "scam" and "trust me").

confidentiality agreements — A written document used by an owner of a literary property when submitting such property to others for review that provides assurances to such owner that the party to which such project has been submitted will not disclose to others any information regarding the project (see "non-circumvention clause," "non-disclosure agreement" and "submission release").

confidentiality provision — A clause in a broader written agreement that serves the same purpose as the confidentiality agreement (see "confidentiality agreement").

confidential private placement offering memorandum — (see "offering memorandum").

confirmation letter — A letter commonly sent to subscribers (investors) accepted by the management of direct participation programs (i.e., by the general partners of limited partnerships or the manager of a manager-managed LLC offering), confirming the investor's (unit holder's) acceptance as investors into the entity and confirming the number of units purchased by such unit holders and the number of units accepted by management (see "limited liability company" and "limited partnership").

conflicting dates — A situation that occurs when a single film distributor plans to release more than one film at or about the same time, thus dividing the time, skill and efforts of the distributor's marketing staff between such films. This is of special concern to independent producers who contract with a distributor on an acquisition or rent-a-system basis and the distributor is not careful to allow for adequate separation in release dates between one of its own films and the independent producer's film. The independent producer's concern in such instances relates to whether his or her film will receive the marketing support it would ordinarily receive but for the conflict and whether the distributor's records as to what amounts were expended on behalf of each film are accurate (see "acquisition deal" and "rent-a-distributor").

conflicts of interest — Situations in which regard for one duty leads to disregard of another or might be reasonably expected to do so. Conflicts of interest may be actual or potential. On some issues the film producer and distributor's interests are the same or similar, whereas with regard to other issues, a distributor representing a producer's film, for example, will inevitably be confronted with numerous conflicts of interest that are inherent in the relationship. Some distributors, for example, will seek a representation from the producer in the distribution deal to the effect that the producer knows the distributor is not only distributing other films, but other films similar to the producer's film. It would seem that a distributor would not want to vigorously distribute two similar films that appeal to the same or similar target audiences at the same time and a producer should probably avoid such a conflict or allowing the distributor that freedom. Conflicts of interest also commonly occur with talent agents and entertainment attorneys representing multiple clients. In addition, a "Conflicts of Interest" section may appear in a securities offering disclosure document (see "conflict waivers," "Code of Professional Responsibility" and "ethics").

conflict waivers — Release agreements that clients of attorneys may be asked to sign in the event the attorney represents several clients involved in the same transaction thus raising conflict of interest issues. In such an agreement the attorney will disclose the potential conflict, recommend that each of the client's obtain independent counsel of their own choosing and ask for the clients' knowing consent if the client chooses to proceed without independent counsel (see "Code of Professional Responsibility" and "ethics").

conform — In filmmaking, the term "conform" means to match the film negative and all dupes to the editor's current work print. In a legal sense, the term means to reproduce an exact copy of a document that is often certified to by an authorized individual (see "certify").

conglomerate — A group of corporations engaged in a variety of businesses that are controlled by a single corporate entity. The shares of a corporate conglomerate, however, are still owned and therefore controlled by individuals, other corporations or other entities. For this reason, traditional Hollywood management has been able to maintain control over the film industry even though most of the major Hollywood studio/distributors are divisions of corporate conglomerates (see "corporation" and "subsidiary").

congratulatory advertising — A public announcement of sympathetic pleasure directed to a person or entity on account of success or good fortune expressed by means of broadcast or print media (see "trades").

conscious parallelism — In antitrust law analysis relating to an allegation of a conspiracy in restraint of trade, the phrase conscious parallelism refers to the same or similar business practices under circumstances that logically suggest joint agreement. The courts have never held that a showing of parallel business behavior alone conclusively establishes a conspiracy. Thus, in order to show conspiracy, a plaintiff has to demonstrate similar business behaviors that the parties were aware of to infer an agreement and additional circumstances that logically suggest joint agreement as distinguished from individual action. There seems to be a considerable amount of conscious parallelism in the motion picture industry although it is difficult to prove in a court of law and even more difficult to find anyone with the courage to complain (see "antitrust laws," "bidding war," "blacklisting," "blind bidding," "net profit participation," "price fixing" and "video/DVD revenue reporting").

consent — Approval of what is done or proposed by another (e.g., certain matters covered in a distribution deal may require the written consent of the other party; see "consent to service of process" and "waiver").

consent and release — A form agreement used when a producer or production company produces a motion picture based upon or involving the life or incidents in the life of a real person and that gives the producer or production company such person's consent to portray such person in the film and releases such producer or production company from certain claims that the person may have based on such portrayal (see "release").

consent decree — An agreement of the parties in a litigated matter that is made under the sanction of, and approved by, the court not as the result of a judicial determination, but merely as their agreement to be bound by certain stipulated facts. A consent decree is not appealable (see "Paramount Consent Decree of 1948").

Consent Decree of 1948 — (see "Paramount Consent Decree of 1948").

consent to service of process — A legal document providing a securities issuer's consent to the filing of any notices of litigation against such issuer with a designated state official in the state where the issuer proposes to offer or sell securities instead of with the issuer, wherever such issuer is located. Such consents are typically required of an issuer of securities to be provided to the state securities regulatory authorities in each state in which such issuer proposes to offer or sell its securities (see "blue sky laws," "conditions and limitations" and "notice filing").

consideration — The inducement to a contract, something of value given in return for performance or promise of performance by another, for the purpose of forming a contract. Consideration is one element of a contract that is generally required to make a promise binding and to make the agreement of the parties enforceable as a contract. As an example, the consideration paid by a distributor for the rights to distribute a film may be in the form of advances, guarantees, profit participations or royalties or a combination thereof (see "advance," "contract," "contingent compensation," "guarantee," "participations" and "royalties").

consolidated financial statement — A written record of the financial status of a business organization, including a balance sheet and an income statement (operating statement or profit and loss statement) that brings together all assets, liabilities and operating accounts of a parent company and its subsidiaries. Such a financial statement may also include a statement of changes in working capital and net worth (see "balance sheet," "corporation" and "net worth").

consortium — A group of companies formed to promote a common objective or engage in a project of benefit to all the members of the group. The relationship normally entails cooperation and a sharing of resources, sometimes even common ownership (contrast with "cartel"; see "professional association" and "trade association").

conspiracy — A combination of two or more persons to commit a criminal or unlawful act or to commit a lawful act by criminal or unlawful means; or a combination of two or more persons by concerted action to accomplish an unlawful purpose or some purpose not in itself unlawful but committed by unlawful means. Motion picture exhibitors have generally failed in attempts to convince the courts that blind bidding was a conspiracy in restraint of trade in violation of the Sherman Antitrust Law partly because of the difficulty in showing a conspiracy. For the same reason, Hollywood apologists often raise the conspiracy issue in the face of criticism of the business practices of the major studio/distributors, even if not alleged, simply because it tends to shift the discussion from the studio business practices to whether a conspiracy can be proved. In this sense the conspiracy issue serves as a red herring or smokescreen (see "antitrust laws," "combination in restraint of trade," "Hollywood apologist," "illegal combination," "red herring," "restraint of trade" and "smokescreen").

conspiracy in restraint of trade — (see "combination in restraint of trade").

conspirator — One involved in a conspiracy; one who acts with another, or others, in furtherance of an unlawful transaction (see "combination in restraint of trade").

constructive notice — Notice other than actual notice that is accepted in law as a substitute for actual notice (see "consent to service of process").

construing — The interpretation of a document (see "contract").

consultant — One who has a high level of expertise on a particular topic and provides professional advice or services relating to his or her area of expertise. Consultants are often hired by movie producers to advise on technical matters (e.g., courtroom procedure, historical details, space technology, etc.; see "litigation").

consultant employment agreement — The written contract between a motion picture producer and a person who makes his or her expertise in a certain area available for a fee or some other form of valuable consideration. From a film budgeting standpoint, consultants are generally considered above-the-line (see "above-the-line" and "above-the-line employment agreements").

consultation — The seeking or giving of professional advice. Many film distribution agreements provide that the distributor is obligated to consult with the film's producer regarding various matters relating to marketing the film, distributor editing and so forth. However, there is rarely any effective way for the producer to enforce such consultation rights. Producers should try to be more clear in exactly what is expected of the distributor when consulting with the producer (see "consultation rights").

consultation rights — The power or privilege to discuss a certain matter. In motion picture distribution agreements provisions are commonly made for certain issues to be determined in the future by one or the other of the parties. Some of those decisions may be made in the sole discretion of specified parties. Others may require mutual approval while still others may be made by a specified party who has an obligation to at least discuss the matter with the other party. This privilege held by the non-decision making party to discuss the matter is referred to as a consultation right. As an example, a studio production-financing/distribution agreement may provide the studio with a right of consultation with respect to locations for producing the film. It may also provide the production company with a right of good faith consultation with respect to

the film's distribution pattern and ad campaign for the initial U.S. theatrical release. With respect to the production company's right of consultation, however, the distributor will likely provide that its decision is final, although no such corresponding provision may be included with respect to the studio's consultation right (see "discretion," "mutual approval" and "sole discretion").

consumer purchase market — Retail sales of products to the general public. The term is most used to describe the sales of videocassettes or DVDs as opposed to rental transactions (see "sell-through market").

contact print — A positive or negative film that is made by placing a piece of exposed film in contact with unexposed film and exposing the duplicate a frame at a time in a lab printer (see "contact printing").

contact printing — The process of making a positive print directly from the working negative (see "contact print").

contact sheets — The preliminary printing of multiple still photography shots for review and selection of the most desirable shots for actual use in film publicity and advertising (see "delivery items" and "production stills").

Content Scramble System (CSS) — A technology created by the movie industry to control access to digital video disc (DVD) media. CSS is not a copy protection system, but rather an access control system: it prevents the playback of discs on "unauthorized" devices (i.e. devices lacking decryption keys that the movie industry provides, for a fee, to preferred manufacturers). Ironically, pirates can still make duplicates of CSS-scrambled DVDs, and these pirated copies will play normally in authorized DVD players. CSS does not prevent piracy (see "Digital Millennium Copyright Act").

contingencies — Pre-conditions to a contract (i.e., particular events or circumstances that must occur, before other obligations created by the contract are owed). In a production-financing/distribution agreement for example, the distributor may condition its obligations undertaken pursuant to the agreement on obtaining satisfactory clearance of the production company's chain-of-title to the rights relating to the motion picture (see "chain-of-title," "clearance" and "production-financing/distribution agreement").

contingency or contingency reserve — Money set aside in a film budget for unanticipated costs (i.e., to help prevent the film from going over-budget). Traditionally a film budget contingency equals 10 percent of the production budget excluding the cost of insurance and the completion bond, although some completion guarantors may require a higher contingency reserve on some films (same as "production contingency").

contingent compensation — Remuneration that is not owed or paid unless and until a specified event occurs (e.g., a salary bonus paid only if a film generates a specified level of distributor gross receipts; see "contingent participations," "contract of adhesion," "contractually defined profits," "creative accounting" and "net profit participation").

contingent deferments — All or part of salaries that are paid on a delayed basis and only upon the occurrence of a specified event (e.g., film rentals, distributor gross receipts or net profits reaching a certain level; see "deferments or deferrals," "fixed deferments," "percentage participation" and "points").

contingent liabilities — Potential financial susceptibility such as a pending lawsuit, a judgment under appeal and/or a disputed claim (see "litigation").

contingent participations — A percentage of gross or net revenues that are not due and payable unless and until a specified event occurs (e.g., a gross participation may not be paid until a film's gross receipts reach a specified level of breakeven and net profit participations will not be paid unless and until the film's revenue stream actually reaches net profits according to the distributor's accounting; see "contingent compensation," "contract of adhesion," "contractually defined profits," "creative accounting" and "net profit participation").

continuities — Material written to link program elements but that is not written by the script's writer (see "continuity").

continuity — The consistency of the look and sound of each shot in the film. Also, the uninterrupted and dramatically structured sequence of events in a film or tape production that maintains the continuous and seemingly uninterrupted flow of action of the story (also called "action continuity"; see "sequence").

continuity breakdown sheets — Film production forms on which all pertinent information regarding the visual and audio requirements of each scene in a film such as costumes, special effects, stunts, vehicles, props and special sound equipment are recorded during the production of a film. This information is an important reference for production personnel who are concerned with the continuity of the film (see "continuity").

continuous supply of product — An uninterrupted flow of motion pictures. The ability to provide a continuous supply of quality motion pictures is an extremely important element of the leverage or bargaining power that a producer or production company brings to the table in negotiations with a distributor. Also, a distributor must possess this same ability in order to effectively collect film rentals from or negotiate settlements with exhibitors. During times when credit and capital markets are constricted some distributors encourage producers to utilize their distribution facilities on a rent-a-system basis partly in an effort to keep enough product flow in the distributor pipeline to maintain a stronger bargaining position in relation to the exhibitors (see "product" and "rent-a-distributor").

contract — A promise, or set of promises, for breach of which the law gives a remedy, or the performance of which the law in some way recognizes as a duty. The essentials of a valid contract are: parties competent to contract, a proper subject-matter, consideration, mutuality of agreement, and mutuality of obligations. A contract is a transaction involving two or more parties whereby each becomes obligated to the other, with reciprocal rights to demand performance of what is promised by each respectively. In filmmaking, contracts generally are used in acquiring the rights to a story and/or screenplay, between the producer and each of the members of the creative team, between the producer and the film's distributor(s) and between the distributor and all other entities involved in distributing or exhibiting the film. The terms of the contract between a film's producer and distributor are critical in

determining whether a producer and/or investors participate in a film's profits. On the other hand, certain parties in the film industry are notorious for not implementing the actual language appearing in the contract. Legal systems in Europe and Asia have different criteria for what makes a contract (see "breach of contract," "deal points," "distribution agreement," "remedy" or "remedies" and "terms").

contract of adhesion — (see "adhesion contract").

contract player— An actor employed under an agreement for a term of at least ten out of thirteen weeks and that may not specify any role, picture or series (see "actor").

contractual breakeven — A point in a motion picture's revenue stream that is defined by agreement to constitute breakeven. Since there are many ways to define breakeven in film distribution agreements and certain breakeven points may never be achieved due to the effect of the so-called "rolling breakeven," it may be advantageous for all profit participants at whatever level to negotiate a contractually defined breakeven for purposes of triggering the payment of bonuses, escalations or various levels of participation (see "artificial breakeven," "breakeven," "cash breakeven," "first breakeven" and "rolling breakeven").

contractual incentives/disincentives — Provisions included in the agreements between a studio or other film production company that is financing the production of a feature film and the film's producers and/or director to encourage such persons to complete the film on time and within budget (see "double add-back," "leverage" and "penalty-free cushion").

contractually defined profits — A reference to the fact that the terms "profit," "gross profit," "net profit" and other important terms in a film distribution agreement are actually subjective terms and that their meaning may vary somewhat in each film deal depending on how the term is specifically defined in that contract. In other words, there is no industry standard definition for such terms since no one individual or organization has the authority to impose such definition on two individuals or entities negotiating a contract containing those terms. Producers should carefully review these definitions and reduce the overly expansive language, while also trying to keep such concepts simple, so there is less question about how to apply the terms (see "adhesion contract," "contractually defined terms" and "subjective terms").

contractually defined terms — Words or phrases the meanings of which are agreed upon in a written agreement and whose meanings may be different than their meanings in a different context (see "commonly understood," "contractually defined profits" and "terms of art").

contractual overhead — A motion picture distributor's expenses that cannot be directly allocated to a specific motion picture distributed, but that are deducted from gross receipts as distribution expenses for the films the distributor releases by authority of a provision in the distribution agreement relating to each film. Nearly all if not all major studio/distributors impose such contractually defined overhead charges on the producers of films they distribute, thus it may be fair to assume that few, if any, feature film producers have the bargaining power to eliminate such charges (see "administrative overhead," "advertising overhead," "contract of adhesion," "level playing field" and "overhead").

contractual quagmire — A phrase used to indicate that a particular transaction requires an overly burdensome and complicated amount of documentation. Some point out that from a contractual point of view, it is sometimes so difficult to coordinate the various concerns of a bank, completion bond company, the film's producer and the various media and territorial distributors when negotiating, drafting and attempting to coordinate multiple pre-sale agreements that a contractual quagmire may occur (see "default disaster," "pre-sales" and "splits rights basis").

contractual theater overhead — (see "house nut").

contribution — In direct participation programs, any money, property or services rendered, or a promissory note or other binding obligation to contribute money or property, that an investor contributes to the entity (i.e., usually a limited partnership or manager-managed LLC) as capital in that investor's capacity as an investor pursuant to an agreement between the investors and management, including an agreement as to value (see "direct participation program," "limited liability company" and "limited partnership").

control figure — The dollar amount of a theater's gross box office receipts stipulated within the license agreement which, if not attained during a specified period of time, allows the exhibitor or the distributor to terminate the film's exhibition by that exhibitor (see "holdover figure").

controlled availability — The practice of manipulating and/or withholding the renting, selling or licensing of motion pictures to exhibitors such that a motion picture is made available to an exhibitor after that film's true availability. Distributors who choose to engage in such practices surely may be able to influence the exhibitor's choice of films that are exhibited. If an independent producer's film is being distributed by an independent distributor, such practices engaged in by the major studio/distributors would have a tendency to limit the available theaters for the independent producer's film. On the other hand, if the independent producer's film is being distributed by a major studio/distributor, the independent producer may benefit from that distributor's "special" clout, but also may be involved in an actionable conspiracy (see "availability" and "conspiracy").

controlled distribution — Securities terminology for a limited offering of securities by the owners of the securities themselves or an offering of securities by an issuer through a broker/dealer acting as an underwriter for such issuer pursuant to a formal underwriting arrangement (see "distribution" and "uncontrolled distribution").

controlled theater — A cinema over which a distributor has power or influence with respect to the choice of movies exhibited therein, usually due to an ownership interest held by the distributor or by virtue of such distributor's market power. The major studio/distributors have historically been able to maintain effective indirect control of the production of movies through the control (and in some instances direct ownership of) first-run theaters. Harold Vogel's book *Entertainment Industry Economics* presents a very revealing chart relating to the question of domination of box-office performance by key U.S. movie theaters (the information in the chart apparently first appeared in *Variety* and was originally based on

the work of Art Murphy). The chart shows that 50 percent of the U.S. screens generate 67 percent of box office gross and that 75 percent of the U.S. screens generate 90 percent of box office gross. Thus, regardless of the quality of their movies (granted such movies will always meet certain minimum standards), the major studio/distributors merely have to control access to the right 75 percent of motion picture screens in the U.S. for their films to generate 90 percent of the box office gross. And, as can be seen from the information reported herein under "Market Share," the movies distributed by the major studio/distributors have consistently generated in excess of 90 percent of the box office gross for many years. Experienced net profit participation auditors report that "controlled theaters" are generally more than fair in their settlements with their own exhibitors, but on the other hand, they can afford to be since the distributor of a controlled theater (in the partial ownership sense) is also now participating in the "house nut" and "concessions" at such theaters (see "antitrust laws," "blind bidding," "box office gross," "concessions," "day and date," "first-run theater," "house nut," "major exhibition chains," "market power," "market share," "Paramount Consent Decree of 1948" and "settlement").

controller or comptroller — Chief accountant of a company who is responsible for preparing financial reports and supervising internal audits (see "chief financial officer").

control group — A limited number of individuals having a unifying relationship and the ability to exercise restraining or directing influence over the conduct of a particular industry (see "Hollywood control group").

control of a picture — The authority or power to make the final creative decisions with regard to a motion picture. A concept that may play an important role in the choice of the form of film finance, since it is generally accepted that some producers may lose creative control of their picture when it is financed by a studio (see "creative control").

control person — A person who is able to affect the actions or policies of the issuer or an underwriter or others in a securities offering, through the ownership of stock, position, by contract or otherwise (see "control stock," "holding company" and "working control").

controls — Certain required deadlines, procedures, reports or limitations imposed by a studio/distributor on a feature film production company whose film's production costs are being financed by the studio/distributor. Such controls will typically be set out in the production-financing/distribution agreement (see "approvals").

control stock — Shares of a corporation owned by shareholders having a controlling interest in the corporation (see "holding company" and "working control").

conversion — In a tort law context, the wrongful deprivation of another's property (i.e., without his or her authorization or justification). In the context of a film distribution deal, the term "conversion" refers to a specific kind of distribution expense (i.e., costs, discounts and expenses incurred in obtaining remittances of foreign receipts to the U.S., including costs of contesting imposition of restricted funds that are generally treated as off-the-top distribution expenses; see "off-the-top expenses" and "tort").

convertible securities — Corporate financial instruments that are exchangeable for a set number of another form of corporate ownership (i.e., common stock, at a pre-stated price). Convertible securities usually take the form of preferred stock or debt instruments such as bonds. They are most appropriate for investors who want higher income than is available from common stock, together with greater appreciation potential than regular bonds offer. From the issuer's standpoint, the convertible feature is usually designed as a sweetener, to enhance the marketability of the stock or bond (see "debt").

cooling off period — The interval of time (usually twenty days) between the filing of a preliminary prospectus with the SEC and the offer of the securities to the public (see "acceleration," "effective date," "public offering," "registration" and "waiting period").

co-op-ads — (see "cooperative advertising").

cooperative advertising — Film advertising and promotion in which the costs are shared between the distributor and exhibitor or other entity and generally calculated on a weekly basis. The exhibitor's contribution toward the total cost of the ads is either a pre-determined fixed amount set out in the contract between the distributor and exhibitor (but decreasing from week to week) or a negotiated formula based on mutually agreed ad expenditures. The distributor's contribution may be a fixed amount or a percentage arrangement similar to that used for film rentals. Expenditures for cooperative advertising are more advantageous from a tax standpoint since such costs can usually be deducted in the year in which they are incurred, whereas national advertising may have to be capitalized and amortized over the period in which the major portion of gross revenue from the picture is recorded. Unfortunately distributors and exhibitors commonly negotiate and settle their accounts relating to several motion pictures, thus it is often difficult to determine exactly what portion of cooperative advertising costs incurred by a distributor should be allocated to a given producer's film, or whether such allocations are accurate. The producer's auditor should have the authority to examine exhibitor/distributor contracts and the records relating to such shared expenses (see "amortization," "capitalization," "FASB Statement No. 53" and "participation").

co-producer — A person or entity joining with another to produce a motion picture or television picture (see "co-producer credit").

co-producer credit — The acknowledgment or recognition on the motion picture screen awarded to producers of a film who shared producer responsibilities (see "co-producer" and "produced by credit").

co-production — A film produced through the cooperation of and with substantial contributions of two or more production companies (see "international co-production").

co-production deal — A film production arrangement wherein two or more production entities share in the cost of production, typically on a 50/50 basis (see "co-production financing" and "joint venture").

co-production financing — A sharing between two or more entities of the responsibilities relating to the financing of a film production; distributor-financiers may make co-production deals with one or more parties for one or more territories so that the risks associated with financing the production of the film will be spread amongst several parties. Numerous items relating to decision-making authority on various production questions must also be negotiated in order to avoid conflicts on such issues inherent in co-production relationships (see "financing" and "international co-productions").

copy — The written selling message of an ad (see "body copy").

copyright — A bundle of rights associated with the works of artists and authors giving them, among other things, the exclusive right to publish, copy, distribute or otherwise use their works or determine who may do so. A work that was created (fixed in tangible form for the first time) on or after January 1, 1978, is automatically protected from the moment of its creation and is ordinarily given a term enduring for the author's life plus an additional seventy years after the author's death. In the case of "a joint work prepared by two or more authors who did not work for hire," the term lasts for seventy years after the last surviving author's death. For works made for hire, and for anonymous and pseudonymous works (unless the author's identity is revealed in Copyright Office records), the duration of copyright will be ninety-five years from publication or one hundred and twenty years from creation, whichever is shorter. It is illegal for anyone to violate any of the rights provided by the copyright law to the owner of copyright. These rights, however, are not unlimited in scope. Sections 107 through 121 of the 1976 Copyright Act establish limitations on these rights. In some cases, these limitations are specified exemptions from copyright liability. One major limitation is the doctrine of "fair use," that is given a statutory basis in section 107 of the 1976 Copyright Act. In other instances, the limitation takes the form of a "compulsory license" under which certain limited uses of copyrighted works are permitted upon payment of specified royalties and compliance with statutory conditions (see "copyright infringement," "fair use," "first sale doctrine," "fixed work," "patent," "plagiarism," "public domain," "trademark," "transfer of copyright ownership" and "work made for hire").

copyright assignment — A written agreement that is used to transfer to a purchaser, all of an owner's right, title and interest in a specific literary property that has already been copyrighted. A so-called short form copyright assignment is usually used for recording such transfer with the U.S. Copyright Office. The short form sets out only the most basic information relating to the identity of the parties (assignor and assignee) along with a description of the literary property (see "assignment" and "transfer of copyright ownership").

copyright certificate — The physical documentation provided by the U.S. Copyright Office as evidence of the registration of material for copyright purposes (see "copyright registration").

copyright deposit — A non-returnable submission of material to the U.S. Copyright Office for the purpose of registering such material for copyright purposes. The copyright deposit requirements vary depending on the item being copyrighted (see "copyright").

copyright infringement — The unauthorized use of copyrighted material (see "fair use").

copyright license — The right granted that gives a person or entity permission to publish, copy, distribute or otherwise use their works or determine who may do so (see "copyright" and "license").

copyright owner — The holder of the exclusive right to publish a creative work or determine who may publish such work (see "copyright").

copyright ownership — The possession of rights conferred by copyright registration (see "copyright registration").

copyright proprietor — (same as "copyright owner").

copyright registration — A formal filing for a claim to copyright protection with the U.S. Copyright Office. Copyright transfers, renewals and security interests may also be registered (see "copyright deposit").

copyright report — A written study, usually prepared by attorneys or copyright specialists in Washington D.C. as to the copyright status (i.e., the ownership of previously copyrighted material) of a specific literary property (book, play, motion picture, television series, rights in a character, etc.) in which someone wants to acquire rights (see "copyright search").

copyright search — An examination of the copyright status (i.e., the ownership of previously copyrighted material) of a specific literary property (book, play, motion picture, television series, rights in a character, etc.) in which someone wants to acquire rights (see "copyright").

copyright search report — (same as "copyright report").

copyright transfer — (see "copyright assignment").

corporate bond — A debt instrument issued by a private corporation. Corporate bonds are securities. They are typically taxable, have a par value of $1,000 and have a term maturity (i.e., they come due all at once and are paid out of a sinking fund accumulated for that purpose). If registered, they may also be traded on major exchanges, with prices published in newspapers (see "bond," "debenture," "debt instrument," "indenture" and "sinking fund").

corporate conglomerate — (see "conglomerate").

corporate financing — The raising of funds for general corporate purposes by debt or equity means. In the context of film finance, the funding of film projects through the vehicle of a corporation (e.g., by selling shares in a film production company organized as a corporation). In the film business, general corporate financing may be utilized to fund a slate of films, including acquisition, development, production and distribution (see "financing" and "single-picture financing").

corporate formalities — The required activities in putting together a corporation and preserving its corporate status, including organizational and regular board meetings (supported by minutes), annual shareholders' meetings (also supported by minutes), authorizing and issuing stock and maintaining other corporate records (see "corporation").

corporate investment — A term used to describe situations in which a corporation or corporations make direct investments of funds in a film project (i.e., fully or partially underwrite the cost of producing a film, typically because there is some sort of tie-in between the film and a product the corporation markets; see "product placement" and "promotional tie-ins").

corporate opportunity — A situation in which a person who has a close relationship with a corporation takes advantage of the special knowledge he or she thereby acquires for personal gain. The term refers to a legal doctrine that directors or others invested with a fiduciary duty toward a corporation may not appropriate for their own benefit and advantage a business opportunity properly belonging to the corporation (see "fiduciary" and "insider trading").

corporate stock — An equity or ownership interest in a corporation usually created by a contribution to the capital of the corporation. Its unit of measurement is the share and the owner of one or more shares of stock in a corporation is entitled to participate in the corporation's management and profits, and in distribution of assets upon dissolution of the company (see "security" or "securities," "share" and "shareholders").

corporation — An association of shareholders (or even a single shareholder) created under statute and regarded as an artificial person by courts, having a legal entity entirely separate and distinct from the individuals who compose it, with the attribute of continuous existence or succession, and having the capacity to take, hold and convey property, sue and be sued, and exercise such other powers as may be conferred on it by law, just like a natural person (see "C-corporation," "corporate financing," "perpetual existence," "natural person" and "S-Corp").

Corporation for Public Broadcasting (CPB) — A source organization for limited film production funds. The CPB may ask for a minimum number of air plays over a specified period of time on the Public Broadcasting System for a film it helps to finance (see "free television").

cost accounting — The branch of accounting concerned with providing the information that enables management of a firm to evaluate production costs (see "budget").

cost amortization — (same as "amortization"; see "accounting principles and practices").

cost basis — The original price of an asset, used in determining capital gains. It usually is the purchase price (see "capital gain").

cost capitalization — (same as "capitalization"; see "accounting principles and practices").

cost of capital — The rate of return a business could earn if it chose another investment with equivalent risk (i.e., the opportunity cost of the funds employed as the result of an investment decision). In considering studio financing, factors to be included in estimating or calculating the cost of capital and comparing such costs between alternative film finance methods should include, when applicable in a given instance, all studio charges that do not directly relate to production, bank interest and commitment fees. In investor financed securities offerings such costs should include where applicable: the expense of creating sales commissions to broker/dealers, legal and accounting fees, disclosure document costs, marketing costs and notice or other filing fees (see "opportunity cost").

cost of money — (see "cost of capital").

cost of opening — The film distribution expenses including the costs of prints and ads necessary to exhibit a film for the first week of its initial run (see "rising production costs").

cost recovery — A procedure of allocating costs against revenue on a dollar for dollar basis to the point where costs are recovered. Additional proceeds would then be treated as revenue (see "accelerated cost recovery" and "depreciation").

cost reports — Film production accounting prepared by the production manager or production accountant that set out the costs per budget category to the date of the report, the expenditures per category made during the most recent week and estimates the per category costs for finishing the film with totals. In addition to being important to the producer in controlling costs, such reports are generally required by a lender and completion guarantor when a production loan is involved (see "cash flow schedule").

cost to complete — At any given time after the start of principal photography, the amount of funds per film budget category needed to finish the motion picture (see "projections").

costs to date — The amount of funds that have been spent on each film budget category to the date of the cost report (see "cost reports" and "cost to complete").

costume designer — The film production person responsible for the complete costume breakdown; the purchase or design and production of all costumes, color sketches or outline sketches with color samples attached, including drawings or necessary descriptions of detail and its application; all selections from existing costumes whether purchased, promoted, rented or chosen from a performer's personal wardrobe; the supervision of all necessary fittings and alteration of the costumes; the selection of all necessary fabrics and trims; the design or selection of all costume accessories; and the shopping, if necessary, for period costumes and costume accessories; all in accordance with the production design established by the director and the production designer (see "art director").

costumer and wardrobe supervisor — A film production employee engaged in packing, unpacking, re-packing, sorting, hanging, cataloguing, dressing, pressing, cleaning, spot cleaning, dyeing, fitting, remodeling, repairing, sewing, altering, distributing and maintaining all the items of wardrobe and wardrobe accessories and assisting in the dressing of and making of changes for performers. The duties include any work related to the above, as well as any work related to the use, control and disposition of the wardrobe for its efficient and artistic utilization (see "costume designer").

cost/value trend — The tendency for the ratio between expenses and potential revenue to determine a course of action. For example, some industry analysts suggest that the cost/value trends among various markets and media in the motion picture industry argue against the fractionalization of and pre-selling of rights because as film production and distribution costs increase, the percentage of revenue generated through a film's domestic theatrical release is reduced in relation to other media or territories and as the value of cable and video rights increases, the more likely the domestic theatrical distributor will insist on including the cable and video rights as part of the domestic theatrical distribution deal (see "fractionalizing," "pre-sales" and "split rights basis").

cottage industry — A small informally organized group of productive or profit-making enterprises. The film industry is partly made up of a large number of cottage industries. As an example, the small group of profit participation auditors represent a cottage industry that has developed within the film industry (see "economic microcosm" and "profit participation auditor").

counter cyclical — A reference to the tendency of an industry to experience economic cycles that run counter to the economic cycles of other industries (see "cyclical industry," "recession-proof" and "recession-resistant").

counter recessionary — An economic phenomenon that results in a more favorable performance for a certain business or industry during difficult economic times (see "counter cyclical" and "recession resistant").

counterparts clause — A contractual clause usually found in the miscellaneous clauses section of a contract providing that two or more copies of the contract may be signed separately by individual signatories and that all of these signed contracts will be considered as one. This clause makes it more convenient for persons required to sign contracts to do so without all being physically present at the same time or actually signing the same document (see "contract").

counting rules — A securities concept commonly appearing as one of the conditions or limitations of federal or state transactional exemptions from the securities registration requirement that specifies how to count certain investors for investor numerical limitations purposes (e.g., Regulation D Rules 505 and 506 only permit thirty-five unaccredited investors but unlimited accredited investors). Pursuant to the Regulation D counting rules, however, foreign purchasers are not counted, nor are relatives, spouses or relatives of the spouse of a purchaser who has the same principal residence as the purchaser (also called "purchaser counting rules"; see "accredited investor," "foreign purchasers," "investor numerical limitations" and "Regulation D").

coupled films — Films that are marketed together as a package (see "allocation issues," "block booking," "tentpole strategy" and "tying arrangement").

coupled with an interest — A contractual phrase providing that the authority granted in a contract is given to the agent for consideration and that in circumstances where not recognizing such authority would result in an injustice, the courts will imply authority so as not to mislead another (see "power of attorney").

counsel — An attorney appointed to advise and represent an individual or entity in legal matters. Also the act of giving advice as a result of consultation (see "code of professional responsibility").

covenant — An agreement or promise to do or not to do a particular thing (see "warranty" or "warranties").

covenant not to compete — A contractual provision through which a party or the parties to a contract promise to refrain from conducting business or professional activities of a nature similar to those of the other party or parties for a reasonable period of time and in a limited geographical area (also called "non-compete clause"; see "non-circumvention clause" and "non-disclosure agreement").

covenant of good faith and fair dealing — A contractual agreement or promise to conduct one's business dealings with another in good faith and fairly (i.e., to conduct such business dealings honestly, in fact); to observe reasonable commercial standards of fair dealing in the trade and not to deny the existence of the contract. Some states provide that the covenant of good faith and fair dealing is implied in every contract executed in that state (see "good faith" and "warranty" or "warranties").

coverage — In motion picture cinematography, additional shots to augment the master shot, such as single, cutaway shots, closeups or tight two-shots. It is from the master shot and coverage (or cover shots) that the editor builds scenes. In the most general sense, coverage or cover shots are alternate depictions of portions of a film (i.e., scenes shot from different camera angles, thus providing differing points of view of the same action; see "cover shot").

coverage (development) — The process of review and comment used by most studio systems in the development of screenplays, whereby a submitted screenplay is assigned to a reader who reads the screenplay and provides development notes (i.e., coverage) for evaluation by the studio's director of acquisitions and other development executives to aid them in determining whether the project should be acquired or approved for the next stage in development or "greenlighted" for production financing (see "development," "development notes," "reader" and "story analyst").

cover shot — An extra take of a scene that is printed and available for use if the initially preferred take is for any reasons ultimately not selected to appear in the completed film for any reason (see "coverage" and "take"; same as "insurance take").

crawl — A list of credits that moves up the screen, often superimposed over a live-action background (see "creeper titles").

creative accounting — A derogatory term commonly used to refer to the accounting practices of the major studio/distributors that may include everything from sharp negotiating tactics used in conjunction with drafting a film's distribution agreement to actual dishonest practices in reporting and dividing up the revenues generated by a given film. The supposed negotiations relating to the deals impacting how film revenues are allocated often result in agreements weighted heavily in favor of the distributor as opposed to the producer and other net profit participants. Although mistakes and misapplications of contractual terms do appear to occur quite often in the industry, sometimes what is called creative accounting is no more than the film distributor following the terms of the negotiated distribution deal that were clearly disadvantageous to the producer in the first place. Thus, in some instances what producers call creative accounting is merely the result of their own lack of preparation for the distribution negotiation process (or more often, their lack of negotiating leverage). Independent producers, must therefore work harder to improve their (or their representatives') negotiating skill and leverage including insisting on broad auditing rights (see "account number," "adhesion contract," "allocation," "anticipated expenses," "apportioned expense," "bad debt," "combination ad," "commingling of funds," "cross collateralization," "deal memo," "direct distribution expenses," "discretion," "facilities allocation," "front end load," "GAAP," "improperly claimed expenses," "kickback," "overhead," "rolling break-even," "settlement transactions," "standard contract," "studio accounting practices," "subjective terms," "sue-us," "underreported rentals" and "usury").

creative control — The power and authority to make decisions with respect to a film being produced and with regard to significant qualitative aspects of the film (i.e., the appearance and content of the final feature film product). Creative control is often a major point of negotiation between a producer and director and sometimes between a producer and distributor/financier. The issue comes up in the context of a financing/distribution agreement with respect to editing rights (i.e., whether the distributor has the right to make editing changes, have final editing rights or produce the final cut of a movie). Such rights, to some extent, depend on the parties' relative bargaining strength and the stature, as well as the rights of the producer and/or director as between them. The producer may or may not be able or willing to give any editing rights to the distributor, but some editing changes may be required as per government regulation or in order to get a contractually required motion picture rating. If granted, such rights should be subject to a producer's right of approval, rather than just unlimited editing rights (also called "artistic control"; see "creative differences," "creative elements," "editing rights" and "waiver of droit moral").

creative decisions — Determinations relating to the artistic aspects of a feature film. Financing/distribution agreements generally will make some provision for who has the authority to make creative decisions with respect to various versions of the film as between the distributor, producer and director. Such agreements may also provide a mechanism for the parties to communicate their objections to the exercise of certain cutting rights of another party (see "editing rights" and "final cut").

creative demands — The pressure to successfully compete with other films in the marketplace with respect to any and all elements of a film. Such pressure, real or perceived, may help to explain why in some major studio/distributor releases film elements like new and heretofore unseen special effects sometimes overpower the rest of the movie to the point of distraction (see "creative control").

creative department — A major administrative unit of the typical motion picture studio/distributor that is primarily responsible for evaluating proposed motion picture projects, reviewing and evaluating script submissions and recommending which films the studio will develop and/or produce (see "business affairs department," "legal department," "production department" and "studio").

creative differences — Disagreements among producer, director, cinematographer, principal actors or other above-the-line personnel relating to elements of a film. Sometimes, such persons so strongly disagree with respect to a given motion picture element that they cannot or choose not to continue working together. Thus, "creative differences" are often cited as the reasons for quitting or being fired and sometimes serves as a "catchall" excuse for such action (same as "artistic differences").

creative elements — Those aspects of a film or filmmaking that require the power or ability to produce from imaginative skill (see "creative talent").

creative financing — Methods of funding films that involve new, different or unusual investment vehicles, techniques or combinations thereof (e.g., mixing equity from third parties with bank loans or arranging multiple pre-sales in foreign markets). It may be fair to observe that too many independent producers spend too much time and effort trying to come up with ever more creative methods of film finance when their collective interests would be better served through an effective association of independent film producers with its focus on reforming the many unfair, unethical, unconscionable, anti-competitive, predatory and/or illegal business practices of the major studio distributors (see "hybrid security" and "multiple pre-sales").

creative producer — A term used by some in the industry to distinguish between a producer who is significantly involved in artistic aspects of producing a motion picture as opposed to an executive producer who may be primarily responsible for obtaining production financing and in related business matters, and on the other hand, a line producer who is more directly involved with the logistics of actual production (see "executive producer," "line producer" and "producer").

creative talent — Screenwriter, producer, director, actors, actresses and others who participate in the creative process (see "creative producer").

credit — Loans, bonds, charge-account obligations and open-account balances with commercial firms. Also, available but unused bank letters of credit and other standby commitments as well as a variety of consumer credit facilities (see "distributor credit").

credit balance — An account balance in the customer's favor (see "credit").

credit contractionary environment — An economic climate in which it is difficult for businesses to obtain loans (see "credit" and "lender financing").

credit issues — Questions relating to screen credits (e.g., where the credit will appear in relation to the film's title, whether the credit will appear on a separate card and what size type will be used; see "credits").

credit lines — Established lending relationships in which a borrowing entity may have been pre-approved up to a specified limit or pre-qualified to obtain loans from a lender (see "lender financing").

creditor — One to whom money is owed by a debtor; one to whom a financial obligation exists. A producer who borrows money from a bank for the production of a film is a debtor to that creditor bank (see "credit").

credit requirements — The feature film billing notices that are either mandated by an individual employment agreement or the applicable rules of a given union or guild (see "minimum credit requirements").

credits — The listed names and positions of the cast, crew, staff and others involved in a given film or TV production that are seen at the beginning and/or end (same as "billing"; see "prominence").

credit statement — A written statement to be provided by the producer of a film to the distributor setting out all main-and-end title billing, paid-advertising billing and all requirements regarding paid advertising (same as "billing statement").

credit titles — (see "credits").

creeper titles — An out-of-date reference to the listing of actors, producers, directors and others involved in a film that was accomplished through the slow rotation of the listing in front of the camera with the use of a drum that was not visible (see "crawl" and "title").

crew — A film's crew is composed of those who work "behind the camera" in the technical and production positions, such as sound-persons, camera-people, grips and so forth. The term differentiates these people from the cast (see "cast," "operational staff," "production staff" and "staff").

crew agreement — The employment contract for persons who perform the technical and production tasks (i.e., behind the camera), in the making of a feature film (see "employment agreement").

crew/cast agreement — A rather simplified form of combined employment contract used by ultra-low budget filmmakers for the employment of all production personnel, technicians and actors. Such an agreement is designed to simplify and expedite the paper work involved in contracting with such persons and may involve the use of a form agreement with numerous blanks to be filled in (see "employment agreement").

crime — Any act that the government has determined is injurious to the public and therefore prosecutable in a criminal proceeding (see "rules" and "white collar crime").

critic — Persons usually employed by newspapers, television stations or other media who screen newly released movies and provide their subjective views and comments on the movie for the public's information (see "blurbs," "industry critic," "positive review" and "review").

critic's review — The comments and reactions of a movie critic as such appear in a newspaper column, in a television segment, on the Internet or other media (see "critic").

crony — A close and long-standing friend; pal (see "cronyism").

cronyism — Partiality to close and long-standing friends (i.e., cronies), especially as evidenced in the appointment of such persons to political or other jobs without regard to their qualifications (see "discrimination," "favoritism" and "nepotism").

cross-collateralization — An accounting practice used by and which benefits distributors whereby distributors offset their losses in one market against profits in another or on one film against another. In a worldwide distribution deal the studios typically seek to cross-collateralize profits and losses among territories. With cross-collateralization the producer can only share in the profits of one territory to the extent that the profits of that territory, exceed the combined losses of all other territories worldwide. In situations where multiple films of a single producer or production company are being distributed by a single distributor, the distributor may seek authorization in the distribution agreement to cross-collateralize the financial performance of each of such films with the others. That practice should be negotiated by and between the producer and distributor. In some instances, no provision is made in the distribution agreement regarding cross-collateralization (at any level) and thus the

distributor may choose to use its discretion with regard to this issue. In still other instances, the producer must carefully monitor the activities of the distributor to be certain that it is not effectively cross-collateralizing the financial performance of the producer's film with the performance of the films of other producers. Licensees of film packages may also cross-collateralize the results of the exhibition of such films in foreign territories (see "allocation," "creative accounting," "cross-collateralization of markets," "cross-collateralization of slates," "de facto cross-collateralization," "discretionary cross-collateralization," "overage," "unrecouped expenses" and "unauthorized cross-collateralization").

cross-collateralization of markets — The offset of the distribution results from one market area against the results of another market area (see "cross-collateralization").

cross-collateralization of movie slates — The offsetting by the distributor of the economic results of all of the motion pictures produced by a single production company that has contracted for such pictures to be distributed by a distribution entity (see "cross-collateralization" and "cross-collateralization of markets").

cross-collateralization provisions — The language in a film distribution agreement that authorizes the distributor to offset the profits of one movie against the profits of another movie or authorizes the distributor to offset the profits of a movie in one market against the profits of the same movie in another market. Since producers often have multiple picture arrangements with studios, their profits from one picture may be cross-collateralized against the losses of the same producer's other pictures being distributed by the same distributor, but a net profit participant other than the producer should not be subject to the distributor's cross-collateralization with the producer (i.e., the net profit participant should thus be excluded from the producer's net profit definition; see "net profit participant").

crossover film — A feature film that was originally targeted for a narrow specialty market but which achieves acceptance in a wider market (see "breakout" and "crossover potential").

crossover potential — The prospects for a film to attract a much larger movie-going audience than originally anticipated (see "crossover film").

cross plugs — Promotional references to a film in several different media such as novelization of the screenplay, licensing the film's title for use by others, pre-release merchandising, on the Internet, etc. (see "advertising").

cross purchase agreement — (same as "buy/sell agreement").

cultural differences — Characteristics that distinguish one society or extended social group from another. Such differences may create obstacles for many forms of film finance that require international cooperation and can form arbitrary employment obstacles for persons who do not share the same cultural characteristics of the dominant group in a particular domestic industry such as the film industry (see "control group," "foreign currency deal," "foreign equity investment" and "foreign tax deal").

culturally based — A partiality toward a specific society or segment of society. Films that are culturally biased toward U.S. society or one segment or another of U.S. society may not be received as well overseas. On the other hand, a film that provides a favorable portrayal of the culture of another country, even as a sub-theme, may facilitate the raising of funds in that country (see "favorable portrayal").

culture promotion — The promotion of a specific culture, religion or way of life through the movies; what many in the film industry recognize as an important sub-theme of movies, second only to entertainment. Foreign governments more commonly recognize (or openly acknowledge) the value of motion pictures as promoters of culture, whereas, Hollywood studio executives tend to hide behind the smokescreen that movies are merely entertainment (see "favorable portrayal," "hidden agenda," "movies with a message," "patterns of bias" and "unfavorable portrayal").

cumulative rights — A contractual phrase meaning that rights granted or created pursuant to a contract are additional to each other and not exclusive of one or the other (see "contract").

cumulative voting — The corporate procedure that permits shareholders, who generally are entitled to one vote for each share held, to accumulate their votes for any one directorial candidate in corporate elections to the board of directors. The method improves minority shareholders' chances of naming representatives to a corporation's board of directors (see "minority interest" and "shareholder").

cure — In legal terms, to correct a legal error or defect; to free from something objectionable or harmful; to rectify or remedy. In contracts, to correct a breach. Contracts will often provide an opportunity for a defaulting party to cure the problem within a certain number of days after notice of the default (see "breach of contract").

currency — Something that is in circulation in a given country as a medium of exchange including coins, paper money, government notes and bank notes (see "currency conversion" and "devaluation").

currency conversion — The exchanging of the monies of one country for an equivalent amount of another country's funds (see "currency" and "devaluation").

currency deals — (see "foreign currency deal").

currency exchange — (same as "currency conversion").

currency exchange rate — (see "exchange rate" and "exchange rate movements").

current assets — Cash, accounts receivable, inventory and other holdings that are likely to be converted into cash, sold, exchanged or expensed in the normal course of business, usually within a year (see "financial statement").

current economic realities — A realistic appraisal of the present business environment. In antitrust law, some of the major studio/distributors previously subject to the Paramount consent decree have successfully argued that current economic realities in the entertainment industry present significantly changed circumstances and that such circumstances should be considered by the U.S. District Court judge supervising the consent decrees to re-allow studio ownership of theaters (see "Paramount Consent Decree of 1948" and "TriStar Case").

current liabilities — Debts incurred by the reporting entity as part of normal operations and expected to be repaid during the following twelve months (e.g., accounts payable, short-term loans and that portion of long-term loans due in one year; see "financial statement").

custodian — One entrusted with guarding and keeping property or records (see "bankruptcy" and "trustee").

customarily kept by the distributor — A reference to the type and manner in which a film distributor maintains its books and records, in its usual manner. Some distribution agreements will establish such a loose standard for the distributor to comply with in meeting its obligations to keep accurate books and records relating to the distribution of a film. If such language is used, and the distributor has not heretofore kept any records, such language may not impose any additional obligation on the distributor. Such language should be eliminated from distribution agreements in favor of a more responsible standard (see "customary").

customary — Commonly practiced, used or observed (i.e., the provisions that are usually found in motion picture production documentation). With respect to a film distribution agreement (and other motion picture documentation), producers must recognize that the use of such vague and subjective terms are just that "vague and subjective." Their use imposes very little on the studio/distributor and such standards of conduct can only be enforced after the fact, if at all. Such vague standards as "customary practices," "long-standing and well-established practices in the industry" or "customary terms and conditions for agreements of this nature in the motion picture industry" may often appear in so-called short form feature film production documentation or deal memos along with a statement of the intention of the parties to negotiate, draft and sign a more complete written agreement to include such terms at a later date. However, even though there may be a certain level of unanimity regarding the type of provisions that ought to be included in the same or similar feature film related agreements, the specific wording, the application of such terms or their interpretation by the courts in any given circumstance is by no means standardized. In addition, some view the use of such vague standards by the major studios as a means of continuing their dominance and control over the rest of the industry. Whenever possible, such terms should be negotiated out of the agreement and replaced with a more definite standard of conduct (see "customary terms," "deal memo" and "reasonable and customary").

customary terms — The provisions that are usually found in motion picture production, financing and distribution documentation (see "customary," "deal memo," "letter agreement," "short form agreement" and "standard contract").

custom duties — Fees or tolls imposed by the sovereign law of a country on imports or exports (see "distribution expenses").

customs inspection — The examination of goods being imported or exported into or out of a country by the agency authorized to collect duties, tolls or imposts imposed by the sovereign law of the country. Unfortunately, the customs officials of some countries are corrupt and permit the unauthorized copying of U.S. made motion pictures during the customs inspection. One producer reported that he saw videocassettes of his previously unreleased motion picture already on sale at a local bazaar while traveling from the customs offices to his hotel on a visit to a foreign country for the purpose of exhibiting his film in its world premiere at a local film festival (see "piracy").

cut — (see "edit").

cutouts — (see "trims," "outakes" and "second take").

cutter — (see "editor").

cut-through endorsement — A provision often found in completion guarantees that allows the lender or financier to look beyond the completion bond company to the financially responsible insurance company or group that ultimately backs the completion guarantor for payment on a claim (see "completion guarantor").

cutting edge deals — Agreements drafted and negotiated by the most sophisticated attorneys and business executives in an industry incorporating the most advanced contractual provisions and taking advantage of the most current developments in the industry (see "contract" and "standard contract").

cutting rights — (same as "editing rights"; see "final cut").

cutting room — The physical room or facility where a film is edited (see "edit").

cyclical industry — A distinct group of productive enterprises, the film industry in this case, that experiences economic cycles. The movie business is generally considered to be a cyclical industry (see "economic cycles" and "out-of-favor Indies").

cyclical theory — A statistical theory adhered to by some in the film industry suggesting that at some point in the future, film genre that are not currently popular will again be favored by the movie-going public (see "genre").

D

dailies — Printed film scenes delivered daily from the laboratory of film materials shot on the preceding day. The dailies are generally reviewed and approved by the director and others before a particular set is struck (also called "rushes").

Daily Variety — An entertainment industry trade publication that is published daily and reports on developments in the motion picture, television, stage, home video and cable industries (see "trades" and "variety").

daily contract for theatrical motion pictures — A standard Screen Actors Guild contract used for the employment of performers on a daily basis. Additional clauses not part of the standard form may be inserted into these contracts (see "minimum free lance contract for theatrical motion pictures").

damage — A legal wrong that causes injury to another, either in his or her person, rights, reputation or property (same as "injury"; contrast with "damages").

damages — Monetary compensation that the law awards to a person or entity who has been injured by the action of another (contrast with "damage"; see "remedy" or "remedies").

day and date — A concept used in making a film available for exhibition that requires that one theater's run of a film be controlled by (i.e., identical to) another theater's run of that same film. This relationship usually exists in the negative sense (i.e., forbidding the controlled theater's exhibition of a film until the controlling theater is able to exhibit that same film). However, "day and date" may be used in a positive sense (i.e., compelling the controlled theater to exhibit a film simultaneously with the controlling theater's run of that same film; see "controlled theater").

day and date release — The simultaneous (same day, same date) release of a motion picture in two or more theaters in a given market. The phrase may also be used to refer to the simultaneous opening of a movie in two or more markets (see "day and date").

day player — An actor or actress hired to work on a daily basis and who is involved in only a few scenes or has only several lines (i.e., a player employed by the day, other than an extra, stunt person, professional singer or airline pilot; see "actor," "bit player" and "extra").

day player contract — (see "daily contract for theatrical motion pictures").

DBA — Acronym for "doing business as," a phrase used to indicate that an unincorporated individual (or individuals) are conducting a business under a fictitious name (see "fictitious name" and "sole proprietorship").

"D" counties — The A.C. Nielsen Company designation for sparsely populated, mostly rural counties in the U.S. (i.e., counties that do not fit within the Nielsen definitions of "A," "B" or "C" counties; see "'A' counties," "ADI Market," "'B' counties," "'D' counties" and "Nielsen Media Research").

deal — Slang for contract or agreement (see "contract," "deal memo" and "deal points").

deal breaker — An issue being discussed in contract negotiations that if not agreed to will prevent an agreement from being reached on the overall contract. The term is also sometimes applied to an individual (i.e., a "deal breaker" as opposed to a "deal maker"; see "deal points").

dealer — A person or entity engaged in the business of buying and selling securities for his or her own account (i.e., engaged in the purchase of securities and their resale to customers). The activities of securities dealers are regulated by the Securities and Exchange Act of 1934 (see "broker," "broker/dealer," "investment adviser," "NASD," "SEC" and "underwriter").

deal memo — A shortened version of a contract (i.e, a brief memorandum of the most important negotiated terms between contracting parties). For example, a distribution agreement between a production company and a film distributor may initially utilize a letter agreement format, that theoretically covers the main points (deal points) agreed to by the parties, such as salary, time schedule, screen credit and percentage participation in the film's net profits, if any. Deal memos may also be used in contracting with performers and others critical to the production of a movie. Deal memos are often used by the major studio business and affairs departments to get the film production process underway on a given film, with the intent that the studio's legal department will ultimately negotiate and draft a more complete agreement. For smaller independent producers and distributors, the deal memo may not be necessary or even desirable, since these smaller entities do not have the bureaucracy of a major studio that often slows the negotiating and drafting process, and in fact the deal memo may be dangerous for the smaller production company since the more detailed provisions of the full contract may be much more burdensome or onerous for the producer and may even conflict with the original provisions of the deal memo (see "long form distribution agreement").

deal memorandum — The more complete title for deal memo (see "deal memo").

deal points — An informal and general reference to the most important terms of a contract (e.g., in a film distribution agreement: date, parties, term, territory, consideration, fees and expenses, identity of film, definitions of terms, provisions for production financing, ownership of picture and copyright, length, quality standard, screenplay identification, language, title clearance, MPAA rating and delivery terms; see "deal memo," "distribution agreement" and "distribution checklist").

deal terms — A more formal and specific reference to the provisions of an agreement. Also, the heading for a major section of some feature film distribution agreements, a section that may include provisions relating to contingencies, picture specifications, basic elements, production/delivery requirements, delivery specifications, controls/approvals/obligations, production company's right of consultation, financing, consideration, rights, notices and payments and special provisions (see "deal points" and "distribution agreement").

debenture — A general debt obligation backed only by the integrity of the borrower and documented by an agreement called an indenture. An unsecured bond is a debenture (see "bond," "debt" and "indenture").

debt — Money, goods or services that one party is obligated to pay to another in accordance with an expressed or implied agreement. Debt may or may not be secured. Also, the general name for bonds, notes, mortgages and other forms of paper evidencing amounts owed and payable on specified dates or on demand. Both the lender and the producer should be careful to ensure that what is intended to be a loan to be used for production funds for a feature film can be fairly characterized as debt and not characterized as an equity investment. If the transaction is characterized as some form of equity participation, the "lender" actually becomes an investor whose investment is at risk and thus there may be no obligation for the producer to repay the loan. Although that may sound favorable to the film's producer, it may also result in the producer having sold an unregistered security to a passive investor (thus triggering securities compliance problems), and may result in the creation of an entity (e.g., joint venture or association) that may generate unfavorable tax consequences. The factors that determine whether a transaction creates debt or equity include: (1) whether or not the loan is a non-recourse loan or a recourse loan (i.e., a non-

recourse loan secured only by the film is more likely than a recourse loan to be considered an equity investment); (2) whether a fixed repayment date has been established; (3) whether the loan is secured; (4) whether the rate of interest on the "loan" is tied to the amount of profits earned by the film (i.e., if the interest rate increases with the level of profits, that increases the chances that the transaction would be characterized as an equity investment); (5) whether the "lender" exercises substantial control over the production (i.e., the more control exercised by the lender the less likely the transaction would be characterized as a loan — on the other hand, the more control exercised by the "lender" the less likely the transaction would be characterized as a security); (6) whether the "lender" subordinates (i.e., takes a second position to third parties with respect to payments made from the film's revenues); and (7) whether another lender would have loaned funds on the same or similar basis (see "bank," "collateral," "equity," "interest" and "lender financing").

debt capitalization — (see "foreign debt capitalization programs").

debt financing — The funding of a project or the activities of a company through the issuance of one or more debt instruments (see "debt instrument").

debt instrument — Written promise to repay a debt; document that serves as evidence of a debt such as promissory notes, bills, corporate bonds, notes, banker's acceptances, certificates of deposit, commercial paper, debentures or indentures (see "debt financing" and "equity").

debt loads — The burden of a company's financial obligations. If a company's debt is so great that the cash required to meet its obligations to make payments of principal and interest during any given period can only be met by siphoning off cash flow normally allocated for other important obligations, serious financial consequences may follow (see "bankruptcy," "debt-to-equity ratio," "debt device" and "financial management").

debtor — One who has the obligation of paying a debt; person or business that owes money (see "creditor" and "debt").

debt retirement — Repayment of a debt (see "debt").

debt security — Security representing money borrowed that must be repaid and having a fixed amount, a specific maturity or maturities and usually a specific rate of interest or an original purchase discount (e.g., a bill, bond, commercial paper or note; contrast with "securities"; see "collateral").

debt service — Cash required in a given period of time, usually one year, for payments of interest and current maturities of principal on outstanding debt (see "debt" and "interest").

debt-to-equity ratio — In corporate finance, the total liabilities of the corporation divided by the total of shareholders' equity. The ratio may give some indication of the extent to which an owner's equity can cushion creditors' claims in the event of the corporation's liquidation (see "debt" and "equity").

debt-to-net-worth ratio — For individuals, the total liabilities of the individual divided by such individual's net worth. These ratios are sometimes used by lenders and other prospective creditors in determining whether to

make loans or extend credit to such individuals (see "net worth").

deceased persons — Human beings who are no longer living. Aside from living persons, even dead persons (through their personal representatives or heirs) may have a protectable "right of publicity," especially where there is a considerable amount of fictionalization in a film being produced about such a deceased person. Releases from the proper living persons may have to be obtained in such circumstances (see "clearance," "defamation" or "defamation of character," "libel," "privacy, right of" and "releases").

decision-making continuum — A reference to the producer and distributor decisions relating to film distribution alternatives (i.e., at one end of the spectrum, the producer merely submits a property to a major studio/distributor for development and the film is produced on an in-house production/distribution basis. In this instance, the major studio/distributor obtains worldwide rights to distribute the film, bears all of the financial risk (although it is also significantly involved in shaping the quality of the product) and the distributor fees will be their highest (approximately 30 percent to 40 percent depending on the market and media). On the opposite end of the spectrum, the producer approaches the distributor with an already financed and completed film in addition to some or all of the prints and ads money needed and offering the distributor the opportunity to distribute the film in the domestic market only on a rent-a-system or rent-a-distributor basis. There is little or no financial risk for the distributor in that situation and its distribution fees are thus the lowest under those circumstances (approximately 12 percent to 15 percent). In between are the production-financing/distribution arrangements between a distributor and an independent producer, negative pickup and other third party production lending arrangements, the pure acquisitions and other variations on production financing, distribution funding, financial risk, creative control and distribution fees (see "acquisition distribution agreement," "distribution alternatives," "in-house production," "lender financing," "negative pickup," "production-financing/distribution agreement," and "rent-a-distributor").

deductions — Amounts allowed to taxpayers under the Internal Revenue Code as offsets against gross income or adjusted gross income (see "income," "loss" and "proportionate share of deductions").

deem — A verb meaning to think of as true. Film distribution agreements often provide that certain things may be deemed to be so by the distributor and such provisions are examples of distributor discretion that should be examined for reasonableness. From the independent producer's point of view, a more objective method for determining the truth or circumstances involved in any matter dealt with in a film distribution transaction is likely to be more preferable and therefore should be negotiated where possible (see "contract of adhesion" and "discretion").

de facto cross-collateralization — The unauthorized arbitrary allocation of gross receipts to a motion picture marketed as part of a package either to networks, cable, syndication markets or foreign territories. Such allocations effectively cross-collateralize the profits or losses of one movie with the profits or losses of other movies in the package (see "cross-collateralization," "cross-collateralization of

markets," "cross-collateralization of slates," "discretionary cross-collateralization" and "unauthorized cross-collateralization").

de facto strike — An unofficial and unauthorized work stoppage designed to force an employer to comply with employee demands (see "guild," "production slowdown," "strike" and "union").

defamation or defamation of character — The publication of anything injurious to the good name or reputation of another, or that tends to bring such person into disrepute. A defamation designed to be read is a libel; an oral defamation is a slander. There is no legal cause of action called defamation; libel and slander may be founded on defamation, but the right of action itself is libel or slander. A motion picture may defame a person, thus insurance is often obtained by producers to cover this risk (see "clearance," "libel," "slander" and "tort").

default — A failure to discharge a duty (e.g., failure of a debtor to make timely payments of interest and principal as they come due); some omission to do that which ought to have been done by one of the parties to a contract (see "breach of contract" and "interest").

default disaster — A phrase used to describe the potential situation when a motion picture licensee who pre-bought rights, decides to forfeit its deposit (if any), refuse to pay a promised advance and forego exhibition of the film in its territory after seeing the completed picture and determining that it is much worse than expected. This is particularly problematic if the original pre-sales contract was used by the producer as collateral to obtain a production loan. In that event, the bank may demand that the producer repay the loan and the producer may have to seek payment from the distributor. If the producer fails to repay the loan, the bank might foreclose on the film negative if it took a lien as further collateral, or attach the film and its proceeds even if it did not have an original lien (see "bank," "lender financing," "negative pickup," "pre-sales" and "split-rights basis").

defendant — The person defending or denying a legal complaint; the party against whom relief or recovery is sought in a legal action or law suit. In a civil proceeding, the defendant is one who is sued and is called upon by the complaint to make satisfaction for a wrong alleged by the plaintiff (see "action," "litigation," "plaintiff," "sue us" and "suit").

deferments or deferrals — All or a portion of salaries or compensation for cast, crew or others providing property or services for the production of a movie paid (by agreement) on a delayed basis after the property and/or services have been provided and usually after the release of the film. If such deferments are to be paid out of monies generated by the exhibition of the film they are also by definition contingent upon the film earning enough money to pay such deferments. In a studio financed production deal it is preferable from the producer's point of view (if possible) to have the deferments treated as distribution expenses as opposed to production overhead, since distribution expenses are not recouped until after the film is in distribution, whereas a studio's production overhead will be considered an interest-bearing production expense from the time it is incurred. Also, the distribution deal should clearly set out who pays such deferments as between the distributor and producer (see "contingent deferments," "fixed deferment," "percentage participation," "producer's share," "production cost deferments" and "points").

deferments schedule — A list, usually included as an exhibit to a film production-financing/distribution agreement, setting out the names, amounts and classes (if any) of deferred compensation to be paid to persons or entities who provided products or services in the production of a feature film (see "deferments" or "deferrals" and "pari passu").

deferral of taxes — Postponement of tax payments from the current year to a later year (see "deferral structures" and "income tax").

deferral structures — A reference to the structuring of a specific transaction, such as an advance payment, so as to delay the date of payment for tax purposes while still providing access to the cash in advance. Such tax deferral techniques include the use of a refundable deposit, standby letters of credit and payor/payee loans (see "advances," "deferral of taxes" and "refundable deposit").

deficiency letter — Written notice from the SEC to a prospective issuer of securities in a public offering that the registration statement and/or preliminary prospectus needs to be revised in ways specified in the letter (see "issuer," "private placement," "prospectus," "public offering" and "SEC").

delayed reduction of negative costs — (see "interest").

deleveraging — The reduction of a company's debt in relation to equity in the firm's capital structure. The more long-term debt a company has, the greater its financial leverage (see "financial management" and "leverage").

delinquency — Failure to make a payment on an obligation when due (see "debt" and "interest").

delivered answer print — (see "answer print" and "delivery").

delivery — In legal terminology, a voluntary transfer of title or possession from one party to another. The term is often defined in a film distribution agreement as a schedule that lists the physical items to be provided by the producer to the distributor (through the lab or otherwise) and sets the deadlines for such items to be delivered. Delivery is usually defined as a series of objective events and does not rely on distributor approval. Producers should watch out for the distributor who tries to insert subjective approval language in the delivery mechanism. Also, producers should examine the delivery schedule carefully with all providers of items on the list (e.g., film lab and E&O insurance carrier, to make certain that each item can be provided). Also, see that the delivery schedule is presented in chronological order for the convenience of those obligated to meet its requirements. Draft the delivery schedule so that it can be a useful and working document, not something that is signed and forgotten. Also, distributors sometimes want access to the producer's original delivery materials, but the producer may want to insist that those original materials being provided through a lab remain at the producer's laboratory, assuming that the producer actually selected the film lab. Producer's should also not fail to budget for the costs associated with delivery since such costs may be substantial (see "breach of contract," "laboratory access letter" and "laboratory letter").

delivery costs— Those expenses specifically associated with delivering the required materials to the distributor. For financial planning purposes, the producer must not overlook his or her projection of the costs relating to providing the delivery materials (see "delivery materials").

delivery date — The date or dates on which the required elements specified in the distribution agreement (i.e., in the delivery schedule that may be attached as an exhibit to the distribution agreement) are to be delivered to the distributor or made available to the distributor through the lab. Generally, delivery is defined by the specific distribution agreement that provides the producer with a means to objectively comply with his, her or its obligations under the distribution agreement (see "delivery schedule").

delivery date acceleration — A rarely used provision in a film distribution deal that may permit the distributor to move the date for delivery of certain items forward in the event that the producer is in breach of specified provisions of the agreement (e.g., in exercising the producer's or distributors cutting rights, he or she does not comply with the distributor's release schedule or bidding and distribution requirements; see "delivery date").

delivery items — The specific items slated to be delivered by the producer to the distributor pursuant to the film distribution agreement's delivery schedule (see "delivery materials," "delivery schedule" and "major delivery items").

delivery materials — The film related items required to be delivered to the distributor, including the laboratory access letter, attached as an exhibit, so the distributor will have access to the film materials, a delivery schedule and list of film credits. The specific items listed for delivery typically include final screenplay and shooting script, publicity material, credit statement, black and white photographs, color photographs, final answer print, original picture negative and composite optical soundtrack negative, interpositive, television cover shots and scenes, internegatives, main and end titles, music, dialogue and sound items, film and soundtrack materials, screen credits, dialogue, action continuity, laboratory letter, MPAA certificate, certificate of insurance, residual information, title and copyright reports, soundtrack album materials, work print and out-takes (see "delivery requirements" and "delivery schedule").

delivery requirements — A provision in a film distribution agreement that sets out the actions to be taken and the items to be delivered to a film's distributor pursuant to the distribution agreement. The delivery requirements section of a film distribution agreement must be carefully drafted so that the distributor will not be able to refuse delivery of the completed film on subjective grounds. In addition, if the delivery requirements provision is not carefully drafted, a negative pickup agreement may not be acceptable to a lender, investors or other motion picture financiers (see "delivery materials," "delivery schedule" and "negative pickup agreement").

delivery schedule — A list (usually an exhibit to a film distribution agreement) that sets out the items to be provided by a film's producer to the distributor (much of which is provided through the lab) and provides the deadlines for such delivery (see "delivery," "laboratory access letter" and "objective delivery requirements").

demand — The quantity and quality of movie or movies that the general public or a projected audience wants to or will pay to see at any given time (i.e., the collective desires of the general public or projected audience to see a given movie, a specific type of movie or a unique combination of elements in a movie). Studio executives are presumed to have some ability in anticipating such audience demand, however, in 1983 longtime studio executive David Picker

was quoted in William Goldman's book (*Adventures in the Screen Trade*) stating: "If I had said yes to all the projects I turned down, and no to all the ones I took, it would have worked out about the same." Thus, the above-stated presumption may not be accurate in many instances and the Hollywood insider stranglehold on key studio executive positions for more than one hundred years cannot be justified (see "elements" and "projected audience").

demand loan — Loan with a set maturity date, after which the lender may call for repayment at any time (see "debt," "interest" and "lender financing").

demand note — The loan instrument that by its express terms is payable immediately on an agreed-upon date of maturation without requiring any further demand. The maker of the note acknowledges his, her or its liability as of the due date; also included are those instruments payable on sight or upon presentation or for which no time for payment is stated (see "debt" and "interest").

demographics — The statistical characteristics of a specific human population, such as a movie audience or movie audiences generally. Such characteristics typically include (among other things) age, sex, income and level of education (see "marketing research," "profile" and "projected audience").

depreciation — A deduction allowed to a taxpayer representing a reasonable allowance for the exhaustion, obsolescence, wear and tear of tangible property used in a trade or business, or tangible property held for the production of income. The depreciation deduction is allowed for the loss of value of tangible assets due to wear, use, etc., as well as obsolescence and passage of time. Where property is entitled to depreciation, a more rapid deduction method (more rapid than straight-line depreciation) may be permitted (see "accelerated cost recovery," "amortization," "deduction," "expense," "income forecast method," "Section 181 of IRS Code," "straight-line depreciation" and "tax benefits").

derivative distribution rights — Film distribution rights relating to remakes and sequels for both film and television (see "ancillary rights" and "sequel").

description of business — Another name or title for a major section in a securities disclosure document providing information (i.e., disclosures) relating to the industry in which the business is to be conducted, competition, operational information and so forth. The description of business section of a securities disclosure document may contain some of the same or similar information as a business plan but the two documents are not the same are not intended to be used for the same purpose (see "plan of business," "private placement offering memorandum" and "securities disclosure document").

descriptive titles — Titles of films that, to some extent, describe what the film is about (see "movies with a message" and "title treatment").

designated market area — The Nielsen audience-market classification that designates a certain market area in which local television stations have partial or complete dominance over stations from other market areas. The concept is similar to Arbitron's ADI and is sometimes used in film distribution to designate

a geographical area of a film's release (see "ADI Market").

designator — One who designates (see "designee").

designee — One who is designated, (i.e., appointed to serve; see "designator").

detailed budget breakdown — An item by item analysis of a film's budget that may be some twenty-five or more pages in length (see "budget," "use of proceeds" and "top sheet").

detailed cost reports — (see "cost reports").

devaluation — The lowering of the value of a country's currency relative to gold and/or the currencies of other nations. Devaluation can also result from a rise in value of other currencies relative to the currency of a particular country (see "currency," "currency conversion" and "exchange rate").

development — In the broader sense, the initial stage in the preparation of a film. In this sense, development includes formulating and organizing the idea or concept for the movie, the acquisition of rights to the underlying literary work or screenplay, preparing an outline, synopsis and/or treatment and writing, polishing and revising the various drafts of the script, attaching elements to the script and seeking production financing. In the more narrow sense, this same term means those activities relating specifically to taking an idea or concept and turning it into a finished screenplay. Note that in either case, it may be necessary to spend some money on such activities, particularly packaging, thus some form of film financing may be required to fund the activities of the development stage (see "development process," "development stages," "packaging," "preliminary/development offering," "pre-production" and "step deal").

development financing — Arranging, acquiring or raising funds to finance the activities relating to the first stage in the life of a film (i.e., development in the broadest sense; see "development," "development deal," "investment contract," "investor financed development offering," "investor financing agreement" and "loan").

developmental funds — The monies required to pay the expenses associated with the earliest stage in the process of making a film, the development stage (contrast with "seed money"; see "development," "investor financed development offering," "investment contract," "preliminary investors" and "venture capital").

development company — A film company that specializes in developing motion picture properties (see "development").

development deal — Typically, an agreement by a studio or production entity to provide early funding for a producer during the development of a motion picture project or projects. Development funds may also be provided to directors or screenwriters. The major studios commonly fund the development costs of many screenplays that are never approved for production and those costs are recouped from the budgets of the movies that are produced as part of the studio's overhead charge. To the extent that studio development activities are inefficient, as they are widely believed to be, such overhead charges imposed on other films are unreasonable (see "creative accounting" and "overhead").

development expenses — In the broadest sense, the costs associated with the earliest stage in the preparation of a motion picture project. Development expenses might include optioning or acquiring the screenplay or an underlying property, attorney and/or accounting fees, screenwriter compensation, research costs, preliminary budget preparation, packaging costs and expenses associated with seeking production financing. In the more narrow sense, development costs are those directly associated with the development of the script (see "development money investment agreement," "investor financed development offering," "investment contract" and "preliminary/development offering").

development fee — A specified amount of money agreed to be paid to a producer or production company by a motion picture production financing source, (e.g., a studio, for activities relating to the development of a motion picture project). If the project proceeds to production any development fee payment may be deducted from other producing fees to be paid to the production entity ("development").

development hell — A situation in which a film project enters the studio development process, but never actually gets production funding and never actually is made available to other production companies because it is not placed in turnaround (see "development process," "turnaround" and "turnaround hell").

development financing — Raising the money to pay for the development activities relating to a film or films. In recent years, the major studios have used corporate funds or funds raised by various other means. Independent producers are more likely to use the investor financed development offering as the developmental financing vehicle, although corporate funds (for production companies organized as a corporation), or even loans may provide development financing (see "development," "development risk," "investor financed development offering," "investment contract" and "step deal").

development money investment agreement — A written contract, that may utilize a letter format, between an active investor and a feature film producer to provide funding of development activities associated with the picture (see "investment contract," "investor financed development offering," "investor financing agreement," "preliminary/ development funds" and "preliminary/ development offering").

development notes — A report on a review of a screenplay draft that is being developed by a film studio or production company that analyzes the script's storyline, plot structure, characters, scenes, etc. and makes suggestions on how the screenplay can be improved. This analysis may play a role in determining whether the project is approved for production (see "coverage," "green light," "reader" and "story analyst").

development process — The series of activities, procedures and changes that take a script idea or concept and ultimately lead to a finished screenplay (see "idea," "concept," "outline," "synopsis," "treatment," "first draft," "polish," "revision," "rewrite" and "shooting script").

development risk — The possibilities that the investment of time, skill and money in the development of a screenplay will be lost (i.e., production funds for the film will not be forthcoming and the film will not be produced).

Since hundreds of scripts are developed each year for each film that is actually produced, the development risk is considerable, therefore financiers of development costs may reasonably expect a higher rate or return on their investment (i.e., anywhere from two to five times the amount invested). In the alternative, such investors will want to continue to participate in the film's profits without limiting their upside potential (see "development financing" and "production risk").

development stages or steps — The specifically identifiable phases a motion picture script goes through during development, including idea, concept, outline, synopsis, treatment, first draft, polish, revision, rewrite, final screenplay, shooting script, etc. Few of the film projects in development actually are taken through the full series of development steps. A studio development deal, for example, may have a total possible cost of $950,000, but the first step of the deal may only cost $100,000, and the project may receive no financial commitment beyond that. In that situation, the producer may have to decide whether to seek a reversion of rights and continue to develop the project on his or her own or to get the project into turnaround (see "development process," "reversion right" and "turnaround").

DGA — (see "Director's Guild of America").

DGA basic agreement — The employment agreement for motion picture directors that has been approved by signatory production companies and the Director's Guild of America on behalf of its director members. The agreement provides minimum standards for the employment of directors relating to compensation, benefits, residuals, working conditions and other important issues (see

"Director's Guild of America" and "signatories").

dialogue — Spoken words in a film or screenplay (see "dialogue replacement," "screenplay" and "script supervisor").

dialogue director — The film production person responsible for reviewing lines with actors prior to a take (see "dialogue").

dialogue track(s) — The audio track(s) of a motion picture sound track that only contain spoken material. The dialogue tracks exist only as separate tracks until the final mix of music, sound effects and dialogue into a composite sound track (see "music track" and "sound effects track").

dialogue replacement — The re-recording of conversation between two or more characters on the soundtrack of a motion picture. Dialogue may need to be replaced for several reasons (i.e., the original recording on location may have produced poor quality sound or specific words or phrases may no longer be appropriate). In replacing dialogue, the actors have to lip sync their own voices and in some instances the voices of others. Actor employment agreements should provide for such contingencies (see "automatic dialogue replacement," "employment agreement" and "looping").

digital media — Any form of information stored in the computer, including data, voice and video. Also, an storage device that holds digital data, including hard and optical disks and USB drives (see "digital music player,""media player," and "USB device").

digital music player — Hardware or software that plays audio files encoded in MP3, AAC,

WMA or other audio formats. There are several software-based music players that play audio files in a desktop or laptop computer, such as iTunes, RealPlayer and Windows Media Player. On the hardware side, countless handheld players use flash memory or a hard disk to hold songs downloaded from the user's computer. Low-capacity units with only 128MB of flash memory hold approximately thirty songs in the MP3 format. Flash-based players with 4GB of memory can store a thousand titles. Hard disk models can handle up to fifteen thousand tunes and more. Apple's iPod has clearly been the industry leader in portable music players (see "digital media" and "media player").

Digital Millennium Copyright Act (DMCA) — A complex and controversial piece of legislation passed by the U.S. Congress in 1998 that purportedly was designed to bring copyright law up to date with the development of digital media. Among other things, the DMCA outlaws the manufacture of, or "trafficking" in, technologies capable of circumventing so-called "technical protection measures" used to restrict access to copyrighted works. Ostensibly this provision of the DMCA was designed to discourage the (already) illegal pirating of protected material, but the law also has some rather sweeping side effects. In particular, it effectively eviscerates the long-standing "fair use" exceptions to copyright. If a publisher can use technology to enforce where, when and how a copyrighted work is accessed, and if the law bars consumers from circumventing such technologies, even with products they have legally purchased, then the provisions of "fair use" become irrelevant (see "content scramble system," "fair use" and "piracy").

digital video — An optical media format that can be used for data storage. It can be used for movies and offers high video and sound quality (see "digital video disc" and "high definition television").

digital video disc (DVD) — An optical disc storage media format that can be used for data storage, including movies with high video and sound quality. DVDs resemble compact discs since their physical dimensions are the same (120 mm/4.72 inches or occasionally 80 mm/3.15 inches in diameter) but they are encoded in a different format and at a much higher density. All DVDs, replicated (factory pressed), recorded (burned), video, audio, data or otherwise are DVD-ROM discs, though many refer to a "DVD-ROM" as a pressed data disk only. A DVD with properly formatted and structured video content is a DVD-Video. DVDs with properly formatted and structured audio are DVD-Audio discs. Everything else (including other types of DVD discs with video) is referred to as a DVD-Data disc. From an historical perspective, the use of DVD's did not take off quite as fast as some of the early predictions, but it has sold faster than the videotape, CD and laserdisc formats. In fact, before the third anniversary of the availability of the DVD as of March 2000, the DVD had become the most successful consumer electronics entertainment product ever. As of the fall of 2003, 16 million DVD-Video players had been shipped in the U.S. adding to an existing installed base of 73.3 million. In addition, more than 27,000 DVD-Video titles were available in the U.S. at the time and that number has certainly increased since. When DVD players became available in early 1997, Warner and Polygram were the only major movie studios to release titles. Additional titles were available from small publishers. The other studios gradually joined the DVD camp. Dreamworks was the last significant studio to announce full DVD support. Paramount, Fox, and Dreamworks initially supported only Divx, but in the summer of 1998 they each announced support for open DVD. Eventually, DVD player sales exceeded VCR sales in 2001. DVD recorders are expected to hasten the death of VCRs once the price difference is small enough. DVDs have many advantages over tapes, such as no rewinding, quick access to any part of a recording and fundamentally lower technology cost for hardware and disc production. By 2010, VHS may be as dead as vinyl records were in 2000 (same as "DVD-ROM").

diligence — Attention to the matter at hand. Due diligence or reasonable diligence is that diligence that is required by the circumstances, the rendering of which prevents liability for negligence. This standard of conduct is a relative one, and is determined by considering the facts of each particular case. In the context of a securities offering, such as a film limited partnership or manager-managed LLC, the phrase due diligence refers to the securities underwriter's or participating dealer's obligation to verify independently the facts and representations provided by a seller or issuer of securities. The objectives of such "due diligence" are to develop confidence that the offering document contains full and fair disclosure and that the prospective investors have a shot at an economic benefit (see "due diligence").

dilution — A reduction in the value of corporate shares through the issuance of additional shares or the exercise of rights relating to convertible securities, warrants or stock options (see "corporation").

direct advertising — Advertising, such as the mailing of flyers or mass e-mails, directed to individuals within a specific target group (see "advertising" and "projected audience").

direct charges — Expenses that apply specifically to a given activity, such as production or distribution (see "direct distribution expenses" and "overhead").

direct costs — Expenses specifically related to the production of a given motion picture (contrast with "indirect costs and expenses" and "production overhead").

direct distribution expenses — All costs and expenses incurred, paid, payable or accrued, in connection with the distribution, advertising, exploitation and turning to account of a motion picture. The largest two items relating to the release of any picture are advertising/publicity and print costs. Other direct expenses may include, but are not limited to, such things as checking and collection costs, certain taxes and freight. Items like trade-association fees and assessments, guild payments, along with market research should be considered indirect or at most, allocated amongst several films that benefit from such expenditures. Generally direct distribution expenses are specifically defined or described in some detail in a section of the distribution agreement or in an exhibit to the distribution agreement. Claimed or exaggerated distribution expenses often form the primary focus of producer audits. If the distribution agreement limits distributor expense deductions to direct expenses, the profit participant auditors will be concerned with ferreting out indirect expenses that are claimed by the distributor as direct expenses. Specific categories of direct expenses that the distributor may deduct should be itemized. Other "indirect expenses" such as the distributor's general administrative overhead and similar internal costs, should be regarded as a normal cost of doing business for the distributor and not recoupable from the picture's proceeds or at least the producer should negotiate for as small a percentage of such expenses to be charged to the picture as possible. It may also be useful to establish some relationship between that percentage and the number of films distributed by the distributor in the course of a year. Otherwise the producer should be certain that the word "direct" is inserted in front of the general description of what kind of expenses are to be deducted as distribution expenses (see "creative accounting" and "contractually defined terms").

direct government subsidies — (see "government subsidies").

director agreement — (see "DGA basic agreement" and "director's employment agreement").

director commitment — A promise from a motion picture director that he or she will direct a certain motion picture. Such commitments may range from informal, oral "hand-shake" deals to written director employment agreements that contain full pay and play provisions (see "letter of intent," "letter of interest," "nominal payments," "pay or play" and "pay and play").

director (corporate) — One who sits on a board of directors of a corporation and who has the legal responsibility of exercising control over the officers and affairs of the entity. A director has a fiduciary duty to the corporation and to its stockholders to manage the affairs of the corporation in a manner that is consistent with the shareholders' interests. Any breach of this fiduciary duty may subject a corporate director to personal liability to both the shareholders and the corporation (see "fiduciary" and "shareholders").

director deferment — A portion of a motion picture director's salary, the payment of which is delayed by agreement. Such deferments are usually paid out of the film's revenue stream and with investor financed independent films, after investor recoupment (see "deferment").

director (film) — In the film industry, the person who is generally regarded as the primary creative force behind a motion picture and who oversees its entire artistic production. Also, the person who controls the action and dialogue in front of the camera and who is therefore responsible for interpreting and expressing in a film the intentions of the screenwriter and producer as set out in the screenplay. The director is usually hired by the producer (see "auteur," "collaborative process," "creative control," "final cut," "hyphenate" and "producer").

director of photography (DP) — The film production title and credit given to the cinematographer, who is responsible to the film's director for achieving optimum photographic images for the film (i.e., lighting, framing and shooting the film, in collaboration with the director). The DP usually does not actually run the camera (the job of the camera operator) but the DP oversees everything having to do with the camera and lighting (e.g., selecting the camera and lighting equipment, supervising the camera and lighting crews and determining the lighting pattern and exposure for each scene; see "cinematographer").

director's cast list — The list of a film's cast prepared by the director during the film's pre-production and for filing with the appropriate unions/guilds, if involved (see "director" and "guild").

director's cut — A completed motion picture consisting of the audio and visual elements chosen by the director. A director's cut is sometimes used as a sneak preview (see "creative control," "final cut," "other versions" and "sneak preview").

director's development deal — A financing commitment by a studio or other production company to finance the costs of a film project being developed by a director as opposed to a producer (see "development deal").

director's employment agreement — The written contract between the feature film director and the producing entity that sets out the terms and conditions pursuant to which the director is to provide directing services for a given motion picture (see "above-the-line employment agreements," "loan-out agreement," "straight employment agreement" and "three-party agreement").

Directors Guild of America (DGA) — The film industry trade union for directors, assistant directors and production managers. Through the collective voice of more than thirteen thousand members that the DGA represents, the Guild seeks to protect directorial teams' legal and artistic rights, contend for their creative freedom, and strengthen their ability to develop meaningful and credible careers (see "director" and "industry groups").

director's promotional budget — Monies allocated for the promotion of a film by the film's director (see "director" and "promotional activities").

director's questionnaires — Questionnaires circulated by a corporation's counsel to directors, officers and 10 percent stockholders seeking information about such individuals, the company and their relationships with the company for the purpose of gathering data that must be disclosed in securities registration statements (see "corporation," "insider," "insider trading," "public offering" and "securities").

directory advertising — The kind of movie advertising typically run by exhibitors in newspapers every day that usually contains only the title of the films being shown, the theater's name, address and phone number along with the times at which each film is to be exhibited (see "display advertising").

direct participation program — An investment opportunity structured so as to allow the investors to participate directly in the cash flow and tax benefits of the underlying investment. Such programs are usually organized as limited partnerships or more recently as manager-managed limited liability companies (LLCs). The use of these investment vehicles as tax shelters in the U.S. has been significantly limited by tax legislation affecting passive investments. On the other hand, the use of such investment vehicles for raising some or all of the development or production funds for low and ultra-low budget feature and documentary films and as a means for spreading the risks associated with such projects amongst a large group of passive investors remains fairly consistent (see "active investors," "limited liability company," "limited partnership" and "passive investors").

direct-to-video release — A feature film produced without any intention of seeking a foreign or domestic theatrical release or that goes into video/DVD release because it was unable to attract a theatrical distribution deal. Generally, such features are low or ultra-low budget productions. Some production companies target

their productions for this specific market so as to avoid the much talked about theatrical distributor/exhibitor accounting and business practices that tend to result in very few instances of net profit participations for producers and/or other net profit participants (see "business practices," "creative accounting," "DVD" "theatrical release" and "video/DVD revenue reporting").

dirty dupe — A black and white copy of the spliced, scratched and dirty work print (i.e., a work print that has not been timed ; see "work print").

disadvantage — An unfavorable condition. Each form of film finance offers certain advantages and certain disadvantages. There is no single "best way" to finance a feature film for all motion picture producers. Independent producers should be extremely cautious and/or avoid altogether the film finance consultants who vigorously advocate a single form of film finance while claiming there are no disadvantages (see "advantage," "availability analysis," "financing" and "pro and con analysis").

disbursement — In investor financing, the paying out of money in the discharge of a debt or an expense, as distinguished from a distribution to investors (see "cash distributions").

disbursing agent — The entity or individual responsible for paying the debts or expenses out of a fund on behalf of others. The film distributor usually acts as the disbursing agent for feature films and therefore has the power and authority to interpret all contract provisions relating to the payment of profit participations to others. Most film industry observers seem to agree that all of the major studio/distributors have a problem with arithmetic and all of their errors seem to be in favor of the distributor. However, some of those so-called creative accounting problems are not based on poor math, but an interpretation of contract provisions not favorable to third party profit participants (see "creative accounting" and "revenue stream").

discharged — In bankruptcy, the release of the debtor from most of his, her or its debts (see "bankruptcy").

disclosure — The release by corporations, limited partnerships or other entities seeking to raise money through some form of securities offering of all information, positive or negative, that might bear on an investment decision, as required by the securities laws (see "anti-fraud rule" and "securities").

disclosure document — The written and bound information that is required by the federal and state securities laws to be provided in advance to prospective purchasers of securities. The securities disclosure document associated with a private placement (exempt offering) is typically called an "offering memorandum" and the securities disclosure document associated with a public/registered offering is typically referred to as a "prospectus" (see "industry overview," "offering circular," "plan of business," "private placement offering memorandum," "preliminary prospectus," "program highlights," "prospectus," "red herring" and "use of proceeds").

disclosure requirement — The information required to be provided by the issuer of a security to prospective investors in the form of a disclosure document pursuant to a specific form of registration or exemption from registration (see "disclosure document").

discount — An entertainment lending institution's reduction from the stated amount provided for in a distribution or pre-sale agreement, resulting in the amount of cash such lender is willing to advance to a film producer based on the contractual commitment. Such cash advance is always less than the amount stated in such agreements (see "bank," "lender financing," "negative pick-up," "pre-production financing," "pre-sales" and "split rights deal").

discounted cash flow — The value of future expected cash receipts and expenditures at a common date, calculated using net present value or internal rate of return. Discounted cash flow is a factor in analyses of both capital investments and securities investments (same as "present value" and "time value of money").

discounting — In film, the practice of paying or lending a film producer an amount in cash less a certain per cent against the future value of a distribution contract and/or pre-sale commitment (e.g., a lender may require that the producer provide so-called "bankable" commitments equal to 115 percent of a film's budget in order to lend the producer 100 percent of the monies required to produce the movie; see "bankable," "lender financing," "negative pickup," "pre-sale commitment" and "split rights deal").

discounts — A reduction in price. Such reductions are often negotiated and/or awarded by exhibitors and other feature film licensees to distributors on a given picture or they are sometimes based on the volume of pictures provided by the distributor. Distributors often seek to exclude the value of such discounts in profit participation calculations, arguing that the distributor's activities are responsible for earning such credits. However, without the feature film or films made available to the distributor by the producer and other profit participants, the distributor would not be in a position to either negotiate or receive such discounts. Producers may therefore want to negotiate a fair provision in the distribution agreement that includes the value of such discounts in the profit participation calculations (see "kickback" and "rebate").

discretion — The power or right to choose between alternative courses of action or inaction. Many film distribution agreements are currently drafted so as to include numerous situations in which the distributor is allowed to exercise its discretion, sometimes even its "sole unfettered discretion" (as if there is a higher level of discretion than "discretion"). Such distributor discretion may relate to the manner and extent of the film's release and the markets selected, as well as the theaters in each such market, to sales methods, policies and terms, to the right of the distributor to refrain from commencing distribution or discontinuing distribution in any country or place at any time and to allocating license payments among films marketed as a package. In negotiating with distributors, independent producers should seek to eliminate unnecessary, undesired or potentially troublesome distributor discretion. Producers may want to pay particular attention to the provisions that include the following words or phrases which indicate someone, usually the distributor, is being allowed to exercise its discretion: "allocation," "apportion," "best efforts," "customary," "customarily," "deem," "discretion," "good faith," "industry standards," "latitude," "reasonably," "reasonably deem," "reasonable efforts," "usual" and "usual

and customary manner." All of such terms have been used in film distribution agreements. When such a word or phrase is used, the producer may want to determine who's discretion is involved and then consider whether it is possible to negotiate and draft language that provides a more objective standard with which to comply. Some discretion will almost always be necessary, but discretion can also be an invitation for abuse. Since film distributors have a well-documented one hundred-year history of abuse of discretion the elimination of such distributor discretion may be essential to the preservation of the rights of all profit participants (see "creative accounting," "latitude" and "trust me").

discretionary cross-collateralization — The offsetting of motion picture profits by a distributor between markets or films in situations where the distribution agreement does not address the practice (i.e., such cross-collateralization is left to the discretion of the distributor; see "cross-collateralization," "cross-collateralization of markets," "cross-collateralization of slates," "de facto cross-collateralization" and "unauthorized cross-collateralization").

discretionary funds — A small percentage of a mutual fund, trust, pension or other fund which, at the discretion of the fund manager, may be invested in a broad range of securities even high risk investments such as motion picture production. Some so-called Hollywood money middle men, finders and/or scam artists, have been known to request an up front payment from producers seeking to access such supposedly existing discretionary funds for production financing, for the purpose of using such monies to pay what in effect might be considered a commercial bribe to an asset manager who would then divert some of the discretionary funds under his or her management toward payment of the production costs of the motion picture. Unfortunately, once the up front payment is made, the financial go between and his principal disappear (see "asset management," "commercial bribery" and "scam").

discrimination — The treatment of someone differently on a basis other than merit; the unequal treatment of parties who are similarly situated. Federal law prohibits discrimination on the basis of race, sex, nationality, religion and age in matters of employment, housing, education, voting rights and access to public facilities. Also, states or any government bodies may not engage in actions that result in discrimination on grounds of race, sex, nationality, religion or age (see "anti-Semitism," "bias," "blacklisting," "cronyism," "nepotism," "prejudice," "problem producer," "reciprocal preference," "relationship driven business" and "reverse discrimination").

disgruntled investor — An investor who becomes unhappy about an investment for any reason, even reasons not directly related to the investment, since unhappy people can always come up with reasons for regretting an investment decision. Disgruntled investors often request that their money be refunded (see "rescission" and "rescission offer").

display advertising — Advertising in newspapers and magazines that features art work or other information relating to a specific film (see "directory advertising").

display art — The illustrations used in print advertising. Display art often includes title art, body copy and the billing for a movie (see "display advertising" and "title art").

dispute resolution provision — A clause in a contract that sets out an agreed upon method for resolving disagreements between the parties to the contract. In film industry agreements, such provisions are extremely important for the following reasons: no single person can make a commercial feature film alone, disagreements often occur among various contributors to a film project and such disagreements usually need to be resolved quickly in order to take advantage of the availability of certain skilled persons committed to the project or to avoid the loss of vast sums of money already invested (see "arbitration," "arbitration clause" and "expedited arbitration").

disqualifiers — A list of conditions typically imposed on the use of both state and federal, registered and exempt securities offerings that disqualifies the issuer from relying on a given form of registration or exemption if certain persons associated with the issuer have violated certain, (mostly securities related) rules, laws or orders in the past five years. Because of these issuer disqualifiers, it is important for any issuer of a security (e.g., a film limited partnership and its general partners, or a manager-managed LLC and its manager) to be very familiar with the backgrounds of the people involved in helping to raise money for the offering (also called "bad boy rules," "issuer disqualifiers"; see "finder" and "issuer").

dissolution — The end of the legal existence of an entity. The process is governed by statute in most states (see "liquidation" and "winding up").

distant locations — Union terminology for out-of-town locations on which a film's production employees are required to remain away and to be lodged overnight (see "nearby locations").

distributable cash — A defined term in a direct participation program offering (e.g., limited partnership or manager-managed LLC offerings) that typically sets out what deductions, if any, will be made from program gross revenues before arriving at the actual cash to be distributed to the investors, for example: all funds received by the entity from its activities minus (a) all operating expenses of the entity, including, if any, all remaining unreimbursed offering expenses and expenses incurred by the entity in connection with the distribution and exploitation of the pictures and the ancillary rights thereto; (b) such reserves as the management deems necessary in accord with good business practice to cover future entity expenses; (c) all costs of production of the pictures that have not been supplied by the entity, by a completion guarantor or by any pre-sales or other similar agreements (such as, for example production funds obtained through loans); and (d) any deferments or percentage participations that are contractually committed to be paid out of gross entity revenues. Some limited partnerships use the term "net partnership receipts" to described the same or similar concept. The corresponding terminology for an LLC would be "net LLC receipts" (see "cash distributions," "gross partnership revenues," "limited liability company," "partnership expenses" and "partnership net receipts").

distribute — The act of selling or licensing a motion picture in various markets or media [see "distribution (film)"].

distributing syndicate — In securities offerings, a group of brokerage firms or investment bankers that join forces in order to facilitate the distribution of a large block of securities (see "selling group").

distribution (film) — The selling or licensing of a motion picture in various markets or media along with the advertising and promotion of the film. This process includes negotiating with exhibitors and licensees, determining the number of prints to be ordered from the lab (or arranging for the digital exhibition of the picture), planning and implementing the advertising and promotional campaign, transporting the prints to the theaters for exhibiting (if prints are still used) and collecting film rentals or other revenue from the exploitation of the film in all markets and media (see "distributor" and "sub-distributor").

distribution (finance) — A payment in cash or in property by an entity to the owner or owners of such entity (e.g., a corporate dividend to its shareholders is a corporate distribution, the payment of a portion of limited partnership net receipts to its limited partners is a partnership distribution and the payment of an LLC's distributable cash would be a distribution for a manager-managed LLC; see "corporation," "limited liability company" and "limited partnership").

distribution (securities) — The offer and sale of securities to prospective investors (see "controlled distribution," "offering" and "uncontrolled distribution").

distribution activities — In addition to the activities known as "distribution strategies," a film distributor is responsible for the collection of gross receipts, for computing all deductions from gross receipts and disbursing funds to participants (see "disbursing agent," "discretion" and "distribution strategy").

distribution advance — Money paid by a film distributor to a film's producer as partial consideration for certain rights to distribute the film with some or all of such payments made either at the time the distribution agreement is signed and/or upon delivery pursuant to the distribution agreement's delivery schedule. In either case, such advanced sums are generally recoupable from the distributor's gross receipts generated by the exploitation of the film (see "advance" and "delivery").

distribution agreement — The contract between a film's producer and its distributor through which the distributor commits to distribute the film in specified territories or throughout the universe, for a set period of time (sometimes in perpetuity), and that defines the other important terms including how and when each party is to be compensated (see "deal memo," "deal points," "distribution checklist," "license agreement," "long form distribution agreement," "production agreement," "minimum rating" and "rent-a-distributor").

distribution alternatives — The various ways that are available to release and distribute a motion picture. From an analytical perspective, there appears to be five major ways in which U.S. made motion pictures are distributed: (1) films referred to as in-house productions are developed, produced and distributed by the major studio/distributors or independent production/distribution entities that have the capacity to manage an in-house production, (2) films financed by the major studio/distributors using the production-financing distribution agreement will arrange for their affiliated distribution arm to distribute the film, (3) distributors providing distribution agreements and guarantees to film producers prior to production of the film so that those distribution agreements and guarantees can be taken to a bank or banks to be used as effective collateral

for some form of lender financing will distribute the film when complete (e.g., negative pickups and foreign pre-sales), (4) distributors acquire the rights to distribute an already completed film through an acquisition distribution agreement or (5) the rent-a-distributor situation in which an independent producer finances both the production and distribution costs, only using the distribution facilities of a distributor to distribute the film for a reduced distribution fee. When none of those more common forms of distribution are available, an independent producer may utilize some form of self-distribution (see "acquisition distribution agreement," "four walling," "in-house production," "negative pickups," "production-financing/distribution agreement," "rent-a-distributor" and "self-distribution").

distribution approach — The plan and strategy of a producer for distributing a film. A discussion of a producer's distribution approach is often an integral part of the discussion appearing in an film securities offering disclosure document (see "business plan," "disclosure document" and "distribution strategy").

distribution campaign — The overall plan and strategy for distributing a film, including advertising, promotion, number of prints (unless distributed digitally) and the release pattern (see "advertising" and "release pattern").

distribution channels— The worldwide combination of sub-distributors, foreign sales agents, and others involved in the distribution of a film that a given movie distributor utilizes on a regular basis (see "sub-distribution").

distribution checklist — A listing of the deal points to be negotiated and provided for in a film distribution agreement or a list of the activities to be undertaken in the process of distributing a film(see "deal memo," "deal points" and "distribution agreement").

distribution commitment — An agreement or pledge to provide a domestic or foreign theatrical release for a film; also agreements or pledges to provide certain specified aspects of such distribution (e.g., a specified level of expenditures for prints and ads). Producers should seek to negotiate reasonable commitments with distributors and actively monitor their implementation (see "prints and ads commitment" and "theatrical release").

distribution costs — (see "direct distribution expenses" and "distribution expenses").

distribution expenses — The costs involved in distributing a film. Generally included are expenses relating to advertising and publicity, conversion, checking, claims, collections, copyright and royalties, other versions of the film, insurance, trade dues, licenses, prints, taxes and transportation. Distribution expenses are usually deducted from the distributor's gross receipts after the distributor deducts its fees. Profit participation auditors report that distributors often exaggerate or inflate such distribution expenses (see "creative accounting," "direct distribution expenses," "pension fund contributions" and "theatrical releasing costs").

distribution fee or distributor's fee — The contractual amount that the company distributing a motion picture or television film charges for its distribution and related services. Such amounts are usually deducted out of the distributor's gross receipts and will typically vary from 30 percent to 40 percent, depending on the market and media. In the less common rent-a-distributor deal, the distribution fee may be in the 12 percent to 15 percent range. The distribution fee is intended to compensate the distributor for its selling efforts and the maintenance of its home office, branch offices, world-wide sales organization and the use of monies for releasing costs. Distribution fees are usually divided into two major categories: theatrical/non-theatrical and ancillary rights (see "decision-making continuum," "gross receipts," "outright sales," "rent-a-distributor" and "royalty fee basis").

distribution guarantee — A promise by a feature film distributor to pay a specific amount of money to or for the benefit of a film producer as consideration for the distributor's right to distribute the film. Such a distribution guarantee may be used by the film's producer as effective collateral to support a bank loan, or a producer may be able to use the distribution guarantee as a way of reassuring prospective investors that the film will be distributed (see "advance" or "advances," "guarantee" and "pre-sale guarantee").

distribution partnerships — Limited partnerships formed and funded for the purpose of raising money to pay for the print, advertising and other expenses incurred in distributing a motion picture or motion pictures. Traditionally, such P&A investors would participate in a movie's revenue stream before production money investors and certain of the expenses incurred by the partnership might qualify as deductions in the year incurred. Such direct participation programs may also be structured as manager-managed LLCs (see "cooperative advertising," "limited partnership" and "limited liability company").

distribution pattern — (see "release pattern").

distribution plan — The strategy a producer develops for acquiring a distributor for his or her film or the method to be utilized by the distributor in releasing a film (see "choosing a distributor," "release pattern," "release sequence").

distribution reports — Monthly summaries of information relating to the distribution of a film commonly required by a production lender. Such reports typically include release dates, print and advertising budgets, an itemization of gross film rentals, distribution fees, distribution expenses and the percentage participations of the producers and others (see "lender financing").

distribution rights — The legally enforceable interests in the distribution of a feature film that may include theatrical, ancillary and non-theatrical markets (see "rights").

distribution risk — From the point of view of the producer, investors and/or financiers, the term "distribution risk" may refer to the danger that a film will not get a distribution deal (i.e., not be distributed theatrically or at all). From the point of view of the distributor, the term may refer to the danger that, if released theatrically, the film may not recoup its acquisition and releasing costs (see "lender risk elimination," "risk," "risk disclosure" and "risk factors").

distribution strategy — The overall plan employed by a film's distributor in its release. Elements of the plan usually include the advertising and publicity strategy, timing of the release (i.e., what is the optimum time during the year, in which markets or cities and in what order and how to release), along with the activities involved in preparing and handling the bidding process with exhibitors and negotiating the terms of exhibition when necessary (see

"distribution activities" and "distribution approach").

distribution term — The period of time during which a film's distribution or licensee has the right to distribute the film in a given territory or media. Major studio/distributors often seek distribution rights in perpetuity (see "term" and "territory").

distribution territories— The geographical areas within which a distributor organizes its sub-distribution activities in the United States and the world. Major studio/distributors will often seek distribution rights through the universe, but in other instances distributors may split the domestic territory from international territories (see "split rights deal" and "territory").

distributions — In the context of a direct participation program as with a limited partnership or manager-managed LLC, any cash or other property distributed to investors, creative talent or third parties on account of their interest in the investment vehicle or agreements therewith. The term "distributions" usually will not include any payments to the entity management in the form of management fees, organization fees, production fees, selling fees or reimbursement for goods or services provided to the entity, assuming such payments are excluded pursuant to the limited partnership agreement or LLC operating agreement (see "distributable cash").

distributor — Any person or entity engaged in the business of renting, selling or licensing motion pictures to exhibitors; the person(s) or entities operating between the producer and exhibitor of motion pictures who obtain rights to the film, arranges for its exhibition, sends such film to exhibitors, sometimes through sub-distributors and collects film revenues and distributes such revenues to any profit participants based on their individual agreements. A distributor will typically deduct a distribution fee and distribution expenses at some pre-determined point from the film's revenue stream. The distributor is also generally responsible for the promotion of a film. To the extent that a producer has a choice of distributors, factors often considered important in the producer's selection of a distributor include amount of advance, extent of rights conveyed, cross-collateralization, guaranteed marketing commitment, input and/veto power over artwork and theater selection in top markets, track record, frequency of accounting statements, audit rights, producer's participation in promotion, marketing strategy, the deal, distributor's leverage with exhibitors, potential conflicts with other films the distributor is handling, turnaround provision and personal chemistry (see "creative accounting," "choosing a distributor," "direct distribution expenses," "law of supply and demand," "sub-distributor" and "track record").

distributor commercial — A promotional message (e.g., previews of other films to be released by the same distributor or any paid appearance of a product, commodity or service, as in product placements arranged by the distributor). The distribution agreement provision relating to distributor commercials should limit such commercials to before or after the exhibition of the film, unless product placements arranged by the distributor are approved by the producer and the distributor's product placement fee is included in the distributor's gross receipts for purposes of calculations involving the producer and other participants (see "commercials" and "product placement").

distributor commitments — (see "distribution commitment" and "financing").

distributor credit — Any extension of payment terms offered by the distributor to sub-distributors and/or exhibitors on indebtedness owed to the distributor by such entities. An abuse of such extensions delays payment to the producer and other profit participants (see "settlement transaction").

distributor credit-worthiness — The ability and willingness of a distribution company to pay its debts and other financial obligations in a timely manner. The credit-worthiness of a distributor who provides a negative pickup distribution agreement and distributor guarantee to a producer is a major consideration for the lender in the determination of whether to lend motion picture production funds to that producer using the distributor guarantee as collateral. From the lender's point of view, the risk relating to the credit-worthiness of the distributor is the only risk the lender is willing to assume in a negative pickup deal (see "lender financing," "lender risk elimination" and "negative pickup").

distributor/exhibitor split — A reference to the ratio of sharing as between the film distribution company and the theater in net box office earnings after the theater's overhead is deducted. The deal between the distributor and exhibitor may provide that the split changes each week that the film remains in the theater and generally the percentage going to the theater would increase each week (see "box office gross," "film rentals," "house nut," "ninety/ten deal" and "sliding scale").

distributor financing — Production financing for a film either partially or wholly provided by the film's distributor (see "financing").

distributor guarantee — (see "distribution guarantee").

distributor incentives — Provisions in a motion picture distribution agreement that tend to stimulate the distributor to more aggressively distribute a motion picture (i.e., to open the picture in the better theaters and to provide ample prints and ads expenditures). Production lenders sometimes require such incentives (e.g., having the distributor put up at least a quarter to one half of the film's production budget, letting the distributor keep higher distribution fees in the deal and/or having the distributor keep other rights to exploit besides domestic theatrical; see "distribution commitment").

distributor release campaign — The film distributor's strategy relating to the exhibition of a film and its implementation. The release campaign may include plans relating to advertising and publicity, the release date, the distributor's prints and ads commitment, the film's release pattern and its release sequence in all markets and media (see "advertising," "publicity," "release date," "release pattern" and "release sequence").

distributor rentals — (see "film rentals," "gross receipts" and "rentals").

distributor revenue — The total income (money or value received by a motion picture distributor) generated by the exploitation of a given film or received by distributors collectively for all films distributed during a given period (see "revenue recognition and reporting").

distributor's assumption agreement — A provision in the distribution agreement through which a film distributor takes possession of or lays claim to a feature film while also providing that the producer takes on the responsibility for certain liabilities of the distributor that are incurred by the distributor as a result of its distribution of the producer's film (see "assumption agreement" and "leverage").

distributor's film rentals — (see "film rentals" and "gross receipts").

distributor's gross receipts — A term that is usually defined in the distribution agreement and which typically refers to the total amount of money received by the distributor from all sources for the exploitation of a film (contrast with "film rentals").

diversification — The spreading of investment risk by putting assets into several categories of investments (e.g., stocks, bonds, money market instruments and precious metals, or into several industries, or into a mutual fund, with its broad range of stocks in one portfolio); at the corporate level, by entering into different business areas, as conglomerates do and in film by investing in more than one film (same as "spreading risk"; see "exotic investment product," "portfolio," "slate of pictures"and "risk factors").

diversity — With respect to business organizations or an industry like the film industry, the term diversity refers to a collective mixture of people of different so-called "races," ages, ethnicity, gender, regional origin, religion, cultures, sexual orientation, physical characteristics and other differentiating factors. For its one hundred year history, Hollywood has not been very diverse at any level, and as an American institution it has failed miserably in providing for diversity at the top (see "discrimination," "diversity casting incentives," "Hollywood control group" and "nepotism").

diversity casting incentives — A Screen Actors Guild program designed to increase acting opportunities for members of four so-called "protected groups." The program only applies to the SAG Modified Low Budget and Low Budget Agreements, but allows producers of such films to increase their budgets from $625,000 to $937,000 for the modified low budget films and from $2,500,000 to $3,750,000 for low budget films. A producer can demonstrate the required level of diversity by meeting specified criteria: (a) a minimum of 50 percent of the total speaking roles and 50 percent of the total days of employment are cast with performers who are members of the following four protected groups: (1) women, (2) senior performers (sixty years or older), (3) performers with disabilities, or (4) people of color (Asian/Pacific Islander, Black, Latino/Hispanic and Native American Indian) and; (b) a minimum of 20 percent of the total days of employment is cast with performers who are people of color. Although SAG must be commended for creating such a program to encourage diversity in casting the program falls short of meeting the real world needs of the Hollywood-based U.S. film industry in two important ways: (1) the film industry has been dominated for one hundred years by a small segment of a U.S. national minority (see "Hollywood control group" and "Hollywood insiders") and this small group has discriminated at all levels of the industry, but most particularly at the top executive levels, against all others including many groups not "protected" by the SAG diversity casting incentives (including such groups as Christians, Muslims, Catholics, Mormons, Whites from the South, Asians and Arabs) and (2) SAG does not even have jurisdiction to address the most critical form of discrimination in the U.S. film industry, the subtle forms of discrimination (nepotism, cronyism, favoritism, blacklisting, etc.) that have effectively prevented most of the industry's top level positions from being occupied by Hollywood outsiders (see "Hollywood outsiders," "low budget agreement," "modified low budget agreement"and "Screen Actors Guild").

divest or divestiture — To deprive or dispossess, especially of property, authority or title. In a legal sense, divestiture is a remedy, by virtue of which a court of law may order an offending party to rid itself of property or assets before that party would normally have done so. The purpose of divestiture is to deprive a defendant of the gains of his, her or its wrongful conduct and the remedy is commonly used to enforce antitrust laws. A court, however, will generally not invoke this rather extreme remedy unless it finds divestiture to be both necessary and practicable in preventing monopoly or restraint of trade. In 1948 after ten years of litigation, the major studio/distributors at that time were ordered to divest themselves of their theater holdings (i.e., vertical integration was deemed to be anti-competitive). The term divestiture may also refer to a corporation's orderly distribution of large blocks of another corporation's stock, that were held as an investment (see "antitrust laws," "combination in restraint of trade," "monopoly," "oligopoly," "Paramount Consent Decree of 1948," "restraint of trade" and "TriStar Case").

dividend — Distribution of corporate profits or earnings to the corporation's shareholders, prorated by class of security and paid in the form of money, stock or company products or property. The amount is decided in the discretion of the corporation's board of directors and is usually paid quarterly. Dividends must be declared as income by the recipient and thus are taxable in the year they are received. If the top level executives (i.e., management in a corporation) are able to control, manipulate and/or fool the corporation's board of directors, they may be able to successfully siphon off more of a corporation's revenue stream for their own compensation and the benefit of their cronies as opposed to allowing a larger amount of such corporate revenue to flow through to the corporate shareholders. For this reason, simply because a corporation consistently pays reasonable dividends to shareholders does not mean that management is competent or honest. It may mean that the company is making so much money that management can take excessive amounts for its own compensation, and with respect to the film industry specifically, allow additional excessive amounts to be paid to talent, their agents and entertainment attorneys who are all friends with corporate management while still paying the reasonable dividends (see "double taxation" and "limits on dividends").

division — An administrative or operating unit of a business (e.g., a corporation). In the film industry a studio may be a division of a larger corporate organization that has other divisions relating to feature film production, film distribution, a video/DVD company, publishing, cable television interests, a record company, etc. (see "corporate conglomerate").

division of gross receipts — The heading of a provision typically found in feature film distribution agreements that sets out what deductions the distributor will take from its gross receipts (e.g., distribution fees and distribution expenses), what the distribution fee percentages will be in each market, at what point any producer advance will be recouped and whether the distributor will participate in the balance (see "direct distribution expenses" and "net profits").

DMA — (see "designated market area").

DOCU/DRAMA — A film using actors which re-creates events that supposedly actually occurred (see "documentary").

documentary — A film or video presentation of actual events using the real people involved and not actors (see "docu/drama").

documentation — Furnishing, authenticating or supporting with written documents (see "loan documentation").

document-intensive business — A commercial activity requiring extensive contract negotiations and drafting of written agreements between many related parties. The motion picture business is a document-intensive business (see "entertainment industry").

dog and pony show — A somewhat irreverent reference to the sales presentation made by representatives of securities issuers to prospective investors or in other business related presentations (see "pitch" and "road show").

Dolby noise reduction — Any of a series of licensed noise suppression formats that yield an improved signal-to-noise ratio (i.e., a film sound system that minimizes noise level and allows for cleaner recording and greater fidelity; see "Dolby stereo" and "sound tracks").

Dolby sound — (see "Dolby noise reduction" and "Dolby stereo").

Dolby stereo — A licensed release print format in which four tracks of sound are derived through a process of encoding and decoding of the audio material contained on stereo optical tracks (see "Dolby noise reduction").

domestic contracts — The written agreements between U.S. distributors and film producers that U.S. banks may consider lending against (see "foreign contracts," "negative pickup").

domestic co-production — (see "co-production").

domestic corporation — A corporation doing business in the state in which it was incorporated. In all other states in the U.S., such a corporation's legal status is that of a foreign corporation. For that reason alone, it is not always advantageous to incorporate in a state other than the state in which a corporation is physically based and actually doing business, since many states require that foreign corporations register to do business where such business is actually being conducted (see "alien corporation" and "foreign corporation").

domestic distributor — A film distribution company that distributes films in the U.S. and Canada (see "distributor").

domestic number one hit — The top grossing film compared to other films during at least one week, which is one of the traditional time periods used for comparing the exhibition performances of feature films (see "blockbuster," "hit" and "tentpole film").

domestic pickup — A feature film, the distribution rights to which are acquired after the film is completed, through the means of an acquisition distribution agreement and that is only to be distributed pursuant to such agreement in the domestic theatrical marketplace (contrast with "negative pickup"; see "acquisition distribution agreement," "decision-making continuum," "distribution alternatives" and "worldwide pickup").

domestic receivables — Monies owed to a producer or distributor from domestic sources. Both domestic and foreign receivables from approved obligors are included in the borrowing base formulas used by entertainment lending banks (see "borrowing base formula" and "lender financing").

domestic rights — The authority to distribute a feature film in the U.S. and Canada (see "theatrical distribution").

domestic theatrical admissions — The number of people who buy tickets to see feature films exhibited at theaters in the U.S. and Canada during a given period of time (e.g., a year; see "box office gross" and "theatrical admissions").

domestic theatrical distribution contract — The agreement between a film's producer and distributor relating to the distribution of the film in U.S. and Canadian theaters (see "theatrical distribution").

domestic theatrical market — For U.S. produced films, the United States of America, the District of Columbia and Canada and their territories and possessions including Bermuda, the Bahamas and Puerto Rico (see "domestic rights").

domestic theatrical release — A motion picture exhibition pattern encompassing the U.S. and Canada (see "release pattern").

domestic version — A reference to the cut of a film that is released in the U.S. and Canada as contrasted with a version that may differ and which is released in foreign markets or that is prepared for television (see "cultural differences" and "other versions").

domicile — The place where an individual or entity has his, her or its permanent home or principal establishment, to where, whenever such individual or such entity's management is absent, it is their intention to return (see "foreign banks" and "foreign corporation").

dominant media conglomerates — The largest and most influential corporations in the communications industries including feature film production, distribution and exhibition, network television, cable television, radio, newspaper, magazines, book publishing, etc. When the Reagan administration eased regulatory restraints (i.e., adopted a policy of less government regulation — specifically a relaxation of the enforcement of the U.S. antitrust laws in the entertainment industry), the dominant media conglomerates including the major U.S. studio/distributors regained control over some of the most important theater chains. These exhibitor circuits are not only the largest in terms of the total number of theaters and screens, but are also the most strategically located in the leading film markets (see "antitrust laws," "communications industry," "entertainment industry," "number of screens," "major exhibition chains," "Paramount Consent Decree of 1948" and "TriStar Case").

double add-back — A commonly used over-budget penalty included in agreements for studio production financing of a film that permits the studio to recoup from the film's producer or director twice the amount of the overage prior to breakeven on the film. Notwithstanding the fact that unreasonable contractual penalties may not be enforceable, this studio over budget policy raises a question as to whether such over budget costs, when added twice, bear interest and overhead charges the second time around. Also, a determination has to be made as to whether the increased costs are due to certain factors excluded from the calculations relating to the question "was the over budget threshold exceeded." Distribution agreements sometimes exclude such costs as losses covered by insurance, losses caused by events of force majeure, changes initiated by or approved by the studio, third-party breaches, currency fluctuations, union increases and/or lab increases (see "budget overages," "force majeure clause," "interest-bearing," "over-budget penalty," "overhead," "penalty-free cushion" and "withholding").

double bill or double billing — (see "double feature").

double booking — An exhibitor's renting, purchasing, licensing and/or scheduling for exhibition on a certain date of more films at its theater than the theater has screens on which to exhibit the films. Occasionally the exhibitor will not even exhibit the extra film (i.e., does not split the screen) but rather postpones the extra film's run to a later date. Sometimes this postponement occurs too late in time for the exhibitor's competitors, who have been contractually prohibited by the distributor from exhibiting the film until after the exhibition at the preferred theater (see "day and date" and "exhibitor").

double distribution fees — Full distribution fees paid to both the film's distributor and its sub-distributor, in situations in which a film's distributor utilizes the services of a sub-distributor in certain markets or territories. In such situations, the film's producer and other profit participants are being subjected to distribution fees from both entities, portions of which are redundant. The producer should seek to have the primary distributor absorb some or all of the distribution fee of the sub-distributor within its own distribution fee retaining the balance as a supervision fee or have the fees of the sub-distributor passed through without markup. In the alternative the producer may seek to negotiate a minimal override for the primary distributor on the distribution fees of sub-distributors (see "override," "pass-through," "supervision fee," "sub-distributor" and "sub-distribution").

double feature — The exhibition of two motion pictures in the same theater (one after another) for which patrons are only charged the price of a single ticket. During the Great Depression motion picture theater ticket sales fell significantly and the "double-feature" was created by independent exhibitors in an effort to re-attract audiences. The distributor of such a pairing must allocate (based on a pre-determined formula, at the distributor's discretion or otherwise) the film rentals generated by the joint exhibition of the films between the two films for purposes of calculating payments due to profit participants, if any (see "allocation issues," "combo engagement," "creative accounting," "discretion" and "settlement transaction").

double scale — The payment of twice the union minimum salaries established for film cast or crew members by the applicable union or guild (see "scale").

double taxation — Taxation of corporate earnings at the corporate level, then again at the individual level as stockholder dividends (see "corporation," "direct participation program," "limited liability company," "limited partnership," "pass-through vehicle" and "S-Corp").

double week — A variation on the distributor/exhibitor deal referred to as the 90/10 split in which the distributor reduction in its percentage share is effected every two weeks instead of every week (see "ninety/ten deal").

downside exposure — (same as "downside risk" and "downside protection").

downside protection — Elements of a film finance package that are designed to reduce the risk of loss for the film's investors or financiers (e.g., well known actors, a completion guarantee, pre-sales and/or a domestic theatrical distribution commitment may be considered downside protection; see "downside risk," "upside potential" and "safety hedges").

downside risk — The dangers of an investment producing negative results; an estimate that a security will decline in value (also called "downside exposure"; see "downside protection" and "upside potential").

draft script or screenplay — A preliminary version of a completed screenplay. Union definitions call for a complete draft of a script in a mutually agreed form to a length to be specified by the producer (see "polish" and revision").

drama-logue — A casting newspaper that regularly publishes announcements that describe producers' casting requirements and information about how actors may apply for those roles (see "BackStage.com," "casting" and "CastPages.com).

dramatic — Relating to a composition involving interesting or intense conflict of forces, intended to portray life or characters or to tell a story through action and dialogue and designed for film, radio, television or theatrical performance (see "docu/drama" and "screenplay").

dream — A goal or purpose ardently desired (see "chasing a dream" and "pied piper").

droit moral — French for moral right (see "moral rights").

dry mortgage — An arrangement whereby a motion picture is the sole collateral for a production loan and the loan is repayable only from the proceeds of distribution of the motion picture. Production lenders usually require secondary sources of loan and interest repayment (see "collateral" and "lender financing").

dual listing — A security that is listed on more than one exchange, thus increasing the competition for bid and offer prices as well as the liquidity of the securities (see "broker/dealer" and "securities").

dual regulation — Securities law requirement that the offer and sale of securities must comply with both federal and state laws and regulations (in each state in which securities are to be offered or sold) and to the extent that such regulatory provisions conflict, the more burdensome standard must be adhered to. Provisions of the National Securities Markets Improvement Act of 1996 ("NSMIA"), however, allow federal securities laws to pre-empt state law in certain circumstances (see "blue sky," "NSMIA" and "securities").

dub — To copy a film, videotape or audio recording (see "dupe," "looping" and "mix").

dubbing — The act of synchronizing the lip movements of an actor with a voice not originally recorded in synch for a motion picture. The voice may be that of another actor and it may be speaking another language (see "automatic dialogue replacement," "dub" and "looping").

due diligence — In the offering of securities, such as corporate stock, limited partnership interests or units in a manager-managed LLC, the investigation conducted by counsel, the managing underwriter in an underwritten securities offering, a managing broker/dealer, selling broker/dealer firms and accountants, for the purpose of demonstrating a reasonable basis for believing that the statements contained in the registration statement, prospectus or other securities disclosure document (e.g., a private placement offering memorandum) are true and that no material facts have been omitted. Sufficient due diligence at the start of such an offering may help such persons avoid liability if in fact it is subsequently established (e.g., by a disgruntled investor) that the issuer of such securities engaged in securities fraud in the conduct of such offering (see "creative accounting," "diligence," "initial public offering," "stock fraud" and "underwriter's questionnaire").

due diligence kit — A notebook, typically in the form of a three ring binder with index tabs, containing information developed by an issuer of securities for review by a prospective selling broker/dealer firm that is conducting a due diligence investigation of the issuer of the securities to determine whether such broker/dealer will participate in the issuer's securities offering. The information is designed to aid the broker/dealer in its investigation of the issuer and the offering and some of the information in the due diligence kit will overlap disclosures ultimately found in the offering disclosure document (see "due diligence").

due diligence meeting — A meeting conducted by the underwriter of a new offering at which brokers can ask representatives of the issuer about the issuer's background and financial reliability and the intended use of the proceeds of the offering. Brokers who recommend new offerings without very careful due diligence work may find it more difficult to successfully defend lawsuits if the issuer is subsequently sued by disgruntled investors (see "disgruntled investor" and "due diligence").

dues and assessments — The charges levied by the Motion Picture Association of America (MPAA), the Association of Motion Picture and Theatrical Producers (AMPTP) and other industry groups for their work in representing the interests of their respective segments of the motion picture industry. These dues payments are allocated to each film based on a percentage of the gross receipts generated by the film. Thus, such payments are considered a distribution expense and are paid prior to any payments to net profit participants. The MPAA distribution companies reportedly extract these dues allocations from theatrical revenues generated by MPAA distributed films whereas the percentage used is based on the anticipated revenues from television, video and theatrical distribution. Thus, producers should seek to negotiate a cap on the amount of dues charged to a given film (see "professional association" and "trade association"; also see "residuals" and "royalty payments").

dummy — A straw person, a sham. For example, a dummy corporation is a corporation that has no business purpose other than to provide protection from liability or from the disclosure of the names of the principal or principals behind its activities. In some instances, a general partner of a limited partnership may be no more than a "dummy" for the limited partners (see "limited partnership" and "piercing the corporate veil").

dupe — A duplicate. As a verb, dupe means to copy a film or tape recording (see "dub" and "optical dupe").

dupe negative — Copy of a film with the light and dark parts in approximately inverse order to those of the original photographic subject. A dupe negative is produced by printing from a positive film (i.e., it is made from a fine grain master positive or interpositive and is used to strike release prints; see "internegative").

duress — Action by a person that compels another to do what he or she would not otherwise do. Duress is a recognized defense to any act, such as a crime, contractual breach or tort, that must be voluntary in order to create liability for the person committing the act (see "blacklisting" and "contract of adhesion").

duty — Obligatory conduct owed by a person to another person (see "tort").

DVD — (see "digital video disc").

DVD-ROM — (same as "digital video disc").

earnings and profits — Generally, a tax term referring to the income of a corporation or other entity which, if distributed to its shareholders or investors respectively, would constitute a dividend (or cash distribution) to the distributee shareholder or investor (see "corporation," "limited liability company" and "limited partnership").

earnings before taxes — Corporate profits after interest has been paid to bondholders but before taxes have been paid (see "corporation").

earnings per share — That portion of a corporation's profit allocated to each outstanding share of common stock. The figure is calculated after paying taxes and after paying preferred shareholders and bondholders, if any (see "corporate stock" and "corporation").

earnings-price ratio — The relationship of earnings per share to a corporation's current stock price. It is used in comparing the relative attractiveness of stocks, bond and money market instruments (also called "earnings yield"; "corporate stock").

earnings statement — (see "income statement").

earnings yield — (see "earnings-price ratio").

ease of integration — The relative difficulty of achieving vertical integration in an industry. Another component of the U.S. Justice Department's six-part test relating to vertical mergers (see "antitrust laws," "merger guidelines," "Paramount Consent Decree of 1948" and "TriStar Case").

economic abuses — Unfair, exploitative or offensive business practices. Federal and state governments have a legitimate interest in eliminating economic abuses that are harmful to its citizens (see "antitrust laws," "anti-competitive business practices," "blind bidding" and "business practices").

economic cycle — The interval of time during which a recurring succession of economic events or phenomena is completed. World and national economies as well as the movie business are said to be cyclical in nature (i.e., trends tend to repeat themselves; see "cyclical industry" and "out-of-favor indies").

economic life — The period during which a property will yield a return on investment (see "economic cycle" and "rate of return").

economic microcosm — A smaller unit of a larger industry (e.g., the feature film industry is a smaller unit of the larger entertainment and communications industries, or on an even smaller scale, it may be said that the so-called "A" level deals and those involved in such transactions in one way or another exist in their own microcosm of the feature film industry). Other microcosms of the film industry include profit participation auditors, production accountants, entertainment attorneys, screenwriters, equipment rental houses and so forth (see "A-level motion picture," "cottage industry" and "profit participation auditor").

economic reprisal — A retaliatory act by a business or industry segment. In response to the passage of anti-blind bidding statutes in various states, some of the major studio/distributors have reportedly threatened from time to time to take their lucrative location filming to non-regulatory states (see "anti-blind bidding statutes," "blind bidding," "economic abuses," "location filming" and "non-regulatory states").

economic war zone — An industry in which various factions are battling for dominance and/or survival. It would appear that some in the film industry will use whatever tactics are necessary to win the Hollywood wars (see "antitrust laws," "blind bidding," "creative accounting," "industry groups," "market power," "number of screens," "predatory practices," "reciprocal preferences" and "unethical business practices").

Edgar — The SEC's electronic data gathering, analysis and retrieval system. Most public/registered offerings effected pursuant to SEC regulations must be filed electronically using the EDGAR system (see "regulation S-T").

edit — To select, arrange and assemble film, videotape or audio tracks (i.e., prepare for projection or playback or to make the film ready for its final sound mix). Also, to creatively arrange the elements of a motion picture for presentation in the most desirable sequence based on the subjective opinion of the editor, director, producer or whoever has ultimate creative control over the project at the time the film is being edited (see "creative control," "cut," "final cut" and "pan and scan").

editing rights — A negotiated provision in feature film distribution agreements that sets out the authority of the distributor to edit a picture after it is delivered to the distributor by the producer (see "creative control," "final cut" and "droit moral").

editing room assistant — A person engaged in and about the editing room, film library and vault, whose duties may include splicing, patching, rewinding, coding film and carrying materials to and from the editing room, library and splicing machines (see "assistant editor" and "editor").

editor — The person responsible for assembling the raw material of a motion picture into a coherent whole. An editor will take the film through several stages: from an assembly to a rough cut and then to a fine cut, while typically delegating the preparation of music and sound effects tracks to a specialist in sound editing (see "cutter" and "supervising editor").

editor's work track — A sound print that usually contains all of the sound tracks (including sound effects, original sound and dubbed sound), but generally does not include the final musical score, which in many situations is added to the finished film [see "work print (sound)"].

effective — The declaration by the SEC that a registration statement in a public securities offering is complete and that the offering to prospective investors can commence (see "acceleration" and "public offering").

effective date — The date on which a securities public offering is approved by the SEC and the appropriate state regulatory authorities for sale to the public (see "quiet period" and "waiting period").

effects track(s) — [see "sound effects track(s)"].

electrical reproduction — The reproduction of an image or sound by means that utilize electricity (see "mechanical reproduction").

electrical transcription — A recording (as on magnetic tape or phonograph record) made for later broadcast (see "cassette").

electronic media buys — Purchases of advertising time on radio and television. Industry analysts report that the total cost of electronic media buys has increased 30 percent to 40 percent in the last several years and threatens to climb further. Such price increases make it increasingly more difficult to open a feature film on a wide basis because of the high cost of national electronic media support (see "advertising" and "distribution costs").

electronic press kit — An audio and/or video version of motion picture promotional materials that is sent out to radio or television stations in the market in which a movie is being promoted. An electronic press kit may contain audio or video taped presentations of stories for possible inclusion in news programming, interviews and any other information that might interest the press regarding the movie being promoted (see "press kit").

elements — The various components that go together to make a movie (e.g., the concept, the screenplay, producer, director, director of photography, cast and crew, the distribution deal or distributor and publicist). Also, units of original edited reversal or negative film, as well as sound tracks that are used to make the composite print. Most commonly when someone is talking about the "elements" of a film, they are generally referring to the script, the director and the lead actors (see "concept," "idea," "investment letter of intent" and "package").

embargo — A legal prohibition upon commerce (i.e., a common carrier or public regulatory agency order prohibiting or restricting freight transportation; see "restricted currencies").

employee — One who works for and under the supervision of another, usually for a salary and in a position below the executive level; a hired person who is subject to the control of the hirer as to the means, method and details of performance. Film producers, for example may be considered employees on studio in-house productions, whereas in production-financing, negative pickup, acquisition and rent-a-distributor distribution deals, the producer would more likely be considered an independent contractor (see "distribution alternatives," "freelance employee," "independent contractor" and "Producers Guild of America").

employer — One who hires, uses or engages the services of other persons for pay. An employer need not actually exercise the right of control over the means, the method and the details of an employee's performance. The AMPTP represents the major studio and certain other production company employers with respect to guild issues (see "Alliance of Motion Picture and Television Producers," "employee," "guild" and "independent contractor").

employment agreement — A contract that governs the hiring and work of an employee. With respect to motion pictures, employment agreements may be used for both above-the-line and below-the-line personnel ("above-the-line employment agreements," "below-the-line employment agreements" and "deal memo").

employment verification — A requirement in employment agreements that makes any offer of employment contingent upon the prospective employee's ability to prove his or her identity and employment eligibility as required by the Immigration Reform and Control Act of 1986 and obligates the prospective employee to complete, execute and deliver certain forms relating to employment eligibility verification along with documentation of the prospective employee's employment eligibility (see "employment agreement").

encumbered — Owned by one party but subject to another party's valid claim (see "claim," "clearance" and "title").

encumbrance — A burden on title or a charge on property; a third party's lawful interest in property that diminishes the value of that property and impairs the transfer of marketable title (see "chain of title" and "clearance").

end credits — (see "end titles").

end-title billing — (same as "end titles")

end titles — The list of cast and crew who worked on a motion picture that runs at the conclusion of a film or tape (see "main and end titles").

end users in the foreign marketplace — A term referring to foreign entities, such as television networks, entertainment consortiums, foreign conglomerates or foreign theatrical and home video distributors who purchase rights to exploit U.S. made films in foreign markets. Some of these entities are capable of financing a domestic film production and/or distribution company and may do so in exchange for product flow and participation in world-wide revenues (see "foreign distribution").

engagement — The exhibiting of a film in a movie theater where admission is charged and afterwards, film rentals are paid to the film's distributor (see "exclusive engagement" and "run").

enjoin — To command or instruct another, with appropriate authority, either to do a specific act or to refrain from doing a certain act (see "injunction").

enterprise — A business firm; a term often applied to a newly formed profit-seeking venture (see "business plan," "securities disclosure document" and "venture capital").

entertainment — Something diverting or engaging, particularly a public performance that is designed to be amusing or to cause the time to pass agreeably. Although movies are often promoted as mere entertainment, they go beyond entertainment by communicating ideas in a powerful way and offering visual models for behavior (see "communications," "communications industry," "entertainment industry," "idea," "movies with a message," "multi-cultural society" and "propaganda").

entertainment attorney — A lawyer who has expertise in the field of entertainment law. The entertainment industry generally includes movies, radio/television, live theater, music and print publishing. Common areas of law involved include antitrust, copyright, contract, defamation, labor, music, obscenity, tort and trademark (see "securities attorney").

entertainment banker — A banker, bank or bank division with specialized knowledge of the entertainment industry and that holds itself out as being interested in making loans for entertainment related projects, including feature film production (see "bank," "interest" and "lender financing").

Entertainment Data, Inc. — An on-line computerized data gathering and data base service (owned by A.C. Nielsen since 1997) for the motion picture industry that tracks box office performance, lists films in release with release dates, stars, genre and box office grosses to date, the pictures released in a single month coupled with a display of releases and grosses for the same month in the prior year, provides information on scheduled releases including title, stars, major credits and synopses and permits comparisons of genres in the marketplace, release patterns and market share (see "baseline").

entertainment industry — A distinct group of productive enterprises involved in the creation of programs primarily for the amusement and diversion of the public. The entertainment industry includes motion pictures, television, theatre, recording, music publishing, video and literary publishing (see "communications industry," "marketplace of ideas" and "propaganda").

entertainment investment banker — An investment bank that specializes in or has a department providing banking services relating to the funding of entertainment projects (see "investment bank" or "investment banker").

entertainment portfolio — The combined holdings of a bank involved in entertainment lending or the similar holdings of a corporate conglomerate or investor (see "bank," "corporate conglomerate" and "lender financing").

entertainment stocks — The shares of corporations that are significantly involved in the entertainment industry and which may be traded on the New York Stock Exchange, the American Stock Exchange, the NASDAQ Stock Exchange and/or over-the-counter. Current information relating to such stocks is regularly reported in the trades [see "entertainment industry," "exchange," "over-the-counter (OTC)" and "trades"].

entire agreement clause — A provision included in many contracts (e.g., film distribution agreements), providing that the agreement constitutes the entire agreement and supersedes and cancels all prior negotiations, undertakings and agreements, both written and oral, between the parties with respect to the subject matter of the agreement. The clause may provide further that no officer, employee or representative of either party has any authority to make any representations or promises not contained in the written agreement and that neither party has signed the agreement in reliance on any such representations or promises. Producers negotiating with various representatives of distributors should make notes of any oral representations made by such persons and systematically see that such representations are incorporated into the distribution agreement, otherwise, if this "entire agreement clause" is included, such oral representations are likely to be worthless (same as "entire understanding clause"; see "deal memo" and "oral representations").

entire understanding clause — (same as "entire agreement clause").

entity — Generally in commerce, a term meaning a business which is in a form that has a distinct existence separate from its owners. Thus, under this definition a corporation, a limited partnership and an LLC would be considered entities but a sole proprietorship would not. For accounting purposes an entity is more broadly defined as any unit, existing or to be formed, for which financial statements could be prepared in accordance with generally accepted accounting principles or another comprehensive basis of accounting. Pursuant to this definition, an entity can be an individual, partnership, corporation, trust, estate, association or governmental unit (see "corporation," "joint venture," "person," "partnership" and "proprietorship").

entrepreneur — A person who takes on the risks of starting a new business. Often, venture capital is used to finance the start-up in return for a piece of the equity. Once an entrepreneur's business is established and organized as a corporation, shares may be sold to the public as an initial public offering, assuming favorable market conditions exist or develop. Independent films, however, are commonly financed as projects (i.e., the investment vehicle is either a limited partnership or manager-managed LLC; see "business plan," "enterprise," "limited

partnership," "limited liability company," "securities" and "venture capital").

equal likeness — A clause in actor employment agreements providing that if anyone else's photograph or likeness appears in paid advertisements relating to the motion picture, a photograph of the actor of equal size and prominence must also appear in such advertisement (see "employment agreement" and "perks").

equipment insurance — Insurance covering all risks of direct physical loss, damage or destruction to film production company owned or leased miscellaneous equipment, including cameras, camera equipment, sound, lighting, editing equipment, grip equipment and projectors. Coverage can be extended to mobile equipment vans and studio location units (see "insurance" and "miscellaneous equipment insurance").

equipment rental — The hiring or leasing for a fee of various motion picture production machinery, tools or gear during the limited period of production for which it is needed. Renting movie production equipment eliminates the need for many production companies to purchase and maintain such equipment during times when films are not being produced (see "equipment rental houses").

equipment rental agreement — The contract between a film production company and a motion picture equipment rental facility that sets forth the terms and conditions under which the rental facility will permit the production company to use motion picture production equipment owned by the rental facility in the production of a motion picture (see "equipment rental" and "equipment rental houses").

equipment rental houses — Businesses that specialize in providing all sorts of film production equipment to production companies on a rental basis (see "equipment rental agreement").

equitable remedy — The means employed to enforce or redress an injury other than remedies at law (see "action," "action-at-law," "injunction" and "specific performance").

equity — The interest or value that an owner has in property, over and above any liens against it. For corporations, the ownership interest possessed by shareholders (i.e., stock as opposed to bonds), for limited partnerships, the profit sharing interests of the partners and for a direct investment in a film project, the percentage participation interest in the back end (i.e., a defined stage of the film's revenue stream; contrast with "debt"; see "back end," "limited partnership," "ownership," "percentage participation," "share" and "shareholder"). In law, the term means fairness (i.e., that equity will derive a means to achieve a just result when legal procedure or remedies are inadequate; see "equitable remedy," "action-at-law," "injunction" and "litigation").

equity financing — Raising money by offering ownership interests in an entity (e.g., shares of common or preferred stock for a corporation, limited partnership interests for a limited partnership or units in an LLC) or percentage participations in a film's revenue stream. Equity financing of a feature film enables the producer to finance the film unhampered by studio executives or the oversight of a completion guarantor's representative (if the producer so chooses) but investors may be active or passive depending on the structure of the deal (see "active investors," "creative control," "equity," "investor financing," "lender financing," "passive investors," "studio financing" and "risk capital").

equity financing contract — A funding agreement through which investors provide monies for a project or for a company's use in exchange for an ownership interest in the entity, typically through corporate stock, limited partnership interests, units in an LLC or a direct investment in the project (see "equity" and "equity financing").

equity investment — A direct investment for an ownership stake in a for-profit business venture as opposed to debt that requires pre-arranged repayment with interest, but without profit or loss participation for the lender (see "debt," "equity" and "interest").

equity investment fund — A sum of money set aside for a specific purpose involving an ownership interest (e.g., to help finance the completion of feature motion pictures, wherein the fund's contribution to a picture allows the fund to gain an ownership interest in the picture; see "completion fund" and "loan").

equity kicker — Offer of an ownership position in a deal that involves loans. In return for that equity kicker, the lender is likely to charge a lower interest rate on the loan. Convertible features and warrants are offered as equity kickers to make securities attractive to investors (see "sweetener").

equity participants — Individuals or entities that contribute funds for the production of a movie and/or toward its theatrical releasing costs in exchange for an ownership position in the producing and/or distributing entity (see "equity" and "investor").

equity security — Any security that provides an ownership interest (see "equity" and "security").

errors and omissions insurance — Financial protection that covers legal liability and defense for a film production company and other named insureds against lawsuits alleging unauthorized use of titles, format, ideas, characters or plots; plagiarism, unfair competition or breach of contract and failure to obtain requisite releases. E&O coverage also commonly protects against alleged libel, slander, defamation of character or invasion of privacy. The producer usually pays for such coverage, at least initially, but if the coverage is expanded to include possible distributor error, the distributor should pay for some or all of the coverage for the distribution period. Also, when errors and omissions insurance is provided, there is no longer any need for the distributor to withhold sums of money from distribution proceeds to cover such claims, unless there is a possibility that such claims may exceed the limits of the insurance coverage. Also, the producer should discuss the E&O requirements as set out in the distribution deal with his or her insurance agent or carrier to make sure the distributor is not obligating the producer to provide coverage that is not available in the current marketplace (see "excess insurance coverage," "insurance" and "privacy, right of").

errors and omissions policy — The insurance agreement relating to errors and omissions risks (see "errors and omissions insurance").

errors and omissions renewals — The extension of the coverage period for an existing errors and omissions insurance policy through the payment of the premium. In the context of a film distribution deal, the distributor often provides that it is not responsible for such renewal, but in the event the producer does not renew, the distributor may renew and can deduct the premium cost as a distribution expense. On the other hand, if the errors and omissions of the distributor are also covered by the policy the distributor should pay a portion of the premium (see "distribution expenses" and "errors and omissions insurance").

escalating contingent compensation — Remuneration to be paid to persons who provide products or services for use in the production of a motion picture that is paid in progressively higher percentages or amounts following receipt of specified levels of distributor gross receipts or any other specified triggering mechanism (see "bonus," "contingent compensation" and "front-end compensation").

escalation — Language in employment agreements that provides for an increase in a participant's net or gross profit participation in the event that the box office gross or the distributor's gross receipts rise to certain pre-designated levels. Also, clauses in distribution agreements that permit the distributor's distribution fees to escalate under certain circumstances (see "escalating contingent compensation").

escalation point — That place in a motion picture's revenue stream at which a participant's participation percentage increases or a distributor's distribution fees increase (see "distribution fee," "escalating contingent compensation").

escrow — Money, securities or other property or instruments held by a person or entity who is not a party to a transaction (third party) for future delivery to a party upon the occurrence or non-occurrence of a specific event or events.

Escrow accounts are commonly used by independent producers to provide assurances to the agents for actor/actresses that the agreed upon compensation will be paid when due. Escrows have also been used when raising production monies through the vehicle of a limited partnership or manager-managed LLC to hold investor funds until the minimum offering amount is achieved. However, most states do not require the formal escrow of investor funds for private placements, thus, an interest-bearing, segregated bank account can serve the same purpose (see "impound," "private placement," "segregated, interest-bearing account," "third-party escrow" and "trustee").

escrow account — An accounting relationship with a financial institution under a particular name usually evidenced by a deposit against which withdrawals may be made under certain circumstances as set out in the escrow agreement (see "escrow").

escrow agent — The financial institution through which an escrow account is established. Some such institutions prefer to be referred to in the documents that establish the relationship as escrow holders, thus ostensibly avoiding the implications of an agency relationship (see "escrow holder").

escrow agreement and instructions — The written contract between the party that is placing money in escrow and the escrow holder that sets out the terms and conditions under which the escrow holder agrees to act as such and provides instructions to the escrow holder for the maintenance and closing of the escrow account (see "escrow" and "escrow holder").

escrow holder — A financial institution that maintains escrow accounts but which prefers not to be referred to as an escrow agent (see "escrow agent").

escrow of fixed compensation — A common requirement for obtaining a firm commitment from an important actor, actress or director to work in a proposed motion picture meaning that their agreed upon salary has to be deposited into an escrow account before they will commit to the picture. The agents representing actors, actresses and directors who are in demand will insist on some such provision before taking their principals off the market for the time period during which their services are to be required (see "escrow account").

estimated use of proceeds — (see "use of proceeds").

ethical — Conduct that is consistent with the standards followed in a business or profession (see "ethics").

ethical malaise — A phrase used to describe the low ethical standards and conditions prevailing in the Hollywood film community. In a guest column written by Los Angeles attorney Eric Weissman in October of 2004, Mr. Weissman admitted that an "ethical malaise hangs over the entertainment business." He reported that more than ever these days, the news contains allegations of abuses and criminal behavior by industry professionals. Citing just a few examples, he pointed to the Los Angeles City Attorney's lawsuit against the PR firm Fleischman Hillard over fraudulent billing; the indictment of Franchise Pictures for fraudulent production budgets; and the indictment of Entertainment Industry Development Corporation head Cody Cluff for embezzling public funds. Weissman lamented the years of bad publicity for studio accounting practices pointing out that such practices put pressure on talent to make demands for huge up-front salaries. He added that some entertainment industry clients are so insecure that some agents ask for money under the table payable directly to them in addition to the 10 percent that was paid to the agency, so that the client will be assured of personal special representation. He also indicated that he has heard of entertainment attorneys who, in return for the promise of top flight services, will pocket monies for themselves under the table in addition to what was being paid to the firm (see Erik Weissman article cited in this book's Selected Bibliography along with the book *Hollywood Wars*).

ethics — The discipline dealing with what is good and bad and with moral duties and obligations; the principals of conduct governing an individual or a group; the standards followed in a business or a profession (see "Code of Professional Responsibility," "conflicts of interest" and "unethical").

evidence of insurance — A certificate of insurance provided by the insurance carrier serving to demonstrate that a specific policy of insurance (e.g., producer's liability) is currently in effect and the premium has been paid for a specified term. Such evidence of insurance is generally a perquisite to obtaining a motion picture completion bond (see "certificate of insurance," "completion bond," "insurance," "lender financing" and "negative pickup").

exact interest — Interest calculated on a 365-day year. Studio/distributors providing production financing often prefer to use ordinary interest since it results in higher interest payments on the negative cost of the picture in the final accounting period (see "interest" and "ordinary interest").

excerpts — Passages or film clips selected or copied for use in another film (see "license of stills/excerpts").

excess insurance coverage — Insurance protection above the limits of the basic policy for which an additional premium will be charged (see "errors and omissions insurance," "insurance," "primary insurance" and "reinsurance").

excessive interest — (see "interest").

exchange — A regional office of the larger film distributors. These offices are responsible for supplying the distributor's motion pictures to exhibitors in the region where the exchange is located. The delivery arrangements relating to cans of 35mm film will change as more theaters are equipped to project digitized movies (see "digital media," "major studio/distributors" and "sub-distribution").

exchange controls — A country's regulations relating to the exchange of foreign currencies (see "currency conversion").

exchange rate — The measure or value of currencies traded between various countries (see "beneficial exchange rate").

exchange rate fluctuations — (see "currency conversion" and "exchange rate movements").

exchange rate movements — Changes in the value of a country's currency relative to the currency of other countries. Such changes may significantly affect the value of foreign film rentals (see "currency conversion" and "floating exchange rate").

exclusions— A term used and defined in some distribution agreements to be the amounts of all adjustments, credits, allowances (other than advertising allowances), rebates and refunds, given or made to sub-distributors, exhibitors and licensees that are excluded from accountable gross. Also, monies in the nature of security deposits, advances or periodic payments are not included in accountable gross until they have actually been earned (such as by the exhibition of the film) or forfeited. In other words, some distribution deals will allow the distributor to not count and therefore not be obligated to include in its net profit calculations, certain items that otherwise might be included in gross receipts. Such exclusions must be carefully reviewed by the entertainment attorneys representing any net profit participant for reasonableness. The term may also be used in describing what costs are to be excluded in determining whether or not the cost of a production has exceeded a specified percentage (e.g., 110 percent of the approved production budget; see "accountable gross," "adjusted gross," "approved production budget" and "gross receipts").

exclusive engagement — A method of releasing a feature film in which the film is opened in a single theater (or possibly more than one screen in a given theater complex) in any given major city or market. The contractual arrangement with the exhibitor usually provides the distributor with an option after a specified period of time to keep the film at that theater for a long exclusive run or to widen the release of the film in that city based on the film's performance (see "engagement," "mini-multiple," "run" and "special handling").

exclusive ground transportation — A provision sometimes requested in the employment agreements for actors, actresses and others that requires the production company to provide a vehicle and a driver for the sole use of that artist in getting to and from the set of a motion picture in production or to and from the airport when the artist is required to fly to an out of town location (see "perk").

exclusive opening — (see "exclusive engagement").

exclusive run — (see "engagement," "exclusive engagement" and "run").

execute or execution — The signing, dating and sealing (if applicable) of a contract or agreement making it valid (see "acknowledge" and "certify").

executive officer — The president, any vice president in charge of a principal business unit, division or function (such as sales, administration or finance), any other officer who performs a policy making function, or any other person who performs similar policy making functions for the issuer of a security (see "chief executive officer").

executive producer — For independent productions, an individual or individuals who provide something very important to the production of the motion picture, such as providing or obtaining production funding, obtaining a commitment from a big name star or director or packaging some or all of the project. At the major studio lots the executive producer is often the producer in charge of the logistics of production, a staff producer working for the studio and keeping track of schedules, budgets and all general production areas. In the context of an investor financed independent production, the executive producer is likely to be the person or persons designated by the investment vehicle's management to receive the executive producer screen credit for services rendered in the organization and funding of the entity, preparation of the offering memorandum, conduct of the offering and/or in otherwise arranging for the production of a film or films. The term also refers to such person's screen credit (see "employee," "line producer," "packaging" and "producer").

executive producer fee — A payment or payments made to the executive producer(s) of a film, out of the film's budget for services rendered in helping to arrange for the production financing of a film or films and/or for other administrative duties associated with a given film (see "executive producer").

exemption — A deduction allowed to a taxpayer because of his, her or its status as a taxpayer rather than because of specific economic costs or expenses incurred during the taxable year (see "exempt security," "income tax" and " transactional exemption").

exempt offering — (see "private offering").

exempted security — A security that is not required to be registered under the provisions of the Securities Exchange Act. This term may include both exempt securities and exempt transactions (see "exempt security" and "exempt transaction").

exempt security — A security that is not required to be registered under the provisions of the Securities Exchange Act because of the type of security it is, as opposed to the type of transaction in which such security is offered or sold (e.g., securities listed on a national securities exchange, securities issued or guaranteed by the U.S., any state, any political subdivision of a

state, or any agency of such governmental entity or any security issued by and representing an interest in or a debt of any bank organized under the laws of the U.S.; see "transactional exemption").

exempt transaction — A securities offering that is exempt from the securities registration requirements because of the manner in which the securities are offered or sold as opposed to the type of securities involved (e.g., an SEC Regulation D offering does not permit advertising or general solicitation). Regulation D is a federal transactional exemption and most states provide compatible exemptions as limited offering or small offering exemptions (also called "transactional exemption"; see "exempt security" and "private offering").

exhibit — To show a motion picture to the public for a charge (see "exhibitor").

exhibition — A public showing of a feature film for a charge (see "exhibitor" and "major exhibition chains").

exhibition contract — The agreement between a film's distributor (or producer who is self-distributing) and the theater or theater chain that sets out the terms of a film's exhibition at such theaters (see "distributor/exhibitor split").

exhibitor — The owners or operators of movie theaters or the actual theaters that exhibit feature films; also any person engaged in the business of operating a movie theater (see "major exhibition chain").

exhibitor chain — Motion picture exhibition companies that own and operate theatres at multiple locations. Major exhibitor chains include AMC, Century Theaters, Cinemark USA,

Cineplex-Galaxy, Landmark Theatres, Loews Cineplex Entertainment, Mann Theatres, National Amusements, Northeast Cinemas LLC, Pacific Theatres and Regal Entertainment Group. Following the Reagan administration easing of regulatory restraints, the major studio/distributors have regained a certain level of ownership and control over some of these major exhibition chains (see "exhibitor" and "major exhibition chains").

exhibitor circuit — (same as "exhibitor chain").

exhibitor financing — The partial or complete funding of the production costs of a motion picture by a theatrical exhibitor. Although exhibitors often complain about the quality of the films that are made available to them for exhibition, they seldom risk their own capital in the effort to improve on that quality. Occasionally, however, a theatre circuit may involve itself in production financing (see "major exhibitor chains" and "NATO").

exhibitor's bid — (see "bid").

exhibits — Documents added to a securities disclosure document such as a prospectus (for public/registered offerings) or a private placement offering memorandum (for private/exempt offerings) that supplement the disclosures already appearing in the disclosure document which is to be given in advance to prospective investors. Certain exhibits are required by the securities laws (e.g., a Regulation D offering refers to Regulation S-K, which in turn, requires that the exhibits listed in Item 601 be included; see "Regulation D" and "Regulation S-K").

exit poll — A market research technique in which moviegoers are interviewed after they have seen a motion picture and as they leave the theater in an effort to gauge the audience's reaction to the picture (see "focus groups").

exotic investment product — A strikingly different, unusual or high-risk investment vehicle or opportunity. Relative to other financial or investment products ordinarily handled by securities broker/dealer firms, the financing of an independent feature film through means of an investor financed direct participation program (i.e., limited partnership or manager-managed LLC) is considered exotic (see "investor financing" and "risk factors").

exotics — (same as "exotic investment product").

expedited arbitration — An even quicker resolution of a dispute than that normally provided by regular arbitration. Lenders sometimes require a provision for expedited arbitration in the inter-party agreement, specifically with respect to disputes over whether delivery has been effected. The lender wants a quick resolution as to whether completion and delivery have been properly made so that it can collect from either the distributor or the completion guarantor (if it is determined that completion and delivery have not been properly made (see "arbitration," "completion guarantor," "inter-party agreement," "lender financing" and "negative pickup").

expend — To pay out or spend (see "expenses").

expense — As a verb, to deduct a cost item in order to reduce tax liability (see "capitalize" and "expenses").

expense allowance — A pre-paid stipend or reimbursement privilege for out of pocket expenses incurred by an employee, such as an actor or director, while involved in the production of a film (see "perk").

expenses — Costs that are currently deductible as opposed to capital expenditures that may not be currently deducted but which either must be depreciated or amortized over the useful life of the property or may not be deducted at all (see "amortization," "capital expenditure," "capitalization" and "depreciation").

exploit — As commonly used in the motion picture business, to manipulate and/or capitalize on a given feature film; also to make productive use of the talent of others for one's own advantage. Hollywood insiders have often been accused of exploiting outsiders to the industry (see "Hollywood insiders," "maximum exploitation" and "traffic in").

exploitation — All of the advertising, publicity, merchandising, licensing and promotion of a motion picture, and in a broader sense, any use of a film, sound track album or other product for one's own profit or advantage. In this latter sense, many independent producers, creative talent, profit participants and others in the industry with inadequate leverage are regularly exploited by film distributors, studio executives, agents and entertainment attorneys in what may be described as a winner-take-all economic system (see "inferior bargaining position," "leverage" and "maximum exploitation").

exploitation film — A feature motion picture that contains obligatory or gratuitous sex, violence, horror, catastrophic events or a combination of any or all of such themes and that has little socially redeeming value. The exploitation film blatantly advertises and uses these themes to attract unsophisticated audiences. Such films typically enter and exit the theatrical market more quickly than other feature films (see "genre," "production value" and "theme").

exploitative approach — A film advertising campaign designed to appeal to the traditional themes of exploitation films, sometimes to the point of misleading prospective moviegoers about the nature of the film (see "exploitation film").

export capabilities — The ability of a country or an industry within a country to sell goods in other countries. Some entertainment industry analysts expect the export capabilities of the U.S. film and television industries to experience a steady decline in the years ahead (see "foreign market").

exposed film — The acetate-based, emulsion-coated strip of plastic with perforations on the edges (that is used to make photographic images) that have been subjected to light but not yet processed (see "film").

express representation — A statement set out in words (see "implied representation" and "representation").

exterior — Any motion picture scene shot out of doors (see "back lot" and "location").

external financing — Funds brought in from outside the corporation (e.g., a bank loan, proceeds from a bond offering or cash from venture capitalists). External funds supplement internally generated cash flow and are used for business expansion, as well as for seasonal working capital needs (see "internal financing").

extortion — The illegal taking of money by anyone who employs threats or other illegal use of fear or coercion in order to obtain the money, and whose conduct falls short of the threat to personal safety required for robbery (e.g., the use of the threat to use violence in order to collect interest or the debt itself). For example, if a distributor's representative suggested or implied that a profit participant might be "blacklisted" if such profit participant did not forego a lawsuit or settle a lawsuit for less money than is owed that threat might be considered a form of extortion (see "blacklisting," "loan sharking" and "racketeering").

extra dividend — Corporate dividend paid to shareholders in addition to the regular dividend (see "corporation").

extra expense insurance — An insurance policy that will reimburse a production company or producer (the insured) for any extra expense necessary to complete principal photography of an insured movie production due to the damage or destruction of property or facilities (props, sets or equipment) used in connection with the production (contrast with "completion bond"; see "insurance").

extra release — An agreement between feature film producers and persons who may appear in a recognizable manner in a film (and who have not otherwise provided their authorization for such appearance). The extra release authorizes the appearance and thus eliminates the risk of future claims against the production company or its assigns (see "release").

extras — Non-speaking atmosphere talent; actors and actresses who have no spoken lines in a movie (unless as part of a group) and who are generally not called upon to make any gesture that would set such actors or actresses apart from the other extras (see "atmosphere," "background cast," "bit player" and "screen extras guild").

extrinsic event — Outside of or not a part of an occurrence or happening. For example, pursuant to the terms of some film distribution agreements, costs caused by an extrinsic event may be excluded from the determination as to whether the production costs of a motion picture have exceeded the specified percentage (e.g., 110 percent of the approved production budget; see "force majeure clause").

facilities allocation — The apportionment of studio or distributor operating expenses among the studio's various components for the purpose of charging such expenses against a given film's costs. In studio/distributor financed films, the producer should consider negotiating to exclude such indirect costs from the permissible distribution expense deductions or to place a limit on the percentage of such allocations or in the alternative, carefully reviewing such allocations to make certain they are reasonable. If facilities allocations are made by an independent distributor, such expense allocations are no different than studio overhead (see "contract of adhesion," "creative accounting," "inferior bargaining position," "market power" and "overhead" or "overhead costs").

facilities arrangements and agreements — Film production deals that make locations and/or studios available for shooting films in a certain locale either at no cost or at significantly reduced rates in order to attract or increase business for the facility (see "facilities subsidies").

facilities deals — Film finance transactions in which crews, locations, local cast, studio facilities, cameras or some combination thereof are offered for a reduced rate and to cover a certain percentage of a film's below-the-line costs. Such deals are sometimes offered by local studios trying to stimulate business for their facility (see "foreign below-the-line deals").

facilities lessor — The person or entity who leases his, her or its facilities (e.g., a studio sound stage) to a film production company. As well as sometimes serving as production financiers and distributors, the major studio/distributors sometimes also serve as facilities lessors (see "major studio/distributor" and "studio").

facilities subsidies — Film production deals offered by governments (usually foreign) that make locations and/or studios available in their jurisdiction either at no cost or significantly reduced rates (see "facilities arrangements" and "foreign government grants and subsidies").

fair competition — The conduct of rival businesses in an impartial, unbiased and equitable manner. The court in the case resulting in the 1948 Paramount consent decrees determined that the only means of promoting fair competition within the motion picture industry was to order divestiture of the ownership of theatrical exhibition from the production/distribution side of the business. Although some in the film industry feel such prohibitions against vertical integration should remain in place, the federal government has apparently backed away from its earlier position due to what the major studio/distributors claim are changed circumstances (see "antitrust laws," "blind bidding," "block booking," "major exhibition chains," "merger guidelines," "Paramount Consent Decree of 1948," "political influence," "TriStar Case" and "unfair competition").

fair market value — The price at which an asset or service passes from a willing seller to a willing buyer, assuming that both are rational and have a reasonable knowledge of all relevant facts relating to the sale (see "law of supply and demand" and "market value").

fair use — In federal copyright law, the use of copyrighted materials in a manner that does not constitute an infringement of copyright and without the required payment of royalties; a permitted use by copying and acknowledgment. The fair use exception to copyright infringement is a privilege in others than the owner of the copyright to use the copyrighted material in a reasonable manner without the owner's consent, not withstanding the exclusive rights granted to the owner by the copyright. Whether a use is considered a fair use depends upon the purpose and character of the use, the nature of the copyrighted work, the amount and substantiality of the portion used, and the effect of the use upon the market value of the copyright. Important factors include whether the copied material was creative or research-oriented; the status of the user (reviewer, scholar, critic, journalist, compiler, parodist, etc.); extent of use (both qualitatively and quantitatively); the absence of an intent to plagiarize as evidenced by proper acknowledgment and the original contribution of the user (see "copyright" and "plagiarism").

FASB — (see "Financial Accounting Standards Board").

FASB Statement No. 34 — A set of accounting principles and guidelines promulgated in 1980 by the Financial Accounting Standards Board for use by the film industry and relating to the capitalization of interest costs. FASB Statement No. 34 requires that interest costs be capitalized as part of the historical cost of acquiring certain assets. To qualify for interest capitalization, assets must require a period of time to get them ready for their intended use (e.g., assets intended for sale or lease that are constructed as discrete projects, such as motion pictures). Interest capitalization is required for those assets if its effect, compared with the effect of expensing interest, is material. If the net effect is not material, interest capitalization is not required. Prior to 1980 interest costs of a motion picture studio were written off as incurred (i.e., deducted in the year incurred). Under FASB Statement 34, such costs must be capitalized and then charged in the studio's accounting as part of the negative cost (see "capitalization," "expense," "interest" and "FASB Statement No. 53").

FASB Statement No. 53 — A set of accounting principles and guidelines promulgated by the Financial Accounting Standards Board that relate to financial reporting by producers and distributors of motion picture films. Such guidelines cover three key areas: (1) expense versus capitalization policies, (2) product availability and revenue recognition concepts and (3) estimation procedures and profit or loss determination. FASB Statement No. 53 provides that producers and distributors who license film exhibition rights to movie theaters generally must recognize revenue when the films are shown (i.e., that all film exploitation costs for prints, advertising, sub-distribution fees, rents, salaries and other distribution expenses that are clearly to benefit future periods should be capitalized as film-cost inventory and amortized over a period in which the major portion of gross revenue from the picture is recorded). This method of accounting must be applied to national advertising, but local and co-operative advertising expenditures are generally closely tied to local grosses and are thus normally taken as a deductible expense in the year incurred because they usually do not provide any benefits in future periods (see "capitalize," "expense," "interest" and "revenue recognition and reporting").

FASB Statement No. 96 — A set of accounting principles and guidelines promulgated by the Financial Accounting Standards Board that relate to financial reporting by producers and distributors of motion picture films and more specifically to the difference between what a company records in its books as a tax liability and what it actually has to pay in taxes. Previously, a company could record a column called "deferred taxes" but that option is no longer available. Now, tax liability is only recognized when it actually takes effect. These rules are designed to prevent film companies from carrying an excessive value on their movies a fairly common practice (see "creative accounting," "Financial Accounting Standards Board" and "tax").

faulty stock, camera and processing insurance — An insurance policy that covers loss, damage or destruction of raw film or tape stock, exposed film (developed or undeveloped), recorded videotape, sound tracks and tapes caused by or resulting from fogging or the use of faulty developing, faulty editing or faulty processing and accidental erasure of videotape recordings (see "exposed film" and "insurance").

favorable portrayal — A positive depiction in a motion picture (see "bias," "hidden agenda," "marketplace of ideas," "negative portrayal," "patterns of bias" and "propaganda").

favoritism — In an employment context, showing a bias toward a particular individual for some arbitrary reason other than merit (see "discrimination" and "nepotism").

favored nations clause — A provision in a contract meaning the contracting party will be given treatment on a par with that provided others with whom the other party deals. In entertainment agreements the clause may be used to denote a level of profit participation, the size and placement of billing, the caliber of dressing rooms or motor homes on location and other such matters (see "pari passu," "perks" and "percentage participation").

feature — The principal attraction playing in a movie theater; a full-length dramatic film (not documentaries or film shorts) made primarily for entertainment and commercial theatrical release. Feature-length made-for-television films or tapes are often referred to as TV films, movies-of-the-week or TV specials and may have a slightly longer running time than the typical ninety minutes of a feature film. Some in the industry define a feature as any motion picture, regardless of topic, that is longer than 4,000 feet (see "feature length" and "pre-feature entertainment").

feature film — (see "feature" and "feature length").

feature film fund — Private or government monies set aside for the purpose of financing some or all of the development or production costs of certain feature films that meet the requirements of the fund (see "completion fund" and "Telefilm Canada").

feature film limited partnership — A film financing vehicle through which passive investors (the limited partners) typically provide some or all of the production monies for producing one or more motion pictures. Like corporate stock, interests in limited partnerships are securities, thus the federal and state securities laws may apply, including the anti-fraud provisions. In recent years, the film limited partnership has often been portrayed in a negative light by many broker/dealers, financial commentators, investment advisors and certainly film industry professionals who have expertise in other forms of film finance, ostensibly because investors have not fared well, with their investments in such film financing vehicles. In some specific instances, it is entirely possible that greedy general partners or others help to create a situation in which excessive up front fees or expenses are deducted from the offering proceeds (i.e., the monies raised through such limited partnership offerings), thus not leaving enough of such funds to actually produce the movie promised or envisioned. It is also possible that such excessive up front payments to key people do not leave enough profit participation incentive to provide adequate motivation for the producer to negotiate a distribution deal that treats such passive investors fairly (i.e., in some circumstances the producer may have a conflict of interest with such investors). It might just as accurately be pointed out, however, that the industry and distributor practices cited elsewhere in this book probably play an even more significant role (in most feature film limited partnership situations) in actually determining whether such investors recoup or see a reasonable profit on their investment. If, in fact, any feature film distributor engages in very many

of the business practices described herein, it is not likely that any profit participant including limited partnership investors are going to see any share of such profits. In this sense, the problem is not with the investment vehicle, but distributor practices (see "business practice," "creative accounting," "disclosure document" and "stock fraud").

feature length — A full-length motion picture that is seventy minutes, plus. Feature films today generally do not run less than ninety minutes and are typically between ninety to one hundred and twenty minutes. Exhibitors typically do not like longer motion pictures because they want to bring in new ticket-buying audiences as often as possible so they will spend more money on popcorn and other concessions, an important source of revenue for exhibitors (see "feature" and "running time").

feature motion picture or feature film — (see "feature").

featured player — A principal actor or actress who does not have a starring role in a motion picture but is a main character. The featured player will generally have higher billing and will receive greater compensation than a day player (see "actor," "bit player" and "star").

featurette — A behind-the-scenes look at the making of a given movie presented on film or video. Movie featurettes are made primarily for use on television for the purpose of promoting the movie on which it is based (see "feature length" and "film short").

federal ID number — An identification number that pursuant to IRS (federal) rules must be obtained by every business that pays wages to one or more employees. Such number must be used on the business' income tax return. The federal ID number is also typically required by a bank, along with the business entity's formation documents in order to open a bank account in the name of the business. Obtaining a federal ID number is an administrative task (not a legal task) and merely involves the submission of an application to the IRS (see "employer" and "Internal Revenue Service").

federal tax discussion — A discussion of the material federal income tax issues and/or consequences of investing in securities offerings structured as direct participation programs (e.g., film limited partnerships or manager-managed LLCs). The discussion forms a major section in the securities disclosure document and can only be provided by tax counsel and/or accountants (same as "tax discussion"; see "securities disclosure document" and "tax opinion").

Federal Trade Commission (FTC) — Federal administrative agency established in 1914 for the purposes of preventing misrepresentation and fraud in advertising, protecting consumers against unfair methods of competition and deceptive business practices and investigating and curbing violations of the antitrust laws. The agency's Bureau of Competition is responsible for the enforcement of the antitrust laws and it generally accomplishes its goals through civil remedies (i.e., its authority to order the offender to "cease and desist" from a prohibited practice). If its order is disobeyed, the FTC must then go to federal court to seek enforcement (see "blurbs," "business practices," "conduct restrictions," "fraud" and "U.S. Justice Department").

fees — A charge for a service. The distribution fee is typically the first deduction from the distributor's gross receipts and may range from 30 percent to 40 percent depending on the market and media. Subsequent to its fee, a film distributor will then typically deduct all of its distribution expenses incurred in distributing the film (see "distribution expenses," "location fee," "location permit," "permits" and "taxes").

festivals — (see "film festivals").

fictionalization — The act, process or product of converting a non-fictional literary work into fiction (i.e., a story invented by imagination; for example, taking a story based on an actual incident and writing a screenplay by changing the characters, the plot and details enough to justify its status as an original work of fiction; see "clearance," "docu/drama," "novelization" and "release").

fictitious name — The name of a business that is different than the name of the business' owner. The concept of doing business under a fictitious name is referred to in many states as a "DBA" (doing business as). Most state laws require that any individual or individuals conducting a business under a name other than their own must register to do business under such name. The fictitious name filing is effected through the county clerk's office or as a service provided by a local business journal/paper (see "DBA," "fictitious name filing" and "sole proprietorship").

fictitious name filing — An application that is to be completed and placed among the records of the county courthouse of the county in which an unincorporated business is conducting its operations under a name other than the name of the business' owner. Entities such as corporations, limited partnerships and LLCs, other common forms of doing business besides the sole proprietorship, must clear their proposed names with the secretary of state in the state of formation (see "DBA," "fictitious name" and "sole proprietorship").

fiduciary — A person or entity having a legal duty, created by his, her or its undertaking, to act primarily for the benefit of another in matters connected with an undertaking (i.e., a person in a position of trust and confidence). General partners of limited partnerships are considered fiduciaries in their relationship with the limited partner investors. The same is true of the manager of an LLC. Under certain circumstances, feature film distributors may also be considered fiduciaries on behalf of all net profit participants (see "conflicts of interest," "general partner," "good faith," "limited partnership" and "LLC manager").

fifty/fifty first dollar split — A feature film distribution deal that consists of an equal 50/50 split of the distributor's gross receipts from the first dollar with no advance paid to the producer. This is a rare but desirable variation of the feature film distribution agreement from the producer's standpoint. The theory here is that since the producer financed the film and the distributor is financing the distribution, they are taking an approximately equal risk and should therefore share equally from first dollar (see "fifty/fifty net deal" and "first dollar").

fifty/fifty net deal — One of the negotiated divisions of net profits between a film producer and distributor. Such a division of revenue is generally made after the distributor deducts its fee and expenses. Such a deal is rarely seen today (see "fifty/fifty first dollar split," "first dollar gross deal," "modified gross deal," "seventy/thirty deal" and "sliding scale").

filing fees — Payments required to be made to state and federal securities regulatory authorities in public or private securities offerings. In public offerings fees (referred to as registration fees) are generally required to be paid to the SEC, the NASD and to each state in which such securities are to be offered. In private placements, such fees are referred to as "notice filing fees"). Pursuant to Regulation D, for example, no notice filing fee is required to be paid to the SEC (with the Form D submission), but many states will require a notice filing fee be submitted along with other documents that are part of the required notice filing (see "blue sky laws," "conditions and limitations," "Form D," "NASD," "notice filing," "private placement," "public offering," "Regulation D" and "SEC").

film — Raw stock used either for negative or positive prints, or in a larger sense, a portion of or the total finished motion picture production (in this latter sense, the same as "motion picture"; see "exposed film").

film buyer — A representative of an end user of feature films in the foreign marketplace who is responsible for negotiating the purchase of licensing rights to feature films for exploitation in the foreign territories and/or media represented (see "booking agent," "end users in the foreign marketplace," "foreign distribution" and "foreign sales agent").

film clip — (see "clip").

film clip license — An agreement between one party (usually a production company) and the owner of the copyright to a motion picture or television program, permitting the use of a brief segment of the motion picture or television program in a subsequent film or program. Such agreement grants permission to use the film clip in the second film (see "clip," "license of stills/excerpts" and "release").

film commissions — Governmental agencies created primarily for the purpose of attracting film production activity to their jurisdiction (whether it be at the national, regional, state, county or local level) and in assisting filmmakers with the logistics of their local shoot, partly by acting as a liaison between the film company and the local community. Film commissions commonly promote the suitable film production locations within their jurisdiction to the film community, provide free location scouting services and publish or promote directories of local production facilities and services. Such film commissions seldom engage in the activities relating to facilitating the independent financing of the production and/or distribution costs associated with feature films, which in the long term, may tend to generate films that provide more favorable portrayals of the local area than those produced by outside financing sources and production entities with few if any local personal ties. Such governmental or quasi-governmental agencies are also generally not permitted to become involved in the issue of anti-blind bidding legislation (see "anti-blind bidding statutes," "blind bidding," "economic reprisal," "film festivals," "lobbying," "location filming" and "regulatory states").

film credits — (see "credits").

film exchanges — Regional film distribution centers from which many films are distributed to individual movie theaters in the region. Also companies that purchase leftover, unopened cans of raw stock from the major studios and in turn, sell to producers for less than the manufacturer's charges (see "distributor," "exchange" and "sub-distributor").

film elements — (see "elements").

film festivals — Special commercial, social and cultural events featuring the showings of numerous films that may be based on a specific theme such as comedy or politics. Such festivals ordinarily take place in one city or location over a period of several days, may include film related seminars, workshops, dinner programs and are usually climaxed by the presentation of commendations, awards and prizes (see "Cannes Film Festival," "Sundance Film Festival," "Telluride Film Festival" and "Toronto Film Festival").

film laboratory — (see "lab").

film laboratory agreement — (see "laboratory film processing agreement").

film library — [see "catalog (library)"].

film library values — (see "library values").

film licensing terms — (see "licensing terms").

filmmaker — One who directly and individually handles and/or supervises all of the production steps necessary to create and produce a complete motion picture (see "collaborative process," "director" and "producer").

filmmaker's return — Another term for producer's net or producer's net profits (i.e., what is left for the filmmaker or the filmmaker's share of net film profits after deferrals, investor obligations and other debts are paid; see "gross receipts," "net profits" and "producer's share").

film market — A gathering of motion picture producers and distributors for the purpose of buying, selling and/or licensing film product. A film market is often associated with a film festival (see "American film market," "MIFED" and "Cannes Film Festival").

film package — A group of films that are being financed together or films being sold as a group to various media (e.g., independent television stations or foreign territories; see "allocation issues," "packaging" and "television syndication").

film package financing — The funding of multiple films or the activities relating to the packaging of a given film or the packaging of films for television syndication purposes (see "packaging").

film rating system — (see "MPAA" and "ratings").

film rentals — The money owed and/or paid by a theatrical exhibitor to a distributor under a film's lease agreement (i.e., the monies paid by the exhibitor and/or earned and due to be paid to the distributor as rental fees for the right to license a film for public showing). Authorities do not seem to agree on this issue of "owed" versus "paid", thus most film distribution agreements do not even use the term "rentals" but instead use and contractually define the broader concept of "gross receipts." Film rentals are generally computed weekly on a consecutive seven-day basis (Wednesday through Tuesday or Friday through Thursday, depending on the day on which the film first opens in the market). Film rentals as between the distributor and exhibitor are negotiable and may be determined by several different methods, including a 90:10 basis, sliding scale, fixed percentage, minimums (floors) that relate specifically to the gross box-office receipts and a flat-fee basis that is a predetermined, unchanging amount. In many

distributor/exhibitor contracts, the film rentals earned will change from week to week, with the distributor's relative share generally decreasing and the exhibitor's share increasing from the first through subsequent weeks. This means that an exhibitor tends to make more money off of the films that stay in their theaters the longest (i.e., the so-called "blockbusters"). Quite often the exhibitor and distributor will negotiate a settlement amount for film rentals that is actually less than the actual amount owed by the exhibitor. The term also refers to the accumulated film rentals for a given film from all theaters in a market or all markets (also called "distributor film rentals" and "gross rentals"; contrast with "gross receipts"; see "fiduciary," "gross film rentals," "percentage rentals," "selling subject to review" and "settlement transaction").

film rental percentages — The division of box office receipts between the exhibitor and distributor following deductions for a second feature and cartoon, if any, for the exhibitor's expenses (contractual theater overhead) and expressed as a percentage of the remaining box office net. While the major studio/distributors are able to extract distribution terms for a major motion picture that calls for the payment of 70 percent and more of the box office receipts (in a film's initial weeks of release), the industry average for all pictures is pegged at about 35 percent to 45 percent of box office receipts, depending on the type of motion picture and its distributor (see "collection," "house nut," "gross receipts," "rentals," "selling subject to review" and "settlement transactions").

film schools — Colleges and universities that offer a degree program in film. Some of the better known film schools include New York University, the University of Southern California and the University of California at Los Angeles. On the other hand, there may be as many as six hundred or so film schools in the U.S. at any given time and they reportedly graduate some 26,000 students each year. Also, only 5 percent to 10 percent of those graduates apparently end up making a living in their chosen career field. It may be possible that both the industry and the film schools are actively misrepresenting the promise of career opportunities in the film industry; that they are misleading some 23,400 individuals annually and persuading them to pretty much waste their undergraduate studies on subjects that are not likely to be of much value in their lives. The film industry, college and university administrations and their professors all have a self-serving reason for actively or passively encouraging this fraud on unsuspecting students (see "chasing a dream," "law of supply" and "demand" and "pied piper").

film short — The DGA defines a short as any motion picture that when released is 2,700 lineal feet or less in length on 35mm, or 1,080 lineal feet or less in length on 16mm film. The WGA defines a short as a motion picture that when released is 3,600 lineal feet or less in length. In some distributor/exhibitor deals a percentage deduction from box office receipts is taken by the exhibitor for showing the film short (see "feature length" and "short film agreement").

film splitting — (see "product splitting").

film starts — The number of films for which principal photography has begun in a given geographical area (i.e., in a city, county, state, region or country); a kind of statistic typically kept by film commissions (see "film commissions").

film stock — Unexposed and unprocessed rolls of film that come in standard roll-lengths of 100, 200, 400, 1000 and 2000 feet (see "film").

film subsidies — A grant by a government to a film producer or production company to assist in the production of a film (i.e., for a film project deemed advantageous to the public or in the public interest; see "foreign subsidies," "government subsidies" and "grants").

final answer print — (see "answer print").

final cost statement — In the context of a production-financing/distribution agreement, the last accounting of expenses associated with the production of a motion picture as determined after all of the studio's departments and the production company have reported their costs on the picture to the studio's comptroller. The final cost statement is submitted by the studio to the production company and any bonus due the production company or others based on the size of the remaining balance in the production account is paid (see "bonus," "production account" and "rising production costs").

final cut — The last fine-tuning of a motion picture immediately following acceptance of the fine cut version, wherein the sound is mixed and the picture conformed and made ready for the lab to run off the answer print. The final cut is the finished version of the work print to which the negative is conformed in order to strike the release prints that are to be exhibited in theaters. Who has the ultimate authority to approve this version of a film is a significant negotiating point between producers and directors and also between producers and distributors. Many film distribution agreements provide that the distributor has sole discretion to edit the film as it sees fit. Producers generally want to limit the rights of distributors to edit the film without the producer's approval to certain situations (i.e., to meet censorship and MPAA rating requirements; see "answer print," "creative control," "discretion," "editing rights" and "marketplace of ideas").

final cut director — A motion picture director who has the ability to negotiate a provision in a distribution agreement authorizing him or her to control the final editing of the film for all or certain specified versions of the picture (e.g., for the domestic theatrical release; see "editing rights" and "final cut").

final draft — The last version of a completed screenplay prepared by the screenwriter(s) prior to the shooting script and any directorial changes (see "draft script or screenplay," "polish," "revision" and "shooting script").

final judgment — The decision of a trial court that prevents the relitigation of the same matter. The finality of a judgment may be overturned on appeal, however, and in that situation the matter can then be returned to a trial court for redetermination of some or all of the issues involved. Many feature film distribution agreements require the producer to reimburse the distributor for legal fees if the producer files a lawsuit against the distributor but fails to obtain a final judgment against the distributor. The producer may want to consider making such a requirement reciprocal, but even more important and if possible, the producer may want to eliminate the "final judgment" requirement altogether since most lawsuits are settled prior to "final judgment" and substantial legal fees may have been incurred by the distributor (see "litigation" and "sue us").

final marketing outlet — The retail level of a business. In the feature film theatrical business exhibition is the final marketing outlet. From 1940 to 1948 (most of the years during which the Paramount case was being litigated) the major studio/distributors of that period produced about 62 percent of the films and distributed approximately 71 percent of the domestic films released. The major studio/distributors gained effective indirect control of feature film production through their control of first run theaters. By monopolizing the final marketing outlet they successfully curtailed entry by independent producers. The Paramount consent decree was partly intended to weaken the market dominance of the major studio/distributors. But, more recently the U.S. Justice Department enforcement of antitrust laws have been relaxed in the entertainment industry) the feature films distributed by the current group of major studio/distributors and their subsidiaries generate about 96 percent of the domestic box office gross in any given year, as much if not more dominance of the marketplace than prior to the Paramount Consent Decree (see "barriers to entry," "MPAA Cartel," "major exhibition chains," "merger guidelines," "number of screens," "Paramount Consent Decree of 1948" and "TriStar Case").

final print — (same as "release print").

final prospectus — The portion of the effective registration statement delivered in advance to all prospective purchasers of securities in a public/registered offering (see "disclosure document," "prospectus" and "red herring").

final screenplay — (same as "shooting script"; see "first draft," "polish" and "revision").

final shooting script — A completed film script that has been broken down and re-organized in accordance with the manner in which the film will be shot (same as "shooting script").

finance charges — Any charge for an extension of credit including interest, service or carrying charges, loan fees or finders fees, fees for credit investigations and charges protecting the creditor against default. Finance charges are also subject to state prohibitions against usury (see "interest" and "usury").

Financial Accounting Standards Board (FASB) — An independent, Connecticut-based entity or board, formed in 1973, that makes the rules for accountants relating to establishing and interpreting generally accepted accounting principles. The FASB succeeded and continued the activities of the Accounting Principles Board (see "creative accounting," "FASB Statement No. 34," "FASB Statement No. 53," "FASB Statement 96" and "GAAP").

financial condition — (see "financial position").

financial forecasts — Prospective financial statements that present, to the best of the responsible party's knowledge and belief, an entity's expected financial position, results of operations, and changes in financial position at some point in the future. A financial forecast is based on the responsible party's assumptions reflecting conditions it expects to exist and the course of action it expects to take. A financial forecast may be expressed in specific monetary amounts as a single point estimate of forecasted results or as a range, where the responsible party selects key assumptions to form a range within which it reasonably expects, to the best of its knowledge and belief, the item or items subject to the assumptions to actually fall. When a forecast contains a range, the range should not be selected in a biased or misleading manner (e.g., a range in which one end is significantly less probable than the other; see "assumptions," "computer model," "financial projections," "limited use," "partial presentations," "profit projections," "pro forma financial statements," "prospective financial statements" and "responsible party").

financial institution — An organization that collects funds from the public to place in financial assets such as stocks, bonds, money market instruments, bank deposits or loans (see "bank" and "lender financing").

financial leverage — (see "leverage").

financial management — The direction of the fiscal aspects of a business. Some financial analysts say that the commonly held notion that the primary reason for most of the recent film production company bankruptcies is the failure of their motion pictures to perform at the box office is false. Instead such analysts point to improper financial management (e.g., increasing debt during good times, rather than decreasing debt) as one of several reasons for such failures. Other reasons cited include the failure to use sophisticated computerized financial modeling on a continuous basis and the abandonment of successful actions (while substituting new, untried ideas, without first piloting them with limited financial commitments). Other industry observers suggest that improper financial management may be irrelevant in an industry that is so dominated by a few major players who have long-standing reputations for engaging in numerous questionable business practices (see "anti-competitive business practices," "barriers to entry," "business practices," "computer model," "conscious parallelism," "creative accounting," "debt," "financial modeling" and "reciprocal preferences").

financial modeling — The design and manipulation of mathematical representations of an economic system or corporate financial applications so that the effect of various proposed changes can be studied and forecast (see "computer model," "financial forecasts," "financial projections" and "mental modeling").

financial performance — The effectiveness and achievements of an individual or entity in business world, specifically as such performance relates to fiscal matters (see "bottom line" and "profit margin").

financial position — The status of a firm's assets, liabilities and equity accounts as of a certain time, as shown on such firm's financial statement (also called "financial condition").

financial projections — The hypothetical results of an investment in a film in the event that certain stated assumptions prove accurate. Financial projections are estimates (based on reasonable assumptions) of the future financial results of an investment and its activities relating to the production, distribution and exploitation of a film or films. Financial projections are prospective financial statements presenting one or more hypothetical courses of action for evaluation based on the responsible party's assumptions reflecting conditions it expects would exist and the course of action it expects would be taken, given one or more hypothetical assumptions. The estimate of financial results may be based on assumptions that are not necessarily the most likely. In a film offering, such assumptions may include, among other items, assumed numbers for domestic theatrical box office gross, exhibitor's take, distribution

fees and expenses, projected revenues from all other markets, expenses of the investment vehicle, including deferments, if any, along with the various percentage participations of the investors and others. The SEC provides guidelines for financial projections used in conjunction with public/registered offerings (see "box office comparables," "financial forecasts," "limited use," "partial presentations," "profit projections," "pro forma financial statements," "prospective financial statements" and "responsible party").

financial resources — The available means to capitalize or finance the activities of a business. The major studio/distributors have traditionally possessed the financial resources to distribute a sufficient number of films each year to satisfy the exhibition needs of the most important theater chains, to fund their films' costly advertising and promotional campaigns, to maintain nation-wide distribution networks and to bear the large losses that films sometimes generate. The actual production costs of many of the films distributed by the so-called majors, however, may be wholly or partly borne by others (see "barriers to entry," "capital-intensive business" and "major exhibition chains" and "major studio/distributors").

financial risks — The possibilities associated with the investment of funds in a business activity that such funds will not be recouped or will not be returned in sufficient amount to justify the original investment (see "lender risk elimination" and "risk factors").

financial standings — The rankings of corporate fiscal attributes by industry analysts including total revenue, operating margins, net income, long-term debt, return on investment, current assets, current liabilities and cash flow margins (see "industry analysts" and "Paul Kagan Associates, Inc.").

financial statement — A written record of the financial status of an individual, association or business organization, including a balance sheet and an income statement (operating statement or profit and loss statement). The financial statement may also include a statement of changes in working capital and net worth (see "balance sheet" and "net worth").

financial supermarket — A large brokerage firm that offers a wide variety of financial services and investments to a wide variety of clients (see "boutique").

financiers or financing source — Persons or entities that raise or provide development, production and/or distribution monies or financing for a given movie or movies. A movie financier or financing source may be active or passive with respect to his, her or its involvement in the project. Financiers may be investors. The use of financing from a passive financier or investor usually indicates that a securities offering is involved and thus compliance with the federal and state securities laws is mandated. Major motion picture studio/distributors may serve as facilities lessors and distributors as well as financiers (see "investor," "broker/dealer," "finder," "securities" and "studio").

financing — The techniques or activities involved in obtaining or raising the monies required to pay the expenses incurred in the various phases of a business (e.g., the stages of motion picture development, production and/or distribution). The most substantial blocks of feature film financing are typically provided through [1] studio financing, which in a broader sense is distributor (or as some prefer "employer") financing, [2] lender financing (typically requiring bankable pre-sale and/or distributor commitments; also some production money lenders are not banks), [3] co-production or joint venture financing in which two or more industry individuals or entities combine funds to finance the production of films in which the co-production or joint venture parties are actively involved, [4] passive investor financing provided through various securities vehicles such as corporations, limited partnerships or manager-managed LLCs offered to the investing public either through public/registered or private/exempt offerings, or [5] various forms of international financing. A limited number of grants are also made available through some organizations but are generally not significant dollars relative to the costs of producing a feature film for theatrical release (see "bank loan," "co-production financing," "corporation," "distributor commitments," "distributor financing," "joint venture financing," "limited partnership," "outside investors," "passive investor financing," "pre-sales," "public offering" and "private offering," "production-financing/distribution agreement," "single picture financing," "split rights deals" and "studio financing").

financing date — The date on which the production company receives its requisite production financing for a given picture. Sometimes this date is used in calculating the producer's delivery date in a distribution agreement (see "delivery" and "start date").

financing entity — The individual or firm that is putting up the production costs for a motion picture. An industry financing entity rarely commits to production financing without a substantially developed package (i.e., a completed screenplay and attached director and lead actor, along with a detailed production budget and shooting schedule). On the other hand, groups of individual passive investors who are not part of the film industry may, in some circumstances, be willing to provide financing for low-budget features without all of the above-described elements in place (see "financing," "manager-managed LLC," "limited partnership" and "package").

financing fees — Monies paid to the financing entity that provided or arranged for the production financing for a motion picture (see "financing," "financing entity," "finder's fee" and "executive producer fee").

financing options — The alternative forms of film finance (see "financing").

financing unit — A separate entity, typically a subsidiary corporation, created primarily for the purpose of raising capital for the production of the movies of the parent corporate film production company. Such a separate corporation may be able to sell its stock (thus raising production funds) and participate in a joint venture with the parent producing entity without diluting the ownership interests of the parent's shareholders (see "corporate stock," "dilution" and "equity").

finder — A person who brings together the buyer and seller in a transaction. Many state securities laws place severe restrictions on the payment of any form of transaction-related remuneration to persons who are not licensed as NASD/SEC securities broker/dealers (i.e., finders, in certain transactions involving the offer or sale of securities). No such restrictions are involved in active investor (i.e., non-securities) transactions. Recently, the California legislature has, in effect,

codified its case law relating to finders and made the applicable provisions even more strict. Section 1029.8 of the California Code of Civil Procedure now authorizes an action for rescission of the sale or purchase of a security resulting from sales activities for which a broker/dealer license is required. In addition, under existing California law, an unlicenced person who causes injury as a result of engaging in specified activities for which a license is required is liable for treble the amount of assessed damages. Thus, utilizing the services of unlicenced persons (i.e., in finders) in the sale of a security does not appear to be a good idea in California. Other state laws may be similar (see "active investor vehicle," "business plan," "finder's fee," "passive investor vehicle," "private offering" and "securities").

finder agreement — The written contract between a feature film producer (or production company) and a person (or entity) who is not licensed as a securities broker/dealer that sets out the terms and conditions under which such person/entity may participate in the finding of funds for a film project or film production entity (see "finder").

finder sales — A method of raising funds for business ventures including film projects and one of three methods of marketing securities, although a misnomer since the actual sale in securities transactions must be conducted through the issuer (i.e., the finder's activities should be strictly limited to merely bringing the buyer and seller together). In addition, in most states no transaction-related remuneration can be paid to finders for the sale of a security (see "active investor vehicle," "broker/dealer sales," "finder," "issuer sales," "passive investor vehicle" and "securities").

finder's fee — A negotiated fee or commission paid to an individual or organization for "finding" what the other party needs or desires. In the film industry such a fee may be paid for finding a buyer for the purchase of a literary property or finding a financier for the production of a film. If a security is involved (i.e., passive investors), many state laws severely limit the activities of such finders and/or the payment of such fees to persons who are not licensed as securities broker/dealers (see "active investor vehicle," "finder," "finder agreement" and "passive investor vehicle").

fine cut — A more refined version of the work print and the version that follows the rough cut. At each successive stage in the editing of a film, the cutting is refined and unnecessary footage is eliminated (see "work print").

fine-grain — Film emulsions in which the grain size is smaller or finer than the older type emulsions commonly employed prior to the mid-'30s. Fine-grain film is usually slower (requiring more exposure) than other films (see "film" and "film stock").

fine-grain dupe — A dupe negative made from a master positive that was taken from the original black and white negative. Also a dupe negative made directly by using the contact reversal-printing process from the original black and white negative (see "fine-grain," "negative" and "print").

fine-grain master positive — The film processing step (in black and white) that comes after the original black and white negative. This processing step both protects the original and allows printing of optical effects (see "fine-grain" and "optical effects").

finishing fund — (see "completion fund").

firm — A broad term describing a business entity and including a corporation, partnership or proprietorship (see "corporation," "entity," "person" and "natural person").

F.I.R.M. — The Film Industry Reform Movement, a film industry Web site created for the purpose of encouraging a critical look at business practices of the Hollywood-based U.S. film industry (see "adhesion contract" and "unconscionable").

firm commitment — A securities offering in which the underwriter agrees to purchase the entire offering and resell it to the public (see "all or none," "best efforts offering," "broker/dealer," "selling concession" and "underwriting spread").

firm lease agreement — A film lease agreement that is not subject to adjustment (see "selling subject to review" and "settlement transaction").

first-answer print — The first conformed and sound-mixed composite print prepared by the film laboratory. This print is checked by the lab timer and the film's producer and/or director for correct and satisfactory color timings, sound-printing and synchronization (see "collaborative process" and "print").

first assistant camera person — The film production person responsible for maintaining and cleaning all elements in the camera package, setting up the camera with the appropriate lens and filters for each shot, and setting the lens stop and focus for each shot (see "cinematographer" and "director of photography").

first assistant director — The person whose work on a film involves specifically managing the pre-production preparation, including organizing the crew, securing equipment, breaking down the script (or story board) and preparing the strip-board and shooting schedule. During production he or she assists the director with respect to the on-set production details, coordinates and supervises crew and cast activities and organizes and facilitates the flow of production activity [see "director (film)" and "second assistant director"].

first dollar — The earliest monies that a film generates following its release (i.e., typically, the first monies received by the film's distributor). Distributors will seek to draft a distribution deal that will allow them to deduct their fees and expenses from these first monies. Also, gross profit participants, if any, by definition will have a right to take their percentage from these earliest funds (subject to contractually defined deductions). Others who may seek to negotiate a participation in such first monies (but rarely succeed) include investors (possibly until recoupment), deferred salaried talent, lenders and film labs. The term "first dollar" can also be used in relation to other specific entities with an interest in a film's revenue stream (see "adjusted gross," "fifty/fifty first dollar split," "gross receipts" and "net profit").

first dollar deal — Generally, a type of distribution agreement providing that revenues generated from the exploitation of a film are divided amongst the participants starting with the very first dollars returned to the distributor (i.e., after settlement with the exhibitors but before any distributor fees or expenses are deducted). In the current marketplace, first dollar deals occur rarely, if ever (see "first dollar gross deal" and "net deal").

first dollar gross — (see "first dollar," "first dollar deal" and "first position gross").

first dollar gross deal — A specific and rare distribution deal providing that the producer gets approximately 25 percent to 30 percent of the distributor's gross until a multiple of print and ad expenditures is reached, at which point the producer's share escalates to approximately 65 percent (see "modified gross deal" and "net deal").

first draft — The first complete version of a motion picture screenplay in continuity form including full dialogue. A first draft is usually longer than the final draft (see "polish" and "shooting script").

first draft script breakdown — (see "first draft," "production board," "production breakdown" and "shooting script").

first-generation dupe — A reversal print made from a reversal-stock original or master tape, often for the purpose of producing further prints or tapes, that are known as second-generation dupes (see "print").

first look deal — A studio development deal in which the studio provides development financing or other assistance to a producer on a film project or projects in exchange for the studio having the right of first refusal on further development, production and/or distribution of the film (see "housekeeping deal," "overall deal" and "right of first refusal").

first monies — (see "first dollar" and "first dollar deal").

first negotiation right — (see "right of first negotiation").

first option — (same as "first look deal").

first position gross — A share of the gross receipts or total revenues from a given source or stage in a movie's revenue stream, such as film rentals or home video/DVD, which is accounted for before distribution fees, distribution expenses, negative costs or other gross participations are deducted. First position is generally considered to be the most sought-after participation in a movie deal but it is seldom awarded by movie studio/distributors, except to a handful of the most-recognized talent in the industry. To the extent that anyone other than the distributor is participating in distributor gross receipts in a first position, chances for that film generating net profits are substantially diminished (also called "first dollar gross"; see "gross receipts" and "video corridor").

first-run — The initial exhibition of a motion picture in a designated geographic area for a specified period of time (i.e., the opening cycle in the exhibition of a motion picture or the first release of a film in a major market area). The "first run" of a motion picture usually is booked as a single feature (except at drive-ins), and as the release of the movie continues (or earlier if the picture does not perform well) it may be double billed in so-called sub-run markets (see "booking," "double-bill," "first-run date" and "first-run theater").

first-run date — The specific period of time during which a motion picture is initially exhibited in major market areas (see "first-run" and "first-run theater").

first-run syndication — The initial showing of a motion picture in the off-network market (see "off-network" and "television syndication").

first-run theater — A theater that primarily exhibits films on the films' initial exhibition (i.e., usually the better theaters in the major market areas; see "final marketing outlet," "first-run" and "first-run date").

first sale doctrine — A legal doctrine that imposes a limit on a copyright owner's exclusive distribution rights of a literary property that has been copyrighted. The doctrine states that the lawful owner of a copy or the literary property itself may sell, rent or otherwise dispose of that copy or property without the authority of the copyright owner and that in the absence of any contrary contractual restrictions, this owner (e.g., a video rental store that contracted with the copyright owner for a videocassette or DVD of a movie) may resell it or rent it without any further financial obligation to the copyright owner (e.g., the producer or distributor). This doctrine has permitted the video stores to rent film videos and DVDs repeatedly without paying further compensation to the video distributor/wholesaler (see "copyright," "pay-per-transaction" and "video rights agreement").

first theatrical release — The initial distribution of a feature film to theaters (see "theatrical release").

fiscal — Of or pertaining to financial transactions (see "fiscal year").

fiscal year — Any twelve-month period used by a business as its fiscal accounting period (see "fiscal").

five o'clock look — An unethical business practice allegedly engaged in by some distributors who wait until the exhibitor bids for the first-run of an about-to-be-released film are in, then the distributor calls an exhibitor to whom the distributor would like to award the movie and reports the highest bid received for the film to that point from the favored exhibitor's competitors. The distributor then allows that exhibitor to come in late with a higher bid and awards the first-run of the movie to the late (and highest) bidder. Such a practice obviously favors the financially stronger theatre chains (see "bid," "blind bidding," "closed bidding," "conduct restrictions," "predatory practices," "selling subject to review" and "unethical business practices").

fixed asset — Tangible property used in the operations of a business but not expected to be consumed or converted into cash in the ordinary course of events; normally represented on a company's balance sheet as the fixed asset's net depreciated value (see "asset" and "capitalize").

fixed bonus — A specific and negotiated amount of compensation that is awarded to a person who provides services in the production of a motion picture, if the film generates a specified level of gross revenues at the domestic theatrical box office or achieves a specified level of distributor gross receipts (see "contingent compensation" and "escalating contingent compensation").

fixed capital — The amount of capital permanently invested in a business (see "capital").

fixed costs — Expenses that remain constant regardless of sales volume (e.g., executive salaries, interest expense, rent, depreciation and insurance costs; see "direct distribution expenses" and "overhead").

fixed deferment — A specified amount of all or some of agreed upon compensation (i.e., not

based on a percentage), that is to be paid after the services for which the payment is being made have been performed and after the time at which such compensation might otherwise be paid. Typically, deferrals on investor financed independent films are paid out of the film's revenue stream after the investors have recouped (see "contingent compensation," "contingent deferments," "deferments" or "deferrals" and "percentage participation" or "points").

fixed installments — Periodic payments of a specific amount of money. Pursuant to the terms of a production-financing distribution agreement, a studio/distributor may advance funds to the production company for the production of a picture up to the total of the approved production budget, and if required thereafter, up to and including the contingency, in fixed installments and consistent with a cash flow schedule mutually approved by the production company and the studio/distributor (see "approved production budget," "cash flow schedule," "contingency" and "mutual approval").

fixed price — In a public offering of new securities, the price at which investment bankers in the underwriting syndicate agree to sell the issue to the public. In contract law, a type of contract where the price is preset and invariable regardless of the actual costs of production (see "price fixing," "public offering" and "securities").

fixed rate loan — A loan in which the interest rate does not fluctuate with general market conditions (see "lender financing").

fixed work — In copyright terminology, a work is fixed in a tangible medium of expression and therefore is copyrightable when its embodiment in a copy or phono record, by or under the authority of the author, is sufficiently permanent or stable to permit it to be perceived, reproduced or otherwise communicated for a period of more than transitory duration (see "copyright" and "fair use").

flat dollar payments — Disbursement of a specific amount of money. Some executives of the major studio/distributors and other industry spokespersons who consistently champion the studio view on industry issues complain that union and guild requirements calling for flat dollar payments as residuals on syndicated programming (as opposed to the percentage residuals paid for the same programs carried on basic pay cable) have contributed to a declining syndication market. These spokespersons suggest that the unions and guilds should bring this component of their required residual payments into alignment with current economic realities by modifying their residual packages and converting their flat dollar payment requirements into payments based on percentages of revenue (see "collective bargaining agreements," "guild," "residuals" and "syndicated films").

flat fee or flat rate — A set and unchanging amount of money or fee paid for services rendered or for a product. In a film context, a flat rate most often appears in the negotiations between producers and cast or crew. No overtime is paid on a flat rate as opposed to weekly or hourly rates (see "flat rentals" and "outright sale").

flat rentals — Compensation paid by a film's exhibitor to the distributor on a weekly basis at a pre-determined amount (i.e., not based on a percentage of the film's box office; see "film rentals" and "percentage rentals").

flat sale — A term used in certain feature film distribution agreements that is contractually defined to refer to a license for theatrical exhibition of a motion picture for a period in excess of two years for a territory or area in consideration of the payment of a specified amount of money not fixed by a percentage of the buyer's receipts. As thus defined, flat sale does not apply to the customary manner in which motion pictures are licensed to most exhibitors in the U.S. and Canada but is more typical of motion picture rights sales in most of the foreign markets, although not necessarily the top foreign markets (see "outright sale").

flat world-wide distribution fee — A fixed percentage charged by a feature film distributor for distributing a film in all media throughout the world. Such fees are associated with rent-a-system transactions and the percentages tend to fall in the 15 percent to 20 percent range (see "rent-a-distributor").

flip-flop — A sudden reversal as in direction or point of view. In the context of investor financed independent film, that point when special allocations of tax attributes between the producer group and the investors terminate and the producer group's profit-sharing percentage usually is increased substantially (see "limited partnership," "manager-managed LLC" and "payout").

float — Amount of unrestricted securities of a given issuer publicly available for trading (see "public offering").

floating exchange rate — The movement of a foreign currency exchange rate in response to changes in the market forces of supply and demand. Currencies strengthen or weaken based on a nation's reserves of hard currency and gold, its international trade balance, its rate of inflation and interest rates and the general strength of its economy (see "exchange rate movements").

floor — A lower limit. In the context of a distributor/exhibitor agreement, the minimum percentage of box office gross the distributor is entitled to receive regardless of the exhibitor's operating expenses (i.e., a minimum weekly percentage of a film's gross box office receipts that the film's lease agreement guarantees the distributor will receive as film rental regardless of the theater's house allowance). Floors may be subject to adjustment (i.e., reduced over the course of the film's engagement), and may range from 70 percent to 25 percent. Also, in negotiating with a bank for a loan, a producer may seek a floor and a ceiling on interest rates to fix the financing costs within a certain range. Producers may also seek to negotiate a gross floor in the distribution agreement or if third party participations are being deducted from net profits (or the producer's share), the producer may want to insert a floor to keep such participations from falling below a specified percentage (see "box office gross," "ceiling," "film rentals," "gross floor," "hard floor," "house nut" and "soft floor").

flowery language — Rhetorically elegant words. Such words tend to exaggerate or embellish the facts. If included in a securities disclosure document subject to the anti-fraud rule, they may be misleading. Thus, they should be removed in favor of a more objective and factual description (see "anti-fraud rule" and "puffery").

flow-through vehicle — (Same as "pass-through vehicle").

flyers — Advertising circulars for mass distribution (see "advertising" and "direct advertising").

focus groups — A gathering of people for the purpose of reviewing and discussing their reactions to a motion picture or its proposed advertising campaign (e.g., focus groups are sometimes used to determine which feature film poster design is more appealing or best represents the film being marketed; see "advertising campaign").

foley stage recording — The registering of artificially created motion picture sounds on tape in a specially designed recording studio that has facilities to project picture and sound simultaneously while recording new sounds that are being created by the so-called foley artists. The foley stage is a large room with various types of floor surfaces and other objects used to create most of the sound effects for a motion picture (see "sound effects").

force majeure clause — A provision in contracts that is intended to excuse a party from performance of its obligations in the event that such performance is prevented by forces outside the control of such party. Typically, such events or forces are partially specified and may include strikes, labor disturbances, acts of God, etc. and then will include a catch-all phrase at the end (e.g., "...or other force majeure"). The provision may provide for the suspension, extension or termination of the agreement if the event of force majeure continues beyond a specified period of time (see "abbreviated force majeure clause").

forecasting — Projecting current trends using existing data (see "computer modeling," "financial forecasts," "financial projections" and "pro forma").

foreign banks — Banks headquartered outside the U.S. (see "lender financing" and "split rights deals").

foreign below-the-line deals — Film finance transactions in which a foreign government offers to provide the crew, locations, local cast, studio facilities, cameras or some combination thereof to cover a certain percentage of a film's below-the-line costs. In exchange, the foreign government will typically ask for distribution rights in its own country (and sometimes in neighboring countries) and that a significant portion of the film be shot in the host country. U.S. producers who have taken advantage of these programs report that the film stock is generally not included, the cameras are generally not that good and it is best for producers to take their own lighting (see "facilities subsidies").

foreign competition — Business rivals based outside the United States. The experience of other U.S. industries in recent years has convinced some observers that the motion picture industry is not immune from the impact of reduced productivity and foreign competition (see "reduced productivity").

foreign contracts — The written agreements between foreign theatrical distributors or representatives of other foreign film markets and movie producers that banks may consider lending against. Generally, U.S. banks are not as willing to lend against such foreign contracts because it is more difficult to determine the credit-worthiness of such foreign distributors and more difficult to perfect the U.S. bank's security interest in the foreign collateral (see "domestic contracts").

foreign corporation — A corporation chartered under the laws of a state other than the one in which it is conducting business (also called "out of state corporation").

foreign currency deal — Film financing arrangement in which a foreign country (e.g., an Eastern European nation) will offer to provide goods and production services for below-the-line costs for a small amount of so-called hard currency (i.e., U.S. dollars). Such deals, however, usually mean that the film's producer will have to successfully negotiate through a difficult and archaic bureaucratic system, that the technical production expertise and equipment made available is not up to par, that living standards may be unacceptable to many of the film's above-the-line personnel and that extraordinary logistical problems will be created. Producers experienced with these sorts of arrangements suggest that to justify the deal, location desirability must be the more important consideration over saving money (see "exchange rate" and "facilities subsidies").

foreign debt capitalization programs — Financial arrangements formally adopted by numerous third-world countries that owe large amounts of debt to foreign banks which encourage the purchase of the foreign country's debt at a significant discount and exchanging it for foreign currency to be used for film production activities in the foreign country. A U.S. producer seeking to take advantage of such programs must contact the U.S. office of an official representative of such foreign country and complete an application. Once approved, the foreign currency is contributed to a corporation incorporated in that foreign country, the stock of which is owned by the U.S. producer (see "debt").

foreign distribution — The theatrical licensing, exploitation and/or sales of a film in markets outside the market in which the film was produced. For U.S. produced films, foreign distribution involves theatrical exhibition and/or sales outside the U.S. and Canada (see "domestic theatrical release," "foreign markets," "foreign pre-sales" and "foreign sales agents").

foreign equity financing — Film funding provided by foreign sources (non-U.S.) in exchange for an ownership interest or profit participation in the film or films financed, or an ownership interest in the entity producing such film(s). In addition to requiring an equity participation in the film's receipts, foreign equity investors may also require that the rights relating to the exploitation of the film in certain territories be reserved for them (see "financing").

foreign equity investment — A movie financing arrangement in which the motion picture producer actually co-ventures the production with a foreign partner (i.e., the foreign investor becomes the financial and/or creative partner of the domestic producer). When such foreign partners are industry insiders in their home market, they often can provide expertise in exploiting the film or films in that territory and in guiding a particular film production through complex governmental bureaucracy. Thus, movies that are at least considered a part domestic production in such foreign countries may be accorded some favoritism when such a foreign partner is aboard (see "financing" and "international co-production").

foreign exchange services — Banking services relating to the exchange of foreign currencies (see "currency conversion").

foreign facilities deals — (see "foreign below-the-line deals").

foreign film — From the perspective of someone who is primarily involved in the U.S. film business, films produced by a production entity based outside the U.S. (see "foreign corporation" and "production company").

foreign film rental — The money owed and/or paid to a film's distributor under the various film licensing agreements relating to the exploitation of the motion picture in foreign territories (see "film rentals" and "restricted currencies").

foreign financing — Film funding of all types (debt and equity) originating from foreign (non-U.S.) sources (see "financing").

foreign government grants and subsidies — Specific donations by non-U.S. governments to filmmakers to assist in the production of a film that is deemed advantageous to the country or a given locale within the country that is served by that government (e.g., production of the movie will provide jobs and help the economy in a given area or the movie will provide favorable publicity for the locale; see "facilities subsidies").

foreign licensing deal — A movie distribution agreement with a foreign entity and providing for the exhibition of a movie in a foreign territory (see "foreign market").

foreign market — Non-domestic geographical area of demand for films. Films are usually sold on a country by country basis outside the U.S. and Canada and all rights (i.e., television, video/DVD, etc. are included; see "domestic theatrical market").

foreign ownership — Possession and title held by non-U.S. based individuals or entities; in a business context, top level management and title to a company's assets held by persons or entities based in a non-U.S. country. Major U.S. studio/distributors have been purchased in recent years by Canadian, Italian, French, Australian and Japanese interests, however, some have relinquished their interests in a relatively short period of time (see "corporate stock" and "equity").

foreign potential — The prospects of a film with regard to its appeal to foreign audiences. Certain types of films do better in foreign markets than others (see "action/adventure," "genre" and "physical comedy").

foreign pre-sales and agreements — Contracts to provide cash advances or commitments (hopefully bankable or lendable commitments) to purchase a film for distribution in a given foreign market provided prior to the film's completion (see "foreign sales agents" and "pre-sales").

foreign production problems — Common difficulties that arise in the production of a feature film at non-U.S. locations (e.g., restrictive regulations relating to cast, crew and the script, language barriers, frequent delays, unstable governments, riots, civil war and less than adequate housing facilities for the cast and crew; see "international co-production" and "pro and con analysis").

foreign purchasers — For purposes of compliance with the federal Regulation D securities registration exemption, offers and sales of securities to foreign persons made outside the U.S. effected in a manner that will result in the securities coming to rest abroad may be excluded from the Regulation D numerical limitation on the number of investors (see "counting rules" and "Regulation D").

foreign receipts — Monies earned by exploitation of a film outside the U.S. and received by the distributor. It is important for the producer and other profit participants to clarify at what point foreign receipts are to be included as part of the distributor's gross receipts (i.e., when profit participants will receive the benefit of the collection of foreign receipts that could but have not been remitted to the U.S.; see "foreign tax credits" and "remitted or remittable").

foreign receivables — Monies owed to a producer or distributor from non-domestic sources (see "domestic receivables").

foreign revenues — The total income produced by the exploitation of feature films outside the domestic marketplace. Although foreign revenues have grown in recent years, that growth appears to be leveling off ("revenue sources").

foreign sales — (see "foreign distribution").

foreign sales agents — Persons or entities authorized to sell rights and to exploit a film on behalf of the producer on a country by country or market by market basis in the non-domestic territories. Most foreign sales agents do not cross-collateralize the profits of a single film between markets. However, any group of films sold as a package to a foreign territory may raise allocation issues that are effectively the same as cross-collateralization. Typically foreign sales agents will charge a 25 percent fee if an advance is given to the producer but a 15 percent fee if no advance is provided (see "cross-collateralization," "foreign distribution" and "foreign sales representative").

foreign sales representative — The person or entity authorized by a film's distributor or producer to sell rights to the film and exploit the film in foreign markets; a broader term than "foreign sales agent" including both "foreign sales agents" and "foreign distributors" (see "cross-collateralization," "foreign distribution" and "foreign sales agents").

foreign subsidies — Film subsidies granted by foreign governments (i.e., not any governmental unit within the U.S.). Such subsidies usually require that most of the film be shot in the subsidizing country, using almost exclusively native technicians, facilities and actors (see "Film subsidies," "foreign tax shelters," "government subsidies," "grants," "international co-productions" and "pro and con analysis").

foreign tax credits — Dollar for dollar deductions from an individual or entity's U.S. income tax for the payment of foreign taxes levied by countries as a remittance or gross receipts tax. Foreign taxes generally represent the largest part of the distribution expense item "taxes." Distributors often pay such taxes, then deduct such payments from their gross receipts as a distribution expense (meaning that the producer and other net profit participants have actually paid the taxes) while the distributors still claim the foreign tax credit against their U.S. tax liability. Producers may want to see that the distribution agreement provides that either the distributor should not deduct the payment from gross receipts or the foreign tax credit should be passed on to the producer group ("creative accounting," "fraud" and "unethical business practices").

foreign tax deals — Tax benefits offered by a foreign country to filmmakers from other countries as an incentive to shoot the movie in

that country; such deals usually require that the majority of the film be shot in the offering country and, in some cases, that the key actors, creative personnel and the producer must be from that country (see "foreign production problems," "international co-productions" and "tax shelters").

foreign taxes — An assessment levied pursuant to the authority of a non-U.S. governmental entity on a person or property for public purposes including support of the government (see "foreign tax credit").

foreign tax shelters — A transaction based on foreign law (i.e., non-U.S.) and structured so that foreign taxpayers reduce their tax liability by engaging in activities that provide deductions or tax credits to apply against their tax liability (see "abusive tax shelter," "big five," "international tax attorney" and "tax shelter").

foreign television license fees — Payments made for the rights to show U.S. produced television programming in non-U.S. territories (see "foreign territories").

foreign territories — All portions of a territory not included in the domestic marketplace (i.e., from the perspective of a U.S. filmmaker, outside the U.S. and Canada; see "foreign market").

foreign theatrical — The market for films exploited through exhibition in theaters located in countries other than the U.S. and Canada (see "foreign territories").

foreign version — A motion picture that has been changed in some way for release in foreign markets. Generally, the change consists of adding sub-titles or dubbing in the foreign language, but may also include other changes (e.g., to meet local governmental censorship requirements; see "cultural differences" and "other versions").

format — The width to height ratio of a motion picture as it is projected on the screen (see "aspect ratio" and "pan and scan").

Form 1-A — Regulation A offering statement pursuant to the Securities Act of 1933 (see "Regulation A" and "securities").

Form D — The federal Regulation D notice filing form that is used by issuers of securities to provide notice to the SEC that an offering claiming a Regulation D exemption from securities registration is being relied upon. The form must be filed with the SEC within fifteen days of the first sale in the offering and at other times set forth on the form itself. Most states will also accept the SEC's Form D to meet the state's notice filing requirement pursuant to a state's limited offering exemption considered compatible with the federal Regulation D, although a few states require notice filings to be effected prior to the offer or sale of securities in their state (see "blue sky laws," " notice filing requirement" and "Regulation D").

Form S-1 — The general purpose federal form for securities registration (for public offerings) prescribed by the SEC under the Securities Act of 1933. An unlimited amount of money can be raised pursuant to an S-1 offering, extensive disclosure is prescribed and the prospectus and registration statement must be filed with the SEC in Washington D.C. (see "Form SB," "prospectus," "public offering," "registration statement," "Regulation A" and "SCOR)."

Form SB-1 — Registration statement under the Securities Act of 1933 for securities to be sold to the public by certain small business issuers seeking to raise $10 million or less. This form allows an issuer to provide information in a question and answer format, similar to that used in Regulation A offerings, however, most issuers find that the Q&A format results in a less than adequate selling document as compared to a well-drafted prospectus. Unlike Regulation A filings, Form SB-1 requires audited financial statements (see "Form SB-2" and "Regulation SB").

Form SB-2 — A form of securities registration under the Securities Act of 1933 for securities to be sold to the public by certain small business issuers seeking to raise capital in any amount. If a company is a "small business issuer," it may register an unlimited dollar amount of securities using Form SB-2, and may use this form again and again so long as it satisfies the "small business issuer" definition. One advantage of Form SB-2 is that all its disclosure requirements are in Regulation S-B, a set of rules written in simple, non-legalistic terminology. Form SB-2 also permits the company to: provide audited financial statements, prepared according to generally accepted accounting principles, for two fiscal years. In contrast, Form S-1 requires the issuer to provide audited financial statements, prepared according to more detailed SEC regulations, for three fiscal years; and include less extensive narrative disclosure than Form S-1 requires, particularly in the description of the business, and executive compensation (see "Regulation SB" and "small business issuer").

Form 10-K — The annual report required by the SEC of every issuer of a registered security, every exchange-listed company and any company with five hundred or more shareholders or $1 million or more in gross assets (see "publicly held" and "public offering").

formula deal — A film licensing agreement between a distributor and a circuit of theaters in which the license fee of a given feature is determined, for the theaters covered by the agreement, based on a specified percentage of that feature's national box office gross. The formula deal effectively cross-collateralizes the financial performance of the film among the various theaters at which it is exhibited. The results of film formula deals have been found to be an unreasonable restraint of trade. If a major studio/distributor also owns certain exhibitors it may be more difficult to prevent them from effectively utilizing formula deals as between their internally controlled distributor and exhibitor (see "antitrust laws," "cross-collateralization," "major exhibition chains," "Paramount Consent Decree of 1948," "TriStar Case" and "vertical integration").

formula for computing net profits — A negotiated provision that often appears as an exhibit to a production/financing distribution agreement and sets out the manner in which net profits on a film are calculated (also called "net profits formula").

for profit — A business created and conducted for the purpose of making money in addition to the services and/or products provided (see "hobby" and "non-profit").

founders — The people who organize, create and originally control a business entity (see "corporate stock," "corporation," "founder's shares" and "shareholders").

founder's shares — Corporate stock issued to the corporation's organizers, and often carrying special privileges (see "corporate stock," "corporation," "founder" and "shareholders").

four-run break — A release pattern in which a film is made available to only four theaters within a specified geographical area (see "two-run break" and "three-run break").

four-wall or four-walling — A technique used by some distribution companies and/or producers for exhibiting their film or films in which the distributor or producer handling his, her or its own distribution offers the theater(s) a pre-set negotiated price or flat weekly rental fee for the use of the theater. The rental fee is thus guaranteed to the exhibitor regardless of the film's revenue intake at the box office. This fee is for the use of the "four walls" of the theater. The distributor or producer pays all advertising expenses and usually hires personnel to be at each theater for supervision and nightly collection of all monies taken in at the box office. Through this method, the exhibitor has eliminated certain risks in that rental income is guaranteed, however, the exhibitor is foregoing the opportunity to show other movies during that same period. The distributor or producer incurs a greater risk but is also in the position, should the film be successful, of reaping the benefits of 100 percent of the monies taken in at the box office, less advertising, administrative and rental costs. Revenues from concession sales may be negotiable. If the film is being four-walled by its producers, four-walling is a form of self-distribution (see "distribution alternatives" and "self-distribution").

four-wall advertising — A specific advertising approach used to support a film's four-wall engagement that consists entirely of local advertising, the purpose of which is to achieve a high frequency of impressions among the film's potential audience in the local market just prior to the film's exhibition at a local theater (see "four-wall" and "four-walling").

four-wall engagements — (see "four-wall").

four-wall exhibition agreement — The contract between the theater owner and the distributor or producer in which the theater owner agrees to allow the distributor or producer to exhibit a film in the theater based on a pre-set negotiated price or flat weekly rental fee to be paid for the use of the theater. The rental fee is thus guaranteed to the exhibitor regardless of the film's revenue intake at the box office. This fee is for the use of the "four walls" of the theater (see "four-wall").

fractionalized rights — In film distribution, the stripping or separating out of various territories and/or markets from the domestic theatrical distribution (i.e., not making some or all of the ancillary rights available to the domestic theatrical distributor; see "fractionalizing" and "split-rights basis").

fractionalized sales — (see "fractionalized rights," "fractionalizing" and "split-rights basis").

fractionalizing — The separate selling of the various distribution rights to a film (e.g., domestic theatrical, foreign theatrical, video and cable; see "multiple pre-sales" and "split-rights basis").

fractured rights — (see "fractured rights deal").

fractured rights deal — A film finance and distribution transaction, commonly utilized in the 1980's, in which the film's producer pre-sold domestic video and international rights, then engaged a distributor to distribute in the domestic theatrical marketplace for a fee. Sometimes the producer also retained all domestic television rights. The pre-sales would typically cover all of the production and some or all of the domestic releasing costs for the picture, leaving the producer's share of theatrical revenues and television rights for potential net profits. Fractured rights deals worked (1) before video became a significant revenue source for the major studio/distributors (thus the studios did not demand to participate in the video revenue stream at that time); (2) independent video companies were still paying substantial fees for video rights, (3) more banks were prepared to loan money to support these deals and fund production, (4) the funds supplied by independent video companies and outside banks were sufficient to cover production costs and a significant portion of domestic releasing costs. The fractured rights deals of the 1980's are generally no longer available. They have been replaced by the split rights deals or distributors demand worldwide rights (see "lender financing," "pre-sales," "rising production costs" and "split rights deal").

franchise — A special privilege granted to an individual, entity or group; also the right given to a private person or corporation to market another's product within a certain area. Thus, motion picture theaters that have an exclusive contractual arrangement to show the pictures of a single distributor are operating through a franchise granted by that distributor (see "franchise agreements").

franchise agreements — A film licensing agreement, or series of licensing agreements, entered into as part of the same transaction, in effect for more than one motion picture season and covering the exhibition of features released by one distributor during the entire period of the agreement. Such agreements typically protect the exhibitor by prohibiting the exhibition of that distributor's films within the geographical market of the exhibitor and protect the distributor by committing the exhibitor to book the distributor's films. In recent court hearings relating to the requests of certain distributors to be relieved of the Paramount consent decree conduct provisions in dealings with exhibitors, the U.S. Justice Department has taken the position that franchise agreements are not necessarily anti-competitive in the current marketplace (see "antitrust laws," "conduct restrictions," "Paramount Consent Decree of 1948" and "TriStar Case").

franchise picture — A motion picture that is expected to be a blockbuster and generate a series of sequels, along with video game and merchandising opportunities (see "blockbuster," "merchandising" and "sequel").

franchise tax — A tax generally imposed by the states upon corporations and somtimes other entities as a tax upon the net income of the corporation attributable to activities within the state or on the net worth of the corporation located in the state (see "corporation").

franchised sub-distributor — A defined term in some film distribution agreements referring to a person or entity, other than the distributor, who is licensed by the distributor to distribute or sub-license a film for exhibition in a particular geographic area outside of the domestic territory. The agreement creates an obligation for such person or entity to account for or report to the distributor the amount of any income or expense of such distribution or sub-licensing, regardless of whether any amounts payable to the distributor by such person or entity for such licenses are fixed, on a percentage, guaranteed or

other basis, or computed or determined in any other manner or by any combination of any of the foregoing. The major studio/distributors usually do not use such sub-distributors in the domestic territory (see "outright sale" and "sub-distributor").

fraud — Intentional deception resulting in injury to another. Elements of fraud are (1) a false and material misrepresentation made by one who either knows it is false or is ignorant of its truth, (2) the maker's intent that the representation be relied on by another and in a manner reasonably contemplated, (3) the recipient's ignorance of the falsity of the representation, (4) the recipient's rightful or justified reliance on the representation and (5) proximate injury to the recipient. Fraud usually consists of misrepresentation, concealment or nondisclosure of a material fact, or at least misleading conduct, devices or contrivance. If in fact, a given feature film distributor actually engaged in a significant amount of the conduct described in this book, it is likely that such distributor has intentionally deceived and caused an injury to all of the profit participants involved in the deal, thus, such distributor may well have committed some form of actionable fraud (see "adhesion contract," "anti-fraud deal," "block booking," "creative accounting," "overreaching," "predatory practices," "racketeering," "RICO," "scam" and "white collar crime").

free and clear — Unencumbered title to property (see "title").

free enterprise system — An economy structured around unfettered choice (i.e., businesses are free to choose what products they will make, consumers are free to choose what they will buy and prices are generally left to fluctuate with supply and demand in an openly competitive market). Free enterprise has traditionally been one of the basic underlying economic principles of the U.S. economy. Unfortunately, some businesses, if not limited by government or law suits, will use unfair, unethical, unconscionable, anti-competitive, predatory and illegal business practices to gain a competitive edge over competitors, often to the detriment of the consuming public and other less powerful interests in a given industry. That appears to be the case in the Hollywood-based U.S. film industry today (see "anti-competitive business practices," "antitrust laws," "greed," "combination in restraint of trade," "law of supply and demand," "marketplace of ideas," "predatory practices," "role of government," "unethical business practices" and "unfair competition").

freelance employee — A person who is not regularly employed by a business but who agrees to perform duties for compensation. For film union purposes, those who are employed for a period of less than sixteen weeks are considered freelance employees (see "employment agreement" and "independent contractor").

free television — Broadcast television programming that is supported by television commercial sponsors (i.e., the exhibition of a program on home type television receivers without any specific charge required of the recipient either for the program or for the channel on which the program is received and without originating the program on a cable facility; see "basic pay cable," "pay cable" and "pay-per-view").

frequency of payments — How often compensation is disbursed. Frequency of payments can be an important issue as between producers and distributors when the distributor

or its studio affiliate provides financing for a motion picture project and is thus charging interest on the negative cost of the film, particularly since in the studio production-financing/distribution deal, the distributor typically deducts its distribution fees and distribution expenses from gross receipts, then deducts interest payments from the revenue stream before the negative costs start to be recouped (see "interest" and "production-financing/distribution agreement").

fringe benefits — Compensation other than salary paid to persons who work on the production of film. Fringe benefits generally are not paid in the form of cash but may include life insurance, vacation pay, health, welfare and pension benefits, free screenings of a movie, Christmas bonuses, car-pooling, etc. Some distributors have reportedly over-stated the amount of fringe benefits paid to unions or guilds and then deducted the inflated amount from the distributor's gross receipts as distribution expenses, or even worse, as film production costs on which interest charges accumulate (see "creative accounting" and "unethical business practices").

fringe player — A person who does not actively participate in the activities of the entertainment community's mainstream (see "'A' title," "bankable actors," "economic microcosm," "independent producer," "major exhibition chains," "major studio/distributors" and "star").

front end cash compensation — Money paid for services to be performed and either paid upon the signing of a written agreement or as of the start of the services. Similar to an advance except that front end cash compensation may or may not be recoupable out of the film's revenue stream (see "contingent compensation").

front end load — The sales charge applied to an investment at the time of initial purchase. A front end load may also be that portion of the capital contributed by investors in a direct participation program such as a film limited partnership (or manager-managed LLC) that constitutes offering costs, including management fees, syndication costs (offering selling costs), legal fees, accounting fees, disclosure document printing (or copying) and binding, commissions and marketing costs. Generally, such costs should not exceed approximately 15 percent of the offering proceeds, since the larger front-end load reduces the amount that ultimately may be available to produce the film (i.e., the asset that may result in income or gain). The concept of front end loading also describes the efforts of stars, directors, producers and other creative personnel, in studio, bank or investor financed films, who demand higher compensation to be paid at earlier stages of production or at earlier stages of the revenue stream, thus making less revenue available for subsequent profit participants (see "creative accounting," "gross participations," "leverage," "net profits," "participant" and "up front").

full audit — (see "audit").

full disclosure — The requirement to set forth in writing all material facts relating to a securities transaction. All securities transactions (i.e., the sale of securities) impose certain disclosure obligations on issuers (see "anti-fraud rule," "disclosure document" and "securities").

fully distributed — A new securities issue that has been completely resold to the investing public (i.e., to institutions, individuals and/or other investors as opposed to broker/dealers; see "securities").

fully negotiated agreement — A contract the terms and provisions of which have all been considered and treated by the parties (also sometimes referred to as a "Long Form Agreement" although most long form agreements in the film industry are not actually fully negotiated since very few negotiating parties have equal leverage thus are forced to accept certain provisions on a take it or leave it basis; see "adhesion contract," "deal memo," "letter agreement," "player agreement" and "short form agreement").

fund — To provide monies to finance the development, production and/or distribution activities of a feature or documentary film. As a noun, a pool of money, some of which may be available for use in meeting the production or distribution costs of a film (see "financing" and "venture capital").

fundamental analysis — An approach to the analysis of the balance sheet and income statements of companies used by analysts in an effort to forecast the future stock price movements of the companies. Such analysis considers past records of assets, earnings, sales, products, management and markets in the attempt to predict future trends in these indicators of a company's success of failure. By appraising a firm's prospects, analysts assess whether a particular stock or group of stocks is undervalued or overvalued at the current market price (see "corporate stock," "fundamentals" and "technical analysis").

fundamentals — The basic characteristics of a company considered by financial analysts in determining investment prospects. Among other things, fundamentals include past records of assets, earnings, sales, products, management and markets. A statement that the fundamentals of the movie business have never been better suggests that such companies are strong and the climate for investing in such firms is favorable, although a distinction must be made about which segment of the industry is favored since, for example, there can be a significant difference among the conditions of the major studio/distributors, independent producers, independent distributors and individual entities within each such segment of the industry (see "corporate stock," "fundamental analysis," "Paul Kagan Associates, Inc." and "publicly held").

funding — The raising or providing of monies to finance a film project (see "financing").

funding sources — All of the places where feature film producers may go to find financing for the development, production and/or distribution of motion pictures. Such sources have traditionally included the major studio/distributors, other established film production companies, independent distributors, film, television and cable organizations, other ancillary market entities, banks and other lenders, private investors, joint venture investors, family and friends, etc. In the course of any given year there may be some six hundred motion pictures released theatrically in the United States. There may be hundreds more feature films that were actually produced but did not get a theatrical release. All of these were financed in some manner. No one has apparently been able to take the time or make the effort to do what would be necessary to determine what financing methods were used by each of these production companies and for several reasons: (1) there are so many films produced each year, (2) many are produced by small companies that come together just to produce that one film and then their principals go on to other things and they may be hard to find, (3) even if located and they

were willing to be questioned about their film's financing, many film production company executives, both large and small, have been known to mislead others about their actual costs and funding sources and (4) some of these entities would not disclose their method of financing, even if subpoenaed before a Congressional investigating committee. Thus, no one really knows how many films were financed in a given year as in-house studio productions, through the use of a production-financing distribution agreements, as negative pickups or other forms of lender financing, as fractured rights deals, as split rights deals, with collateralized bank loans, using foreign territorial pre-sales, as joint ventures (domestic or formal international co-productions), with corporate stock or debt offerings, through public or private limited partnerships or LLCs, with active or passive investors, with domestic facilities deals, through grants, using foreign below-the-line deals, through foreign tax shelters, as foreign equity financing or foreign currency deals, through self-financing techniques, family and friends or money laundering schemes. Such a research project, possibly conducted by a professional association of independent producers, for example, would provide the industry with important information (see "financing").

fund-raising process — The activities associated with arranging for the production financing of a motion picture (i.e., the manner, means and procedures involved in acquiring capital; see "financing," "investor financing," "lender financing," "offering" and "venture capital").

fund-raising proposals — Propositions relating to the acquisition of financing for a project (e.g., development or production financing for a motion picture; see "business plan," "development financing," "disclosure document," "investment contract," "investor financing agreement," "financing," "joint venture agreement" and "limited partnership offering").

funds for releasing costs — The money required to pay for the expenses associated with the release of a motion picture, principally for prints and advertising costs, although as digital releases become more common, the cost of prints will be eliminated. All other things being equal, a producer who approaches a distributor with a completed motion picture including well known talent, with funds for releasing costs and with worldwide rights still available should be in the best possible bargaining position with respect to negotiating the terms of a distribution deal. On the other hand, in the film industry it still may be unreasonable to expect a distribution agreement, even under the above-described circumstances to be fair to both parties in all its provisions (see "advertising," "decision-making continuum," "prints," "releasing costs" and "rent-a-distributor").

G

gap financing — A form of lender financing on a film for which the pre-sale of territorial rights has yet to cover the entire budget (i.e., funds are still needed to produce the film and there are also unsold territorial rights in some of the top ten markets). In that sense, gap financing is merely an extension of the pre-sale financing technique, in which the bank loans are partly based on the good faith estimates made by an experienced foreign sales agent that distribution deals to distribute the film in the remaining unsold territories among the more important foreign countries will come to fruition (see "foreign sales agent," "lender financing" and "pre-sale financing").

GAAP — Acronym for generally accepted accounting principles (see "creative accounting," "generally accepted accounting principles").

gaffer — The chief electrician in a film production. The film production person responsible to the director of photography for the safe and efficient execution of the lighting patterns outlined by the director of photography (see "director of photography" and "gaffer's best boy").

gaffer's best boy (or best girl) — The first assistant electrician. The film production person responsible for assisting the gaffer in the performance of his or her duties and for supervising the operation of the lighting and electrical equipment (see "gaffer").

gauge — A measurement term used to describe the width of positive film. For feature films, the gauge is usually 35mm and sometimes 70mm. Also, some low-budget feature films have been shot in 16mm and blown-up to 35mm, although as the technology advances more and more low budget films are being recorded on high-definition or digital video (see "film," "high-definition" and "thirty-five millimeter").

generally accepted accounting principles (GAAP) — Conventions, rules and procedures that define accepted accounting practice. These basic guidelines and procedures were originally set forth in the U.S. by the Accounting Principles Board of the American Institute of Certified Public Accountants. That board was replaced in 1973 by the Financial Accounting Standards Board (FASD), an independent self-regulatory organization Financial statements included in a securities registration statement must be prepared in accordance with GAAP, as well as the SEC's own accounting standards. Major studio/distributors generally do not restrict themselves to the use of generally accepted accounting principles (see "contractually defined terms," "creative accounting," "FASB" and "Regulation S-X").

general partner — In the context of a general partnership, one or more individuals or entities that are jointly and severally responsible for the debts of the partnership. In the context of a limited partnership, the person or entity named as the general partner (i.e., management) in the opening recital of the partnership agreement, together with any other person who becomes a general partner of such partnership pursuant to the limited partnership agreement. In a limited partnership, an individual general partner's liability to partnership creditors is not limited. In a film partnership the general partner is generally the producer or the person who put the deal together (or an entity controlled by such person) and is responsible for control and management of the partnership's activities. A general partner of a limited partnership may be an individual or a corporation (see "corporation," "limited liability company," "limited partnership" and "manager").

general partnership — A partnership without limited partners (i.e., an unincorporated association of two or more persons doing business as co-owners for profit). A general partnership is a contract of two or more competent persons to place their money, effects, labor and skill, or some or all of them, in lawful commerce or business and to divide the profit and bear the loss in certain agreed upon proportions. Partners in a general partnership are individually liable for the debts of the partnership and assets individually owned will be subject to execution to satisfy any such debt when partnership assets are insufficient. A general partnership (like a limited partnership) is not subject to income taxes; rather its partners

are directly taxed individually on the income, taking into account their share of partnership gains and losses. A joint venture is a specialized form of general partnership (see "partnership," "investor financing," "joint venture," "limited liability company" and "limited partnership").

general release — A motion picture that is exhibited in a large number of theaters (some consider five hundred theaters as a general release) and throughout the country (i.e., in most of the major U.S. markets). On the other hand, releases to more than three thousand theaters are not uncommon for the hoped-for blockbusters (see "limited engagement," "mini-multiple," "print," "release pattern" and "wide release").

general solicitation — Activities relating to the offer and sale of securities, by whatever means, that involve contact by an issuer or its representatives with prospective purchasers with whom the issuer has no pre-existing relationship (e.g., mass-mailings, cold calls, Internet spam and unqualified visits to issuer Web sites). A general solicitation is prohibited pursuant to both state and federal exemptions from the securities registration requirements but is permitted in a public/registered offering (see "cold calls," "limitations on manner of offering," "MAIE," "private placement," "public offering" and "solicitation").

general theatrical release — (see "general release" and "theatrical release").

general use — Widely disseminated or relied upon. With respect to prospective financial statements in accounting, a reference to the use of such statements by a person with whom the responsible party is not negotiating directly (e.g., in an offering statement of an entity's debt or equity interests). Because recipients of prospective financial statements distributed for general use are unable to question the responsible party directly, the presentation most useful to them is one that portrays, to the best of the responsible party's knowledge and belief, the expected results. Thus, technically, only a financial forecast is appropriate for general use (see "financial forecasts," "financial projections" and "limited use").

generation — Each progressive step in the film preparation process starting from an original negative going through a release print. As the process moves away from the original, each generation will typically show some slight loss in quality (see "answer print," "release print" and "work print").

genre — A distinctive type or category of literary composition and a particular type of motion picture, for example, action/adventure, love story, comedy, romantic comedy, western, science fiction (sci-fi), horror/fantasy or murder/mystery (see "exploitation film," "movies with a message" and "theme").

geographic market — The area where a particular product is sold. Film licensing agreements between a film distributor and an exhibitor will typically describe the geographic market that will be exclusive to the exhibitor (see "foreign market" and "territory").

glamour industry — A business that is considered to be fascinating and exciting to the general public. The film industry is such a business and this factor is often cited as an underlying reason for investor interest in the industry, at least for individual investors (i.e., some of these investors are partially motivated to invest in movies because of the so-called "cocktail chatter" value of such investments). In

other words, such investments are more interesting to talk about than other investments typically found in an investor's portfolio (see "investor motivation").

global communication — An expression that recognizes that due to increasingly advanced technologies information intended for mass audiences commonly flows throughout the world (i.e., from a communications standpoint, the world is shrinking). Such developments inevitably contribute to conflicts between disparate cultures. Dominant film industry entities can contribute to or help alleviate such conflict should they choose to (see "cultural differences," "culturally biased," "culture promotion," "patterns of bias" and "propaganda").

global environment — A reference to the trend toward more international financing of the production and distribution of feature films based partly on the realization that films are often produced for a world-wide audience ("global integration," "internationally competitive" and "transnational cartelization").

global integration — The combining of businesses on an international scale (see "horizontal integration" and "vertical integration").

globalization — The increasing integration of economies around the world, particularly through trade and financial flows. The term sometimes also refers to the movement of people (labor) and knowledge (technology) across international borders. ["Globalization: Threat or Opportunity?" IMF Staff Issues Brief, April 12, 2000 online at http://www.imf.org/external/np/exr/ib/2000/o41200.htm] Globalization cannot, however, be limited to economies, trade, financial flows, the movement of people, knowledge and technology. It also brings about cultural conflicts in areas of language, politics, religion and traditions. The globalization that has had such a profound effect on other U.S. industries over the last few decades has now belatedly reached the film industry. ["The Migration of U.S. Film & Television Production,"U.S. Department of Commerce Study on Runaway Production, March, 2001, page 59] In the past few years a global commercial-media market has emerged. ["The New Global Media, Robert W. McChesney, *The Nation*, November 29, 1999] What is being sought, is the creation of a global oligopoly. It happened to the oil and automotive industries earlier this century; now it is happening to the entertainment industry. ["The New Global Media, Robert W. McChesney, *The Nation*, November 29, 1999] The global media market has come to be dominated by the same eight transnational corporations that rule U.S. media: General Electric, AT&T/Liberty Media, Disney, Time Warner, Sony, News Corporation, Viacom and Seagram, plus Bertelsmann, the Germany-based conglomerate. ["The New Global Media, Robert W. McChesney, *The Nation*, November 29, 1999]

global media presence — Communications industry interests throughout the world (see "communications industry," "entertainment industry" and "internationally competitive").

global recession — A worldwide economic downturn (see "global environment").

go ahead — The approval of a motion picture project for production (see "green light" and "pass").

goal — An end toward which effort is directed (see "dream").

going private — Changing public ownership of a corporation to private ownership either by the company's repurchase of shares or through purchases by an outside private investor (see "corporate stock," "private placement" and "publicly held").

going public — The process of offering equity ownership interests in an entity (e.g., a corporation's shares) to the public through a public/registered offering for the first time, thus shifting the company's ownership from one or a few private investors (e.g., stockholders) to a base that includes a large group of public investors. Such an offering is referred to as an initial public offering (IPO) and the corporate shares (or other entity interests such as limited partnership of LLC units) are said to have market value (see "corporate stock," "initial public offering," "market value," "public offering" and "publicly held").

good distributor — A subjective term which from an independent producer's point of view suggests at least some of the following: a feature film distributor who does not abuse the disparity in bargaining power as between the producer and distributor at the negotiating table (i.e., does not offer unconscionable distribution terms on a take it or leave it basis), is enthusiastic about distributing the motion picture it has committed to distribute, develops a credible marketing plan for the film, can afford the expense of adequately promoting the motion picture, will make reasonable prints and ads commitments, will honor in good faith the consultation rights of the producer, does not unreasonably interfere with or limit the audit rights of the producer and other net profit participants, will fairly respond to the discovery of accounting discrepancies, does not engage in unethical business practices and otherwise has a good track record with other producers. Such entities are rare in the Hollywood based U.S. film industry. (see "adhesion contract," "allocation issues," "anti-competitive business practices," "audit rights," "blacklisting," "conduct restrictions," "creative accounting," "Paramount Consent Decree of 1948," "problem producer," "sue us," "TriStar Case," "unconscionable contract" and "unethical business practices").

good faith — Being loyal and conscientious with respect to one's duty or obligation (i.e., a total absence of any intention to seek an unfair advantage or to defraud another party); an honest and sincere intention to fulfill one's obligations. Film distribution agreements often turn to this rather vague standard which can only be applied after the fact. When possible, such terms should be replaced in the distribution agreement with a more precisely defined standard of conduct (contrast with "bad faith"; see "covenant of good faith and fair dealing").

good faith consideration — Something of value given by one party in return for a performance or a promise of performance by another, for the purpose of forming a contract without any intention to seek an unfair advantage or to defraud the other party (see "consideration" and "good faith").

good film — A subjective term which in the final analysis means a film that its intended audience enjoyed and appreciated. From the standpoint of distributors and film financiers, a good film is a film people will pay enough money to see to make the venture profitable. Note however, that different participants in a film's revenue stream

participate in profits before others (see "blockbuster," "bomb" and "hit").

good title — (see "clearance," "clear title," "just title" and "title").

good will — An intangible but recognized business asset that is the result of such features of an ongoing enterprise as the production or sale of reputable brand name products, a good relationship with customers and suppliers and the standing of the business in its community. Goodwill can become a balance sheet asset when a going business is acquired through a purchase transaction in which the price paid exceeds the net asset value. A distributor's reputation for providing a continuous flow of quality films is an important aspect of its goodwill with exhibitors. Also, the preservation of a feature film production and/or distribution company's goodwill is an important concern in selecting merchandising partners (see "asset," "merchandising agreement," "merchandising rights," "mergers and acquisitions" and "rent-a-distributor").

governing law clause — A contractual provision usually found in the miscellaneous provisions section of a contract that names the state under whose laws any dispute arising pursuant to the contract is to be resolved (see "arbitration clause," "contract" and "dispute resolution provision").

government subsidies — Grants by a government (city, county, state, federal or foreign) to filmmakers to assist in the production of a film that is deemed advantageous to the community served by that government (e.g., production of the movie will provide jobs and help the economy in a given area or the movie will provide favorable publicity). In contrast to foreign governments, the U.S. government has tended to avoid such subsidies and has not recognized the value of motion pictures for cultural promotion purposes, choosing instead to leave the pursuit of such "hidden agendas" to the private sector (see "film subsidies," "foreign subsidies," "grants," "hidden agenda" and "marketplace of ideas").

"G" rating — An MPAA rating indicating that a motion picture has been approved by the MPAA's Classification and Rating Administration for general audiences (i.e., in the opinion of the MPAA ratings board there is nothing contained in the film that would offend parents if the film were viewed by children; see "MPAA" and "ratings").

grace period — The period of time provided in most loan contracts and insurance policies during which default or cancellation will not occur, even though a payment is past due. Also a negotiated provision in some long-term loans whereby repayment of principal does not begin until some point well into the life of the loan. A borrower will sometimes accept a higher interest rate for a longer grace period (see "debt," "insurance" and "lender financing").

grantee — One to whom a grant is made. The grantee in a film distribution agreement is the distributor (see "grant of rights" and "grantor").

grant of rights — The awarding of power or privilege to someone who is justly entitled. In a motion picture contractual context, grant of rights refers to the power or privilege of developing, producing and exploiting a literary property, screenplay and/or movie. Such rights are granted to producers in the acquisition of literary properties, to distributors by producers through the distribution agreement and to sub-distributors and others through various licensing agreements. The phrase "grant of rights" also refers to the provision in such agreement which sets out what rights are being granted. Generally, in a film distribution deal, such rights will cover markets, changes to the title, the use of music on a soundtrack, dubbed versions and trailers, re-editing, advertising and publicizing the picture, use of excerpts, use of the names and likenesses of cast members, commercials, publishing a novelization, adding the name and trademark of the distributor, merchandising, music, publishing and radio rights, remakes and sequels, assignment of producer's rights and warranties from the producer not to encumber the rights granted nor grant the same rights to others. The producer is typically required to confirm that this provision accurately sets out the grant actually being made (see "grant of rights provision" and "license").

grant of rights provision — The paragraph (or paragraphs) in a film-related acquisition of rights, distribution or licensing agreement that sets forth the type of rights and the extent of those rights provided (see "grant of rights").

grantor — One who makes a grant. The grantor in the film distribution agreement is generally the film's producer or the production entity (see "grantee" and "grant of rights").

grants — Motion picture production funds, generally provided for only a portion of a feature film's budget, made available through government agencies, private foundations, special interest groups, educational research organizations or the media. Each grant source may impose unique requirements and restrictions regarding the awarding of its grant (e.g., only to individuals, only to non-profit organizations or only in a specific field of interest; see "film subsidies," "foreign subsidies" and "government subsidies").

graphics— The visual components of a print advertisement including the type styles used, logos, drawings and the ad's border (see "logo").

grassroots campaign — Advertising campaign that uses flyers, posters, stickers, etc. to promote special screenings which in turn seek to build word of mouth for a specific film in the local community (see "word-of-mouth" and "outreach campaign").

graylisting — A form of discrimination based on age (i.e., age bias). Screenwriters have complained about the youth-driven agents and executives who run the U.S. television and film companies saying such persons have an obsession with youth and that it has become a factor in deciding whether a scriptwriter can write (see "bias," "blacklist," "discrimination," "patterns of bias" and "prejudice").

greed — An inordinate or reprehensible desire to acquire money and things. Although no scientifically conducted study is cited to support the statement, it would appear that there is adequate informal evidence to support a conclusion that greed is a motivation that seems to occur frequently in the film business. When a motion picture like *Coming to America* grosses more than $300 million worldwide but does not reach net profits it may be fair to assume that "greed" was involved in the negotiation or implementation of that distribution deal somewhere along the line. When the number one box office hit at the time for Warner Bros. (*Batman*) achieved $253.4 million in distributor gross receipts as of September, 1990 but based on the distributor accounting still showed a deficit of $35.8 million it may be fair to conclude

that someone taking off-the-top was being greedy in that deal. In that specific situation, the movie's star Jack Nicholson reportedly received $50 million in total compensation. Now for the poor and working people of this country, that may appear obscene. It would not be unreasonable for them to boycott every movie Jack Nicholson makes in the future because his $50 million is enough for a life time and it came out of somebody's else's share. In the meantime the movie-goers have to pay for all of this greed. The motion picture *Rain Man* reportedly grossed more than $400 million, but according to an MGM/Pathe accounting statement for the period from November 1990 to February 1991 it was still more than $27 million away from breaking even (see "boycott," "breakeven," "Buchwald Case," "creative accounting," "gross receipts," "inferior bargaining position," "leverage," "market power" and "net profits").

green band trailer — A movie trailer that has been edited for showing to general audiences (see "red band trailer" and "trailer").

green light— The authority or permission from a studio to produce a motion picture being financed by the studio. Few, if any, other entities in the film industry are in a position to "green light" a movie since the financing may come from several different sources (see "go ahead," "green lighting films" and "pass").

green lighting films — Granting approval for a film project to proceed from development to production (see "green light").

grip — A general term for a crew member who provides labor on the set of a motion picture (see "key grip").

gross — (see "box office gross").

gross audience — The total number of viewers that combined media advertising generates for a movie (see "advertising").

gross box office and box office receipts — (see "box office gross").

gross corridors — Percentage participations in the gross receipts of a specific market or medium as opposed to an across-the-board gross participation in all of the distributor's gross receipts (see "gross receipts," "percentage participation" and "video corridor").

gross deal — In the context of a film distribution contract, a profit participation for the producer or others in the distributor's gross receipts as opposed to a participation in net profits (see "adjusted gross," "film rentals," "gross" and "net profits").

gross film rentals — The distributor's share of the gross box office before distribution fees and costs (advertising, prints and promotion expenses) are deducted by the distributor (also called "gross rentals"; see "gross receipts").

gross floor — A negotiated minimum level of back end participation in a movie's revenue stream regardless of the number or amount of distributor or other deductions from its gross receipts. This device ostensibly permits a producer or other person relying on a percentage participation in net profits to receive at least this minimum (i.e., gross floor) regardless of how many gross points are awarded to others or distributor deductions are otherwise made from gross receipts. It may be necessary to include such a gross floor to preserve some profit participation for the producer and others participating in the producer's share. In light of the reported figure that only about 5 percent of

movies using the major studio/distributor net profits formula ever reach breakeven (i.e., generate net profits), it would seem to be quite essential for every producer to insist on at least some small percentage of a gross floor until distribution deals begin resulting in more films that generate net profits (see "floor," "gross participants" and "gross receipts").

grossing potential — A theater's historical ability, with films comparable to the film whose exhibition at that theater is being considered, to generate box office receipts and, consequently, film rentals; also the prospective box office gross for a given film (see "box office comparables" and "financial projections").

gross or gross income — In general terms, the total amount of income generated by a property before deduction of any expenses (see "box office gross," "distributor's film rentals" and "gross receipts").

gross participants — Persons or entities who are able to negotiate a percentage interest in a motion picture distributor's gross receipts. Generally, only a very few high-powered actors, directors and producers have the kind of leverage that will permit such participations. Without a gross floor being negotiated by a net profit participant, a single gross participant may eliminate the possibility of a movie's revenue stream ever generating net profits for anyone. It would be better for the producer to stand up for the interests of all net profit participants at the time of negotiating for high priced star talent and refuse to grant gross points. For example, it would be difficult to believe that every net profit participant on the all-time box office champ for Warner Bros. *Batman* would not resent the fact that Jack Nicholson's agent, in addition to getting him a reported up front fee advance of

$6 million, was successful in negotiating one of the richest deals in Hollywood history: 15 percent of the gross with an escalator clause that boosted Nicholson's take to as high as 20 percent the more money the film took in. Thus, Nicholson's earnings alone accounted for more than $50 million of *Batman's* production costs according to industry sources and along with the distributor's fees and expense reimbursement provisions pretty well eliminated all possibilities that net profit participants on that film will ever see another dime. In another example, when Richard Dreyfuss and his agent reportedly asked for gross points in the film *Close Encounters of the Third Kind* producer Julia Phillips reportedly refused to cave in and thus gave all net profit participants on that film a better shot at realizing additional compensation (see "average negative cost," "gross participations" and "split rights deals").

gross participants — Persons or entities who have negotiated or are awarded a percentage participation in a movie's gross receipts or other defined level of a movie's revenue stream at some stage of gross and prior to net receipts or net profits. Without a gross floor being negotiated by a net profit participant, a single gross participant may eliminate the possibility of a movie's revenue stream ever generating net receipts or net profits (see "gross floor").

gross participations — Percentage interests in the distributor's gross receipts earned through the exploitation of a motion picture (see "gross participants," "gross receipts," "minimum guarantee" and "net profit participation").

gross points — (see "gross participations").

gross positions— (see "gross participants").

gross proceeds at first breakeven — (see "gross proceeds after breakeven").

gross partnership revenues — (see "partnership gross revenues").

gross per screen — A commonly used standard of motion picture performance that measures, for comparison purposes, the amount of box office gross generated by a given movie over the course of a specific period of time. Unless specifically stated, the time period is one week (see "box office gross").

gross points — Percentage participations in film rentals as opposed to net profits (see "points").

gross proceeds — (see "gross receipts" and "gross rentals").

gross proceeds after breakeven — A defined stage in a motion picture's revenue stream (in this case the distributor's gross receipts) that may trigger a bonus or escalation as soon as the gross receipts reach a specified form of breakeven (see "actual breakeven," "bonus," "breakeven," "cash breakeven," "escalation," "first breakeven," "gross receipts" and "second breakeven").

gross proceeds of the offering — The aggregate total of the original invested capital of the investors (i.e., the total amount of money to be raised in a direct participation program offering). Such offerings are typically structured as limited partnership or manager-managed LLC offerings. However, the term could also apply to an offering of corporate shares. For a film offering, the gross proceeds would equal the film's budget including above-the-line, production period, post-production and other expenses, plus the offering costs. Film offerings may also include such non-budget items such as "marketing to distributors," "LLC maintenance" and "profit participation auditor" (also called "offering proceeds" or "proceeds of the offering").

gross profit — Generally, net sales less the cost of goods sold. This is not a term commonly used in the film business (see "gross receipts" and "net profits").

gross profit participant — One who has a right to participate on a percentage basis in the gross receipts of the distributor as generated by a movie. Gross participations are not likely to be based on actual gross receipts, but some form of adjusted gross (see "adjusted gross," "first dollar" and "gross points").

gross receipts — A contractually defined term in motion picture distribution agreements, generally referring to all monies actually received by the distributor (or its subsidiaries or affiliates) from the exploitation of any rights granted pursuant to the distribution agreement, from all sources, stated in U. S. dollars, and not subject to forfeiture or return, including non-returnable advances and guarantees. The major areas from which gross receipts are derived include home video/DVD, theatrical revenue or "film rental," non-theatrical, pay television, network television, television syndication and ancillary rights. Producers must be careful to clarify whether and to what extent any advance and/or guarantee is to be included in gross receipts. The studio/distributors will generally take the position that advances should not be included in gross receipts until earned, in other words, the distributor will want to deduct an amount equal to any advance that has been paid to the producer from monies received by the distributor and will not want to consider such amounts as part of gross receipts for any calculations based on gross receipts (contrast

with "film rentals" and "gross rentals"; see "contractually defined term").

gross receipts tax — A government levy based on total sales (see "foreign tax credit").

gross rentals — The aggregate amount of the film distributor's share of monies paid at theater box offices computed on the basis of negotiated agreements between the distributor and the exhibitor. Note that gross receipts refers to amounts actually received and from all markets and media, whereas gross rentals refers to amounts earned from theatrical exhibition only, regardless of whether received by the distributor (also called "gross proceeds"; see "gross receipts").

gross revenues to the partnership — (see "partnership gross revenues").

gross revenues to the LLC — (see "LLC gross revenues").

gross to distributor basis — A manner of reporting film earnings that is the equivalent to distributor's gross receipts; film earnings are sometimes reported on this basis in the trades (see "box office gross" and "gross rentals").

guarantee — Agreement that a specific sum of money will be paid when conditions specified in the contract are met. In film, a guarantee is a sum of money which is payable regardless of a film's performance in the marketplace. It most typically appears as a dollar amount of minimum film rental that the exhibitor promises to pay the distributor regardless of the amount of film rental earned by the distributor under the film's lease agreement. Generally, a guarantee is paid prior to the film's exhibition (payable up front in installments or in a lump sum at a specific date).

Such sums are advance payments against the producer's or distributor's share of any profits but are not refundable (contrast with "guaranty" and "guaranty agreement"; see "advance" or "advances," "distributor guarantee," "pay or play," "personal guarantee," "pre-sale guarantee" and "release commitment").

guarantee clause — A provision in a contract, note or other agreement that creates an obligation of some kind, that commits the guarantor to perform the obligation, pay the debt, etc. in the event of a failure to do so by the original obligor (see "guaranty," "completion bond" and "surety").

guarantee deal — (see "distribution guarantee" and "guarantee").

guarantor reinsurance — Part of a guarantor's risk may be shared with an insurance company so as to spread the risk and allow the original guarantor to assume responsibility for a greater possible loss. A commensurate portion of the fee or premium is also shared with the reinsurer (see "completion guarantor," "cut-through endorsement" and "reinsurance").

guarantor's fee — The fee charged by the completion bond company for providing its over-budget protection. Such fees have historically ranged from 2.5 to 6 percent and sometimes have included a share in the film's profits. Due to a more competitive environment, some completion bond fees as low as 1.5 percent have been reported (see "completion guarantor").

guaranty — An agreement or promise to answer for the debt, default of miscarriage of another. One giving a guaranty agrees to perform the act promised to be done or properly done by another person if that person does not fulfill his, her or its obligation (see "completion bond" and "surety").

guaranty agreement — An undertaking by any person to pay the debt or perform the contract or duty of another, even when that person remains liable on the underlying obligation. The agreement sets forth the parties' rights and duties, in conditional or absolute form. For example, a film lab may require a guarantee from the principal owner or owners of its customer, particularly if such customer is a small independent film production company (see "guaranty" and "surety").

guild — Labor organization (i.e., an association of workers who do the same or similar kinds of work). The word guild is used in the names of most of the performing arts unions (e.g., Screen Actors Guild, Directors Guild of America, American Guild of Variety Artists and the American Guild of Musical Artists, but other guilds include the American Federation of Television and Radio Artists and the American Federation of Musicians). Trade unions are generally limited to skilled or semi-skilled workers who have learned crafts. These organizations bargain collectively on behalf of their members with single employers, business firms, or associations of employers. Then the guild will restrict the rights of its members to work for companies that have not signed the union's basic agreement. The unions set up working rules relating to work standards, wages, hours and credits and other matters, arrange for membership meetings and social functions, call strikes when deemed necessary, issue bulletins, and in some cases offer legal advice and apprenticeship/intern openings for those starting in the particular discipline of the union. The crafts people and artists working at the major studios are nearly all union members and thus their salaries are typically higher than those paid non-union crafts people. In independent, "off-the-major-studio-lot" film and tape productions the employees are often a mix of union and non-union. The unions are supported financially primarily through membership dues. The Producers Guild of America is a misnomer since producers are management by nature and thus producers should be organized as a professional association (see "professional association" and "trade association").

guild agreements — The film union contracts between film producers and unions representing different segments of motion picture labor that set out working rules relating to work standards, wages, hours and credits and other matters for the members of such guilds (see "guild").

guild requirements — Film union rules relating to work standards, wages, hours, credits, etc. that producers must comply with in order for the members of specific guilds to properly be employed on such producer's film (see "guild").

guild/union flight accident insurance — A type of insurance that provides motion picture/television guild or union contract requirements for aircraft accidental death insurance to all production company cast or crew members (see "insurance").

hard floor — A percentage that is not subject to further reduction (e.g., a minimum percentage gross participation of 20 percent). As a variation of the concept, a hard floor might be negotiated for net profit participations while a soft floor is used for gross participations (see "floor" and "soft floor").

hard to audit expenses — Costs that are difficult to verify. Many of the film distributor distribution expenses deducted from the distributor's gross receipts in order to arrive at net profits are difficult to verify or judge as to reasonableness. For this reason alone, it might better serve the overall film community for the entire system relating to the deduction of distribution expenses to be abandoned in favor of negotiated across-the-board gross participations for all participants (see "direct distribution expenses").

HDTV — The acronym for high definition television, the newest standard in television and video. It offers higher resolution, better color, and better audio. There are both analog and digital versions of HDTV; a television transmission standard that is replacing the systems previously in use. HDTV provides improved video images, a new format for producing films and potentially a new market for films. HDTV proponents claim that it offers images equal in quality to 35mm film. The U.S. TV system (NTSC) presently uses 525 lines of resolution. HDTV uses no less than 1,000 lines. The Japanese have adopted a 1125 line standard or format (see "high definition television" and "video format").

headline — A catchy phrase or word, usually set in boldface and larger type and placed above the body copy of an ad or article. Headlines are designed to grab the attention of the reader (see "advertising," "body copy" and "sub-head").

hedge funds — An investment partnership or mutual fund that uses selling short to hedge long positions in stocks. If stock selection is correct, the stocks sold short decline more in a falling market than the stock owned, and the stocks owned appreciate more in a rising market than the stocks sold short. The objective is to generate trading and investment profits no matter what the direction of the general market. A perfect hedge is one that eliminates the possibility of future gain or loss. Many of the film industry investment funds referred to as "hedge funds" are not hedge funds at all (see "mutual fund").

heirs — Technically, those to whom statutory law appoints to inherit an estate should the ancestor die without a will. However, as commonly used, the term often includes those who inherit by will or deed as well as by operation of law (see "assigns," "personal representative" and "successor").

hertz — A unit of frequency equal to one cycle per second; abbreviated Hz (see "sound").

hiatus — A break in an activity or a lapse in continuity (see "gross participants").

hidden agenda — Plans of things to be done or intentions that are not apparent or divulged. Filmmakers make movies for many reasons. Making money, becoming famous, earning the respect of professional peers, providing entertainment and communicating important ideas would seem to be high on anyone's list of the typical reasons why movies are made, although the order of importance certainly may differ amongst individuals. The feature film, as a communications medium, with its large screen, color technology, special effects, lighting techniques, exquisite photography, incredible sound, excellent talent on and off the screen, is also, without question, one of the most effective forms of communicating ideas that the world has yet devised. It would indeed be naive for anyone to assume that the communication of ideas is not an important motive for any serious filmmaker or filmmaking concern. A feature film also affords a unique opportunity for those who control or dominate the process of decision-making as to which movies or ideas are included in motion pictures, to insert such ideas or select and actively promote the movies that best express the views, interests, cultural perspectives and prejudices held by those decision-makers (see "bias," "favorable portrayal," "government subsidies," "marketplace of ideas," "patterns of bias" and "unfavorable portrayal").

hidden contingency — A budgeting technique that incorporates an extra 10 percent into each and every budget category of a film budget (see "budget overruns," "completion guarantor" and "contingency").

high concept — A film idea, concept or plot that can be described in a very few words (see "hook" and "hype-worthy").

high definition television — (see "HDTV").

highest leverage position — Circumstances that provide an individual or entity with the maximum amount of bargaining power or strength. People who have something you want have power over you. For example (all other elements being equal), a producer who approaches a distributor with a quality motion picture in the can along with prints and ads money is likely to be able to negotiate more favorable terms for the distribution deal than a producer who approaches a distributor seeking production and distribution funds for a movie yet to be produced. The producer in the first situation above also eliminates most of the opportunities for the distributor's so-called "creative accounting" (see "creative accounting," "decision-making continuum," "funds for releasing costs" and "rent-a-distributor").

high net-worth individuals — Persons whose assets significantly exceed their liabilities. Banks are usually quite willing to make loans to such individuals (see "accredited investor," "lender financing" and "net worth").

hit — A subjective term for which no precise definition is available but which is applied to motion pictures that are well received by the general public and do well at the box office. A "hit" film may be popular with the public, but not necessarily a financial success for all persons or entities who participated in the production or distribution of the film. Also, in the view of some industry analysts poor financial management is a more significant contributing factor to the many film production company failures than the lack of so-called "hit" motion pictures (see "blockbuster," "bomb," "creative accounting," "domestic number one hit," "financial management," "gross receipts," "net profits" and "successful film").

hobby — An activity not engaged in for profit (see "hobby losses," "for profit" and "non-profit").

hobby losses — A loss incurred by a taxpayer in an activity not engaged in for profit. In general, hobby losses are deductible only against income generated by the hobby (see "for profit," "non-profit" and "tax deduction").

holdback periods — A time frame within which a film cannot be released in a given media or market. If the distributor is given a broad grant of rights in the distribution agreement, the distributor will want to make its own internal decisions regarding appropriate sequential distribution in various media in a given territory. The producer, on the other hand, may want to seek a holdback schedule in order to ensure that the picture has an opportunity for maximum revenues in each territory or medium of exploitation. If the producer has reserved certain rights, the distributor may seek holdback provisions. Typical holdback periods might include: video/DVD rights: nine to twelve months after initial theatrical release; cable and pay tv: three months after start of video/DVD

distribution; free television: two years after initial theatrical release (see "release sequence").

hold harmless — Protect from loss or liability; indemnify; guaranty. In contract law, the phrase is used to signify a commitment by one party to make good or repay another party to an agreement in the event of a specified loss (see "indemnify").

holding company — A corporation that owns enough voting stock in another corporation to influence its board of directors and therefore to control its policies and management. A holding company need not own a majority of the shares of its subsidiaries or be engaged in similar activities. Typically a holding company is not an operating company (see "affiliate," "parent corporation" and "subsidiary corporation").

holdover — An exhibitor's keeping of a film for exhibition beyond the minimum period of exhibition time stipulated in the license agreement. A holdover may occur either by reason of the exhibitor's voluntary action with the distributor's consent or by operation of the license agreement's holdover clause (same as "carryover").

holdover clause — A clause within a feature film license agreement that requires the exhibitor to continue exhibiting a film beyond the film's minimum period of exhibition time, such requirement being triggered by the film achieving its holdover figure. A holdover clause may provide that the exhibiting theater's clearance is reduced during the holdover (same as "carryover clause"; see "clearance," "holdover figure" and "exclusive engagement").

holdover figure — The negotiated weekly minimum dollar amount of money taken in at a theater's box office that a film must reach in order to be held over for the next week (i.e., a dollar amount of a theater's gross box office receipts that, if equaled or exceeded from the film's exhibition during a specific period of time, requires or permits the exhibitor to continue to exhibit that film for an additional week). This figure is mutually agreed on by the exhibitor and distributor when the terms under which the film will be played are originally established and set out in the distributor/exhibitor agreement. The holdover figure is an objective standard and provides a means for either the distributor or exhibitor to insist that the picture continue if the figure was achieved or, if not, cease to be shown in that specific theater (same as "carryover figure"; see "control figure").

Hollywood — Hollywood is a district in Los Angeles, situated west-northwest of downtown L.A. off the 101 Freeway. It is considered to be the historical center of the U.S. film industry and the word is often used to refer to the industry as a whole. Of the remaining so-called major studio/distributors, Paramount is still in Hollywood on Melrose. Sony Entertainment, including Columbia and TriStar, is in Culver City. Warner Bros. and Disney are in Burbank. Universal is in Universal City near Studio City. Twentieth Century Fox is in Century City. Many of the ancillary industries (such as editing, effects, props, post-production, and lighting companies) remain in Hollywood, along with many sites of interest to tourists. The central repository for most books about the film industry (the Samuel French Bookshop) also remains in Hollywood on Sunset Boulevard.

Hollywood accounting — (see "creative accounting").

Hollywood apologist— Someone who speaks or writes in defense of the Hollywood-based major studio/distributors whenever the business practices of such studios come under criticism. Someone who defends the Hollywood-based U.S. film industry, which has been dominated for approximately one hundred years by a small group of so-called major studio/distributors (see "anti-competitive business practices," "anti-Semitic sword" and "business practices").

Hollywood control group — A relatively small group of people who mostly share the same religious/cultural background and have utilized hundreds of unfair, unethical, unconscionable, anti-competitive, predatory and illegal business practices to gain and maintain control of the most powerful positions (including those occupied by major studio executives, top producers and directors, entertainment attorneys, some talent and agents) in the Hollywood-based U.S. film industry for approximately one hundred years (see "Hollywood insiders").

Hollywood insiders — The same as "Hollywood Control Group." A majority of the Hollywood insiders are mostly politically liberal (although some may share the views of the so-called Neo-Cons with respect to international affairs), not very religious, Jewish males of European heritage. The group as defined is much too narrow to suggest or imply that "Jews control Hollywood" since such a statement would be misleading (i.e., the much broader, more diversified and more general so-called Jewish community does not control Hollywood). Nor does this accurate observation regarding the Hollywood control group suggest or imply that these men engage in the business practices described here because they are Jewish. Instead, this definition assumes that they behave just as anyone else would under the same or similar circumstances (i.e, they engage in the cited business practices because such practices tend to permit this small group of individuals to retain control or power over an important communications industry that generates huge amounts of money and very likely influences the beliefs and behavior of millions of moviegoers worldwide; see "culture promotion," "Hollywood outsiders" and "propaganda").

Hollywood outsiders — People who have come to Hollywood over the years and worked in the film industry at some level but do not share the same religious/cultural background of the Hollywood insiders. Some of the more well known Hollywood outsiders include D.W. Griffith, Joseph P. Kennedy, William Randolph Hearst, Orson Welles, Howard Hughes, Robert Altman, Kirk Kerkorian, Dino De Laurentiis, David Puttnam, Ted Turner, Rupert Murdoch and Mel Gibson. Corporations that qualify as Hollywood outsiders include CBS, Coca Cola, TransAmerica, Westinghouse, Sony and Matsushita (see *Hollywood Wars — How Insiders Gained and Maintain Illegitimate Control Over the Film Industry*).

Hollywood Reporter — (see *"The Hollywood Reporter"*).

home run — Slang for a large gain by an investor in a short period of time. As applied to film finance, the phrase refers to a film project that performs really well in the marketplace (i.e., is a huge financial success). Investors in independent films may be partly motivated by the possibility that a film may hit a financial home run (see "upside potential").

home video — The presentation of a film in private homes on a television screen by means of rented or purchased video cassettes or DVDs

(see "DVD," "video" and "video/DVD revenue reporting").

home video rights — The rights associated with the exploitation of a film in the home video market (see "DVD," "home video royalty" and "video/DVD revenue reporting").

home video royalty — A share of the proceeds from the sale or rental of motion picture videocassettes or DVDs paid by the video wholesaler to the distributor. In contrast to feature film sub-distribution in other media, film distributors handling the distribution of motion pictures on videocassettes or DVDs accept mere royalties from the wholesalers instead of the balance of the wholesale proceeds minus a modest sub-distribution fee. Royalty payments are traditionally much smaller than other forms of percentage participations. Before this rapidly diminishing revenue stream generated by home video reaches the producer, the distributor will also typically deduct its negotiated distribution fee. This system was designed by the major studio/distributors who, in many instances, own significant and/or controlling interests in the video/DVD wholesalers, thus these major studio/distributors get to participate twice in the video/DVD revenue stream and are able to minimize the dollars that ultimately flow past the distributors to the producer and other net profit participants (also called "royalty on home video"; see "conflicts of interest," "fiduciary," "twenty percent rule," "unethical business practices" and "video/DVD revenue reporting").

homogenous films — Motion pictures that are the same or similar. During the early years of the motion picture industry, the major studio/distributors produced a large volume of films that were very similar (i.e., they were designed to and did appeal to the same mass audience, thus exhibitors had little need to pre-screen each motion picture offered). With today's more fractionalized audiences and film's of widely varying quality that appeal to separate but more narrow audiences there is a greater need for exhibitors to pre-screen the product they are asked to exhibit (see "anti-blind bidding statutes," "audience fractionalization," "blind bidding," "heterogenous product" and "mass audience").

hook — Something unique that will set a film project apart, that can be expressed succinctly and that will tend to attract the attention or gain the interest of a target audience. In a motion picture context, a "hook" may be utilized by a writer, producer or director pitching a project in search of production financing, a "hook" may be emphasized by a producer who seeks a distributor and the distributor's marketing department will utilize a "hook" to help make the film stand out from the other movies competing for attention, to get prospective moviegoers into the theater and to stimulate favorable word-of-mouth. In these situations, the "hook" for a movie may be a unique storyline, someone's first film, an ultra-low-budget production, great special effects, a major star, etc. (see "advertising," "marketing department," "pitch" and "primary audience").

horizontal integration — A consolidation of business entities at the same level within an industry (e.g., the motion picture business basically has three levels, production, distribution and exhibition). Thus, if two production companies merge, that is an example of horizontal integration. On the other hand, if a production company and a distribution entity merge that is an example of vertical integration (see "merger guidelines," "Paramount Consent Decree of 1948," "TriStar Case" and "vertical integration").

horizontal merger — The combination of two or more companies at the same level within an industry. Mergers typically occur in three ways (1) through a pooling of interests, where the accounts of the respective companies are combined; (2) through a purchase, where the amount paid over and above the acquired company's book value is carried on the books of the purchaser as goodwill; or (3) through a consolidation where a new company is formed to acquire the net assets of the combining companies (see "goodwill," "horizontal integration," "merger guidelines" and "vertical integration").

horizontal price fixing — Price fixing engaged in by those in competition with each other at the same level in an industry. For example, if exhibitors conspired to fix prices at a certain level that would be an example of horizontal price fixing. On the other hand, if an exhibitor and a distributor conspired to fix prices, that would be an example of vertical price fixing (see "antitrust laws," "price fixing" and "vertical price fixing").

hot issue — A public offering of securities where the securities, after their initial sale to the public, are resold in the open market at prices substantially higher than the original public offering price. The NASD defines a hot issue as a securities issue in which the aftermarket price is 10 percent or higher than the original price. The SEC definition, on the other hand, requires that the market be looked at thirty to sixty days later and that factors leading to the rise in price be examined (see "corporate stock," "public offering" and "publicly held").

house — A motion picture theater (see "house manager" and "house nut").

house allowance— A specified dollar amount, agreed to as between a film's distributor and exhibitor, and deducted from a film's gross box office receipts, before the distributor's film rentals for the film are calculated (same as "contractual theater overhead").

house expense — (see "house nut").

housekeeping deal — A motion picture development deal between a production company and a major studio/distributor in which the studio agrees to pay the overhead expenses of the production company in exchange for the first opportunity to acquire the right to produce and distribute any film projects developed by the production company (see "first look deal," "independent producer" and "overall deal").

house manager — The person in charge of a movie theater ("house") who manages the operation of the theater, runs the theater's logistics and supervises ticket sales. Sometimes the house manager also owns or is a co-owner of the theater (see "house nut").

house nut — A negotiated dollar amount as between a film's distributor and its exhibitor that represents the estimated expenses during the course of a week for the film exhibitor (i.e., the amount it supposedly costs an exhibitor to operate a theater for a week). In a typical exhibitor/distributor agreement the distributor would split the balance of the box-office gross (in accordance with the agreed upon percentages between them) after the house nut has been deducted by the exhibitor (i.e., the exhibitor deducts the amount of the "house

nut" before the distributor/exhibitor split of the balance). This negotiated figure may range from $5,000 a week to $35,000 a week depending on the theater (same as "contractual theater overhead," "weekly house allowance" and "weekly house expense"; see "box office gross," "concession sales," "controlled theater" and "distributor's film rentals").

house overhead allowance — (same as "house allowance").

hybrid security — A security that combines features of debt and equity (e.g., of both bonds and stocks; see "bond" and "stock").

hype — Publicity and advertising, including personal and television talk-show appearances and Web sites, along with newspaper and magazine articles, designed to promote and publicize a film. Film producers often hire publicists to create hype within the film industry in an effort to add value to a film in production prior to negotiating a distribution deal (see "buzz," "publicist" and "publicity").

hype-worthy — A film concept or project that can be effectively advertised and publicized (see "high concept").

hyphenate — A single individual who performs the work and obtains the screen credit for two positions in the production of a film (e.g., producer-director or writer-director; see "actor," "director," "producer" and "screenwriter").

hypothecation — In banking, the pledging of property to secure a loan. Hypothecation does not transfer title, but does transfer the right to sell the hypothecated property in the event of default. In the securities field, hypothecation is the pledging of securities to brokers as collateral for loans made to purchase securities or to cover short sales (see "collateral," "lender financing," "pledge" and "secured debt").

hypothetical assumptions — Facts or statements taken for granted and upon which financial projections may be based (i.e., assumptions are used in the preparation of financial projections to present a condition or course of action that is not necessarily expected to occur, but is consistent with the purpose of the projections). In order for the financial projections to be credible, the assumptions upon which they are based must be reasonable relative to what generally occurs in the marketplace (see "financial projections" and "key factors").

Hz — The abbreviation for hertz (see "hertz").

IATSE — (see "International Alliance of Theatrical and Stage Employees").

idea — A formulated thought or opinion; a mental image or formulation of something seen or known or imagined; a pure abstraction, or something assumed or vaguely sensed. In theory and in filmmaking, the idea is more narrow in scope than a concept, thus the concept is considered the initial step in creating a movie. Many persons both in and out of the film business recognize that ideas are the film industry's most important article of commerce and that the motion picture is one of the most powerful methods for communicating ideas that human beings have yet devised. Since ideas have always and will always be powerful motivators of human conduct it is hardly credible for anyone to claim that movies are merely entertainment (see "concept," "culture promotion," "marketplace of ideas," "patterns of bias," "propaganda" and "theme").

ideas originating with producer — Language in a development deal between a studio/distributor and an independent production company that provides a mechanism for dividing film projects (at their earliest stages) between the entities at the end of the present contractual relationship (i.e., those ideas or motion picture concepts that

originated with the production company as opposed to the studio/distributor can be retained by the production company to the exclusion of the studio/distributor; see "development deal," "first look deal," "housekeeping deal," "overall deal" and "term deal").

IFIDA — (see "International Film Importers and Distributors of America" and "industry groups").

IFP/West — Formerly the West coast chapter of the Independent Feature Project, a film industry organization that changed its name to Film Independent or FIND (see "FIND" and "independent feature project").

illegal — Behavior that is against the law (i.e, that can result in the imposition of either criminal or civil sanctions). Criminal sanctions include prison sentences and fines. Civil sanctions include damages, liability and injunctions (see "remedy").

illegal combination — Two or more persons or entities who join together to commit an illegal act (e.g., the joining together of two competing companies in an industry to alter the competitive balance in their favor is an illegal combination in restraint of trade; see "combination in restraint of trade").

illegal trade practice — A custom in a business that is against the law (e.g., the fixing as between competitors of film licensing terms, runs, clearances and minimum admission prices or the use of unconscionable provisions in film industry contracts; see "adhesion contracts," "antitrust laws," "Buchwald Case," "price fixing," "reciprocal preferences" and "splitting arrangements" and "unconscionable").

illegal use of motion picture— A broad concept referring to any unauthorized exhibition of a film by exhibitors or individuals, including piracy (see "copyright" and "piracy").

illiquid — A reference to a firm that lacks sufficient cash flow to meet current and maturing obligations. With respect to investments, illiquid means not readily convertible into cash (i.e., assets for which there is no ready market and which therefore may take some time to sell; see "cash" and "liquid asset").

illusory promise — A promise so indefinite that it cannot be enforced or which, by virtue of provisions or conditions contained in the promise itself, is one whose fulfillment is optional or entirely discretionary on the part of the promisor. Since such a promise does not constitute a legally binding obligation, it is not sufficient as consideration for a reciprocal promise and thus cannot create a valid contract (see "adhesion contract," "contract" and "unconscionable provision").

implied representation — A statement that is not explicitly written or made but which can be reasonably determined by deduction or inference from known facts and circumstances

(see "express representation" and "representation").

immediate window — The opportunity to exhibit a film in one medium shortly after it is exhibited in another medium (e.g., on basic cable following the network airing; see "release sequence" and "window").

import permits — Written authorizations provided by sovereign governments allowing an individual or entity to bring in a product from a foreign or external source. Motion picture distributors generally must obtain import permits in order to bring a film into a given country for exhibition in that country (see "foreign distribution").

impound — A condition required in certain securities offerings in which the investor funds received are placed in an escrow account (i.e., impounded, and not released to the issuer of the securities until the amount needed has been raised). If the minimum amount is not received, all impounded funds are returned to the subscribers (see "escrow").

improperly claimed expenses — A distributor accounting practice in which the distributor wrongfully or unfairly allocates certain of its incidental expenses or general costs to a specific film, exaggerates its distribution expenses or charges duplicate costs to two separate films or completely fabricates distribution expenses that are allocated to a film, all for the purpose of preventing the involved film or films from going into net profits or reducing the films' net profits, so as to, in turn, reduce the net profit participations to be paid to others by the distributor (see "creative accounting," "overreported travel," "studio accounting practices" and "unethical business practices").

incentive payments — Compensation awarded to persons or entities for helping to produce above-average or better than expected results (see "contingent compensation").

incestuous share dealing — The buying and selling of the corporate stock of one company by another company and vice versa for the purpose of creating tax or other financial advantages (see "reciprocal preferences").

income — An economic benefit; money or value received (see "net income").

income forecast method — An accounting procedure, more specifically a method of depreciation (i.e, the recovery of cost through tax deductions), more commonly used for films prior to the enactment of Section 181 of the IRS Code that helps to ensure acceleration of deductions against film revenues. It is computed by multiplying the capitalized cost of the film by a fraction with a numerator equal to the net receipts (gross receipts less current deductible costs and distribution fees) from the film for the taxable year in question and a denominator equal to the total estimated net receipts from the film. Such estimates must be reasonable or they may be challenged by the IRS (see "accelerated cost recovery," "net receipts," "Section 181 of the IRS Code," "straight-line depreciation" and "tax benefits").

income statement — A financial statement for a business entity that gives operating results for a specific period; also referred to as an earnings report, operating statement and profit-and-loss statement. Such statements normally cover twelve months of operations with interim statements at quarterly periods in current fiscal or calendar years (see "profit and loss statement").

income tax — An annual tax imposed upon income received, reduced by the allowable deductions and credits (see "foreign tax credits" and "Internal Revenue Service").

income tax effects — The results of a transaction with regard to federal income taxes (see "income tax").

incorporate — To form a corporation; to organize and be granted status as a corporation by following procedures prescribed by law. Incorporating is controlled by state law in the state of incorporation and typically involves the drafting and filing of articles of incorporation with the state's secretary of state, purchase of a corporate kit in which to maintain the corporation's records, preparation of the initial minutes in support of the first shareholder's meeting and the first meeting of the board of directors, the drafting and acceptance of corporate bylaws, the physical issuance of corporate shares and the noting of such issuance in the stock transfer ledger (see "corporation").

indemnification — An agreement between two parties whereby one agrees to pay the other if the other incurs certain expenses. In a securities offering, a form of intended reimbursement to an underwriter by an issuer for payment by the underwriter to a customer/investor who successfully litigates issues relating to the purchased securities sold by such underwriter. Also, the process of protecting or compensating someone or an entity against hurt, loss or damage and/or compensating them for any incurred hurt, loss or damage (i.e., an exemption from incurred penalties or liabilities; see "insurance" and "liability").

indemnification provision — Language in a contract providing that one party will pay the other if the other incurs certain expenses (see "indemnification").

indemnify — To secure against loss or damage that may occur in the future, or to provide compensation for or to repair loss or damage already suffered; also to insure or to save harmless (see "hold harmless").

indemnity — The obligation or duty resting on one person to make good any loss or damage another has incurred or may incur by acting at his, her or its request or for his, her or its benefit. Typically a film distribution agreement will require that the producer or production company provide such an indemnity to protect the distributor (i.e., agree to indemnify the distributor for any breach of the producer's warranties and representations). On the other hand, there is usually no reciprocal indemnification provision in favor of the producer nor are there extensive distributor warranties typically found in such agreements making the indemnity provisions of such contracts one-sided (see "adhesion contract," "unconscionable," "warranty" or "warranties" and "representations").

indenture — A written agreement that sets out the terms under which bonds or debentures may be issued. Terms include the amount of the issue, the interest rate, the maturity, the property pledged as collateral, if any, and certain covenants including any provision for a sinking fund. An independent trustee, usually a bank or trust company, is named to oversee the issue of the bonds, to collect and pay interest and principal and to protect the bondholder's rights as specified in the indenture (see "bond," "debenture" and "sinking fund").

independent audit rights — The authority to conduct an examination of the books and records separate from an authorized entity (e.g., in a film distribution agreement, the distributor may undertake the responsibility for paying directly to third party participants any portion of the production company's share of gross or net proceeds as assigned by the production company, provided that no such third party has an audit right other than that granted to the production company; see "audit," "audit rights" and "broad audit rights").

independent checking company — A business that can be hired by a producer or distributor to verify the number of paid ticket purchasing moviegoers in attendance at showings of a given movie and which is not the checking service normally used by the major studio/distributors (see "attendance checking," "checker," "checking and collection costs," "puffed numbers" and "skimming").

independent contractor — One who makes an agreement with another to do a piece of work while retaining control of the means, method and manner of producing the result (see "employee" and "freelance employee").

independent contractor agreement — The written contract between a feature film producer and a person providing services in the production of a motion picture when such services are being rendered on an independent contract basis as opposed to on an employee basis pursuant to an employment agreement (see "independent contractor").

independent distributor — A motion picture distributor not affiliated with one of the major studio/distributors (see "American Film

Marketing Association," "independent producer" and "major studio/distributors").

independent feature film — Ostensibly, any motion picture not produced by a major studio/distributor. Unfortunately, not all sectors of the film industry agree as to the definition of an independent film. The Independent Film & Television Alliance claims that a film is independent if more than fifty percent of its financing comes from sources other than the major studio/distributors. This definition lacks clarity in the sense that it does not indicate whether the financing is for development, production or distribution or all three phases in the life of a film. In any case, the IFTA definition does focus on how the film is financed. The IFTA goes onto indicate that independent productions cover all budget ranges and genres and are aimed at wide, as well as niche, audiences. Another industry association, not so directly tied to film finance and production, chooses to use a less objective and even more difficult to apply definition of independent film. The Film Independent group (FIND — formerly IFP/West or IFP/LA) takes the position that an independent film is one that exhibits uniqueness of vision, contains original, provocative subject matter, was produced using an economy of means (with particular attention paid to total production cost and individual compensation) and then requires only that some unstated percentage of financing come from independent sources. That means that at the discretion of FIND, films financed by the major studios or their subsidiaries can compete for FIND awards, which may be precisely the purpose of such a vague definition. It allows FIND to include more well known stars in their annual awards ceremony, thus making the organization appear more glamorous and meaningful. In the process, however, FIND is literally inviting the major studio/distributors to gobble up even more of the attention and marketplace desperately needed by independent filmmakers, thus, as an organization, FIND can hardly be said to effectively represent the interests of independent filmmakers. Both of these definitions seem to be succumbing to the power of the Hollywood major studio/distributors. After all, if a film is 50 percent financed by a major studio/distributor or affiliate it is most likely going to be released, at least in the domestic marketplace, as a major studio/distributor or affiliate release, thus for all practical purposes it is not an independent film, in the ordinary sense of the words. When major studios put up half of the production financing for a film, they tend to have a say in how the film is made. To be more precise in determining whether a film is an independent film, it may be relevant to determine which of the three phases in the life of a film have been financed without the aid of any of the so-called major studio/distributors. In other words, if an independent producer has been responsible for raising the funds to develop, produce and distribute a motion picture, that is clearly an independent film. If, on the other hand, an independent producer has financed the development phase, but has used the assistance of a major studio/distributor and/or one of its subsidiaries in financing the production phase, in addition to the distribution of the film, it would not be accurate to call that an independent film (even though it was developed independently). Still further, if an independent producer raised the financing for the development and production phase, then merely looked to a major studio/distributor or affiliate/subsidiary to release the picture (i.e., the distributor was only responsible for the costs of distribution and acquired the rights to distribute the film as a pure acquisition), that may be considered an independently produced film, that was merely released by a major studio/distributor or affiliate/subsidiary (see "independent producer" and "major studio/distributors").

independent feature project (IFP) — A non-profit membership organization dedicated to promoting quality American independent feature filmmaking and supporting the efforts of individual filmmakers (artists and technicians) through educational programs, publications, services and awards. IFP chapters exist in New York, Chicago, Minnesota, Seattle and Phoenix. IFP/West or IFP Los Angeles was formerly affiliated with IFP, but severed those ties when it changed its name to FIND. IFP Members include producers, directors, writers, crafts people, distributors and movie industry executives. The IFP has rarely functioned as an advocacy group and even if it attempted to do so, it would probably have difficulty obtaining a consensus relating to a single important advocacy issue from its diverse membership and corporate sponsors. In other words, one of the weaknesses of the organization is that it seeks to serve too many segments of the film industry, thus, in all fairness, it does not serve any of those interests adequately, certainly not the interests of independent producers (see "conflicts of interest," "FIND," "IFP/West" and "Producers Guild of America").

independent film — (see "independent feature film" and "independent production").

Independent Film and Television Alliance (IFTA) — A non-profit trade association with one hundred and fifty plus company members. The IFTA is concerned with production and distribution of independent English language titles internationally. The IFTA's predecessor organization, the AFMA or "the Alliance" was established in 1980 as the American Film Marketing Association ("AFMA"). Its first members were a group of distributors and sales agents whose main goal was to expand the independent film business by creating a world-class trade show, the American Film Market (AFM). Today, the association has evolved into the trade association for the independent film and television industry worldwide, while the AFM concurrently has become the largest international film market in the world. The association adopted its new name in 2004, in recognition of its global membership and its mission to promote the independent industry throughout the world. IFTA's membership includes companies from twenty-two countries, spanning production, distribution and financing of independent film and television programming. Collectively, its members produce more than four hundred independent films and countless hours of television programming each year and generate more than $4 billion in distribution revenues annually. Since 1980, more than fifty percent of the Academy Award™ "Best Picture" winners have been films produced or licensed globally by IFTA member companies. IFTA serves as the voice and advocate for the independent film and television industry worldwide. The organization is committed to building and protecting its members' ability to finance, produce, distribute and market independent films and television programs around the world. Together with the Independent Film & Television Export Alliance (the Export Alliance), the Alliance speaks out on matters of critical importance, including the elimination of trade barriers, the impact of new technology on traditional business models and the need to foster broad-based growth of the industry around the world. Where appropriate, IFTA actively lobbies national and international government officials in regard to measures affecting the independent industry. The IFTA website is located online at http://www.ifta-online.org/.

independent filmmaker — A person who has an idea for a film and develops the idea into a concept and/or obtains the rights to an existing literary property, or other necessary underlying rights), raises or arranges for raising the funds with which to develop, package, and produce the film, maintains substantial creative control throughout the making of the film, and ultimately arranges for marketing and distribution (see "filmmaker" and "producer").

independently distributed film — A motion picture that is distributed by a company that does not rent, sell or license its films through a major motion picture distributor (see "independent distributor," "independent feature film," "market power" and "market share").

independent market share — The percentage of domestic theatrical box office gross garnered by the films distributed by independent distributors collectively as opposed to the percentage of box office gross of the films distributed by the major studio/distributors. The independent distributor market share only averaged about 7 percent of the box office gross prior to the round of acquisitions and mergers of the top independent distributors by the major studio/distributors in the '90s. Those actions narrowed the market share of independent films even further to about 4 percent of domestic box office gross (see "market share").

independent producer — In the narrowest sense, individual producers or film production companies that do not work for the major studio/distributors (i.e., are not studio employees). Some make the further distinction

that independent producers or production companies generally do not own their own production studios and are not likely to be a continual source of motion pictures for exhibitors. However, many producers who qualify as independent producers using these criteria have contractual relationships with the studios that provide for at least some partial studio financing of these independent producers' feature film projects and provide substantial authority for the studio to approve certain significant elements of the film. Since 1971, independent producers have produced more than half of the films made in the United States. Unfortunately, of the thousands of feature films that are produced each year in the U.S. only something in the neighborhood of six hundred get any kind of theatrical release, about half of those are self-distributed by the company that produced it and typically less than one hundred and fifty of the others are distributed by the major studio/distributors (the MPAA companies). While some of the MPAA company releases are produced by independent producers, the MPAA company releases (including subsidiaries) generate about 97 percent of the domestic theatrical box office gross each year. On the other hand, profit participation auditors who work in the field on a daily basis estimate that only 5 percent of the MPAA films released each year achieve net profits [see "acquisition," "financing," "housekeeping deal," "output deal," "overall deal," "producer," "production-financing/distribution agreement," "right of first refusal" and "spec (speculation)"].

independent production — Technically, TV or film production not financed by a major studio/distributor. However, today studios often finance all of a so-called independent producer's overhead, research and development, production and distribution costs in exchange for owning the rights to distribute the film throughout the world in all media, and in that context, "independent" is used to indicate the producer is not on the studio's permanent payroll. Independent productions not financed by studios or other production companies that are not signatories to the various guild agreements may involve non-union cast and crew. Generally, films produced as independent productions are lower budgeted films than studio produced films (see "independent feature film").

independent production company — A company that specializes in producing feature films and that is not associated with a major studio/distributor except sometimes contractually for a limited term (see "major studio/distributors").

independent production partnerships — A reference to several joint venture feature film production entities, not directly associated with the major U.S. studio/distributors that have been created in years past with massive funding from foreign sources. The term could also apply to any feature film limited partnership or manager-managed LLC that is not closely affiliated with a major/studio distributor (see "foreign equity financing," "joint venture," "limited liability company" and "limited partnership").

independent specialty distributors — Small entrepreneurial film distributors who specialize in distributing the lower-budgeted so-called art films or "B" projects (see "art film," "art theater," "'B' movies'"" and "calendar house").

independents — (see "independent distributor," "independent producer" and "independent production company").

independent theater — A theater not owned or operated by a large theater chain (see "blind bidding" and "major exhibition chains").

indirect costs and expenses — Expenses incurred by a film distributor that are not defined in the distribution agreement as direct distribution expenses (see "direct distribution expenses," "overhead," "overhead costs" and "production overhead").

individual film forecast method — (see "income forecast method").

inducement agreement — A less formal written inducement agreement typically in letter form (see "inducement agreement").

inducement letter — A written agreement signed by an individual artist/performer, stating that such artist/performer has a binding agreement with his or her loan-out company and agrees to be bound by and perform all provisions of the loan-out (or lending) agreement executed as between the loan-out company and the motion picture production company that is hiring the artist through the use of a loan-out agreement (see "lending agreement," "loan-out arrangement" and "loan-out company").

industry analysts — Persons, usually specialists in financial matters or in the news media, who observe, collect data, study and report on trends in the entertainment field. Unfortunately for the independent sector of the film industry, most of such studies and reports relate to that segment of the film industry represented by the large publicly held corporations known as the major studio/distributors. In addition, the information that is developed is generally proprietary and the reports are quite expensive. Academics and industry associations do not tend to engage in extensive studies of the film industry partly because the industry is notorious for not cooperating with such efforts and much of the information that is reported in the trades is unreliable. Further, these same groups tend to shy away from the more difficult issues of discrimination, lack of diversity at the top, patterns of bias in motion picture content, ethical problems, anti-competitive activities and so forth (see "broker/dealer," "Paul Kagan Associates, Inc." and "trades").

industry assessments — The prorated dues, fees or other costs required of member companies to support the activities of industry trade groups such as the MPAA, MPEAA, IFTA, etc. Such costs, clearly indirect expenses, are typically included in the definition of distribution expenses in film distribution agreements. Thus, independent producers whose films are released by MPAA companies are being charged for support of an industry trade organization whose policies are consistently opposed to the interests of independent producers. One might think that independent producers would eventually catch on and form a narrowly focused association of independent film producers that could also be supported partly by a fair share of such industry assessments (see "direct distribution expenses," "distribution expenses," "dues and assessments" and "industry groups").

industry critic — An individual who provides analysis and information that is critical of the film industry or a segment of the industry. Film critics are somewhat rare because of the fear of retaliation (see "blacklisting," "critic," "discrimination" and "industry analysts").

industry groups — A broad term including all film or entertainment related organizations such as trade associations, professional associations,

unions and guilds. Industry groups include the MPAA, the MPEAA, the Academy of Arts and Sciences, AMPTP, AFI, IFTA, FIND, IFIDA, IFP, and the numerous guilds (see "American Society of Association Executives," "association projects," "lobbyists" and "professional association").

industry overview — A section of a securities offering disclosure document that is required to be included when the securities are being offered and sold to persons with little knowledge of the industry in which the business seeking financing functions. The overview relates to the industry generally and not to the specific project(s) being funded. Typically, a motion picture industry overview will include an explanation of the various stages of film production (development, pre-production, principal photography and distribution) and a description of the route the money, if any, will take in getting back to the investors, including the ranges of fees or percentages typically deducted along the way and by whom (see "disclosure document" and "investor financing").

industry profit margins — The average difference between gross sales and net profits for an industry as a whole or a significant portion of an industry (e.g., the major studio/distributors in the motion picture business). Industry analysts have reported that industry profit margins for the major studio/distributors have remained below 10 percent in recent decades. Of course, it is clearly foreseeable that the excessive executive salaries and extreme talent compensation packages paid by the major studio/distributors would tend to hold down their profits (see "profit margin" and "profitability").

industry trades — (see "trades").

inferior bargaining position — Economic and other circumstances that result in less leverage for one party when negotiating a transaction. With few exceptions, independent feature film producers in the current industry environment have little or no real negotiating power when it comes to determining the terms of the film distribution deal. First, the basic economic law of supply and demand is working against the independent producers (i.e., there are too many films being produced each year and not enough willing and capable film distributors available to distribute those films). Thus, even though the available distributors may be willing to negotiate on certain aspects of the distribution deal, as to any given issue, distributors pretty much have the power to say "take it or leave it, we'll move on to the next film." Of course, many independent producers foolishly believe that by producing a "great" film all of their problems associated with their inherent "inferior bargaining position" will go away. Unfortunately, by concentrating most if not all of their time, energy and skill on the creative side of the film business equation as opposed to the business side of the business, many independent producers end up winning the "film" but losing the "deal" (see "adhesion contract," "arm's length," "creative accounting," "exploitation," "law of supply and demand" and "leverage").

inflation — An increase in the volume of money and credit relative to available goods resulting in a substantial and continuing rise in the general level of prices (see "inflation indexed cap").

inflation indexed cap — A ceiling on payments that may move up or down with the rate of inflation (see "inflation").

in-flight version — A feature film edited so as to make it suitable for exhibition on airplanes, specifically with respect to the exhibitor's time and rating requirements (see "non-theatrical" and "other versions").

information requirements — Securities disclosure regulations relating to the type of information required to be furnished to prospective purchasers of securities under an exemption from registration such as Regulation D or a specific form of registration (e.g., Regulation A, Form S-1 or Form SB-1; see "disclosure document," "Regulation D" and "securities").

infringement of copyright — (see "copyright infringement," "fair use" and "plagiarism").

infringement suit — A federal court law suit brought against someone who is alleged to have used copyrighted material in an unauthorized manner (see "copyright," "fair use" and "plagiarism").

in-house — A motion picture developed and produced by and within the organization of a producer/distributor as opposed to a film produced by an independent producer and acquired by the distributor for distribution (see "acquisitions," "distribution alternatives," "negative pickup," "production-financing/distribution agreement" and "rent-a-distributor").

initial actual breakeven — Another contractually defined breakeven point in the revenue stream of a motion picture, that commonly means that point at which net proceeds are reached (see "actual breakeven," "artificial breakeven," "breakeven," "cash breakeven," "net proceeds" and "rolling breakeven").

initial incorporation — One of the so-called active investor investment vehicles in the sense that a small group of people may form a new corporation without having to conduct a full-fledged securities offering. The founding shareholders are considered active in the sense that they choose who will serve on the corporation's board of directors (see "investment vehicle").

initial distribution — The first release of a completed motion picture for viewing by the general public; also the first release of a video/DVD (see "release," "re-release" and "re-issuing costs").

initial public offering (IPO) — A corporation's first offering of stock to the public through a registered/public stock offering (contrast with "primary distribution"; see "corporate stock," "penny stock," "pricing amendment," "publicly held" and "public offering").

initial release — (see "initial distribution").

initial release budget — The planned and categorized expenditures associated with a film's first distribution (see "distribution expenses" and "initial distribution").

initial U.S. theatrical release — The first distribution of a motion picture in the United States. Some distribution agreements provide that the distributor will consult in good faith with the production company regarding the distribution pattern and ad campaign for the initial U.S. theatrical release, provided, however that the distributor's decisions with respect thereto will be final (see "advertising campaign," "release pattern" and "right of consultation").

injunction — A judicial remedy granted for the purpose of requiring a party to do or refrain from doing or continuing to do a particular act or activity. The injunction is a preventive measure that guards against future injuries rather than affording a remedy for past injuries. Many film distribution agreements contain language prohibiting a producer from seeking to enjoin the release of the film regardless of the distributor's alleged wrongful conduct. In other words, the only available remaining remedy is to sue for damages after the fact (see "enjoin," "litigation" and "remedy" or "remedies").

injury — Any wrong or damage done to the person, rights, reputation or property of another (see "crime," "damage" and "tort").

in kind — To return something of the same or similar type or quality to that which was received, though not necessarily the identical article (see "restitution").

in perpetuity — To exist forever; perpetually. Many film distribution agreements are not outright purchases of a completed film, but merely a license to distribute. However, the distribution term may be in perpetuity (see "term").

inside information — Corporate affairs that have not yet been made public. SEC rules restrict the ability of a corporate insider to trade on the basis of such information (see "insider" and "insider trading").

insider — In the corporate world, a person with access to key corporate information before it is announced to the public. Every officer and director of a corporation and any person who owns more than 10 percent of the stock of that corporation is an insider. In a more general sense, a person who is in a position of power in a business or industry (see "control person," "Hollywood insiders" and "principal stockholder").

insider's game — A competitive industry viewed as a contest between rival factions and run by a restricted inner circle of people, admission into which may be limited by arbitrary considerations. These so-called "insiders" in the film industry are also sometimes referred to as being "members of the club." Although different people may use varying criteria for defining who or how many people are actually "members of the club," in a general sense these "club members" are the top level owner/executives of the major studio/distributors and the top actors, actresses, producers and directors in the industry along with their agents and entertainment attorneys (see "economic war zone," "Hollywood control group," "level playing field," "member of the club," "reciprocal preferences" and "relationship-driven business").

insider trading — The illegal buying or selling of corporate stock by a corporate officer or other corporate insider who profits by his or her access to information not available to the general public (see "corporate opportunity," "fiduciary," "inside information," "insider" and "securities").

insert — A filmed close-up of short duration, edited into a film sequence to help explain some part of the action or to assist in the film's continuity (see "action," "close-up," "continuity" and "sequence").

insolvency — A financial condition in which an individual or entity is unable to meet his, her or its obligations as they mature in the ordinary course of business or has liabilities that exceed his, her or its assets at any given time (see "bankruptcy").

installment sale — A sale made with the agreement that the purchased goods or services will be paid for in fractional amounts over a specified period of time (see "interest").

institutional advertising — Advertising sponsored by or carried on behalf of large or significant organizations in a given society or culture (e.g., banks, insurance companies, labor unions, universities, etc.; see "advertising").

institutional investor — An organization that trades large volumes of securities, usually an insurance company, investment company or bank (see "bank" and "investor").

instrumentation — In music, the theory and practice of composing, arranging or adapting music for a group of instruments of different kinds. Also, the term is sometimes used to refer to the list of instruments that a work is scored for (see "conducting" and "orchestration").

instrument of transfer — The legal document that conveys the title of property and/or rights to the new owner (see "chain of title" and "title").

instruments — Legal documents in which some contractual relationship is given formal expression or by which some right is granted (see "contract").

insurable interest — That relationship with a person or thing that will support the issuance of an insurance policy. A person or entity is usually regarded as having an insurable interest in the subject matter insured when such person or entity will derive pecuniary (i.e., of or related to money) benefit or advantage from its preservation, or will suffer pecuniary loss or damage from its destruction (see "insurance," "insured" and "insured risk").

insurable risk — Any possibility of loss relating to the production of a motion picture that may be insured against. Production lenders and completion guarantors will not assume responsibility for such risks and will require that the producer obtain available insurance to protect against loss (see "insurance," "insurance coverages" and "lender risk elimination").

insurance — A financial arrangement or agreement (insurance policy) between an individual or company (the insured) and a financial institution (insurance company, insurance carrier or insurer) whereby the insurer agrees to compensate the owner of the insurance policy in the event of the destruction or loss of, or injury to, a specified person or thing in which the policy owner has an insurable interest. The policy owner pays premiums as consideration for the insurer's commitment. In a broad economic sense, insurance transfers risk from individuals to a larger group. Motion picture insurance premiums for various coverages, excluding the completion bond, generally equal about 3 percent of a film's budget (see "claims made policy," "completion bond," "insurance policy," "policy," "premium" and "reinsurance").

insurance backed schemes — An adjunct element of a film financing plan used by some producers in the mid to late '90s that involved the purchase of insurance to help protect against the risk of loss on a slate of films that was being financed through bank loans and in most instances involving gap financing. Most of the deals ended in massive litigation involving the producers, distributors, banks, insurance brokers, insurance companies and reinsurers. The basic concept was that even though the risk of a single film making a profit was not good, spreading that risk over a slate of films somehow improved those risks. Allegedly, however, some of the producers substituted their weaker film projects into the package after it was funded, thus increasing the risk of loss (see "GAP financing," "insurable risk," "lender financing" and "pre-sale financing").

insurance carrier — An insurance company (see "insurance").

insurance coverages — The various kinds of insurance policies and occurrences for which insurance is designed to provide financial protection. Motion picture insurance may include coverage for the camera and processing; cast; comprehensive liability; completion guaranty; errors and omissions; extra expense; faulty stock, props, sets and wardrobe; guild/union flight accident; miscellaneous equipment; negative film and videotape; property damage liability and worker's compensation. A producer's insurance policy may incorporate all or some combination of these coverages (contrast with "completion bond"; see "insurable risk" and "producer's insurance policy").

insurance policy — The actual document serving as the contract between the insurance company and the insured and stating the agreement terms (see "certificate of insurance" and "claims made policy").

insurance premium — The consideration paid by the insured to the insurance company for the insurance policy and the coverages it provides (see "insurance coverages").

insurance take — (see "cover shot").

insured — The person or entity protected by an insurance policy; usually, the person/entity who contracts for a policy of insurance that indemnifies him, her or it against loss, although the policyholder (owner) may not be the same as the insured in some cases (see "additional insureds" and "insurance").

in synch — A technical phrase stating that the sound and the picture in a film are properly timed (i.e., synchronously joined; see "composite" and "synchronism").

intangible — Abstract; having no physical material body. In its intangible form a motion picture is viewed as a collection of rights that may be sold or licensed in their entirety or piece by piece. As noted earlier, copyright protection is available for works fixed in tangible form, not for intangible ideas (see "commodity," "intangible assets," "product" and "tangible asset").

intangible assets — Rights or non-physical resources that are presumed to represent an advantage to the firm's position in the marketplace. Such assets include copyrights, patents, trademarks, goodwill, computer programs, capitalized advertising costs, organization costs, licenses, leases and import and export permits (contrast with "tangible assets").

integration — In securities law, a concept used for determining whether a given offering is a separate offering, and thus may qualify for an available exemption from registration, or

whether it is part of a larger offering and must be treated as such for regulatory purposes. The Regulation D integration provision requires that all sales that are part of the same Regulation D offering must meet all of the terms and conditions of Regulation D. However, offers and sales that are made more than six months before the start of a Regulation D offering or are made more than six months after completion of a Regulation D offering will not be considered part of that Regulation D offering, so long as during those six month periods there are no offers or sales of securities by or for the issuer that are of the same or a similar class as those offered or sold under Regulation D, except for other specified exempt offers or sales. The SEC considers the following factors in determining whether offerings should be integrated for regulatory purposes: whether the offerings (1) are part of a single plan of financing, (2) involve the same class of security, (3) are made at or about the same time, (4) involve the same type of consideration and (5) are made for the same general purpose. For example, an investor financed development offering followed by what the producer/issuer thought was a separate investor financed production money offering may be treated as a single offering (i.e., integrated) for securities regulatory purposes (see "offering" and "Regulation D").

inter-client confidentiality — Attorney ethics require that a lawyer not reveal information relating to representation of a client unless the client consents after consultation, except for disclosures that are impliedly authorized in order to carry out the representation. This ethical prohibition sometimes presents problems for the entertainment attorney who represents several clients, all of whom may be involved in the same film production (see "Code of Professional Responsibility," "conflicts of interest," "ethics" and "representation of multiple clients").

intercut — A film editing technique in which different sequences of action are alternated between each other to make them appear to be happening concurrently in the movie (see "edit").

interest — Consideration or compensation paid for the use of money loaned; the cost of using money, expressed as a rate per period of time, usually one year, in which case it is called an annual rate of interest. In studio financing (i.e., in a production-financing/distribution deal), interest on the negative cost is typically deducted from the distributor's gross receipts after the distribution fee and expenses, but before recoupment of the negative cost). Interest issues may create problems for independent producers at several levels: (a) Interest Plus Profit Participation—Distribution agreements involving at least partial studio or distributor financing of the negative cost of a film often allow the distributor to charge interest on its unrecouped negative cost in addition to permitting the studio or affiliated distributor to retain a substantial if not overwhelming interest in net profits. If a distributor deducts a substantial distribution fee, is allowed to recoup its distribution expenses and is paid a fair rate of interest on its borrowed funds, why would anyone except those who have no power to prevent it, allow the same distributor to also participate in the film's net profits? (b) Interest Rates That Are Excessive—The interest rate charged by the studio is often not in proportion to the actual cost of funds. Studios have been known to charge interest rates of 20 percent to 30 percent. If anything, since the studio affiliated distribution company is also able to obtain compensation in the form of its distribution

fees, the affiliated studio acting as a financier should charge less than the market rate for interest on the borrowed funds; (c) Interest on Advances—The studio/distributors may take the position that advances should not be included in gross receipts until earned, in other words, the distributor will want to deduct an amount equal to any advance that has been paid to the producer from monies received by the distributor and will not want to consider such amounts as part of gross receipts for any profit participation calculations which start with a gross receipts figure. At the same time, the studio/distributor may seek to charge interest on such advances. The producer and other profit participants may want to take the position that if advances are excluded from gross receipts, no interest should be charged on such amounts; (d) Interest on Monies Not Spent—Interest is sometimes charged on monies not yet spent by the distributor (e.g., in preparing an earnings statement for a film, the distributor may accrue the print and advertising costs incurred but not yet paid so that an interim participation statement will not show a profit). This accrual of expenses also reduces the amount of gross receipts that could be used to reduce negative costs and thereby also reduce interest charges. In other words, the studio may seek to calculate interest on negative costs from the point at which such expenses are incurred (as an accounting entry), whereas the producer may prefer to have such interest calculated as of the time such expenses are actually paid by the studio; (e) When Interest Charges Stop—Studios may also seek to continue charging interest on the negative costs of a film until the end of the accounting period in which payments reducing the negative cost total and/or interest are received by the studio, whereas the producer and other net profit participants may insist that interest charges stop when such payments are actually received by the studio and not wait until the end of the accounting period, however many months that might involve; (f) Interest on Negative Cost Balances—In calculating this interest on the studio's unrecouped negative costs, all direct distribution costs and fees are typically first deducted from gross receipts as expenses of distribution, thus significantly decreasing the amount of gross receipts, if any, that may apply toward recoupment of the studio's contribution toward production costs. Thus, at many early stages of earnings statements, no recoupment of negative costs is achieved and the interest charges simply continue to accrue. In contrast, with a bank financed motion picture production, the bank will recoup its loaned amount (including the negative cost, plus interest and fees) before the distributor deducts its distribution fee and expenses. If a studio wants to act like a bank and charge interest on borrowed funds, then it ought to also allow a priority position for the recoupment of negative costs so as not to unfairly extend the repayment of the loaned amount thus increasing the total interest charges. In such situations, the studio/bank is guilty of self-dealing; (g) Interest on Overhead—In many instances, even some or all of the indirect distribution costs, the normal costs of doing business as a distributor that are not specifically tied to a particular film being distributed (i.e., overhead), are also deducted from gross receipts as distribution expenses and again, are not available for recoupment of the negative cost. Other items of overhead may be inappropriately characterized as production costs, thus interest may also be charged by a studio or distributor on some of these indirect distribution expenses; (h) Simple vs Exact Interest—Studio/distributors also may use a form of simple interest, based on a 360 day year, instead of exact interest (based on a 365 day

year) and that practice, particularly when dealing with substantial amounts of money in the form of negative costs, will result in the payment of a greater amount of interest to the studio/distributor for that final partial interest bearing term and (i) Interest on Gross Participations—A variation on the practice of charging interest on monies not actually spent in which the distributor for a major studio/distributor financed motion picture categorizes gross participations as production costs (as opposed to distribution expenses) and thus charges interest and overhead on such participations (see "actual interest," "adhesion contract," "creative accounting," "exact interest," "FASB Statement No. 53," "greed," "loan," "overhead," "overhead costs," "prime rate," "production-financing/distribution agreement," "production overhead" and "usury").

interest bearing — An account or charge that yields a fee for the cost of using money. In film, the term usually refers to the studio's practice of charging interest on the studio's overhead surcharge and treating such interest as a production expense of the film. With respect to distribution and production expenses, it is important that a clear distinction be made between the two since if an expense is categorized as a production cost it will bear interest and overhead on studio financed films (see "creative accounting," "interest," "production costs" and "production-financing/distribution agreement").

interest on advances — (see "interest").

interest on gross participations — (see "interest").

interest on monies not spent — (see "interest").

interest on negative cost balances — (see "interest").

interest on overhead — (see "interest").

interest on production costs — (see "interest").

interest on the surcharge — Interest charged by a studio on the overhead fee it extracts from a studio financed production (same as "interest on overhead"; see "interest bearing," "overhead," "overhead costs" and "overhead surcharge").

interest plus profit participation — (see "interest").

interest rate risk — The possibility that a fixed-rate debt instrument will decline in value as a result of a rise in interest rates (see "lender risk elimination").

interests of limited partners — The aggregate interests of all limited partners in their respective capacities as limited partners in the current profits derived from business operations of the partnership (see "majority-in-interest" and "unit").

interests of members — The aggregate interests of all member/investors of manager-managed LLCs in their respective capacities as members in the current profits derived from business operations of the LLC (see "limited liability company," "majority-in-interest" and "unit").

interim credit facility — A loan or some form of credit extended to an organization during a period of transition (i.e., until the organization's permanent financing for its primary activity is obtained; similar to "bridge financing"; see "commercial paper").

interim dividend — A corporate dividend declared and paid before annual earnings have been determined, generally on a quarterly basis (see "corporate stock" and "dividend").

interim relief — A temporary interruption of court imposed restrictions. In the last several decades, most of the distributors and theater owners subject to the Paramount consent decrees have sought interim relief from the application of those decrees (see "conduct restrictions," "merger guidelines," "Paramount Consent Decree of 1948," "TriStar Case" and "vertical merger").

interim statement — A financial report covering only a portion of a fiscal year. Public corporations supplement their annual reports with quarterly statements informing shareholders of changes in the balance sheet and income statement, as well as other corporate developments of interest to shareholders, the business community and the public (see "annual report").

interlocking directorates — Corporate boards of directors whose members serve as directors on more than one corporate board (see "corporate conglomerate" and "corporation").

internal financing — Funds produced by the normal operations of a firm, retained by the firm and used to finance future operations (see "external financing").

internal rate of return (IRR) — A method of calculating the return on an investment (i.e., the discount rate that equates the yearly economic benefits to the present value of the investment); the rate that will discount future cash flows from an investment to an amount that equals the amount invested. Thus, it results in a net present value of zero — see "adjusted rated of return," "discounted cash flow," "rate of return," "required rate of return" and "return on investment").

Internal Revenue Service (IRS) — The U.S. government agency responsible for collecting nearly all federal taxes including personal and corporate income taxes, social security taxes and excise and gift taxes. The IRS administers the rules and regulations of the U.S. Department of the Treasury and investigates and prosecutes tax illegalities (see "income tax").

International Alliance of Theatrical and Stage Employees (IATSE) — The parent organization of some one thousand plus local unions in North America representing every branch of film production, including stage hands, makeup artists and wardrobe handlers, as well as employees in film distribution and exhibition (see "guild").

international buyers — Individuals or entities who acquire licensing rights to motion pictures for exploitation in foreign territories (see "territory").

international co-production and agreements — A source of film financing in which two or more entities from different countries contribute a portion of production financing and in exchange receive a share of profits from exploitation of the film, all pursuant to the terms of treaties between the involved countries. Most European countries, as well as Canada and Australia, have formal co-production treaties relating to financing and producing films. The U.S. has not. Satisfaction of the requirements of an international co-production may yield financing benefits, such as subsidies, television quota benefits, tax benefits, and certain in-kind

investments. Also in such transactions facilities such as studios, scenery, staff, etc., may be provided in order to obtain foreign currency (see "co-production financing," "foreign production problems" and "nationality test").

International Film Importers and Distributors of America (IFIDA) — An assembly of independent producers and distributors that was listed in the MPAA publication about the history of the MPAA Ratings Board, as one of the three industry organization partners in the creation of the movie rating system. The rating system replaced its predecessor the Production Code Administration in November of 1968. Unfortunately, after numerous inquires, this author has been unable to find anyone at the MPAA, MPEAA or NATO who knows anything about this organization. It is also not listed in the Los Angeles or area telephone listings. Thus, it appears likely that the organization no longer exists, in which case its current status should be noted in the above referenced MPAA publication because otherwise it is misleading to suggest that any association of independent producers is currently supporting the MPAA Ratings Board (see "industry groups," "MPAA" and "Production Code Administration").

internationally competitive — Effectively able to vie for business throughout the world. On the one hand it appears reasonable for the major studio/distributors to use their political influence to persuade the U.S. government to relax its enforcement of the antitrust laws in the entertainment industry in an effort to free the these entities from restrictions that impair their ability to compete in a global marketplace. On the other hand, if such relaxed enforcement increases the competitive stranglehold of the major studio/distributors on the domestic industry and makes it even more difficult for the many thousands of independent, small business persons to survive (whether they be production companies, distributors, exhibitors or otherwise), then there needs to be a better balancing of interests in the domestic industry. Also, certain domestic film industry organizations have traditionally worked together in the foreign distribution of films anyway, thus there may be no need to permit vertical integration in the domestic marketplace in order to create more strength for U.S. companies in the foreign marketplace (see "antitrust laws," "Paramount Consent Decree of 1948" and "TriStar Case").

international participations — Percentage interests in some level of a motion picture's revenue stream generated through a film's foreign exhibition (see "foreign equity financing" and "gross participations").

international tax attorney — A lawyer with expertise relating to the tax laws of foreign countries (see "entertainment attorney" and "securities attorney").

international tax shelter/incentives — (see "foreign tax shelters" and "foreign subsidies").

internegative — A negative made from the original film negative and using reversal film stock (see "dupe negative" and "reversal film stock").

inter-party agreement — An agreement among the lending entity, the film distributor and the producer in a negative pickup transaction, which, among other things, provides that the distributor's interest in the revenues generated from the exploitation of the film is subordinated to the interest of the bank in repayment of the bank's loan and the payment of its interest charges. On the other hand, if an investor-

financed limited partnership or member-managed LLC financed the production costs of a motion picture such entities would not be granted a similar first position by the film's distributor (see "investor financing," "lender financing" and "negative pickup").

interpolating — Inserting between other things or parts (e.g., interpolating additional film footage; see "edit" and "final cut").

interpositive — A positive print of a film produced from the original negative that is used to produce duplicate ("dupe") negatives. An interpositive is not used for projection (see "print").

interstate offering — A securities offering made or that may be made to residents of more than one state (see "intra-state offering").

in the can — The exposed film, ready to go to the lab; or that filming is completed (see "acquisition distribution agreement," "can" and "rent-a-distributor").

intra-state offering — A federal exemption from the SEC securities registration requirement that may be made by an issuer organized under the laws of a given state, doing its principal business in such state, and offered solely to bona fide residents of that same state with substantially all of the proceeds of the offering remaining in the state. Such an offering would still need to comply with the applicable state registration or exemption requirements. This federal exemption is primarily used to fund local businesses such as restaurants. It would not be appropriate for financing a film since the market for a film generally includes the entire universe (see "blue sky laws," "interstate offering," "private offering," "public offering" and "securities").

in turnaround — The film development status in which the developing studio or production company decides not to continue developing the property or decides not to go into production on the film, thus making the property available for acquisition by others (see "development" and "turnaround").

invasion of privacy — The wrongful intrusion into a person's private activities by other individuals or by the government including the unauthorized use of a person's name or likeness, the unauthorized disclosure of private facts and false depiction of the voice of a person (see "right of publicity" and "tort").

investment — Using capital in an effort to create more money, either through income-producing vehicles or through more risk-oriented ventures designed to result in capital gains. The term investment may also refer to the amount invested or the property purchased (contrast with "loan"; see "debt," "investor financing" and "securities").

investment adviser — A person or entity who for compensation engages in the business of advising others regarding investing in, purchasing or selling securities. The activities of such persons are regulated by the Investment Advisers Act of 1940. It is generally illegal for the sellers of securities to provide compensation to investment advisors unless the investment advisor is also licensed as a broker/dealer and the compensation is fully disclosed to all parties (see "broker," "broker/dealer," "dealer" and "finder").

investment bank or investment banker — A broker who acts as an underwriter of securities. The investment banker can act as principal by buying the entire issue from the issuer or as an agent by selling the offering on a "best-efforts" basis. In either case, the investment banker sells the issue to other dealers who together with the lead investment banker have formed an underwriting syndicate. Members of the syndicate in turn sell the shares to the investing public and/or to institutional investors (see "broker," "broker/dealer" and "selling group").

investment club — A group of people who pool their assets in order to make joint investment decisions. Choices of which investments to make are made by a vote of members. Pursuant to Regulation D an investment club investment in a Regulation D offering would be counted as one investor so long as such entity was not organized for the specific purpose of acquiring the securities offered (see "National Association of Investment Clubs" and "Regulation D").

investment community — Individuals and/or entities who invest or may invest in a given industry such as the entertainment industry (see "investor financing").

investment contract — A form of investor financing that does not always involve the creation of an entity (like a joint venture, limited partnership, LLC or corporation) but which does involve a contractual relationship between the so-called "contract administrator" and the investor group. An investment contract is otherwise defined as an investment in a common enterprise in which the investors hope to make a profit primarily off the managerial efforts of others. An investment contract is a security and a direct investment, thus compliance with federal and state securities laws is required, and the investors do not enjoy the limited liability of the investor/owners of limited partnership or LLC interests or of corporate stock. A limited partnership is a form of investment contract and thus also a security (see "financing," "investor financing," "investor financing agreement," "preliminary/development disclosure document," "preliminary/development offering," "preliminary/development funds" and "security" or "securities").

investment grade bonds — Corporate bonds with high ratings (see "bond" and "junk bonds").

investment group — An association of individuals or entities brought together for the purpose of investing in a project or venture. The term "investment group" is more commonly applied to higher levels of investment than the term "investment club" (e.g., several companies may come together to form an investment group and in the process create a new entity such as a corporation or joint venture, but the original group may be referred to as the investment group (see "foreign equity investment" and "investment club").

investment income — Money or value received from securities and other non-business investments (e.g., dividends, interest, royalty income and capital gains on stocks). Under the Tax Reform Act of 1986, investment income earned by passive activities, such as a limited partnership, must be treated separately from other passive income; also called portfolio income (see "passive income" and "passive loss").

investment letter of intent — A letter from a financial backer of a motion picture stating the intention of the financier to provide production funding for the picture that the producer can use to help in assembling the various elements required to produce a film. An investment letter of intent is also used in the private placement of new securities between the issuer of the securities and the purchaser establishing that the securities are being bought as an investment and not for resale. This purchaser representation is often included in the subscription agreement that the investor signs. Under SEC Rule 144A, a purchaser of such restricted securities may eventually resell them to the public if certain specific conditions are met including a minimum holding period of at least two years (see "elements" and "private offering").

investment memorandum — (same as "offering memorandum").

investment pool — The combination of resources for a common purpose or benefit (see "blind pool," "limited partnership" and "limited liability company").

investment tax credit (ITC) — A federal U.S. tax credit provided by the tax code that allowed feature films to be recognized as capital assets having a useful life of over three years, thus making films eligible for a 6 2/3 percent credit (based on the total negative investment) assuming that more than 80 percent of the picture was produced in the U.S. The ITC was considered to be a significant form of government subsidy for the film industry (i.e., the ITC had been a major selling point for film financing deals structured as limited partnerships). However, the ITC was repealed as part of the Tax Reform Act of 1986. In repealing the ITC, it would appear that any advantage a U.S. based film industry had in producing movies in the U.S. (i.e., keeping production dollars at home, was severely limited). A producing entity's decision to incur negative costs abroad may have made more economic sense because of lower foreign production costs and particularly if other governments offered tax incentives or other accommodations to attract the film production business. In 2004, Congress passed the American Jobs Creation Act of 2004, containing a new tax incentive for the film industry that was codified as Section 181 of the IRS Code (see "Section 181 of the IRS Code," "selling point," "tax benefits" and "tax credit").

investment vehicle — A contract or entity in which investors can invest. The non-securities (active investor) investment vehicles include the investor financing agreement, the joint venture agreement, the initial incorporation scenario and the member-managed LLC. The securities (passive investor) investment vehicles include the existing corporation, the limited partnership and the manager-managed LLC (see "corporation," "initial incorporation," "investor financing agreement," "joint venture," "limited liability company" and "limited partnership").

investor — A person or entity that commits money in order to earn a financial return. In addition to investing in the stocks of the publicly held corporations known as the major studio/distributors, investors may also provide development, production and/or distribution funding for a given movie project or projects. Unlike financiers, investors do not generally raise funds but only invest. The same active/passive distinction that applies to financiers, also applies to investors. Generally, the raising of funds from passive investors involves the sale of a security and thus requires compliance with the federal and state securities

laws (see "financiers" or "financing source" and "financing").

investor day on the set — A special day set aside on the set of a motion picture during principal photography in which the investors are invited to visit the set. A commonly used technique in low-budget filmmaking for films financed through direct participation programs such as limited partnerships or manager-managed LLCs that helps to glamorize the investment for the investors (see "investor financing").

investor financed development offering — Individuals or entities that provide capital for the development phase of a film, including costs of acquisition of underlying rights, development of the script, packaging and activities involved in seeking production financing (see "development").

investor financing — A broad category of film finance (i.e., the funding of a motion picture project or projects) wherein one or more individuals or entities provide the capital for the endeavor with the hope of making a profit. Generally, the distinction between active and passive investors forms the basis for distinguishing between a non-securities and securities investment offering, respectively. Interests in investor financing agreements and joint ventures, whose investors are generally actively involved in the management of the endeavor are typically not considered securities. Corporations, limited partnerships and manager-managed LLCs, whose investors are generally not actively involved in the management of the endeavor are typically considered securities, and thus must be offered in compliance with applicable federal and state securities laws (see "financing," "preliminary/development funds" and "financiers" or "financiers" or "financing source").

investor financing agreement — A written contract between a project manager (e.g., a feature film producer) and a financing source. If the financing source is an active investor or a so-called industry partner who provides production monies in addition to some other service such as distribution in a given medium or territory, such an arrangement probably does not involve a security. However, if such investors provide their financing and otherwise play a passive role with respect to the project, the federal and state securities laws probably apply to the transaction which then would more properly be characterized as some form of investment contract (see "preliminary/development offering," "investment contract," "development money Investment agreement," "joint venture," "limited liability company" and "limited partnership").

investor motivation — The underlying incentives that prompt individuals or entities to contribute to the financing of certain business activities such as the development, production and/or distribution of a feature film. Such factors may include: (1) interest in supporting the filmmaker's career, (2) attraction to the glamour of the film industry, (3) a feeling that the investment has a certain amount of "cocktail chatter" value, that is, it's more interesting and fun to talk about than most boring investments, (4) a desire to spend time on the set and rub elbows with the cast and crew, (5) a desire to use this investment as an opportunity to learn about how the film industry works, so that he or she can get more involved in the future, (6) helping a son, daughter, niece or nephew appear as an extra in the movie, (7) appearing in the movie as an actor or actress themselves, (8) gaining an opportunity to (in rare and unusual circumstances) direct the movie, (9) wanting to get his or her script produced, (10) benefitting a local economy by bringing the movie there to be shot on location, (11) wants to see one or more of the messages being communicated by the movie on the screen, (12) the hope that the movie will make money for its investors and/or (13) specific tax benefits (see "adjusted rate of return," "glamour industry," "internal rate of return," "profit margin," "profit motive," "rate of return," "return of capital," "return on invested capital" and "Section 181 of the IRS Code").

investor numerical limitations — Federal and state securities law limitations imposed on the use of exemptions from the securities registration requirements that limit the number of investors who may purchase securities in such offerings (e.g., Regulation D Rules 505 and 506 limit sales to no more than thirty-five non-accredited investors, but permit sales to an unlimited number of accredited investors; see "accredited investor," "counting rules" and "Regulation D").

investor relations activities — Activities conducted by an issuer of securities relating to keeping the investors informed about their investment. Such activities may include meetings, telephone conferences, newsletters, letters, e-mails and Web sites, although issuers conducting exempt offerings (i.e., private placements) have to be careful not to use the Internet for a general solicitation (see "investor day on the set" and "investor financing").

investor sophistication requirements — Federal and/or state securities offering investor suitability requirements relating to the background, experience and education of a prospective investor (e.g., Regulation D Rule 506 requires that immediately prior to the sale, the issuer must reasonably believe that each non-accredited investor, either alone or with his or her purchaser representative, must have such knowledge and experience in financial and business matters that he or she is capable of evaluating the merits and risks of the prospective investment; see "accredited investor," "investor suitability standards," "purchaser representative" and "Regulation D").

investor suitability standards — Federal and state securities rules that those selling sophisticated and potentially risky financial products, such as the direct participation programs like limited partnerships and member-managed LLCs, must follow to ensure that investors have the financial means to assume the risks involved (also called "investor sophistication requirements," "purchaser representations," "suitability questionnaires" and "suitability rules").

invitation to bid — A written or oral solicitation or invitation by a distributor to one or more exhibitors to bid or negotiate for the right to exhibit a motion picture (see "bid" and "blind bidding").

IPO — Initial public offering by a corporation of its stock (see "initial public offering," "mezzanine level" and "securities").

irrevocable — Incapable of being revoked; unalterable (see "irrevocable letter of credit").

irrevocable letter of credit — A financing transaction in which a bank issues to a borrower a letter authorizing the borrower to draw on the bank for a stated amount for a specified period, guaranteeing to accept the drafts on the bank if they are made and providing that such authority

cannot be revoked (see "letter of credit" and "standby letter of credit").

irrevocability — The quality or state of being irrevocable (see "irrevocable").

irrevocability appointed — An appointment that is not revocable (see "power of attorney").

IRS — (see "Internal Revenue Service").

isolated ancillary rights — The rights to exploit a film in any single geographical or technological market other than theatrical distribution in the domestic market. Any such ancillary right that is likely to be worth a significant sum of money will probably be demanded by the domestic theatrical distributor as a pre-requisite for its commitment to distribute a film (see "ancillary rights," "fractured rights deals" and "split rights deals").

issue — To authorize, execute and deliver shares of stock or other securities for sale to the public. Also, the term "issue" may be used to refer to the securities themselves (see "issuer" and "issuer sales").

issued and outstanding — Shares of a corporation, authorized in the corporate charter, that have been physically delivered to and are being held by the corporation's shareholders (see "corporation" and "stock").

issuer — An entity selling its own securities. For example, a corporation selling its shares is the issuer of stock. Also, a limited partnership selling its units or interests is an issuer, as is a manager-managed LLC selling its units or interests (see "issuer sales").

issuer disqualifiers — (see "disqualifiers").

issuer sales — An offering of securities conducted directly by the issuer without the use of underwriters or broker/dealers. Persons conducting such sales on behalf of an issuer (1) must not be subject to a statutory disqualification, (2) cannot be compensated in connection with their participation by the payment of commissions or other remuneration based either directly or indirectly on transactions in securities, (3) cannot at the time of their participation, be an associated person of a broker or dealer, (4) must primarily perform or intend to perform at the end of the offering, substantial duties for or on behalf of the issuer otherwise than in connection with transactions in securities, (5) cannot have been brokers or dealers, or associated persons of a broker or dealer, within the preceding twelve months and (6) cannot participate in selling an offering of securities for any issuer more than once every twelve months (see "broker/dealer," "broker/dealer sales," "broker/dealer selling agreement," "disqualifiers," "finder sales," "issuer" and "underwriter").

it's only money — A rationalization that some distributors and others in the film industry use when excusing the business practices engaged in by many in the film industry and described herein. They're expressing the view that the film business is merely a game, that many of the disputes that occur only relate to money and that's not important. The truth is that in most instances, the money being squabbled over represents several years of people's lives, expertise and effort as well as their dreams and that many of the film industry professionals whose rights are trampled because "it's only money" (that has in many instances been wrongfully taken from them), end up with drinking problems or some other dysfunction due to the dilemmas in which they find themselves (i.e., they don't feel they can sue the distributor and still be able to get another job in this town). Again, it is extremely important for producers and others to check the credits on other films distributed by a prospective distributor and inquire as to the distributor's attitude toward such things as fairness and honesty in business transactions (see "blacklisting," "business practice," "creative accounting," "insider's game," "sue us" and "winner-take-all").

J

jacket (or box) — The carton or covering of an album, videocassette, DVD or audio tape package used to protect and market such mechanical reproductions (see "cassette").

Japanese money — In past decades, many billions of dollars have been invested in the American film industry by Japanese owned concerns. A great deal of speculation has occurred relating to the question of how such investments might impact the domestic film industry and how such investments might turn out for the investors. If the distributor and/or industry practices described herein become or continue to be prevalent, it would be surprising if the investment of Japanese monies in the domestic film industry had any significant impact whatsoever on the domestic industry and equally surprising for the Japanese investors to fare any more favorably than other groups or individual Hollywood outsiders that have invested in the Hollywood-based U.S. film industry in the past (see "creative accounting," "insider's game" and "mass exodus").

joint venture — A business undertaking by two or more parties in which profits, losses, and control are shared. A joint venture is a combination of two or more persons who jointly seek a profit from some specific business venture without designating themselves as an actual partnership or corporation. Although technically a form of general partnership, a joint venture usually connotes an enterprise of a more limited scope and duration. Investors in both joint ventures and general partnerships have joint liability for debts and torts. In film joint ventures the parties may contribute various elements, including financing and non-monetary contributions such as the screenplay, an underlying property or a fully packaged project. The joint venture agreement serves to document the transaction (see "corporation," "financing," "general partnership," "liability," "limited liability," "limited partnership" and "limited liability company").

joint venture agreement — The written contract between individuals or business entities engaged in a joint venture that sets out the terms of their joint business endeavor including who contributes what and their profit participation (see "joint venture").

joint venture financing — (see "financing," "investor financing" and "joint venture").

judgments — The determinations of courts of competent jurisdiction on matters submitted to such courts (i.e., for a final determination of the rights of the parties to lawsuits; see "final judgment" and "litigation").

junk bonds — Corporate debt instruments with a low credit rating issued by companies without extensive track records of sales and earnings, or by companies with questionable credit strength. Junk bonds are more risky and pay higher returns than investment grade bonds (see "bond," "debt financing" and "investment grade bonds").

junket — A trip to the location of a film during principal photography sponsored by the film's producing entity and/or distributor for the working entertainment press and during which key cast and crew of the film are made available for photo sessions and interviews. Such film production junkets are designed to generate publicity for the film (see "buzz," "press tour" and "publicity").

junking costs — Expenses incurred in discarding the accumulated scrap associated with the production or distribution of a film. Such costs are generally included in the list of distribution expenses in film distribution agreements (see "distribution expenses" and "scrapping prints").

jurisdiction — A geographical territory in which there is a sovereign power or a governmental authority to govern or legislate. Thus, a jurisdiction may be a country, state, county or city. Also, in film labor matters, the term jurisdiction may relate to whether a particular union or guild has the authority to deal with a given matter (see "collective bargaining agreement" and "guild").

Justice Department — (see "U.S. Justice Department").

just title — An ownership claim to property that is supportable against all other legal claims (also called "clear title," "good title" and "proper title"; see "clearance" and "title").

K

K-1 — (see "Schedule K-1" and "taxable year").

Kagan Associates — (see "Paul Kagan Associates, Inc.").

key — In film distribution and exhibition, a geographical area in which a film is released for theatrical exhibition. Keys are further classified on the basis of population as major keys, ordinary keys or sub-keys (see "break," "key cities," "major key," "ordinary key" and "sub-key").

key art — Art work used in posters and ads for a motion picture (see "advertising").

key art showcase cities — The major markets for art films in North America, including Los Angeles, Washington D.C., San Francisco, Seattle, Boston, Chicago, Toronto and New York (see "art film").

key cities — Cities that are cultural and media centers, larger and generally more lucrative film exhibition markets (see "key").

key crew agreements — The employment contracts for the most important members of a film's production crew. Copies of such agreements are often part of the documentation required for review by a completion guarantor (see "completion bond" and "crew").

key factors — Accounting terminology for the significant matters on which an entity's future results are expected to depend. Such factors are basic to the entity's operations and thus encompass matters that affect, among other things, the entity's sales, production, service and financing activities. Key factors serve as a foundation for prospective financial statements and are the bases for the assumptions (see "hypothetical assumptions" and "prospective financial statements").

key grip — The film production person responsible to the director of photography for supervising all grip crews who assist the gaffer during lighting procedures and to maneuver the camera unit during moving shots. Grips also aid various production departments such as sound, electrical, wardrobe and property in the moving and handling of their equipment (see "crew" and "grip").

key personnel — Other than the cast, the most important people involved in the production of a film are generally considered to be the producer, director, line producer, director of photography and production accountant (see "cast" and "crew").

key trends — Where an industry seems to be heading on important issues. Unfortunately, the Hollywood trade press will sometimes publish reports regarding what are characterized as trends, but the articles in fact do not provide enough evidence to support the claim (see "trend").

kickback — A form of bribery; a practice in which the seller of goods or services gives back to the purchasing agent of those goods or services a portion of the purchase price in order to induce the agent to enter into the transaction. In most commercial transactions, kickbacks are illegal and prohibited by criminal commercial bribery statutes. The principal of the purchasing agent may also have a cause of action against the agent to recover the amount of the bribe. Also for tax purposes, amounts paid as kickbacks or bribes generally are not deductible. Producers and their auditors have to watch for indications of such arrangements in all of the distributor's relationships with the providers of services for which the distributor pays and then deducts the full cost as a distribution expense (e.g., outside advertising agencies, film labs, trailer production firms, exhibitors in co-operative advertising arrangements, distributor employees and facilities, distributor editing, censorship approvals, checking services, screening expenses, industry assessments, residuals and banking costs). It may also be difficult to distinguish between kickbacks and discounts or rebates in some situations (see "creative accounting," "discount" and "rebate").

lab (laboratory) — A company specializing in developing exposed motion picture stock, for both image and optical sound. Film laboratories make, process or develop the camera negative, positive work prints from the negative, black and white dupes from the work print, interpositive prints from the original negative and internegative prints from the interpositive, color reversal internegatives from which release prints are made, the optical sound track, color and density corrections from scene to scene within the film (timing) and release prints for distribution. Many labs also have full post-production videotaping facilities for tape-to-tape, film-to-tape or tape-to-film transfers (see "lab charges" and "laboratory access letter").

lab charges — The fees and expenses imposed by the film laboratory for developing the exposed film, making prints, and performing the other services provided by the lab (see "laboratory" and "laboratory deferments").

lab effects — Optical images that can be added to film during lab processing and printing (e.g., pushing light, printing for night effect and sepia-toning black-and-white stock; "lab").

labels — Brands of commercial recordings issued under a name that is usually trademarked (see "sound track albums").

laboratory access agreement — (same as "laboratory access letter").

laboratory access letter — A letter signed by a film's producer authorizing the film laboratory to deliver to the distributor or its designee at any time during the term covered by the applicable distribution agreement any of the items described in the distribution agreement's delivery schedule (see "delivery schedule" and "lab").

laboratory acknowledgment — A provision commonly found in laboratory access letters providing that by signing the laboratory access letter the laboratory agrees to be bound by the instructions and directions contained in that letter and acknowledges that it has received negative and sound materials of at least standard commercial quality which are suitable for making commercially acceptable release prints and dubbed and sub-titled versions of such prints (see "laboratory access letter").

laboratory deferments — The delayed payment (by agreement) of some or all of the compensation due to a film lab for its work in processing film (see "deferments" and "lab").

laboratory film processing agreement — A contract between the depositor of film elements with the film laboratory (the production company, owner or distributor) and the lab that contains the terms relating to processing the film and for compensating the lab (see "lab" and "lab charges").

laboratory letter — A letter issued by a film laboratory upon completion of a film stating that the finished film is of acceptable commercial quality, that the script was substantially adhered to and that the agreed-upon cast members appeared in their proper roles. Upon receipt of the film and this laboratory letter, the distribution advance, if any, will be released to the producer or lending institution to pay back some or all of a production loan (see "lab" and "negative pickup").

laboratory pledge holder agreement — An agreement between a lending bank and a film lab that is often used in film financing situations involving bank loans, to minimize the laboratory's ability to interfere with the bank's right to enforce its security interest in the film negative. The agreement typically provides that the laboratory holds the negative as a trustee for the lender and includes language that protects the bank against the laboratory's creditors. It may also limit or waive the common-law or statutory lien a laboratory might impose on a film negative in the event that the film production company does not pay for lab services on other films of the same production company at the same lab (see "lab").

labor-intensive business — A business that requires a large pool of workers; an industry in which labor costs are more important than capital costs (see "capital-intensive business").

larceny — The taking of another's property unlawfully with the intention of depriving the owner of its use (same as "theft"; see "racketeering" and "RICO").

laser disc — A video recording and playback device that is covered by a reflective plastic coating and uses a low power laser beam to read audio and/or video information encoded in a series of microscopic depressions or tracks on the disc. Such discs can only be played on one side, but the tracks on a laser disc are spaced much more closely than those found on an audio record (see "compact disc," "record" and "technological developments").

Latin — A source language for English, French, Spanish and other languages. Some Latin phrases are still used in legal documents, although it would be preferable to eliminate their use and focus on making such documents more understandable to those who read them (see "caveat emptor").

latitude — Freedom of action or choice. Most of the film distribution agreements offered in the current marketplace give the distributor a great deal of latitude with respect to matters relating to the distribution of the film and in the distributor's handling of monies resulting from the exploitation of such film (see "creative accounting," "contract of adhesion," "contractually defined terms" and "discretion").

launch — The commencement of a motion picture release (see "release").

launch windows — Periods of times during which a film may be exhibited in a given market (e.g., theatrical, foreign, video, pay-tv, television network and syndication; see "optimum release pattern" and "release sequence").

law of supply and demand — A basic economic principle providing that to the extent the supply of goods or services is greater than the demand for such goods and services, all other things being equal, the market price for such goods and services will be lower than if the demand was greater than the supply. In the film industry, this law is always at work. For example, there are clearly more talented actors, actresses and directors available for work on motion pictures than there are motion pictures produced in a given year, thus without the support of their respective unions, the compensation for the working actors, actresses and directors would likely be significantly less than it is. In addition, since there are more motion pictures produced each year than there are capable distributors willing to distribute such films (i.e., with available release slots), the distributors are in the stronger bargaining position with respect to the terms of the distribution agreements. In the U.S., the exhibitors have also built so many theater screens that the distributors tend to have the advantage in negotiating the terms of their exhibition agreements, although a significant fluctuation in the number of films distributed in any given year may have an impact on the bargaining power between such parties. Also, as mentioned elsewhere in this book, some distributors are entering or re-entering the exhibition arena, thus eliminating any question of arm's length negotiation, disparity of bargaining power or the impact of the law of supply and demand as between the distributor and exhibitor in such situations. This presentation of the concept is, of course, an over-simplification, but the law of supply and demand does underlie and influence most of the negotiations between the parties named in this paragraph and many others in the film industry. It would also appear, however, that based on the compilation of reported industry and distributor practices contained herein, certain distributors may have leveraged this basic economic advantage into an abusive dominance which could under certain circumstances be criminal. As indicated above, the disparity in bargaining power between distributors and others in the industry is partly based on this law of supply and demand, however, industry interest groups, such as unions, guilds, professional or trade associations, or even film schools, seem to be either unaware of the critical need to take steps to reduce this great disparity and unaware of the impact such legitimate action might have on the economic fortunes of the smaller numbers remaining in the field, or in the alternative, they are unwilling to take such actions. It is important to note that the antitrust laws do apply to the activities of such groups and that any measures taken to reduce the numbers of available suppliers of specified services in given field must comply with such laws (see "antitrust laws," "buyer's market," "inferior bargaining position," "market value," "negotiate," "predatory practices" and "soft market").

lawsuit — (see "action," "litigation" and "suit").

laziness — A human affliction described as a disinclination to work. When it comes to negotiating a custom film distribution agreement that actually fits the interests and needs of two individual parties (the distributor and producer), laziness sometimes plays a part, particularly with the smaller, understaffed film distribution companies. Working through a twenty or thirty page film distribution agreement and making changes requested by a producer is quite tedious. As with the production of any lengthy and complicated document, distribution agreements are often primarily based on some prior distribution agreement either previously used by the present distributor or some other distributor, and as such, may contain numerous provisions that simply do not apply to the transaction being currently negotiated. The term laziness may also apply to producers who allow the financial prospects of their film and all who share in the transactions as profit participants to be controlled by a document whose provisions went largely unnegotiated (see "contract of adhesion" and "negotiate").

lead — The primary acting role in a screenplay or teleplay. There can be two leads — the male and the female (see "principals" or "principal player").

lead bank — (see "participation loan").

lead lender — (see "participation loan").

lead line — A descriptive phrase or sentence used in the advertising and promotion of a film that elaborates on the title of the film (see "hook").

lease — A contract through which one party called the lessor relinquishes his, her or its right to immediate possession of property while retaining ultimate legal ownership or title (see "lessee," "lessor" and "title").

legal department — A major administrative unit of the typical motion picture studio/distributor that is primarily responsible for negotiating the details of and drafting the long form agreements on behalf of the studio with producers, directors, talent and writers or their respective agents (see "business affairs department," "creative affairs department," "deal memo," "long form agreement," "production department" and "studio").

legal opinion — Although there may be many types of legal opinions, in film finance the term may refer to a statement provided by an attorney relating to the legality of the issuance of securities in a public/registered or private/exempt offering (see "corporate stock," "federal tax discussion," "limited partnership," "public offering" and "tax opinion").

legal proceedings — A required disclosure in securities offerings through which the issuer provides information regarding any material pending legal proceedings, other than ordinary routine litigation incidental to the business of the issuer, to which the issuer is a party or to which any of its property is subject (see "disclosure document" and "securities").

legend — In securities terminology, an all-caps, bold face statement or paragraph (usually some sort of disclaimer) required to be prominently displayed in a required securities disclosure document (prospectus or offering memorandum) as a condition of relying on an available federal or state exemption from the securities registration requirement or in the use of a specific form of registration (see "conditions and limitations," "investor suitability requirements," "private placement," "public offering" and "purchaser representations").

legs — An attribute of a film in release meaning it has strong ongoing and continuing audience appeal and that its positive word-of-mouth assures a long play in theaters (see "word-of-mouth").

lender — Individual or firm that extends money to a borrower with the expectation of being repaid on a date certain, usually with interest. In the event of a corporate liquidation, lenders are paid before stockholders receive distributions (see "debt" and "lender financing").

lender financing — The funding of the production costs of a motion picture through some form of loans. Some lending organizations that regularly lend movie production funds are not organized as banks, however, most of such loans come from the entertainment lending divisions of banks located in Los Angeles or New York. Lender financing transaction for motion pictures include the worldwide negative pickup, the domestic negative pickup, international negative pickup, foreign pre-sales, gap financing, super-gap and insurance backed schemes (see "bank loans" and "inter-party agreement").

lender legal fees — Compensation paid out of the loaned funds to attorneys who represent the bank or lender in a production loan transaction, thus adding to the principal the producer has borrowed and increasing the amount of interest earned by the bank. It is in the producer's interest to seek a cap on such fees, although some banks will not permit the imposition of a ceiling (see "cap," "cost of capital," "lender financing" and "negative pickup").

lender risk elimination — Banks and other lenders who regularly lend monies to motion picture producers for the production costs of a movie or movies generally attempt to assign, neutralize or eliminate all of their non-credit risks in the transaction including title risk, insurable risks, completion and delivery risk, box office risk, cash-flow risk and currency risk. Thus, the only remaining risk for the lender in such transaction relates to the credit-worthiness of the distributor furnishing the distribution guarantee (see "bank loans" and "insurable risk" and "interest rate risk").

lending agreement — (see "loan-out agreement").

lending standards — The criteria a bank establishes and follows in making film production loans (e.g., a certain percentage of a film's budget must be secured by distribution and other contracts and/or other collateral, the producer and director must have a successful track record and a completion bond must be in place; see "completion bond" and "track record").

lessee — One who holds an interest in property by virtue of a lease (see "lease" and "lessor").

lessor — One who grants a lease to another, thereby transferring an exclusive right of possession and use of certain property which is subject to the lease and subject only to the rights expressly retained by the lessor in the lease agreement (see "lease" and "lessee").

letter agreement — (see "letter of agreement").

letter of agreement — A short written agreement in letter form. This shorter form of agreement (i.e., more brief than a so-called fully-negotiated or long-form agreement), does not usually contain all of the terms and provisions of the more complete agreement and is used to shorten the negotiation process so that pre-production or production on a motion picture may begin. Such agreements usually recite that at some time in the future, other terms and provisions will be negotiated and added to or incorporated within the short form agreement. It may be important to set a specific deadline for completing and signing the long-form agreement, because if a dispute arises before the longer agreement is in effect, the dispute will have to be resolved based on the provisions of the shorter agreement. In contrast, some argue that it is better to forego the more detailed agreement since many parties in the film industry do not have the bargaining power to actually conduct arm's length negotiations resulting in a fully-negotiated agreement with the other party anyway (similar to "short form agreement"; see "contract of adhesion," "deal memo," "letter of intent," "long form agreement" and "standard contract").

letter of credit (LC) — A financing transaction in which a bank issues to a borrower a letter authorizing the borrower to draw on the bank for a stated amount for a specified period and guaranteeing to accept the drafts on the bank if they are made. A letter of credit is not a standby letter of credit if it may be drawn upon in the absence of default in payment of the underlying evidence of indebtedness. Limited partners in some film partnerships are asked to obtain such letters, which may be used as security for partnership loans. Also, some foreign distributors offering pre-sale contracts may be required to put up U.S. dollar denominated letters of credit before their contracts will be discounted by U.S. banks (see "irrevocable letter of credit," "negative pickup," "split rights deal," "standby letter of credit" and "U.S. dollar denominated letters of credit").

letter of intent (completion guarantor) — A letter of intent issued by a feature film completion guarantor confirming that it is prepared, in principle, to grant a guarantee of completion, subject to certain conditions. The following conditions are generally included: that the completion guarantor is satisfied with the budget, script, shooting schedule and delivery requirements; that the financing for the approved budget (including an agreed upon contingency reserve) is in place; that all agreements for the acquisition of rights, and the employment of all creative elements and key personnel are available; and that other items

including but not limited to insurance, studio, and location agreements, etc., are satisfactory (see "pre-production").

letter of intent (general legal) — A written communication setting out a preliminary understanding of the parties. Such a letter is generally not considered a contract (i.e., does not constitute a binding agreement and creates no liability as between the parties). Rather, it is an expression of the tentative intentions of the parties; an agreement to agree. In other words, a contract to make a contract is not a contract. However, if a formal writing is contemplated by the parties and the letter of intent is properly drafted, a binding contract may arise between the parties before this latter writing is executed as long as there has been a meeting of the minds concerning the essential elements of the writing (see "contract").

letter of intent (film) — A written communication from a director, actor, actress or other person (or company) who has been invited to be involved in the production or distribution of a film, expressing the intent of such person (or company) to perform whatever services he, she or it has been asked to perform on that movie contingent upon certain specified conditions being met (e.g., agreement on mutually acceptable compensation, production monies being raised and/or no contractual commitments that would interfere with such person's or company's availability at the time they are needed to work on the film). A letter of intent expresses a higher level of commitment than a letter of interest but may or may not be legally binding depending on the language used [see "letter of intent (general legal)," "letter of interest" and "pre-production"].

letter of intent (securities) — A negotiated agreement between an underwriter and a corporation seeking a public offering of its securities that sets out the amount of the issue, calls for preparation of a registration statement and formation of an underwriting group, states the proposed maximum and minimum offering price and the maximum percentage for underwriting discounts and determines how expenses will be allocated (see "broker/dealer," "corporate stock," "public offering," "securities" and "underwriter").

letter of intent to acquire literary property — A party's statement of his, her or its intention to purchase a literary work under certain stated circumstances. Such letters are often given or requested to indicate the purchasing party's level of interest in the property (see "letter of intent/film" and "letter of intent/general legal").

letter of interest — A written communication from a person who has been approached regarding the possibility that they might play some role or perform some function relating to the production of a motion picture, that expresses their interest in participating in the project pending its further development, funding of the film and/or after further talks at a later date. A producer, for example, may want to obtain letters of interest or so-called letters of support from a distributor while seeking funding for a project. Although some in the industry suggest that such letters are "worthless," it would be more accurate to say that such letters are not intended to be binding, but they do show that the producer has identified certain film distributors, that the producer has presented the film project to such distributors and the distributors were at least interested enough to say in writing (if this is what they said) that when the project is funded and produced they would like

to see it to determine at that time whether they would have any interest in distributing the completed film (also sometimes called "letters of support"; see "letter of intent").

letter of support — (same as "letter of interest").

level playing field — An expression which, when used with respect to a particular industry, such as the film industry, refers to whether the rules of the game are the same for all of the players, or whether the environment ("field") in which the business is conducted provides a fair opportunity for all to participate on an equal basis. Some industry observers suggest that the primary reason for most of the failures of the independent production and distribution companies in recent years relates to this issue of the "level playing field" and not "lack of hits" or "poor financial management" as others might suggest (see "anti-competitive business practices," "antitrust laws," "blind bidding," "contract of adhesion," "creative accounting," "financial management," "hit," "leverage," "reciprocal preferences" and "unethical business practices").

leverage — In the context of film industry negotiations, the power to control or influence others. The concept is extremely important in determining the outcome of negotiations as between film distributors and producers. A different form of leverage, financial leverage refers to the amount of debt a company has in relation to its equity. The more long-term debt the company has, the greater the financial leverage. Some industry observers point out that the extensive use of financial leverage was not part of the business culture prior to the 1970's and suggest that most failures of feature film production companies are associated with excessive use of financial leverage (see "clout," "computer modeling," "contract of adhesion," "debt," "equity," "financial management," "law of supply and demand," "level playing field," "most favored nations clause," "pari passu" and "power").

levy — To raise or collect; to seize or assess. Also an amount levied (see "dues and assessments," "foreign tax credits" and "tax").

liable — The state of being obligated according to law (see "liability" and "limited liability").

liability — An obligation to do or refrain from doing something; a duty which eventually must be performed. Also an obligation to pay money; signifying money owed, as opposed to an asset. The term is also used to refer to one's responsibility for his, her or its conduct, such as in contractual liability or tort liability (see "corporation," "joint venture," "limited liability," "limited partnership" and "tort").

liability insurance — Insurance that protects a film producer against the risks involved in engaging in various activities that may generate pecuniary obligations (see "errors and omissions insurance," "insurance" and "property damage liability insurance").

liability limitation — A contractual provision that limits the responsibility or exposure of a given party for certain risks or obligations. If, for example, a film distributor assumes the burden of protecting a film's copyright against infringement, it may also incur some potential liability if it fails to act conscientiously in the protection of such copyright. Thus, the distributor may seek a provision in the distribution agreement which limits its liability for its own conduct in attempting to protect the film's copyright. The producer, particularly if the distribution rights granted are limited, may want to negotiate to see that such limits do not protect the distributor against willful misconduct or gross negligence and possibly even negligent conduct, because such limits may not provide enough incentive for the distributor to act conscientiously to protect the copyright (see "copyright infringement," "errors and omissions insurance" and "liability").

libel — A tort consisting of a false and malicious publication made or printed for the purpose of defaming one who is living (see "defamation," "defamation of character," "public figure," "slander" and "tort").

library — [see "catalog (library)"].

library values — The monetary worth of a collection of films owned by a movie distributor or production company (see "asset value").

license — A right granted that gives a person or entity permission to do something which he, she or it could not legally do absent such permission (i.e., a grant of permission by the licensor for the licensee to do a particular thing, to exercise a certain privilege or to carry on a particular business). In film, license agreements typically include the agreement between a film's producer and distributor and the agreements between the distributor and other parties that outline the rights and limitations relating to the use of the film and the profit split or consideration. Film license agreements are thus used for granting film distribution, theatrical exhibition, home video, television, merchandising and other film rights. A film license is generally characterized by a time limitation and conveys control but not ownership of such rights (see "assign," "copyright license," "distribution agreement," "grant of rights," "licensee," "mechanical license" and "release").

license agreement — The contract between a distributor and an exhibitor for the exhibition of a motion picture by the exhibitor. Also, any of the agreements as between the distributor of a film and sub-distributors, territorial distributors and others (such as video companies) who obtain rights to exploit a feature film from the distributor. Although, technically the distribution agreement itself, as between the production company and the film's distributor is a license agreement, it is more commonly referred to as a "distribution agreement" (see "distribution agreement" and "license").

licensed media — A provision in a film distribution agreement that sets out the specific forms of communication vehicles through which the motion picture may be distributed and/or exploited (e.g., theatrical, non-theatrical, free and pay television and home video; see "licensed term" and "licensed territory").

licensed term — The number of years that a distributor, sub-distributor, territorial distributor has to exploit a film (e.g., seven years commencing from the delivery of the picture; see "licensed media," "licensed territory" and "perpetual rights").

licensed territory — The geographical area in which a distributor or sub-distributor is authorized to distribute a film (e.g., in the United States and Canada, including their territories and possessions, the military installations of such countries wherever situated, and on ships and airlines flying the flag of the U.S. or Canada; see "licensed media," "licensed term" and "sub-distributor").

licensee — One to whom a license has been granted. A film distributor, sub-distributor, exhibitor and other parties who are licensed to exploit a film in any manner may all be licensees (see "distributor," "exhibitor," "sub-distributor" and "video companies").

license fees — The compensation paid to a licensor for the grant of rights provided in a licensing agreement (see "licensed territory" and "licensee").

license for merchandising agreement — (see "merchandising agreement").

license of stills/excerpts — A written agreement between a feature film producer and the owner of a prior motion picture that provides the producer with the owner's permission to use excerpts or stills from the earlier movie. Such licenses are primarily used for the purpose of avoiding the possibility of future claims (e.g., copyright infringement; see "clip," "excerpts," "film clip license" and "production still").

license period — (see "licensed term").

licensing agreement — Any of the written agreements executed by and between a film's producer and distributor as well as between the distributor and other parties granting the producer's or distributor's permission for such parties to exploit the film in a specified manner and for consideration (see "license" and "merchandising agreement").

licensing process — The activities engaged in, the procedures used and the negotiations involved while a feature film distributor is contracting with exhibitor's and sub-distributors for the exploitation of a film. Typically, the final print of a film is not available for screening at the beginning of this process (as between the distributor and exhibitor) thus, the exhibitors often have to make their offers based on a very sketchy information provided by a distributor. Such information usually only includes the names of the principals involved in the film and a brief synopsis of the plot. Some exhibitors complain that such a small amount of disclosure relating to a film does not allow them to adequately assess a film's potential profitability or its suitability for their particular patrons (see "anti-blind bidding statutes," "blind bidding," "licensing terms," "locked picture" and "trade screening").

licensing term — The provisions of feature film agreements authorizing the exploitation of a film, including in a distribution deal, contingencies, picture specifications, consideration, rights, financing arrangements, credit provisions, representations and warranties, indemnification, etc. In the licensing agreements between the distributor and exhibitors or sub-distributors, such terms might include the length of the run (term), territory, media, rights and fees. Film rental fees are usually calculated on a weekly basis and a floor, if any, declines each week during the run until it reaches a specified minimum. Consequently, it is generally to the advantage of the exhibitor to secure successful films with longer runs since the exhibitor typically retains a larger percentage of the box office gross as the run is extended ("floor," "long-run engagement" and "run").

licensor — One who grants a license (e.g., a producer who retains ownership rights in a film may grant a license to a distributor). A distributor may in turn grant a license to a sub-distributor or exhibitor (see "licensee").

lie, cheat and steal syndrome — The signs and symptoms of a pattern of business practices and behavior that seem to occur regularly in the film industry and can be characterized by a lack of basic honesty or ethics and motivated by greed. Producers should always check with other producers that have done business with a distributor in the past before going forward with a distribution agreement (see "business practices," "contract of adhesion," "creative accounting," "greed," "insider's game," "predatory practices," "proclivity for wrongful conduct," "reciprocal preferences" and "unethical business practices").

lien — A charge, hold, claim or encumbrance upon the property of another as security for some debt or charge; not title to property but a charge upon it. The term connotes the right that the law gives to have a debt satisfied out of such property (see "claim," "clearance," "encumbrance" and "title").

limitation of liability — A ceiling on the amount of money an investor in a corporation, limited partnership or LLC is responsible for paying as a result of a lawsuit against the entity. Generally such investor liability is limited to the amount of the investor's investment (see "cap," "ceiling," "liability" and "limited liability" and "limited liability company").

limitations on resale — A securities limitation typically imposed pursuant to federal and state exemptions from the securities registration requirements providing that following the initial sale, such securities cannot be resold unless they are registered with the SEC and in each state where sales are anticipated or, in the alternative, are separately qualified for available exemptions from registration (see "conditions and limitations").

limitations on manner of offering — Securities restrictions typically imposed pursuant to federal and state exemptions from securities registration requirements (e.g., that neither the issuer nor any person acting on its behalf may offer or sell such securities by any form of general solicitation or general advertising, including but not limited to (1) any advertisement, article, notice or other communication published in any newspaper, magazine, or similar media or broadcast over television or radio and (2) any seminar or meeting whose attendees have been invited by any general solicitation or general advertising; see "broker/dealer sales," "cold call," "conditions and limitations," "finder sales," "general solicitation," "issuer sales" and "Regulation D").

limited engagement — A phrase used in conjunction with a film's exhibition that suggests that a motion picture is to be exhibited at that theater for a shorter time than usual (see "general release," "mini-multiple" and "wide release").

limited liability — The limitation placed on the amount an investor can lose resulting from a lawsuit against the entity invested in or other loss suffered by such entity. Liability for corporate shareholders, limited partnership investors and investors in LLCs is generally limited to the amount such investors invested (see "corporation," "liability," "limitation of liability," "limited liability company" and "limited partnership").

limited liability company — An entity and fairly recently authorized form of doing business that combines ownership and management characteristics of both the corporation and the limited partnership. The LLC is a flow-through tax vehicle similar to the LP. It can be managed in a democratic style similar to a general partnership (member-managed LLC) or in a more corporate style with management by designated managers (see corporation," limited partnership," "member-managed LLC" and "manager-managed LLC").

limited offering exemption (LOE) — The term generally applied to the state transactional exemptions from the securities registration requirement that are somewhat compatible with the federal Regulation D exemption (see "conditions and limitations," "small offering exemption," "Regulation D" and "ULOE").

limited partners — Purchasers of interests or units in a limited partnership offering who are accepted as unit holders by the partnership's general partner(s). A limited partner is a partner in a limited partnership whose liability to partnership creditors is limited to the amount of his, her or its investment in the partnership, any additional amounts he, she or it may be obligated to contribute under terms of the partnership agreement and his or her share of undistributed partnership earnings. A limited partner may lose his, her or its limited liability status by participating beyond a permitted level in the control of the partnership (same as "unit holders" in many partnerships although it is possible to be a unit holder and not be a limited partner in situations where a unit is subsequently transferred and the general partner has not yet approved the new unit holder as a limited partner (see "unit holder" or "unit purchaser" and "silent partner").

limited partnership— A state regulated form of doing business which is a special form of partnership that has both general and limited (or silent partners). A limited partnership is an entity created by two or more persons and having one or more general partners and one or more limited partners. The activities of the limited partnership are controlled primarily by the partnership agreement between the general partners and the limited partners and pursuant to the state's limited partnership act. A limited partnership is an entity in which one or more persons, with unlimited liability (the general partners) manage the partnership, while one or more other persons only contribute money, property or their past services for interests in the limited partnership (called limited partners). The limited partners have no right to participate in the day-to-day management and operation of the business and assume no liability beyond their contribution. Interests in limited partnerships are securities, therefore the federal and state securities laws must be complied with in raising funding for a film using the financing vehicle of a limited partnership. The various state partnership acts provide a producer/general partner with more flexibility in structuring the deal as between the general and limited partners than corporate statutes provide (see "corporation," "creative control," "financing," "general partner," "joint venture," "lender financing," "offering," "passive investor financing," "securities" and "syndication").

limited partnership agreement — The written agreement between the general partner(s) and limited partner(s) in the creation of a limited partnership. A written limited partnership agreement is generally required by state law as part of the process of forming a limited partnership. Such agreement also defines and controls the relationship as between the parties. To the extent an issue is not provided for in the limited partnership agreement, the applicable state's limited partnership act will typically control. A common misconception held by some independent feature film producers is that a limited partnership agreement is all that is needed to raise money by means of a film limited partnership. The limited partnership agreement by itself is not enough to either create a limited partnership or to make offers and sell interests in the limited partnership. The creation of the limited partnership entity requires a filing with the secretary of state in the state in which the limited partnership is being organized and compliance with other provisions of that state's limited partnership act. In addition, the offer and sale of interests in limited partnerships requires compliance with both the federal and state securities laws, which in turn mandate, among other things, the written disclosure of all material aspects of the transaction to prospective investors (see "anti-fraud rule," "disclosure document," "limited partnerships," "offering memorandum," "prospectus" and "security" or "securities").

limited partnership investment agreement — (see "limited partnership agreement").

limited release — The exhibition of a motion picture in a small, specific area or nationally with a limited number of prints (e.g., fifty or less). Sometimes the limited release is used for test marketing (i.e., to sample audience reaction to a film), to limit the risk of financial loss on a given film or as part of a regional release pattern (see "general release," "mini-multiple," "print," "release pattern" and "wide release").

limited review — An accountant's review of financial statements that does not rise to the level of a full audit. In certain circumstances, a limited review, which is less expensive than a full audit, may be sufficient to provide a financier, investor group, producer or net profit participants with an adequate level of comfort (see "accountant's opinion" and "audit").

limited use — An accounting term used with regard to prospective financial statements and referring to the use of such statements by the responsible party alone or by the responsible party and third parties with whom the responsible party is negotiating directly (e.g., negotiations for a bank loan, submission to a regulatory agency) and meaning that the financial statement is to be used solely within that entity. Third-party recipients of prospective financial statements intended for limited use can ask questions of the responsible party and negotiate terms directly with it. Any type of prospective financial statements that would be useful in the circumstances would normally be appropriate for limited use. Thus, the presentation may be a financial forecast or a financial projection (see "general use," "financial forecasts," "financial projections," "prospective financial statements" and "responsible party").

limits on dividends — In bank lending, barriers imposed by the lending bank on a corporation's ability to pay dividends to its shareholders. However, such a limit or barrier on dividends in a loan agreement may help a company avoid an IRS tax imposed on the unreasonable accumulation of retained earnings (see "corporation" and "lender financing").

line of credit — A bank's moral commitment, as opposed to its contractual commitment, to make loans to a particular borrower up to a specified maximum during a specified period. Bank lines of credit may be based solely on the financial statements and quality of the people associated with a film production or distribution company and such funds may provide working capital to buy scripts, turn novels into screenplays and scout site locations, among other things (also called "bank lines" and "lender financing").

line producer — The supervisor of below-the-line elements of a film during its production. The line producer is generally an employee of the production company and is primarily responsible for seeing that the film is completed on time and within the prescribed budget. In some situations, a line producer may report to a production manager but on other pictures, particularly lower-budgeted projects, the responsibilities of the production manager and line producer may be combined into one job. A completion guarantor may insist that a line producer with an excellent track record be hired for a certain film before it will approve the bond for that picture (see "completion guarantor," "creative producer," "executive producer," "producer," "production manager" and "unit production manager").

liquid asset — Cash or something that is easily convertible into cash. A corporation's liquid assets may include cash, marketable securities and accounts receivable. An investor in an illiquid investment such as a privately placed limited partnership is required to have substantial liquid assets that would serve as a financial cushion if the illiquid investment does not work out favorably (see "illiquid" and "investor suitability standards").

liquidate — To settle; to determine the amount due, and to whom due, and having done so, to extinguish the indebtedness. Also, to sell; to reduce the value of an object or an asset to its cash value. To liquidate a business means to assemble and mobilize the assets, settle with the creditors and debtors, and apportion the remaining assets, if any, among the owners (see "asset value" and "bankruptcy").

liquidating dividend — A distribution of assets in the form of dividends from a corporation that is going out of business (i.e., in the process of liquidating; see "corporate stock" and "liquidate").

liquidating value — Projected price for an asset of a company that is going out of business (also called "auction value"; see "liquidate").

liquidation — The dismantling of a business, paying off debts in order of priority and distributing the remaining assets in cash to the owners. Involuntary liquidation is covered under Chapter 7 of the federal bankruptcy law (see "bankruptcy," "corporate stock," "dissolution" and "winding up").

liquidator — In a limited partnership context, the person or persons who liquidate the partnership pursuant to the partnership agreement (see "limited partnership" and "liquidation").

listed security — A security that has been listed for trading on one of the stock exchanges or that has been listed with the SEC (see "publicly held" and "stock exchange").

listed stock — Corporate stock that is traded on an organized stock exchange. Such companies must satisfy the requirements of the exchange on which their stock is traded in addition to those of the SEC (see "publicly held," "Securities and Exchange Commission" and "stock exchange").

listing — A paid entry in a regular list of movies playing locally that is published in a newspaper or magazine (see "advertising").

listing requirements — Rules that must be met before a stock is listed for trading on an exchange (see "listed stock").

literary material — Writings that may be used as the basis for a feature film including stories, adaptations, books, treatments, scenarios, continuities, teleplays, screenplays, dialogues, scripts, sketches, plots, outlines, narrative synopses, routines and narrations (see "literary property," "property" and "underlying rights").

literary property — A literary work upon which a motion picture may be based. The term is more narrow than underlying property since the latter may include literary as well as other material on which a motion picture may be based (see "literary materials," "literary works," "novel," "option," "purchase" and "underlying property").

literary works — (see "literary material").

litigants — The parties involved in a lawsuit or litigation (see "action" and "litigation").

litigation — Lawsuit, a controversy that is presented to a court, at least through the initial filings (see "action," "arbitration," "final judgment" and "mediation").

litigation budget — The monies required to initiate, maintain and pursue a lawsuit. Such budget may include filing fees and other court costs, investigatory expenses and attorney fees. In addition to auditing funds, an independent producer may need to set aside some funds to cover litigation costs in the event a dispute arises with respect to a film's distribution and the distributor's accounting for profit participations (see "audit" and "litigation").

litigation disclaimer — A contractual clause, usually found among the producer warranties in the film distribution agreement, that is a general disclaimer by the producer that there is any litigation pending that could impair distribution of the picture. The producer may want to obtain corresponding representations and warranties from the distributor along with indemnification (see "indemnification" and "warranty").

live stage production — A theatrical presentation involving live performers (see "live stage rights").

live stage rights — The authority to exploit a version of a film presented as a theatrical presentation involving live performers (see "live stage production").

living expenses — The ordinary costs of maintaining a person away from his or her home while on location or other assignment relating to the production of a motion picture (see "budget," "exclusive ground transportation," "perks," "rising production costs" and "transportation costs").

LLC — (see limited liability company).

LLC articles of organization — The initial document required to be filed with the secretary of state in the state in which a limited liability company is being formed (see "LLC operating agreement").

LLC distributable cash — LLC gross revenues minus any deductions authorized by the LLC's operating agreement (same as LLC net profits).

LLC gross revenues — All monies earned by and received by the LLC for LLC activities (e.g., the production and distribution of a feature film).

LLC manager — The individual, individuals, entity or entities designated in the operating agreement to manage the operations of a manager-managed limited liability company.

LLC operating agreement — The contract between the manager(s) of a limited liability company and its member/investors that sets forth the rules for operating the company.

loan — The delivery of a sum of money to another under contract to return an equivalent amount at some future time with or without an additional sum agreed upon for its use (i.e., interest). The characterization of a transaction as a loan or some other type of borrowing has significance in ascertaining whether usury laws apply to the amount of interest being charged, or in the alternative in determining whether the transaction should be more properly characterized as some form of equity investment that may also involve the sale of a security (contrast with "investment" and "security" or "securities"; see "bank loan," "debt" and "interest").

loan documentation — All of the documents prepared by the lending institution relating to a loan and the documents required to be provided by the producer in obtaining a loan (see "loan").

loan-out agreement — The written contract between an individual artist and a company that sets out the terms and conditions of the relationship which has been created for the purpose of hiring out the services of the artist to third parties through the company (also called "lending agreement"; see "inducement letter," "loan-out arrangement," "loan-out company" and "straight employment agreement").

loan-out arrangement — The agreement between an individual artist and a corporation owned by such artist whereby such company provides the artist for employment through the company to third party employers. The concept originally developed to take advantage of certain tax laws that favored such arrangements, however, not all of those tax benefits are still in effect, thus the desirability of creating such an arrangement for a given artist depends on an analysis of the impact of the current tax laws on the special circumstances of a specific individual (see "inducement letter," "loan-out agreement" and "loan-out company").

loan-out company — A corporation or other entity owned by an individual artist that contractually furnishes the services of such individual to a third party (e.g., a motion picture production company; see "loan-out agreement" and "loan-out arrangement").

loan-out corporation — (see "loan-out company").

loan sharking — The practice of lending money at usurious rates of interest. Many states have laws that render usurious interest, and in some instances even the underlying debt, uncollectible (see "extortion" and "usury").

lobby card — A standard size poster used for display in a movie theater lobby or outside the theater. A lobby card is smaller than a one-sheet (see "one-sheet," "poster" and "sell-sheet").

lobbyists — Persons engaged in the business of seeking to persuade public officials, especially legislators to pass laws that are favorable and to defeat those that are unfavorable to their interests or the interests of their clients, or to assist in the drafting of acceptable provisions for such legislation. Lobbyists usually work for professional or trade associations, labor groups, corporations or other organizations whose interests may be affected by a given piece of legislation. The activities of lobbyists are regulated by statute in most jurisdictions (see "association projects," "industry groups," "MPAA," "Paramount Consent Decree of 1948," "political influence," "professional association" and "TriStar Case").

lobbying — Activities engaged in by persons (lobbyists) in an attempt to persuade legislators (and in some cases government regulators) to pass or vigorously enforce laws or regulations that are favorable to their interests or the interests of their clients, or to defeat, amend or not vigorously enforce those laws or regulations that are unfavorable. The activities of lobbyists are generally regulated by statute, and contrary to what is often suggested in the press, there is nothing wrong with lobbying per se. Lobbyists merely represent the interests of organized interest groups and most significant interests are represented by lobbyists. If a significant interest is not represented by lobbyists, it should be. In the motion picture industry some segments of the industry (e.g., major motion picture producers and distributors) are well represented by their trade associations, which vigorously lobby on behalf of the interests of their member companies while other segments of the same industry (e.g., independent producers) are not organized at the industry level in a manner that will permit the effective advocacy of their interests with respect to important issues. Thus, certain laws, government regulations and/or the enforcement of such laws and regulations are not likely to be favorable to the interests of the unrepresented group. That in fact may be the case with respect to questions relating to the enforcement of the federal antitrust laws, (specifically vertical integration), blind bidding, block booking, the motion picture rating system, the membership policies of certain industry associations, controlled theaters, etc. Some in the industry consider it foolish for independent producers to try to function in an industry without an effective advocacy group representing their interests at the industry level and that the circumstances for the independent producer are likely to continue to deteriorate without such representation (see "antitrust laws," "association projects," "contract of adhesion," "creative accounting," "industry groups," "lobbyists," "major exhibition chains," "marketplace of ideas," "market share," "MPAA," "number of screens" and "political influence").

local stations — Television stations that broadcast programming within a limited geographical area (see "syndication").

locomotives — High profile, 'A' level" motion pictures that are part of a package of films sold in syndication or in foreign territories. These "locomotives" drive the package (i.e., motivate buyers to purchase the package of films just to get access to these few good pictures; see "allocation issues," "package" and "syndication").

location — Any place, other than the studio lot, where films may be shot. The term is also used to refer to the geographical site of a motion picture theater (see "right of consultation" and "set").

location accountant — A person hired by a production company, a producer or a payroll service company and assigned to work on a film's location and to generate regular written reports that account for all the money spent while the film is being shot on location (see "completion guarantor," "production

accountant" and "production-financing/distribution agreement").

location agreement — The written contract between a feature film production company and the owner of a specifically identifiable site or building that is to be used in or portrayed in a movie (see "stage agreement").

location fee — The consideration or compensation paid for the use of a site and the facilities thereon in the process of shooting a motion picture (see "location permit").

location filming — The shooting of scenes for a motion picture at any place other than on a studio lot or in a studio sound stage. Many states in the United States have established film commissions that aggressively compete to attract location filming and the accompanying expenditure of funds for their state. In reaction to the passage of anti-blind bidding statutes in some states, certain major studio/distributors once threatened to (and may have in some instances) restricted their location filming to states that have not passed such legislation (see "anti-blind bidding statutes," "blind bidding," "economic reprisal," "film commission," "lobbying," "location," "location list," "location permit" and "state legislatures").

location list — A record or inventory of sites that are available and suitable for shooting scenes for a film on location (see "location manager").

location manager — The film production person responsible for all film logistical matters relating to the use of film shooting sites other than the studio lot. Generally, the location manager will help to identify the locations that are called for by a given script, scout the locations, take or acquire location photographs, analyze and evaluate the suitability of various locations, budget the cost of using the prospective locations, consult with the film's director, producer and production designer regarding the use of such locations, and then after locations are chosen, arrange for needed releases and negotiate the terms for the use of such locations. The location manager also is responsible for making the arrangements for location permits, parking, catering, necessary police and fire personnel and other matters relating to the specific locations (see "location list" and "location permit").

location permit — Licenses often required and granted (usually for a fee) by local governmental units for the privilege of going onto private or government owned property to shoot scenes for a movie (see "location filming" and "location manager").

location scout — An individual who seeks to identify appropriate sites for shooting a film on location and investigates the appropriateness of such sites for scenes to be included in a given film project. A location scout may also serve as the location manager, or work with the location manager.

locked picture — A work print of a finished film of such quality that screening prints may be made therefrom for viewing by potential exhibitors (see "blind bidding," "licensing process," "trade screening" and "work print").

LOE — Acronym for limited offering exemption (see "limited offering exemption" and "securities").

logistics — The procurement, maintenance and transportation of material, facilities and

personnel (see "location filming" and "location manager").

logline — A very brief (one to three line) teaser synopsis of a movie script; something similar to the descriptions of a films typically found in *TV Guide* (see "synopsis").

logo — A signature design or device that is unique and identifiable with a certain product or company. Logos may appear on literature, letterhead, in advertising and in a film. Logos may also include trademarks or service marks (see "service mark" and "trademark").

long form agreement — Contracts that are (at least in theory) fully negotiated and contain all of the terms and provisions intended by the parties thereto. Long form film distribution agreements, for example, relating to the licensing of feature films, are negotiated by and between the film's producer and a distributor (or their legal representatives) and usually include long lists of delivery items, detailed lists of what will be considered distribution expenses, extensive producer warranties, the laboratory access letter and an instrument of transfer. Sometimes, negotiators will initially opt for a letter agreement, deal memo or short form agreement in order to save time, although such a tactic involves certain risks if a dispute on a question not covered by the shorter form of agreement arises before the long form agreement is signed (see "deal memo," "distribution agreement," "fully-negotiated agreement," "letter of agreement" and "short form agreement").

long form distribution agreement — A motion picture distribution agreement that has been fully negotiated and contains all of the terms and provisions intended by the parties thereto. (see "distribution agreement" and "long form agreement").

long-run engagement—An extended exhibition of a motion picture at a theater. The run of most feature films exhibited in the domestic theatrical market do not extend beyond one or two weeks. The very successful films may run as long as ten weeks or more. Distributors have been known to extract twelve week minimum guarantees from exhibitors as part of the licensing terms of certain hoped-for blockbusters (see "licensing process," "licensing terms" and "run").

long-term debt — A liability that is not due for more than a year. Generally, interest payments will come due on long-term debt periodically, typically on a quarterly, semi-annual or annual basis (see "long-term financing").

long-term financing — Liabilities not repayable within one year and of an equity nature (see "debt," "equity" and "long-term debt").

looping — The synchronization of separately recorded film dialogue with its corresponding film image (see "automatic dialogue replacement," "dub" and "synchronization").

loss — Tax term for the excess of expenses over income in a tax year. An individual can deduct only those losses that are incurred in his, her or its trade or business, in a transaction entered into for profit (as opposed to a hobby), or as a result of a casualty or theft (see "capital loss,"

"deductions," "net operating loss" and "passive investment losses").

lot — The grounds of a studio, including administration buildings, production offices, standing sets, sound stages, dressing rooms and all structures, streets and fencing associated therewith (see "on-the-lot deal" and "studio").

low-budget agreement — A Screen Actors Guild agreement that permits its actor members to work on films being produced for less than $2,500,000 for a day rate of $504 dollars or a weekly rate of $1,752, with six day work weeks (with no premium), no consecutive employment (except on overnight locations) and reduced overtime rates. Such rates may change from time to time per SAG rules (see "modified low budget agreement," "screen actors guild," "short film agreement," "student film agreement" and "ultra-low budget agreement").

low-budget films — Generally, feature films in the $1 to $3 million dollar range. However, SAG defines a low budget feature, for purposes of its low budget features agreement to be a feature-length motion picture, intended for theatrical exhibition, at a total production cost not exceeding $2,500,000 or (see "big-budget films," "low budget agreement" and "medium-budget films").

lyricist — One who writes the words to a song (see "music").

lyrics — The words of a song (see "lyricist" and "music").

M

made-for-television product — Feature films made specifically for showing on television and without a theatrical release (see "movie of the week").

made-for-video — Feature film specifically produced for release to video markets only (i.e., without a theatrical or television release; see "direct to video release" and "video companies").

Mafia — Originally, a Sicilian secret criminal society, but a term that is sometimes currently used to describe a secret organization composed chiefly of criminal elements engaged in controlling racketeering, peddling of narcotics, gambling, prostitution and other typically illicit activities throughout the world. Some writer/researchers have alleged that significant Mafia connections and influence have long existed in the capital intensive motion picture industry, but as with antitrust law violations, such allegations have been difficult to prove. In the context of the film industry, the term is sometimes used to describe the Hollywood insider group as the "Jewish Mafia" suggesting that the small group of politically liberal, not very religious, Jewish males of European heritage who have held about 70 percent of the top major studio executive positions for the past one hundred years have gained and maintain that dominance over the industry through the continued use of hundreds of well documented, unfair, unethical, unconscionable, anti-competitive, predatory and/or illegal business practices [Sources: Dan E. Moldea's *Dark Victory*; *Who Really Controls Hollywood* and *Hollywood Wars — How Insiders Gained and Maintain Illegitimate Control Over the Film Industry*; see "antitrust laws," "extortion," "mob controlled distribution company," "money laundering," "movies with a message," "organized crime," "political influence," "racketeering," "RICO," "theft" and "white collar crime").

magazine article — A periodical containing miscellaneous prose compositions usually forming an independent part of the publication. Magazine articles may serve as the basis for a motion picture screenplay (see "clearance" and "underlying property").

magnetic film — An iron oxide coated (light sensitive) strip of plastic, perforated with sprocket holes and containing a thin magnetized audio track that is used for recording sound material in synch with the visual film images, all of which are used to produce negative and positive motion picture prints with sound (see "film").

mag-optical track — Film with multiple sound tracks, one or more of which is magnetic and at least one of which is optical. At the time it was first introduced, the mag-optical track permitted virtually all theaters to exhibit such films regardless of the playback technology the theaters were using. However, the system is no longer in common use (see "optical sound track").

MAIE — (see "model accredited investor exemption").

main and end titles — The titles and credits at the beginning and end of a film (see "end titles").

main elements — (see "elements").

mainstream audience — A broad, general audience, targeted by most commercial film releases (see "projected audience").

maintaining a market — The making of a market by a securities broker/dealer over a long period of time (see "making a market" and "market makers").

main-title billing — All credits appearing at the beginning of a film (see "main and end titles").

major distributors — (same as "major studio/distributors").

major exhibition chains — The largest theater owners who control the most theaters and screens in the best locations. Although ownership interests change from year to year, the major exhibition chains include Regal Entertainment Group, AMC, Cinemark USA, Inc., Carmike Cinemas, Inc., Cineplex Entertainment LP, National Amusements, Inc., Century Theatres, Kerasotes Theatres, Hollywood Theatres, Marcus Theatres Corp., Empire Theatres Limited (see "Exhibitor"). Following the Reagan administration easing of regulatory restraints, the major studio/distributors have regained a certain level of control over some of these major exhibition chains (see "number of screens," "Paramount Consent Decree of 1948," "TriStar Case" and "vertical integration").

major foreign markets — The countries outside the U.S. that currently provide the greatest demand for domestic theatrical entertainment product (i.e., Japan, Germany, Italy, United Kingdom, France, Spain and Australia; similar to "prime foreign territories"; see "foreign market").

majority — The status of a person who has reached the age established by state law for such person to be held legally responsible for his or her actions. The required age may differ among jurisdictions and even with a jurisdiction for different purposes (see "minor" and "minority").

majority-in-interest — In film and other limited partnerships or manager-managed LLCs, more than 50 percent of the interests of limited partners or LLC members, unless otherwise provided for in the partnership or operating agreement (see "interests of limited partners," "limited liability company," "limited partnership" and "unit").

majority shareholder — A corporate owner of shares who controls more than half the outstanding common shares of that corporation (see "principal stockholder," "sole shareholder" and "working control").

major key — A geographical area, relatively well-defined and denoted by a concentrated population (generally of approximately one hundred thousand or more) within a metropolitan setting, by the geographical area's historical ability to produce film rental income for distributors and by the geographical area's media advertising umbrella. An exchange area's major keys generally break a first run movie simultaneously (see "first-run," "first-run theater" and "key").

major markets (U.S.) — New York, Chicago and Los Angeles (see "markets").

major-owned screen — Exhibition outlets (i.e., theatrical screens owned by the major studio/distributors; see "major exhibition chains" and "number of screens").

majors — (see "major studio/distributors" and "major exhibition chains").

major studio/distributors — An unofficial entertainment industry designation that may change from time to time and refers to the largest and most powerful film studio, producer/distributor entities. Objectively speaking, they are "majors" because their film releases garner a major portion of the domestic box office gross in a given year, usually a double digit percentage of market share for each such company. From an exhibitor's perspective, a "major" is any distributor that can provide long-term consistent output of predictably high quality feature films. Generally these so-called "majors" maintain distribution sales offices in the major exchanges in the U.S. and operate sub-depots that function as shipping offices for prints and related promotional materials in the remaining territories. Some industry analysts also include ownership of production studios as an integral part of the definition of "major." In recent years, the "majors" have been generally considered to be the MPAA companies Sony (Columbia Pictures/TriStar), Walt Disney (Buena Vista), Paramount, Twentieth Century Fox, Universal and Warner Bros. Some of the majors have also acquired a number of other successful independent distributors in recent years and have re-entered the exhibition arena during this period of relaxed U.S. Justice Department policy toward certain possible antitrust law violations (see "insider's game," "lobbying," "major exhibition chains," "market share," "member of the club," "MPAA," "number of screens," "political influence," "studio," "studio financing," "studio lots" and "vertical integration").

make-up artists/hair stylists — Film crew who prepare, style, mix and/or apply all facial, body or hair cosmetics; style and/or apply all head, body and facial wigs, hair pieces and transformations in consultation with the producer. Such persons style, cut and/or color hair; perform prosthetic work, including preparation, styling, lab work and application; and consult when the producer elects to engage a consultant for an unusual effect in make-up and/or in hair style (see "cast," "crew," "operational staff," "production staff" and "staff").

making a market — The maintaining of a firm bid and offer price by a securities broker/dealer on a given security by standing ready to buy or sell round lots at publicly quoted prices. A managing underwriter typically makes a market for its client's stock (see "market maker," "maintaining a market" and "round lot").

management — The combined areas of policy and administration for a business. Also the people who make the decisions and provide the supervision necessary to implement the business owners' objectives. In some instances when a major studio/distributor has been acquired by a corporate conglomerate the studio's management team has pretty much stayed in place or has simply been replaced by other Hollywood insiders (see "corporation," "mergers and acquisitions," "officers" and "shareholders").

management fee — A fee or compensation paid for services rendered in connection with the management of a business activity. In film limited partnerships and manager managed LLCs, such fees may be paid to the general partner/producer or manager/producer or to others and may be based on a percentage of offering proceeds during the first year and on a percentage of partnership or LLC gross receipts in subsequent years. Such fees may also be waived by the general partner/manager since such persons of the owners of such entities are often compensated for also serving as producers, directors, writers and otherwise (see "limited liability company" and "limited partnership").

manager-managed LLC — A passive investor investment vehicle in which one or more managers manage the operations and activities of a business organized as an LLC and the member/investors are not involved in helping to make management decisions. Units in manager-managed LLCs are generally considered to be securities and therefore their sales must comply with the federal and state securities laws. LLCs are formed by preparing and filing articles of organization with the secretary of state and the drafting and approval by the members of an LLC operating agreement (see "limited liability

company," "member-managed LLC" and "securities").

managing broker/dealer — Another less formal term for managing underwriter used to describe a broker/dealer firm that takes the lead in organizing a selling group of broker/dealers put together for the distribution of a security in a best efforts offering (see "best efforts," "managing underwriter" and "selling broker/dealer").

managing broker/dealer agreement — The contract between the issuer of securities and the managing broker/dealer setting out the terms under which the managing broker/dealer will organize a selling group of broker/dealers and distribute such securities (see "managing broker/dealer," "selling broker/dealer" and "underwriting agreement").

managing underwriter — The leading and originating investment banking firm of an underwriting group organized for the purchase and distribution of a new issue of securities (also called "syndicate manager"; see "managing broker/dealer" and "underwriter").

manipulation — The buying or selling of a security to create a false appearance of active trading and thus influence other investors to buy or sell shares. Both civil and criminal penalties may apply to this activity (see "corporation," "insider trading," "publicly held," "securities" and "stock exchange").

manner of offering limitation — (see "limitations on manner of offering").

marginal pictures — A subjective term used to describe feature films that are not necessarily expected to be major successes at the box office but still could be financially successful for a distributor (see "blockbuster" and "hit").

marketability — The speed and ease with which a particular security may be bought and sold (see "securities").

marketable security — Security that is of reasonable investment caliber and can be easily sold on the market (i.e., any security for which, as of the date of disposition, there was a market on an established securities market or otherwise; see "securities").

marketable title — Ownership rights that a reasonably well-informed purchaser would, in the exercise of ordinary business prudence, be willing to accept (see "bad title," "clearance" and "title").

marketing — In film distribution, the combined activities of the sales and advertising departments (or outside advertising consultants) of the film distributor. The sales department books pictures into theaters, determines when a film will open, what the release pattern will be and upon what terms the film will be exhibited. The advertising and publicity departments seek to increase the awareness of a film among prospective movie goers and their interest in seeing a film (see "advertising" and "publicity").

marketing campaign — A specific plan or strategy designed to promote awareness of a motion picture and to motivate the general public to go see it (see "advertising campaign," "marketing strategy," "publicity" and "release strategy").

marketing department — The major administrative division of the typical film industry studio/distributor that is primarily responsible for planning and implementing the distribution of motion pictures (see "advertising," "business affairs department," "creative affairs department," "distributor release campaign," "legal department," "marketing," "production department," "release pattern," "release sequence" and "studio").

marketing research — The systematic collection and analysis of demographic and other information relating to potential movie-going audiences used in making motion picture marketing decisions (see "demographics").

marketing strategy — This term may apply to several different situations, including a producer's plan for promoting a film to distributors, the distributor's plan or method used in advertising and promoting a film to exhibitors, the plans of sales agents in marketing to prospective licensees in the ancillary markets and the concepts and plan for selling a movie to the public (i.e., advertising and promoting a motion picture so as to create demand amongst film goers to see the film; see "marketing," "marketing campaign" and "release strategy").

marketing to distributors — The activities undertaken by a film producer in seeking on or more distributors for a completed film. Typically, producers use three methods for marketing a completed film to distributors: (1) hiring a screening room and inviting distributors and their representatives to a screening; (2) seeking to screen the film at various film festivals; and/or (3) reproducing DVD copies of the film and sending them to prospective distributors. Each of these methods costs money, thus, independent producers should allocate some funds to cover such costs (even though these expenses are not considered part of the film's production budget). Also line item sometimes included as a non-film budget item in the estimated use of proceeds section of a film limited partnership or manager-managed LLC offering that sets forth an amount of funds to be used to promote a completed independent film to potential prospective distributors (see "estimated use of proceeds," "producer's representative," and "use of proceeds").

market maker — Securities broker/dealers who create opportunities to buy and sell (i.e., make a market) for a given security (see "making a market," "maintaining a market" and "underwriting").

marketplace of ideas — The worldwide environment in which formulated thoughts or opinions may be expressed. Because of the presumed (or well-established) importance of the motion picture as a vehicle for the expression of ideas, the obvious power of this form of communication and the fact that movies are often exhibited worldwide, it is vitally important that all significant human interests whether based on racial, cultural, religious, socioeconomic, political or other factors be concerned about the use and abuse of the motion picture medium as a means for advocating any of such interests. In other words, all of these interest groups should be concerned as to whether their views are consistently portrayed in a positive or negative fashion through feature films. Thus, to the extent that an industry such as the motion picture business is dominated by a particular interest group that consistently espouses a biased point of view on numerous issues that are presented in films, and to the extent that such an interest group utilizes the practices described in this book to perpetuate its dominance of the industry, other interest groups, including government, may justifiably take action which is both designed to

"level the playing field"and to broaden the points of view expressed through the motion picture medium. Taking such action would inevitably strengthen democracy and the marketplace of ideas (see "antitrust laws," "hidden agendas," "insider's game," "level playing field," "market share" and "movies with a message").

market power — The ability to control or dominate a specific level of an industry (e.g., wholesale or retail). Generally, in the application of the antitrust laws to the film business, market power may be presumed from the fact that the product involved (i.e., motion pictures are copyrighted). However, in recent years, the U.S. Justice Department has taken the position that if a market is not otherwise susceptible to market power wielded by a single firm or a coordinated group of companies, even significant increases in barriers to entry in that market are unlikely to adversely affect competition in the marketplace (see "antitrust laws," "barriers to entry," "merger guidelines," "MPAA," "Paramount Consent Decree of 1948," "political influence," "TriStar Case" and "vertical merger").

markets — Geographical or technological areas of demand for film product, including theatrical and ancillary markets (see "ancillary markets," "foreign territories" and "theatrical market").

market share — The percentage of industry sales of a particular company, product or segment of an industry. In recent years, independently distributed feature films only generated a yearly average percentage of domestic theatrical box office gross in single digits). That means the MPAA company and subsidiary/affiliate distributed films (some of which were produced by independent producers) generated an average of more than 92 percent of the domestic box office gross. One of the more puzzling of motion picture industry phenomena is the rather common occurrence at the annual Academy Awards for independently produced films to win a disproportionate share of the more important awards (e.g., best picture, best director, best actor, best actress and best screenplay), particularly since many of those same award-winning films are not as commercially successful as many of the films produced by the major studio/distributors. Some industry observers would quickly dismiss that anomaly as the result of differences between movies that are targeted for the large mass audience (commercial product) and those that are designed to be small films tailored for a limited but more discriminating audience (not commercial). Another factor in how well these two categories of films are received at the box office may have nothing to do with whether such pictures are quality award winners or merely commercial, but have more to do with which distributors have the market power to get their films shown at theaters, to spend the money to advertise and promote their pictures and the leverage to collect film rentals from exhibitors. Besides, the more artistic award-winning independently produced films, after receiving all of the free publicity and promotion associated with the Academy Awards, are suddenly now more "commercial" and those distributed by the major/studio distributors before the awards can be re-released (or continued in release) to take advantage of their new profit-making potential (see "Academy Awards," "blind bidding," "blockbuster strategy," "cartel," "controlled theater," "major exhibition chains," "market power," "oligopoly," "political influence," "prints and ads commitment" and "settlement").

market value — The price that goods or a property would bring in a market of willing buyers and willing sellers, in the ordinary course of trade (see "law of supply and demand").

marquee — The signboard, usually cantilevered and often lighted, which is most commonly situated in front of a theater, typically above the entrance and box office. It has movable letters that spell out the names of the current and/or coming attractions and the featured performers (see "marquee value" and "star").

marquee value — Actors and actresses who have names that are recognizable to the theater-going public and who have some level of drawing power or so-called "box office appeal" (see "box office appeal," "marquee value" and "star").

mass advertising campaign — A film marketing and promotion program that is directed to the general public primarily through radio, television and newspapers (see "advertising" and "advertising campaign").

mass audience — A large cross section of society (see "blind bidding," "homogeneous films" and "projected audience").

mass exodus — A phenomenon seen in the executive suites of the Hollywood-based major studio/distributors from time to time, when a group of Hollywood insider executives leave a studio en masse or threaten to leave, either when new ownership of the studio is acquired by Hollywood outsiders or is being threatened.

mass marketing — A commercial marketing approach for films that provides high visibility in all media and in many theaters (see "direct advertising," "homogeneous films" and "projected audience").

master agreement — A licensing agreement or "blanket deal" covering the exhibition of features in a number of theaters, usually comprising a circuit (see "circuit" and "formula deal").

master limited partnership (MLP) — A limited partnership formed under state partnership law where the limited partnership interests are publicly traded (e.g., on the New York Stock Exchange or "over the counter"). Unless a securities registration exemption applies, interests in MLPs are required to be registered. The term "master limited partnership" originates from the structure of the entity. Partnership interests are issued to a "master" limited partner who then arranges for the sale of the units to the public (also called "publicly traded partnership"; see "limited partnership").

master positive — A positive film with special photographic characteristics that make it suitable for serving as a master from which a series of dupe negatives can be printed while minimizing any loss of quality (see "print").

master scene — A primary dialogue or action scene in a motion picture in which the characters are developed or the plot is advanced (see "master shot" and "scene").

master script — The final shooting script from which all others are duplicated (see "screenplay" and "shooting script").

master shot (or master scene) — A complete movie scene covering all dialogue and action in the widest and longest shot. Into this scene are added cutaway shots, close-ups, medium shots, etc. All of these shots are called coverage or cover shots. Sometimes the problem of matching physical action is handled by simultaneous multi-camera filming/taping. However, the master shot is the scene to which all else is referenced in editing and to which all other action must be synchronized or matched (see "scene").

material — Important, necessary or substantial (see "anti-fraud rule," "breach of contract," "material breach" and "material tax issue").

material breach — In contract law, a breach that is substantial and operates to excuse further performance by the aggrieved party. A material breach impairs the value of the contract and gives rise to an action for breach of contract (see "breach of contract" and "material").

material fact — Securities terminology for information of reasonably sufficient importance to be disclosed to investors in a securities offering (i.e., a fact which, if called to the attention of a reasonably prudent investor, would tend to influence, either positively or negatively, the investor's judgment relative to buying or selling the securities of an issuer; see "anti-fraud rule" and "disclosure document").

material tax issue — Any federal income tax issue relating to a tax shelter that would make a significant contribution toward sheltering, from federal taxes, income from other sources by providing deductions in excess of the income from the tax shelter investment in any year, or making available tax credits to offset tax liabilities in excess of the tax attributable to the tax shelter investment in any year (see "tax shelter," "tax opinion" and "tax shelter registration").

maximum offering proceeds — The highest amount of money being sought in a mini-maxi securities offering (see "mini-maxi offering").

mechanical exploitation — The highest level of profit or advantage that may be gained from the exhibition or related activities and products associated with a motion picture (see "exploitation," "foreign distribution," "live stage rights," "merchandising," "product placement," "tie-ins," "video rights agreement" and "wide release").

mechanical interest allowed by law — The highest percentage of interest that is permitted to be charged by lenders pursuant to state usury laws (see "actual interest," "interest," "prime rate" and "usury").

mechanical license — Written authority granted by the owner of a copyright, or such owner's agent, to reproduce copyrighted material for designated consideration. Copyright law provides that any composition may be mechanically reproduced once the owner of the copyrights has used or permitted the use of the composition for mechanical reproduction (see "license agreement").

mechanical reproduction — Reproduction by machine or tools as opposed to reproduction by electrical means (see "compact disc," "electrical reproduction" and "phonograph").

mechanical rights (royalties) — The rights to reproduce and to distribute copyrighted materials to the public. Mechanical royalties are paid to obtain such rights, usually on a per-copy basis (see "copyright" and "royalties").

media — The means of communication that reach the general public, such as radio or television; the plural form of medium. Media is a generic word that includes the specific medium of the press (see "communications industry" and "entertainment industry").

media buys — The purchase of motion picture advertising time and space on television and radio and in newspapers and magazines. Advertising is generally the single largest expenditure incurred in the distribution of a motion picture. Independent producers who use the facilities of unaffiliated distribution entities must carefully monitor and vigorously audit distributor practices relating to media buys to make sure the distributor is not simply charging off its most expensive media buys in time or space on the independently produced picture, as opposed to other movies it may be distributing at the same time or while recording the less expensive time for its own motion pictures (regardless of which advertising cost was actually tied to which movie). Also, independent producers must be very careful as to which distribution personnel, if any, gets charged against the costs of such advertising and which personnel are simply absorbed into the distributor's fee. Generally, the time of distributor marketing department employees should not be separately charged to a motion picture, particularly if an advertising overhead charge is imposed (see "advertising," "advertising overhead" and "creative accounting").

media mix — The combination of communication outlets chosen to advertise a given film (see "advertising").

media player — Software or hardware that "plays" audio, video or animation files. In the Windows world, Windows Media Player, the media players from RealNetworks (RealOne, RealPlayer, etc.) and Apple's iTunes are widely used. Most media players include the functions of digital jukeboxes for organizing a user's music collection and also provide Internet radio. When the word "portable" is used with "media player," it refers to a handheld device (see "portable media player").

mediation — A form of alternative dispute resolution (i.e., a method of settling disputes without going to court and through the use of a neutral third party who serves as mediator between the parties; see "arbitration," "litigation" and "negotiation").

medium — (see "media").

medium-budget films — As of the publication date of this dictionary, motion pictures with budgets in the neighborhood of $8 to $15 million dollars, although these figures may vary from year to year (see "big-budget films" and "low-budget films").

megaplex — A motion picture theater in which two or more screens under the same ownership are housed in one structure utilizing a common lobby, ticket sales booth and concession counter. As the number of screens in such facilities has grown, the term megaplexes has come to mean facilities with sixteen screens or more, whereas multiplexes have eight to fifteen screens (see "major exhibition chains," "number of screens" and "overflow").

member of the club — A reference to the fact that Hollywood is an insider's game and the insiders make up what is sometimes referred to as a "club"(see "insider's game," "MPAA," "relationship driven business" and *The Club Rules — Power, Money, Sex, and Fear — How It Works in Hollywood*, Paul Rosenfield, Warner Books, 1992).

member-managed LLC — An active investor investment vehicle organized as an LLC in which each of the member/managers actively participate in making the important management decisions. The number of member-managers is limited as a practical matter, to the extent that larger numbers make it difficult to keep all of the member-managers actively involved in management. The ownership units of such vehicles are generally not considered securities. LLCs are formed by preparing and filing articles of organization with the secretary of state and the drafting and approval by the member-managers of an LLC operating agreement (see "limited liability company" and "manager-managed LLC").

members — The investor owners of a manager-managed LLC (see "limited liability company").

memorandum of agreement — A written outline of some intended agreement or an instrument drawn up in brief form. The phrase is sometimes used as the title of a complete agreement that has been memorialized in writing. The term is often used as the title of entertainment industry contracts (e.g., memorandum of agreement to co-finance theatrical motion pictures; see "contract" and "deal memo").

mental modeling — Projecting the financial results of a company without the aid of a computer (see "computer model" and "financial management").

merchandise and publishing royalties — Percentages of revenue paid for the authority to use and exploit property rights relating to products, names and events appearing in or used in connection with a motion picture as well as property rights relating to published materials (see "maximum exploitation" and "merchandising").

merchandising — The manufacture, distribution, licensing, selling or other exploitation of characters, names and events appearing in or used in connection with a motion picture (e.g., in the form of T-Shirts, books, posters, jewelry, games, dolls and/or toys; see "allied rights" and "goodwill").

merchandising agreement — The licensing contract between a production company, as the owner of the property rights associated with a feature film, and a manufacturer and/or distributor that has the capability of producing and distributing licensed products based on the characters or objects portrayed in the motion picture (same as "license for merchandising agreement").

merchandising rights — The rights to manufacture, distribute, license, sell or otherwise exploit characters, names and events appearing in or used in connection with films beyond the motion picture market (e.g., in the form of T-Shirts, books, posters, jewelry, games, dolls and/or toys). Such rights on certain movies may be very valuable (see "merchandising").

merchandising tie-ins — Cooperative promotional campaigns connecting specific merchandise with a given film (contrast with "product placement"; see "promotional tie-ins").

merchantable — An item fit for sale in the usual course of trade, at usual selling prices. A merchantable item shall be of ordinary marketable quality, bring the average price, be lawful merchandise, be good and sufficient of its kind and be free from any remarkable defects (see "sale of goods statutes").

merchant bank — A financial institution that engages in investment banking, counseling and negotiating in mergers and acquisitions and a variety of other services, including securities portfolio management and the acceptance of foreign bills of exchange (see "bank," "investment bank" and "investment banker").

merger — The combining of two or more companies (see "mergers and acquisitions," "merger guidelines" and "vertical integration").

merger guidelines — A six-part analytical framework set forth by the U.S. Justice Department in 1984 for use as a guide in analyzing the competitive effects of a proposed vertical merger in the motion picture business which is based on the U.S. Justice Department's analysis of Clayton Act cases. The guidelines are summarized as follows: (1) Does the contemplated merger significantly foreclose other competitors (e.g., exhibitors) from access to motion pictures or access on competitive terms? (2) Does the proposed merger significantly foreclose other competitors (e.g., distributors) from access to theaters or a substantial portion of theaters? (3) If actual competitors are not likely to be foreclosed from access to motion pictures on competitive terms, does the proposed action nonetheless effectively force actual or potential competitors to enter or continue in the distribution or exhibition business on a vertically integrated basis? (4) If vertical integration is effectively required in order to enter or continue in the business, how difficult is to it to achieve vertical integration? (5) If vertical integration is required, and if there are significant barriers to such integration, is the market otherwise conducive to (i.e., will it allow) non-competitive performance? and (6) Does the proposed vertical merger have offsetting positive benefits for the economy by creating efficiencies? (see "antitrust laws," "barriers to entry," "Clayton Act," "internationally competitive," "market share," "Paramount Consent Decree of 1948," "political influence," "TriStar Case" and "vertical integration").

mergers and acquisitions — Activities relating to the combining of two or more companies and/or the purchase of companies. Such activities often involve and therefore must be conducted in compliance with the securities laws since most companies involved in mergers and acquisitions are corporations and corporate shares are securities. Some attorneys and investment bankers specialize in the very complex transactions relating to mergers and acquisitions. Also, since mergers or acquisitions could result in an illegal restraint of trade, proposed mergers or acquisitions of certain companies in the same or related industries may have to first be approved by the U.S. Justice Department antitrust law division (see "antitrust laws," "merger guidelines," "Securities and Exchange Commission" and "U.S. Justice Department").

message movie — A motion picture in which the themes o ideas being communicated are apparent. All movies communicate one or more messages (i.e., underlying themes or ideas), thus it is difficult to distinguish a motion picture in which the message is more apparent (i.e., a message movie) from one whose message is more subtle and therefore perceived as entertainment. On the other hand, entertainment has always served as a useful mechanism for the communication of propaganda (see "culture promotion," "marketplace of ideas," "movies with a message" and "propaganda").

mezzanine level — In venture capital terminology, stage of a company's development just prior to its going public. Venture capitalists investing at this point generally have a lower risk of loss than at previous financing stages and can hopefully look forward to earlier capital appreciation as a result of the market value gained through a subsequent initial public offering (see "IPO," "second round" and "venture capital").

micro-budget film — (see "ultra-low budget").

mid-week box office — The Mondays, Tuesdays and Wednesdays of each week, which traditionally have generated the lowest number of theater admissions. A major studio/distributor once proposed that the nation's movie theater operators offer their releases at a discount on Tuesdays in an effort to boost mid-week attendance at the theaters. The proposal was reportedly greeted with reluctance by many of the largest exhibitors (see "box office gross").

MIFED — An international film market held in Milan, Italy in the fall (Mercato Internazionale Filme e Documentario). At this market, representatives of various entities in the film industry meet to exhibit and view films, to promote proposed films and to discuss the possible financing, acquisition and/or distribution of such films (see "American film market," "Cannes Film Festival" and "film market").

mime — To act a part with mimic gesture and action usually without words (see "actor" and "bit player").

mini-majors — An arbitrary, unofficial and probably outdated term used to describe a second tier of feature film producer/distributors. Some analysts use the lack of production studio facilities as a criterion for separating "mini-majors" from "majors." The list changes from time to time depending upon how such entities fare in the movie marketplace. Such labels are often used by investment analysts and the trade press in describing various entertainment companies. In recent decades, most of the previous mini-majors were merged with other entities, acquired by the major studio/distributors or went out of business. Also in recent years, *Variety* has discontinued the use of the term as a category for statistical reporting purposes in its annual list of films distributed by major studio/distributors and independents (see "independent distributor," "independent producer," "major studio/distributors," "studio lots" and "trades").

mini-maxi offering — A securities offering with a stated minimum of offering proceeds and a maximum. Such an offering might permit a filmmaker to seek a minimum (enough to produce one film) and a maximum (enough to produce several films) in a multiple film offering, or produce a single film in a different way. Also, an underwriting arrangement with a broker/dealer requiring that the broker/dealer sell a stated minimum of securities on an all-or-none basis and the balance on a best-efforts basis. Issuer sales (i.e., without the participation of broker/dealers) may also be used to raise funds in such offerings using a mini-maxi format. The required estimated use of proceeds section of a mini-maxi offering must disclose the estimated use of proceeds for both a minimum and maximum column, as well as explain how a level of offering proceeds somewhere in between the two will be handled (see "disclosure document" and "use of proceeds").

mini-multiple — A feature film release pattern in which the film is exhibited at a number (more than an exclusive engagement and less than a wide release) of quality theaters in strategic geographic locations (see "exclusive engagement," "general release," "limited engagement" and "wide release").

minimum — In film exhibition, the lowest acceptable weekly rental payment to be paid by a film's exhibitor to the distributor as a percentage of such film's box office gross at a theater (same as "floor").

minimum admission prices — A specified amount (per the exhibition agreement between a theater chain and a distributor) below which motion picture theater ticket prices may not fall. One of the conduct restrictions of the Paramount consent decree was designed to prevent the major studio/distributors from conspiring to fix minimum admission prices among the theaters they either owned or controlled (see "controlled theater," "Paramount Consent Decree of 1948" and "price fixing").

minimum advance — (see "advance").

minimum credit requirements — The feature film billing notices specified in the applicable union or guild basic agreement for its members or in an individual employment agreement. The credit should be specified in the employment agreement if a union/guild agreement does not apply or if the individual being hired is to receive credit beyond the union/guild minimum (see "credit requirement" and "guild").

minimum film rental — A reference to what is probably the most common film rental split between distributors and exhibitors (i.e., the 90/10 deal). Pursuant to this arrangement, the distributor would be paid 90 percent of the box office receipts after the theater's overhead has been deducted, but not less than an agreed upon minimum percentage of the total box office (a floor) for the film's first week or two of exhibition. Then the distributor's percentage share would be reduced each subsequent period for the film's run (see "ninety/ten deal" and "sliding scale").

minimum free lance contract for theatrical motion pictures — The Screen Actors Guild standardized contract to be used by producer signatories to the Producer-SAG agreement in hiring performers on a weekly basis. Additional clauses that are not part of the standard form may be inserted into such contracts (see "daily contract for theatrical motion pictures").

minimum gain — A technical accounting concept used in a limited partnership context, meaning the excess of the outstanding principal balance of any non-recourse debt of the partnership over the partnership's allocable share of the adjusted basis of the project for federal income tax purposes (see "limited partnership").

minimum guarantee — A commitment to pay no less than a specified amount out of revenues generated. Motion picture licensing arrangements for the major foreign territories typically utilize this method of compensation, although any fee advances paid, if any, would be deducted from the minimum guarantee (see "outright sale").

minimum offering proceeds — The lowest amount of money to be raised in a securities offering structured as a mini-maxi offering. The minimum must be enough to permit the conduct of business activity that could result in a profit for investors. In the context of a movie offering, that may mean enough to produce the movie for the lowest possible budget, or if a development offering, the lowest amount of funds needed to pursue a development strategy. Typically, the issuer in such offering cannot spend any of the investor funds until the minimum has been reached (see "mini-maxi offering").

minimum rating — A commitment made by a feature film producer to a distributor and/or financiers that the film being produced will receive an MPAA rating not worse than a specific rating (e.g., not more restrictive than an "R" rating). Such commitments are often required in film distribution agreements and if the producer fails to deliver the agreed upon rating, the distributor may be relieved of its obligation to pay monies or release the picture. Such situations which involve an MPAA member distributor and an independent producer may raise the question relating to the inherent conflict of interest involved in rating films through the facilities of an MPAA sponsored organization (see "CARA," "distribution agreement," "financing," "independent producer," "MPAA" and "ratings").

minimum requirements — A phrase and provision associated with an output distribution agreement that establishes certain standards or conditions (e.g., relating to budget, rating, running time, subject matter, etc.) for the motion pictures to comply with before the distributor will be obligated to distribute films under the agreement (see "output deal" and "output distribution agreement").

minimum wage sales — Salary minimums set by the various film related unions and guilds (see "compensation schedules," "double scale" and "scale").

minor — A person who is not old enough to be held legally responsible for all of his or her actions (e.g., entering into contracts), and/or who is not legally entitled to the rights held by citizens generally (e.g., voting). In most states, a minor is a person who has not yet achieved his or her eighteenth birthday but many states have set a higher legal age for the purchase of alcoholic beverages. Feature film producers must give special consideration to performers who are minors and, since laws relating to the employment of minors are generally promulgated by the states, must be aware of what the specific requirements are in the state in which some or a portion of a motion picture is to be shot. Such state laws typically impose a ceiling on the number of hours each day that a minor may work, provide educational or schooling requirements and in some cases, require court approval of the minor's contract (see "location filming," "majority," "minority" and "state legislatures").

minority — The status of a person who has not yet reached majority (i.e., legal age). A person who has not yet reached majority is not old enough to be held legally responsible for all of his or her actions (e.g., entering into contracts) and/or legally entitled to the rights held by citizens generally (e.g., voting). In most states the age of majority is now eighteen, however, some states have set a higher legal age for the consumption and purchase of alcoholic beverages (see "minor" and "majority").

minority interest — The interests of shareholders who, in the aggregate, own less than half of the common shares of a corporation (see "corporate stock," "corporation," "shareholders" and "working control").

mirrors of society — A reference to the belief that movies reflect real life. Some writers and/or observers of Hollywood movies falsely claim that movies merely mirror what actually occurs in society, while others more accurately point out that movies sometimes portray images of things that have never occurred and may never occur (e.g., science fiction, action/adventure and horror genres). In addition, it may be more accurate to observe that movies actually tend to a great extent to mirror the values, interests, cultural perspectives and prejudices of their makers, and that the real "makers" of the films released by the major studio/distributors are the top studio executives who actually have the power to green light and/or acquire movies for production and/or release, after all, their choices are what end up on the screen (see "patterns of bias").

miscellaneous equipment insurance — An insurance policy that covers against all risks of direct physical loss, damage or destruction to cameras, camera equipment, sound, lighting and grip equipment, owned by or rented to the production company. Coverage can sometimes be extended to mobile equipment vans, studio location units or similar units upon payment of an additional premium (see "equipment insurance").

mix (mixing) — The process of combining a number of separate sound tracks of dialogue, music or sound effects onto a single track with optimum balance. "Mixing" is also sometimes referred to as "re-recording" and "dubbing" (see "dubbing").

mixed dialogue — The spoken words of two or more actors and/or actresses blended together on a single track. The term also applies to mixed music and mixed sound effects (see "mix").

mixing — [see "mix (mixing)"].

mixing facility — The physical plant where the mixing of movie sounds occurs [see "(mix (mixing)"].

mob — (see "Mafia").

mob-controlled distribution company — A film distribution company controlled by organized crime. An independent production company once reportedly licensed a small independent distributor to distribute its film but shortly after exploitation of the film was completed in the primary markets the distributor filed for bankruptcy and the production company was never paid its portion of the film's revenues. Subsequent investigations revealed that the distributor had been set up specifically for that purpose. It is interesting to note that in any given year more than 50 percent of U.S. feature film distributors only distribute one film and approximately fifteen to thirty feature film distribution companies cease distributing films for one reason or the other. Even the possibility that this may occur makes it imperative that producers investigate the distributors with whom they do business (see "choosing a distributor" "Mafia," "money laundering," "racketeering," "RICO," "track record" and "white collar crime").

model accredited investor exemption (MAIE) — A model state level securities law promulgated by NASAA in 1997 that exempts from registration and sales/advertising filing requirements those offers and sales of securities (not more than $1,000,000) issued to accredited investors only. The term "accredited investor" is defined at Regulation D, Rule 501, with a listing of entities and individuals possessing substantial assets and/or net worth. Pursuant to the MAIE,

securities may only be sold to persons reasonably believed by issuers to be accredited investors who are purchasing for investment and not for resale. These state exemptions are generally not available to issuers in the development stage of their business or to issuers and affiliates who have been subject to various "bad boy" disqualifying provisions. Issuers of such securities may use any means to generally announce the proposed offering but unless permitted by the state securities administrator, the information contained in the announcement has to be restricted to the (1) name, address and telephone number of the issuer; (2) name, price and aggregate amount of the offered securities; and (3) brief descriptions of the offered securities and issuer's business. In addition, a statement must be included that indicates (1) the securities will be sold only to accredited investors; (2) no money or other consideration will be solicited or accepted by means of the general announcement; (3) the securities have not been registered with or approved by the SEC (or any other state agency); and (4) the securities are being offered and sold under an exemption to the securities registration requirement. To qualify for the exemption, states typically require issuers to file, within fifteen days after the first sale of the securities in the state, a notice of transaction, a consent to service of process, a copy of the general announcement and a fee (see "NASAA," "Regulation D" and "Rule 504").

model agreement — A sample contract that may be drafted by an industry organization for educational purposes. Unlike the unions and guilds, professional and trade associations are not allowed to bargain collectively on behalf of their members, but there is no reason that seminars and other educational programs cannot be properly conducted (in compliance with the antitrust laws that apply to such association activities) so as to meet the needs of association members with respect to the study and understanding of certain key industry agreements which significantly effect their livelihood. For example, the IFTA (formerly the AFMA) has model distribution agreements with terms and provisions from which its members may choose when drafting their own distribution agreements for the distribution of feature films. It has also long been recognized in the film industry that the terms and provisions of the film distribution agreements used by the major studio/distributors are remarkably similar regardless of whether their association (the MPAA) was actively involved in that phenomenon or not. Since many of the terms and provisions of the feature film distribution agreements being used today are not favorable to the independent feature film producers (and other net profit participants), there may be some value for such producers in re-organizing an effective association and include the development of a model distribution agreement, the terms of which are more favorable to independent producers, among the projects the association undertakes (see "association projects," "conscious parallelism," "contract of adhesion," "industry groups," "lobbying," "Producers Guild of America," "professional association," "squeaky wheel gets the grease" and "standard contract").

modeling — The envisioning of the future operation of a company (see "computer model," "financial projections" and "mental modeling").

modeling services — Financial management consultants who specialize in or offer computerized financial modeling assistance (see "computer model," "financial management,"

"mental modeling," "modeling" and "real model").

modified gross deal — A film distribution deal in which the producer gets an advance and the distributor recoups some negotiated multiple of that advance plus its distribution fees and expenses off the top before splitting the remainder with the producer (see "first dollar gross deal" and "net deal").

modified low budget film — A Screen Actors Guild designation for a film being produced on a budget of less than $625,000 dollars (see "modified low budget agreement").

modified low budget agreement — A Screen Actors Guild agreement that permits its actor members to work on films being produced for less than $625,000 for a day rate of $268 dollars or a weekly rate of $933 dollars with six day work weeks (no premium), no consecutive employment (except on overnight locations), and reduced overtime rates (see "low budget agreement," "Screen Actors Guild,""short film agreement," "student film agreement" and "ultra-low budget agreement").

monetary advances — With respect to motion picture pre-sales, the consideration paid to a feature film producer by an entity acquiring distribution rights in a given medium or territory at the time the agreement is signed or upon delivery of the film. Such advances may take a form that is readily convertible into cash (i.e., monetary advances or bankable commitments that may be used by the producer as collateral for a discounted bank loan; see "collateral," "pre-sales" and "split rights deal").

monetary damages — Compensation, in the form of money, awarded by a court of law to one who has been injured by the action of another (contrast with "damage"; see "injury" and "remedy" or "remedies").

monetized trade surpluses — The excess of goods and services provided by one country to another converted into money. The monetized trade surplus of Japan in previous decades permitted Japanese business entities to purchase significant ownership interests in U.S. based companies including major studio/distributors (see "global integration," "globalization" and "Japanese money").

money laundering — The funneling of money obtained by illegal means through an apparently or previously legitimate operation. For example, consider this reported scenario in the film industry: a drug dealer agrees to pay the production costs of a feature film in exchange for the rights to distribute that film in a single foreign territory where that drug dealer controls a chain of theaters. It is then possible for the drug dealer and his exhibitor associates to inflate the theatrical box office admission figures and send what appears to be a legitimate but inflated distributor's share of the box office gross back into the U.S. as laundered money. In any given year in which five hundred or more feature films are distributed in the U.S., with the source of the production financing for many of such films unknown or difficult to determine, it is quite likely that such practices are continuing to occur (see "capital-intensive business," "Mafia," "mob controlled distribution company," "movies with a message," "racketeering," "relationship driven business," "RICO" and "white collar crime").

monopolize — To obtain or create control over the production and distribution of a product or service by a single company or a group of firms

acting in concert (see "antitrust laws" and "monopoly").

monopoly — Control of the production and distribution of a product or service by one firm or a group of firms acting in concert; a market condition where all or nearly all of an article of trade or commerce within a community or district is brought within the control of one person or company, thereby excluding competition or free traffic in that product. Monopolization is prohibited by the federal U.S. statute called the Sherman Act. Conviction can lead to criminal penalties and divestiture. The offense of monopoly has two elements: (1) the possession of monopoly power in the relevant market, and (2) the willful acquisition or maintenance of that power as distinguished from growth or development as a consequence of a superior product, business acumen or historical accident (see "antitrust laws," "cartel," "oligopoly" and "transnational cartelization").

moral rights — The right of an author or artist to object to or prevent the distortion, mutilation or other alteration of his or her work which is detrimental to the author or artist's honor or reputation. Although the term is widely recognized in civil law countries, as currently codified in the U.S. Copyright Act, federal moral rights legislation covers only certain works of the visual arts, and specifically excludes protection for motion pictures. Nevertheless, a right analogous to a moral right has been recognized in this country in several situations in which the integrity and reputation of an artistic creator were protected by the courts. The express grounds on which common law protection has been given include libel, unfair competition, copyright and the right of privacy. Several states also have their own state statutes relating to moral rights. Feature film distributors often include a provision in the distribution agreement that results in the waiver of such rights by the producer (see "common law," "droit moral," "editing rights," "moral rights waiver," "lobbying" and "tort").

moral rights waiver — (see "waiver of moral rights").

moratorium — A legally authorized period of delay in the performance of a legal obligation or the payment of a debt (i.e., a waiting period set by an authority, for example, a moratorium on principal and/or interest for a period of time; see "balloon payment" and "moratorium statutes").

moratorium statutes — A law enacted by a legislature that authorizes periods of delay in the performance of a legal obligation or the payment of a debt (see "bankruptcy," "moratorium" and "restricted currencies").

most favored nations clause — A contractual clause by which each signatory grants to the other the broadest rights and privileges that it accords to any other entity with which it deals. In film contracts with multiple percentage participants, this provision ensures that one participant's terms will be no less favorable than those of any other participant of like standing. Thus, this clause is crucial to those participants who find themselves in the same category (e.g., net profit participants). If two such participants are supposed to be paid a specified percentage of net profits but the definitions of net profits in their respective agreements differ, without the most favored nations clause, one may prevent the other from being paid at that level or at all (see "assumption agreement," "leverage," "pari passu," "profit" and "percentage participation").

most favored nations treatment — To be dealt with in a manner that is just as favorable as others in the same position (see "most favored nations clause" and "pari passu").

motion picture — A series of pictures projected on a screen in rapid succession with people and objects shown in successive positions slightly changed so as to produce the optical effect of a continuous picture in which the objects move. For purposes of delivery, this term is often a defined term in film distribution agreements. As an example, for a feature film, each picture will often be required to be between ninety (90) and one hundred twenty (120) minutes in length. The definition may also require that each picture, when delivered, will be completely finished, fully edited and titled and fully synchronized with language dialogue, sound and music and in all respects ready and of a quality, both artistic and technical, adequate for general theatrical release and commercial public exhibition. Each picture will consist of a continuous and connected series of scenes based on a specific screenplay and shall be suitable for exhibition to the general public in any and all domestic and foreign markets. Such picture will be produced utilizing the English language on 35mm film in color. To the extent that the above described version of each picture is not suitable for U.S. network broadcast or does not comply with such network standards and practices, cover shots, alternate scenes or another version of each picture suitable for such broadcast shall be delivered to the distributor (same as "film" or "movie").

motion picture association accountants — Accountants or accounting firms that specialize in or have expertise in areas relating to the movie industry (e.g., production accounting, film financing and auditing; see "production accountant" and "profit participation auditor").

motion picture association acquisition/ distribution agreement — (see "acquisition/ distribution agreement").

Motion Picture Association (MPA) — The Motion Picture Association is the international counterpart of the MPAA. It was formed by the MPAA in 1945 as the Motion Picture Export Association of America (MPEA) and changed its name to the MPA in 1994. Through the MPEA (now MPA), the MPAA sought to respond to the rising tide of protectionism resulting in barriers aimed at the importation of American films into other countries. The president and chief executive officer of the MPAA is also the chairman and chief executive officer of the MPA. The MPAA is also a sister association of the AMPTP (see "Alliance of Motion Picture and Television Producers" and "Motion Picture Association of America").

Motion Picture Association of America (MPAA) — A movie industry association organized to promote the international dissemination of American films and to upgrade imported films. The organization was founded in 1922 as the trade association for the American film industry, but it has evolved into an advocate for major producers and distributors as opposed to the independent producers and distributors. Its members include the major studio/distributors. One of the MPAA's functions is the assigning of audience ratings. The MPAA also maintains a strong lobbying arm that constantly monitors both the federal and state legislative branches for proposed bills or provisions in bills that are considered unfavorable to the interests of the MPAA companies. The MPAA also monitors and works to eliminate certain alleged exhibitor practices (e.g., product splitting, piracy and the illegal use of motion pictures). MPAA company activities involving vertical integration, block booking, tying arrangements, dominance of market share, association membership policies and anti-competitive business practices may raise questions regarding how these companies came to dominate the industry (see "illegal use of motion picture," "lobbying," "MPA," "MPEAA," "NATO," "piracy," "product splitting" and "ratings").

motion picture exhibitor — (see "exhibitor").

Motion Picture Export Association of America (MPEAA) — (see "Motion Picture Association").

Motion Picture Industry Encouragement Act — A Jamaican statute passed in September, 1991, that grants film companies set up to film in Jamaica nine years of income tax exemption on profits or gains earned in the production of a motion picture. The entire production need not be filmed in Jamaica. U.S. stockholders of such film companies would not be subjected to U.S. tax under terms of a previous treaty between the two countries that precludes double taxation. The act also grants relief from customs duties on equipment, machinery and materials for the building of studios or for use in motion picture production, so long as those items are not available locally in Jamaica (see "government subsidies" and "tax benefits").

motion picture insurance — Customized packages of insurance policies covering risks associated with movie production, including insurance for the cast, negative film and videotape, props, sets and wardrobe, animal mortality, equipment, bad weather, extra expense, property damage liability, errors and omissions, non-owned aircraft, water craft, workers compensation, comprehensive general liability, auto liability and union and guild flight accidents. Insurance costs usually account for approximately 3 percent of a film's budget and that does not include the completion bond fee which is not actually a form of insurance (see "completion bond," "insurance" and "surety").

motion picture laboratories — (see "laboratory").

motion picture marketplace — (see "film market").

move-over — A movie exhibitor/distributor term meaning to move a film out of one theater into another (i.e., to transfer a film's showing from a theater to another theater within the same competitive theater area, for that film's subsequent run, without that film's subsequent run having been made available to any other theater). A move-over right is a privilege given by a distributor to an exhibitor/licensee to move a picture from one theater to another as a continuation of the run at the licensee's first theater (see "move-over clause").

move-over clause — A provision in a distributor/exhibitor agreement that permits the exhibitor to exhibit a film at another theater under certain specified circumstances (see "move-over").

movie — Another name for motion picture and feature film (see "motion picture").

movie house — Another name for motion picture theater (see "exhibitor").

movie lender — A bank that lends production and/or distribution funds to movie studios and/or production companies (see "financing" and "lender financing").

movie of the week — A made for television movie produced specifically for a slot in an ongoing series of movie presentations on television, or a motion picture selection aired as part of such an ongoing series (see "made-for-television product" and "pilot").

movies with a message — Motion pictures in which a moral, social or other statement predominates over the entertainment value of the movie. All movies have one or more messages and financiers, producers, screenwriters, directors, actors and others in the industry have long recognized and used the medium as one of the most effective means yet devised by humanity for the communication all sorts of ideas. However, if the message is too strong or seems out of place, it may be resented by and distracting to the audience which presumably goes to the movies primarily to be entertained. The Oliver Stone movie "JFK" could be considered an example of a strong "message movie." Some might even suggest that the real message coming out of that motion picture was not designed to convince the movie-going audiences that a conspiracy was involved in the assassination of a U.S. President (which many people already believed anyway), but instead to divert attention from one suspect group (the mob) and direct it toward others (the CIA and the highest levels of the U.S. government), while simultaneously suggesting that the same conspiracy was also involved in the killings of Bobby Kennedy and Martin Luther King. If allegations that elements of the mob were really the moving force behind the killings of the Kennedy brothers and that the mob has connections with the motion picture industry are true, this might help to explain why the motion picture took that particular editorial slant (see "approvals," "controls," "creative control," "culture promotion," "favorable portrayal," "final cut," "funding sources," "hidden agenda," "in-house production," "Mafia," "marketplace of ideas," "negative pickup," "patterns of bias," "production-financing distribution agreement" and "unfavorable portrayal").

MOW — (see "movie of the week").

MPAA — (see "Motion Picture Association of America").

MPAA cartel — A reference to the extraordinary influence that the member companies of the Motion Picture Association of America exert over the film industry, in addition to their dominance of the industry in terms of market share (see "antitrust laws," "barriers to entry," "bidding war," "cartel," "conscious parallelism," "major exhibition chains," "market power," "market share," "MPAA," "Paramount Consent Decree of 1948," "transnational cartelization," "TriStar Case" and "vertical integration").

MPAA certificate — The certificate for a film's designated rating issued by the MPAA's Code and Rating Administration (same as "MPAA code seal"; also called "certificate of code rating").

MPAA code seal — A certification that a film, its trailers and advertising have been made and rated in conformity with the regulations and standards of the MPAA (same as "MPAA certificate").

MPAA rating — (see "ratings").

MPAA Rating Administration — The MPAA department that classifies completed motion pictures as being suitable for different audiences

(see "Motion Picture Association of America" and "ratings").

MPAA rating and certificate — The certificate for a film's designated rating issued by the MPAA's Code and Rating Administration. The rating of a movie may significantly affect the number of people who may see a given movie. Since the MPAA rating is provided by a board of MPAA employees, there is an unethical built-in conflict of interest in the rating of films produced by non-MPAA member production companies. This conflict of interest should not be tolerated by independent producers. A professional association of independent feature film producers and the existing IFTA (formerly the AFMA), which represents independent distributors should start an alternative and improved movie rating system or become partners with the MPAA in sponsoring the movie rating system, to, at least, remove the appearance of this conflict of interest. Also, a movie's distribution agreement may provide for a specified MPAA rating, and if that rating is not obtained, the obligation on the part of the distributor to distribute the film may have been eliminated. Thus, the producer must be careful not to commit to producing a movie that cannot achieve the rating called for in the distribution agreement (see "independent producer," "MPAA," "MPAA code seal").

MPEAA — (see "Motion Picture Export Association of America").

multi-cultural society — A community, nation or other broadly defined group of people in which a variety of distinctive traditions, institutions, relationship patterns, collective activities and interests co-exist. The United States is clearly a multi-cultural society. Given that ideas are the most important commodity of the motion picture business and that the feature film is one of the most effective, if not the most effective means of communication yet devised by human beings, it is of critical importance to a multi-cultural society that all significant cultural and other interest groups within that society have a fair opportunity to express their most important commodity (their ideas) through one of our most effective means of communication (the feature film). To this end, both the federal and state governments in the U.S. have an obligation to its multi-cultural citizenry to assure such fairness and equal opportunity in the marketplace of ideas (see "communication," "communications industry," "culture promotion," "entertainment," "entertainment industry," "idea," "marketplace of ideas," "movies with a message" and "propaganda").

multi-national corporation — A corporation that has production facilities or other fixed assets in at least one foreign country and makes its major management decisions in a global context (see "corporate conglomerate").

multi-part series — A succession of television presentations that are all portions of the same overall program (see "television series").

multi-picture financing — The funding of the production and possibly distribution expenses associated with more than one film. Corporate financing for a studio or film production company is generally multi-picture financing, sometimes with joint venture partners. Limited partnerships, manager-managed LLCs or lender financing may also be used to raise funds for multiple pictures (see "single-picture financing" and "slate of pictures").

multiple — In film exhibition, the situation in which more than one exhibitor or theater is involved in the simultaneous showing of a film in a given market (for an explanation of the way the same term is used in corporate finance (see "price/earnings ratio").

multiple film offering — A film investment vehicle seeking to raise enough money to produce and/or distribute more than one motion picture (see "mini-maxi offering" and "slate of pictures").

multiple picture distribution agreement — A feature film licensing contract that covers more than one movie (see "output deal" and "overall deal").

multiple-picture slate — A film production company's planned program of film production involving more than one film (see "output deal" and "slate of pictures").

multiple pre-sales — Pre-production commitments to license a film in more than one market (e.g., several foreign markets, video and pay cable; see "creative financing," "fractionalizing," "negative pickup," "pre-sales" and "split rights basis").

multiple representation — (see "conflicts of interest," "inter-client confidentiality" and "representation of multiple clients").

multiple screen movie house — (see "multiplex").

multi-plex — A motion picture theater in which two or more screens under the same ownership are housed in one structure utilizing a common lobby, ticket sales booth and concession counter. Multiplexes are facilities with eight to fifteen screens. Megaplexes are those with more than sixteen screens (see "major exhibition chains," "number of screens" and "overflow").

multi-screen complex — (see "megaplex" and "multiplex").

multi-tiered audience — A film audience of different types of people who are attracted to the film for different reasons. It may sometimes be necessary to reach such an audience through differing forms of advertising, promotion and publicity (see "advertising" and "projected audience").

music — Vocal or instrumental sounds having rhythm, melody or harmony (see "lyrics").

music agreements — Contracts relating to the music and music rights associated with a motion picture. On pictures that are being bonded, copies of all existing music agreements must be furnished to the completion guarantor for its review (see "completion bond" and "music").

musical score — (see "score" and "scoring").

music clearance — The process through which permission is obtained from either or both of (1) the owner or owners of a song (the person or people who wrote it) or (2) the master recording (the people who recorded it), so that an individual, group or entity may use that song in a movie. Music Clearance can be a complicated process (see "clearance" and "publish").

music cue — Music written to accompany a specific portion of a film (see "music cue sheets").

music cue sheets — Listings by film reel of the places on the film where various musical contributions begin and end, also showing the composer and publisher. The music cue sheets are used in licensing and in determining royalties (see "music" and "music cue sheets").

music director — The person responsible for seeing that music is composed and/or selected for a motion picture and is orchestrated and copied. The music director also supervises the actual scoring sessions, and in some cases may conduct them (see "music").

music editor — A film post-production person engaged in assembling and synchronizing music film tracks for the purpose of re-recording (see "editing").

music mixer — The person responsible for controlling, balancing and combining a number of separate music sound tracks and achieving the best musical sound for a given film. The music mixer is typically a member of a team of re-recording mixers who prepare the final sound for a film during its post-production (see "mix").

music publisher — One who controls the rights in a musical composition to license for performances, mechanical reproductions and synchronizations and to print, publish and sell sheet music (see "publish").

music rights — The power and authority to use and otherwise exploit the music associated with a movie. Such rights are sometimes referred to as music publishing rights (see "synchronization license" and "synchronization rights").

music track(s) — The audio tracks containing only music. These tracks only exist as separate tracks until the final mix of music, sound effects and dialogue into a composite sound track (see "dialogue track" and "sound effects track").

mutual approval — The sanction of one or more parties to a transaction or with respect to specific issues that arise as part of a given transaction. For example, a production-financing/distribution agreement may call for the mutual approval of the production company and the distributor in selecting the actors and actresses engaged to play roles set forth in the distribution agreement if persons already pre-approved are not ultimately used for any reason (see "approvals," "discretion" and "right of consultation").

mutual fund — A sum of financial resources collected and managed by an investment company that raises money from investors and invests it in stocks, bonds, options, commodities or money market securities. These funds offer investors the advantages of diversification and professional management. For these services they charge a management fee, typically 1 percent or less of assets per year. A limited partnership or manager-managed LLC investing in one or more feature films could not accurately be referred to as a mutual fund (see "hedge funds").

mutual participation — Language in an agreement that sets out the circumstances under which parties to the agreement (and possibly others) will take part in a specified common activity in the future. For example, in a production-financing/distribution agreement the distributor may provide that if it determines to exercise its theatrical derivative distribution rights granted in the distribution agreement, the distributor, the production company and certain associated artists must then negotiate with each other for their mutual participation in the theatrical production and the terms of such participation will be no less favorable to the production company and the associated artists than those contained in the distribution agreement (see "production-financing/distribution agreement").

name-actors — On the screen talent whose names are recognizable by much of the movie-going public and whose inclusion in a film may tend to provide some level of box-office draw for the film (see "marquee value" and "star").

name-dropping — Including the names of very important people in a conversation or other communication for the purpose of impressing the person receiving the communication. A technique financial analysts suggest has been successfully used by the large public feature film limited partnership offerings in recent decades that raised monies for films produced and distributed by major studio/distributors with well-known stars. Investors appeared to be more willing to invest in such vehicles even though the performance record of such large major-studio offerings has not been impressive from an investment perspective. The disappointing performance of such film partnerships from the investor perspective has also contributed to the perception that feature film limited partnerships are not useful financing vehicles for certain types of motion pictures (see "investor motivation" and "limited partnership").

named perils insurance policy — An insurance policy that limits coverage to the risks specified in the policy (see "claims made policy" and "insurance").

narration — The reciting of the details of a story (see "narrative" and "novel").

narrative — The story itself (see "narration," "novel," "story line" and "treatment").

narrow release — The platformed distribution of a motion picture (i.e., begun in a few theaters in the hope that favorable word-of-mouth will allow a wider distribution in the weeks ahead). The risks of such a release pattern are high, since if the picture does not make it initially, it will generally not be booked into other theaters, which calls for a more expensive advertising campaign, that in turn, typically adds value to the ancillary rights, particularly pay television and video (see "platformed" and "release pattern").

NASAA — Acronym for North American Securities Administrators Association (see "blue sky laws," "securities" and "uniform limited offering exemption").

NASD — Acronym for National Association of Securities Dealers (see "broker/bealer" and "National Association of Securities Dealers").

NASDAQ — The acronym for National Association of Securities Dealers Automated Quotations, a national automated quotation service for over-the-counter securities. The operation is supervised by the NASD and input is provided by hundreds of over-the-counter market makers (see "market makers," "NASD" and "securities").

national advertising campaign — A movie marketing and promotional strategy and plan that is implemented across an entire country, particularly in the U.S. It may involve television, radio, newspaper and possibly other media advertising buys. Such campaigns take time to plan and implement and have to be timed to coordinate with the release of the motion picture. Distributors feel that this coordination of timing is critical because national advertising campaigns may also involve numerous tie-ins that stimulate maximum exploitation of a motion picture's profit potential during the first few weeks of its exhibition in the domestic theatrical marketplace (see "advertising," "blind bidding," "merchandising," "tie-ins" and "trade screening").

National Association of Investment Clubs — An association based in Royal Oak, Michigan, that helps investment clubs get established (see "investment club" and "investment group").

National Association of Securities Dealers (NASD) — The professional/trade organization that is authorized and partly responsible for enforcing the SEC rules and regulations relating to investment banking and securities broker/dealer activities in the U.S. In an IPO or other public/registered securities offering, the NASD reviews copies of the registration statements and underwriting agreements to determine whether the underwriting compensation fits within the NASD's guidelines as to what is fair and reasonable (see "broker/dealer," "over-the-

counter market," "private securities transaction" and "SEC").

National Association of Theater Owners (NATO) — The trade organization for feature film exhibitors. NATO headquarters is in North Hollywood (see "exhibitor" and "major exhibition chains").

national circuits — Motion picture theater chains with theaters generally across the U.S. Included among the national circuits are AMC, Century Theatres, Cinemark USA, Cineplex-Galaxy, Landmark Theatres, Loews Cineplex Entertainment, Mann Theatres, National Amusements and Regal Entertainment Group (see "major exhibition chains").

National Do Not Call Registry — A federal program that allows citizens to register their phone numbers so that telemarketers are prohibited from calling the registered numbers. The National Do Not Call Registry gives citizens a choice about whether to receive telemarketing calls at home. Most telemarketers are not supposed to call a registered number once it has been on the registry for thirty-one days. If they do, the individual can file a complaint at the national registry Web site. There is no cost for registering a home or mobile phone, and the registration is effective for five years (see "telemarkerters").

nationality test — Requirements of the formal international co-production treaties that relate to the content of a film, where it is shot and who is involved. Under such tests, films will typically be required to use a local director, script, writer and source material, local stars, local crews and, in some cases, the film will have to be shot in the local language. Also, creative and financial contributions from each of the countries involved will generally have to be more than 30 percent, studio shooting and lab work will have to be carried out in one of the countries, local producers must be credited on screen and all the actors and creative elements must come from one of the two treaty countries (see "foreign production problems" and "international co-productions and agreements").

national marketing strategy — A motion picture advertising and publicity campaign that involves media buys throughout the country. The advent of television has provided feature film distributors with an efficient, although increasingly expensive, medium for promoting a wide release (see "narrow release," "releasing costs" and "wide release").

national release — Distribution of a film for exhibition in theaters throughout the U.S. (see "regional release pattern" and "wide release").

national reviewers — Film critics who are read or listened to by a national audience (see "blurbs," "industry critic" and "critics").

National Securities Market Improvement Act (NSMIA) — A federal securities law passed by Congress in 1996 providing that U.S. securities offerings that are national in character will be regulated only at the federal level by the SEC, not by the states. Thus, some aspects of state ("Blue Sky") law regulation has been removed from certain offerings. NSMIA, added to the 1933 Securities Act as Section 18, preempts state registration requirements with respect to certain transactions exempt under the Securities Act, including (among others) private placements pursuant to rules issued under Section 4(2) of the 1933 Securities Act (i.e., transactions exempt under Rule 506 of Regulation D). NSMIA provides for the exemption from state regulation

of certain offerings of "covered securities." Included among the "covered securities" are offers to qualified purchasers (now considered synonymous with the accredited investor concept as defined in Regulation D) and offerings made pursuant to the Regulation D, Rule 506 safe harbor. However, the states still retain the right to require notice filings and can bring enforcement actions with respect to fraud or deceit, thus the anti-fraud rules still apply to such offerings (see "anti-fraud rule," "private offering exemption," "Regulation D" and "Rule 506").

NATO — (see "National Association of Theater Owners").

NATO/Showest — An international convention and trade show of film exhibitors, distributors, suppliers and vendors that is held annually, usually in February in Las Vegas (see "trade association").

natural person — A human being, as opposed to artificial or fictitious "persons" or things such as corporations, limited partnerships or limited liability companies (see "corporation" and "entity").

NC-17 — The newest copyrighted MPAA rating established in September of 1990 to replace the X-rating (which was not copyrighted by the MPAA and was therefore available for use by anyone) and indicating that no children under the age of seventeen should be admitted. The NC-17 rating does solve the problem of unauthorized use of the "X" rating by pornographers (since the MPAA had failed to copyright the "X" rating), but some states or local communities will still not admit persons under twenty-one to such films and some newspapers will still not carry advertising for an

NC-17 rated film. This rating change also does not address the concerns of parents and independent producers relating to a more detailed rating system which distinguishes between violence, sex and language. Nor does this rating change deal with the inherent conflicts of interest in having an MPAA sponsored organization rating the films produced by non-MPAA member production companies (see "independent producer," "MPAA," "MPAA rating" and "certificate").

nearby locations — Union terminology for film locations on which employees are not lodged overnight but return to the studio or home at the end of a day's work. All work performed away from a studio is considered on location (see "distant locations" and "location filming").

necessary expense — For tax purposes, an expense is necessary if it is appropriate and helpful rather than necessarily essential to the taxpayer's business. To be deductible as a trade or business expense, an expenditure must be both ordinary and necessary in relation to the taxpayer's trade or business (see "deductions," "ordinary expense" and "tax benefits").

negative — Film with the light and dark parts in approximately inverse order to those of the original photographic subject. The term is used to designate any of the following: raw film stock specifically designed for a negative image, the negative image itself, the negative raw film stock that has been exposed but not yet processed and film that has been processed and that bears a negative image (see "exposed film," "original picture negative," "original sound negative" and "picture negative").

negative cash flow — The business situation in which a business spends more cash than it

receives through earnings or other transactions in any given accounting period (see "cash flow," "cash flow cycle" and "positive cash flow").

negative costs — The total of all of the various costs, charges and expenses incurred in the acquisition, development and production of a motion picture, in all its aspects prior to release (i.e., to produce the final negative). These include such items as facilities (sound stage, film lab, editing room, etc.) and raw material (set construction, raw-film stock, etc.). Typically such costs are segregated as pre-production, above-the-line production-period costs and below-the-line costs and post-production-period costs. Negative costs are also distinguished from distribution, sub-distribution and exhibition costs. When a studio/distributor finances the production costs of a film, there may be a tendency for the distributor to characterize some of what are actually distribution costs as production costs, with the result that interest being incurred by the production cost side is inflated. The term "negative cost" for a studio/distributor not only may include the out-of-pocket production expenses but also a non-allocated overhead percentage charge that may range from 10 percent to 15 percent (see "distribution expenses," "interest," "overhead," "production costs" and "rising production costs").

negative cutting (or negative matching) — The cutting of the original negative of a film to match the edited positive, shot-by-shot and frame-by-frame (see "edit").

negative film and videotape negative insurance — An insurance policy that covers against all risks of direct physical loss, damage or destruction of raw film or tape stock, exposed film (developed or undeveloped), recorded videotape, sound tracks and tapes up to the amount of insured production cost (see "insurance").

negative insurance — (see "negative film and videotape insurance").

negative pickup — The contractual commitment made by a distributor to a producer to purchase or license feature film distribution rights from the producer and to pay an agreed upon purchase price ("pick-up price") when the distributor picks up the negative after delivery of the completed picture. The commitment is usually made prior to the completion of the film. The money is usually not paid to the producer until the film is finished, but if the negative pickup deal is with a distributor that meets the criteria of entertainment lenders (e.g., typically a major studio/distributor or other credit-worthy distributor). The producer may be able to take the agreement to such a bank where it can be discounted (i.e., for a fee paid to the bank, converted into an amount of cash less than the face value of the distributor's guarantee). Such funds may then be used to pay for some or all of the production costs of the film. From the perspective of the producer, the negative pickup is a form of lender financing that also involves arranging for distribution. Sometimes, the term "negative pick-up" is used to refer to a sale or license of distribution rights at any time, even after completion of the film. However, that transaction is more accurately referred to as an "acquisition" or "pure acquisition" which is documented by an acquisition/distribution agreement. Thus, referring to a distributor's acquisition deal as a "negative pickup" is misleading (see "acquisitions," "pickups," "pickup price," "production-financing/distribution agreement" and "split rights basis").

negative pickup deal — (see "negative pickup" and "negative pickup distribution agreement").

negative pickup agreement — A contract between a film's producer and a distributor in which the distributor commits to distribute the film and provides such commitment prior to the completion of the film. The producer is then able to take the agreement to a bank and obtain a production-money loan using the distributor's agreement as effective collateral for the loan (see "negative pickup distribution agreement" and "acquisition/distribution agreement").

negative pickup distribution agreement — Technically a misnomer, since there is no significant difference between an acquisition/distribution agreement and this so-called negative pickup distribution agreement except that the negative pickup transaction takes place prior to completion of the film. Thus, a negative pickup actually refers to a form of film finance as opposed to a separate type of distribution agreement (see "acquisition/distribution agreement," "negative pickup," "production-financing/distribution agreement" and "theatrical distribution contract").

negative portrayal — An unfavorable depiction of someone or something in a motion picture (same as "unfavorable portrayal"; see "positive portrayal" and "hidden agenda").

negligence — Failure to exercise that degree of care that a person of ordinary prudence (a reasonable person) would exercise under the same or similar circumstances (see "liability" and "tort").

negotiate — To confer with another party to a proposed agreement for the purpose of arriving at a settlement as between the parties with regard to the issue or issues of concern. In film exhibition, to rent, sell or license motion pictures without bidding (see "arm's length," "bid," "contract of adhesion," "good faith," "leverage," "market power" and "overreaching").

negotiated contractual definitions — A phrase that refers to terms used in certain motion picture industry agreements, such as film distribution contracts, the meanings of which have been specifically bargained for or settled on after some discussion between the parties to the contract. Some spokespersons for the major studio/distributors are fond of explaining that most if not all of these alleged "creative accounting" practices are really the result of disappointed net profit participants who did not understand the effect of the contractually defined terms in their agreement. It is probably more accurate to observe that most of these terms, whose defined meanings in film industry contracts sometimes vary considerably from the meanings of the same terms as used in the agreements of other industries, are not negotiated at all, and if they are negotiated, the negotiations are between parties with such a disparity in bargaining power that there is an absence of any meaningful choice on the part of the weaker party (see "contract of adhesion," "contractually defined terms," "contractually defined profits," "creative accounting," "inferior bargaining position" and "unconscionable contract").

negotiated cushion — A provision in a production-financing/distribution agreement that sets an upper limit (i.e., an amount over and above the film's approved production budget) that has to be exceeded before the film will be considered over budget and any over-budget penalties kick in (e.g., 10 percent of a film's budget or 10 percent of below-the-line costs; see "double add-back," "over-budget penalty" and "penalty-free cushion").

negotiated deal — As between exhibitors and distributors, an exhibition agreement that is negotiated as opposed to one that was accepted on bid. In the event that a distributor rejects all bid offers submitted by exhibitors for the right to license a film for exhibition within a market, the branch office of the distributor will, in turn, either re-bid the picture suggesting different terms or send out a notice to all exhibitors by which it offers to negotiate openly in an effort to award the film to the theater that offers the most attractive negotiated terms. Such negotiations between film distributors and exhibitors may have the same negative results on prospective net profit participants as the settlement transactions between the same distributors and exhibitors (see "bid," "blind bidding," "five o'clock look" and "settlement transactions").

negotiated offer — (see "negotiated deal").

negotiated underwriting — An underwriting of a new securities issue in which the spread between the purchase price paid to the issuer and the public offering price is determined through negotiation rather than multiple competitive bidding. This spread represents the compensation to the investment bankers participating in the underwriting (see "purchase group," "syndicate" and "underwriter").

negotiation — The discussions with others relating to the settlement of or agreement on a matter. Also, the practice of renting, selling or licensing motion pictures in the absence of bidding (see "bid," "blind bidding," "boilerplate," "contract of adhesion," "standard contract" and "unfair negotiating tactics").

nepotism — In an employment context, favoritism shown to a relative (e.g., hiring an employee because of his or her relationship to the employer instead of purely on the merits). The Hollywood-based major studio/distributors have long been known to have engaged in rampant nepotism through the one hundred year history of these companies. Nepotism is a form of discrimination (see "bias," "discrimination," "favoritism," "insider's game," "member of the club," "prejudice," "reciprocal preferences" and "relationship driven business").

net — Generally, the figure remaining after all relevant and appropriate deductions have been made from the gross amount of revenues (see "net assets," "net profit" and "net worth").

net assets — The difference between a company's total assets and liabilities (also called "owner's equity" or "net worth").

net box office after overhead — In calculations relating to the distributor/exhibitor deal for a film's theatrical run, the balance of box office gross following deductions by the exhibitor for a second feature, cartoon or other pre-feature entertainment, if any, and deduction for the negotiated house nut (see "film rentals," "gross receipts," "house nut" and "net box office receipts").

net box office receipts — In calculations relating to the distributor/exhibitor deal for a film's theatrical run, the balance of box office gross following deductions by the exhibitor for a second feature, cartoon or other pre-feature entertainment, if any, but before deduction for the negotiated house nut (see "gross receipts,"

"house nut" and "net box office after overhead").

net capital gain — The amount by which an individual or entity's net long-term capital gain is more than his, her or its net short-term capital loss. The tax rates that apply to net capital gains are generally lower than the tax rates that apply to other income and are called the maximum capital gains rates. For 2005, the maximum capital gains rates were 5, 15, 25 or 28 percent. If an individual's capital losses exceed capital gains, the excess is subtracted from other income on the tax return, up to an annual limit of $3,000 ($1,500 if married and filing separately).

net current assets — The difference between current assets and current liabilities (also called "working capital").

net deal — A film distribution deal in which the distributor recoups all its costs and collects all distribution fees before giving the producer all or a negotiated and specified percentage of the remainder of the film's revenues or net profits. Typically, the distributor first deducts its distribution fee (a percentage of its gross receipts), then recoups the expenses incurred in distributing the film. Also, if a studio/distributor that finances the production cost of a film inflates its distribution fees, includes its overhead as part of the negative cost of a film, takes its distribution fees and expenses prior to deducting interest on the negative cost and applying any revenues toward the reduction of the negative cost charges, while also permitting an actor or director to participate in some form of the film's gross receipts, it is very unlikely that the film will ever generate any net profits for anyone else (see "adhesion contract," "creative accounting," "first-dollar gross deal," "modified gross deal," "net profits" and "overreaching").

net film rental — Revenue from a film's theatrical release after distribution fees and costs are deducted from the distributor's gross film rentals (i.e., what remains of gross film rental after distributor fee percentages in various media and markets, as well as distribution and merchandising costs are deducted; see "net").

net income — Generally, the sum remaining after all expenses have been met or deducted; the income in excess of costs. The term is synonymous with net earnings and with net profit or net loss, depending on whether the figure is positive or negative (see "income," "profit," "receipts" and "revenue").

net income and net losses — IRS terminology for all income or losses of a limited partnership or manager-managed LLC for any taxable year determined before taking into account any depreciation and not including any income, gain or loss realized in connection with a capital transaction or upon termination of such flow-through entity (see "income tax").

net operating loss (NOLS) — Tax term for the excess of business expenses over income in a tax year. Under the tax loss carryback, carry forward provisions, NOLs can (if desired) be carried back or forward for a certain number of years (see "loss").

net points — (see "net profits," "net profit participant," "points" and "talent participations").

net proceeds — Generally, the amount (usually cash) received from the sale or disposition of property, from a loan, or from the sale or issuance of securities after deduction of all costs incurred in the transaction. In computing the gain or loss on a securities transaction for tax purposes, the amount of the sale is the amount of the net proceeds. In the film industry, the term "net proceeds" is also sometimes used as a contractually defined term to mean the same as the more commonly used phrase "net profits" (see "breakeven," "gross receipts," "initial actual breakeven" and "net profits").

net proceeds of the offering — Gross proceeds of a corporate stock, limited partnership or manager-managed LLC offering minus the offering expenses incurred and to be paid by the entity in connection with organizing the entity and in offering shares or units to prospective purchasers, so long as the deduction and payment of such expenses are authorized and to the extent such expenses are not limited by the applicable agreements (see "gross proceeds of the offering").

net proceeds to participant — Assuming this is the deal and the specific film distribution agreement uses this terminology, the term "net proceeds to participant" refers to a defined term in some film distribution agreements referring to the balance of the motion picture's revenue stream remaining after deducting off-the-top expenses, distribution fees and other distribution expenses. Such a participant may be considered a gross participant since he or she is getting the balance of gross receipts minus the specified deductions, or in the alternative, a net profit participant since the described calculations come pretty close to being the same as the calculations for determining net profits in a lender-finance negative pickup transaction. On the other hand, in a studio financed production-financing/distribution arrangement and in investor financed productions, the interest and negative costs of the picture still have to be deducted from the film's revenue stream before arriving at net profits (see "gross participant," "net profits" and "off-the-top expenses").

net profit before participations — Another variation on the term "net profit" implying that there have been no gross participations in the deal and that "net profits" are being determined before any participations are to be paid. Generally speaking, percentage participations may be paid out of gross receipts, net profits, the producer's share or some other defined point in a film's revenue stream (see "producer's share").

net profit definition — The manner in which the term "net profit" is defined in a film distribution and other film industry agreements (see "net profits").

net profit formula — The method for arriving at net profits, typically taking into consideration such concepts as distributor gross receipts, distribution fees, distribution expenses, adjusted gross and the net profits definition (also called "formula for computing net profits"; see "net profits").

net profit(s) — This term is generally defined in a film's distribution agreement and other film industry agreements that provide for a net profit participation (i.e., its definition is contractual). Generally speaking, in a net deal, net profits are the amount of gross receipts remaining after deducting distribution fees, distribution expenses, interest on negative costs, negative costs (plus overhead) and specified deferments and gross participations, if any. Net profits is not a static concept and is continually subject to recalculation from one accounting period to another to take into consideration additional

distribution fees and expenses even after net profits were first achieved. On the other hand, the fact that the net profit definition is contractual is rather meaningless in an environment where one party (the distributor) has so much more leverage than the other party (the production company) that there are no really meaningful negotiations taking place (see "gross receipts," "net points," "rolling breakeven" and "talent participations").

net profit participant — Any party who has a contractual right to be paid a percentage of a film's net profits (see "first dollar," "gross receipts," "net points," "net profits" and "profit participation").

net profit participant association — A proposed association of net profit participants formed for the purpose of protecting the interests of all net profit participants, including producers, executive producers, directors, screenwriters, actors, actresses, financiers and investors, with a particular focus on accounting practices of the feature film distributors as such practices effect contingent compensation (see "association projects," "business practices," "contract of adhesion," "creative accounting," "industry groups," "MPAA" and "professional association").

net profit participation — A form of percentage participation in a motion picture's revenue stream that has been characterized by some as "the customary form of participation" although it has not always been so, nor is it likely to continue to be, since more and more prospective net profit participants within the industry understand how unlikely it is for a film to generate net profits (see "first dollar gross deal," "fifty/fifty split," "modified gross deal," "seventy/thirty split," "fifty/fifty net deal" and "net deal").

net profit participation schedule — A list, usually accompanying a distribution agreement as an exhibit, that sets out the names and percentage participations of persons who are to receive net profit participation payments (see "participant" and "participation").

net receipts — Sometimes used in place of net profits and also contractually defined (e.g., an amount equal to the sum remaining after deducting from gross receipts, first, the distributor's fees, and, second, all distribution expenses). In each distribution agreement in which distribution expenses are being deducted, careful attention should be given to what constitutes a distribution expense. Sometimes this definition appears as an exhibit to the distribution agreement. Net receipts in a limited partnership or manager-managed LLC context may be the same as gross revenues to the entity minus authorized deductions (sometimes referred as "distributable cash" in the flow-through entities; "limited partnership," "manager-managed LLC" and "net profits").

network — A national television corporation that owns and operates or affiliates with independently owned television stations across the country and transmits through such stations regularly scheduled series, news, drama, sports and other programming commissioned to be produced by others or produced by the network itself. Networks sell air time and programming to sponsors and pay compensation to their affiliate stations to carry its scheduled national programming. The television broadcast networks in the U.S. include ABC, CBS, NBC, Fox and PBS (see "cable," "network television" and "Public Broadcasting System").

network broadcast — A television program transmitted over the airwaves and originated by one of the television networks in the U.S. such as ABC, CBS, NBC, PBS or Fox (see "network").

network standards and practices — (see "standards and practices").

network television — The market for films on the ABC, NBC, CBS, PBS and Fox affiliated broadcast stations (see "Public Broadcasting System").

network television film license agreement — The contract between a film's producer or distributor and a television network for the broadcast of a film on so-called free television (see "free television," "network" and "network television").

net worth — The excess of assets over liabilities (same as "net assets" and "owner's equity").

new delivery technologies — Newly developed forms of presenting a motion picture for viewing. Over the years, new technologies have included video recorders, videocassette, cable television, satellite delivery, pay-per-view capability, digital video discs (DVDs), laser discs, the Internet, iPods (see "technological develop-ments").

new equity — Capital raised by selling additional ownership interests in a business. Based on the fairly common references appearing from time to time in the film industry trade press regarding various creative forms of financing resorted to at one time or another by major studio/distributors, certain segments of the film industry and its deal-makers seem to take special pride in putting such deals together. On the other hand, it is quite possible that if the financiers or investors involved in the creative film financing deals of several years ago (or of the last decade for that matter) had received reasonable returns there probably would be no need to be so creative, for the capital needs of the film industry would be either met by earned revenues or by those same financiers and investors coming back to invest again (see "creative accounting," "equity," "profit margin" and "rising production costs").

newspaper — A paper that is printed and distributed, usually on a daily or weekly basis, and that contains news, articles, opinion, features and advertising. The concepts upon which motion pictures are based have sometimes come from newspaper articles (see "idea," "clearance," "concept" and "underlying material").

news release — A misnomer since only the press can determine whether, on any given day, an item is of sufficient interest and/or importance to be considered news (see "media" and "press release").

new technologies — A reference to all sorts of new technological developments that may have an impact on the entertainment industry, not just those relating to the delivery of such entertainment (see "new delivery technologies" and "technological developments").

Nielsen Media Research — A service that tracks the television and media viewing habits of homes across the country. Nielsen data describes American audiences and influences television programming (same as "A.C. Nielsen Company"; see "Arbitron Ratings Company").

ninety-ten deal — The distributor/exhibitor split of net box office revenues in the first week or two. In one variation of the 90/10 deal, after the theater's nut (weekly operating expense) is deducted from gross box office, the distributor receives 90 percent of the remaining box-office receipts and the exhibitor 10 percent for the first week of a film's exhibition and then the distributor's share is reduced by 10 percent each week for the remainder of the run until a minimum distributor percentage is achieved (e.g., 35 percent). In another variation, the minimum starts out at 70 percent (although the distributor percentage share is still 90 percent, and the minimum is reduced proportionately along with the distributor's share each week until the lowest floor level is achieved (see "double week," "floor," "minimum film rental" and "sliding scale").

no-action letter — A letter requested from the SEC in which the SEC agrees to take no civil or criminal action with respect to a proposed securities related activity as factually described in the letter to the SEC and asking for the SEC staff's opinion (see "securities and exchange commission").

nominal payments — The disbursement of small or modest amounts of money. A compromise tactic used by some independent feature film producers in obtaining contingent commitments from directors or actors that can be used in demonstrating to prospective financiers and/or investors that a substantial movie package is in place (i.e., only awaiting production financing). Depending on the specific agreement, such payments would probably not be recouped by the producer if financing fell through (see "letter of intent," "letter of interest," "pay and play" and "pay or play").

non-allocated overhead percentage charge — (see "overhead").

non-assessable stock — Corporate stock purchased from the issuer at full par value or more per share. Fully paid stock cannot be assessed to pay debts of the issuer in the event of bankruptcy or liquidation and is, therefore, non-assessable (see "corporate stock" and "corporation").

non-circumvention clause — A provision in a contract designed to prevent one or the other party, or both, from utilizing information gained or relationships developed as a result of their original agreement in pursuing other business opportunities without the other party (see "covenant not to compete" and "non-disclosure agreement").

non-compete clause — (see "covenant not to compete").

non-disclosure agreement (or revision) — An agreement or provision in a larger contract by one party not to reveal information presented to such party by another (see "covenant not to compete," "non-circumvention clause," "submission release" and "trade secret").

non-exclusive election — Securities concept referring to the fact that an issuer choosing to avail itself of one of the Regulation D exemptions from securities registration (Rule 504, 505 or 506) does not preclude itself from also relying on other available exemptions, such as Sections 4(2) or 4(6)of the Securities Act of 1933, if the conditions and limitations imposed on the use of those exemptions are complied with (see "limited partnership," "manager-managed LLC," "Regulation D" and "securities").

non-marketable security — A security that cannot be sold on the market such as certain government bonds and notes. It can only be redeemed by the holder. Also, a security that is not of investment quality (see "marketable security" and "security").

non-owned aircraft liability insurance — Insurance providing coverage when aircraft are used in connection with a film's production (see "insurance").

non-performance — In contract law, the failure to fulfill an obligation. The non-performance must be material and substantial to justify suspension of another's return performance (see "breach of contract," "consideration" and "material breach").

non-profit — An incorporated organization chartered for purposes other than money-making activities. Such organizations are generally engaged in charitable, educational or other civic or humanitarian activities (see "hobby" and "for profit").

non-public offering — (same as "exempt offering" and "private offering").

non-recourse — Without personal liability (i.e., the individual owners of an entity obtaining a non-recourse loan are not personally responsible for paying the loan back). An obligation that is nonrecourse does not provide a tax basis for federal taxation purposes for individuals, partnerships or LLCs except in limited cases (see "basis," "lender financing" and "limited partnership").

non-recourse debt — In a limited partnership context, any debt secured by a film (being funded by a limited partnership), with respect to which none of the partners have any personal liability as determined under Treasury Regulations issued under Section 752 of the Code (see "non-recourse" and "recourse debt").

non-recourse loan — A loan for which the borrower has no personal liability. Such loans, however, may be secured by specific assets of the borrower (see "recourse loan").

non-refundable deposit — (same as "nominal payments").

non-refundable guarantee — A contractual promise that a specific sum of money will be paid when certain conditions are met and once that sum is paid, the person or entity that makes the payment does not have the right to recoup such payment out of subsequent revenues (see "advance" and "guarantee").

non-regulatory states — States within the United States that have not adopted anti-blind bidding statutes (see "anti-blind bidding statutes," "blind bidding," "economic reprisal," "lobbying" and "trade screening").

non-resident aliens — Persons who are not citizens of the United States who also do not reside within the borders of the U.S. A non-resident alien may not be a shareholder in an "S" corporation (see "S Corp").

non-returnable advance — A payment made prior to a specified event and that may or may not be recoupable. If recoupable, such a payment can only be recovered from future earnings. In either case, the recipient of the payment is under no obligation to return the payment. Studios often obtain advances or guarantees from exhibitors, thus the issues relating to whether and to what extent an advance or guarantee is included in the distributor's gross receipts (since advances, even if labeled "non-returnable," are subject to certain adjustments as between the exhibitor and distributor). The major studio/distributors prefer not to include advances in gross receipts until they are earned (see "advance" or "advances," "distribution guarantee," "guarantee," "non-refundable guarantee" and "recoupment").

non-theatrical — The term does not mean all distribution other than theatrical but refers instead to a relatively specialized market of institutionalized users as opposed to the general public. The market includes in-flight airplanes, hotels, the Red Cross, trains and ships, schools, colleges and other educational institutions, libraries, governmental agency facilities, military installations, business and service organization clubs, shut-in institutions, retirement centers, prisons, museums, film society facilities, churches, offshore drilling rigs, logging camps, and remote forestry and construction camps. The non-theatrical market may also be divided into domestic and foreign (see "allied rights," "ancillary markets" and "theatrical release").

non-theatrical distribution rights — The authority to sell and/or license a film in the ancillary markets (see "distribution rights" and "non-theatrical").

non-theatrical distribution license agreement — A contract between a film's producer and a specialized distributor for distribution of the film in the specialized market of institutional users as opposed to the general public (see "license agreement" and "non-theatrical").

non-union film — A feature film production that does not fall within the jurisdiction of any applicable guild agreements. The term is also sometimes used to refer to films that are being produced with SAG actors (pursuant to SAG rules) but with non-union below-the-line personnel (see "artificial pickup," "development," "guild," "negative pickup," "Screen Actors Guild" and "union").

non-union production — (see "Article Twenty" and "non-union film").

non-theatrical film rental — Motion picture distributor receipts generated by the exploitation of a movie in the non-theatrical markets (see "non-theatrical").

non-voting stock — Corporate stock that does not empower the shareholder to vote on corporate resolutions or the election of directors. Preferred stock is usually non-voting stock (see "common stock").

no-par stock — Corporate stock issued with no stated value on the stock certificate. New issues of stock used to be commonly issued as par value stock, but this practice has generally been abandoned since states started taxing corporations based on par values. Today, par value is more likely to be arbitrarily set as a low value or the stock will be issued as no-par stock when allowed by state law. In accounting for stock issues, the par value is carried as a separate item with the balance of stock issue proceeds carried as capital surplus (see "corporate stock" and "corporation").

no-par value stock — (see "no-par stock" above).

North American Securities Administrators Association — An organization made up of state securities regulators who meet periodically and promulgate model state securities laws, industry disclosure guides and regulations designed to provide uniformity in the implementation of state securities laws and to achieve the consumer protection goals of securities regulation at the state level (see "blue sky laws," "NSMIA," "SEC" and "ULOE").

no strike, no lockout clause — A provision in certain guild basic agreements providing the guild's agreement (on behalf of its members) that during the term of the basic agreement, the guild will not call or engage in any strike, slowdown or stoppage of work affecting theatrical or television motion picture production against the production company signatories to the basic agreement (see "guild" and "strike").

note — (same as "promissory note").

notice and cure period — A negotiated period of time (e.g., ten days), during which a breaching party to a contract has to correct the breach following notice by the non-breaching party (see "notice and cure provision").

notice and cure provision — A clause in an agreement providing that in the event a breach of a contractual provision occurs, the breaching party may have a specified period of time to correct the breach, following written notice by the non-breaching party (see "notice and cure period").

notice filing — With respect to securities offerings, the presentation of the document or documents prescribed by law with the appropriate securities regulatory authorities for the purpose of notifying such authorities that a security is to be or has been offered or sold in the regulated jurisdiction. The SEC's Regulation D requirement that five copies of a completed

Form D be filed with the SEC within fifteen days of the first sale of a security in a Regulation D offering is a form of notice filing. Most states that make available a private placement type exemption (limited offering exemption) from the state securities registration requirements typically require some form of notice filing either before or after the sale of such securities. Most such states also accept the SEC's Form D, with the state signature page signed. A consent to service of process and a filing fee are also typically required. A notice filing is not the same as and should not be confused with a securities registration (see "blue sky laws," "limited liability company," "limited partnership," "registration" and "securities").

notice filing fee — The charges imposed by the state securities regulatory authorities that must accompany the notice filing and consent to service of process in a private placement offering (see "blue sky fees," "filing fees" and "registration fee").

notice filing requirement — Federal and state securities law requirements that a notice be filed with the appropriate securities regulatory authority of the offer or sale of a security within the applicable jurisdiction (e.g., the federal Regulation D exemption from securities registration requires that a notice on Form D be filed with the SEC within fifteen days of the first sale in the offering). Some state notice filings for exempt offerings are required to be filed in advance of any offer in the state (see "Form D," "blue sky law reporter" and "Regulation D").

notice of assignment — A form used by a secured party (e.g., a lending bank) to give notice to the payor (i.e., the person or entity obligated to make payments) to make such payments directly to the secured party. The notice of assignment is used when the proceeds of a specific contract (e.g., a film distribution agreement) are assigned as security for an obligation (i.e., the obligation of a feature film producer who borrows production money from a bank to repay the loan; see "security agreement").

notice of sale — The form or document required to be filed with the SEC at the federal level and with many state securities regulatory authorities at the state level before or after offering or selling a security in such jurisdictions. The event that triggers the notice filing and the timing of the filing will vary from jurisdiction to jurisdiction (see "notice filing requirement").

notice of tentative writing credits — A Writer's Guild of America form used by producers in notifying all writers who participated in the writing of a screenplay for a motion picture of the statement of credits proposed to be used by the producer (i.e., the tentative credits for "story by" and "screenplay by" are listed on the form). Each participating writer then has a specified number of days (usually ten) to object to the proposed credits if such writer is not satisfied with the credit assigned to him or her. The notice is usually provided at the same time the writers are provided with a copy of the "shooting script" (see "Writer's Guild of America").

notices provision — A common clause in contracts that sets out the addresses of the parties to the agreement and provides instructions for sending important written communications to such parties (see "contract").

novel — A literary form characterized by a long and complex original prose narrative that deals with human experiences as related through a connected series of events. Novels sometimes serve as the basis for screenplays (see "literary property").

novelization of a screenplay — The converting of a motion picture script into a short literary version of the script (up to 7500 words, not a full-blown novel). The novelization of a screenplay provides another possible avenue for exploitation of a motion picture to a film's producer/distributor (i.e., the licensing of such rights may generate additional revenue from a motion picture project; see "merchandising" and "novel").

novelization rights — The authority to convert a motion picture script into a long and complex original prose narrative (i.e., novel; see "novel" and "novelization of a screenplay").

NSMIA — (see "National Securities Market Improvement Act").

nudity clause — A negotiated provision in actor/actress employment agreements that specifies when, if and under what circumstances an actor or actress may be filmed in the nude (see "nudity rider").

nudity rider — An amendment or addition attached to a performer's employment agreement for the purpose of obtaining the prior approval of the actor/actress in situations where such performers are appearing in a feature film that calls for such actor or actress to be nude or semi-nude (see "nudity clause" and "rider").

nudity/sex scenes — A typical heading for the paragraph in a performer's employment agreement that sets out the contractual provisions relating to nudity and/or the performer's appearance in sex scenes. If the producer intends to obtain a nudity waiver, the contract should be drafted to limit allowable nudity and/or sex scenes (or to provide for the use of a double where appropriate) according to the performer's requirements. The contract should also prohibit the use of nude scenes in trailers, music videos, still photographs, etc. unless the performer provides his or her written consent (see "nudity rider" and "nudity waiver").

nudity waiver — A full or partial release signed by an actor or actress providing that such person intentionally and voluntarily has given up, relinquished or surrendered his or her right to object to being photographed in the nude (see "nudity rider").

number of screens — The total count of the whitish, matte, beaded or metallic surfaces on which the motion picture is projected in theaters in the United States or other jurisdictions. The number of screens in the United States in 2005 was 38,852, with 709 of those existing at drive-in theaters. Thus, hypothetically assuming the major studio/distributors and their subsidiary/affiliates considered in the aggregate have twenty-eight films in release (on average) in any given week and average 1,000 prints per film, that means those films being distributed by the major studio/distributors would take up 28,000 screens in the U.S. or 72 percent of the available screens), thus preventing the films being distributed by independent distributors from exhibiting their films on those same screens. Also, interestingly enough, this hypothetical 72 percent of screens is very close to the percentage of screens reported at the entry "Market Share" herein which points out that it only takes a selected 75 percent of the theaters in the U.S. to generate more than 90 percent of the box office gross. In addition, as also pointed out at the entry "Market Share" herein, for the last decade or so, the MPAA companies (i.e., the major studio/distributors) have succeeded in grabbing a 92 percent plus market share of U.S. theatrical box office receipts (see "blind bidding," "blockbuster strategy," "controlled theater," "major exhibition chains," "market power," "market share" and "relationship-driven business").

numbers game — A term referring to the fact that certain transactions are predominantly influenced by the applicable numerical variables and that persons involved in such transactions must be aware of such variables (i.e., must play the odds). For example, if a film producer were to conduct a general solicitation of prospective investors, in the context of a public/registered securities offering and used cold calls (i.e., telephone calls to prospective investors with which the producer and other upper-level management of the production company had no pre-existing relationship), experienced telephone solicitors suggest that eventually such telephone calls will settle into a fairly dependable ratio of calls to sales, which then makes such a calling operation a numbers game (i.e., if the producer calls enough people, he or she will raise the money needed). In addition, the concept is relevant to the producer's choice between available forms of film finance (e.g., a banking executive recently indicated that only about 1 in 200 of the producers who approach the bank seeking production financing succeeded in getting a loan). A spokesman for an international bank, active in financing films on a splits rights basis, estimates that approximately sixty-five U.S. made films each year are financed in this manner, that's some sixty-five films out of about two thousand a year. On the other hand, not even the studio executives responsible for reviewing submitted screenplays know how many such scripts are considered by the studios in the course of a given year, thus determining the odds against obtaining studio financing on a project are simply not known, although clearly enormous (see "availability analysis," "number of screens" and "pro and con analysis").

numerical limitation on investors — (see "investor numerical limitations").

nut — (see "house nut").

objective — Something toward which effort is directed. Also, expressing or dealing with facts or conditions as perceived without distortion by personal feelings, prejudices or interpretations (see "bias," "dream" and "goal").

objective delivery requirements — Quantifiable and time-specific standards that must be met by a film's producer in delivering various elements of a completed feature film to a distributor. Such delivery requirements should not be based on some subjective approval of the distributor, thus producers should avoid language in the distribution agreement that calls for an artistic judgment by the distributor (see "delivery schedule").

obligor — Generally, one who has an obligation, such as an issuer of bonds, a borrower of money from a bank or another source or a credit customer of a business supplier or retailer. In a loan situation, an obligor is legally bound to repay the debt (to the obligee), including interest, when due (see "debt" and "lender financing").

obscene material — Material which, taken as a whole, appeals to the prurient interest and lacks serious literary, artistic, political or scientific value. Matter so classified is not protected by the "free speech" guarantee of the First Amendment to the U.S. Constitution. Material is considered "obscene" when (1) the subject as a whole appeals to the prurient interest of the average person, using contemporary community standards, (2) the work depicts or describes in a patently offensive way sexual conduct proscribed by state statute and (3) the work as a whole lacks serious literary, artistic, political or scientific value. The issues of how "local" the community must be and by whose standards obscenity is to be determined are set out in statutes but it has been held that "contemporary community standards" is a sufficient jury instruction without specifying the geographical extent of the community (see "censorship," "pornography" and "prurient").

obstruction of justice — The impeding of those who seek justice in a court of law, or those who have duties or powers of administering justice. The offense includes attempting to influence, intimidate or impede any juror, witness or officer in any court regarding the discharge of his or her duty, as well as the actual impeding of the due administration of justice (see "racketeering" and "RICO").

off-balance sheet partnerships — Film financing vehicles, such as limited partnerships or manager-managed LLCs that raise money not reflected on the balance sheets of the controlling production company or studio (see "corporation," "limited liability company" and "limited partnership").

offer — A manifestation of willingness to enter into a bargain, so made as to justify another person in understanding that his, her or its assent to that bargain is invited and will conclude it. The offer creates a power of acceptance permitting the offeree by accepting the offer to transform the offeror's promise into a contractual obligation (see "contract").

offer for sale — (see "sell").

offering — In the context of a manager-managed LLC or limited partnership, the offer and sale of interests or units in the entity made either in reliance on available exemptions from registration under the 1933 Act and compatible state securities laws (i.e., private offerings), or as a public offering (i.e., registered with the SEC and in each state in which offers or sales are to be made; see "limited liability company" and "limited partnership").

offering ceiling — A limit on the total amount of money that can be raised pursuant to a specific type of securities registration or exemption (see "ceiling," "private placement" and "registration").

offering circular — An alternative phrase used in describing securities disclosure documents. The SEC's Regulation A disclosure document is specifically referred to as an offering circular as opposed to a prospectus (also see "disclosure document," "offering memorandum," "prospectus," "Regulation A" and "preliminary offering circular").

offering date — The date on which a distribution of securities is first made available for sale to the public (see "securities").

offering expenses — The organizational and syndication expenses incurred in organizing the entity and selling the securities in a securities offering, such as a corporate stock, manager-managed LLC or limited partnership offering. Generally, the offering expenses in a private placement should not exceed approximately 15 percent of the aggregate offering proceeds, including broker/dealer commissions and due diligence expenses. For offerings sold through issuer sales, the offering expenses should be no higher than 4 percent to 5 percent (even less for offerings over 1 million dollars). Some states impose a ceiling on such amounts in private offerings. NASD guidelines limit broker/dealer commissions in a public offering to 10 percent plus .5 percent for bona fide due diligence expenses and limits offering expenses to 15 percent of the offering. Such offering expenses are not part of a film's budget, thus, when setting forth the use of proceeds for a film offering, the offering expenses should be set out separate from the film budget items (see "commission," "gross offering proceeds," "organizational expenses," "proceeds of the offering" and "syndication expenses").

offering memorandum — A securities disclosure document (e.g., in limited partnership, corporate stock or manager-managed LLC offerings) usually associated with a private placement offering (i.e., an offering that is being conducted in reliance on available exemptions from the federal and state securities registration requirements). This is the document provided to potential investors in privately placed securities offerings such as film limited partnerships or manager-managed limited liability company offerings. It normally contains information on the proposed investment, the terms and conditions under which it is offered, the risks involved, the federal tax consequences of the investment, financial projections, various information concerning the general partner or manager and the management's relationship to the venture, certain required legends and purchaser representations, among other disclosures. The term is sometimes confused with the term "prospectus" although most securities practitioners reserve the term prospectus for the securities disclosure document used in association with public/registered offerings (see "private placement offering memorandum," "offering circular," "memorandum" and "prospectus").

offering price — The price per unit at which a new or secondary distribution of securities is offered for sale to the public (also called "public offering price" (see "offering").

offering proceeds — (see "proceeds of the offering").

officers — Persons empowered by a corporation's bylaws and by statute to perform the duties of their offices and to execute contracts and other instruments on behalf of the corporation. A corporation's day-to-day operations are supervised and conducted by its officers and employees [see "corporate stock," "corporation," "director (corporate)" and "shareholders"].

official nationality — (see "nationality test").

off-network — Other than on the four major free television organizations, CBS, ABC, NBC and Fox. The phrase is sometimes used to refer to

television syndication as in the "off-network syndication market" (see "syndication").

off-network syndication market — (same as "television syndication").

off-network television productions — Television programming produced especially to be shown on local television stations or cable (see "off-network," "off-network syndication market" and "syndication").

offset rights — The authority to adjust accounting records to compensate for a credit or loss incurred by a second party. In the film distribution agreement the distributor may seek offset rights to adjust the accounts as between the producer and distributor. Also, if a distributor/exhibitor agreement provides for offset rights the exhibitor is able to deduct co-op advertising or other expenses owed to the exhibitor by the distributor from distributor rentals which would have otherwise been paid to the distributor. Lending banks will typically require that the distributor's offset rights be waived so as to better ensure more rapid payment to the bank. It would make sense for any entity providing production funds (e.g., a film limited partnership or manager-managed LLC) to also request that the distributor's offset rights be waived until the financing entity has recouped its investment (see "distribution agreement," "lender financing," "license agreement," "limited partnership" and "negative pickup").

offshore — (as used in the U.S.) Any financial organization with headquarters outside the country (see "offshore banks").

offshore banks — Banks headquartered outside the U.S. (see "offshore").

offshore companies — Business organizations with headquarters outside the U.S. (see "offshore banks").

offshore entity— Any business organization that is headquartered outside the U.S. (see "offshore").

offshore territories — (see "foreign market").

off-the-bottom expenses — Another contractually defined term sometimes used in feature film distribution agreements to describe another category of distributor expense deductions that are taken by the distributor after payment of gross participations, if any, but before net profits. For example, in a distribution arrangement where production costs are provided by a limited partnership, manager-managed LLC or a third party financier (other than a bank/lender) the distributor may want to first deduct from gross receipts its distribution fee, then any off-the-top expenses, then gross participations, if any, then off-the-bottom expenses and remit some or all of the balance to the producer's group that is responsible for providing the partnership or financier with recoupment of the negative costs plus whatever return they contracted for. This same financing entity may also be responsible for dividing up the balance of the net profits as between deferrals, net profit participations and the producer's share. On the other hand, if a bank or lender were involved in a negative pickup situation, the negative costs plus interest and fees would be paid by the distributors to the bank or lender upon delivery of the film from the producer to the distributor, then as revenues were generated by the exploitation of the film, the distributor might take its distribution fees, off-the-top expenses, pay gross participations, if any, take off-the-bottom costs and remit some or all of the balance to the producer's group as net profits. In the studio financed production-financing/distribution arrangement, the distributor typically takes its distribution fees first, then off-the-top expenses, pays gross participants, if any, takes off-the-bottom costs, deducts interest payments, then recoups the negative cost and finally, if anything is left, remits some negotiated percentage of the balance to the producer group as their share of the film's net profits (see "lender financing," "limited partnership," "negative pickup," "off-the-top expenses," "production-financing/distribution agreement" and "when the money's paid").

off-the-top deductions — (see "off-the-top expenses").

off-the-top expenses — Contractually defined feature film distribution costs that represent the first group of expenses deducted by the distributor from the distributor's gross receipts. Off-the-top expenses typically include licenses and taxes, checking and collection costs, any expenses associated with converting foreign currency into U.S. dollars, residual payments, trade dues, assessments and local advertising. The major studio/distributors rather uniformly deduct their distribution fees first (i.e., they base the percentage calculation on the largest pool of money received by the distributor, 100 percent of the distributor's gross receipts), then they deduct off-the-top expenses, if any, before paying any contractual gross participations out of this remaining fund which may be labeled "accountable gross" or "adjusted gross." Some independent distributors may deduct certain distribution expenses off-the-top before computing their distribution fee. Note that a lower distribution fee percentage is most likely to result in higher distribution fees if the fee calculation is applied to the larger pool of money (i.e., before the off-the-top expenses are deducted). Other distributors may want to deduct all distribution expenses off-the-top and then divide up the balance between participants pursuant to pre-agreed percentages (see "accountable gross," "adjusted gross" and "fifty/fifty net deal").

oligopoly — An industry in which a few large sellers of substantially identical products dominate the market; a market situation in which a small number of selling firms control the market supply of a particular good or service and are therefore able to control the market price. An oligopolistic industry is more concentrated than a competitive one but is less concentrated than a monopoly (see "antitrust," "cartel," "market share" and "monopoly").

oligopolistic industry — A business that is dominated by a few large sellers of products (see "cartel" and "oligopoly").

omissions — Things neglected or left undone. In the context of a securities offering, material disclosures not included in the disclosure document (see "anti-fraud rule" and "errors and omissions insurance").

omnies — Extras in a film who speak only atmospheric words as part of a group (see "bit player" and "extras").

one-line description — The briefest possible written representation of a proposed motion picture screenplay that is sometimes used by experienced screenwriters, directors or producers to submit (i.e., pitch) a concept to studios or other production companies for development funding (see "basic story outline," "synopsis" and "treatment").

one-picture license — (see "single-picture license").

one sheet — A standard size (27 inches by 41 inches) color movie poster that is used for display at theaters and in other locations. The one sheet usually contains the basic elements from which a film's newspaper ads are made, including a graphic design such as a photograph or drawing, a custom title treatment, a lead line to accompany the title, credits for principal cast and crew and any outstanding quotes from critical reviews (see "lobby card" and "sellsheet").

online casting services — Web sites on the Internet that provide news and casting information for actors, along with places where actors can connect with the nationwide performance community (see "Back Stage.com" and "CastPages.com").

ongoing costs — Expenses that continue to accrue. For example, in the context of a film distribution deal any of the distributor expenses that are based on some percentage of a defined portion of the film's revenue stream would be considered ongoing costs, so long as there was no ceiling on such expenses. Thus, residuals, taxes, trade association dues, gross profit participations and even interest up to a point all might be considered ongoing costs. This concept helps to explain why after a motion picture achieves net profits for one accounting period, it may not be in net profits as of the next accounting statement (i.e., these ongoing costs may have increased substantially during the next accounting period; see "gross receipts" and "net profits").

on spec (speculation) — The production of a motion picture with no negative pickup or distribution deal in place (i.e., the producer is speculating that the film will be good enough to attract a distribution deal). Also, producers without funds often seek the assistance of writers, attorneys, accountants and others in the development or financing of a film project and ask that such services be provided on spec (i.e., without being compensated on a current basis). In addition, screenwriters sometimes write screenplays on spec hoping to submit or sell the script when it is completed or have a production company option the script (see "bidding war," "independent producers" and "spec").

on-the-lot — Film industry jargon meaning a production company has a presence (e.g., an office) at one of the major studio/distributor or large production company facilities (i.e., on the studio lot) typically because the production company has a first-look and/or development deal with the studio/production company (see "development deal" and "first-look deal").

on-the-lot deal — Arrangements between production companies and major studio/distributors with sound stages and other related physical facilities permitting the production company to maintain an office on the lot at the studio and to engage in the development of film projects. The studio may provide some additional financial support for the activities of the production company. In exchange, the studio gets a first-look opportunity to distribute all films developed by the production company.

open check — The monitoring of ticket sales at a motion picture theater's box office in which the person doing the checking (i.e., the checker) identifies himself or herself to the theater manager and asks permission to monitor the conduct of the theater's box office personnel.

Such observation enables the checking entity, usually the film's distributor (or on behalf of the distributor), to compare box office receipts on the day checked with a day in which ticket sales were not observed (see "blind check," "checker" and "distribution expense").

opening — The commencement of public exhibition for a film. A film's producer and distributor will typically want to create a special event for a film's opening with the film's director and stars present. As the old film industry joke goes: "Movies are like parachutes, if they don't open, you die." (see "distribution expenses," "premiere" and "promotional activities").

opening date — The day on which a film's public exhibition commences (see "release date").

operating margin — The difference between the revenues of a business and expenses of operating the business, excluding income derived from sources other than the business' regular activities and before income deductions. Reportedly the major studio/distributor operating margins have been quite low in recent decades (see "profitability," "profit margin" and "rising production costs").

operating performance — An analytical and judgmental term used in evaluating the overall accomplishments and behavior of a business. A business' operating performance is usually evaluated with respect to its financial results (see "bottom line" and "financial standings").

operating profit (or loss) — The difference between the revenues of a business and the related costs and expenses, excluding income derived from sources other than its regular activities and before income deductions [also called "net operating profit (or loss)," "operating income (or loss)" and "net operating income (or loss)"].

operating statistics — (see "financial standings").

operational staff — Those hired to work on a film because the worked performed in relation to the production of a motion picture is considered practical as opposed to creative. Operational staff includes camera, sound and stunt persons, grips, drivers and others. Sometimes these categories are simply referred to as production staff and/or crew (see "cast," "crew," "production staff' and "staff').

opinion makers — Influential people from various walks of life (arts, media, politics, etc.) who may be available to help spread favorable word-of-mouth about a film prior to its opening. The term does not include film critics and feature writers (see "critic," "industry critic" and "sneak preview").

OPM — (see "other people's money").

opportunity cost — Generally, the highest price or rate of return an alternative course of action would provide (see "adjusted rate of return" and "cost of capital").

optical dupe — A duplicate film negative printed in an optical printer and typically containing optical effects (see "dupe").

optical effects — Modifications of the photographic image as filmed in a motion picture camera, produced in an optical printer (see "optical printer").

optical house — A company that specializes in customized optical printing and/or special effects for motion pictures (see "optical effects").

optical print — A film with positive images produced on an optical printer (i.e., other than by contact printing; see "optical house" and "optical effects").

optical printer — A film camera and projector that operate in combination to reproduce photographic images on film that has already been processed. The optical printer is used to add images or to enlarge or reduce the existing images (see "optical effects").

optical soundtrack — A sound track optically recorded onto photographic film. It is read (played back) on an optical sound reader (see "mag optical sound track").

optimum release pattern — A movie distribution plan that is expected to or produces the most favorable results in terms of attendance (see "launch windows" and "release pattern").

option agreement — (see "option").

option or option contract — Generally, a binding promise by which the owner of property agrees that someone else has the privilege of buying the property at a fixed price within a stated period of time. In film, a negotiated written agreement that provides to the option purchaser who pays an option fee the exclusive right to develop, finance, produce or sell the property (i.e., a script) during a specified period of time. The option contract typically specifies a given date by which the property is to be in production, funding is secured, the outright purchase takes place or the option is renewed for an option renewal fee. Otherwise, the option and associated rights will expire and the rights to the property will revert to the original owner. The option agreement is typically one of the first steps in the development of a property into a motion picture (also referred to as "option agreement"; see "acquisition agreement," "acquisition of story rights," "clearance" and "development").

option period — With respect to a literary property, the period of time provided by contract within which the party holding the option right has to exercise that right (i.e., the length of time during which a producer who has optioned a literary property has to secure financing to produce the property, to find a purchaser, to purchase rights to the property or renew the option as per the option agreement; see "option/purchase agreement").

option/purchase agreement — A contract between a producer or production company and a writer that sets out the terms and conditions for the holding of an option right or specified right to make a motion picture based on the literary property and if specified contingencies are met, the outright purchase of the property (also called "option/acquisition agreement"; see "option period").

oral representations — Spoken statements (as opposed to written) made to influence action. In negotiating contracts it is important to incorporate any related oral representations into the written agreement. In film distribution situations, statements regarding the manner in which the distributor intends to distribute a given film are often made orally in various conversations between a film producer and representatives of the distributor. The problem occurs when such statements are not included in the written memorialization of the parties' negotiations (i.e., the written distribution

agreement). The problem is made worse because most film distribution agreements contain a so-called "entire agreement" clause (see "contract of adhesion," "distribution agreement," "entire agreement clause," "good faith" and "negotiate").

orchestra — A large ensemble of musicians who perform on a collection of instruments in which strings are prominent, thereby distinguishing it from the band or wind ensemble (see "conducting" and "symphony orchestra").

orchestration — The art of scoring for different instruments from a musical sketch (see "instrumentation," "orchestra" and "scoring").

orchestrator — The person who takes the composer's or arranger's sketch and assigns parts to the various voices and/or instruments (see "arranger" and "orchestra").

order of appearance — A method of listing the screen credits of the performers in a film in which the performers' names are listed in the order that they appeared on screen (i.e., chronological order as opposed to alphabetical or some other order; see "credits" and "order of credits").

order of credits — The manner in which screen billing is organized. The front credits usually run as follows: distributor, producer/production company presents a (name of director) film, followed by the name or names of the principal stars, then the film title (see "billing," "order of appearance" and "top billing").

ordinary course of business — According to the common practices and customs of commercial transactions; the usual and necessary activity that is normal and incidental to a business.

Occasional isolated or casual transactions are not frequent or continuous enough to constitute the ordinary course of business. This is a phrase that is commonly seen in feature film distribution agreements when the parties have failed to negotiate more specific language. The phrase "ordinary course of business" is a very vague standard of conduct for business practices. It is not a precise standard that can be applied in advance. It is merely a standard that can be applied after the fact, in arbitration or litigation, by bringing in various persons with expertise in the industry to explain what is usual and customary with respect to such practices. Thus, the distributor using this language in its distribution agreement has a lot of leeway pursuant to such language to do whatever it desires, on a given issue, knowing that it may take a complaint from the other party and either an arbitration proceeding or a trial and court judgment to firm up the standard of conduct. The distributor knows that the producer is not likely to sue anyway and if the producer sues, the distributor will most likely settle out of court for an amount less than what was contractually due. Producers may want to consider negotiating such language out of the distribution deal wherever possible and replacing it with a more clear standard of conduct (see "contract of adhesion," "inferior bargaining position," "market power," "subjective terms" and "sue us").

ordinary expense — For tax purposes, an expense that is customary or usual within the experience of a particular trade, industry or community. To be deductible as a trade or business expense, an expenditure must be both ordinary and necessary in relation to the taxpayer's trade or business (see "necessary expense" and "tax benefits").

ordinary income — Income from the normal activities of an individual or business, as distinguished from capital gains from the sale of assets. For tax purposes, ordinary income is the income subject to being taxed at the highest rates as opposed to capital gains which may be taxed at lower rates. Generally, only capital losses may be deducted against capital gains and only ordinary income may be offset by the other deductions (see "capital gain" and "income").

ordinary interest — Simple interest based on a 360-day year, unlike exact interest that is calculated using a 365-day year. Film distributors charging simple interest on the negative cost of a film will collect more interest for that final partial accounting period than if exact interest were being charged. Such amounts could be substantial in light of the recent increases in film production costs (see "exact interest" and "interest").

ordinary key — A geographical area with the attributes of a major key but with a metropolitan population of approximately 50,000 to 80,000 (see "key" and "major key").

organized crime — A syndicate of professional criminals who primarily rely on unlawful activities as a way of life (see "discrimination," "extortion," "fraud," "larceny," "Mafia," "racketeering," "RICO" and "white collar crime").

organizational expenses — Expenses paid or incurred in connection with the organization of a limited partnership, manager-managed LLC or other new business. Unless a Section 181 election is made, such expenses are not deductible but must be amortized over a sixty month period beginning with the commencement of the business. They are costs that are incidental to the creation of the entity, chargeable to a capital account and of a character that, if spent incident to the creation of an entity having an ascertainable life, would be amortized over that life. They must be incurred during the period beginning at a point which is a reasonable time before the entity begins business and ending on the date prescribed by law for filing the entity's return (determined without regard to extensions) for the taxable year the entity begins business. Included are legal fees for services incidental to the organization of the entity, such as negotiation and preparation of the organizational agreement and preparation and filing of the certificate of organization, accounting fees for establishing the entity accounting system and necessary filing fees (see "amortization," "Section 181 of the IRS Code," "start-up costs" and "syndication expenses").

organization fees — Fees paid as part of an entity's organizational expenses (see "organizational expenses").

original — With respect to a screenplay, one that has not been adapted from an article, book, play, existing movie or other source material (see "certificate of authorship," "chain of title," "clearance" and "screenplay").

original cost — All costs associated with the acquisition of an asset (see "asset").

original invested capital — The amount in cash contributed to the capital of a limited partnership or manager-managed LLC by the unit holders and the general partners or managers, if any such general partner/manager cash contributions are made (see "capital").

original issue — The initial sale or issue of a security (see "issuer" and "securities").

original Paramount defendants — The film industry companies that were sued for antitrust law violations by the U.S. Justice Department in 1938, resulting in the Paramount Consent Decree of 1948. The defendants fall into three groups: (1) the producer/distributor/exhibitor defendants (Paramount, Loews, RKO, Warner Bros. and 20th Century Fox), all of which produced motion pictures but distributed and exhibited their own films through subsidiary or affiliate companies, (2) the producer/distributor defendants (Columbia and Universal) both of which produced films and distributed their own films through subsidiaries and (3) a single distributor defendant (United Artists) which was engaged only in distribution (see "controlled theater," "major exhibition chains," "market share," "number of screens," "Paramount Consent Decree of 1948," "political influence" and "TriStar Case").

original picture negative — The film that is initially exposed in the camera and subsequently processed (see "exposed film" and "negative").

original screenplay — The film script that is created by a writer or writers from his or her or their or others' concept and story and not adapted from a book, play or other literary work (also see "original" and "screenplay").

original score — (see "composer's original score," "score" and "scoring").

original sound negative — Film that is initially exposed in a film recorder (see "negative" and "original picture negative").

Oscars — The nickname given to the copyrighted statuettes awarded annually through the Academy Awards ceremonies for outstanding achievement in numerous areas of expertise in the film industry (see "Academy Awards," "Academy of Motion Picture Arts and Sciences," "insider's game," "market share" and "member of the club").

other people's money (OPM) — A reference commonly made by entrepreneurs of all kinds, including film producers, who use funds provided by investors or others to start or build their business. The concept is related to the idea of spreading the risk in the sense that the risks associated with starting or building a business are shared with others. The phrase may be used with reference to investor financing or lender financing (see "investor financing," "lender financing" and "studio financing").

other versions — Different edited copies of a feature film for use in various markets or territories; also a sub-section in certain feature film distribution agreements that specifically sets out the requirements relating to different edited copies of a film either for the purpose of protecting a producer or distributor's cutting rights or to establish the distributor's requirements for different copies of the same film. For example, besides the domestic theatrical version of a movie, other versions may be edited for U.S. free television, airline in-flight use, syndication, pay and cable television and the United Kingdom (see "creative control," "delivery requirements" and "final cut").

outakes — Rejected versions of the same basic film shots that are edited out of (i.e., not used in) the completed version of the film; footage shot but not selected for the final cut of a film (see "cutouts" and "take").

outline — A preliminary treatment of a concept for a film (i.e., a rough sketch of the filmmaker's intended approach to the film's subject including

some description of the principal characters and basic story elements in 5,000 words or less; see "synopsis" and "treatment").

out-of-favor Indies — A phrase used by industry analysts to refer to independent producers who as a group may be less favored than the major studios for film finance purposes during certain parts of the industry's economic cycles. The industry is currently so dominated by the major studio/distributors that it is difficult to foresee when and if independent distributors and/or producers will ever be back in favor regardless of any so-called economic cycles. Thus, the phrase "out-of-favor indies" may describe a permanent state of affairs for independent filmmakers in the U.S. (see "cyclical industry," "economic cycle" and "market power").

out of state corporation — (see "foreign corporation").

output arrangements — (see "output deal").

output deal — A contract through which one entity promises to deliver its entire output to another and the other party promises to accept the entire output supplied (e.g., a distribution arrangement between a production company and a distributor in which the distributor commits in advance to distribute the films produced by the producer). The term also refers to a licensing agreement in which a pay television entity commits to present whatever films a studio produces (see "independent producers" and "output distribution agreement").

output distribution agreement — A contract between a feature film production company and a film distributor providing that so long as the films produced by the production company meet certain specified minimum requirements, the distributor agrees to distribute all of such films (see "minimum requirements" and "output deal").

outreach campaign — (see "grass roots campaign").

outright sale — A term defined in some distribution agreements as a license to any person, by the distributor or any franchised sub-distributor, to distribute the film for theatrical exhibition, in a particular geographic area and for a particular period of time (other than any such license for a period of less than one year for theatrical exhibition in a part of any country), without any obligation of such person to account for or report to the distributor or such franchised sub-distributor the amount of any proceeds or expenses of such distribution or sub-licensing. Thus, in the motion picture industry, an "outright sale" does not refer to a true sale, but instead to the license of a right for a flat fee instead of an ongoing percentage of profits. Flat fee arrangements are commonly employed with certain territories and particular media (e.g., some foreign territories). The outright sale provides a lump-sum payment or payments and minimizes the distributor's expenses since it will not have to monitor sub-distribution and provide periodic accounting statements for those territories. However, there can be a significant difference between what a distributor is paid by a foreign sub-distributor for the rights to exploit a motion picture in a given territory on an outright sale basis and what the distributor may have been able to earn on the film if it distributed the film in such territory through its own facilities (in the event that such facilities existed). The producer may want to seek limits on the distributor as to the territories and media in which such types of sales may be

made (i.e., the producer may want to seek to insert language in the distribution agreement that prohibits outright sales by the distributor in the major foreign territories including France, the United Kingdom, Germany, Australia, Japan, Spain and Italy; see "flat sale," "franchised sub-distributor" and "receipts").

outs — (see "outakes").

outside director — A member of a corporation's board of directors who is not an employee of the company. Such directors are usually paid on a per meeting basis for such service (see "corporation," "officers" and "shareholders").

outside investors — Individuals or entities who invest money for the production of films on a project or multiple-film basis through limited partnerships or manager-managed LLCs and who are not shareholders, directors, officers or employees of the producing entity (see "financing").

outside offered projects — In the context of a film distribution agreement in which the distributor has a right of first negotiation for an individual artist's next theatrical film, the term "outside offered projects" refers to proposed motion pictures not developed by the artist but with respect to which the artist is offered employment in the capacity of producer, director, player and/or writer. The distribution agreement may provide that the artist negotiate exclusively with the distributor in good faith with respect to their mutual participation in the production and distribution of the artists's next theatrical motion picture project. The agreement may further provide that if no agreement is reached within 30 days after such negotiations have commenced, neither party shall have any further obligations to the other with respect thereto (see "right of first negotiation").

outside production company — A feature film producer or producing entity that is independent from a major studio affiliated production company (see "independent producer").

outside the pot — Ancillary revenue that is not included in the distributor's gross receipts. In some feature film distribution agreements the distributor will separate out certain ancillary revenues from the gross receipts revenue stream that is subject to participations. In those situations, participants may want to negotiate a participation in that separate revenue stream or eliminate the exclusion (see "ancillary rights," "gross receipts" and "retroactive basis").

outsider's viewpoint — The perspective of someone who is not from the same country, region or a particular group in control of a given business or industry. The U.S. film industry, for example, has from time to time, produced motion pictures focusing on purely American social phenomenon or events with directors from other countries, pointing out that it is sometimes most revealing to look at ourselves as others see us. This book represents another example of this approach to the search for truth (see "insider's game," "marketplace of ideas" and "member of the club").

outstanding — Unpaid; not yet presented for payment; also stock held by shareholders and shown on the corporation's balance sheets under the heading of capital stock issued and outstanding (see "accounts receivable" and "settlement transaction").

outstandings — Among film distributors and exhibitors, the money for advertising expenses or film rentals that the distributor owes the exhibitor or the exhibitor owes the distributor. If the distributor and exhibitor disagree as to the correct amount due on a given film or several films from the same distributor, such amounts may remain unsettled for a period of time and may have to be settled on the basis of a compromise figure relating to more than one film. This practice can have an adverse impact on a movie's profit participants if the settled amount is not properly allocated amongst the films in the group (see "creative accounting" and "settlement").

outstanding security — A security that is held by an investor and which has not been redeemed or purchased back by the issuing corporation (see "corporate stock" and "corporation").

overage — The amount an exhibitor exceeds a film rental commitment to a distributor on a given film. Exhibitors sometimes use excess film rental earned in one circuit theater to fulfill a rental commitment defaulted by another. Also, foreign distributors usually retain a distribution fee computed from the first dollar of film rental in the foreign territory and recoup their guarantees and distribution costs before any additional amounts, known as overages, are payable to the sales agent. The term may also be used to describe the amount that production costs have exceeded a film's budget (see "creative accounting," "foreign distribution," "foreign sales agent," "split rights deal" and "underage").

overages — Film production costs that exceed the amount provided in the prepared budget (see "over-budget").

overall deal — An arrangement with a studio/distributor entered into by an independent producer in which the studio supplies funds to finance the development of the independent producer's film projects and to cover the independent producer's overhead for a specific period of time. In exchange the studio/distributor gets a right of first refusal on the projects developed by the independent producer (same as "housekeeping deal" although broader than a "first look deal").

overall term deal — (see "overall deal").

over-budget — Exceeding the planned expenditures for a film (see "budget" and "over-budget penalty").

over-budget penalty — A form of financial punishment or forfeiture imposed by a studio when a producer of a studio financed film goes over budget. While the terms forfeiture and penalty are often used interchangeably, the generic term "penalty" includes forfeiture and the term "forfeiture" in a more narrow sense relates to a loss of real or personal property, while a penalty most often relates to the loss of money. In either case, the major studio/distributors will try to avoid the use of these particular words in describing their over-budget policy relating to the production of a motion picture, since contract law may not allow unreasonable penalties to be enforced in commercial transactions (see "double add-back," "negotiated cushion," "over-budget policy," "penalty-free cushion" and "withholding").

over-budget policy — The established practice and procedures of a motion picture studio acting as a film financier for a picture with regard to the production costs of the picture exceeding the approved production budget (see "double add-back," "negotiated cushion," "over-budget penalty," "penalty-free cushion" and "withholding").

overhead or overhead costs — Generally, the costs of operating a business that are not directly associated with the production or sale of goods or services; also called indirect costs and expenses or production general expenses (i.e., a charge typically levied by a motion picture studio, generally within the range of 10 percent to 25 percent of the movie's production costs or budget, and designed to cover the studio's overhead). Such overhead costs are attributed to accountants, lawyers, studio executive salaries and their expenses, rental of sound stages or other studio facilities such as dressing facilities, vehicles, telephones, office space and equipment, secretaries salaries, story-abandonment costs and general administrative costs relating to the production area or other costs of doing business that are all absorbed by the studio's various productions. The actual accounting entry for such costs is referred to as the overhead surcharge. Since it is expressed as a flat percentage, it has no relation to actual costs. Interest is usually charged on the overhead surcharge in P-F/D agreements and the overhead surcharge amount is generally deducted prior to the calculation of net profit participations, thus adding significantly to the amount that must be recouped by the studio before a motion picture can realize net profits. Studios have also been known to charge an overhead fee on other expenses which are in themselves overhead. Producers may be able to avoid some overhead costs by avoiding the studio/distributors or by negotiating a smaller percentage for such charges, by specifically listing the deductible charges or in the alternative, by closely monitoring such charges for reasonableness (same as "production overhead" and "non-allocated overhead percentage charge"; see "creative accounting," "interest," "production overhead" and "overhead surcharge").

overhead surcharge — The actual accounting entry made by the studio in studio financing of the production of a film that covers the studio's general or indirect (i.e., overhead) costs (see "distribution expenses," "overhead" or "overhead costs" and "production overhead").

overflow — Moviegoers who choose to see a movie other than their first choice because the movie they came to see is sold out. Such a phenomenon occurs most commonly at megaplex and multiplex theaters (see "megaplex" and "multiplex").

overpayment — An amount of money either paid to the producer by the distributor or credited to the producer's account and reflected on the earnings statement, that is in excess of the proper amount. A provision is often found in film distribution agreements that allows the distributor to deduct equivalent amounts from future producer payments or demand repayment of overpayments already paid to the producer (see "distribution agreement").

overreaching — In commercial law, taking an unfair advantage over another through fraudulent practices or abuse of superior bargaining power; synonymous with fraud. Contracts that are the product of overreaching in an unequal bargaining context may be unenforceable today under modern concepts of fraud or the unconscionability doctrine. It is very likely that all distribution agreements with the major studio/distributor are guilty of overreaching (see "contract of adhesion,"

"negotiate," "submission release" and "unconscionable contract").

overreported travel — Another of the wrongful studio accounting practices sometimes complained about by producers in which the studio inflates the travel expenses associated with the production of a film being produced in conjunction with the studio (see "improperly claimed expenses," "kickbacks" and "studio accounting practices").

override — A commission taken by a film's primary distributor on the distribution fee charged by a sub-distributor. In a situation where an independent distributor utilizes the distribution services of a major studio/distributor for actual distribution, instead of an absorption or "pass through" arrangement, some distributors will charge an "override" (e.g., 10 percent to 15 percent, of the amounts received from the actual theatrical distributor; see "absorption approach," "double distribution fees," "pass-through," "supervision fee" and "sub-distribution").

override approach — (see "override").

overscale — Salaries that are paid to actors and others that exceed the union minimums (see "guild" and "union").

overseas receptivity — The manner in which U.S. produced films are received by the movie-going public or television viewers in foreign countries (see "culturally biased," "culture promotion" and "marketplace of ideas").

over supply of product — More production or output of items destined for a commercial market than demand for the same item. In the motion picture industry, for example, there are more feature films produced each year than there are willing and capable distributors to distribute such films. That over supply of films is partly responsible for a market condition that puts producers (generally) at a disadvantage when it comes time to negotiate the terms of a distribution deal, and distributors tend to take advantage of the producers' lack of leverage (see "inferior bargaining position" and "law of supply and demand").

over-the-counter (OTC) — A method or mechanism for trading securities that are not listed and traded on an organized stock exchange (see "corporate stock," "over-the-counter market," "penny stock" and "pink sheets").

over-the-counter market— A securities market created by dealers who primarily handle trading in securities that are not listed stocks on an organized stock exchange. OTC trading differs from exchange trading in that transactions are carried out through a computer network and negotiations with a number of dealers, called market makers, as compared to the single specialist, single location auction market mechanism used for listed securities trading. The market maker acts as principal in the transaction that involves the dealer as buyer and seller from his or her own inventory (see "broker/dealer," "market makers," "National Association of Securities Dealers" and "stock exchange").

owner — The person who has legal title to property (e.g., the owner of a script; see "clearance" and "title").

owner's equity — (same as "net assets" and "net worth").

ownership— A person's or entity's exclusive right to possess, enjoy and dispose of a thing (e.g., all or a percentage equity interest in the copyright, gross receipts and expenses of a motion picture (see "equity").

ownership interest — In a limited partnership or manager-managed LLC context, the interest of each partner/member in the partnership or LLC (see "equity" and "limited partnership").

P&A — (see "prints and ads").

package — As a noun, the total presentation of the basic elements needed to do a film or TV series or special. Such a film package minimally consists of a script, a budget, a shooting schedule and often commitments by a star or stars and a director. Such a package can also be enhanced by including agreed-upon deferments from the lab, performers or director, and having part of the funding already raised or agreed upon. As a verb, package means to put together the various elements of a film (script, director, actors, producer, etc.) which make a film project more marketable to potential financiers, producers and/or distributors. In the broadest sense, some level of packaging is inherent in the process of producing and financing a motion picture, and the process of packaging generally costs money. Thus, some level of financing must occur prior to production financing. However, some agents, talent agencies, entertainment attorneys and others engage in packaging activities and utilize some of their own clients, with the intent of maximizing their own fees on the packaged film project. In this more narrow sense, packaging may be considered somewhat unethical or illegal and have a negative connotation, in that these "packaged" films are not "cast" rather, they are "packaged" for the benefit of the packaging entity instead of "cast" for the purpose of bringing together the most desirable combination of elements that are likely to result in the best motion picture. Certain "packaged" elements of a film may also prove to be unacceptable to a financing source and may thus become a detriment to the production of a given film (see "casting," "elements," "financing entity," "pay or play" and "syndicated films").

package fee — The compensation paid by a buyer and received by the person responsible for assembling a group of films for sale as a package or a film project with assembled elements (see "elements" and "package").

package sales — More than one film sold as a group for a lump sum. Distributor's sometimes will seek to make outright sales of a picture in certain territories as part of package of several films for a fixed price. Films may also be licensed as part of a package for television (network or syndication). The producer may want to seek to impose reasonable limits on the distributor's ability to sell or license a producer's picture as a package unless a reasonable mechanism is established for providing a fair valuation of such picture compared to the others in the package. If left to the discretion of the distributor, the film in the package that has the fewest or no profit participation obligations may wind up being allocated the most value (see "allocation," "outright sales," "sub-distributor" and "syndication").

packaging — The activities relating to putting together a film package (i.e., attaching actors and a director to a script and offering to a production entity as a package — not separately; see "package," "package fee," "packaging agent" and "tying arrangement").

packaging agent — A motion picture talent agent who goes beyond the traditional services relating to representing the interests of his or her talent clients by obtaining employment and puts together a film package specifically with roles for the talent represented. Such activities not only impinge on the traditional role of the producer but also may be illegal (see "package," "package fee" and "tying arrangement").

packaging attorney — Entertainment lawyers who bring together the various elements of a film project and assist in obtaining either production financing for the project and/or attaching the elements to the project (see "elements," "executive producer," "package," "packaging" and "producer's representative").

packaging service — A person or entity (not an agent or attorney) who holds themselves out as having expertise relating to the assembling of feature film elements for the purpose of obtaining production financing and provides such services to independent producers (see "package," "packaging agent" and "packaging attorney").

packaging services agreement — An agreement between a film's producer and a packaging services company through which the packaging services company agrees to perform certain services relating to the packaging of the film project (see "package" and "packaging service").

PACs — (see "political action committees")

page — A means of time measurement for a screenplay. A screenplay page, in running time, averages about sixty seconds. For principal photography, a given number of pages are typically scheduled on a specified shooting day (see "screenplay").

paid ads — (see "advertisement" and "advertising").

paid advertising — (see "advertisement" and "advertising").

paid-in capital — The capital received by a corporation from investors in exchange for stock, as distinguished from capital generated from earnings or capital that has been donated (see "capital").

paid media — All forms of paid advertising (see "advertising").

pan and scan — A process used in presenting feature films on television in which the film's wide-screen dimensions are pared down to fit the smaller ones of the TV screen. The process involves cutting off some of the wide-screen film images on the edges or editing back and forth between subjects that would have appeared together in the frame on the larger movie screen. Many filmmakers are opposed to the technique saying it distorts the original film's intent. However, the vast majority of films released on videotape and subsequently to pay-TV, basic cable and free-TV outlets use the process (see "edit" and "moral rights").

panning/scanning — (see "pan and scan").

paper profit (or loss) — Unrealized capital gain or capital loss in an investment or portfolio; calculated by comparing the current market prices to the prices at which those assets were originally bought. Such profits and losses become realized only when the securities are sold [see "realized profit (or loss)"].

par — Equal to the nominal or face value of a security. Par value for a corporation's common stock is set by the company issuing the stock. Par value generally does not have any relation to market value (see "no-par stock" and "stated value").

parallel business behavior — The similar conduct of businesses with respect to specific business practices. In the film business, for example, exhibitors have sometimes alleged that the practice of blind bidding, which is engaged in by most of the major studio/distributors, is a conspiracy in restraint of trade, a violation of the federal Sherman Antitrust Act. However, U.S. courts have never held that a showing of parallel business behavior alone conclusively establishes a conspiracy. In order to prove conspiracy, the plaintiff exhibitors would have to show conscious parallel business behavior to infer an agreement, but they need to show additional circumstances that logically suggest joint agreement, as distinguished from individual action that happens to be the same. Other examples of distributor parallel business behavior may include the many unconscionable contract provisions in distribution agreements (see "bidding war," "blind bidding," "conscious parallelism" and "twenty percent rule").

Paramount Case — (see "Paramount Consent Decree of 1948").

Paramount Consent Decree of 1948 — The popular name for the final judgments handed down by the U.S. District Court for the Southern District of New York, with respect to each studio/distributor or motion picture related defendant (Loew's, Paramount, Columbia Pictures, United Artists, Universal, American Theatres, Warner Bros., 20th Century Fox and RKO) in the U.S. v. Paramount Pictures case. A separate judgment was issued for each of the nine defendants, and although similar, the judgments were not identical. Generally, the decrees prohibited certain trade practices (e.g., block booking, unreasonable clearances), and with respect to some of the defendants, but not all, the decrees mandated that the defendant distributors divest themselves of all motion-picture theater holdings and prohibited the acquisition of theaters in the future. The decrees sought to put an end to so-called vertical integration, through which the motion-picture companies produced, distributed and exhibited their film products to the public. The intention was to provide competing theaters an equal opportunity to license motion pictures for commercial presentation. Since the Reagan presidency, however, and partly due to the effective lobbying effort of the MPAA, the U.S. Justice Department has relaxed its enforcement of the antitrust laws as applied to the major movie studios and vertical integration is once again on the rise. This trend does not favor independent producers, and, in order to combat the resulting increased control of the major studio/distributors over all levels of the industry, independent producers must organize a permanent professional association and seek to protect their long term economic interests by making sure the current administration, the Justice Department and Congress is aware of the effects of the major studio/distributors' re-entry into movie exhibition (i.e., the effects vertical integration has on independent producers; see "antitrust law violations," "block booking," "clearance," "lobbying," "market power," "market share," "merger guidelines," "number of screens," "original paramount defendants," "political influence," "squeeze out," "tracks," "TriStar Case" and "vertical integration").

Paramount decrees — (see "Paramount Consent Decree of 1948").

parent corporation — A company that owns or controls subsidiaries through the ownership of voting stock. A parent company is usually an operating company in its own right. In situations where the parent company has no business of its own, the term "holding company" is often preferred (see "affiliate," "corporation," "holding company" and "subsidiary").

pari passu — A Latin phrase meaning pro rata and concurrent. The phrase is used often to describe the relationship between investors and/or profit participants in a film and when such persons are to recoup their investment or receive their contracted for payments of deferments or profits (see "Latin," "profit" and "profit participant").

parking — A temporary placement of securities, in a public offering, by a broker/dealer, with favored customers who buy at the offering price but resell in the aftermarket at prices generally higher than the initial offering price (see "broker/dealer," "public offering" and "securities").

partial financing — A portion of the development or production funds for a feature film have been raised, are in place or are committed. In the current marketplace for the financing of feature films, it is often helpful to spread the risk (i.e., to use more than one source) for the high risk production financing, and of course, it is generally helpful when approaching a prospective financing source if at least part of the financing is already in place (see "financing," "investor financing," "lender financing" and "studio financing").

partial presentations — An accounting term for financial presentations that do not meet the minimum presentation guidelines of the AICPA or other authoritative accounting organization (see "prospective financial statements," "financial forecasts," "financial projections" and "pro forma financial statements").

partial secondary offering — An offering of securities by both the company and stockholders (see "corporate stock," "corporation," "offering" and "securities").

partially amortized loans — (see "balloon payment").

participant — A term defined in some distribution agreements as any person entitled to receive contingent compensation, as distinguished from fixed compensation (see "contingent compensation," "gross receipts," "net profits" and "profit participation").

participation — A share in the profits of a film; contingent compensation as distinguished from fixed compensation. Also, as between a film's distributor and exhibitor, the weekly dollar sharing on the part of each for cooperative advertising expenditures on a film in a given market (see "profit participation" and "cooperative advertising").

participation loan — A loan made by more than one lender and serviced (administered) by one of the participants, called the lead bank or lead lender (see "debt" and "lender financing").

participation rate — The percentage of a specified portion of a motion picture's revenue stream (i.e., gross receipts or net profits, that an individual or entity is to receive as some or all of his, her or its contribution to the project; see "gross receipts," "net profits" and "participation").

participations in gross receipts — A percentage interest held by an individual or entity in that portion of a motion picture's revenue stream defined as distributor's gross receipts (see "gross receipts," "interest" and "participation").

participatory debt instrument — A hybrid security that in addition to debt features also provides equity participation (i.e., the right to participate with common stockholders in additional distributions of earnings under specified conditions; see "corporate stock," "debt," "equity" and "security" or "securities").

parties (to the contract) — Those individuals or entities who negotiate and sign a binding agreement (e.g., the distributor and producer who sign a film distribution agreement). In some such agreements, the producer is referred to as the grantor or the licensor and the distributor is referred to by a shortened form of its name or as grantee or licensee. Use of the terms distributor and producer would help make it easier for all persons who may review a distribution deal to keep the parties straight (see "grantor," "licensee" and "grantee").

partners — Typically defined in a limited partnership context to include the general

partners and all unit holders (i.e., limited partners) in the limited partnership. Reference to a partner in such a limited partnership refers to any one of the above (see "general partners," "limited partnership" and "profit-sharing ratio").

partnership — A general term that may include both general and limited partnerships; a legal but unincorporated relationship and form of doing business that has been created between two or more persons who contractually associate in the conduct of a trade or business and agree to share in the profits and losses of the enterprise. For tax purposes, the term "partnership" includes any syndicate, group, pool, joint venture or other unincorporated organization through or by means of which any business, financial operation or venture is carried on and that is not, within the meaning of the tax code, a corporation, trust or estate (see "corporation," "general partnership," "joint venture," "profit sharing ratio" and "limited partnership").

partnership agreement — An agreement, generally prepared by the general partner's securities attorney, that serves as the basic underlying legal document relating to and regulating the relationship between a limited partnership's general partners and limited partners (i.e., any valid written agreement of the partners as to the affairs of a limited partnership and the conduct of its business, including all amendments thereto). Such agreements must be drafted in accordance with the specific provisions of the state limited partnership act of the state in which the partnership is being created (also sometimes called "articles of partnership"; see "joint venture agreement" and "limited partnership").

partnership certificate — Documentary evidence of the ownership of an interest in a limited partnership, setting out the number of units owned. Partnership certificates are not required to be used in marketing limited partnerships since the offering memorandum, a copy of the subscription agreement and an acceptance letter from the general partner would ordinarily be kept by the investor as evidence of ownership (see "certificate of limited partnership" and "stock certificate").

partnership contribution to negative cost — A concept relating to films financed partially by funds provided by a limited partnership that refers to what percentage of a film or films' production and/or distribution costs the partnership has provided. Such percentage will be used in determining what profits, if any, will be paid to the partnership. Such deals are usually structured as joint ventures between the limited partnership and a studio/distributor or production company (see "joint venture," "limited partnership" and "when the money's paid").

partnership expenses — The costs incurred in organizing, maintaining and selling the interests in a partnership. Generally, in a film limited partnership, the general partners will be authorized in the partnership agreement to deduct monies to pay for on-going partnership expenses such as the annual preparation of the partnership K-1's, from partnership gross receipts before arriving at net partnership revenues which may be referred to as distributable cash (see "distributable cash," "offering expenses," "Schedule K-1" and "syndication expenses").

partnership gross revenues — The total amount of revenue received by the partnership from all sources for partnership activities including with respect to a film limited partnership the distribution, exhibition and exploitation of the partnership's films (same as "gross partnership revenues" or "gross revenues to the partnership"; see "limited liability company" and "limited partnership").

partnership net — (see "partnership net receipts").

partnership net receipts — The remaining portion of partnership receipts after specified deductions are taken from partnership gross revenues. Some limited partnerships and manager-managed LLCs use the term "distributable cash" to mean the same thing. Partnership net receipts are the funds distributed amongst the partners pursuant to the pre-recoupment and post-recoupment profit-sharing ratios (see "cash distributions," "distributable cash," "profit-sharing ratio" and "payout").

pass — A declination (e.g., an indication from a studio or other production company that they do not wish to participate in the production, financing or development of a given motion picture project submitted to them). Unfortunately, a "pass" sometimes means the studio executives will proceed with their own version of the same project without the people who originally submitted it. The studios simply run the concept or early draft of the script through a series of additional screenwriters, make whatever changes they choose and produce the film anyway, knowing that it will be difficult, time-consuming and expensive for the original submitting party to prove theft or copyright infringement, and even if they do, the damages will likely be nominal (see "go ahead," "green light," "sue us" and "theft of ideas").

passive activity — Any activity that involves the conduct of a trade or business and in which the taxpayer/investor does not materially participate. Losses and credits from passive activities are limited by the tax laws (e.g., passive losses can only be deducted from passive income). In a limited partnership or manager-managed LLC context, the passive activity limitations apply to each partner/member's share of any loss or credit attributable to passive activity of the partnership/LLC. Such limitations do not apply to the entity itself (see "internal revenue service," "investor financing," "passive investors," "securities" and "tax shelter opinion").

passive activity loss — The amount by which the aggregate losses from all passive activities exceed the aggregate income from all passive activities for the tax year (see "passive activity" and "passive income").

passive income — Income from business activities in which a taxpayer does not materially participate, such as a limited partnership or a manager-managed LLC, as distinguished from income from (1) wages and active trading or (2) business and investment income, such as dividends and interest. Pursuant to the Tax Reform Act of 1986, losses and credits from such passive activities are deductible only against income and tax from passive activities, although one passive activity can offset another and unused passive losses can be carried forward from year to year (see "deductions," "passive activity" and "passive loss").

passive investment losses — Expenses that exceed annual income from an investment in which the investor is not actively involved (e.g., limited partnership or manager-managed LLCs; see "limited liability company," "limited partnership" and "loss").

passive investors — Persons who invest in trade or business activities in which such investors do not materially participate (e.g., limited partners or members of a manager-managed LLC; see "active investors," "investor financing" and "securities").

passive investor financing — (see "financing," "limited partnership" and "passive investors").

passive investor vehicles — A business financing instrument or structure involving contributors of funds who are not active in any significant way in the management of the business. Passive investor vehicles include limited partnerships, manager-managed LLCs, existing corporations and investment contracts or profit participation agreements (see "passive income" and "securities").

passive loss — (same as "passive activity loss").

pass-through — In film sub-distribution situations, the charging of the sub-distributor's fee against a film's rentals without a markup or override by the primary distributor (see "absorption arrangement," "double distribution fees," "override," "sub-distribution" and "supervision fee").

pass-through arrangement — (see "pass-through").

pass-through vehicle — An investment vehicle such as a limited partnership or manager-managed LLC that does not pay federal income taxes on the vehicle's income at the entity level. Such taxes are not paid until the entity's income is passed through to its investors and the investors then pay federal income taxes at the individual level (see "direct participation program").

past performance — A concept used by producers to illustrate to prospective distributors and/or investors how well a proposed film may perform at the box office by comparing such future performance with the actual performance of films with similar budgets and genres that have already been distributed (see "box office comparables," "similar pictures" and "track record").

patent — A government grant of a right to exclude others from the making, using or selling of an invention during a specified time period. Thus, a patent constitutes a legitimate monopoly and is designed to give the inventor a fair opportunity to recoup his, her or its costs in developing the item and possibly to make a profit, so as to encourage invention (see "antitrust laws," "copyright," "monopoly" and "trademark").

patron — In art circles generally, a wealthy or influential supporter of an artist or writer, but in a film context, anyone who purchases a movie ticket and thus supports its production and exhibition with a small contribution (see "boycott" and "investor").

patterns of bias — The consistent repetition of outlooks or prejudices (e.g., researchers have determined that Hollywood movies tend to portray certain populations in our diverse society in a stereotypical or negative manner and such consistent portrayals constitute patterns of bias. Such patterns may change over time (see "favorable portrayal," "hidden agenda," "mirrors of society," "prejudice" and "unfavorable portrayal").

Paul Kagan Associates — Media analysts specializing in financial and investment research who present seminars and publish newsletters, studies and reference books for cable tv, pay tv, broadcasting, motion pictures, tv program syndication, home video and home shopping (see "industry analysts," "major exhibition chains" and "*Show Biz News*").

pay and cable television version — An edited copy of a feature film that is suitable for exhibiting on pay cable and basic cable (see "other versions").

pay and play — A contractual commitment from a motion picture production company or studio to not only pay the agreed upon compensation to an artist (producer, director, actor, etc.) but to actually produce the picture and utilize the services of the artist therein. The pay and play arrangement is particularly important for the artist who takes a developed project to a production company and for situations in which the artist's compensation is principally contingent compensation (contrast with "pay or play"; see "nominal payments").

payback — The method and manner of returning money loaned to or invested in a venture (see "interest" and "rate of return").

payback period — The length of time needed to recoup the cost of a capital investment (see "payback").

pay cable — The system for transmitting television signals and programming by wire to the homes of fee paying subscribers (see "cable TV").

payee — Any person to whom a debt should be paid; one to whose order a negotiable instrument, such as a bill of exchange, note or check, is made payable (see "payer").

payer (or payor) — One who pays a debt or is obligated to pay a debt under a promissory note or other financial instrument (see "payee").

pay or play — A contractual obligation between the producer and generally actors or directors providing that the producer will pay a stated amount whether or not the services of the actor or director are performed or required. Such commitments are made by producers in order to obtain corresponding commitments from talent in packaging a film which in turn helps to procure production funding for the project. Such commitments from talent may also be obtained in some circumstances with nominal non-returnable payments based on a percentage of the total salary. The "pay or play" arrangement does not commit the producer to utilize the services of the artist, thus if the project falls through the artist may not only incur some down-time in his or her career and lose a specific opportunity to appear in what was obviously a desirable vehicle but also is cutoff from receiving any contingent compensation related to the project (see "financing," "nominal payments," "packaging" and "pay and play").

pay-or-play commitments — (see "pay or play").

payout — That point in time when an amount invested in a limited partnership or manager-managed LLC has been recouped through cash distributions (i.e., the point in time when the aggregate unreturned capital contributions of the investors in such direct participation programs have become zero). Payout generally is accompanied by a reallocation of the rights to income or cash flow among the participants in an investment (same as "recoupment"; see "post payout sharing ratio" and "pre-payout sharing ratio").

pay-per-transaction — A video/DVD distribution system that requires consumers to pay each time a video or DVD is rented as opposed to each viewing (contrast with "pay-per-view"; also see "first sale doctrine").

pay-per-view — A cable television delivery method wherein the subscriber is billed only for specific programs (i.e., a cable service that makes available to a subscriber an individual movie, sporting event or concert on payment of a fee for that single event; contrast with "pay-per-transaction"; see "cable television" and "subscription television").

pay-per-view rights — The authority to exhibit a motion picture or other program on a pay-per-view basis (see "pay-per-view").

payroll management — (see "payroll and production accounting").

payroll and production accounting — Accounting services relating specifically to movie cast and crew payrolls and production expenses. Such services may include pre-production budgeting, auditing services, preparation of final cast lists, payroll job cost data, final job cost reports and federal and state tax reports along with the computation and payment of residuals and the coordination of union contracts (see "production accountant").

payroll service — (see "payroll and production accounting").

pay television — Subscriber-paid-for television, generally the first pay television window (time period during which a film may be exhibited on pay television) that is presented in an uncut and uncensored format. Pay television includes satellite-delivered pay cable, over-the-air-subscription TV and standard cable (see "cable television").

pay television license agreement — The contract between a film's producer or distributor and a provider of television programming paid for by subscribers (see "pay television revenue").

pay television output arrangement — An agreement between a production company or studio and a subscriber-paid-for-television service such as HBO or Showtime for the pay television service to purchase all of the programming produced by the production company or studio, so long as certain requirements are met (see "output deal").

pay television revenue — Income generated through subscriber-paid-for television (see "free television").

pecuniary — Relating to money and monetary affairs; consisting of money or that which can be valued in money (see "monetary advances," "monetary damages" and "remuneration").

penalty clause — A provision commonly found in contracts, borrowing agreements and savings instruments that provides for penalties in the event a contractual promise is not kept, a loan payment is late or a withdrawal is made prematurely (see "prepayment penalty").

penalty formula — A predetermined formula for reducing the producer's profit participation if the production goes over budget (see "over-budget policy" and "penalty-free cushion").

penalty-free cushion — A percentage of a film's budget (negotiated by the producer with a studio providing production financing) that would have to be surpassed before the film would be considered over-budget and penalties (typically in the range of 5 percent to 10 percent), are imposed (see "budget overages," "double add-back," "penalty formula" and "withholding").

penny stock — Corporate shares that generally sell for less than one dollar per share, although the price may rise to as high as ten dollars per share after the initial public offering. Penny stocks are generally traded over-the-counter (see "corporate stock," "initial public offering," "over-the-counter" and "security or securities").

penny stock offering — The offer and sale of securities relating to low priced corporate stock (see "penny stock" and "securities").

pension fund contributions — Payments made by a film producer or distributor out of a film's budget or from the revenues generated by a film to the retirement funds of the various unions or guilds whose members were involved in the production of the film (see "distribution expenses" and "guild").

per annum — With respect to a year. The major studio/distributors in the film business generally will distribute about fifteen to twenty-five motion pictures per annum (see "number of screens," "rent-a-distributor" and "release slots").

percentage allocated — That portion of a specific fund that is to be apportioned among two or more participants (see "allocation issues," "block booking" and "double bill").

percentage interest — In limited partnership and manager-managed LLC terminology, the respective interests of each investor in the entity and/or its revenue stream (see "limited liability company," "limited partnership" and "percentage participation").

percentage participation — The percentage or fraction thereof of any of several defined levels of a movie's revenue stream (film rentals, gross receipts, adjusted gross, accountable gross, net receipts, net profits, LLC's gross revenues, general partner's net receipts, etc.) in which persons or entities have an interest. The financial interests of persons or entities in a film's revenues, receipts or profits, expressed as percentages and designated by the person or entities authorized to award such participations (distributor, executive producer or producer and in the context of a film limited partnership, possibly the general partner or the manager in a manager-managed LLC). Thus, a person making a contribution to the production or distribution of a given film may negotiate for a percentage of such specified level. A percentage participation differs from deferred compensation (see "contingent compensation," "contingent deferment," "deferment" or deferrals," "fixed deferment," "points," "profit participation" and "talent participations").

percentage rentals — Film rentals paid by a film's exhibitor to the distributor based on a negotiated percentage of the film's box office (see "film rentals" and "flat rentals").

percentage sale — A film rental agreement between a motion picture distributor and an exhibitor that is based on a negotiated percentage of the film's performance at the box office (see "film rentals" and "percentage rentals").

perfectionist director — An overly fussy director who wastes film and the time of cast and crew trying to make every shot perfect. Such directors can be responsible for time and budget overruns and are often avoided by producers (see "auteur," "budget," "collaborative process," "director" and "prima donna").

performance — The fulfillment of a duty or obligation; a promise kept. The term refers especially to completion of one's obligation under a contract (see "duty" and "contract").

performance record — How an individual or entity has performed in the past. In the context of film limited partnerships or manager-managed LLCs, the results of operations of such an entity from an investment perspective (see "past performance," "prior performance" and "track record").

performer employment agreement — A general term referring to written contracts by and between feature film production companies and actors or actresses (see "employment agreement" and "player agreement").

performers — Actors and actresses in film productions who have speaking, dancing or singing parts. Extras and walk-ons are not considered performers (see "featured player" and "supporting player").

perk — A fringe benefit or privilege or profit over and above a salary. The word is an abbreviation for perquisite. Perks often are important negotiating points in employment agreements for the services of actors and actresses. Such negotiated perks may include exclusive ground transportation, the right to retain the artist's wardrobe at the end of the shoot (or to purchase at a negotiated percentage of the producer's cost), for the production company to cover the actor and loan-out company, if any, on the errors and omissions, general liability and worker's compensation insurance policies for the film, to receive invitations to film festivals and celebrity premieres for the film (with a guest), a complimentary copy of the film on video/DVD (or laser disc), a "workout" personal trainer during principal photography (or before if important for the role), use of the studio's corporate jet, for the studio to rent the actor's own motor home (if he or she owns one) and hire a driver to get it to the location, employment of the artist's assistant(s), providing per diem, airfare and credit, if appropriate, a nanny for the artist's children and/or a security person, dialogue coach and/or translator (see "rising production costs").

permanent financing — Long term corporate financing by means of either debt (bonds or long-term notes) or equity (common or preferred stock; see "corporation," "financing," "investor financing" and "lender financing").

permits — Governmental licenses granting permission for a film production company to shoot a portion of a film within the governmental unit's jurisdiction (see "location permit").

perpetual existence — An important corporate characteristic that permits the corporation to continue in existence forever as opposed to a sole proprietorship which is limited by the natural lifetime of its owner and a partnership that can exist only so long as the contractual relationship remains in effect among the parties (see "choice of entity," "corporation," "partnership" and "sole proprietorship").

perpetual rights — The legal power and authority to exploit a film without limit in terms of time (i.e., for an infinite period); forever (see "distribution term" and "term").

perpetuity — Until the end of time (i.e., forever). Feature film distributors, particularly in situations where a studio/distributor provides funding for both the production costs of a motion picture and the distribution expenses will want to obtain a grant of distribution rights in perpetuity, effectively adding that film to its library of films even though copyright ownership may stay with an independent production company (see "distribution term").

per se violations — An infraction of the law that does not require extraneous evidence or support to establish the existence of the infraction. In antitrust law, certain types of business practices are considered per se restraints of trade. Since proof of the conduct alone proves a violation of the Sherman Antitrust Act, there is no need to prove any injury to competitors, that would otherwise be a necessary element in an antitrust action. Price fixing, for example, is a per se violation of the federal antitrust laws (see "antitrust laws," "conduct restrictions," "minimum admission prices," "Paramount Consent Decree of 1948," "price fixing" and "Sherman Antitrust Act").

person — In law, an individual or incorporated group having certain legal rights and responsibilities, thus, an individual, partnership, limited partnership (domestic or foreign), trust, estate, association, corporation or other entity may be referred to as a person (see "natural person").

personal appearance tours — A series of publicity appearances by actors and directors, a certain number of which are commonly contracted for between the producer and distributor (see "promotional activities").

personal guarantee — A guarantee for which the guarantor is personally liable (see "guarantee" and "guaranty").

personal liability provision — Language in an agreement (e.g., a loan), providing that an individual may be held personally responsible for repayment of the debt or other obligation. A film producer may seek to set a limit on his or her personal liability and/or exempt specific assets (see "liability" and "limited liability").

personal manager — A person who manages the affairs of another. In the entertainment industry, the personal manager is generally intimately involved with career development and the creation of a favorable public perception for their clients. Their focus is generally more directed toward the day-to-day activities of their clients than those of agents. Some personal managers combine several roles such as that of lawyer, personal manager and film and television producer (see "agent," "business manager," "entertainment attorney," "personal representative" and "producer's representative").

personal release — A written document signed by an individual whereby such individual gives up some claim, right or interest to the person against whom the claim, right or interest could have been enforced. In film, personal releases are generally obtained from all persons whose names or likenesses may appear in a movie (see "clearance," "release" and "title").

personal representative — A person who represents another in the affairs of that other person, under a power of attorney or due to the incapacity of the principal through death, incompetency or infancy (see "assigns," "heirs,"

"personal manager," "producer's representative" and "successor").

personal security — An obligation to repay a debt evidenced by a pledge, note or bond in contrast to collateral security. Evidences of debt that bind the creditor to the debtor, not the debtor's collateral (see "collateral," "debt" and "recourse loan").

P-F/D agreement — (see "production-financing/distribution agreement").

PGA — (see "Producers Guild of America").

"PG" rating — An MPAA rating indicating that a motion picture has been reviewed by the MPAA's Classification and Rating Administration, and that parental guidance is suggested (i.e., in the MPAA's opinion, the film may contain some material parents might not like for their young children; see "ratings").

"PG-13" rating — An MPAA rating indicating that a motion picture has been reviewed by the MPAA's Classification and Rating Administration and that parents are urged to be cautious since the film may contain some material that may be inappropriate for pre-teenagers (see "ratings").

phantom income/gain — Taxable income or gain that exceeds cash flow or distributable cash in a limited partnership or manager-managed LLC. In other words, since such flow-through vehicles are not taxed at the entity level but may be authorized to make certain deductions from the entity's gross revenues, the amount of cash distributed to investors may not be as great as the amount of revenues that the individual investor is credited with for tax purposes (i.e., the individual investor may have a tax liability on his or her share of the revenues received by the entity but not actually passed on to the individual investor; see "income tax," "limited liability company" and "limited partnership").

phonograph — An instrument by means of which sounds can be mechanically recorded and reproduced (see "compact disc" and "music").

phonograph record — A disc with spiral grooves carrying recorded sound for phonograph reproduction (see "phonograph").

photograph— A picture or likeness obtained through the art or process of producing images on a sensitized surface by the action of light or other radiant energy (see "film" and "photoplay").

photoplay — Another name for screenplay or script, although seldom used anymore (see "screenplay").

physical comedy — A genre of film of light, amusing or humorous characters that utilize facial expression, bodily action or gestures and/or other prop, scenery or action-based humor as opposed to mental humor. Such comedies have tended to fare better in foreign markets over the years as opposed to the more subtle forms of comedy (e.g., so-called relationship movies; see "foreign potential" and "overseas receptivity").

physical production department — A somewhat redundant phrase most commonly used by film industry personnel who are associated with the major studio/distributors to refer to the studio's production department and to clearly distinguish that department from the studio's creative department (see "creative department" and "production department").

physical properties — Tangible possessions or effects. The phrase is sometimes used as a catch-all phrase in the "security interest" paragraph of a studio distribution agreement indicating that in order to secure the studio's advance of production funds to an independent production company for the production of a film, the production company assigns to the studio as security, all of its right, title and interest in the picture, all associated copyrights, all negatives, film, tape and other physical properties created or acquired for the picture (see "security agreement" and "security interest").

pickup — Scenes or shots filmed after the completion of a film's principal photography in order to fill in any gaps in the film's continuity (see "pickups").

pickup deal — (see "pickups").

pickup distribution deal — (see "acquisition distribution agreement" and "pickups").

pickup photography — (see "pickup").

pickup price — The consideration agreed to be paid by a motion picture distributor to a film's producer upon completion and satisfactory delivery of the film to the distributor pursuant to the terms of a negative pick-up distribution agreement. The term is also used by some in the industry to indicate the price paid for a film purchased pursuant to an acquisition distribution agreement. Sometimes the pick-up price will approximate the negative cost of the picture (see "acquisition distribution agreement" and "negative pickup").

pickups — Films acquired for distribution by a distributor on an acquisition distribution basis after such films are completed. Some in the industry erroneously use the term to describe a negative pickup or the term negative pickup to describe such an acquisition when the negative pickup is a technical term describing a specific form of lender financed film production, using a distribution agreement and guarantee as collateral for the loan. The negative pickup transaction is clearly different from a "pickup" or distributor "acquisition" deal (see "acquisition distribution agreement," "negative pickup" and "pickup price").

picture (s) — (see "motion picture").

picture editor — The film production person actually engaged in the editing and/or cutting of positive prints of a motion picture into proper sequence and story form (see "sound editor" and "supervising editor").

picture mix — The combination of feature films that make up the slate of a motion picture production or distribution company. From a financial management point of view, the varying combinations of low, medium and high budget pictures in different genres provide varying financial risks and opportunities that need to be analyzed using financial modeling techniques (see "computer model," "financial management," "financial projections" and "mental modeling").

picture negative — Film that, after exposure to a subject or positive image and subsequent processing, produces a negative picture image on the film (see "exposed film" and "negative").

picture print — Processed film with a positive image and no sound track (see "print").

picture release negative — A film negative that has been conformed to the work print and from which release prints are struck (see "answer print" and "release print").

picture specifications — The required characteristics and elements of a motion picture to be delivered to a financing studio or distributor pursuant to a production-financing/distribution agreement. Such specifications may include the requirement that the approved basic elements be used in the film, such as the specifically identified underlying material or screenplay and specified director, producer and principal cast members. Also, such specifications will require that the final budget not exceed the approved production budget. Production specifications generally also include a start date, production schedule, locations, along with the identification of the production company's attorney and the studio's production executive(s). Delivery specifications may also include a delivery date and a specified film lab. In addition, certain controls, approvals and obligations may be set out in the agreement along with the production company's right of consultation relating to the film's distribution pattern and ad campaign for the initial U.S. theatrical release (see "delivery requirements").

piece of the action — Equity participation in an economic endeavor (see "equity," "investor financing" and "profit participation").

pied piper — In the context of the motion picture business, a reference to the allure of the much publicized glamour, fame and fortune associated with the industry. Just as the "Pied Piper" of the children's fairy tale, films that are exhibited in almost every community in the country and in many across the globe, entice the "children" of the world to come to the center of American filmmaking Los Angeles (see "chasing a dream" and "film schools").

piercing the corporate veil — The process of imposing liability for corporate activity, in disregard of the corporate entity, on a person or entity other than the offending corporation itself. Generally, the corporate form of doing business isolates both individuals and parent corporations from liability for corporate misdeeds. However, the courts will ignore the corporate entity and strip organizers and managers of the corporation of limited liability in certain circumstances (e.g., under capitalization, commingling or misappropriation of funds and other assets, failure to obtain authority to issue stock, disregarding legal formalities, etc.) In so doing the court is said to be piercing or lifting the corporate veil (see "alter ego doctrine," "corporation," "ultra vires activities" and "undercapitalization").

pilot — Typically a ninety minute or two hour Movie of the Week (MOW) that is produced as a hopeful forerunner to a television series (see "television series" and "television special").

pink sheets — Daily publications of the National Quotation Bureau that detail the bid and asked prices of thousands of over-the-counter equity stocks. Brokerage firms subscribe to the pink sheets, named for their color, because the sheets not only give current prices but list market makers who trade each stock (see "broker/dealer," "market maker," "over-the-counter" and "securities").

pipeline — A reference to the established relationships and the film distributor's organization that takes a film from the producer and lab to its exhibitors (see "blockbuster strategy," "distribution channels," "reciprocal preferences" and "relationship driven business").

piracy — The commercial appropriation, reproduction and distribution of property in contravention of the protections provided by copyright, patent, trademark or trade secret law. Piracy is often committed in foreign territories (i.e., beyond the reach of the owner's jurisdiction). The MPAA and its sister association (the MPA) take a lead role in the prevention of piracy. Domestic exhibitors have occasionally been accused of engaging in such activities (see "Digital Millennium Copyright Act," "jurisdiction," "MPAA" and "NATO").

pitch — A brief oral presentation made to a studio, production company or other source of development or production financing in order to persuade such financing source to become involved in the production of the movie (see "pitch meeting" and "theft of ideas").

pitch meeting — A conference between a person who has an idea or concept for a motion picture (which may or may not exist in any written form) for the purpose of presenting that idea to a representative of a development or production financing source (e.g., a production company or studio; see "idea," "concept," "copyright infringement," "outline," "pitch," "screenplay," "synopsis," "theft of ideas," "treatment" and "submission release").

plagiarism — Appropriation of the literary composition of another and passing off as one's own the product of the mind and language of another. The offense of plagiarism is known in the law as infringement of copyright and usually only occurs when the work allegedly copied is protected by copyright. The offense may also refer to copying uncopyrighted or "public domain" works without giving credit to the work being copied (see "copyright," "fair use" and "public domain").

plaintiff — The one who initiates a civil lawsuit (see "defendant," "litigation" and "original Paramount defendants").

plan of business — Another name or title (along with "description of business") for a major section in a securities disclosure document providing information (i.e., disclosures) relating to the industry in which the business is to be conducted, competition, operational information and so forth. The plan of business or description of business section of a securities disclosure document may contain some of the same or similar information as a business plan but the two documents are not the same and are not intended to be used for the same purpose. In venture capital and other business financing situations, some people use this phrase to refer to the document (more commonly known as a "business plan") prepared by the entity seeking funding and presented to prospective providers of capital that contains a description of the intended business, the principal products to be produced and the principal markets for and methods used in distributing such products. The use of a business plan alone may be adequate for non-securities (active investor) financing vehicles. In a securities offering (with large groups of passive investors), more than a business plan is required (i.e., the information normally included in a business plan forms only one of many required sections of the securities disclosure document and the contents of the securities disclosure document are determined by the SEC's disclosure guidelines that apply to the specific offering contemplated). The plan of business for a feature film limited partnership or manager-managed LLC (securities offerings) usually covers proposed activities, significant current statistics regarding the movie industry, management information including narrative biographies of key people involved, information on the film or films including history of rights acquisition, screenplay synopsis, production information, marketing and promotion plans, distribution approach, box office comparables, completion bond arrangements, if any, and other financing arrangements, if any (see "business plan," "disclosure document," "private placement offering memorandum," "securities disclosure document" and "venture capital").

plan of distribution units — A required section of the disclosure document in a securities offering that discusses how the securities will be marketed (i.e., through issuer sales or broker/dealer sales; see "corporate stock," "limited liability company," "limited partnership" and "securities").

platformed — A motion picture that has been exhibited in a few theaters for the purpose of building an audience for the picture before expanding its exhibition to more theaters (see "platforming," "release pattern" and "rollout").

platforming — A method of releasing a film in which the film is opened in a single theater or a small group of key theaters in a major territory with the specific intention of widening the run to numerous theaters either in one step or in phases after the film has established itself (see "platformed," "wide release" and "word-of-mouth").

platform release — (see "platformed" and "platforming").

play — When used as a verb and in the context of motion picture exhibition, the term "play" has the same meaning as "exhibit." On the other hand, a play, as in "live stage play" may form the basis of a screenplay (see "exhibit," "live stage play" and "underlying property").

play date — The actual calendar date on which a motion picture opens in a market or nationwide; the actual full-length public showing of a film in its domestic theatrical release (see "break," "engagement" and "prime theatrical play dates").

player — Another term used for actor, actress or performer. The term is also sometimes used as slang for someone very much involved in the thick of the action in the film industry (see "actor," "actress" and "bit player").

player agreement or player deal memo — A short form contract for a performer that serves as the memorandum of the minimum negotiated terms between the production company and performer concerning provisions usually most essential to the performer (i.e., compensation, credit and reimbursement of expenses). The form is often used to establish the central deal points when production is about to be commenced and the production company needs the performer to provide his or her services right away. It may also serve as the basis for the preparation of a subsequent long form performer agreement (see "deal memo," "fully negotiated agreement," "performer employment agreement" and "short form agreement").

playing time — (same as "playtime").

playoff — The distribution of a film after key openings (see "release pattern").

playoff record — Information relating to the dates and locations at which a film has been exhibited (see "playoff").

playtime — The length of a movie's run (i.e., the amount of time, expressed in days, that a film is shown or is expected to be exhibited in a given theater or market from its opening in that market). Playtime may also mean a particular period of the calendar year such as "Christmas playtime" or "summer playtime" (see "run").

pledge — A deposit or transfer of personal property (such as securities or the cash surrender value of life insurance) to a lender or creditor as security (collateral) for an obligation or debt. The terms pledge and hypothecate are similar since neither involves the transfer of title (contrast with "assign"; see "hypothecate").

pledge agreement — An agreement relating to a pledge of personal property to a lender or creditor as security (or collateral) for an obligation or debt (see "collateral," "debt" and "pledge").

plot — The main story line of a screenplay or film. If the plot can be described in a very few words it is considered high concept (see "hidden agenda," "high concept," "one-line description," "synopsis," "subplot" and "theme")

plot point — A turning point in the action of a film's screenplay (see "plot").

points — The percentage of a film's anticipated net profits (or net proceeds) negotiated or awarded to a participant in the production of the film. The term is customarily used to describe a stated percentage of 100 percent of the film's net profits, and if it is being used to describe a percentage of any other stage in a film's revenue stream (e.g., distributor's adjusted gross receipts) that may more accurately be described as a profit participation (see "gross receipts," "net profits," "percentage participation" or "points," "profit participation" and "revenue stream").

polarization — A separation of parts into opposite extremes. Some film industry observers have expressed concern that the industry has become more polarized in recent years, meaning that the differences between the "haves" and the "have nots" (or insiders versus outsiders) have widened. For producers and production companies this means that as compared to independent producers, the resources, capabilities, leverage, market power and market share of the major studios has increased (i.e., the barriers to entry in that level of the industry have increased). It also appears that the same is true for the distribution level of the industry as well as exhibition (i.e., the larger organizations have distanced themselves from their competitors partly through more vertical and horizontal expansion; see "barriers to entry," "independent producer," "market power," "major exhibition chains," "major studio/distributors," "Paramount Consent Decree of 1948" and "TriStar Case").

policy — The written contract of insurance (see "insurable interest," "insurance" and "insured")

policy holder — The person or entity granted an insurance policy (also called "policy owner").

policy loan — A loan from an insurance company secured by the cash surrender value of a life insurance policy (see "insurance").

polish — Revisions of specific scenes in a movie script, but not a complete rewrite; a special stage in the script writing process between drafts that is recognized by the Writer's Guild of America and for which separate compensation is paid (i.e., a polish is a slight revision of a script). A more extensive polish would constitute a revision and a substantial revision would create the next draft. A polish is the writing of changes in dialogue, narration or action in a script, not including a rewrite (see "development," "draft," "first draft," "final screenplay," "revision," "rewrite," "script" or "screenplay" and "shooting script").

Political Action Committee — Government regulated organization created by corporations, professional and trade organizations and labor unions to raise political contributions and contribute to political candidates who may be supportive of the sponsoring group's interests (see "political influence").

political influence — The ability to persuade governmental decision-makers. The most powerful group of companies in the motion picture business, the MPAA, finally realized a long-term goal with the installation of its friend, Ronald Reagan, in the U.S. Presidency during the decade of the 1980s. Reagan did not disappoint the MPAA when he adopted a policy of relaxed federal antitrust law enforcement for the entertainment industry. That policy change made it possible for some of the MPAA companies to re-enter the exhibition arena, become even more vertically integrated than they had been since the 1940's and regain the additional clout in the market place that would allow them to exert even greater control over the exhibition, distribution and production of feature films (generally at the expense of the independent sector). Continuing political influence at the highest levels of government appears to serve as the motivation supporting the massive MPAA, MPAA PACs, studio executive and studio executive spouse political contributions to U.S. Presidential candidates of both major political parties (see "antitrust laws," "association projects," "lobbying," "market power," "MPAA," "Paramount Consent Decree of 1948" and "TriStar Case").

pool — (see "industry pool" and "investment pool").

pooling agreements — Exhibitor agreements with each other and their affiliates by which theaters of two or more of them, normally competitive, are operated as a unit or managed by a joint committee or by one of the exhibitors, the profits being shared according to prearranged percentages. Some of these agreements state that the parties cannot acquire other competitive theaters without first offering them for inclusion in the pool (see "antitrust laws" and "product splitting").

pornography — Books, magazines, films, videos, pictures and other such material depicting sexual acts that appeal to one's prurient interests (see "censorable material," "obscene material" and "prurient").

portable media player — An umbrella term for a variety of handheld devices that play audio and/or video. The device may also serve as a portable photo album and display still images such as GIFs and JPEGs. The term "media player" without the "portable" typically refers to software (see media player), but may refer to the devices mentioned here. Flash-based and disk-based MP3 players, that are audio-only, are the most popular portable media player. An MP4 player refers to a video playback device, that may be combined with an MP3 player and small screen such as the full-sized iPod or be a larger handheld device with a bigger screen such as a portable media center device. Most video players support audio formats as well (see "digital music player").

portfolio — The combined investment holdings of an individual or institutional investor. Investors seek to diversify their portfolios in order to spread the risk and hedge against the risk of loss in one sector of the market as opposed to another (see "corporation," "investor financing," "securities" and "stock").

positive — A film print made from a negative (or stock shot in the camera with reversal film) with the colors appearing in the appropriate places (see "negative" and "print").

positive cash flow — Financial circumstances in which more cash comes in than goes out in a given accounting period (see "cash flow" and "negative cash flow").

positive print — The phrase positive print can be used to mean the raw stock specifically designed for producing a positive image, the positive image itself, positive raw stock that has been exposed but not processed, or processed film bearing a positive image (see "paid advertising").

positive review — A favorable evaluation of a motion picture by a movie critic (see "blurbs," "critic" and "industry critic").

poster — The generic term used to describe printed motion picture display advertisements that are usually in color and that typically contain the basic elements from which movie newspaper ads are made including a graphic design such as a photograph or drawing, a custom title treatment, a lead line to accompany the title, credits for principal cast and crew, and any outstanding quotes from critical reviews. A movie poster may range in size from the 8 ½ by 11 inch sell-sheet to outdoor billboards (see "lobby card," "one sheet," "print" and "sell-sheet").

poster service — A firm that offers guaranteed delivery of movie advertising material to exhibitors (see "poster").

post-breakeven participation — Contractual percentage participations due to be paid after reaching a specified form of breakeven (e.g., net profits; see "actual breakeven," "breakeven," "cash breakeven," "gross participations," "net profits" and "pre-break participation").

post-payout sharing ratio — The percentage ownership interest of a partner in a limited partnership or a member/investor in a manager-managed LLC, following payout or recoupment (see "recoupment," "payout" and "pre-payout sharing ratio").

post-production — The final stage in the preparation of a film prior to delivery to the lab on behalf of a distributor. Post-production activities include editing, looping, the application of music, special effects and titles. The post-production process brings all the elements together to form the finished feature film (see "development," "delivery," "pre-production" and "principal photography").

post-production costs — The expenses incurred in the production of a motion picture in the final stage of production (i.e., following principal photography; see "post-production").

post-production schedule — A listing of the amount of time (usually expressed in terms of weeks) that the various component tasks or stages relating to the production of a film following principal photography will take. For example, the tasks or stages may include laboratory processing, final dubbing, recording sound, scoring and recording music, final cut, director's cut and assemblage or rough cut. This

schedule may appear as an exhibit to the director's employment agreement (see "post-production").

post-production services (or completion services) — Feature film production services provided by post-production companies following principal photography. Such services include looping, sound transfers, lab printing, conforming of original picture, graphics and sound mixing (see "post-production sounds").

post-production sounds — The sounds added to a movie during post-production including dialogue, sound effects and music added by the dialogue editor, sound effects editor, composer and music editor respectively (see "post-production").

post-synching or synchronization — The re-recording of film dialogue or sound in an acoustically proper environment. This post-production technique is used when sound has been recorded unsatisfactorily at the time of shooting or when it was impossible or difficult to record the actual sounds or dialogue while shooting. Post-synchronization is also used to translate a film's dialogue from one language to another (see "automatic dialogue replacement").

potential competitors — Prospective business rivals. The U.S. Justice Department merger guidelines suggest that if a proposed vertical merger effectively forces actual or potential competitors to enter or continue in the distribution or exhibition business on a vertically integrated basis then such proposed vertical merger is less likely to meet with the approval of the Justice Department (see "actual competitors," "merger guidelines," "Paramount Consent Decree of 1948," "TriStar Case," "vertical integration" and "vertical merger").

potential downside — (see "downside exposure").

potential upside — (see "upside potential").

power — The possession of control or influence over others (see "major exhibition chains," "major studio/distributors," "market power," "market share," "merger guidelines," "number of screens," "predatory practices" and "reciprocal preference").

power coupled with an interest — A power over property that is accompanied by or connected with an interest in the property subject to the power. Under the law of agency, when an agent has a power over property and also has a beneficial interest in that property, the principal may not revoke the agent's power until the interest has expired or unless the principal and agent have agreed otherwise (see "agent" and "power of attorney").

power of attorney — A written instrument by which one person, as principal, appoints another as his or her agent and confers upon such agent the authority to perform certain specified acts or kinds of acts on behalf of the principal. Such powers of attorney may be made irrevocable. Often, the subscription agreement in a film limited partnership or manager-managed LLC offering will include a power of attorney which, among other things, authorizes the general partner or manager to sign the limited partnership agreement or LLC operating agreement on behalf of the investor/subscribers (see "agency," "attorney-in-fact" and "proxy").

pre-break participation — Contractual percentage participations due to be paid prior to achieving a specified form of breakeven in a motion picture's revenue stream (i.e., a gross participation). Since gross participations are deducted from gross receipts earlier in the revenue stream, they effectively reduce (and in many instances eliminate) all net profit participations. Anyone negotiating for a net profit participation with a studio on a studio financed film would be wise to inquire as to whether the studio has or intends to award any gross participations on the project. A studio may play a game of semantics and contend that net profits are not being reduced by gross participations since the concept of net profits inherently contemplates certain deductions from gross receipts. Prospective net profit participants (or their representatives) may want to counter that after the applicable breakeven point there should be no separate treatment for gross participants since the gross participation is merely another form of net profit participation expressed in a different way, especially in the case of gross participations that only begin after a specified form of breakeven is achieved and that are calculated on a rolling breakeven basis (see "actual breakeven," "artificial breakeven," "cash breakeven," "gross participations," "net profits," "post-break participation" and "rolling breakeven").

pre-conditions — Requirements that must be met in advance. For example, in a distribution agreement awarding final cutting rights to the director, the distributor may impose certain pre-conditions upon such rights (i.e., the cost of production must not exceed 110 percent of the approved production budget and contingency, the picture as delivered must substantially and materially conform to the approved screenplay, the picture must have a running time of not less than ninety-five nor more than one hundred and ten minutes with a rating no more restrictive than "R," the picture and all major delivery items must be fully delivered on the dates required in the distribution agreement and the director's final cutting rights must be exercised so as not to conflict with the picture's planned release schedule and the distributor's exhibitor bidding practices; see "approved production budget," "blind bidding," "final cut" and "running time").

predatory practices — Aggressive tactics used in conducting business that are designed to exploit or destroy others for the gain of the aggressor business (see "adhesion contract," "cartel," "conduct restrictions," "inferior bargaining position," "polarization," "reciprocal preferences," "take it or leave it" and "unconscionable").

preemptive right — A right giving existing stockholders the opportunity to purchase shares of a new issue before they are offered to others. Its purpose is to protect shareholders from dilution of value and control when new corporate shares are issued (see "offering" and "rights offering").

pre-existing relationship — One of the conditions directly or indirectly required for compliance with the federal and state transactional exemptions from the securities registration requirement in order to avoid a prohibited general solicitation. Generally, a pre-existing relationship includes any relationship consisting of personal or business contacts of a nature and duration such as would enable a reasonably prudent person to be aware of the character, business acumen and general business and financial circumstances of the person with whom such relationship exists (see "finder," "Regulation D" and "subscription application and agreement").

pre-feature entertainment — Programs exhibited at theaters prior to the feature film (i.e., film shorts, cartoons, newsreels, reports on the music industry, "ask a celebrity" presentations, etc.; see "cartoon" and "short").

preferred stock — A class of capital stock that pays dividends at a specified rate and has preference over common stock in the payment of dividends and the liquidation of assets. Generally, preferred stock does not carry voting rights (see "common stock," "dividends" and "stock").

pre-formation interests — Interests (units) in a film limited partnership or manager-managed LLC that are being offered prior to the formation of the entity (i.e., a limited partnership or manager-managed LLC to be formed upon minimum funding). Such interests or units would still be considered securities for purposes of complying with the federal and state securities laws (see "limited liability company," "limited partnership" and "unit").

prejudice — Preconceived judgment or opinion; an irrational attitude of hostility directed against an individual, a group, a race or their supposed characteristics (see "anti-Semitic sword," "anti-Semitism," "bias" "blackball," "discrimination," "insider's game," "member of the club," "nepotism," "patterns of bias," "regional prejudice" and "relationship driven business").

preliminary funding — (see "development funds").

preliminary prospectus — The initial securities disclosure document provided to prospective investors by an underwriter, broker/dealer or issuer relating to a new issue of securities in a public/registered offering (see "disclosure document" and "red herring").

preliminary/development disclosure document — The written information that is required to be disclosed to prospective passive investors in a preliminary/development offering (see "development financing," "disclosure document" and "investment contract").

preliminary/development funds — A term similar in meaning to the venture capital concepts of start-up monies and seed capital but more typically associated with feature film limited partnership or manager-managed LLC offerings raising something in the neighborhood of seventy-five to two hundred and fifty thousand dollars to fund the development of a film or films along with the up front costs associated with preparing subsequent production financing arrangements (see "development money investment agreement," "investment contract," "investor financing agreement," "preliminary investors" and "preliminary/development offering").

preliminary/development offering — A film financing transaction specifically designed to raise funds from passive investors and to pay for the costs associated with the development phase of a film project as well as any expenses incurred in seeking production financing (e.g., through a studio/distributor or a subsequent investor offering). A preliminary/development offering structured as an investment contract for passive investors would generally be considered a securities offering and investment interests sold in such an offering would have to be offered and sold in compliance with the federal and state securities laws. Such offerings are more commonly structured as limited partnership or manager-managed LLC offerings (see "development," "development money investment agreement" and "preliminary investors").

preliminary investors — Individuals or entities who provide development funds for a motion picture project through an investment vehicle such as a limited partnership or manager-managed LLC (see "development funds," "preliminary/development funds," "preliminary/development agreement" and "seed money").

preliminary offering circular — A securities disclosure document that is permitted to be used pursuant to the SEC's Regulation A to allow the solicitation of indications of interest from prospective purchasers prior to the SEC clearance date (see "prospectus" and "Regulation A").

premiere — The first official public showing of a theatrical film in a specific theater, the first airing of a film on television or the screening of the first segment of a new TV series (see "opening" and "premiere benefit").

premiere benefit — The first official public showing of a theatrical film, all or a portion of the proceeds of which are to be donated to a designated charity (see "premiere").

premium — The fee paid to an insurance company for insurance protection (see "insurance").

pre-mix session — The combining of several soundtracks at an early stage in the creation of a composite soundtrack that is designed to make the eventual final mix less complicated (see "soundtracks").

pre-opening advertising — Film advertising carried prior to the opening of a film (see "advertising").

pre-packaged — A feature film project that already has significant elements attached before its producer approaches either a prospective financier or distributor (see "elements" and "package").

prepayment clause — A provision in loan agreements that permits prepayment of the loan at any time without penalty. If such a provision is not contained in the agreement the lender may charge a fee if the loan is paid off before it is due (see "debt," "lender financing" and "prepayment penalty").

prepayment penalty — A fee paid by a borrower to a bank when a loan that does not have a prepayment clause is repaid before its scheduled maturity (see "prepayment clause" and "right of prepayment").

pre-payout sharing ratio — The percentage ownership interest of a partner in a limited partnership or a member in a manager-managed LLC prior to payout or recoupment (see "payout," "post-payout sharing ratio" and "recoupment").

pre-print laboratory work — Activities relating to the preparation of a specific film at the film laboratory and prior to the printing of the camera negative or positive work prints (see "laboratory").

pre-production — The earliest phase of film production (as opposed to development) although there may be some overlap between the two phases. Pre-production, for example, may encompass polishing and breaking down the script for budgeting purposes, preparing story boards, hiring or obtaining letters of intent from creative personnel (including the director and principal cast), establishing shooting locations and shooting schedules, preparing the final budgets, casting, the finalization of creative decisions and such other steps as are necessary to prepare for the actual commencement of photography. The pre-production stage of the film will generally extend from two to three months, although this time period may vary widely from film to film. Principal photography follows the pre-production stage. As a general rule, pre-production activities do not go forward unless production financing is in place, thus, particularly for independent films, sometime before, during or after the development phase, the important activity of film finance must occur [see "development," "letter of intent (film)" and "letter of intent (completion guarantor)"].

pre-production financing — (see "development financing," "negative pickup," "pre-production" and "pre-sale financing").

prequel — A feature film that is released after the original but which actually tells a related story that occurred before the story depicted in the earlier released film (see "remake" and "sequel").

pre-sale — A contract relating to the licensing of motion pictures that is negotiated and signed prior to the completion of the film and often before the start of principal photography. Such agreements are also sometimes used to obtain monetary advances or as a form of security or collateral for a discounted bank loan or to aid in obtaining production financing from financiers or investors. Generally, in order to be "bankable" or "lendable" such agreements must guarantee a specific amount of money by a certain date and the payment of such sum should not be dependent on too many contingencies (see "debt," "lender financing," "monetary advances," "multiple pre-sales," "negative pickup," "pre-sale financing" and "split-rights basis").

pre-sale commitment — (see "pre-sale financing").

pre-sale distribution guarantees — (see "pre-sale financing").

pre-sale guarantee — (see "distribution guarantee," "guarantee" and "pre-sale financing").

pre-sale financing — The funding of a film's production costs through the granting of a license for film rights by a producer to a distributor in a particular media or territory prior to completion of the film. Pre-sales may take the form of funds, guarantees or commitments that may be obtained or used to obtain funds, in addition to other available production financing in the form of cash advances or guarantees paid by domestic or foreign distributors, pay or cable television systems, video cassette producers, television syndicators and/or bank loans obtained by using such cash advances or guarantees as effective collateral. For example, if a producer had a contract for the pre-sale of a movie to a U.S. or foreign distributor, a home video company, a pay TV service or a TV syndicator, the producer might be able to present those contractual commitments to a bank and walk away with a bank commitment to pay cash as per a cash flow schedule (see "monetary advances," "pre-production financing," "pre-sale agreement" and "split rights deal").

pre-sales — (see "pre-sale financing").

pre-screening — Exhibitions of a motion picture or components of the movie conducted in order to get preliminary audience reaction to help the producer and distributor make decisions about what to or what not to include in the final version (see "focus group," "preview" and "screening").

press agent — (see "publicist").

press kit — Part of the basic film advertising campaign package designed to be offered to the media. It generally consists of a portfolio type case containing ad mats, a synopsis of the film's story, cast and crew list, narrative biographies of the director and stars, copies of the film's critical reviews, 8 x 10 stills from the film, running time for the film and suggested publicity articles for adaptation by the local media. The press kit is sent by the distributor to sub-distributors and exhibitors and is designed to give them a feeling for what the film is about while also providing them with the information that reporters and critics may request (see "campaign package," "publicity articles" and "support materials").

press packet — (see "press kit").

press release — A prepared statement released to the news media for their use and consideration in preparing their news reports. Generally, press releases are issued by a company's management regarding events or occurrences it considers noteworthy (see "promotional activities" and "trades").

press tour — An important part of motion picture publicity campaigns in which a film's director and/or stars are made available for local newspaper, magazine and radio/television talk show interviews in the major cities in which the film opens. Generally, the participation of such persons, the number of appearances or the amount of time they are required are negotiable items in the contractual agreements that commit the director and actors to a movie (contrast with "junket").

preview — An advance showing of a film before its scheduled release date, usually to invited groups, like the press or industry executives to help spread good word-of-mouth or to the paying public as part of a test marketing program. Editing changes are sometimes made after such tests (see "screening," "sneak preview," "test marketing" and "word-of-mouth").

price case — A lawsuit in which the plaintiff has the burden of showing that the terms of the litigated agreement are so disparate from market prices that the contract is unconscionable (see "contract of adhesion," "market power" and "unconscionable").

price discrimination — The practice of charging different persons different prices for the same goods or services. When price discrimination is engaged in for the purpose of decreasing competition, for instance, through tying the lower prices to the purchase of goods or services, it constitutes a violation of the Sherman Antitrust Act. Unlawful price discrimination is also specifically covered by the Clayton Act and by the Robinson-Patman Act (see "antitrust laws" and "price fixing").

price/earnings ratio (P/E) — The current market price of a share of a corporation's stock divided by its earnings per share over a twelve month period. The P/E ratio gives investors an idea of how much they are paying for a company's earning power (same as "multiple"; see "corporate stock").

price fixing — Under the federal antitrust laws, a combination or conspiracy formed for the purpose and with the effect of raising, depressing, fixing, pegging or stabilizing the price of a commodity in interstate commerce. The test is not what the actual effect is on prices but whether such agreements interfere with the freedom of traders and thereby restrains their ability to sell in accordance with their own judgment (see "antitrust laws," "horizontal price fixing" and "vertical price fixing").

pricing amendment — The amendment to the registration statement in a public/registered securities offering that includes information regarding the price of the offering, underwriters' compensation, the list of underwriters in the syndicate and the issuer's latest responses to the SEC's comment letter (see "comment letter," "IPO" and "public offering").

prima donna — An extremely sensitive, vain or undisciplined performer. In the case of a film, a prima donna is more likely to be an actor, actress or director and may cause delays or other problems for a production which may translate into higher production costs and possible budget overruns (see "auteur," "collaborative process," "completion guarantor," "director," "final cut," "perfectionist director," "perks" and "star").

primary audience — A specific demographic population to which a movie is believed to have the most appeal and at which such movie is primarily aimed. Similar to "target audience" although target analysis for a film may include several levels of audiences with the primary audience being the main audience to which the film is expected to appeal (same as "target audience"; see "appeal," "audience," "projected audience" and "test marketing").

primary campaign — The initial film advertising and promotional program that is designed around a specific theme and to attract a given audience segment (see "advertising campaign" and "alternate campaign").

primary distribution — The sale of a new issue of securities, as distinguished from a secondary distribution, that involves previously issued securities (same as "primary offering," but contrast with "initial public offering"; see "underwrite").

primary locations — The most important shooting locations to be used in the production of a film. In location scouting, generally the primary locations are sought first, then nearby secondary locations are acquired (see "location").

primary insurance — The basic insurance coverage provided by a policy with its initial ceiling on the amount that will be paid out on any claim or claims under such policy (see "errors and omissions insurance," "excess insurance coverage" and "reinsurance").

primary offering — (same as "primary distribution"; see "underwriting").

prime foreign territories — The United Kingdom, the Scandinavian countries, France, Germany, Italy, Spain, Japan, Turkey and Australia (similar to "major foreign markets").

prime play date — The best calendar date on which to open a motion picture (same as "prime release date"; see "Christmas season," "play date" and "summer season").

prime rate — The interest rate banks charge their most credit worthy customers. Loans to less

credit worthy borrowers are often tied to the prime rate (i.e., a few percentage points above prime; see "actual interest" and "interest").

prime release date — The most advantageous date on which to first open a motion picture, in a particular market and/or nationally (same as "prime play date"; see "Christmas season," "release date" and "summer season").

prime schedules — (see "prime theatrical play dates").

prime theatrical play dates — The actual calendar dates or periods that (based on past performance) tend to produce the largest movie-going audiences for feature films (e.g., Christmas holidays and summer). Successful independent distributors have commonly used the strategy of not releasing their movies during such periods so as to avoid direct competition with motion pictures released by the major/studio distributors (see "antitrust laws," "competition," "market power," "market share" and "play date").

principal — In general, the major party to a transaction or the owner of a privately held business. In the law of agency, a principal is one who has permitted or directed another to act for such principal and subject to his or her direction or control. With respect to investments, the principal is the basic amount invested, exclusive of earnings. In banking and finance, the term refers to (1) the face amount of a debt instrument or deposit on which interest is either owed or earned and (2) the balance of a debt, separate from interest (see "debt," "interest," "lender financing" and "surety").

principal artists' contracts — Employment agreements relating to the services of the feature actors and actresses playing the lead roles (see "employment agreements").

principal assets — The most important property of a company (see "asset").

principal cast members — (see "principals" and "principal players").

principal photography — The actual filming of all scripted material covering most of the speaking parts in a film and the time period during which such filming occurs (see "development," "post-production," "pre-production" and "second unit").

principals or principal players — The main featured actors or actresses in a film who have major speaking parts. Some union definitions specify that a principal player is a performer engaged to speak or mime eleven or more lines of dialogue, or an actor engaged to perform a major role without dialogue (see "guild" and "lead").

principal stockholder — Corporate shareholders who own a significant number of shares in a corporation. SEC rules specify that a principal stockholder is a person who owns 10 percent or more of the voting stock of a publicly held corporation (see "corporation," "insider," "majority shareholder" and "sole shareholder").

principal sum — (same as "principal").

principal talent — The actor(s) and/or actress(es) that play the main characters in the story. Stars are usually the principal talent but principal talent in the picture may or may not be a star (see "star").

print — Copies of a film that are distributed to theaters; the print is a positive made from an original (or dupe) negative that is used for projection. A print is a copy made from the master for the purpose of motion-picture presentation (i.e., the specific motion-picture release). The master is preserved for additional duplication. A distribution company may make only a few copies or some 3,000 plus prints depending on the coverage desired for a particular motion picture. The term print also refers to movie advertising placed in newspapers and magazines and by means of posters (see "general release," "limited release," "poster" and "wide release").

print costs — The expenses incurred in making a film's release prints for theatrical exhibition. The cost of a single print is often in the $2,000 range; thus, if a distributor were to print 2,000 copies of a film, its print costs would equal $4 million. Print costs are one of the major distribution expenses (advertising being the other) and present a significant opportunity for overstating costs or possible kickback arrangements between distributors and laboratories. As more theaters are equipped for digital exhibition, there will be less need for the use of film prints (see "audit," "discounts," "kickbacks," "prints and ads," "rebates" and "release print").

prints and ads (P&A) — The film prints actually distributed to theaters for exhibition and the advertising that promotes the film. The number of prints actually made and used in the release of films varies widely from only a few to more than three thousand and as such can be a major expense in the distribution of a film, usually second only to advertising. On the other hand, a film's P&A expenses do not represent all of the film's distribution expense, thus, it is confusing to use the term "P&A" as if it refers to all distribution expenses (see "direct distribution expenses" and "print costs").

prints and ads budget — The funds allocated to be spent on the costs associated with printing copies of the film for exhibition and the advertising for such film (see "advertising," "print" and "print costs").

prints and ads commitment — The promise by a film distributor or others to expend a certain amount of money on prints and advertising for a movie. Minimum levels of prints and advertising in the theatrical release may also be required by home video companies in order to trigger a particular deal with such companies. In some circumstances, it may also be to the advantage of a film's producer and other net profit participants to place a ceiling on the amount of prints and ads expenses that a distributor may incur in the distribution of the producer's film without the producer's approval (see "distribution commitment" and "print costs").

prints and ads financing agreement — A contract between an independent feature film producer or production company and a financier in which the financier agrees to provide the monies necessary to pay for the prints and advertising of a film in return for a specified payback. Such an agreement with active industry parties (e.g., film labs or distributors) may be structured as a joint venture agreement. On the other hand, if the financier is a passive investor, compliance with the federal and state securities laws may be required. Also, it is important in such agreements that it be made clear whether the term "P&A" is being used to mean "all distribution expenses" as opposed to just the actual costs associated with

the film's prints and advertising (see "prints and ads budget" and "rent-a-distributor").

prior performance — The past results of similar movies. In the context of limited partnership and manager-managed LLC offerings, the past results of operations of the prior offerings and business activities operated by the same management group (see "box office comparables" and "limited liability company" and "limited partnership").

priority of run — (same as "clearance").

priority recoupment — An earlier position in a revenue stream for the recovery of invested or expended funds than another or other positions. Generally, in the current marketplace, distributor paid prints and ads expenditures have a priority recoupment position (i.e., such costs are recovered by the distributor before almost all other deductions from the revenue stream, except for the distributor's fees and possibly the limited off-the-top expenses). On the other hand, in a lender financed motion picture transaction, the lender will contractually impose a priority recoupment position for its principal, interest and fees over all other parties (i.e. the bank is paid upon delivery of the film by the producer to the distributor and does not have to wait to participate in the film's revenue stream). With respect to independent films financed through a film limited partnership or manager-managed LLC, unless the producer successfully negotiates a priority recoupment position on behalf of the financing entity's investors, the investors will have to rely on some portion of the film's net profit participations or some similar specified portion of the revenue stream to recoup their investment (see "distributable cash," "inter-party agreement," "negative pickup" and "when the money's paid").

privacy, right of — A general right to be left alone; a right to live life free from unwarranted publicity; a generic term encompassing various rights recognized to be inherent in the concept of ordered liberty. Invasions of one's privacy constitute a tort for which judicial remedies are available. The four different types of torts are (1) appropriation, or the use of a person's name, picture, or likeness as a symbol of his or her identity without compensation; (2) an intrusion upon a person's physical solitude or seclusion; (3) the public disclosure of private facts; and (4) placing a person in a false light in the public eye by associating this person with beliefs or activities with which this person has no connection (contrast with "publicity rights"; see "clearance," "errors and omissions insurance" and "tort").

private corporation — (see "closed corporation").

private limited partnership — A limited partnership that did not register the offering of limited partnership interests (i.e., securities) with the SEC or with the state securities regulators in each state in which such securities were to be offered and sold but instead relied on available exemptions from such securities registration requirement (see "exempt offering," "private offering," "private placement" and "Regulation D").

private litigation — A lawsuit that does not involve the government (i.e., the parties are civil litigants). In addition to both criminal and civil sanctions that may be pursued in court by the U.S. Justice Department, the federal antitrust laws provide civil remedies for private citizens and/or businesses (see "antitrust laws" and "damages").

privately held corporation — (see "closed corporation").

private offering — (same as "private placement").

private offering exemption — A federal (statutory) exemption from the securities registration requirement provided by Section 4(2) of the Securities Act exempting from registration "transactions by an issuer not involving any public offering." To qualify for this exemption, the purchasers of the securities must: have enough knowledge and experience in finance and business matters to evaluate the risks and merits of the investment (the "sophisticated investor"), or be able to bear the investment's economic risk; have access to the type of information normally provided in a prospectus (i.e., a public offering's securities disclosure document); and agree not to resell or distribute the securities to the public. In addition, an issuer may not use any form of public solicitation or general advertising in connection with the offering. The precise limits of this private offering exemption are uncertain. As the number of purchasers increases and their relationship to the company and its management becomes more remote, it is more difficult to show that the transaction qualifies for the exemption. If an issuer offers securities to even one person who does not meet the necessary conditions, the entire offering may be in violation of the Securities Act. The SEC's Regulation D, Rule 506, was created partly for the purpose of providing a "safe harbor" rule, so that issuers would have more objective standards with which to comply and thereby be assured of compliance with the requirements of this Section 4(2) exemption (see "Regulation D" and "sophisticated investor").

private placement — Generally, any offer or sale of a security (e.g., limited partnership interests, corporate stock or units in a manager-managed LLC) that is not required to be registered with either the state or federal securities regulatory authorities because such offers or sales comply with all of the conditions and limitations imposed on the use of specific federal and state exemptions from the securities registration requirements. The issuer in a private offering is not allowed to advertise or generally solicit. The offering costs associated with a private placement are generally much lower than in a public offering and the offering can generally be "on the street" (i.e., sales can start) sooner (same as "exempt offering" or "private offering"; see "public limited partnership," "public offering," "registered offering," "small offering exemption" and "Regulation D").

private placement offering memorandum (PPM) — The securities disclosure document required by the securities laws in exempt offeringsto be provided to prospective purchasers prior to their purchase and that must fully disclose all material aspects of the transaction and not omit any information that would be an important consideration in a prospective investor's decision as to whether to invest or not (see "anti-fraud rule," "disclosure document," "memorandum," "offering memorandum" and "prospectus").

private securities transaction — A securities transaction in which an associated person (i.e., a person associated with an NASD member broker/dealer firm, for example, a registered representative) sells a security to an investor on behalf of another party (e.g., as part of a private offering of limited partnership interests) without the prescribed participation of the associated person's employer broker/dealer firm. Such transactions are prohibited by the NASD (see "broker/dealer," "due diligence," "NASD," "registered representative" and "supervision").

privatization — The conversion from government control of a business or industry to non-government control (i.e., public ownership and control, for example as in the ownership and control of television in many European countries in recent years; see "foreign market").

pro and con analysis — An objective evaluation of the advantages and disadvantages of the various forms of film finance available to a producer for a given film project. In the world of film finance, producers are confronted with a bewildering array of production funding choices and unfortunately in their written, panel and lecture presentations relating to film finance, many industry professionals with bona fide expertise in a narrow area of film finance tend to stress the advantages of the form of film finance he or she favors without objectively discussing the disadvantages. The producer, on the other hand, must look beyond such self-serving presentations and demand a realistic appraisal of the disadvantages associated with the particular form of film finance being discussed. As the producer's research progresses, he or she will eventually want to be in a position to objectively analyze the pros and cons of several available forms of film finance as applied to a specific film project (see "advantage," "availability analysis," "disadvantage" and "financing").

probable cause — Facts and circumstances within one's knowledge and of which one has reasonably trustworthy information, sufficient in itself to warrant a person of reasonable caution to believe the assertion that has been made (see "bad faith denial of contract").

problem producer — A term used to describe a producer considered by the person applying the label (usually a studio or distributor executive) to be difficult to work with as a film producer or who does not play along with some of the inequities in the studio/distributor dominated U.S. film industry (see "blacklist," "completion guarantor" and "discrimination").

proceeds — In a loan context, funds given to a borrower after all costs and fees have been deducted (see "debt" and "lender financing").

proceeds of the offering — The investor funds raised by means of a securities offering (see "gross proceeds of the offering," "net proceeds of the offering" and "use of proceeds").

proclivity for wrongful conduct — A phrase used by three different judges and/or attorneys over a forty plus period of years to describe the conduct and business practices of the Hollywood establishment: Justice Douglas in the Paramount II appeal, Judge Palmieri in the Warner Bros. purchase of Cineamerica and Los Angeles attorney Pierce O'Donnell in the Buchwald vs Paramount case (see "Buchwald Case," "ethical malaise" and "Paramount Case").

produced by credit — The acknowledgment that appears on the motion picture screen and sets forth the name of the film's producer (see "co-production credit" and "producer").

producer — The person who carries ultimate responsibility for the original shaping and final outcome of a film, although the distributor may insist on certain editing rights that may allow such distributor considerable discretion in changing the film once delivered to such distributor. The producer generally finds and develops a film project, hires the writer or writers, develops the script, hires the director and actors, arranges for financing and oversees the production of the film. For the purposes of antitrust law analysis, the producer or production company is the manufacturer of a product (the film) and the distributor is a wholesaler (there may be different levels of wholesaling involved (e.g., sub-distribution) and the exhibitor is the retailer. Note that the Producers Guild of America has its own elaborate descriptions of producer responsibilities for producer credit purposes (see "collaborative process," "creative producer," "director," "editing rights," "executive producer," "filmmaker," "independent producer," "line producer," "Producers Guild of America" and "studio producer").

producer agreements — All motion picture documentation (i.e., contracts or employment agreements) relating to feature film producers, including executive producers and line producers. Such agreements are usually executed as between the studio or production company and the producer, but such agreements also may be between the producer and other film financing sources and writers (see "independent producer," "producer employment agreement" and "production company").

producer code of credits (PCOC)— A set of job descriptions, guidelines and rules for resolving credit disputes for producers, prepared by the Producers Guild of America after years of research into producing credits and their use within the entertainment industry. In drafting such rules, the PGA attempted to reflect the current realities and responsibilities of the profession. The PCOC consists of four sections. The first three address respectively the three primary producing titles in theatrical motion pictures (Produced by), television series

(Executive Producer) and long-form television (Executive Producer). Collectively, these three titles comprise the Producers Guild of America's Sanctioned Credits. For each of these titles, a detailed job description and list of producing functions is provided; a credited producer must perform a majority of the producing functions listed within the relevant section of the PCOC. While the Producers Guild does not arbitrate subsidiary producing titles, each section also includes a series of credit guidelines to cover the entire producing team. The fourth section comprises the PGA's rules governing the arbitration of credit disputes. This process is based upon the arbitration process utilized in determining eligibility for the Producers Guild Awards (see "Producers Guild of America").

producer credits — The on screen acknowledgment of the persons who performed certain production or financing related functions with respect to a motion picture. Producer credits may include executive producer, producer, line producer, associate producer, co-producer, assistant producer, supervising producer, "a production of" and "produced by." Unfortunately, since no guild or association has jurisdiction to control the granting of producer credits, the producer credit is sometimes used to reward persons who are not really producers at all and has reportedly been used to help some otherwise undeserving persons to become members of the Academy. This aspect of the credits problem, of course, raises questions about the entire membership selection process at the Academy and the credibility of its Oscar winning selections (see "Academy of Motion Picture Arts & Sciences," "Academy Awards," "member of the club," "PGA," "reciprocal preferences" and "relationship driven business").

producer deferment — The agreed upon delayed payment of compensation due a producer. Low budget producers often find it helpful to defer some or all of their fee when seeking financing for their project (see "deferrals" and "producer").

producer/director undertakings — Written promises by a film's producer and director, required by a completion guarantor as a prerequisite to the issuance of a completion bond, (1) providing assurances that the full financing necessary to fund the budgeted cost of the picture (including a contingency amount of usually 10 percent and the completion guarantor's fee) is available to the producer to be spent on the picture, (2) to stay within the budget in casting the film and to limit expenses, (3) by the director that the budget, shooting schedule and post-production schedule are achievable and that the allocation of film stock in the budget is sufficient, (4) that the film's music and related clearances will be obtained within the budgeted amounts, (5) that any delivery requirements pursuant to any distribution agreements and any publicity costs that are in excess of the approved budget will be considered to be distribution costs and expenses and will not be chargeable to the production budget and (6) that legal fees charged to the production budget will be limited to the amounts budgeted (see "completion bond").

producer employment agreement — A contract between the producing entity or production company and the producer that includes provisions relating to the producer's compensation and credit, the producer's rights with respect to the basic property and the producer's responsibility for ensuring that the motion picture is completed (see "independent producer" and "production company").

producer participation alternatives — Other ways for a film's producer to be compensated for his or her services in producing a film besides participating in the distributor's gross receipts. Such alternatives may include the payment of a specified bonus for every increment of distributor gross receipts or box office gross the film generates above a certain level, the payment of a bonus on the sale of a certain number of videocassettes or DVDs, letting the producer retain the rights to exploit a film in a certain territory or medium (e.g., television syndication) or paying the producer with options to purchase stock in the distribution company (see "net profit participant" and "video corridor").

producer's advance — Money paid by a film's distributor to its producer prior to release of the producer's film. Such advances may be paid upon signing of the distribution agreement and/or upon delivery of the picture (see "advance" or "advances" and "up-front distribution money").

producer's approvals and controls — Language negotiated for inclusion in some feature film distribution agreements that provides that the producer of a film has mutual approval (with the distributor) over certain matters relating to distribution (e.g., advertising, marketing and publicity, campaign strategy, release plan and the pricing strategy and advertising campaign for the home video release). This section of the distribution agreement may also provide that the distributor does not have any right to edit, alter or change the picture after the director's final cut, except to add the distributor's logo and releasing credit, and except as legally required for government censorship or time slot requirements, in which event the agreement may provide that the director will have the right to

perform the necessary editing to comply with the censorship or time slot requirements (see "collaborative process" and "final cut").

producer's development deal — A financing arrangement provided to a producer for covering the costs associated with the earliest stage in the production of a motion picture (i.e., the development phase including acquisition of rights, development of the screenplay and packaging activities). The phrase "producer's development deal" is sometimes used to distinguish such transactions from development deals awarded to writers or directors (see "development" and "development deal").

producer's errors and omissions insurance — (see "errors and omissions").

producer's fee — Compensation paid to a film's producer out of the budget of the film for his or her producing services. Also the up front payment to the person who has developed a film project and sells it to a studio for production and distribution. In most situations, the producer's fee is the only compensation a feature film producer will receive for the production of a film, since net profits are rarely generated (see "contingent compensation," "gross receipts," "independent producer" and "net profits").

producer's insurance policy — A special type of insurance contract that incorporates most or all of the various kinds of insurance coverages that relate to the production of motion pictures (see "insurance" and "insurance coverages").

producer's net — Monies received by the producer for the exploitation of a film over and above the producer's expenses in producing such film (see "net profits," "producer's fee" and "producer's share").

producer's net profits — That portion of a film's net profits allocated to the producer (see "net profits").

producer's package — The written presentation prepared by a film producer that describes or otherwise represents the elements of a planned film project and is used in obtaining financing and/or distribution arrangements. Depending on at what stage it is presented to prospective financiers and/or distributors, the package may include some or all of the following items: title report, copyright search report, chain of title documents including certificate of authorship for screenplay, a copy of the copyright registration(s), corporate resolution authorizing the producer to negotiate and sign a distribution deal, final screenplay and shooting script, proposed cast and production credits, synopsis of the script, biographies of key people, feature stories on lead actors and director, production stills, casual cast photos, agreements relating to the film's music, MPAA certificate (if available) and the E&O certificate of insurance (see "choosing a distributor," "distribution alternatives," "financing" and "package").

producer's representative — A person who is authorized by a motion picture producer to act on behalf of the producer in the conduct of the producer's business affairs (e.g., in negotiating script option or acquisition agreements, development deals, personnel agreements, production financing arrangements and distribution agreements). The term is most commonly associated today with the individual who helps the independent producer arrange for distribution of the film. Although not required, many producer's representatives are attorneys. A

producer's attorney, on the other hand, does not become a producer's representative, unless such attorney goes beyond advising the client and the drafting of documents and actually becomes involved in the direct negotiation of the producer's deals with the parties on the other side of the transaction (see "agent" "executive producer," "entertainment attorney," "packaging attorney," "personal manager" and "personal representative")

producer's royalty — Payments to a feature film producer or production company for the rights to exploit certain of the ancillary rights associated with a motion picture (e.g., for the soundtrack album). As an example, the film distribution agreement may provide with respect to producer royalties on the film's soundtrack album that two-thirds of the amount of any advance from the record company acquiring the soundtrack distribution rights in excess of the cost of production of the soundtrack and soundtrack album for the picture (including, but not limited to, producer advances, artists's advances, third party costs and all other costs which are customarily recognized in the phonograph record industry) is payable to the production company for its own account with the remaining one-third payable to the film distributor (see "royalties" and "soundtrack albums").

producer's share — A term defined in some distribution agreements as the accountable gross remaining after the deduction, on a continuing basis, of the aggregate of the distributor's distribution fees, distribution expenses and gross participations, if any. Some distribution agreements provide that third party participations, if any, be deducted from the producer's share. The reasoning used to support this position is that the producer, to a greater or lesser extent, is responsible for the production of the motion picture, including all of the associated costs (i.e., the producer is responsible for negotiating and allowing such third party participations, that may include talent participations since talent is not a party to the distribution agreement between the producer and distributor). Thus, logically (from the distributor's point of view) the producer should pay the costs of these contingent commitments to talent out of the producer's portion of the film's revenue stream (i.e., out of net profits). The producer may readily agree with this analysis since the producer and all other net profit participants are likely to fare better if they are paid on a pari passu basis with the talent as opposed to allowing talent to receive gross participations. In addition, a producer may seek to negotiate an assumption agreement with the distributor obligating the distributor to calculate and pay all contingent compensation with respect to a film. On the other hand, in the studio/distributor financed films, gross participations are sometimes also defined as a production cost and thus the studio/distributor collects interest and overhead charges on these "expenses" which were never actually paid out by the studio/distributor (see "accountable gross," "assumption agreement," "creative accounting," "gross participations," "interest" and "pari passu").

Producers Guild of America (PGA) — An organization created partly for the purpose of correcting the use of inappropriate screen credits for executive producers, producers and associate producers. However, the PGA, unlike the Writers Guild or the Directors Guild, is not recognized as a collective bargaining agency and has no specific legal jurisdiction over the dispensation of credits. In 1983, when the PGA tried to gain such status, the National Labor Relations Board ruled that producers cannot be a union because their jobs are essentially managerial. That appears to be true for independent producers but not necessarily the case with producers who are employees of the major/studio distributors. As a result of the NLRB's decision and the PGA's own narrow focus, independent producers are left without any effective professional association that is exclusively devoted to the vigorous advocacy of the interests of independent producers in whatever forum such interests arise. In order to be more effective at the industry level, independent producers need to organize some form of association of independent feature film producers (much like the IFTA—the trade group primarily representing the interests of independent distributors) in order to protect their interests at the industry level (see "American Academy of Independent Film Producers," "association projects," "FIND," "IFP" and "model agreement").

producers liability insurance — (see "insurance coverages" and "producer's insurance policy").

producing entity — In instances where a film is produced by a production company or other entity as opposed to an individual producer, the production company is said to be the producing entity, although one or more individual principals of the company may receive a producer or executive producer screen credit (see "independent producer" and "production company").

producing for hire — Performing the services of a feature film producer as an employee of a studio or other production company. Under such circumstances the results and proceeds of the producer's work belong to the production company that hired the producer (see "independent producer," "producer" and "Producers Guild of America").

product — Something produced. In film, the result of the combined efforts of all of those persons involved in the production of a motion picture (i.e., the motion picture or finished film itself; see "collaborative process," "commodity," "idea," "intangible" and "tangible asset").

product costs — (same as "negative costs").

product flow — The continuing or uninterrupted movement of motion pictures week after week at movie houses. The ability of a distributor to provide a consistent flow of quality motion pictures to exhibitors gives the distributors greater leverage with such exhibitors in booking films in their theaters and in negotiating the terms of the exhibitor/distributor deal as well as the settlement transaction (see "major studio/distributors," "product source" and "settlement transaction").

product glut — The flooding of a market with goods so that supply exceeds demand. An unusually high number of motion picture films produced and/or available for distribution in a given year. The U.S. film industry appears to be in a continuing state where the number of films produced far exceeds the ability or willingness of distributors to distribute (see "law of supply and demand" and "product shortage").

product integration — Situations where a product is so integrated into the movie that it is partly what the movie is about (see "product placement" and "product plug").

production — A presentation of a story or exposition on film or videotape that has continuity and direction, complete in itself. The general term used to describe the processes involved in making all the original materials that are the basis for the finished motion picture. Also a film in the process of being produced (see "product" and "motion picture").

production account — The bank account into which funds designated to be spent on the production of a motion picture are deposited (see "production" and "production accountant").

production accountant — A member of a film production staff (or an independent contractor) who sets up and maintains the books and payroll system throughout the making of a film. He or she maintains up-to-date, accurate financial records of the costs of producing the film. The production accountant works closely with the production manager and may report to the financing entity. He or she will set up an accounting office, open production bank accounts, review the budget, furnish cost reports, pay all bills incurred by the production, pay the salaries of the cast and crew and handle insurance claims, if any (see "production auditor").

production accounting services — (see "payroll" and "production accounting").

production agreement — A contract between a feature film financier or financing source and a production company setting out the terms under which the production company will produce a motion picture being financed by the financier or financing source. When such agreements are made with a vertically integrated organization such as a major studio/distributor, production agreements are often combined with distribution agreements (e.g., the production-financing/distribution agreement; see "distribution agreement," "financing agreement" and "production-financing/distribution agreement").

production auditor — An accountant who conducts an examination and verification of the production company's accounting documents and supporting data for the purpose of rendering an opinion as to their fairness, consistency, and conformity with generally accepted accounting principles (see "production accountant").

production board — A board with several panels on which separate strips containing sketches of each scene of a film script are placed to aid in scheduling and budgeting (see "shooting schedule" and "story board").

production breakdown — A detailed system of separating each and every element of a film script and then re-arranging them in the most efficient and least expensive manner for filming. The term also refers to a detailed analysis prepared by a film's script supervisor for the purpose of timing the script (see "production board").

production budget — The amount of money itemized by spending category anticipated to be required to produce a film. The production budget will generally include pre-production, principal photography and post-production. Other film related costs such as insurance, contingency reserves and completion bond fees are usually included under an "other" category (see "budget" and "development").

Production Code Administration — An entertainment industry organization that operated from the 1930s until 1968 and approved or disapproved of the content of films until the system was abandoned in 1968 in favor of the so-called MPAA rating system (see "MPAA," "IFIDA" and "ratings").

production company— An organization or business entity that develops and produces feature or documentary films (see "distributor," "independent producer," "major studio/distributors" and "studio").

production comptroller — (see "production accountant").

production contingency — An amount of money, typically 10 percent of the production budget, that is set aside to cover unexpected expenses or budget overages. The percentage might be raised for a low-budget picture being shot without a completion bond. Also, a completion guarantor may require a higher percentage on certain films before agreeing to provide the completion bond (same as "contingency" or "contingency reserve").

production contracts — The written agreements negotiated and signed between a film's producer and all persons or entities providing products or services in the production of a film (e.g., director, cinematographer, actors, actresses, catering and transportation services, etc.; see "contract" and "production").

production costs — The expenses planned or incurred in producing a feature or documentary film (i.e., the expenses incurred in the production of a film negative). Such costs are generally incurred in four stages: story rights acquisition and development, pre-production, principal photography and post-production. The complete production process can take a year to eighteen months. Production expenses may include the cost of the story, salaries of cast, directors, producers, etc., set construction and operations, wardrobe, sound synchronization, editing and any other costs necessary to create a finished film negative. Other components of movie production costs might include (depending on the form of film finance used) residuals, participations, allocated studio overhead, abandonment costs and capitalized interest. Production costs may also include contractual overheads and contractual facility and equipment charges in excess of actual costs, rebates and receipts from sales of props and sets, provision for self-insurance, a completion bond charge, participations before break-even and overhead and deferments, along with actual or imputed interest. The production cost for studio financed films does not mean the studio's cost in providing a certain service or product but what it arbitrarily decides to charge the film for such service or product and the studio markup for such items is often extremely high. It is also very important to clearly define in any production-financing/distribution agreement the distinction between production costs and distribution expenses (and to vigorously monitor the studio's classification of expenses), since a studio financier will typically seek to charge interest on the cost of producing the negative (production expenses) as well as apply the studio's overhead percentage against the production cost total. The producer and other profit participants, therefore, must insist that no expenses that are actually distribution costs be classified by the studio as production costs since such a practice would tend to delay any net profit participation (see "creative accounting," "direct distribution expenses," "gross participations," "interest," "negative costs" and "rising production costs").

production cost deferments — Arrangements for the deferral of some or all of the costs of goods and/or services provided by the suppliers of such goods and/or services so that the payments are not a production cost but rather are paid out of specified receipts before or after investor or financier recoupment (see "deferments" or "deferrals").

production deferments — (same as "production cost deferments").

production department — A major administrative unit of the typical studio/distributor that is primarily responsible for the physical production of a motion pictures being produced by the studio on an in-house basis (see "business affairs department," "creative department," "legal department," "major/studio distributors," "marketing department" and "studio").

production designer — The film production person who works closely with the director and who is responsible for conceiving, planning and supervising the overall visual design of a film (see "art director" and "set designer").

production/distribution agreement — (see "production-financing/distribution agreement").

production entity — The company responsible for the production of a motion picture. The term is used to make a distinction between the production company and the producer who is an individual. Production entities sometimes take the form of a corporation (regular "C" corporation or "S" corp, but may also be fictitious name companies, general partnerships, joint ventures, member-managed LLCs, limited partnerships or manager-managed LLCs (see "corporation," "joint venture," "limited liability company," "limited partnership" and "producer").

production executive — An administrative manager employee of the major studio/distributors who is responsible for overseeing the interests of the studio when it acts as a financier in the production of a motion picture. The studio's production executive will sometimes be named in the production-financing/distribution agreement (see "production-financing/distribution agreement").

production expenses — (see "production costs").

production financing — Funding provided for the production of a film as opposed to development or distribution financing (see "development," "direct distribution expenses" and "distribution alternatives").

production-financing/distribution agreement — A contract between a studio/distributor (or other distributor) and a feature film producer that sets out the terms and conditions under which the distributor will provide production financing for a motion picture in exchange for the right to distribute the film in some or all markets; one of the principal forms of motion picture production financing. The production financing in a P-F/D deal actually takes the form of a loan extended by the studio to the production company. Such studios will usually exercise certain controls and approvals over the production process. As the film is exploited and its revenues are collected by the distributor, the distributor will deduct its fee, its distribution expenses, interest on the loan and then the negative cost of the film before arriving at net profits (also called "production/distribution agreement"; see "acquisition/distribution agreement," "financing," "in-house product," "interest," "negative pickup distribution agreement," "studio financing" and "theatrical distribution contract").

production fund — A sum of money set aside either by governmental or private interests for the purpose of contributing some or all of the monies needed to produce feature films (see "completion fund" and "production financing").

production funds — The monies deposited into a feature film production account to be used in the production of a motion picture. With respect to a studio financed project (i.e., production-financing/distribution agreement) the studio/distributor will typically advance funds to the production company for the production of the picture up to the total amount of the approved production budget, and if required thereafter, up to and including the contingency, in fixed installments and consistent with a cash flow schedule that has been mutually approved by the production company and the studio/distributor (see "production-financing/distribution agreement").

production loans — Funds that are borrowed from a bank or other lending source for the purpose of producing a motion picture (see "collateral," "completion guarantor," "inter-party agreement," "negative pickup," "security agreement" and "split rights deal").

production manager — The film production person responsible to the producer for assembling the budget, organizing the shooting schedule, expediting all aspects of the production and authorizing all expenditures. The production manager supervises the daily production of a film, working directly with the assistant director, producer, and director. He or she relays orders from the director and producer to the assistant director and oversees the signing of contracts, scouting of locations, permit arrangements for all non-studio shoots, catering and daily accounting.

The work of the production manager is similar to and overlaps the responsibility of the assistant director. On some movie sets the production manager is the same as the line producer (see "line producer" and "unit production manager").

production notes — Notes and/or reports made during the filming or taping of all aspects of a film or video production including camera and sound reports, production manager's reports, script clerk's notes, and other similar reports. Such notes are useful during production and in post-production, particularly in editing the film. Production notes are also referred to as production reports (see "production reports").

production office coordinator — The person on a film production who serves as a liaison among the producer, production manager, assistant directors and script supervisor and who is responsible for the set-up and efficient running of the production office for a specific film production (see "production reports").

production overhead — Those costs and expenses incurred by a studio/distributor in the business of producing and distributing motion pictures generally, that cannot be directly charged to specific pictures, regardless of whether or not such facilities or staff are actually used on a given picture. They include such things as rental of sound stages or other studio facilities such as dressing facilities, vehicles, telephones, office space and equipment, secretaries' salaries, studio executives' salaries and their expenses, development and story-abandonment costs and general administrative costs relating to the production area. In view of the fact that distributors are generally permitted to recoup at least 100 percent of their direct distribution expenses and distribution fees for distributing a film in various media and markets, some take the

position that such indirect distribution or other expenses should not be charged against a specific film, either on an actual cost or percentage basis, but rather such studio/distributors should cover such costs as most businesses do with their earned fees. It is particularly troublesome for some to have a studio/distributor finance the production costs of a film, then add such overhead to the negative cost of the film and charge interest on that overhead while delaying recoupment of the negative cost until after distribution fees are collected and distribution expenses are recovered, if ever. Such practices may be considered unconscionable by courts (see "gross participations," "interest," "leverage," "overhead," "overhead surcharge" and "overreaching").

production payroll service — An accounting service that may provide above and below-the-line film production related accounting services (see "payroll" and "production accounting").

production reports — Regular written documentation (usually daily), in production ledgers or on special pads, that indicate acceptable and non-acceptable takes and additional relevant information relating to the specific movie in production. Such pads are pre-printed in a special long, rectangular form with multiple carbons to facilitate the making and distribution of notations relating to each take. Examples of such reports include sound and camera reports. The script supervisor's notes are also generally considered production reports. Production reports are prepared by line producers and unit managers. They contain the work hours for each member of the cast and crew, amount of film stock shot, costs of the shooting day, number of pages filmed, balance of script pages yet to be shot, location and scouting data in brief (i.e., everything essential to the logistics of a movie shoot; see "production manager" and "production notes").

production risk — The danger that a planned feature film production will not be completed, that it will not be completed on time or that it will go over budget (see "completion bond" and "lender risk elimination").

production schedule — The timetable and plan for conducting the principal photography of a motion picture. Such a schedule would include a start date and may be set out in the production-financing agreement (e.g., approximately eleven weeks, comprised of five day work weeks with two holidays off, for a total of fifty-three production days; see "principal photography").

production slowdown — A reduction in the normal work pace of persons involved in the production of a motion picture. Sometimes in the context of employer/employee negotiations unions or guilds use the tactic of a production slowdown to force employers to meet their demands instead of a full scale strike (see "de facto strike" and "strike").

production sound effects — (see "sound effects").

production specifications — The contractual requirements of a film financier with respect to the production of a motion picture being financed. Such specifications may include agreed upon requirements relating to a start date, production schedule and locations along with the identities of the production company counsel and the studio's production executive (see "basic elements," "deal terms," "picture specifications" and "production schedule").

production staff — All of the persons working on a given film shooting assignment who work directly for the studio or production company (i.e., producer, line producer, production manager, production associate, director (in some cases), production secretary and others; see "cast," "crew," "operational staff" and "staff").

production still — A photograph taken during a film's production that is shot with a still camera as opposed to a motion picture camera. A still is usually printed as an 8 x 10 inch black and white glossy or color photograph of an actor or a scene from a film and is used for matching continuity in later shots and for advertising or publicity purposes (see "still photographer").

production unit — A self-contained group consisting of director, camera crew, sound crew, electricians, etc. that works on a sound stage or on location to shoot an assigned motion picture or section of the film (see "unit production manager").

production value — The general appeal of a film due to a certain favorable combination of the film's elements or the appeal of a specific element in such film. Also a reference to the quality of certain aspects of a feature film production (see "audience" and "elements").

product placement — The activities of feature film producers, distributors or their representatives (e.g., product placement firms) in arranging for the appearance of a commercial product in a film for a fee. The practice raises ethical questions with regard to subjecting unsuspecting moviegoers to commercial messages without some form of pre-exhibition disclosure or disclaimer. Notwithstanding the ethical considerations, some studios and producers are able to raise a certain portion of the production funds for producing their movies through product placements. Independently produced films are less likely to benefit unless distribution guarantees can be provided (see "advertising tie-ins," "commercials," "distributor commercials" and "promotional tie-ins").

product plug — Situations where a product appears in a film or other media and there is no economic exchange or consideration paid (see "product integration" and "product placement").

product shortage — A subjective term referring to a significant reduction in the number of feature films produced or distributed in a given year. All other factors being equal, a product shortage tends to improve the bargaining position of feature film producers in relation to distributors, but may also improve the bargaining position of the distributors in relation to exhibitors. Traditionally, the U.S. film industry experiences more product gluts than shortages (see "bargaining position," "bargaining power," "inferior bargaining position," "law of supply and demand" and "product glut").

product source — For distributors, movie production companies are sources of product (i.e., motion pictures). For exhibitors, the distributors are their product source. One of the objectives of production companies and distributors is to be perceived as a continuing source of quality product, because that perception gives them greater negotiating leverage (see "product flow").

product splitting — A film industry practice in which exhibitors allocate among themselves the rights to negotiate for the exhibition of films distributed by motion picture distributors (i.e., a film exhibition practice in which several theaters in a territory informally agree not to bid aggressively against each other for certain films offered by a distributor with the intent of increasing the likelihood that the distributor terms ultimately agreed to by the distributor will be more favorable to the exhibitors). Each theater in a given territory thus would get the chance to license highly desirable films on more favorable terms on a regular rotating basis. Thus, the practice is designed to create a more fair allocation of films among the existing theaters in a given area, to reduce the prices exhibitors have to pay to distributors for the right to exhibit films and as a counter-measure to the distributor practice of blind bidding (same as "film splitting" or "splitting"; see "anti-competitive business practices").

professional association — A membership organization made up of persons engaged in a specific profession who have joined together to promote their mutual interests, through educational programs for members, lobbying activities, industry research and public information programs (see "industry groups," "lobbyists" and "trade association"; contrast with "guild" and "PGA"; also called "professional and trade associations").

professional budget — A film budget prepared for a fee by a specialist in film budgeting as opposed to the film's producer who may or may not have bona fide expertise in the preparation of film budgets (see "budget").

profile — A description of a specific segment of the movie-going public in terms of their demographic and psychographic characteristics, including such factors as age, sex, income, education and life style (see "demographics" and "psychographic").

profit — Generally, the positive difference that results from selling products and services for more than the cost of producing such goods. In film, the amount left over after an exhibitor, distributor, producer or financing entity or group has paid all its bills or expenses. Depending on the deal between each entity, one participant in a movie project will reach profits before others who are participating in the revenue stream at a different level (i.e., later stage). The definitions of net and gross profits will vary from deal to deal depending on what income is included and to be accounted for and what deductions are to be taken against that income before applying a profit participant's percentage to the balance (see "actual breakeven," "artificial breakeven," "breakeven," "most favored nations clause," "pari passu" and "pro rata").

profitability — The quality or state of having an excess of returns over expenditures in a transaction or in a business entity's transactions. The lack of consistent profitability in a business or industry tends to make it difficult to attract capital (see "profit" and "profit margin").

profit and loss statement — (see "income statement").

profit center — A department or area of business within a company or business entity that produces a profit if considered as an independent operation. The most significant profit center for film studios has traditionally been their distribution activities (see "creative accounting," "distribution" and "profit").

profits, losses or credits — IRS terminology for the net income, net loss or credits of a limited partnership or manager-managed LLC, as determined for federal income tax purposes (see "income tax").

profit margin — The difference between a business' gross sales and net profits. The profit margins of the major studio/distributors have been relatively low for many years (see "operating profit" and "profitability").

profit motive — A reason for conducting a business activity. For tax purposes, an essential element in the analysis of whether a trade or business expense is deductible (i.e., to be deductible as a trade or business expense, an expenditure must be paid or incurred in connection with a trade or business and that trade or business must be carried on primarily for profit, as opposed to a hobby for recreation and pleasure). Profit motive is determined by an examination of all the circumstances in the case. There need not be a reasonable expectation that the activity will yield a profit. It is sufficient if it is entered into in good faith with the purpose of making a profit (see "federal tax discussion," "limited partnership," "manager-managed LLC" and "tax opinion").

profit participant — An individual or entity authorized to be paid a stated percentage of a film's revenue stream at a designated point in that revenue stream (e.g., 2 percent of the distributor's gross receipts, 5percent of the film's net profits or 20 percent of the LLC manager's share of the LLC's distributable cash).

profit participation — Any percentage of a film's revenue stream to be paid at a designated point in that revenue stream to an individual or entity involved in the development, financing, production and/or distribution of the movie. Such participations are negotiable and thus may be based on gross receipts, adjusted gross, net profits or other stages in a movie's revenue stream. If reasonable controls and/or limitations are not imposed on the distributor's claim to distribution expenses, the distribution fees are not reasonable and other parties are allowed to participate in the distributor's gross receipts, net profit participations are not likely to occur. Such practices could impact adversely on the financial interests of investors, producers, executive producers, directors, screenwriters, actors/actresses or others who have negotiated a profit participation interest in a given motion picture (see "Association of Net Profit Participants," "net profit participant," "percentage participation" and "points").

profit participation auditor — An accountant (and sometimes attorneys) who are authorized to examine and report on the books of account of film and television distribution entities. Such auditors conduct an inspection of the accounting records and procedures of a film's distributor on behalf of profit participants, for the purpose of verifying the accuracy and completeness of the records. Experienced entertainment attorneys and profit participation auditors recommend that profit participants audit any motion picture that has any likelihood of going into net profits. An audit of studio books for a domestic theatrical release may cost $30,000 or more, but few if any of such audits, do not pay for themselves. Audits of major studios have uncovered millions of dollars in "errors," most of which seem to be in the studio's favor. It may be wise for independent feature film producers to include a line item in their investor-financed offerings (as a non-film budget item) to cover such costs (see "advocate auditing," "audit," "audit rights," "broad auditing rights," "cottage industry," "limited review," "sub-distributor" and "underreported rentals").

profit projections — A prospective financial forecast that implies by its name that a profit, at

some level, will occur, a risky implication at best in motion picture finance (see "financial forecasts" and "projections" and "financial projections").

profit potential — The highest level of earnings for a business transaction that can be reasonably anticipated (see "maximum exploitation" and "profit").

profit-sharing ratio — The ratio in which partners in limited partnerships or members in manager-managed LLCs have agreed to share profits and losses. Profit-sharing and loss-sharing ratios, however, sometimes differ (see "post-payout sharing ratio" and "recoupment").

pro forma — (see "pro forma financial statements").

pro forma cash flow schedule — A prospective financial report prepared by or on behalf of a film's producer, typically at the request of and for the benefit of a bank in a production loan situation, setting out on a weekly basis the amount of money needed to pay for the anticipated production expenses during the pre-production, principal photography and post-production stages of a film production (see "cash flow," "cash flow chart" and "cash flow schedule").

pro forma financial statements — Financial presentations that are designed to demonstrate the effect of a future or hypothetical transaction or event by showing how it might have affected the historical financial statements if it had been consummated during the period covered by those statements (i.e., financial statements that represent proposed events in the form in which they will appear if or when the events actually occur; see "financial forecasts," "financial projections," "partial presentations" and "prospective financial statements").

program highlights — A non-required section of the securities disclosure documents commonly associated with limited partnership or manager-managed LLC offerings that typically takes the form of a one page point by point abstract of the summary of the offering (i.e., listing the main points of the securities offering of interest to an investor; see "disclosure document" and "summary of offering").

programmed music — The generation of music by means of automatic high-speed digital computers (see "music").

progress to production schedule — A feature film development stage planning device that amounts to a projected timetable setting out when the various development steps are expected to be completed (see "development," "draft," "polish," "revision" and "script changes").

projected audience — The total number of persons who are expected to see a given movie in a specific market (see "target audience").

projected cash flow schedule — A prospective financial report prepared by or on behalf of a film production company or producer, at the request of and for the benefit of a studio or other financier, that sets out on a weekly basis the amount of money needed to pay for the anticipated production expenses of a film (see "cash flow" and "pro forma cash flow schedule").

projected overage — A forecast made during the production of a motion picture that estimates how much the actual production costs of the

film will exceed the approved production budget and contingency. Studio production-financing/distribution agreements typically contain provisions that allow the studio to take over the production of a motion picture if, based on the information available (including, but not limited to, the weekly reporting papers furnished by the production company), the studio reasonably believes that the estimated cost of production of the picture will exceed the contingency. In such instances, the studio and production company may engage in efforts to reduce the projected overage by conferring for a stated period (e.g., three days), on a method to reduce the projected overage to a point which will not exceed the contingency. If the studio and production company agree to a reduction plan that will ensure that the contingency will not be exceeded, such reductions may then become part of the approved production budget for the picture. However, if the parties are unable to agree on a reduction plan within the stated period, the studio usually has the right to take over the picture (see "approved production budget," "contingency" and "overages").

project financing — Raising money for a limited term business activity, such as a single motion picture or a multiple-film slate (but limited number of films). The investment vehicles most compatible with project financing are the limited partnership or the manager-managed LLC. Corporate financing is more appropriate for a long-term business strategy (see "single-picture financing")

projection of revenues — An estimated forecast of earnings from a proposed business activity. Most feature film producers and/or production companies do some sort of projection of revenues from a film before committing to do a project (see "computer model," "financial management," "financial projections" and "mental modeling").

projections — (see "financial projections" and "profit projections").

prominence — The style, size and other factors that make a screen credit appear more prestigious (see "billing" and "credits").

promise — A declaration of one's intention to do or to refrain from doing something accompanied by a commitment to do so (see "contract").

promissory note — A written promise committing the maker to pay the payee a specified sum of money either on demand or at a fixed or determinable future date, with or without interest (also called "note"; see "debt" and "lender financing").

promoter — In corporate law, generally anyone who undertakes to form a corporation and to procure for it the rights, instrumentalities and capital by which it is to carry out the purpose set forth in its charter. The SEC defines a promoter as any person who, acting alone or in conjunction with one or more persons, directly or indirectly takes the initiative in founding or organizing the business or enterprise of an issuer of securities or any person who receives 10 percent or more of any class of securities of an issuer on the proceeds therefrom in consideration for services or property. However, a person who receives such securities or proceeds either solely as underwriting commissions or solely in consideration of property will not be deemed a promoter if such person does not otherwise take part in founding and organizing the enterprise (also called "sponsor"; see "corporation").

promotional activities — Film publicity activities geared towards gaining media attention and public interest such as interviews, special screenings for critics, opinion-makers or specific interest groups, public appearances by the director, actors or others involved in the film, sandwich board advertising, T-shirts, comic books, sneak previews and flyers (see "advertising" and "publicity").

promotional campaign — The strategy and planned activities designed to publicize a movie (see "promotional activities").

promotional concept — The primary element of a film that will be utilized in advertising and promoting its exhibition (see "concept").

promotional materials — All of the documents and other items that can be used to obtain publicity for a motion picture including press releases, a description of the film, biographies of key personnel, a list of screening sites, press clippings, recommendations, quotes and flyers, some of which may be posted online at a website for the movie. Such materials may be helpful in stimulating the interest of a distributor in distributing a film or in persuading a potential distributor to at least attend a screening of the film (see "press kit").

promotional quotes — Excerpts from the critical reviews by motion picture critics that are used in the advertising of feature films (see "blurbs," "body copy," "critic's review," "cross plugs," "display advertising," "press kit," "publicity articles" and "puffery").

promotional tie-ins — Advertising campaigns that combine the promotion of a motion picture with a product, such as a soft drink or pizza. Sometimes such products may be subtly or even prominently displayed within the movie for a fee or as part of the tie-in arrangement (contrast with "product placement"; see "promotional campaign").

prompt payment — The timely remittance of amounts due. It is not uncommon for studios or other distributors to hold payments from television and cable sales until actual play dates, even though the funds have been received one or two or more years in advance. Producers may want to negotiate for the prompt payment of all funds due the producer and attempt to define what is reasonably prompt in the case of each type of payment (see "unethical business practices").

propaganda — Ideas, facts or allegations disseminated with the intent of furthering one's cause or of damaging an opposing cause. To the extent that Hollywood movies tend to contain patterns of bias (i.e., consistent negative or stereotypical portrayals of certain populations or consistent positions on certain political or religious related issues) the people who control the process of selecting which movies are to be produced and/or released by the Hollywood major-studio distributors may actually be using this powerful medium for the communication of ideas as propaganda masquerading as entertainment (see "communication," "communications industry," "entertainment," "entertainment industry," "favorable portrayal," "idea," "marketplace of ideas," "movies with a message," "multi-cultural society," "patterns of bias" and "unfavorable portrayal").

proper title — Appropriate or suitable ownership (see "clear title," "good title" and "just title").

property — In general, every species of valuable right or interest that is subject to ownership, has

an exchangeable value or adds to one's wealth. Property describes one's exclusive right to possess, use and dispose of a thing. With respect to film, the word property usually refers to an idea, concept, outline, synopsis, treatment, short story, magazine article, novel, screenplay or other literary form that someone has a legal right to develop to the exclusion of others and that may form the basis for a motion picture. Recognize that some of the above set out property forms (i.e., idea and concept), may be more difficult to protect than others (see "idea theft," "literary materials" or "literary works").

property damage liability insurance — A type of insurance that pays for the destruction of or damage to the property of others (including loss of use of the property) while the property is in the care, custody or control of the film production company and is used or to be used in an insured production (see "liability insurance").

proportionate share of deductions — A reference to the allocation of tax deductions generated by film production activities among equity owners. In a joint venture context, both venturers would receive their proportionate share of such deductions and in a limited partnership or manager-managed LLC, each investor would be allocated his or her proportionate share of tax deductions (see "deductions").

proprietorship — (see "sole proprietorship").

props — Any moveable items seen or used on a motion picture set and used in a particular scene (see "set dressing").

props, sets and wardrobe insurance — A type of insurance policy that covers props, sets, scenery, costumes, wardrobe and similar theatrical property against all risks of direct physical loss, damage or destruction during a film's production (see "insurance").

pro rata — Proportionately allocated in accordance with some standard (e.g., the percentage of interests held by investors in a limited partnership or manager-managed LLC. Such percentages cannot be determined in advance of such offerings since there is no certainty as to how many units will be sold. The pro rata percentages are determined at the end of the offering, after all investors are in and the amount each invested is known (see "pari passu").

prospective financial statements — Either financial forecasts or financial projections including the summaries of significant assumptions and accounting policies. Although prospective financial statements may cover a period that has partially expired, statements for periods that have completely expired are not considered to be prospective financial statements. Thus, pro forma financial statements and partial presentations are not considered to be prospective financial statements (see "financial forecasts," "financial projections," "limited use," "partial presentations" and "pro forma financial statements").

prospective purchasers — In securities terms, people who are offered the opportunity to purchase securities (e.g., units in a limited partnership, interests in a manager-managed LLC or corporate shares). Per the securities laws, such persons must be given a properly drafted securities disclosure document prior to their purchase (see "anti-fraud rule," "disclosure document," "limited liability company" and "limited partnership").

prospectus — A document that discloses financial information about an issuer of securities to prospective purchasers and explains the plans and objectives of the business' undertakings in a public/registered securities offering; also any communication, either written or broadcast by radio or television, that offers a registered security for sale. The Securities Act of 1933 requires the filing of a prospectus, as part of the registration statement, with the SEC and that a copy of the prospectus be provided to each buyer of the securities. The prospectus contains the most important parts of the securities registration statement in a public offering and such document must provide all information relevant to the issue. A prospectus must be written in a clear, unambiguous manner since any injurious misrepresentation constitutes fraud and the complaining party may sue for damage or rescission (see "anti-fraud rule," "disclosure document," "final prospectus," "offering memorandum," "preliminary offering circular," "registration statement," "rescission" and "waiting period").

provision for arbitration — A clause in an agreement that sets out the circumstances under which the parties to the contract will be obligated to take a dispute to an arbitrator for resolution (see "arbitration clause").

proxy — A written authorization signed by one who holds the right to vote on matters to be decided by the ownership of a business entity, such as a corporation or partnership, and that authorizes the holder of the proxy right to exercise the power to vote with respect to the interest of the person who signed the document and had the right to grant such power (see "power of attorney" and "voting stock").

proxy holder — One who has been authorized to cast a vote for another (see "proxy").

prurient — Shameful and morbid interest in nudity, sex or excretion. It is one criteria in determining whether or not something is obscene (see "pornography" and "obscene material").

psychographic — Of or relating to a graph representing the extent to which an individual exhibits traits or abilities as determined by tests or ratings (see "profile" and "target audience").

public accountant (PA) — A person who meets the educational, training, exam and licensing requirements of the state in which he or she practices the profession of accounting (i.e., the recording and summarizing of business and financial transactions along with analyzing, verifying and reporting the results of such transactions), but who was not required to pass the Uniform Certified Public Exam, typically because such accountant had already been practicing for a number of years before such exam and certification program was adopted in that state (see "certified public accountant").

publication rights — The authority to reduce certain information to writing and to make such information known to the general public. Certain publication rights are often granted or reserved in conjunction with a motion picture production (e.g., for the publication of a book about the making of the movie or for the novelization of the screenplay; see "novelization").

Public Broadcasting System (PBS) — A group of some three hundred plus television stations that are loosely affiliated in a relationship somewhat akin to a network (i.e., they share programming) and that carry special educational, documentary, in-depth news and other programs not generally carried by the major TV networks (see "network" and "network television").

public corporation — (see "publicly held").

public domain — Information or literary, artistic or musical work that is available for anyone to use and not subject to copyright protection (e.g., the information or work was not copyrighted or the term of copyright protection has expired; see "copyright").

public exhibition — The showing of a film to a general audience irrespective of whether the audience paid to view the film (also see "commercial public exhibition").

public figure — In libel and privacy law, a person of general fame and notoriety in the community and pervasive involvement in the affairs of society. Case law decisions under the First Amendment require that a public figure must show a defendant acted with actual malice before recovering damages for libel (see "defamation," "libel," "slander" and "tort").

publicist — The person responsible for promotion and publicity of a person or film through all media including radio, television, newspapers, magazines, the Internet etc. A publicist on a film project is referred to as the unit publicist (see "unit publicist").

publicity — Any act or device designed to attract public interest (e.g., information with news value issued as a means of gaining public attention or support). Publicity refers to editorial content as opposed to paid advertising. It is used to promote and exploit a motion picture beyond its advertising (see "advertising," "buzz," "hype," "junket," "marketing" and "promotional activities").

publicity articles — Articles relating to a film that are prepared by the producer or distributor and provided as part of the press kit presented to the media (see "press kit").

publicity material — The physical items utilized in attracting public attention to a given movie, including such things as the final set of cast and production credits, a detailed synopsis of the picture, detailed production notes about making the picture, complete biographies of starring and key feature players, feature stories on key stars and filmmakers and column items or "shorts" (see "column item" and "shorts").

publicity rights — The legal power and authority to publicize a movie, literary property or individual. Also, in privacy law, the right to use or prevent the use of an individual's name, voice or likeness (see "publicity").

publicity still — A still photograph relating to a motion picture and used in promoting the movie (see "photograph").

public limited partnership — A limited partnership whose limited partnership interests are registered for sale with the SEC and in each state in which such interests are offered (contrast with "private placement").

publicly held — A corporation whose shares are available to the public at large and whose activities are regulated by the SEC and the appropriate state securities regulatory authorities (see "public offering" and "securities").

publicly traded — Corporations whose securities are registered with the Securities and Exchange Commission and bought and sold by the general public either through the facilities of an organized stock market or over the counter (see "over-the-counter market," "public offering" and "securities").

publicly traded partnership — (same as "master limited partnership").

public offering — A securities offering that has been registered with the state and federal securities regulatory authorities and which allows the issuer of such securities to advertise and generally solicit prospective investors (also called "registered offering"; contrast with "private offering"; see "cold call," "general solicitation," "limitations on manner of offering," "registration" and "securities").

public offering price — (same as "offering price").

publish — To make known to the general public; to inform one or more persons of a fact or matter that they would not otherwise have reason to know of. In the law of torts, a statement does not constitute defamation unless it is published (i.e., unless it is made known to some third party other than the party making the statement or the party defamed). The act of publishing can involve any form of communication including motion pictures (see "copyright").

publisher — A person or entity that issues and offers for sale books, sheet music or other printed material. Also, in music, the person or entity holding the legal right to record or otherwise exploit a musical work or to license others to do so (see "book," "music clearance," "publication rights" and "publish").

publishing rights — (see "publication rights").

publishing royalty — (see "merchandise and publishing royalty").

puffed numbers — The inflated reports of the performance of a motion picture at the box office. Exhibitor's sometimes exaggerate the box office performance of a film at a specific theater when responding to the inquiries of the trades or various box office reporting services in order to create the impression in the industry that a film is doing better at that theater than it actually is. Distributor's also may "puff" their numbers for industry consumption in order to encourage exhibitors to increase their bids for subsequent runs or to continue an ongoing run. Such reports then mislead prospective net profit participants into thinking that a film may achieve net profits when it actually will not (see "settlement transaction").

puffery — Flattering publicity or extravagant commendation (see "blurbs," "body copy," "critic's review," "cross plugs," "display advertising," "flowery language," "press kit" and "publicity articles").

purchase — To acquire or obtain something through the payment of money or something else of value (e.g., the acquisition of a literary property in exchange for valuable consideration; see "consideration" and "literary property").

purchase agreement — (same as "acquisition agreement" and "rights agreement").

purchase group — A group of investment bankers that, operating under an agreement among underwriters, agrees to purchase a new issue of securities from the issuer for resale to the investing public (same as "underwriting group" or "syndicate"; see "selling group of broker/dealers" and "negotiated underwriting").

purchaser counting rights — (see "counting rules").

purchaser representations — Written statements made by a prospective purchaser of a security to the issuer of such security and made for the purpose of meeting investor suitability requirements for the offering (e.g., regarding the purchaser's intention to purchase such security for his, her or its own investment, the purchaser's state of residence and the purchaser's income or net worth). Such statements generally are made in response to inquiries in the offering subscription agreement. Many state limited offering exemptions require specific purchaser representations as a condition to qualifying for such exemption from that state's securities registration requirement (see "investor suitability standards" and "legend").

purchaser representative — Any person who has such knowledge and experience in financial and business matters that he or she is capable of evaluating, alone or together with other representatives of the purchaser (or together with the purchaser), the merits and risks of a prospective investment and meets other requirements set out in Rule 501 of the SEC's Regulation D. Such purchaser representatives function as financial advisors to the prospective purchaser in a limited partnership, manager-managed LLC or other securities offerings and may help the prospective purchaser meet the offering's investor suitability standards for such offerings (see "investor suitability standards").

pure gross — The gross receipts received by a feature film distributor for the exploitation of a motion picture in all markets and media prior to any deductions whatsoever, including off-the-top deductions (see "gross receipts" and "off-the-top deductions").

pure gross participations — Contingent compensation based on a percentage of and paid out of a feature film distributor's gross receipts prior to any other deductions. Such participations are rarely granted (see "contingent compensation," "first dollar gross," "gross receipts" and "off-the-top deductions").

pyramid scheme — A plan or operation by which a person gives consideration for the opportunity to receive compensation that is derived primarily from a person's introduction of other persons to participate in the plan or operation rather than from the sale of a product by a person introduced into the plan or operation (see "scam").

Q

qualified opinion — An auditor's opinion that accompanies financial statements and calls attention to certain limitations of the audit or exceptions the auditor takes to the statements (see "audit").

quarterly financial results — The fiscal consequences of the operations of a business reported for a three month period of the company's operations (see "financial standings")

quarterly reports — Prepared statements relating to a company's operations and financial results for a three month period. Generally, earnings reports to shareholders of publicly held corporations are made on a quarterly basis and stock dividends are also paid on the same basis (see "annual report").

quiet and peaceful enjoyment — The right to unimpaired use and enjoyment of property leased or conveyed (see "covenant of good faith and fair dealing," "warranties and representations" and "warranty").

quiet period — The period of time during which an issuer of securities in the process of being registered for public offering is restricted by the SEC from putting out promotional publicity. The period generally dates from the pre-underwriting decision to forty or ninety days after the effective date (see "effective date," "prospectus" and "waiting period").

quotas — Limits imposed on the number of products that may be imported into a given country (e.g., limits imposed on the number of American made feature film productions that may be broadcast on European television or exhibited theatrically; see "foreign market").

quota barriers — (see "quotas").

quotes — Excerpts from critical film reviews that are used in advertising a film. Such excerpts are supposed to be specifically approved by the critic prior to use in any advertisement (see "blurbs" and "critic").

R

racketeering — Originally, an organized conspiracy to commit extortion, but the concept has in more recent times, been superseded by RICO (acronym for Racketeer Influenced and Corrupt Organizations act), a federal statute that provides for four punishable racketeering offenses (1) for directly or indirectly investing income derived from a pattern of racketeering activity or through collection of an unlawful debt in any enterprise affecting trade or commerce; (2) for acquiring or maintaining any interest in an enterprise through a pattern of racketeering activity or collection of an unlawful debt; (3) for conducting or participating in the affairs of the enterprise through a pattern of racketeering activity or collection of an unlawful debt; or (4) for conspiring to violate the racketeering provisions. A "pattern of racketeering activity" requires engaging in at least two incidents of racketeering conduct within ten years of each other. Racketeering activity includes among other acts, certain indictable acts under federal and state laws including bribery, embezzlement from pension and welfare funds, extortionate credit transactions, mail fraud, wire fraud, interference with commerce and fraud in the sale of securities. The term "enterprise" in the federal act includes any individual, partnership, corporation or any union or group of individuals associated in fact though not a legal entity.

RICO also makes it unlawful for any person employed by or associated with any enterprise engaged in, or the activities of which affect, interstate commerce to conduct or participate in the conduct of the enterprise's affairs through a pattern of racketeering activity. Criminal violations may result in fines of $25,000 and/or a twenty year prison term and the forfeiture to the United States of any interest or security or contractual right of any kind affording a source of influence over the enterprise. RICO also provides for civil remedies. Any person injured in his business or property by reason of a violation may sue in any federal district court and may recover triple the substantial damages, cost of the suit, including a reasonable attorney's fees. The principal purpose of the act is to strengthen means of preventing money and power obtained from illegal endeavors to corrupt democratic business practices so as to interfere with free competition and to burden interstate and foreign commerce. Essentially, Congress is seeking to halt a pattern of infiltration of business by organized crime. Although most profit participants, including investors in film corporations and individual film investors do not ordinarily think of film distributors as a branch of "organized crime," if in fact, a given distributor engages in a number of the practices described herein, and raises production and/or distribution funds through the sale of corporate stock or other securities, such distributors may have committed securities fraud since the disclosure of such practices would almost certainly be considered material to prospective investors and issuers of securities are under an obligation to disclose all material aspects of any such securities transaction. Thus, a disgruntled investor or other person "wronged" by the activities of a film distributor may be able to establish that the film distributor engaged in numerous instances of racketeering activity (i.e., securities fraud by selling its stock without disclosing that it engaged in anti-competitive and predatory business practices, questionable or unethical conduct, creative accounting or sharp negotiating tactics, all of which may have an adverse impact on the interests of the investor and/or other profit participants; see "extortion," "Mafia," "money laundering," "mob controlled distribution company," "RICO," "theft" and "white collar crime").

radio — The broadcasting industry and the communications device that uses electric waves for the wireless transmission of electric impulses that are converted into sound. Movies are often advertized on radio. (see "broadcast" and "television").

radio spots — Film ads for use on radio; running times for radio spots are usually ten, thirty and sixty seconds. Radio spots are sent to sub-distributors, exhibitors and licensees on cassettes as part of the initial sales package prepared by the distributor of a film (see "advertising").

rate of return — The earnings or profit levels from owning assets or equity positions, expressed as a percentage of the original investment (i.e., the return on the investment).

For common stock, the rate of return is the dividend yield (i.e., the annual amount paid through dividends divided by the purchase price of the stock; also called "return on equity" or "return on invested capital"; see "interest," "real rate of return" and "return on investment").

rate sheet — A photocopied or printed page or brochure showing the costs of various services provided by film production-service companies such as equipment-rental houses, sound-stage facilities, labs, graphics shops and sound-recording studios (also called "price list").

rating — (see "Motion Picture Association of America," "MPAA Rating Administration" and "ratings").

Rating Appeals Board — An organization made up of twenty-two members, men and women from the MPAA and NATO (and formerly from the IFIDA), to which a producer who is for any reason displeased with the rating given his or her movie by CARA may appeal. The Rating Appeals Board sits as the final industry arbiter of movie ratings. Producers still dissatisfied with their movie's rating, however, may bring suit in a proper court of law (see "Rating Board").

Rating Board — A full-time board of seven individuals who are employed by the MPAA and its Classification and Rating Administration to rate movies submitted for rating. Since many of the movies submitted for rating have not been produced by MPAA members, an obvious and built-in potential conflict of interest exists between the MPAA and independent producers (who are not members of the MPAA) in the outcome of such ratings. The MPAA has been rating something in the neighborhood of nine hundred movies each year for the past several years. Some films which sought ratings, however, went straight to video, thus were not theatrical releases (see "MPAA" and "ratings").

ratings— A very general system of movie classification provided by the MPAA for films to be released, utilizing the following letter designations: "G" for general audience (all ages, i.e., a family film), "PG" for parental guidance (i.e., some of the material might not be suitable for children), "PG-13" (some material may be inappropriate for pre-teenagers), "R" for restricted to those of a certain age (this age varies from sixteen to twenty-one, with eighteen being the Motion Picture Association of America's suggested age) and "NC-17" for adults only. The stated purpose of the rating system is to provide advance information to enable parents to make judgments as to whether they want their children to see certain movies. A full-time rating board (employees of the MPAA), composed of seven persons (all who have shared the parenthood experience), headed by a chairman decide on the rating for a given movie by a majority vote. The rating board does not rate films for quality or the lack thereof. The rating board's criteria include theme, language, nudity, sex and violence. Recently, under pressure from people critical of the movie ratings system, the MPAA began offering additional narrative information to supplement the letter ratings and provide more information about why a given movie was given a certain rating. The rating assigned can in some cases significantly increase or decrease the potential audience for a movie and thus impact a movie's potential revenue (e.g., the difference in revenue potential between an "R" rated movie and the previously used "X" rating was substantial). Producers who are not satisfied with the MPAA rating assigned to their film have the right to re-edit the film and re-submit it to the ratings

board or they can release the film without an MPAA rating although most theaters will not exhibit unrated films. Producers also have a right to appeal a rating board decision to the Rating Appeals Board and can of course litigate the question in court. A number of lawsuits were filed in 1989 and 1990 by independent producers challenging the ratings assigned to their movies, particularly the former "X" rating. This prompted the MPAA to adopt the "NC-17" rating, even though some members of the public and exhibitors contend that such a change is merely a substitution of labels and makes no substantive change. Such lawsuits and criticism have also raised the basic question relating to the inherent conflict of interest in a system which allows an MPAA sponsored organization to rate movies produced by its members as well as the movies produced by non-members of the MPAA, although this issue has yet to be resolved. The MPAA has traditionally been opposed to attempts by any governmental entity (or other organization) that tries to set up a system for rating motion pictures as to their content and has used the existence of the MPAA ratings systems (controlled by the MPAA) as an argument against such efforts (see "CARA," "minimum rating," "MPAA," "NC-17," "Rating Appeals Board" and "trailer tags").

ratio — (see "aspect ratio").

raw stock — Film that has not been exposed or processed (see "film").

reader — An agency, film studio or production company story department employee (or freelance reader) who is responsible for reading, summarizing and writing an opinion on literary material submitted to such agency, studio or production company for consideration. The resulting analysis is referred to as coverage or development notes (see "coverage" and "development notes").

real income — Income of an individual, group or country adjusted for changes in purchasing power caused by inflation (see "income").

real interest rate — The current interest rate minus the inflation rate (see "inflation").

realized profit (or loss) — Profit or loss resulting from the sale or other disposal of a security. Capital gains taxes may be due when profits are realized. Realized losses can be used to offset realized gains for tax purposes [see "paper profit (or loss)"].

real model — A reference to computer based financial forecasting or modeling that is done on an ongoing basis and which suggests that such techniques are superior to hard-copy based pro forma financial forecasts that may be done and then forgotten as the business progresses during the forecast period (see "mental modeling" and "financial forecasts").

real rate of return — The return on an investment adjusted for inflation (see "investor financing" and "rate of return").

reasonable and customary — A general standard of conduct for commercial affairs that may only be ascertained on a case by case basis, after the fact, by testimony provided in the context of litigation. A negotiated and more concrete standard of conduct is generally more useful to the parties to a contract and may help to prevent litigation. Such standards are also difficult to establish in the film industry since it turns out that there is often no customary practice (see "subjective terms").

reasonable diligence — (see "due diligence").

reasonable efforts clause — A provision found in film distribution and other contracts that merely obligates the distributor (or others) to put forth reasonable efforts in distributing the film (or in taking other action called for). Less effort is required of the distributor (and others) pursuant to a reasonable efforts clause as opposed to a best efforts clause. If no higher standard of conduct can be negotiated, the producer may prefer the best efforts standard over reasonable efforts (see "best efforts clause").

rebate — In lending, the unearned interest refunded to a borrower if the loan is paid off before maturity. In other commercial transactions, the return by a purchaser to a seller of goods (or provider of services) of a portion of the payment for such goods or services. If a film lab, advertising agency or exhibitor gives a rebate to a distributor because of the volume of business the distributor gives the lab, agency or exhibitor a question may arise as to whether the distributor is obligated to credit a portion of that rebate to the gross receipts of each of the films involved so that the producers and other net profit participants share in the benefits of the rebate. Rebates, like discounts, are often negotiated and/or awarded by exhibitors and other feature film licensees to distributors on a given picture or they are also sometimes based on the volume of pictures provided by the distributor. Distributors often seek to exclude the value of such rebates in profit participation calculations, arguing that the distributor's activities are solely responsible for earning them. However, as with discounts, without the feature film or films made available to the distributor by the producer and other profit participants, the distributor would not be in a position to either negotiate or receive such rebates. Producers may want to seek to negotiate a more fair provision in the distribution agreement that includes the value of such rebates in the profit participation calculations. Even if a producer is successful in negotiating such a provision, it is not unthinkable for a distributor who has a particularly close relationship with a given exhibitor or other film licensee to have the rebate shifted (on paper) to another producer's film and/or included as part of an overall settlement as between the distributor and the licensee, in which case the distributor may have the discretion to allocate the amount of the settlement among various films distributed by the distributor on behalf of several different producers. Also, it may be difficult for an auditor to distinguish between such a rebate and an impermissible kickback (see "discount," "insider's game," "kickback," "reciprocal preferences" and "relationship driven business").

recapture — Tax terminology referring to the forfeiture (or recognition as ordinary income) of tax benefits previously allowed (see "income tax").

receipts — A term defined in some distribution agreements as the rentals, license fees, royalties or other charges received for the license or privilege to exhibit a film (including reissues of the film, but excluding remakes and sequels) or trailers of the film in any way, including theatrical and non-theatrical exhibitions, and exhibitions on or by means of television and including exhibitions by any other process now known or hereafter devised, whether on film or by means of magnetic tape, wire, cassettes, discs or any other devices now known or hereafter devised, but excluding any amounts received from outright sales (see "outright sale").

receiver — Court appointed person who takes possession of, but not title to, the assets and affairs of a business or estate that is in a form of bankruptcy called receivership or is involved in litigation. The receiver collects rents and other income and generally manages the affairs of the entity for the benefit of its owners and creditors until a disposition of the matter is made by the court (see "receivership").

receivership — An equitable remedy used by a court to place property under the control of a receiver so that it may be preserved for the benefit of affected parties who may be involved in litigation (see "bankruptcy," "receiver" and "reorganization").

recession — A downturn in economic activity, defined by many economists as at least two consecutive quarters of decline in a country's gross national product (see "recession-proof" and "recession resistant").

recession-proof — A phrase that has at times been applied to the film business since historically the demand for movies has remained fairly constant regardless of the state of the economy (see "recession" and "recession-resistant").

recession-resistant — The phrase suggesting that a general downturn in the economy will not significantly impact motion picture ticket sales. This phrase has until recent years more accurately described the film business (as opposed to the phrase "recession-proof") but since the 1991 U.S. recession demonstrated that a general downturn in the economy may in fact have an adverse impact on motion picture ticket sales, even "recession-resistant" does not accurately describe the movie business. In today's marketplace there are apparently too many other entertainment options available that were not available in the Great Depression when the myth about the film business being either "recession-proof" or "recession-resistant" was first created (see "recession-proof").

reciprocal preferences — Mutual partiality among competing businesses, an illegal trade practice that violates Section 1 of the Sherman Antitrust Act. In the context of a vertically integrated motion picture industry, a reciprocal preference might take the form of a group of competing distributors/exhibitors, such as the major studio/distributors providing the other major studio/distributor/exhibitors selective contracts for exclusive first runs in their best theaters or at just the exhibitor level with the competing major exhibition chains, each giving some preference to the other's films by organizing splitting arrangements that can help to guarantee the distribution of the best films in their theaters as opposed to the theaters of the smaller independent exhibitors. The concept of reciprocal preferences may also apply to the exhibitor practice of bidding aggressively on films that are distributed by distributors who are fairly lenient when it comes time to settle with the exhibitor (i.e., accept a lesser round-dollar amount for the exhibition of a certain film in exchange for the exhibitor's showing a less desirable film in the past or in the future). At least one major studio/distributor reportedly does not engage in these kinds of settlement transactions and thus does not benefit from this form of reciprocal preference (i.e., it's films are not typically exhibited in the best theaters; see "blind bidding," "major exhibition chains," "major studio/distributors," "Paramount Consent Decree of 1948," "predatory practices," "selling subject to review," "settlement transaction," "split agreement" and "vertical integration").

recision — (alternative spelling for "rescission").

recognizable names — Names of actors, actresses and/or directors who are recognized by a sufficiently large segment of the movie-going public, and therefore their name attached to a movie may serve to attract an audience (see "name actors" and "recognizable stars").

recognizable stars — A somewhat redundant phrase referring to actors or actresses whose names are recognized by a sufficiently large segment of the movie-going public and who are also considered movie stars. Being a star includes being a recognizable name, but not all recognizable name actors are stars (see "name actors" and "recognizable names").

record — A disc with a spiral groove carrying recorded sound for phonograph reproduction (see "laser disc").

record advance — (see "sound track album advance").

recording — The process of affixing live or previously recorded sounds or images on magnetic tape (also see "phonograph").

record of absenteeism — The history or reputation of an actor or actress for being absent from the set of a movie production when his or her services are required, thus slowing the production. Lenders and completion guarantors are wary of actors and actresses who have had such problems in the past (see "completion guarantor" and "lender financing").

record royalties — In the context of the film business, percentage payments paid for the rights relating to and based on the sale of motion picture sound track albums (see "sound track albums").

recoupment — The point at which revenues equal contractually defined expenses (i.e., when the costs and expenses incurred in the production of a film are recovered from the film's revenues). In the context of a film limited partnership or manager-managed LLC, the point at which an investor recovers at least 100 percent of such investor's investment. In such partnerships or LLCs, recoupment is a defined term that is generally that point at which 100 percent of distributable cash paid or credited to the unit holders equals all capital contributions made to the entity; however, in a so-called "investor oriented" film offering, recoupment may be defined as more than 100 percent (i.e., 110 percent, 115 percent, 125 percent of original invested capital; see "advance" or "advances," "breakeven," "payout," "post-payout sharing ratio," "pre-payout sharing ratio" and "non-returnable advance").

recourse — In financing, the ability to pursue a judgment for a default on a note not only against the property underlying the note, but against the party or parties signing the note. If a debt is made nonrecourse, only the property used as collateral for the underlying loan may be reached to satisfy a judgment. Also, the term may be used to mean the act of satisfying a claim (i.e., as in seeking recourse in the courts). Someone failing to obtain the desired result in court might then seek recourse in the legislature (see "recourse debt," "remedy" and "without recourse").

recourse debt — A note, loan, liability or obligation in which the person or entity to whom the debt is owed has the ability to pursue a judgment for a default not only against the property used as collateral but also against the party or parties signing the debt instrument (see "non-recourse debt").

recourse loan — A loan for which an endorser or guarantor is liable for payment in the event the borrower defaults. Also a loan made to a direct participation program such as a limited partnership whereby the lender, in addition to being secured by specific assets, has recourse against the general assets of the entity (see "non-recourse loan" and "personal security").

red band trailer — A movie trailer that can only be shown to an audience that is in the theater to see an "R" rated film, since the trailer itself may contain subject matter unsuitable for general audiences (see "green band trailer" and "trailer").

redeemable security — Any security, other than short-term paper, under the terms of which the holder upon its presentation to the issuer or to a person designated by the issuer is entitled (whether absolutely or only out of surplus) to receive approximately his, her or its proportionate share of the issuer's current net assets, or the cash equivalent thereof (see "redemption" and "stock redemption agreement").

redemption — To regain possession by paying a stipulated price. Some corporations may have a right of redemption with respect to the repurchase of such corporations' outstanding corporate debt or equity securities (see "redeemable security" and "stock redemption agreement").

red herring — A preliminary prospectus (securities disclosure document used in a public/registered offering), relating to the future securities issue and distributed to broker/dealers and prospective purchasers during the waiting period. This disclosure document is called a red herring because a required legend regarding the incompleteness of the information is printed on the cover page in red ink (see "disclosure document," "effective date," "preliminary prospectus" and "waiting period").

reduced distribution fee — A lower than customary charge for providing the services associated with the release of a motion picture. Distribution fees relating to feature films have traditionally averaged about 33 percent depending on the market, media and financial risk undertaken by the distributor. In the so-called rent-a-distributor deal, however, the distribution fee is generally lowered to about 15 percent (see "rent-a-distributor").

reduction — In music, a small version of the original, such as a reduced score. Also, the arrangement of a composition for a smaller number of instruments (see "orchestra").

reduction negative — A negative made from a wider gauge original (e.g., a 16mm negative made from a 35mm original; see "blow-up").

reduction plan — A strategy developed by a studio/distributor financier of a film project and the production company to lower the actual production costs of a motion picture in progress in order to avoid going over-budget and beyond the contingency (see "projected overage" and "take-over").

reel — Metal or plastic wheel on which film is wound for projection and storage purposes. A standard size 35mm reel holds two thousand feet or about twenty-two minutes of film (see "can," "in the can" and "running time").

refundable deposit — Refundable payments made to secure the payor's (e.g., a film distributor) performance of its legal obligations under a contract, including its obligation to make payments under the contract. Courts have held in some cases that refundable deposits, unlike advance payments, are not taxable when received (see "advance payments" and "deferral structures").

regional investment banking house — A broker/dealer firm that provides investment banking services to clients in only a limited number of states in a particular section of the country (e.g., West) as opposed to nationally (see "investment bank" or "investment banker").

regional prejudice — A preconceived judgment or opinion about persons, groups or things based on the geographical area from which they originate (i.e., an irrational attitude of hostility directed against an individual, group or because of the supposed characteristics of the people and items from a given area of a country). Regional prejudice is sometimes used as a theme or sub-theme in motion pictures and appears to be a commonly held attitude of many people in the film industry. Regional prejudice can be just as devastating and/or debilitating as any other form of prejudice and just as wrong. To the extent that motion pictures help to perpetuate such prejudice such activities are harmful to the nation. Hollywood films tend to consistently portray white Southerners in a negative and/or stereotypical manner (see "bias," "discrimination," "favorable portrayal," "patterns of bias," "prejudice," "stereotypical portrayal" and "unfavorable portrayal").

regional release pattern — A method of film distribution in which a film is opened in one or more but a limited number of theaters in a section of the country with the expectation that the film will later be opened in a broader array of theaters across a larger segment of the country, in a pre-set or ad hoc pattern, over a period of time. A regional release is generally less expensive than a simultaneous national release due to the fewer number of prints required and the more limited advertising (see "national release," "release pattern," "selective release," "special distribution" and "wide release").

regional review — A program that seeks to coordinate SCOR or Regulation A securities filings for several states in a region through the state securities regulatory authority of a single lead state in that region. Regional reviews are available in the New England, Mid-Atlantic, Midwest and Western regions (see "Regulation A" and "SCOR").

regional stock exchanges — Organized securities exchanges located outside New York City and registered with the SEC, including Boston, Cincinnati, Intermountain (Salt Lake City), Midwest (Chicago), Pacific (Los Angeles and San Francisco), Philadelphia (Philadelphia and Miami) and Spokane.

registered offering — (see "public offering").

registered representative — A selling agent of a securities broker/dealer firm; commissioned salespersons qualified to take orders for securities from the general public. Such agents must be licensed and in good standing with the SEC, NASD and in each state in which such agents may sell securities. They must also be associated with a broker/dealer firm so that their work can be supervised by the firm. Registered representatives are often referred to as account executives by the broker/dealer firm

employer (see "NASD" and "private securities transaction").

registrar and transfer agent — (see "transfer agent").

registration — In securities law, the process by which an issuer of securities (e.g., corporate stock, limited partnership interests, manager-managed LLC interests, etc.) submits data to the SEC and the securities regulators in each state in which such securities are to be offered and seeks approval for the sale of such securities to the public in such jurisdictions. As a general rule, public/registered offerings are more expensive, time-consuming and complex than private/exempt offerings (contrast with "notice filing"; see "copyright registration," "EDGAR," "private offering" and "public offering").

registration fee — A charge required by the SEC (and the securities regulatory authority in each state) and paid by the issuer of securities in a public/registered offering (see "registration" and "registration filing fee").

registration filing fee — An amount required by the SEC and the applicable state securities regulatory authorities to be paid to such securities regulators in conjunction with the registration of a securities offering. Typically, such fees are equal to one tenth of one percent of the total amount of the offering (see "public offering").

registration statement — A document required by the Securities Act of 1934 that must be submitted to and approved by the SEC prior to a public/registered offering of securities through the mails or in interstate commerce. The registration statement must describe the securities offered and must disclose, in detail, information on the nature of the business including accounting statements, the identity of management and key owners and the purpose of the offering, including the use to be made of the proceeds (see "private offering," "prospectus," "registration" and "waiting period").

regular corporation — (same as "C-corporation").

regular employee — All film employees except those hired as free-lance employees (see "freelance employee" and "independent contractor").

Regulation A — A federal exemption from the securities registration requirement for small securities offerings (not exceeding $5 million in any twelve-month period) provided by Section 3(b) of the Securities Act. Although technically described as an exemption, as a practical matter, Regulation A is a small public/registered offering. An issuer relying on Regulation A must file an offering statement, consisting of a notification, offering circular and exhibits, with the SEC for review and comment. Regulation A offerings share many characteristics with registered offerings. For example, the issuer must provide purchasers with a securities disclosure document (referred to for Regulation A purposes as an "offering circular") that is similar in content to a prospectus. In the alternative, a small company can use the SCOR Form, called Form U-7, to satisfy many of the filing requirements of the SEC's Regulation A exemption, since the company may file it with the SEC as part of the Regulation A offering statement. On the other hand, many issuers find the Form U-7 to be a poor substitute for a properly drafted offering circular, at least in terms of how it is received by prospective investors. Like registered offerings, the securities

can be offered publicly and are not "restricted," meaning they are freely tradeable in the secondary market after the offering. The principal advantages of Regulation A offerings, as opposed to full registration, are: (1) the financial statements are simpler and do not need to be audited; (2) there are no Exchange Act reporting obligations after the offering unless the company has more than $10 million in total assets and more than five hundred shareholders; (3) companies may choose among three formats to prepare the offering circular, one of which is a simplified question-and-answer document; and (4) an issuer may "test the waters" to determine if there is adequate interest in its securities before going through the expense of filing with the SEC. In addition, small businesses offering in several states, may be able to coordinate Regulation A filings through a program called regional review (see "Form 1-A," "offering circular," "preliminary offering circular," "regional review," "SCOR" and "test the waters").

Regulation C — SEC rules providing general requirements for public offerings (see "Form S-1" and "Form SB-1").

Regulation D — A set of three federal exemptions from the securities registration requirements (Rules 504, 505 and 506), promulgated by the Securities and Exchange Commission pursuant to the Securities Act of 1933, that permits the offer and sale of securities without registration so long as the offering is in compliance with a number of conditions and limitations, such as limitations on the amount of money that can be raised, on the number of investors and on the manner of conducting the offering (no general solicitation or advertising), required disclosure of information to prospective investors and notice of sale filing requirements.

In addition, other SEC regulations including Regulation S-K (e.g., Item 601 relating to exhibits) must also be consulted in order to properly comply with Regulation D; see "investor numerical limitations," "investor sophistication requirements," "limitations on manner of offering," "limited offering exemptions," "private limited partnership," "private offering," "Rule 504," "Rule 505" and "Rule 506").

Regulation SB — The SEC's integrated disclosure system for small business issuers of securities (see "Form SB-1" and "Form SB-2").

Regulation S-K — The integrated disclosure rules governing the non-financial portions of forms and reports filed under the Securities Acts. Regulation S-K governs the content of an issuer's disclosure document for both public and private offerings (see "private offering" and "public offering").

Regulation S-T — The SEC's general rules and regulations for electronic filings. Most public/registered offerings are required to be filed with the SEC electronically through the SEC's EDGAR system (electronic data gathering, analysis and retrieval; see "EDGAR").

Regulation S-X — The SEC's accounting standards to be used in the preparation of financial statements for inclusion in a registration statement for a public offering of securities (see "GAAP").

reinsurance — A financial transaction that provides for the sharing of risk among insurance companies (i.e., a portion of an insurer's risk is assumed by other insurance carriers in return for a part of the premium fee paid by the insured). By spreading the risk, reinsurance allows an individual insurance company to insure clients whose coverage would otherwise be too great a burden for the one insurer to carry alone (see "cut through endorsement," "excess insurance coverage," "insurance" and "primary insurance").

reissue — The re-release of a motion picture. The circumstances under which a film may be reissued is sometimes set out in the original distribution agreement (e.g., the film will be re-released in a minimum number of theaters that represents a certain agreed upon percentage of the maximum number of theaters that were used in the original release of the picture, plus a suitable hiatus between the initial release and reissue during which the film was not exhibited in theaters; see "hiatus" and "re-issuing costs").

re-issuing costs — The expenses associated with re-issuing or re-releasing a film (see "initial distribution" and "re-release").

rejection — In banking, the refusal to grant credit to an applicant because of inadequate financial strength, a poor credit history or some other reason (see "lender financing").

relationship-driven business — An industry in which business choices and decisions relating to whether business should be conducted with certain other individuals or entities are based to a great extent on some affinity, link, affiliation or association that may or may not be directly related to the nature of the business. In this sense, such relationship choices might be viewed as another barrier to entry (for antitrust law purposes) to the production, distribution and/or exhibition levels of the motion picture business (see "barriers to entry," "insider's game," "level playing field," "member of the club," "movies with a message," "nepotism," "reciprocal preferences" and "role of government").

release — With respect to movies, the completed film used for general distribution or exhibition; also the act and activities associated with the distribution of a film (e.g., once a motion picture is being exhibited to the public it is considered to be in release or it has been released or it is being exhibited in a certain release pattern; see "launch"). In law, the act or writing by which, or a written document whereby, some claim, right or interest is given up to the person against whom the claim, right or interest could have been enforced. The release clears for use individuals who appear on film (i.e., it may not be safe to use the names, faces or likenesses of any recognizable living persons unless written releases have been obtained and/or other arrangements have been made). A release is not necessary, however, if the person is part of a crowd scene or shown in a fleeting background (see "submission release").

release budget — The film distributor's plan for the coordination of resources and expenditures relating to the distribution of a specific film (see "budget" and "prints and ads budget").

release campaign — (see "distributor's release campaign").

release commitment — The pledges, promises or guarantees of a film distributor relating to the distribution of a given film (e.g., agreements by a distributor to spend a certain amount of money on prints and advertising and/or to release a film in the major population centers in the U.S.). Such commitments are usually required by home video companies before such companies will provide a home video advance or guarantee. The producer should check with video companies in advance to determine what level of release commitment from the distributor in the domestic theatrical release will create value in the property from the video company's point of view. At a minimum, the producer should see that the distribution agreement guarantees a theatrical release. However, distributors will generally resist guaranteeing the type or pattern of release for a picture. They feel that even the use of a broad standard such as "reasonable business judgment" or "best efforts" may invite litigation if the distributor uses incorrect judgment in its selection of a distribution pattern. The producer should, however, seek minimum specific commitments for prints and advertising, particularly for theatrical distribution, since such amounts demonstrate the distributor's commitment to exploitation of the film. For low- to medium-budget pictures, it is not unusual for P&A commitments to equal 50 percent to 100 percent of the film's budget. In addition, to the guarantee of a theatrical release, the producer may seek distributor commitments for producer consultation and approval rights relating to the release pattern, a theatrical release in certain cities and specified limits on distribution expenses. It would seem that if the distributor would work with the producer on such issues and obtain producer approvals of its release plan, there would be fewer grounds for litigation (see "advance" or "advances," "guarantees," "sue us" and "video rights agreement").

release date — The date on which a film first opens, in a given market or nationally (see "blind bidding," "opening date" and "run").

released production — A film that is currently being shown in theaters or on television during its initial distribution (see "release").

release negative — A complete master negative prepared specifically for printing release prints (see "print").

release pattern — The general exhibition plan, strategy or manner in which a certain film is exhibited in a single territory or nationally. The primary goal of such a plan is generally to maximize the number of moviegoers who will pay to see the movie. Factors considered in formulating a release pattern may include the film genre, its MPAA rating, the quality of the film, the most efficient advertising and publicity, the costs of prints, the availability of theaters, the optimum playing time, the anticipated gross potential and expected word-of-mouth (contrast with "release sequence"; see "general release," "limited release," "platformed," "regional release pattern," "rollout," "saturation release," and "wide release").

release print — The final version of a film made from the color reversal negative and ready for distribution to exhibitors (i.e., a composite print made for general distribution). The release print is prepared after the final trial composite or sample print has been approved (see "print costs" and "release negative").

release schedule — A phrase used primarily to refer to the timetable established by each feature film distributor for beginning and conducting the domestic theatrical exhibition of each of its films, as well as the distributor's plans relating to other territories and media. Motion picture distributors often consider the release plans of the films being released by other competing distributors when selecting the optimum time to release a given film (see "release sequence").

release sequence — The planned order in which a motion picture is exhibited in the various

media and territories worldwide. For example, a U.S. made film may be first released for domestic theatrical distribution, then for pay per view, followed by foreign theatrical, home video (DVD), pay television, foreign television, network television and TV syndications. Distributors are constantly changing such release patterns in a continuing effort to maximize the potential revenues generated by a motion picture in all markets (contrast with "release pattern" and "window").

release slots — A limited measure of time or distributor resources that a feature film distributor is able to commit to the distribution of a film. In any one year, most major studio/distributors will not commit to release more than twenty-four or so motion pictures (i.e., they have approximately twenty-four release slots to fill each year or an average of one film released each two weeks or so). On the other hand, the production side of the major studio/distributors is seldom able to produce more than fifteen quality films a year (as either in-house product, on a production-financing/distribution basis or as negative pickups where the studios have significant controls and approvals. Thus, in order to be able to amortize the studio/distributor's ongoing operating costs, many will take in other product to fill those release slots and to maintain their relationships and leverage with the exhibitors as consistent suppliers of quality film product. The additional films will be distributed either on a pure acquisition or rent-a-system basis (see "acquisition distribution agreement," "in-house product," "negative pickup," "production-financing/distribution agreement" and "rent-a-distributor").

release strategies — (see "marketing strategy").

release title — The actual name of the film used during its public exhibition. A film may be developed using a working title or tentative title (see "working title").

releasing cost risk — The possibility associated with distributing motion pictures and funding the accompanying expenses that such costs will not be recouped by the distributor or whoever provides such funds (see "lender risk elimination").

releasing costs — Expenses incurred in putting a motion picture into general or limited distribution. The MPAA reports that the average cost for marketing a major studio release has been in the thirty to forty million dollar range for the past several years (see "rising production costs").

relief — The remedy, assistance or compensation awarded to a complainant by a court, particularly a court of equity, including such remedies as injunction, specific performance and rescission of the contract. The term, however, generally does not mean an award of money damages. Thus, "affirmative relief" is more commonly associated with protection from future harm rather than compensation for past injury (see "damages," "interim relief," "remedy," "rescission" and "TriStar Case").

remake — A full new production and release of a previously made film (see "prequel" and "sequel").

remake and sequel provision — A clause in a feature film distribution agreement that sets forth the circumstances under which the distributor and the other party or parties may participate in a remake of the same motion picture or the production and release of a sequel

to the picture. For example, the following language may be seen in a distribution agreement: "If the distributor determines at any time hereafter to exercise its theatrical derivative distribution rights granted pursuant to this distribution agreement, the distributor, the production company and the producer shall then negotiate with each other in good faith for their mutual participation in a theatrical production based on such rights on terms no less favorable to the production company and the producer than those contained in this agreement. If no agreement is reached within thirty days after such negotiations have commenced, all such rights shall be frozen (see "frozen," "prequel," "remake," "sequel" and "theatrical derivative distribution rights").

remedy or remedies — The means employed to enforce or redress an injury. The most common remedy at law consists of money damages. Other court-imposed remedies include specific performance, restraining orders including injunctions, appointment of a receiver and attachment. Other remedies that do not involve litigation, include lobbying for legislation or taking your arguments to the public (e.g., by advocating an economic boycott or other action by the public; see "damages," "lobbyists," "professional association," "trade association" and "sue us").

remit — To send back (see "remitted or remittable").

remittance tax — A sum of money paid to a foreign government as an assessment on the conduct of business in that country. In feature film distribution, remittance taxes paid by the distributor to foreign governments are typically deducted from distributor gross receipts as a distributor expense (see "foreign tax credit").

remitted or remittable — Already sent back or that which is able to be sent back. With respect to foreign receipts for the exploitation of a motion picture in international territories, the question often arises as to whether a net profit participant should receive the benefit of monies collected in the foreign territory and that could be remitted back to the distributor in the United States but which have not yet been sent back. The typical major studio/distributor definition of the term gross receipts excludes foreign receipts until they are collected and converted into dollars here in the U. S. When the distribution agreement is negotiated, net profit participants may want to take the position that foreign receipts that have been remitted or that are remittable be included in gross receipts (see "foreign receipts" and "net profit").

remuneration — Compensation or payment for a service, loss or expense. Many of the state securities regulations prohibit the payment of any form of transaction-related remuneration to be paid to persons not licensed as NASD/SEC securities broker/dealers or their registered representatives (see "bonus," "compensation," "contingent compensation," "finder," "profit participation," "royalties," "salaries" and "transaction-related").

rent — Compensation for the right to use property. Rent is fixed and certain in amount and payable over a fixed period regardless of the extent of the use of the property (contrast with "royalties"; see "lease").

rent-a-distributor — A method for distributing independently produced films in which the producer provides the financing for all three stages in the life of a movie (i.e., development, production and distribution) but contracts with a distributor to handle the actual distribution of the film. This form of distribution involves the least amount of risk for the distributor since the decision relating to whether or not to distribute is made after the film is in the can and the distributor is not being asked to risk any of its capital on production or distribution. A producer may thus expect the distributor's fee to be at the low end of the spectrum (i.e., about 15 percent) using this arrangement. This distribution method is often criticized on the assumption that such distributors are not likely to make their best efforts on behalf of product in which they have little of their own money invested, particularly when in competition with their own films. Distributors themselves deny that the source of a film has any impact on their level of support. This potential conflict, however, requires an even more careful review of numerous distribution agreement provisions that are effected by the changed circumstances relating to this form of distribution (compare with "acquisition distribution agreement" and "negative pickup"; see "decision-making continuum," "release slots," "releasing cost risk" and "up-front financing").

rentals — That portion of theatrical box office receipts owed by the exhibitor to the distributor; sometimes defined as the amount paid to the distributor after the exhibitor has received its share, a concept similar to the distributor's gross receipts, except that the term gross receipts is much broader (i.e., rentals only applies to theatrical exhibition, whereas gross receipts applies to the distributor's revenues earned in all markets and media). Various authorities seem to disagree as to whether the term "film rentals" means monies owed and received or only monies actually received. In addition, producers may want to indicate in the distribution agreement whether monies received and under the control of the distributor, but still in a foreign territory, should be included as distributor rentals. The actual percentage of box office gross paid to a distributor as rentals may vary wildly from 25 percent to 65 percent, although the average is approximately 45 percent. If that average percentage is approximately correct, then any financial forecasts projecting prospective revenues from the exploitation of a motion picture should not assume a higher percentage for film rentals and should assume an even lower percentage if the distributor is not going to be a major studio/distributor (see "assumptions," "box office gross," "distributor rentals," "financial projections," "foreign receipts," "gross receipts," "house nut" and "remitted or remittable").

rent-a-major — (see "rent-a-distributor").

rent-a-release — (see "rent-a-distributor").

rent-a-system deal — (see "rent-a-distributor").

rent-a-system transaction — (see "rent-a-distributor").

reorganization — In corporate income tax law, a group of transactions including mergers, consolidations, recapitalizations, acquisitions of the stock or assets of another corporation and changes in form or place of organization. The common element in each of these transactions is that if various technical requirements are met, the corporations or shareholders involved may not recognize any gain for income tax purposes and the transaction may take place without generating tax liability (also see "bankruptcy" and "receivership").

repackaging — The development of a new marketing strategy, advertising campaign and title for a previously released motion picture.

Repackaging generally occurs only when a film, in its initial release, performs poorly at the box office and the distributor decides to withdraw it from exhibition and re-release it later as a new film (see "advertising" and "marketing").

repayment sources — The funds, revenue stream or collateral from which a production lender looks to recover its loaned funds, interest and fees. Entertainment lenders typically require at least two sources of repayment (i.e., primary and secondary sources, with the primary source of repayment for a film production loan being payment by the distributor upon delivery of the completed film and the secondary source being the film asset itself as collateral). Other forms of collateral may include pre-sale contracts, letters of credit or other asset collateral (see "revenue sources").

report sheets — Logs or data sheets completed on a daily basis by the camera and sound professionals working on a film shoot. Such reports list each take and note which shots are to be printed and which ones are no good (see "production reports").

representation — A statement; something short of a warranty but sufficient to create a distinct impression of fact conducive to action. Federal and state securities laws often require that prospective purchasers provide certain representations (e.g., relating to their age, state of residence, net worth, annual income and experience with similar investments) to the issuer of the securities prior to their purchase (see "warranty" or "warranties").

representation of multiple clients — The practice among some attorneys, particularly entertainment attorneys serving as the lawyer for more than one client on the same transaction.

Such a situation inevitably raises questions of attorney conflicts of interest (see "conflicts of interest," "conflict waivers," "entertainment attorney" and "ethics").

required rate of return — The return on investment required by sophisticated investors before they will commit money to an investment at a given level of risk. Unless the expected return exceeds this level of required return, the investment will generally be considered unacceptable (see "internal rate of return").

re-recording — The transferring of sound records from one or more films or discs to other films or discs using electrical processes; also the combining of all tracks (i.e., sound effects, dialogue and music, onto one final release-track; see "mix").

re-release — Release of a film for theatrical or television exhibition at any time after its initial distribution has been completed. A re-released film does not require newly incurred production costs (i.e., the primary expense of a re-release is advertising), thus re-releasing a popular film may offer significant profit possibilities. Net profit participants must be sure that revenues generated from the re-release of a film are not excluded from gross receipts in the distribution agreement. The term re-release may also apply to a second release of films on videocassette or DVDs. As a strategy to stimulate secondary sales, the video industry has developed a two-tiered sequential pricing structure. New feature film video/DVDs will typically enter the home video market at a suggested retail price in the sixty to ninety dollar range. Consequently, nearly all of the videocassettes or DVDs sold during this initial release are purchased by video retailers for rental purposes. As certain titles are then re-released months after the initial home video release, they are priced at wholesale prices designed to permit much lower retail prices (typically in the fifteen to thirty dollar range) which in turn stimulates more consumer purchases in this sell-through market (see "re-issuing costs" and "sell-through market," "twenty percent rule" and "videocassette revenue reporting").

re-release showing — (see "re-release").

rerun — The subsequent televising of a specific film or program in a specific market as defined by union or distribution agreements (see "residuals").

rerun fees — Payments made for the exploitation of a film after its initial showing on television (see "rerun" and "residuals").

rescind — To abrogate a contract; to release the parties from further obligations to each other and restore the parties to their status quo ante (prior positions) or the positions they would have occupied if the contract had never been made (see "rescission").

rescission — The cancellation of a contract and the return of the parties to the positions they would have occupied if the contract had not been made (see "prospectus").

rescission offer — An invitation by an issuer of securities to a purchaser to cancel the investment contract and return the amount invested to the purchaser. Rescission offers are sometimes mandated by state or federal securities laws as a civil remedy to correct non-compliance with a securities law or regulation. Many states have explicit rescission offer statutes (see "security" or "securities").

reservation of book publishing rights — A clause in a film distribution agreement that permits the person granting distribution rights to a distributor to retain rights relating to the publication of books or specific kinds of books (e.g., a book about the making of the motion picture; see "publishing rights").

reservation of rights provision — A clause in a film distribution agreement that permits the person granting distribution rights to a distributor to retain all rights not specifically granted to the distributor (see "reservation of book publishing rights").

reserve — Funds kept available by a business to meet future contingencies (see "contingency").

reserved admission engagements — Film exhibitions in which all of the theater seating has been set aside for specific groups or individuals (see "premiere" and "premiere benefit").

reserved rights — Those licensing authorizations that are held back or retained by a person or entity that grants rights relating to the distribution of a motion picture to a distributor. For example, the producer may want to retain all rights not expressly granted to the distributor, including without limitation all remake and sequel rights, the right to license and/or produce television productions (e.g., television series, mini-series, movies for television) based on the picture, all live stage and radio rights and theme park attraction rights, as well as all rights outside the licensed territory and all rights in the licensed territory after the expiration of the licensed term. The producer may also want to add that without limiting the generality of the foregoing, the producer will reserve all publishing rights (including without limitation all screenplay publication, novelization, calendar and comic

book rights (see "reservation of rights provision").

reserve for returns — A deduction by the distributor from video gross receipts to account for the estimated dollar value of videocassettes or DVDs sent back to the distributor from the video wholesaler because they were defective or for other reasons. The distributor may want to hold back as much as 25 percent of the video gross receipts as reserves for video returns. The film producer may want to ask for statistics on such returns to determine whether the percentage is reasonable and/or consistent with the applicable contract provision (see "video/DVD revenue reporting").

reserve or step payments — Funds set aside by a production company for the purpose of periodically compensating producers, writers or directors who have development deals with the production company (see "development deal" and "development stages").

residence sharing relative — Securities law concept that pursuant to Regulation D Rule 501(e) excludes from the numerical count of investors any relative, spouse or relative of the spouse of a purchaser who has the same principal residence as the purchaser (see "counting rules" and "Regulation D").

residual package — That collection of policies and procedures of a given union or guild applied toward the various residuals called for by their respective collective bargaining agreements (see "flat dollar payments").

residuals — Generally, residuals are percentage participations for the exhibition of films or other programs on television (i.e., payments, as to an actor or writer, for each re-run after the initial showing and pursuant to a union agreement). Residuals are generally based on the number of times a film is exhibited on television or as a percentage of revenues from television exhibition and is generally considered a distribution expense for the film's distributor. Thus, from the point of view of the distributor, residuals are costs incurred and payments required under applicable collective bargaining agreements by reason of or as a condition to the use of or the exhibition of a film on television or any other media. The film distribution agreement may provide that to the extent such payments are made to or on behalf of a participant, such payments may be deemed to be a credit against any percentage compensation payable to the participant to the extent not prohibited by the applicable collective bargaining agreement. In addition, such distribution agreements may provide that any payments made to a participant prior to the payment of residuals may be deemed a credit against such residuals to the extent not prohibited by applicable collective bargaining agreements. In either case, the participant may want to see that this provision states that such a credit cannot be deducted a second time against the participant (see "distribution expense," "flat dollar payments," "participant" and "royalties").

residual payments — (same as "residuals").

residuals and royalties provision — Language or a paragraph typically found in a film distribution agreement that provides for the payment of residuals and royalties associated with the picture (e.g., that the distribution company agrees to make all residual and supplemental payments required to be made in the distribution of the picture). Residuals (or residual payments) are percentage participations for television (i.e., payments, as to an actor or writer, for each re-

run after the initial showing and pursuant to a union agreement). Residuals are generally based on the number of times the film is exhibited on television, or as a percentage of revenues from television exhibition. Royalties, on the other hand, are payment to the holder for the right to use property such as copyrighted material (i.e., a negotiated percentage of income paid to an author or composer for each copy of the work sold). A royalty is a share of the product or of the proceeds therefrom reserved by an owner for permitting another to exploit and use his or her property (i.e., the rental that is paid to the original owner of property based on a percentage of profit or production). Royalty is compensation for the use of property, but it is based as to amount entirely upon the use actually made of the property. If residual and royalty payments are defined as a distribution expense they are typically paid prior to net profit participation payments and in certain transactions, prior to the recoupment of the film's negative costs which stops interest from accruing. On the other hand, if they are not paid as a distribution expense, they may have to be paid out of the producer's share. Producers may want to watch for language in a distribution agreement that tries to shift the burden of making such payments to the producer and asks the producer to make such payments out of the producer's share, a tactic that would tend to reduce the producer's profit participation in relation to other profit participants (see "dues and assessments").

responsible party — Accounting terminology for the person or persons who are responsible for the assumptions underlying prospective financial statements. The responsible party usually is management but it can be persons outside of the entity who does not currently have the authority to direct operations (e.g., a party considering acquiring an entity; see "financial projections" and "limited use").

restitution — The act of making good, or of giving the equivalent for, any loss, damage or injury (see "indemnification" and "in kind").

restraining order — A court order granted without notice or hearing, requiring the preservation of the status quo until a hearing can be had to determine the propriety of any injunctive relief, temporary or permanent (see "equitable remedy" and "remedy" or "remedies").

restraint of trade — Illegal restraints interfering with free competition in business and commercial transactions, that tend to restrict production, affect prices or otherwise control the market to the detriment of purchasers or consumers of goods and services. What would otherwise be considered a reasonable restraint of trade may be made unreasonable if they are intended to accomplish the equivalent of an illegal restraint (see "antitrust laws," "conspiracy," "Paramount Consent Decree of 1948" and "Sherman Antitrust Act").

restricted currencies — A foreign currency that is or becomes subject to moratorium, embargo, banking or exchange restrictions, or impediments against remittances to the United States. A producer and other net profit participants may want to clarify in the distribution agreement for a film, whether such funds will be included in the distributor's definition of gross receipts (see "blocked currencies," "embargo" and "moratorium statutes").

restricted funds — (see "restricted currencies").

restricted securities — Securities acquired from an issuer in a non-public transfer, that is, on terms and at a price not offered to the general public through an underwriter or public/registered offering. Since the securities were not part of a public/registered offering and thus not subject to the safeguards of the Securities Act of 1933, such as the registration of the securities and the issuing of a prospectus, their sale to the public is restricted. Under the SEC's Rule 144, restricted securities must be held at least two years prior to their re-sale and may only be sold in small amounts (see "private offering").

retained earnings — Net profits kept to accumulate in a business after dividends are paid (also called "undistributed profits" or "earned surplus"; contrast with "capital").

retroactive basis — The doing of some act in a manner that extends its effect back to a prior time. For example, if a producer of a feature film is also an established producer of soundtrack albums, he or she may be able to negotiate a separate deal for a royalty on the soundtrack recording. If the film distributor is amenable, it is not likely to agree to make such payments until after the motion picture has reached some specified level of breakeven at which time the participation may be awarded on a retroactive basis. Of course, when a participant shares on a separate basis, as described above, the revenue from such a separate source will generally be excluded from the distributor's gross receipts in computing that participant's share of net profits, since if it were included, the participant would be sharing twice in the same revenue. It may be just as reasonable to ask those distributors who have an ownership interest in video wholesalers to use the same reasoning to avoid their double dip in the video revenue stream (see "outside the pot" and "video/DVD revenue reporting").

retroactive escalation fees — (see "retroactive increase").

retroactive increase — A larger payment that is not triggered until a certain event occurs, but which when triggered, permits the recipient to go back to the first revenue dollars relating to the transaction and recoup at the higher rate. Some film distribution agreements provide for distribution fees that escalate retroactively. In such instances, it is important to limit or segregate the revenues from which the retroactive recoupment can be extracted. If the distribution agreement does not address this point, the distributor will most likely take its retroactive increase from 100 percent of the subsequently accruing revenues (i.e., after the triggering event occurs, the distributor will take all of the next revenues to pay for the increase in its distribution fees back to the first dollar). Thus, the susceptible payment corridor from which the retroactive increase is paid should be limited in some reasonable manner (e.g., 50 percent of gross receipts), which allows the production company and other participants to continue receiving their percentage participations while the distributor is recouping retroactively (see "rent-a-distributor").

return — Profit on a securities or capital investment, usually expressed as an annual percentage rate (see "rate of return," "return on equity" and "return on invested capital").

return of capital — The recoupment by an investor of 100 percent of the money invested in a venture. Distributions of cash resulting from the sale of a capital asset or of securities in a portfolio, depreciation tax savings or any other transaction unrelated to retained earnings. Returns of capital are not directly taxable but may result in higher capital gains taxes later if they reduce the acquisition cost base of the property involved. In the context of a limited partnership or manager-managed LLC, unless otherwise provided in the partnership or operating agreement, a return of capital is considered any distribution to a partner to the extent that the partner's capital account, immediately after the distribution, is less than the amount of that partner's contributions to the partnership as reduced by prior distributions that were a return of capital (see "basis," "capital," "capital account" and "return on capital").

return on capital — The amount of money recouped, expressed as a percentage of the money originally invested, over and above that original investment (e.g., a 110 percent return of capital would equal a 10 percent return on capital; see "return of capital").

return of equity — The replacement of an investor's original investment (see "equity").

return on equity — Amount, expressed as a percentage, earned on an investor's original investment (e.g., a company's common stock investment for a given period; see "equity" and "rate of return").

return on invested capital — Amount, expressed as a percentage, earned on a company's total capital (e.g., in a corporate context, its common and preferred stock equity plus its long-term funded debt, calculated by dividing total capital into earnings before interest, taxes and dividends; also called "return on investment" or "ROI"; see "rate of return" and "yield").

return on investment (ROI) — (see "return on invested capital" and "rate of return").

return ratio — The relationship between investment and return expressed as a percentage (see "rate of return").

returns to investors — The money paid to or paid back to investors in a film deal or other investment (see "return of capital" and "return on capital").

revenue — Income from whatever source; that which returns or comes back from an investment (see "income").

revenue chain — (same as "revenue stream").

revenue corridor — A segregated portion of the earnings flowing back from the retail sales source to the various levels of distribution and production. With respect to the revenue stream of a film, the video corridor may be segregated from the theatrical corridor (see "outside the pot," "revenue stream" and "video corridor").

revenue participations — Percentage participations based on a defined stage in a film's revenue stream (see "profit participation").

revenue recognition and reporting — An accounting concept which, as applied to the film industry, means that film producers and distributors cannot recognize revenue from any market or deal until the product is legally made available to the licensee for telecast, exhibition or sub-distribution (e.g., a distributor is not allowed to recognize or record revenue from a fixed non-cancelable pay-TV license during the theatrical run of the movie, since the film will not be available for exhibition in the pay-TV

market until some point in the future; see "accounting principles and practices," "GAAP" and "FASB Statement No. 53").

revenue sharing ratio — In limited partnerships and manager-managed LLCs, the percentage split between the general partner/manager and limited partner/members of profits, losses, cash distributions and other income or losses that result from the operation of the partnership/LLC (see "limited liability company," "limited partnership" and "profit sharing ratio").

revenue sources — The various markets and media in which a feature film may be exploited and which may in turn generate income. Such sources include domestic theatrical, foreign theatrical, domestic home video, foreign home video, pay per view, pay television, foreign television, network television, syndication, non-theatrical, merchandising and sound track albums. Feature film distributors began to typically generate more in domestic wholesale gross revenues from home video than from theatrical sources in the mid-1980s and this pattern has continued since. In addition, foreign theatrical has exceeded domestic in recent years on many films (see "domestic theatrical," "fractured rights," "split rights deal" and "video/DVD revenue reporting").

revenue stream — The income generated by the sale of any product that begins with retail sales and returns through various levels of distribution back to the product source. In the film industry, the monies that flow back from the exhibition of a given film, generally from the exhibitor to the sub-distributors and/or distributor, then to the producer, participants and financier/investors. However, the timing of the various participations in a film's revenue stream will vary considerably depending on how the film was financed (particularly if the financier is also the distributor) and is subject to the terms of the many deals made by potential participants (same as "revenue chain"; see "adjusted gross," "gross receipts," "net profits," "off-the-top," "revenue corridor" and "video corridor").

reverse discrimination — The practice of excluding a classification or race of people who have not been historically discriminated against (e.g., White Anglo Saxon Protestants in the U.S.) from positions that are made available exclusively or primarily to persons or groups that have traditionally been the subject of discrimination, or who otherwise benefit from affirmative action programs. The term has been applied to the practice of reserving positions for minorities in school admissions programs, corporate promotions and rehiring of blacks with less job seniority than whites. The contention that affirmative action violates the equal protection clause of the Fourteenth Amendment and Title VI of the Civil Rights Act has resulted in the expression of different opinions by members of the U.S. Supreme Court. The one hundred-year history of the Hollywood based film industry has also resulted in a form of reverse discrimination in that a small segment of a national minority (i.e., not very religious, politically liberal, Jewish males of European heritage) have been able to occupy most of the important positions in the film industry for that one hundred-year period by discriminating against all others, including African-Americans, Latinos, Native Americans, Irish Americans, Italian Americans, Christians generally and Catholics, Protestants and Mormons specifically, women, Whites from the South and so forth (see "anti-Semitic sword," "bias," "blacklisting," "cronyism," "discrimination," "nepotism" and "prejudice").

reversal film stock — A type of motion picture film that, after it is exposed, is processed to produce a positive image on the same film rather than the customary negative image. If exposure is made by printing from a negative, a negative image is produced directly (see "internegative").

reversal optical — A method of reversing the direction of motion in a movie scene effected by turning the film over and re-photographing it in an optical printer, so that the emulsion side becomes the base side and vice versa (see "optical effects").

reversal print — A print-to-print duplication of a film that is made on special reversal film that transfers a positive to positive image without the use of an intermediate negative (see "print").

reversion provision or agreement — A contractual clause commonly found in option agreements or a separate agreement providing that rights to the literary property which is the subject of the option agreement may automatically revert or be reacquired by the author or owner under specific conditions (e.g., if the option is not exercised within a stated period of time or if exercised, the commencement of principal photography has not begun as of a stated time). The reversion provision is typically associated with the option agreement whereas the turnaround provision is more commonly found in the acquisition agreement (see "substitution clause or agreement," "turnaround provision or agreement" and "reversion right").

reversion right — The power to reacquire the rights to develop, produce, distribute or otherwise exploit a particular literary property under specified circumstances (see "reversion provision or agreement" and "turnaround provision or agreement").

reversionary rights — The interest created by operation of law by a conveyance of property but not transferred by that conveyance, thus reversionary rights remain in the grantor. The reversion of rights to a screenplay provided for in an option agreement depends on the occurrence or non-occurrence of a specific event (e.g., failure to pay a subsequent option payment; contrast with "turnaround provision or agreement").

review — A critical examination of a movie (see "blurbs," "critic," "industry critic" and "positive review").

revision — The script re-writing step beyond a polish but not yet rising to the level of the next draft. Like the polish, the revision is another special stage in the script writing process recognized by the Writer's Guild of America for a separate pay scale (same as "rewrite"; see "draft," "final draft," "polish" and "script" or "screenplay").

revival house — A motion picture theater that specializes in showing films that are no longer in current release (see "calendar house").

revolving line of credit — (see "revolving credit facility").

revolving credit facility — A contractual agreement between a bank and a studio or production company customer whereby the bank agrees to make loans up to a specified maximum for a specified period, usually a year or more. As the studio/production company (borrower) repays a portion of the loan, an amount equal to the repayment can be

borrowed again under the terms of the agreement. In addition to interest, the bank charges a fee for the commitment to hold the funds available (see "credit" and "lender financing").

revolving door — A concept often commonly applied to government and referring to the practice of private citizens, such as attorneys, who go into the service of the government, typically in some regulatory capacity, only to return to private practice following government service and in a position to utilize the expertise and/or contacts gained in government service to enhance their abilities and economic prospects in the commercial marketplace. The problem with this practice typically occurs in the form of conflicts of interest (i.e., the government official makes a government decision influenced by a possible private benefit that might accrue to such individual when he or she becomes a private citizen again). The revolving door concept can also be a problem in an industry like the film industry. When a relatively small but highly visible industry like film, with a high concentration of its participating companies primarily based in one city, like Los Angeles, is dominated by a small number of corporate entities and individual executives, with large monetary rewards floating around, it is not unusual to see people in that industry, studio executives, talent agents and entertainment attorneys, in particular, move from one position to another (in and out of the studios), creating similar opportunities for conflicts of interest. As an example, any independent producer utilizing the services of an entertainment attorney must have to wonder whether that attorney is going to be a film producer or a studio executive next year and thus effectively compete with his or her former client or whether that attorney, who may be hoping to move over and accept a position with a major studio/distributor in the near future, can really vigorously represent the interests of the producer in negotiating a distribution deal with that same distributor. This constant movement back and forth between and among the studios and other segments of the industry does create numerous conflict of interest opportunities, which many in the industry are not even aware of or seem to completely disregard in their blind quest for fame and fortune (see "Code of Professional Responsibility," "conflicts of interest," "ethics" and "greed").

rewrite — The writing of significant changes in plot, story line or interrelationship of characters in a screenplay or teleplay (see "polish" and "revision").

rico — (see racketeer influenced and corrupt organizations).

rider — An amendment or addition attached to another document that makes changes to the original document (see "nudity rider").

right — A claim or title to or an interest in anything that is enforceable by law (see "power" and "title").

right of consultation — (see "consultation rights").

right of first negotiation — The requirement that a prospective transferor (seller) and holder of a right will first negotiate in good faith concerning the purchase of the interest to be transferred with a specified party. If they fail to reach agreement, the transferor can sell his or her interest within a specified period, but at a price no less than the last offer by the specified party. Thus, a right of first negotiation is an agreement

that contractually provides one party with the first opportunity to enter into a subsequent transaction. As an example, a film distributor may want a right of first negotiation to acquire the publication rights to a book (the publishing rights to which have been reserved by a producer), and the distributor may provide in the distribution agreement that if pursuant to such right of first negotiation, the parties cannot agree on terms, then the distributor will have a continuing right of first refusal with respect to any terms less favorable to the producer that the producer is thereafter willing to accept. Also, motion picture exhibitors may enter into agreements that allocate among them the right of first negotiation for films. Under some circumstances a right of first negotiation may be considered an impediment to price competition in the market (see "antitrust laws," "restraint of trade" and "right of first refusal").

right of first refusal — The right of first refusal typically requires a prospective transferring party to secure a bona fide offer for his or her interest and then first offer such interest to another specified party (i.e., the holder of the right on similar terms). If the right is not exercised, then during a specified window period, the transferor can sell for the same or greater purchase price as that offered to the holder of the right of first refusal. Thus, in a feature film context a right of first refusal may be seen as a contractual provision that gives one party to the agreement the power to exercise its right to develop, produce or distribute a film project under certain circumstances and to the exclusion of all others. Such provisions may be found in literary purchase agreements and in studio development deals or so-called overall deals (same as "first look deal"; see "overall deal" and "right of first negotiation").

right of prepayment — In lending, a negotiated right to pay off the entire amount of the loan without a penalty (see "prepayment penalty").

right of privacy — (see "privacy, right of").

right of publicity — (see "publicity rights").

right of rescission — (see "rescission").

rights — Power or privilege to which one is justly entitled. In a motion picture context, rights refer to the power or privilege of developing, producing and exploiting a literary property, screenplay and/or movie (see "discretion," "power" and "title").

rights agreement — (same as "acquisition agreement" and "purchase agreement").

rights granted — (see "grant of rights").

rights granted/reserved — A common heading in a feature film distribution agreement for the provision that sets forth the motion picture rights being granted to the distributor as well as any reservation of rights being made by the person or entity making the grant to the distributor (e.g., a producer; see "grant of rights," "reservation of rights provision" and "reserved rights").

rights offering — Offering of common stock to existing shareholders who hold rights that entitle them to buy newly issued shares at a discount from the price at which shares will later be offered to the public (see "preemptive right" and "subscription right").

right to audit — (see "audit rights").

rising production costs — The seemingly ever increasing expense involved in the making of a motion picture. Many in the film industry have complained for the last several decades about the rising production costs which have been occurring during a period that has witnessed declining theatrical admissions, a slowing of home video cassette/DVD sales worldwide, a leveling off of U.S. made programming sales to Europe and reduced margins of profit. The warning has gone out that this lack of profitability in the film business will make it more and more difficult to attract capital. But it appears that the only thing the business leaders in various segments of the film industry can suggest to lower production costs is for the other guy to quit being so greedy. For example, the studio/distributors complain that the agents and their actor clients need to reduce their up front and gross participation demands. In response the high priced talent agents counter that they will consider such a proposal if the studio/distributors will handle net profit participations more fairly, particularly in the area of home video. This inter-industry economic warfare is unfortunate, in light of what has happened in recent years to other great American industries that could not downshift across the board as the rest of the world became increasingly more competitive and globally integrated (see "budget," "budget categories," "economic war zone," "global integration" and "perks").

risk — In a financial context, the possibility of losing or not gaining value. There are numerous risks associated with the development, production and distribution of a motion picture (see "interest rate risk," "lender risk elimination," "speculation" and "underwriting risk").

risk capital — The money invested in a business venture where such funds are subject to the risks of the enterprise (i.e., risk of loss). Generally, if the investors are passive (i.e., do not materially participate in the management of the enterprise), such an investment involves the offer and sale of a security (see "capital investment," "equity financing," "security" or "securities" and "venture capital").

risk disclosure — The act of informing prospective investors of a securities offering, in writing, about all of the material dangers of an investment in such offering. In securities offerings, certain risks are required to be disclosed so that prospective investors are fairly informed, and the "risk factors" section of the disclosure document is required to be placed in a specific location (i.e., in the forefront of the disclosure document; see "risk factors").

risk factors — In securities offerings, a required discussion of the principal factors that make the offering speculative or one of high risk that must be set forth in the forepart of the disclosure document (see "investor financing," "limited partnership" and "securities").

road show — A feature film theatrical exhibition in which the distributor takes over the operation of the theater. A road show is a public exhibition of a feature in a limited number of theaters, in advance of its general release, at admission prices higher than those customarily charged in first-run theaters in those areas (see "four-wall"). In the context of a securities offering, a road show refers to a multi-city trip by a company's executives, with the broker/dealer, for the purpose of selling the issue through presentations to prospective purchasers and underwriters (see "dog and pony show").

road show exhibition — (see "road show").

Robinson-Patman Act — A federal statute (Section 2(a) of the Clayton Act) that prohibits price discrimination between purchasers of commodities of like grade and quality where the effect of the discrimination may be to substantially lessen competition or tend to create a monopoly in any line of commerce. The illegal discrimination may include payment or acceptance of commissions, brokerage fees or other compensation, payment for services or facilities for processing or sale, furnishing services or facilities for processing or handling, knowingly inducing or receiving discriminatory prices, the discriminatory use of rebates, discounts or advertising service charges or underselling particular localities (see "antitrust laws," "Clayton Act," "kickbacks," "rebates" and "Sherman Antitrust Act").

role — The part played in a film by an actor or an actress as an individual characterization (see "actor").

role of government — The function and activities of the sovereign ruling agency in any given jurisdiction. In a country like the United States where an essentially free enterprise economy is part of the national fabric the role of the federal government is generally minimized, except in situations where private enterprise engages in business practices that reduce or tend to reduce the competitiveness within an industry (i.e., businesses engage in unreasonable restraints of trade, or other civil or criminal violations of the U.S. laws). In the current economic environment, one of the government's regulatory dilemma's relating to the balancing of competitive interests in an industry like the motion picture industry is how to permit combinations of businesses to grow large enough to compete in an increasingly international economy without stifling the small business interests within the domestic industry. However, so long as no organized interest group speaks up for the interests of the small businesses in such an industry, the government is very likely to respond favorably to requests from the larger entities in that industry to allow them the freedom to grow and compete effectively on an international scale. On the other hand, the film's released by the MPAA companies have long dominated both the domestic and international arenas. It addition, it may be possible to allow business combinations for the purpose of international trade without permitting the same combinations in the domestic marketplace (see "antitrust laws," "fair competition," "free enterprise," "industry groups," "global integration," "predatory practices," "money laundering," "movies with a message," "MPAA," "political influence," "restraint of trade," "unfair competition" and "vertical integration").

rollback — A retroactive gross participation that may be negotiated for a top actor, director, producer or writer if the motion picture he or she is involved with earns a certain high level of distributor gross receipts (see "gross receipts," "net profits," "retroactive escalation of fees" and "rising production costs").

rolling breakeven — A point at which a film's revenues are equal to expenses on a continuing basis (i.e., after all appropriate deductions are taken from gross receipts in each accounting period, those persons who have been able to negotiate a percentage or fixed participation at such accounting stages may be paid if the film is in a profit position for the statement period). Too much discretion, latitude, flexibility in the standards of conduct, lack of definition and too

little auditing leeway, etc. in the feature film distribution deal creates an opportunity for the distributor to keep delaying break-even (i.e., rolling it back so that actual breakeven is never achieved) and thus, net profit participants quite often do not receive any money for their net profit participation interests (see "actual breakeven," "artificial breakeven," "breakeven," "cash breakeven" and "creative accounting").

rolling titles — Film credits that move from the bottom to the top of the movie screen; a technique more commonly used for end credits than the main credits (see "crawl").

rollout — A release pattern with scheduled, usually weekly, phases of expanding theatrical exhibition (e.g., a film may open in several key cities or in only one or two — usually New York and Los Angeles), followed one or two weeks later by a number of additional smaller markets, and shortly thereafter by more smaller markets or perhaps the rest of the country (see "platformed" and "release pattern").

rollover — The movement of funds from one investment to another; also a term often used by banks when they allow a borrower to delay making a principal payment on a loan (see "debt" and "lender financing").

room tone — A recording of the existing presence or ambience of an otherwise quiet room. The recording is later mixed in with a film's dialogue track, making the scenes sound more realistic. Room tone may also be used to hide edits, cuts or breaks in the dialogue track (see "mix").

rosters — Lists of union and guild members maintained by the various unions and guilds of their respective members who are available for work (see "guild" and "union").

rough cut — An early stage of editing a film; the version of the work print of a film that follows assembly in the film's progress toward the fine cut stage and completion (i.e., the point at which all the film's scenes are edited together in the desired order for telling the story; see "editor" and "final cut").

round lot — A generally accepted unit of trading on a securities exchange (see "securities" and "stock exchange").

royalties — Payments to the holder for the right to use property such as copyrighted material; negotiated percentages of income paid to an author or composer for each copy of the work sold; a share of the product or of the proceeds therefrom reserved by an owner for permitting another to exploit and use his, her or its property; the rental that is paid to the original owner of property based on a percentage of profit or production. Royalty is compensation for the use of property, but it is based as to amount entirely upon the use actually made of the property (see "commission," "rent," "residuals" or "residual payments," "residuals and royalties provision" and "video/DVD revenue reporting").

royalty basis — The payment of percentage compensation based on the use of property or rights as a royalty as opposed to making such payments in the form of a distribution fee. Unlike other areas of the feature film business, home video revenue percentage participations have been handled on a royalty basis (similar to the record industry) rather than on a distribution fee basis. Royalty payments are traditionally much lower than distribution fees. Also, although the royalty approach is used for determining what goes into the film distributor's gross, the film distributors have, not surprisingly,

generally opted for the distribution fee approach with regard to home video revenue once it reaches the distributor's gross receipts pool (see "distribution fee basis," "royalty" and "video/DVD revenue reporting").

royalty on home video — (see "home video royalty").

"R" rating — An MPAA rating indicating that a motion picture has been reviewed by the MPAA's Classification and Rating Administration, and that attendance is restricted or contains some adult material (i.e., parents are urged to learn more about the film before taking their young children with them; see "ratings").

Rule 504 — One of the three SEC securities registration exemptions provided by Regulation D that specifically exempts the offer and sale of up to $1,000,000 of securities in a twelve-month period. A company may use this exemption so long as it is not a blank check company and is not subject to Exchange Act reporting requirements. Like the other Regulation D exemptions, in general an issuer may not use public solicitation or advertising to market the securities and purchasers receive "restricted" securities, meaning that they may not sell the securities without registration or an applicable exemption. However, an issuer can use this exemption in conjunction with certain small public offerings of securities (i.e., SCOR and MAIE) and investors will receive freely tradable securities under the following circumstances: (1) the issuer registers the offering exclusively in one or more states that require a publicly filed registration statement and delivery of a substantive disclosure document to investors; (2) the issuer registers and sells in a state that requires registration and disclosure delivery and also sells in a state without those requirements, so long as the issuer delivers the disclosure documents mandated by the state in which it registered to all purchasers; or (3) the issuer sells exclusively according to state law exemptions that permit general solicitation and advertising, so long as sales are only made to "accredited investors." Even if an issuer makes a private sale of a security where there are no specific disclosure delivery requirements, the issuer must still provide sufficient information to investors to avoid violating the anti-fraud provisions of the securities laws. This means that all material information must be disclosed and any information provided to investors must be free from false or misleading statements. In addition, an issuer cannot exclude any information if the omission makes the information provided false or misleading (see "accredited investors," "anti-fraud rule," "MAIE," "restricted securities" and "SCOR").

Rule 505 — Another of the three SEC securities registration exemptions provided by Regulation D that specifically exempts offers and sales of securities totaling up to $5 million in any twelve-month period. Under this exemption, an issuer may sell to an unlimited number of "accredited investors" and up to 35 other persons who do not need to satisfy the sophistication or wealth standards associated with other exemptions. Purchasers must buy for investment only, and not for resale. The issued securities are "restricted." Consequently, an issuer must inform investors that they may not sell the securities purchased for at least a year without registering the transaction. An issuer relying on Regulation D, Rule 505 may not use general solicitation or advertising to sell the securities. It is up to the issuer to decide what information needs to be given to accredited investors, so long as the level of disclosure does not violate the anti-fraud prohibitions. But the issuer must give non-accredited investors disclosure documents that generally are the same as those used in the same or similar levels of registered offerings. If information is provided to accredited investors, the issuer must make this information available to the non-accredited investors as well. The issuer must also be available to answer questions by prospective purchasers. Rule 505 requires financial statements certified by an independent public accountant, however, if the company other than a limited partnership or manager-managed LLC cannot obtain audited financial statements without unreasonable effort or expense, only the company's balance sheet, to be dated within one hundred and twenty days of the start of the offering, must be audited; and limited partnerships (and by analogy LLCs) unable to obtain required financial statements without unreasonable effort or expense may furnish audited financial statements prepared under the federal income tax laws (see "accredited investor," "anti-fraud rule" and "Regulation D").

Rule 506 — The third of the three SEC securities registration exemptions provided by Regulation D that specifically creates a "safe harbor" (i.e., more specific requirements that are therefore easier with which to comply) for the SEC's Section 4(2) private offering exemption. If an issuer satisfies the following standards, it can be assured that it is within the Section 4(2) exemption: (1) an unlimited amount of capital can be raised; (2) no general solicitation or advertising may be used to market the securities; and (3) the securities can be sold to an unlimited number of accredited investors and up to thirty-five other purchasers. Unlike Rule 505, however, all non-accredited investors, either alone or with a purchaser representative, must be sophisticated — that is, they must have sufficient knowledge and experience in financial and business matters to make them capable of evaluating the merits and risks of the prospective investment. As with Rule 505, it is up to the issuer to decide what information needs to be given to accredited investors, so long as the level of disclosure does not violate the anti-fraud prohibitions. On the other hand, an issuer must give non-accredited investors disclosure documents that generally are the same as those used in the same or similar level of registered offerings. If information is provided to accredited investors, the issuer must make such information available to the non-accredited investors as well. Under any circumstances, the issuer must comply with the anti-fraud rule. Rule 506 issuers must be available to answer questions by prospective purchasers and the rule's financial statement requirements are the same as for Rule 505. Purchasers of Rule 506 securities receive "restricted" securities. Consequently, purchasers may not freely trade the securities in the secondary market after the offering (see "private offering exemption" and "Regulation D").

Rule 1001 — A federal securities rule promulgated by the SEC that provides an exemption from the registration requirements of the Securities Act for offers and sales of securities, in amounts of up to $5 million, that satisfy the conditions of §25102(n) of the California Corporations Code. This California law exempts from California state law registration offerings made by California companies to "qualified purchasers" whose characteristics are similar to, but not the same as, accredited investors under Regulation D. This exemption allows some methods of general solicitation prior to sales. The California exemption, however, must be paired with the federal Intra-State Exemption, thus is of little use for film offerings (see "California limited offering exemption" and "intra-state offering").

rules — A term with different levels of meanings: (1) a prescribed guide for conduct or action, (2) an accepted procedure, custom or habit and (3) a law or regulation governing procedure or conduct. One of the more common statements made by film industry "insiders" who participate in discussions regarding film finance is "There are no rules." In at least a couple of ways, this may be true (i.e., there is no overall best way to go about financing a motion picture — it really depends on the project — and there are no prescribed guidelines for what works at the box office. But in other ways, this can be an extremely misleading and dangerous statement in that there certainly are a great number of rules when it comes to forming a corporation, creating a limited partnership or manager-managed LLC, conducting a securities offering, running a business, contracting with others, structuring a deal with tax considerations in mind, etc. In that sense, the people who are making the statement "There are no rules" may in reality be saying, "We know there are rules, but we are not going to abide by them because we know that no one who wants to stay in this business will complain and even if they do, their remedies are woefully inadequate, thus, history has shown that we can get away with it." (see "antitrust laws," "blacklist," "code," "conduct restrictions," "conflicts of interest," "crime," "ethics," "extortion," "insider's game," "Internal Revenue Service," "larceny," "merger guidelines," "pro and con analysis," "remedy," "Securities Acts," "sue us," "U.S. Justice Department" and "usury").

run — As a verb in the film industry, "run" means to exhibit a film. As a noun, the term refers to the continuous exhibition of a motion picture in a defined geographic area for a specified period of time or the length of time feature films play in a movie theater, theaters or territory (i.e., successive exhibition of a feature in a given area, first-run being the first exhibition in that area, second-run being the next subsequent, and so on, including successive exhibitions in different theaters, even though such theaters may be under a common ownership or management). Certain distributors have been known to require an exhibitor commitment of up to a twelve week run for a particularly strong motion picture and certain films have been known to continue in a run at certain theaters for as much as fifty weeks (see "break," "playtime," "release date" and "two run break"; contrast with "runs").

runs — The number of continuous, sequential exhibitions of a motion picture in a defined geographic area for a specified period of time or the number of contemporaneous exhibitions of a film within a defined geographic area (contrast with "run"; see "clearances," "licensing terms" and "minimum admission prices").

running time — The total length of time needed to project a film at its normal speed. Feature films usually require a running time of ninety to one hundred and twenty minutes. Exhibitors prefer the shorter running times since that may allow them to bring in one more audience during the course of a day and that increases their concession sales. Many distribution agreements specify a range in which the running time must fall and may make compliance a condition of delivery. Thus, if the producer comes close but fails to come within the prescribed running time, the distributor may be able to use this technical default to avoid its obligations to make payments to the producer pursuant to pre-sale or negative pickup agreements, avoid its obligation to distribute the picture or exercise its editing rights (see "feature length" and "negative pickup").

running time requirements — The outside limit specified by the distributor for the length of a film to be delivered to the distributor. The producer must be certain that he or she can comply with such specific time limits, otherwise the producer runs the risk that the distributor will use the excessive running time of the film as an excuse not to comply with its obligations to distribute the film (see "running time").

rushes — (see "dailies").

S

safe harbor — Generally, a provision in a law that excuses liability if the attempt to comply with the requirements of the law (in good faith) can be demonstrated. More specifically, the SEC's Regulation D was promulgated to provide guidance to issuers of securities who were concerned that conflicting interpretations of the more vague Section 4(2) non-public offering exemption made compliance difficult and therefore more risky (see "integration," "Regulation D" and "securities").

safety hedges — Steps taken by a producer or elements added to a film that help to reduce the downside risk of investing in the film. Safety hedges might include a more commercial script, commitments from recognizable name talent, a distribution deal in place and a completion bond. The more safety hedges a producer can offer a prospective investor, the easier it will be, theoretically, to get a person to invest in a film project. On the other hand, it may be just as effective to sell such an investment based on the theory that the higher the risk, the greater the potential reward. For example, although it is riskier to finance and produce a motion picture without a distribution agreement in place, industry analysts generally agree that a producer is more likely to be able to negotiate more favorable distribution terms for a completed motion picture, as opposed to the terms that may be available for the same movie when the distribution agreement is negotiated prior to completion of the picture (see "downside protection," "downside risk," "negative pickup" and "upside potential").

SAG — (see "Screen Actors Guild").

SAG Final Cast List — The list provided to SAG by a film's producer listing the final cast members selected for a film (see "director's cast list" and "Screen Actors Guild").

SAG nudity waiver — (see "nudity waiver").

SAG producer's agreement — The union agreement movie producers using actors and actresses who are members of the Screen Actors Guild must sign in order to comply with union rules (see "Screen Actors Guild").

SAG ultra-low budget agreement — A Screen Actors Guild contract for independent film productions with a total budget of less than $200,000. All films using SAG low budget agreements must be shot entirely in the U.S. (see "Screen Actors Guild").

sale/lease-back deal — A film investment arrangement in which the film's producer sells the negative to a group of investors and then leases it back over a period of years. If structured properly (and the current law so provides) arrangements may provide tax benefits to the investors and the producer can realize an up-front cash benefit (see "financing").

salable — (see "merchantable").

salary — A fixed and periodic payment for services performed without regard to actual results achieved (see "commission" and "issuer sales").

sale — A contract or agreement by which property is transferred from the seller to the buyer for a fixed price in money, paid or agreed to be paid by the buyer. A sale contemplates a free offer and acceptance, a seller and purchaser dealing at arm's length, and the fixing and payment of a purchase price (see "sell").

sales — (see "distribution").

sales agent — A movie distributor's representative who markets films to foreign territories (same as "foreign sales representative").

sales agent fees — Compensation for the activities of a sales agent (see "distribution fee" or "distributor's fee").

same availability — A manner of making a film available for exhibition so that two or more theaters may not exhibit a certain film before a date certain, on and after which the theaters so tied may exhibit that film regardless of whether all of the others so tied (due to prior commitments or holdovers) can then exhibit that film (see "availability").

same percentage as film rental earned (SPFRE) — A financial arrangement negotiated between a film distributor and exhibitor in which the exhibitor agrees to pay the same percentage of the week's advertising cost for the movie as the exhibitor's percentage of the box office receipts received by the exhibitor in that same week. Producers may want to use a similar concept in negotiating a feature film distribution deal with a distributor, inserting an SPFRE concept in place of the distributor's "discretion" to make allocations among films licensed as a package (see "allocation").

sample advertising campaign mock-up — A full-size presentation, prepared by or on behalf of a film producer, of a suggested movie promotional concept that can often be used to solicit the interest of a production company, distributor or financier for purposes of helping to arrange for production money financing (see "producer's package").

satellite television — Television programming transmitted via a satellite orbiting the earth (see "cable television" and "free television").

saturation booking — Scheduling a motion picture for exhibition in a limited market or area at a large number of theaters and supporting the release with a strong advertising and publicity campaign (see "release pattern").

saturation release — (see "saturation booking").

save harmless — (see "hold harmless").

scale — The minimum wage set by the respective film industry unions and guilds for each individual job category that is performed on a film by union and guild members (i.e., the payment of the minimum salary for a film cast or crew member as specified by the applicable union or guild; see "double scale" and "guild").

scale plus ten — Payment of the minimum union wage plus ten per cent. A common practice in the film industry for actors and actresses in order to cover the fees of their agents (see "scale").

scam — A planned deception in which persons pretending to be engaged in some form of business transaction are actually involved in a ruse designed to separate a victim from his or her money. Among independent feature film producers who are desperately seeking financing for their latest project, the typical pattern is for a money finder, and in some cases, small distributors, to promise full production money funding of the motion picture if the producer will provide a certain amount of up front money to demonstrate to the supposed financing source that the producer is serious. In some instances, it is extremely difficult to distinguish between a legitimate "film finance" operation and a total fraud until after the fact. It may help to get an attorney involved and create a substantial paper trail relating to the transaction while checking to confirm as much information about the parties as possible (e.g., calling the secretary of state's office to determine whether an entity that is purported to be incorporated, is in fact, a corporation in good standing; checking on all other films claimed to have been financed, etc.; see "due diligence," "fraud" and "white collar crime").

scenario — Generally, a sequence of events or an account of a possible course of action or events. In film, an outline or synopsis of a screenplay (see "screenplay").

scene — A single shot or a series of shots that presents some important segment of a screenplay's action or activity. A scene may be filmed with one basic number from end to end, then broken down for coverage into scene numbers, with each sequential number moving up. For example, a full dramatic scene may be composed of several scene numbers and slated and filmed as such in the master scene. Afterwards, coverage shots or cover shots are filmed separately. Thus, a director, or distributor with editing rights, may be able to insert a cover shot at a later time. Scene number and slate numbers are the same (see "final cut," "shot and take").

schedule for production — (see "production schedule").

Schedule K-1 — An IRS form that must be filed annually on behalf of limited partnerships, manager-managed LLCs and other entities which lists each investor's share of income, deductions, credits, etc. (see "Internal Revenue Service," "limited liability company" and "limited partnership").

schedule of net profit participations — (see "net profit participation schedule").

scope of release — How wide a geographical area or how many cities the initial release of a motion picture covers (see "release pattern").

SCOR — A form of securities registration for small businesses promulgated by the North American Securities Administrators Association ("NASAA"), in conjunction with the American Bar Association. SCOR stands for small corporate offering registration. It is intended to be a simplified "question and answer" registration form that companies also can use as the disclosure document for investors. SCOR was primarily designed for state registration of small business securities offerings conducted under the SEC's Rule 504, for sale of securities up to $1,000,000. More than forty-five states recognize SCOR. On the other hand, many issuers find that the Q&A format creates a less than adequate selling document for investors as opposed to the more traditional securities disclosure document. In a further effort to assist small businesses offering in several states, many states coordinate SCOR filings through a program called regional review (see "NASAA," "regional review" and "securities disclosure document").

score — As a noun, the written arrangement of music for a specific performance and medium (e.g., film). As a verb, to compose or to select music to go with a film (see "composer's original score").

scoring — The activity involved in composing, arranging, orchestrating, copying and recording music for a film (see "composer's original score").

S Corp — A corporation that has gained, by election, a special status for tax purposes. It is treated somewhat (but not in all respects) as a partnership since the results of its operations generally are reported by its shareholders and no federal income tax is paid by the corporation. Some states may still impose a tax at the corporate level. Qualification for such status is limited and accordingly not available or advisable for all corporations. For example, only a small business can elect S status; the corporation must be a domestic corporation; it must not have more than seventy-five shareholders; only individuals, estates and certain trusts are eligible to hold stock; non-

resident aliens may not hold stock; with respect to assets and distribution of profits, only one class of stock may be issued; timely filings must be effected to gain the status and the status may be terminated for non-compliance with the rules. Such corporations were formerly called "Sub-S" or "Subchapter S Corporations" (see "corporation").

scrapping prints — The selling of used feature film prints for their salvage value. Although, only a relatively small amount of distributor revenues may be generated through such sales, a producer and other net profit participants may be interested in seeing that the distribution agreement includes such revenue in the definition of gross receipts (see "junking costs").

screen — A whitish, matte, beaded or metallic surface on which the photographic image of a film is projected. A film screen is often perforated in order to transmit sound freely from loudspeakers mounted to the rear of the screen (see "number of screens").

Screen Actors Guild (SAG) — The union that represents actors and actresses (principal performers), sets standards for wages, working conditions and other issues of interest to members and negotiates industry contracts on behalf of its members (see "guild").

screen credits — (see "credits").

screen extras guild — The union that represents film extras (see "extra").

screening — A private showing of all or part of a film, for a selected audience. Generally, no admission is charged (see "preview" and "sneak preview").

screening expense — A cost that may be incurred by the distributor and which is often included as a deductible distributor expense in the distribution agreement (see "distribution expenses").

screening room — A theater with limited seating but equipped with projection equipment and used for showing completed films or films in progress (see "trade screening").

screenplay — The working manuscript for a film (i.e., written dialogue and scene descriptions). The screenplay generally evolves from concept through outline, synopsis, treatment, first draft, other drafts to shooting script (see "original screenplay").

screenplay by — The screen credit provided for the writer or writers of a screenplay (see "written by").

screenplay log — A record-keeping system (either manual or computerized) for keeping track of the screenplays submitted to a production company or studio and what happens to such scripts (e.g., when they first arrive, who checks them out, etc.) Also, a record maintained in film studios or production companies with a significant number of screenplays under development in which the dates and descriptions of all activities relating to the screenplay are noted along with the name of the responsible person (e.g., who receives copies, when synopses are prepared, by whom and when distributed and when various stages of the drafts are received). Sloppy record-keeping sometimes protects the perpetrators of copyright infringement (see "clearance," "coverage," "development," "development notes" and "screenplay").

screens — The plural of screen; also the same as theater in some situations, except that many theaters today have more than one screen (see "megaplex," "multiplex" and "number of screens").

screen splitting — The exhibitor practice of double booking for a single theater screen and exhibiting both of such booked films so that the same film is not exhibited at every one of a theater's daily performances. A separate ticket price is charged to the public for each film's exhibition so that the films are not exhibited as a single-charge double feature. Screen splitting is not to be confused with the splitting of films (same as "splitting the screen"; see "product splitting" and "unethical business practices").

screen test — The performance of a scene by an actor being considered for a part in a film; the scene is from the producer's script, usually in full costume and makeup and recorded on film (see "audition").

screen treatment — (see "treatment").

screen writer — The person who writes a film's screenplay and may have also been involved in writing the story outline, synopsis and treatment (see "screenplay," "spec script," "writer for hire" and "Writer's Guild of America").

Screen Writers Guild — (see "Writer's Guild of America").

script — (see "screenplay").

script breakdown — (see "production breakdown").

script changes — Modifications to a screenplay. Such changes will almost inevitably occur during production of a picture and, if such changes represent substantial departures from the pre-approved script, may create problems with a distributor and/or the completion guarantor. In the event that a distribution agreement was negotiated and signed prior to principal photography, the distributor typically includes a provision providing for script approval. The producer should also include a mechanism for approving subsequent changes and for determining which changes during production require distributor approval, otherwise, the producer risks creating a situation in which the distributor may avoid its obligations under the distribution agreement because of what it considers substantial script changes that have not been approved by the distributor. In addition, when a completion guarantee has been provided, it typically does not cover budget overruns caused by script changes. The producer, however, may want to at least insist on a provision in the completion guarantee that covers script changes prompted by events beyond the control of either the producer or the director ("approvals").

script clearance — (see "clearance" and "clearance procedure").

script log — (see "screenplay log").

script supervisor (or script clerk) — A member of the film production crew and the person responsible on a set or on location for taking detailed notes during production, keeping a record of all scenes and takes, recording such information on the shooting script as scene and take number, camera position, performance continuity, dialogue changes and running time of each shot, and presenting this information in a useful form for the film's editor. The script supervisor is also responsible for recording such information relating to later retakes of the same scene and for bringing continuity discrepancies in an actor's action and/or dialogue to the attention of the director. These notes will be an aid to the director during production and to the editor during post-production (see "screenplay").

scriptwriter's cost — The feature film development and production expenses associated with the compensation paid to the screenwriter (see "rising production costs" and "spec script").

SEC — (see "Securities and Exchange Commission").

SEC attorney — A lawyer who practices securities law (see "securities attorney").

SEC Rule 1001 — (see "Rule 1001").

secondary ancillary rights — The power, privileges and authority associated with a motion picture that is additional to the theatrical exhibition right but not a primary ancillary right such as the right to produce a remake, sequel or television series, but rather the typically less important ancillary rights such as merchandising, soundtrack album, music publishing and live stage play (see "ancillary rights").

secondary audience — A specific demographic population that may be interested in a given movie but which is not necessarily the movie's primary target group (see "appeal," "audience" and "target audience").

secondary campaign — (see "alternate campaign").

secondary cities — Smaller, less lucrative markets, often satellites of key cities (see "major markets").

secondary distribution — Public sale of previously issued securities held by large investors, usually corporations, institutions or other affiliated persons, as distinguished from a new issue or primary distribution, where the seller is the issuing entity (see "publicly held" and "securities").

secondary locations — The less important locations for a film. In scouting locations generally the primary locations are sought first and then nearby secondary locations are acquired (see "location").

secondary offering — An offering of securities by the holder thereof and not the issuer. In other words, if a shareholder of a corporation's stock wanted to sell his or her shares, that would be considered a secondary offering (see "restricted securities").

secondary players — Non-major speaking parts (see "principals" or "principal players").

secondary sales — Reorders of pre-recorded videocassettes or DVDs (see "re-release" and "sell-through market").

second assistant cameraperson — The film production person responsible for loading and unloading film, maintaining all camera department paperwork such as camera reports and shipping labels, preparing the slate for each take, and aiding the first assistant cameraperson (see "cinematographer").

second assistant director — The person involved in the production of a film who assists the first assistant director in conducting the business of the movie set or the location site [see "director (film)" and "first assistant director"].

second breakeven — A contractually defined point in a motion picture's revenue stream when revenues equal costs again (i.e., following the first such occurrence; see "actual breakeven," "artificial breakeven," "cash breakeven," "first breakeven," "gross proceeds at first breakeven" and "rolling breakeven").

second draft — A rewrite of the first draft (contrast with "polish" and "revision").

second feature — The second film when two features are playing on the same bill at a theater (see "double feature").

second round — Intermediate stage of venture capital financing, coming after the seed money (or start-up) and first round stages and before the mezzanine level, when the company has matured to the point where it might consider an initial public offering (see "IPO," "mezzanine level" and "venture capital").

second run — The next continuous exhibition of a motion picture in a designated geographic area for a specified period of time after the conclusion of the film's first run (see "run").

second take — A second filming of the same or similar scene (see "cutouts").

second unit — An additional film production crew (other than the main photographic unit) used for shooting sequences that do not involve principal players but still may require the services of persons whose actions before the camera require direction. Second unit shooting may occur before, during or after principal photography (see "principal photography").

Section 181 of the IRS code — Special Rules for Certain Film and Television Productions at Section 244 of the American Jobs Creation Act of 2004 (later codified as Section 181 of the IRS Code) and which apply to films commencing production after October 22, 2004 and before January 1, 2009. Section 181 provides that if an investment vehicle such as a limited partnership or manager-managed LLC acquires the rights to produce a feature film, each of its investor/taxpayers may elect to deduct his or her pro rata share of 100 percent of the direct and indirect costs of producing the film as an expense for the taxable year in which the costs of production are first incurred, so long as the aggregate cost of the film does not exceed $15 million and 75 percent of the total compensation is paid to actors, directors, producers and other relevant production personnel working on the film is paid for services performed in the United States (see "tax benefits").

section 4(2) offering — (see "private offering exemption").

secured creditor — A creditor who holds security that will cover the amount the debtor owes (i.e., persons or entities that have made loans or extended credit the repayment of which has been guaranteed by the pledge of assets or other collateral). For example, a bank that lends money for the production of a film will almost always insist on being a secured creditor (i.e., will not take an equity position or be at risk with respect to the money it has lent; see "bankable pre-sales commitments" and "collateral").

secured debt — Debt guaranteed by the pledge of assets or other collateral (see "assign" and "hypothecation").

securities — Any financial investment, instrument, arrangement or obligation in which the investors in an enterprise engaged in for profit are passive and have a right to participate in profits; also evidence of a right created in the holder of the security to participate in profits or assets distribution of a profit-making enterprise primarily managed by others. The offer and sale of securities are regulated by both the federal and state governments. One of the primary purposes of the sale of a security is to raise capital for businesses. Common examples of securities utilized for funding film projects are corporate stocks, interests in limited partnerships and manager-managed LLCs. Other securities include notes, stocks, treasury stock, bonds, debentures, certificates of interest or participation in any profit-sharing agreement, collateral-trust certificates, pre-organization certificates or subscriptions, transferable shares, voting-trust certificates, certificates of deposit, or in general, any instrument commonly known as a "security"; or certificates of interest or participations therein, temporary or interim certificates for, receipts for, or warrants or rights to subscribe to or purchase, any of the foregoing; but not currency or any note, draft, bill of exchange, or banker's acceptance which has a maturity at the time of issuance not exceeding nine months, exclusive of days of grace, or a renewal thereof the maturity of which is likewise limited (also referred to as a "security"; contrast with "loan"; see "investment contract," "limited liability company," "limited partnership," "participatory debt instrument," "penny stock," "stock" and "subscription application and agreement").

securities acts — The popular name given to the two major federal statues regulating to the issue of and marketing trade in securities. The Securities Act of 1933 deals primarily with the initial distribution of securities by the issuer, and its objective is to provide full disclosure of facts material to the securities for sale so that investors are able to make informed investment decisions. The Securities Exchange Act of 1934 is designed to regulate post-distribution trading in securities and provides for the registration and regulation of securities exchanges, including disclosure of information about the issue for the purpose of prohibiting fraud and manipulation in connection with the sale or purchase of securities (contrast with "blue sky laws").

securities analyst — An individual, usually employed by a stock brokerage house, bank or investment institution, who performs investment research and examines the financial condition of a company or group of companies in an industry and in the context of the securities markets (see "industry analysts" and "securities").

Securities and Exchange Commission (SEC) — The federal agency empowered to administer the Securities Act and to regulate and supervise the offer and sales of securities (see "NASD" and "securities").

securities attorney — A lawyer who has expertise relating to the federal and state securities laws and practices in that area of the law (see "entertainment attorney," "securities acts" and "blue sky laws").

securities loan — A loan collateralized by marketable securities (see "lender financing").

securities disclosure document — The written information required to be prepared by an issuer of securities or such issuer's behalf by a securities attorney and provided prior to purchase to each prospective purchaser (see "anti-fraud rule," "disclosure document," "offering circular," "offering memorandum" and "prospectus").

security — In investments, any form of profit participation or investment contract in which the investor hopes to make a profit primarily off of the investment managerial efforts of another. The essence of a security is the passive nature of the investor. Units in manager-managed LLCs and limited partnerships are securities, as are shares in a corporation. In lending, the term is also used to describe collateral offered by a debtor to a lender to secure a loan. For example, in a production-financing distribution agreement, the distributor will generally take a security interest in certain items relating to the film in order to secure its advance of production funds to the production company. In other words, the distributor will ask the production company to assign to the distributor as security, all of the production company's right, title and interest in and to the picture (including without limitation, all interest in the results and proceeds of the services of all persons engaged in connection with the picture), whether now owned or hereafter acquired, including, but not limited to, the copyright, all negatives, film, tape and other physical properties created or acquired for the picture (same as "collateral security"; see "equity security" and "securities").

security agreement — The written contract between a feature film producer and a lender providing financing for the producer's motion picture that identifies the collateral offered by the debtor/producer to the lending entity as security for the loan and grants such lender certain rights with respect to the collateral in the event the loan is not repaid by or on behalf of the producer in a timely manner (see "collateral," "notice of assignment" and "studio security agreement").

security interest — An interest in real or personal property that secures the payment of an obligation. In the context of a production-financing/distribution agreement the distributor will generally provide that the security interest granted to the distributor will be prior to all other security interests, other than any security interests in favor of guilds, unions and film laboratories. Also, the distributor will ask the production company to promise to execute and deliver to the distributor all documents the distributor deems necessary or appropriate to perfect its security interest (see "collateral," "debt" and "security").

Security Dealers of North America — A directory of investment banking and brokerage firms in North America published by Standard & Poor's (see "broker/dealer" and "NASD") .

seed money — The earliest funds required for the activities undertaken during the development stage of a business or firm; more often referred to as preliminary or developmental monies in the context of feature films. The term seed money is more typically associated with venture capital fundings (i.e., it is the venture capitalist's first contribution toward the financing or capital requirements of a start-up business). It frequently takes the form of a loan, often subordinated, or an investment in convertible bonds or preferred stock for a start-up corporation (see "development funds," "preliminary investors" and "venture capital").

SEG — (see "screen extras guild").

segregated bank account — A separate bank account and record of financial transactions relating to a given film the funds in which are not co-mingled with any other funds (see "bank" and "production account").

segregated, interest-bearing account — A separate bank account used to temporarily hold investor funds when an independent film is being financed through limited partnership or LLC private offerings and the investors are promised interest on their held funds until a specified minimum offering amount is reached. The investor funds in such an account are not to be co-mingled with any other funds (see "mini-maxi offering" and "minimum offering proceeds").

selective releasing — A method of distributing films, typically utilized by low-budget independent producers or distributors in which a movie receives a limited release in selected cities (i.e., key smaller markets in the U.S.) and the film is then rotated around to other markets (see "regional release pattern").

self-dealing — Transactions in which a fiduciary uses or appropriates the property held in his or her fiduciary capacity for his or her own benefit. Many federal and state statutes prohibit self-dealing (see "arm's length," "conflicts of interest," "RICO" and "video/DVD revenue reporting").

self-distribution — The booking of a motion picture into theaters directly by its producer as opposed to a distributor. Generally, only a small number of theaters would be available to exhibit a self-distributed film. "Four-walling" is a specific form of self-distribution (see "four-wall").

self-financing — The funding of the development and/or production costs of a motion picture with personal funds (see "financing" and "other people's money").

self-insure — To either go without insurance or to set aside a specified amount of money to protect against the risk of loss (see "insurance").

sell — In securities terminology, the terms sell, sale and offer for sale include every disposition or attempt to dispose of a security for value (see "securities").

seller's market — A market situation in which there are more buyers than sellers; the opposite of a buyer's market. Generally speaking, the film distribution arena is a buyer's market. In other words, each year there are many more producers and films produced than there are willing and able distributors or film release slots available (see "buyer's market," "law of supply and demand" and "leverage").

selling agreement — (see "broker/dealer selling agreement" and "selling broker/dealer").

selling broker/dealer — Securities terminology for a broker/dealer firm that has agreed to sell securities on behalf of an issuer of such securities. It is rare for a broker/dealer firm to agree to sell offerings of limited partnership units or manager-managed LLC interests being used to raise financing for independent feature films. Such sales are more commonly conducted through issuer sales (see "broker/dealer selling agreement," "issuer sales," "managing broker/dealer" and "underwriting group").

selling commissions — The transaction-related compensation paid to selling broker/dealers for sales of securities. Such commissions are based on a percentage of the sales price of the investment unit (e.g., 10 percent of the price of a limited partnership unit may be paid to selling broker/dealers out of the offering proceeds once the offering minimum has been attached). As a general rule, selling commissions are not permitted to be paid to finders (i.e., persons not licensed as SEC/NASD broker/dealers or registered representatives) for the sale of securities (see "broker/dealer," "finder's fee," "NASD" and "securities").

selling concession — The discount at which securities in a new issue offering (or a secondary distribution) are allocated to members of a selling group by the underwriters. Since the selling group cannot sell to the public at a price higher than the public offering price, its compensation comes out of the difference between the price paid to the issuer by the underwriters and the public offering price, called the spread. The selling group's portion, called the concession, is normally one half or more of the gross spread, expressed as a discount off the public offering price (see "underwriting spread").

selling expenses — Costs incurred in marketing a securities offering. Because such costs generally are paid from the investors' capital, their status for tax purposes may be important. Prior to enactment of Section 181 of the IRS Code, certain costs, such as syndication costs, were not deductible for tax purposes (see "Section 181 of the IRS Code" and "syndication expenses").

selling group — Group of investment bankers or securities broker/dealer firms organized by the purchase group, including members of the purchase group, whose purpose is to distribute a new issue of securities (also called "selling syndicate"; see "broker/dealer," "investment bank" or "investment banker," "purchase group" and "underwriter").

selling point — A positive element or factor relating to an investment deal that is considered helpful in marketing the program; something about an offering that might encourage an investor to invest (see "investment tax credit," "offering expenses," "Section 181 of the IRS Code" and "tax benefits").

selling subject to review — A film industry practice as between exhibitors and distributors in which these parties renegotiate the film rental due the distributor after the film's theatrical engagement has been completed. From the distributor's point of view, such a practice may be considered necessary because the film performance at the box office was poorer than expected and the distributor wants to book its next film at the same theater under the best available terms. Unfortunately, for the other gross and/or net profit participants on the first movie, who are not likely to be affiliated in any way with the distributor's next movie in release, this practice is blatantly unfair, because if the distributor accepts a smaller number of film rentals from the exhibitor on the first film just so it can get better terms on a second film, the financial interests of the participants in the first film have been sacrificed for the benefit of the distributor. In the context of a so-called "relationship driven business," it would appear that the relationship that means the most to the distributor is the distributor's relationships with the exhibitors as opposed to its relationship with other gross or net profit participants. This is also a business practice that even if addressed at the negotiating stage of the distribution agreement is most likely to be presented on a take or leave it

basis and if the distributor is confronted by an auditor who questions the practice, the auditor is likely to get the "sue us" response. Thus, instead of "our films did not do well at the box office," this practice and others discussed herein may be one of the real reasons why the major distributors and exhibitors seem to do so well in the business while the smaller production companies and distributors fall by the way side (see "adhesion contract," "creative accounting," "conflict of interest," "predatory practices," "reciprocal preferences," "relationship driven business," "settlement transactions," "sue us" and "unethical business practices").

sell-sheet — An 8 ½" x 11" reduction and reproduction of a movie one-sheet used in promoting and selling a film to investors and distributors (see "lobby card," "one-sheet" and "poster").

sell-through market — The aggregate film viewers who will purchase a videocassette or DVD if the price is attractive enough, as opposed to renting a video at a rental location. Once the number of movie retail locations peaked in the mid-'80s, the major studio/distributors focused on developing a sell-through rather than a rental market for their motion picture videocassettes and DVDs (see "Video/DVD revenue reporting").

semi-annual payments — Compensation paid by a feature film distributor to gross and/or net profit participants twice a year. Most distribution companies make semi-annual payments. Some will seek to limit their payment and reporting obligations to once a year. Fewer still are willing to report and pay on a quarterly basis (see "accounting period" and "audit").

separation of rights — A writer's guild basic agreement provision (Article 16) that sets forth the circumstances under which the writer of an original story (or an original story and screenplay) is permitted to retain the rights to certain separable material (e.g., dramatic rights, publication rights and sequel rights) even though the story and/or screenplay was written while the writer was in the employment of a production company, which has the rights to exploit the story and/or screenplay (see "Writer's Guild of America").

sequel — A literary work continuing the course of a narrative begun in a preceding one; a feature film that is released after the original and tells a related story that occurred after the story depicted in the earlier released film (see "prequel").

sequence — A series of shots with a continuity of location, action, time or story and usually with a beginning, middle and end (see "continuity," "location" and "shot").

series — (see "television series").

series rights — The power and privilege to produce a television series based on the same story (see "television series").

service — Useful labor that does not produce a tangible commodity. In legal terminology, the term service is also used as a short form of service of process. In lending, it may also refer to the payment of interest and any sinking fund obligations on debt (see "debt," "product" and "service of process").

service mark — A mark used in the sale or advertising of services to identify the services of one person and distinguish them from the services of others. Like a trademark, a service mark should be searched, cleared and registered with the secretary of state in the state in which it is being used and with the U.S. Patent and Trademark Office so as to provide constructive notice to subsequent users of the same marks that the marks are no longer available for use (see "trademark" and "trade name").

service of process — In law, service or service of process refers to the delivery of a pleading, notice or other paper in a lawsuit to the opposite party, so as to charge the party with the receipt of it and subject the party to its legal effect (see "consent to service of process").

services clause — A provision in the employment agreements of actors, producers, directors and writers that sets out the duties to be undertaken by the employee on behalf of an employer production company (see "employment agreement").

set — The place where a film is shot. Sets may be exterior or interior (see "location," "set dressing" and "studio").

set construction person — A film production's key carpenter who is responsible for supervising all construction associated with the production including sets, set dressings and scaffolding (see "set").

set design — The plan and overall look of the place and places where scenes for a film are shot (see "set designer" and "set dressing").

set designer — The film production person responsible for the supervision and preparation of all sets and shooting locations as required by the production, as well as the supervision of all set dressings and properties (see "set design").

set dressings — The furnishings that are used to decorate a film set (see "props").

settlement — A conclusive fixing or resolution, usually a compromise, between the distributor and exhibitor or distributor and sub-distributors relating to the amount of monies due to be paid to the distributor for the exploitation of one or more films. Generally, settlements are calculated or negotiated on a weekly basis, at least initially between the individual theater and the branch office of the distributor. As between the distributor and exhibitor, settlement is sometimes used to refer to the percentage retained by the exhibitor. The amount actually settled upon may be 10 percent to 30 percent below what the contractual amount would have been. There is almost never any written communication between the distributor and exhibitor relating to such settlement negotiations (i.e., it's all oral, thus the net profit participation auditor can only compare what was paid with what should have been paid pursuant to the contract between the distributor and exhibitor). These settlements may significantly reduce the chances that a given film will ever reach net profits, thus such negotiations adversely impact on the financial interests of a film's producer and its other net profit participants. For example, a distributor may be willing to settle for less than the money actually owed by an exhibitor on a given film in order to help the distributor obtain more favorable exhibition terms on its next film. Some entertainment attorneys have suggested that these settlement transactions would not hold up in court if challenged because the distributor, in its distribution agreement, generally has contracted to maximize its distribution revenue on the film on behalf of all gross and net profit participants. Few if any producers or other profit participants, however, have chosen to litigate this issue and even when

confronted by profit participation auditors, this appears to be another one of those issues the distributors routinely respond to by saying "sue us" (see "blacklisting," "contract of adhesion," "creative accounting," "Net Profit Participant Association," "outstandings," "problem producer," "selling subject to review" and "sue us").

settlement transactions — Agreements between exhibitors and distributors (or distributors and sub-distributors) that settle their respective accounts and which often cover the receipts, deductions, fees etc. for several movies exhibited by such exhibitor and distributed by such distributor (or sub-distributor). The actual numbers in such transactions are typically rounded off, averaged or compromised, thus making it difficult for a producer of a movie involved in such a transaction to determine what amount paid to the distributor should be properly allocated to such producer's motion picture. This is a form of cross-collateralization which producers should object to. To prevent this problem, the producer should require that the distributor insert "floors" in its agreements with sub-distributors and exhibitors. A "floor" is a minimum percentage of the box office gross receipts, with the floors or percentages varying from territory to territory on a sliding scale over time. In addition, the producer may want to see that a "good faith" standard is inserted as part of the distributor's obligations relating to such settlements (see "audit," "creative accounting," "cross collateralization," "selling subject to review" and "sue us").

seven sheet — Pre-printed paper containing motion picture advertising that is posted on junior panels or mini (outdoor) posters measuring approximately eight feet in width by nine feet in height (see "one sheet," "poster" and "sell-sheet").

seventy/thirty — One of the possible divisions of revenue between a film's producer and distributor in which the distributor receives a 30 percent distribution fee on all revenues (i.e., gross receipts) and the producer receives the remaining 70 percent, minus all distribution costs. That is the same as saying the distributor first deducts a 30 percent distribution fee across the board, then deducts its distribution expenses and the producer group receives what is left, if any (see "net profit participation schedule").

severability clause — A contractual provision usually found in the miscellaneous provisions section of an agreement providing that if any provision of the agreement as applied to either party or any circumstance is adjudged by a court to be void and unenforceable, such provision will in no way affect any other provision of the agreement, the application of such provision in any other circumstance, or the validity or enforceability of the agreement as a whole (see "contract").

SFX — (see "sound effects").

sham transaction — A transaction that will be ignored for tax purposes because it is deemed to have no substance (see "scam" and "transaction").

share — A unit of equity ownership in a corporation. This ownership is represented by a stock certificate, that names the company and the shareholder (see "corporate stock" and "equity").

shared employee salaries — A movie studio accounting concept in which the compensation paid to certain employees of the studio is allocated among the various movies that are being produced at the studio, even though such employees may not actually perform any services that directly benefit a given motion picture (see "overhead" or "overhead costs").

shared talent pool — A reference to the fact that many of the people who are involved in the production of feature films are also some of the same people involved in the production of television shows (see "television and film inter-relationship").

shareholders — The equity owners of a corporation. Shareholders have ultimate control over the existence of a corporation and such control is exerted by voting on the elections of directors and on certain major transactions proposed by the directors and management. Shareholders generally do not otherwise participate in setting policy for the corporation (that's done by the board of directors) or participate directly in the day-to-day management of the corporation or approve ordinary contracts (see "equity" and "stock").

share of stock — (same as "share").

share turnover — A measure of the rate at which corporate stock is bought and sold (see "corporation" and "corporate stock").

shares authorized — The number of corporate shares authorized to be issued by a corporation's articles of incorporation [see "articles of incorporation," "charter," "director (corporate)," "officers" and "management"].

shares outstanding — (see "issued and outstanding").

sheet music — The score of a musical composition printed on large unbound sheets of paper (see "music").

shell corporation — A corporation that is formed without significant assets or ongoing operations. Some banks require that a feature film producer seeking a production money loan as part of a negative pickup or split rights transaction incorporate a shell corporation for the sole purpose of holding the single film being financed as its only asset and to start operations with no liabilities. This helps to insure that the bank will have a first priority claim against all of the assets of the newly formed company (as opposed to any other prospective creditor) as the corporation begins operations. The term "shell corporation" is also sometimes used to describe companies set up for fraudulent purposes (e.g., as fronts to conceal money laundering or tax evasion schemes; see "corporate stock," "lender financing," "Mafia," "mob controlled distribution company," "money laundering," "negative pickup," "securities" and "split rights deal").

shelter — (see "tax shelter").

Sherman Antitrust Act — Federal antitrust statute that among other things, prohibits monopolies, attempts to monopolize and unreasonable restraints of trade. Film industry practices that raise antitrust questions include tying arrangements, discrimination, clearances, block booking, pooling agreements, price fixing, formula deals, master agreements and franchises (see "antitrust laws" and "Clayton Act").

shoot — To photograph a scene, a sequence or an entire film with a motion picture camera (see "shot").

shooting — (see "principal photography").

shooting company — The organization working on a particular motion picture (see "production company").

shooting outline — A sketchily written list of actions and objects to be filmed when a shooting script is not available (see "shooting script").

shooting ratio — The ratio of the length of raw film exposed in shooting a film to the footage actually used in the completed motion picture. A 4:1 ratio would be considered very economical while a 10:1 ratio would be somewhat wasteful (see "principal photography").

shooting schedule — The breakdown and organization of a script or story board, into minutes, hours and days for the shooting time allocated by page, scene or locale for a production to be filmed or taped. The objective is to plan the shooting so as to most efficiently utilize all of the elements involved (see "production board").

shooting script — The final completely detailed version of a motion-picture script in which scenes are grouped in the order most convenient for shooting and without regard to plot sequence; the final working script for a motion picture. It details the film's shots one by one in relation to corresponding dialogue and/or other sound (see "first draft," "final screenplay," "master script," "polish" and "revision").

short film agreement — A Screen Actors Guild agreement that permits both professional and non-professional performers to work on films with budgets of less than $50,000 (thirty-five minutes or less) and defer their salaries, so long as no consecutive employment occurs (except on overnight locations; see "low budget agreement," "modified low budget agreement," "Screen Actors Guild," "student film agreement" and "ultra-low budget agreement").

shorts — A brief written statement of information relating to the promotion of a film (see "pre-feature entertainment" and "publicity material").

short — (see "film short").

short form agreement — An abbreviated contract, often drafted in letter form, that contains only the most important terms and provisions and usually provides that it is the intention of the parties to negotiate a more complete agreement at some time in the future to take the place of the short form agreement (see "contract," "deal memo," "fully-negotiated agreement," "letter agreement," "long form agreement," "player agreement" and "standard contract").

short star list — A very limited number of actors who currently have the recognized ability to attract significant numbers of movie-goers into the theaters that are playing motion pictures featuring such stars (see "star").

short subject — (see "film short").

short term — In accounting terminology, assets expected to be converted into cash within the normal operating cycle (usually one year); or liabilities coming due in one year or less. In investment terminology, an investment with a maturity of one year or less (see "asset").

short-term security — A bond or note that matures in and is payable within a short span of time. Such securities are purchased by institutional investors for income rather than for growth potential (see "short-term").

shot — One continuous take in motion picture filming; the basic component of a motion picture (see "scene," "sequence" and "take").

Show Biz News — A semi-monthly newsletter formerly published as a joint venture by Act II Publishing and Summit Media International in 1989 and 1990 and that focused specifically on the business side of the entertainment industry, looking at Hollywood from the studio executive's perspective. This publication may have revealed too much and was discontinued (see "trades").

signatories — Individual producers or film production companies that have signed union or guild collective bargaining agreements which obligate them to comply with such union's or guild's rules and regulations (see "guild" and "union").

significant barriers — Serious obstacles that impede or separate. In an antitrust law context, the phrase "significant barriers" refers to the serious obstacles that may keep a business from either entering or continuing to do business in a particular field (e.g, feature film distribution or exhibition). Several of the U.S. Justice Department vertical merger guidelines relate to the issue of whether or not a feature film distributor or exhibitor must be vertically integrated in order to enter or continue in the distribution or exhibition business (i.e., to successfully compete in those levels of the motion picture business today). As a means of analyzing proposed vertical mergers in the motion picture business, these guidelines further ask how difficult is it to achieve such vertical integration (assuming it is necessary to succeed in today's marketplace), and if vertical integration is required and there are significant barriers to such integration, is the market otherwise conducive to non-competitive performance. In other words, the U.S. Justice Department has apparently taken the position that in a market not otherwise conducive to single firm market power or coordination among several firms, even significant increases in barriers to entry are unlikely to affect competitive market performance adversely (see "barriers to entry," "merger guidelines," "Paramount Consent Decree of 1948" and "TriStar Case").

significant medium for the communication of ideas — Concept expressed by the U.S. Supreme Court in the case of Burstyn v. Wilson (343 U.S. 495, 1952) in describing the motion picture. In this case, the film industry was asking the court to protect film as free speech. The court stated "It cannot be doubted that motion pictures are a significant medium for the communication of ideas. Their importance as an organ of public opinion is not lessened by the fact that they are designed to entertain as well as to inform." The studio position in the Burstyn v. Wilson case, of course, conflicts with the rather disingenuous arguments made so often in more contemporary times whenever a controversial film is criticized and the studio or MPAA executives resort to the "Well, movies are merely entertainment" defense." (see "idea," "MPAA" and "propaganda").

silent bit — An extra player performing pantomime of such significance that it portrays a point essential to the staging of the scene involved (see "bit player" and "special ability extra").

silent partner — A limited partner in a direct participation program, in which cash flow and tax benefits are passed directly through to the equity owners. Such partners are called silent because, unlike general partners, they have no direct role in management and no liability beyond their individual investment (similar to "members" in "manager-managed LLCs"; see "direct participation program," "limited partners" and "limited partnership").

silver screen — (see "screen").

similar pictures — Films that closely resemble each other in significant respects (e.g., concept, genre and budget). The concept is sometimes used to help others understand what a proposed movie is about (i.e., "It's like this film combined with that film.") and sometimes used to help estimate the projected performance of a proposed film by comparing it to other similar films that have been produced and distributed in recent years (see "box office comparables" and "past performance").

simple interest — Interest calculation based only on the original principal amount (contrast with "compound interest").

simple vs exact interest — (see "interest").

single-picture domestic distribution agreement — A contract between a producer and a feature film distributor that sets out the terms under which the distributor agrees to distribute one motion picture in the U.S. and Canada (see "multiple picture distribution agreement," "output deal" and "output distribution agreement").

single-picture financing — All forms of film finance utilized in funding the production and/or distribution costs of one film (e.g., debt financed by banks against the collateral of distribution guarantees payable on delivery of the picture or single picture limited partnership). As a general rule, a production entity with a multiple slate of motion pictures will have more bargaining power with distributors than a producer who is only seeking distribution for a single picture (all other things being equal). The same general rule is also true for distributors seeking to book their motion pictures into theaters. Investors may also want to spread their investment out over a slate of pictures rather than put all of their investment into a single project (see "corporate financing," "financing," "multi-picture financing" and "slate cross-collateralization").

single-picture license — A feature film licensing agreement authorizing the licensee to exploit a motion picture in one or more specific territories and media (see "single-picture domestic distribution agreement").

single-picture transactions — (see "single-picture financing").

sinking fund — Money accumulated by a corporation on a regular basis in a separate custodial account that is used to redeem debt securities or preferred stock issues. A bond indenture or preferred stock charter may specify that payments be made to a sinking fund, thus assuring investors that the issues are safer than bonds (or preferred stocks) for which the issuer must make payment all at once, without the benefit of a sinking fund (see "bond").

skimming — Stealing at various stages in a film's revenue stream (e.g., by a theater's cashier and door person, the theater owner under-reporting ticket sales to the sub-distributor, the sub-

distributor taking a little off the top before reporting to the distributor or the distributor doing the same before reporting to the producer). It is important for the producer to inquire about and to see that the distributor has vigorous ongoing checking and collection programs (see "audit," "checking services," "insider's game," "reciprocal preferences," "relationship driven business" and "underreported rentals")

slander — A form of defamation; spoken words that tend to damage the reputation of another. Truth is an absolute defense to an action for slander (see "defamation," "defamation of character," "errors and omissions insurance," "libel" and "tort").

slate cross-collateralization — A feature film distributor practice in which the distributor offsets the financial performance of one motion picture against the financial performance of other films produced by the same production company (see "cross-collateralization," "cross-collateralization of movie slates" and "single-picture financing").

slate of pictures — A feature film production company's list of proposed motion pictures that are being developed and are planned to be produced, or the films produced or released by a company during a given year (see "output deal").

sleeper — A film that does surprisingly well at the box office (i.e., a motion picture, initially believed to have only limited audience appeal, that is able to "crossover" to a much broader audience partly because of positive word-of-mouth). A sleeper is a film that becomes a financial success although it had not been expected to be one (e.g., low-budget production brought out with little advance publicity; see "crossover film").

slicks — Standardized display ads for films, printed on glossy paper in various sizes and designed to receive local theater information as needed. Slicks are prepared for use in newspapers and magazines (see "advertising").

sliding scale — A financial arrangement, that in the film business often occurs in the deal between an exhibitor and distributor, in which the exhibitor agrees to pay the distributor a different amount (percentage) of film rental depending on the level of box office gross for the week; typically the greater the weekly box office gross the higher the percentage paid to the distributor as film rental (see "ninety/ten deal").

slots — (see "release slots").

Small Business Administration (SBA) — Federal agency created in 1953 to provide financial assistance (through direct loans and loan guarantees) as well as management assistance to businesses that lack the access to capital markets enjoyed by larger more credit worthy corporations (see "corporations," "start-up" and "venture capital").

small business issuer — A company with limited assets seeking to raise funds from investors through the sale of securities (see "Form SB").

small offering exemption — A term used in some states to describe a transactional exemption that may be available for smaller offerings than those relying on such state's limited offering exemption (see "exempt offering," "limited offering exemption" and "private placement").

smokescreen — Something designed to obscure, confuse or mislead. For example, when studio or MPAA executives state that movies are merely entertainment, as they commonly do in defense of a controversial film, they are overlooking the fact that all movies communicate ideas, that ideas have always and will always influence human behavior, thus, movies influence the behavior of some audience members. In other words, they are using the "movies are merely entertainment" scam as a smokescreen (see "culture promotion," "marketplace of ideas," "patterns of bias," "propaganda" and "theme").

SMPTE — (acronym for "Society of Motion Picture and Television Engineers").

SMPTE time code — A film, video and audio industries standardized code (a digital signal) used to enable audio and video playback equipment to lock together in synch. The code is also used in audio and videotape editing to define specific moments on a tape (see "Society of Motion Picture and Television Engineers").

sneak preview — An advance showing of a film in a theater either free, by invitation or to a paying audience to test reaction or hopefully to generate favorable word-of-mouth (see "director's cut," "preview," "screening," "sneak preview advertising," "test marketing," "trade sneak" and "word-of-mouth sneak").

sneak preview advertising — Motion picture advertising designed to promote the various kinds of sneak previews (see "director's cut," "preview," "screening," "sneak preview," "trade sneak," "word-of-mouth sneak").

Society of Motion Picture and Television Engineers (SMPTE) — A professional association of sound, camera and film lab technicians who encourage the maintenance of high technical standards in film and television through the presentation of seminars and the publication of books and scientific papers (see "SMPTE time code").

soft floor — In the context of percentage participations, a floor is a minimum percentage beyond which the participation will not fall. However, a "soft floor" refers to a floor situation in which the floor is subject to further reduction under certain circumstances. For example, once a floor is reached, additional participations may be taken off-the-top, thereby effectively further reducing the floor. Floors, both "soft floors" and "hard floors" may also be used in setting the lowest acceptable weekly rental payments to be paid by an movie exhibitor to the distributor. In that case, the floor is a percentage of the total box office gross receipts for the exhibition of the motion picture (see "floor" and "hard floor").

soft market — Market characterized by an excess of supply over demand. The market for the acquisition of films for distribution in the U.S. would have to be considered a soft market since there is a significantly larger number of feature films produced in the U.S. than there are capable film distributors available to distribute such films in any given year (also called a "buyer's market"; see "law of supply and demand").

soft money — Means for paying for the cost of producing a film other than through the direct payment of hard currency. Soft money for film production often takes the form of tax credits, tax allowances, loan supports, box-office rebates, government subsidies, the barter of cheap facilities and/or a combination of benefits accessed through international co-production deals (see "tax benefits")

soft money deals — Film finance transactions involving a mechanism other than the payment of hard currency for production costs (see "soft money").

sole discretion — Latitude of choice within the control of a solitary individual or entity. Certain issues relating to motion picture distribution agreements may specifically be determined in the sole discretion of the film distributor or other parties to the contract. In fact, most film distribution agreements offered to producers in the contemporary marketplace contain so much discretion in favor of the distributor that no matter how aggressive the entertainment attorney representing the producer, the distributor will still have enough discretion per the terms of the contract to handle the financial results of the film's exploitation however it so chooses ("consultation rights," "discretion," "mutual approval" and "unconscionable").

sole proprietorship — An unincorporated business owned and managed by one person, for the purpose of making a profit; a business or financial venture carried on by a single person that is not a trust or corporation. Unlike a corporation or a trust, a sole proprietorship is not a separate taxpaying entity. Instead, its income is taxed directly to the individual proprietor (same as "proprietorship"; see "entity," "and "fictitious name").

sole screen credit — The acknowledgment on the motion picture screen that a single person performed a certain task relating to the production of the film (e.g., wrote the screenplay; see "credits").

sole shareholder — A single individual or entity who owns all of the shares of a corporation (see "majority shareholder" and "principal stockholder").

solicitation — The process of offering and selling a security to a prospective investor (see "general solicitation" and "limitations on manner of offering").

solid word-of-mouth — Favorable reactions from moviegoers to a particular movie that are passed along verbally to other potential moviegoers (see "word-of-mouth").

solvency — The ability to pay all debts and just claims as they come due (see "bankruptcy").

song — A short poem presented within a musical setting (see "lyrics" and "music").

song writer — A person who writes, composes, creates or conceives, alone or in collaboration with another or others, the words and/or music of any original musical composition. Also, one who creates original arrangements of musical compositions in the public domain or with the permission of the copyrights owner (see "lyrics").

sophisticated investor — A concept describing one of the requirements of prospective purchasers of securities offered pursuant to the SEC's statutory private offering exemption [Section 4(2) of the 1933 Act]. Such purchasers must have enough knowledge and experience in finance and business matters to evaluate the risks and merits of the investment. For example, the SEC's Regulation D, Rule 506 exemption imposes this limitation on the nature of the purchasers: "Each purchaser who is not an accredited investor either alone or with his purchaser representative(s) has such knowledge and experience in financial and business matters that he is capable of evaluating the merits and risks of the prospective investment, or the issuer reasonably believes immediately prior to making any sale that such purchaser comes within this description." (see "private offering exemption" and "Regulation D").

sound — The recorded auditory portions of a motion picture including speaking, singing, music and noise (see "sound editor" and "sound effects").

sound album materials — All of those physical items associated with the production of a phonograph record of the music and songs heard as part of a motion picture (see "album" and "album cover").

sound editor — The film production person engaged in supervising the making or creating of sound effects and/or the creating or making of such effects and/or engaged in assembling and synchronizing sound effects tracks for the purpose of re-recording, including the synchronizing of re-recorded dialogue tracks to the action in a motion picture (see "picture editor").

sound effects track(s) — The audio track(s) containing only sound effects. These tracks only exist as separate tracks until the final mix of music, sound effects and dialogue into a composite sound track ("sound effects").

sound effects — All artificially created or natural sounds, other than synchronized voices, narration and music, that may be recorded on the sound track of a film. Prior to re-recording, these effects usually occupy a separate sound track or tracks called sound effects track(s); see "sound tracks").

sound facilities — Physical plants where movie sound is transferred, synced, looped, re-recorded and mixed (same as "sound laboratory").

sound laboratory — (see "sound facilities").

sound laboratory agreements — The contracts setting forth the terms under which a sound laboratory is to provide services relating to the production of a motion picture (see "sound facilities").

sound mixer — The film production person responsible for selecting and operating all sound equipment. This person is called a mixer because during film takes that require the use of more than one microphone, he or she mixes (balances level and equalization) between the microphones (level refers to volume; equalization refers to the relative intensity of various frequencies (e.g., treble, mid-range and bass). The mixer is also responsible for monitoring each recording and keeping accurate records on the sound reports (see "mix").

sound, music, effects and dubbing editor — A combined screen credit sometimes used to described a single individual who creates and/or selects, assembles and synchronizes music and all other sound tracks for the purpose of re-recording; times and cues the picture for scoring; prepares click, tempo and cuing tracks; edits sound and synchronizes the various tracks to the movie's action and dialogue; intercuts playback and dubbed music tracks; and creates or uses available sound effects tracks for the purpose of recording (see "effects editor," "music editor," "sound editor" and "supervising sound editor").

sound stage — A large warehouse type facility that is soundproof, contains rigging for lights and cables, provides a generous supply of electrical power, with a smooth floor surface and is available for rent and use in building film sets and producing films (see "studio").

sound stock — Blank tapes for the recording of sound (see "film stock").

sound track — The physical portion of a film where either magnetically or optically recorded audio material is contained. Also, a recording of the musical score from a film (see "dialogue track," "music track," "sound effects track" and "sound track albums").

sound track album advance — Up front compensation paid to a motion picture producer or other person relating to the acquisition of rights to distribute a sound track album for a film (see "sound track album right approval").

sound track album right of approval — The contractually granted authority to approve or disapprove of certain matters relating to the production of a motion picture soundtrack album. Such a provision may appear in a feature film distribution agreement (e.g., the distributor may want to have approval rights, not to be unreasonably withheld, of the record company with which the sound track album for the picture is placed; see "sound track album advance").

sound track albums — Phonograph records, tape recordings and compact discs that contain selected portions of a movie's musical score. Sound track albums represent another possible source of motion picture related revenue (see "ancillary rights").

sound track distribution rights — (see "sound track rights").

sound track rights — The legal power and authority to exploit the sound track of a motion picture (see "sound track albums").

sources of revenue — (see "revenue sources").

spec — Short for speculation (e.g., a film that is produced by an independent producer for marketing to distributors as a finished film is said to have been produced on spec). In other words, the producer is speculating as to whether a distributor will be interested and as to how much such a producer will be paid for the film by a distributor. Many low-budget independent producers also try to persuade persons who provide all sorts of property and services in the production of movies to provide such property and services on spec (i.e., in exchange for a very speculative percentage participation in the movie's net profits). Screenwriters also may write a script on spec (i.e., without knowing whether anyone will option it); see "net profit participant").

special ability extra — Non-speaking atmosphere talent possessing special ability, such as horse riding, handling livestock, professional or collegiate level athletic ability, skating and/or swimming (see "extra" and "silent bit").

special allocations — The treatment given to shares of income, loss, credits, deductions and/or other financial or tax items in the manner described in the operating agreement for a manager-managed LLC or the partnership agreement of a limited partnership.

special effects — Optical effects or tricks used to portray or suggest a spectacle or occurrence in a film that would ordinarily be impractical or impossible. The basis of such effects are typically artificially constructed, as a rule in a studio separate from the main shooting stages. Special effects may include split screens, matting, models and combination foregrounds and backgrounds (contrast with "sound effects").

special effects technician — The film production person responsible to the director for safely and effectively planning and executing all special effects required for a film production (see "special effects").

special handling — Specific film marketing strategies for what may be quality films but that do not have obvious broad commercial appeal. Such strategies include exclusive runs in a limited number of selected theaters, advertising campaigns that appeal to more artistic sensibilities as opposed to a more "hard-sell" approach and keeping such a movie in the marketplace long enough for it to find its audience through word-of-mouth (see "art film," "exclusive run" and "legs").

specialized distribution — Distribution of a film to a limited target audience, in a smaller number of theaters than a commercial distribution, with limited advertising expenditures and a strong emphasis on publicity and critical reviews to reach a discerning public (see "regional release pattern" and "wide release").

specific performance — An equitable remedy available to an aggrieved party when the party's remedy at law is inadequate, consisting of a requirement that the party responsible for a breach of contract undertake to perform or to complete performance of his or her obligations under the contract (see "equity" and "remedy" or "remedies").

spec script — A motion picture screenplay written by a screenwriter who is not writing such screenplay at the request of an employer production company and without any commitment from any prospective purchaser to purchase the screenplay (see "bidding war," "conscious parallelism," "rising production costs," "spec," "work made for hire" and "writer for hire").

speculation — Assumption of risk in anticipation of gain but recognizing a higher than average possibility of loss (see "risk" and "spec").

SPFRE — (see "same percentage as film rental earned").

spin off — A motion picture based on a new television series that incorporates any continuing character or substantial element from the series (see "television series").

splice — The method used for joining together the ends of two pieces of film so that they do not overlap (see "edit").

split — The increase in a corporation's number of outstanding shares of stock without any change in the shareholders' equity or the aggregate market value at the time of the split (see "corporate stock").

split agreement — An agreement reached by exhibitors that allocates among the exhibitors the rights to negotiate for the exhibition of films distributed by motion picture distributors. A split agreement may be either film-by-film (in which the exhibitors take turns selecting films

for their theaters on a film-by-film basis so that no two theaters in the same competitive theater area play the same film simultaneously) or distributor-by-distributor, in which the exhibitors allocate among themselves the rights to negotiate with particular distributors for the licensing of films at particular theaters (same as "product splitting"; see "antitrust laws," "blind bidding" and "unethical business practices").

split of proceeds — A term that could apply to any division of revenues between business entities or individuals involved in a transaction, but which in the motion picture industry is most often used to describe the percentage sharing between the distributor and exhibitor in the balance of gross box office receipts after exhibitor deductions. For example, a fairly typical exhibitor's bid for a long-run engagement of a film may call for the distributor to receive 90 percent of the box office receipts for the first two weeks after a negotiated fixed sum is deducted for house expenses, then after the third week, the distributor's share would begin to decline until the ninth week when it reaches 25 percent. The distributor's share would remain at the 25 percent level through the balance of the engagement. Using this split of proceeds, the exhibitor benefits most if the film stays at the theater for a long period of time (see "blockbuster strategy," "concessions," "house nut," "ninety/ten deal," "selling subject to review," "settlement transaction" and "sliding scale").

split-rights basis — (see "split rights deal").

split-rights deal — A film finance and distribution transaction in which a film's distribution rights are separated as between domestic and international rights. For example, by keeping international rights on a promising film that is pre-packaged and financed, the producer may be able to sell these international rights on an auction basis to the highest bidder. The total price obtained may exceed the actual costs incurred in making the film. In addition, the domestic and international rights are not cross-collateralized (i.e., uncrossed) with respect to the producer. In the event that the film is well received at the box office either in the domestic marketplace or internationally, the producer may earn more overages than in a crossed situation, such as a worldwide negative pickup or production-financing/distribution deal. The producer may also be able to limit the studio/distributor's term of rights in split rights deals (see "distribution term," "fractured rights deals" and "pre-sales").

split-rights pickups — A variation on the single negative pickup distribution agreement for worldwide rights, in which at least two different distribution commitments are obtained from different entities prior to the production of a feature film with the distribution rights being split along domestic and international lines. These contractual commitments are then taken to a bank or other lending source, where the contracts are discounted and production funds are loaned to the producer (see "negative pickup" and "split rights deal").

splitting arrangements — (see "product splitting" and "split agreement").

splitting the screen — (see "screen splitting").

splitting — (see "product splitting" and "split agreement").

sponsor — In limited partnerships, the general partner who organizes and sells the limited partnership interests. With respect to manager-

managed LLCs, that would be the manager. For film offerings the general partner or manager would typically be the producer or production company (also called "promoter").

spot announcements — (see "commercials").

spot market — That portion of the buying and selling of radio and television advertising time for the promotion of motion pictures where purchases of time are made on a selective basis with a specific target audience in mind. Spot market purchases are generally more expensive per minute than the blanket network buys, but the purchase of significantly fewer properly targeted advertising slots can generate savings and may produce better results (see "blanket network buys," "media mix" and "rising production costs").

spots — (see "commercials").

spreading risk — (see "diversification").

spreadsheet — Ledger sheet on which a company's financial statements, such as balance sheets, income statements and sales reports, are laid out in columns and rows (see "financial statement").

squeaky wheel gets the grease — An old saying meaning those who complain or make their positions known are more likely to get the desired attention and favorable treatment as opposed to those who suffer quietly. In the context of the film industry, for example, the major feature film distributors have a well-organized trade group (the MPAA) that provides an aggressive lobbying service for its member firms. The MPAA is generally opposed to the passage of anti-blind bidding statutes by state legislatures and to date the interests of the major distributors have won out over the interests of the independent exhibitors on that question in most state jurisdictions. In addition, the MPAA has successfully lobbied the recent U.S. presidential administrations for continued relaxation of the U.S. Justice Department enforcement of federal antitrust laws in the entertainment industry with the result that some of the major studio/distributors (MPAA member companies) have been able to further vertically integrate by merging with or acquiring corporate affiliations with exhibition chains. In the meantime, the independent producers whose interests are significantly effected by both these and other issues have failed to organize any effective advocacy group to speak up in these various forums on behalf of their interests (see "anti-blind bidding," "antitrust laws," "blind bidding," "FIND," "IFP," "industry groups," "lobbyists," "major exhibition chains," "model agreements," "MPAA," "Paramount Consent Decree of 1948," "Producers Guild of America," "TriStar Case" and "vertical integration").

squeeze-out — In corporate law, any transaction engaged in by the parties in control of a corporation for the purpose of eliminating minority shareholders. In a more general business sense, the gradual elimination of smaller less powerful competitors through the use of anti-competitive business practices (see "anti-competitive business practices," "antitrust laws," "cartel," "independent distributor" and "major studio/distributors").

stabilization — The purchase of securities by the underwriters for their own account during the distribution of an issue, when the market price is at or below the public offering price, in order to keep the price up so purchasers will buy from the underwriters in the offering and not on the open market (see "securities").

staff — The staff on a motion picture project includes everyone but the performers. The crew is regarded as operational staff and others as production staff, although these categories often overlap (see "cast," "crew," "operational staff" and "production staff").

stage agreement — A contract between a feature film production company and a studio setting out the terms under which the production company may use the studio's stage in the production of a film (see "location agreement" and "studio").

staggered board of directors — Corporate board of directors a portion of whom are elected each year, instead of all at once, so that their terms are alternating (see "corporation").

staging — A phase of film rehearsal for the actors in which the action in a given scene is blocked out (see "blocking").

standard contract — A proposed agreement typically offered by the stronger party to a contract negotiation, which purportedly sets out the provisions preferred by that party. This is an often abused and misused term referring to a document that does not exist in reality in any business transaction involving negotiations. Producers should avoid doing business with distributors who suggest that they have a standard contract or that there is a standard contract for the industry or a segment of the industry. Every material term of a contract should be considered negotiable. By contrast, in those segments of the film industry in which guilds are authorized to represent particular individuals, a standard guild contract actually exists, but no guild has been authorized to negotiate on behalf of feature film producers (see "contract of adhesion," "creative accounting," "customary terms," "model agreement," "Producers Guild of America," "professional association" and "letter of agreement").

standard split — An outdated and/or mythical profit sharing ratio between distributors and producers that was once believed to be 70/30 after the distributor deducted all of its distribution expenses. There is no such standard provision in an industry where each distribution deal is negotiated between the specific parties to each deal. Distributors who suggest that such a standard exists are probably hoping to lull a gullible producer into accepting onerous or burdensome provisions solely based on the suggestion that "everybody else finds these terms acceptable," whereas if such a standard split actually existed it might raise antitrust or more specifically price-fixing concerns. Of course, any producer who accepts the notion of a standard split deserves the deal he or she gets (see "minimum film rental," "ninety/ten deal" and "sliding scale").

standards and practices — The guidelines and procedures imposed by the Standards and Practices Departments of the major free television networks on material presented for broadcast. For example, "R" rated feature films are generally not considered in compliance with these more restrictive free television requirements. Film distribution agreements typically require that additional television cover shots be provided on such movies. If such cover shots are not provided and/or the movie does not meet the networks' standards, the film distributor may avoid its obligation to make payments to the producer, refuse to license the film in that market or (in some instances) may be authorized to edit the film itself. In a broader sense, the term "standards and practices" may

also apply to the similar guidelines and procedures of newer networks and the cable media (see "network" and "other versions").

standard terms and conditions — A major section of the typical studio/distributor feature film distribution agreement which sets out the terms and provisions relating to the distribution of a feature film that the studio considers standard. It is important to recognize that what is considered standard for that studio may or may not be standard for another major studio/distributor or for an independent distributor, regardless of the fact that such provisions are often similar (i.e., have been borrowed from each other over time). For example, it would be a violation of the antitrust laws for competitors like the major studio/distributors, even through the facilities of their trade association (the MPAA) to get together and agree on standard terms and conditions. Thus, the phrase "standard terms and conditions" does not necessarily mean that such terms and conditions are standard in the industry, nor should independent producers allow themselves to be led to believe that is the case. In other words, a distributor's standard terms and conditions should also be negotiable. Generally, the studio/distributor distribution agreement will also contain a provision that says "To the extent any terms or conditions of the Standard Terms and Conditions are inconsistent with the Deal Terms, the Deal Terms shall govern." Thus, the studio is setting out in the "standard terms and conditions" section what it would prefer with respect to certain issues and if producers want something different, they need to speak up during the negotiations and ask that the language in the "standard terms and conditions" section be crossed out, modified or otherwise altered or that different language be included in the "deal terms" section of the agreement that overrules the "standard terms and conditions" section (see "antitrust laws," "deal terms," "major studio/distributors," "MPAA" and "squeaky wheel gets the grease").

standby commitment — In securities, an agreement between a corporation and an investment banking firm or group (the standby underwriter) whereby the latter contracts (for a fee) to purchase for resale, any portion of a stock issue offered to current shareholders in a rights offering that is not subscribed to during the two to four week standby period. In lending, a bank commitment to lend money up to a specified amount for a specific period, to be used only in a certain contingency (see "lender financing" and "securities").

standby letter of credit — A non-negotiable, non-transferable (except together with the evidence of indebtedness that it secures) letter of credit, issued by a bank or other financial institution which serves as a guarantor of the indebtedness secured by the letter of credit. A standby letter of credit is payable only if the payor defaults on its obligation to make payments under the contract (see "letter of credit").

star — A leading actor or actress who is well known and constantly publicized. The star has billing above the feature players and sometimes enjoys credit lettering that is larger than the credit of the director or producer, depending on the status of the star at the time (see "marque value," "name actors" and "prima donna").

star commitment — The pledge or promise of a proposed lead actor for a motion picture, either directly or through an agent, to appear in a specified role in the project, assuming certain conditions are met. Such commitments are often used by producers to help raise production funding for a film. Star commitments come in all "shapes and sizes," from oral commitments between friends to legally enforceable letters of intent and pay or play and pay and play contractual commitments (see "director commitment," "letters of intent," "letters of interest," "nominal payments," "package," "packaging," "pay and play" and "pay or play").

star deferments — Any agreed upon delayed salary arrangement for a lead actor in a movie. Some actors have been known to delay all or a portion of their negotiated salaries to be paid out of first monies received by a studio/distributor or by the producer in order to help in making the limited available production funds for a special project cover the other costs of production (see "contingent compensation" and "deferrals").

star properties — Feature film projects that are considered excellent vehicles for certain high-profile lead actors or actresses. Some industry observers suggest that competition among the major studio/distributors for star properties has resulted in a studio give away of most of the upside potential of such motion pictures to those stars or to the independently financed production companies that sometimes rent the distribution systems of the major studio/distributors for distribution purposes (see "bidding war," "rent-a-distributor" and "star").

start-date — The projected calendar date on or about which the production of a planned motion picture will begin. A "start date" will almost always be included in production-financing/distribution agreements and negative pickup agreements and will, in both cases, signify the beginning of the specified production schedule and the time when production funds begin to flow from the financing source to the production company as per the projected cash flow schedule. Such dates are also important for obtaining the more formal star commitments. On the other hand, setting a start-date for an independently produced film is always risky unless and until the financing is in place (see "delivery date," "production schedule," "projected cash flow schedule" and "star commitment").

start-up — A new business venture. In venture capital terminology, start-up is the earliest stage at which a venture capital investor or investment pool will provide funds to an enterprise, usually on the basis of a business plan detailing the background of the management group along with market and financial projections, all paired with an appropriate investment vehicle. Investments or loans made at this stage are called seed money (see "business plan," "financial projections," "seed money" and "venture capital").

start-up costs — Expenses necessary to start a new business, incurred prior to commencement of active business operations. The extent of such costs and their status for tax purposes are important to an investor, since they may not be currently recoverable as tax deductions. However, if the taxpayer so elects, trade or business start-up expenses may be amortized (i.e., deducted ratably) over a period of at least sixty months beginning with the month the trade or business begins. There are three types of trade or business start-up expenditures: (1) investigatory expenses for seeking and investigating the feasibility of acquiring or establishing an active trade or business, (2) establishing an active trade or business and (3) activities engaged in for profit or for the production of income before the day on which the trade or business begins, in anticipation of such activities becoming an active trade or business. These taxation rules may be different for certain film projects due to the changes included in the new Section 181 of the IRS Code (see "organizational expenses," "Section 181 of the IRS Code" and "syndication expenses").

star vehicles — (see "star properties").

stated value — The assigned value given to a corporation's stock for accounting purposes in lieu of par value (see "no-par stock" and "par").

state legislatures — The branch of state governments that passes state laws. The issue of blind bidding or anti-blind bidding statutes is a matter that is brought before the state legislatures as opposed to the U.S. Congress, thus those proponents and opponents of blind bidding must lobby with state legislators. Also, unless preempted by the National Securities Market Improvement Act, most securities offerings are subject to the jurisdiction of state and federal laws (see "anti-blind bidding statutes," "blind bidding," "blue sky laws" and "lobbying").

state supported funding — (see "government subsidies").

statute of limitations — A law that establishes a time within which parties to a contract or transaction must take judicial action to enforce their rights or else they will be forever barred from enforcing them in court (see "audit," "litigation" and "remedy").

statutory lien — A charge, hold, claim or encumbrance upon the property of another as security for some debt or charge that is imposed or created by statute (see "lien").

stereotypical portrayal — The presentation of people or things in a motion picture in a manner that is consistent with a standardized mental picture that is held in common by members of a group and that represents an oversimplified opinion, prejudiced attitude or uncritical judgment. Hollywood motion pictures are known to contain patterns of bias (i.e., the consistent portrayal of various populations in a stereotypical or negative manner; see "patterns of bias" and "propaganda").

step deal — A form of feature film development agreement between a producer (writer and/or director) and studio/distributor whereby the decisions to proceed are made and payments to the producer (writer and/or director) coincide each stage of development of the film's screenplay. The first step might involve developing an outline of the screenplay, the second step might involve developing a first draft of the script and so forth. The studio will have the right to decline to develop the project beyond any given stage, if it so chooses (see "development" and "turnaround").

still — (see "production still").

still photographer — The film production person responsible to the producer and/or publicist for taking production stills on a movie set or in association with a film production (see "production still").

stock — Negative film that has not been exposed (see "film").

stock — (see "corporate stock").

stock certificate — Written instrument evidencing a share in the ownership of a corporation and showing the number of shares owned, name of the issuer, amount of par or stated value represented or a declaration of no-par value, the rights of the shareholder and signature of the president and sometimes the secretary (see "partnership certificate").

stock dividend — Payment of corporate dividends in the form of stock rather than cash and as additional shares in either the corporation or a subsidiary (see "corporate stock").

stock exchange — A market maintained for the purpose of buying and selling securities (see "publicly held," "regional stock exchanges" and "securities").

stock footage — Exposed film of scenes or past events that can be duplicated and incorporated into a new production. Stock footage is used when needed shots are too expensive, difficult or impossible to recreate (see "film").

stock fraud — In the sale or offer of corporate stocks, the intentional misrepresentation, concealment or omission of the truth, for the purpose of deception or manipulation to the detriment of an investor or prospective investor. It would appear that the failure of any feature film studio/distributor or independent distributor that is publicly or even privately owned by shareholders, to disclose that they engage in many of the practices described herein (if in fact such is the case), might constitute stock fraud. It is also possible that the publication of this list of distributor/industry practices might create a greater need for stock brokers who offer or sell the stocks of studio distributors, independent distributors or other film industry corporations, to conduct more thorough due diligence investigations of such entities before offering their stocks, otherwise the stock brokers themselves may be exposed to greater liability based on their failure to discover and disclose such practices which could be detrimental to the interests of the investor clients of the stock brokers. This compilation may also encourage closer scrutiny by shareholders of the manner in which a film distributor operates and could conceivably prompt shareholder lawsuits in instances where such practices seem to be prevalent and harmful to such shareholders (see "creative accounting" and "due diligence").

stockholder — Individual or organization with an equity ownership interest in a corporation. Stockholders must own at least one share. The shareholders of corporate entities may be individuals or other corporations. Some corporate conglomerates that have purchased equity ownership interests in motion picture production companies and/or distributors where a certain level of autonomy for the existing management remains intact as part of the deal have been somewhat disappointed in the financial results of their investment. In other words, even though the entertainment entity operates at an acceptable level of profitability, for various reasons, the profits do not always seem to flow through to the equity shareholders (also called "shareholder" or "shareowner"; see "corporate stock," "dividend," "greed," "mergers and acquisitions," "profitability" and "rising production costs").

stockholder of record — Common or preferred stockholder whose name is registered on the books of a corporation as owning shares as of a particular date. Dividends and other distributions are made only to shareholders of record (see "corporate stock").

stock market — An organized market where stocks and bonds are actively traded such as stock exchanges or over-the-counter markets (see "corporate stock" and "stock exchange").

stock redemption agreement — A contract between a corporation and an investor for the repayment of a debt security or preferred stock issue at or before maturity, at par or at a premium price (see "redeemable security," "redemption" and "stock").

stonewall defense — A position taken by a prospective defendant in negotiations between parties designed to avoid litigation in which the defendant simply says "see you in court." The tort of "bad faith denial of contract" seeks to provide a recovery based on a defendant's bad faith conduct in asserting a stonewall defense to an ordinary commercial contract (see "bad faith denial of contract," "probable cause" and "sue us").

story — Literary or dramatic material setting forth the characterization of the principal characters and containing cohesive sequences and action constituting a plot or suitable for use in, or representing a substantial contribution to, a final script (see "plot").

story analyst — An employee of a studio or film production company in the story department, who reads and analyzes literary material such as screenplays, treatments, magazine articles and books submitted to the story department and who prepares synopses of such material for review by the story analyst's supervisor who is usually called the story editor. Stories that are to be selected and developed into screenplays by the studio or film production company are reviewed initially by the story analyst (see "coverage," "development notes" and "story editor").

story board — Sketches or drawings of key incidents in the action described by a movie screenplay that are arranged in order on a board or boards and captioned. Story boards often play an important role in preparing a shooting schedule and otherwise in planning for principal photography. Some producers rely more heavily than others on story boards (see "pre-production").

story by — The screen credit awarded the person who developed a film's story but did not write the screenplay (see "screenplay by" and "written by").

story development — (see "development").

story driven — A motion picture or screenplay that has a well-developed story line as one of its strongest elements, as opposed to certain more exploitative fare that places less emphasis on the story and develops a motion picture centered more around violence, sex, nudity or other such factors (see "elements").

story editor — A supervisor of several story analysts in a movie studio or film production company's story department who reviews the synopses prepared by the story analysts and makes recommendations to the company's production vice presidents as to whether the literary property should be acquired and/or developed (see "story analyst").

storyline — The basic points that form the continuity of a screenplay (see "narrative").

straight employment agreement — The written

contract made directly between an individual (e.g., a feature film director), and the motion picture production company that is hiring such individual, without the intervention of a third entity such as a loan-out company (see "lending agreement" and "three-party agreement").

straight-line depreciation — Method of depreciating (recovering the cost through tax deductions) a fixed asset whereby the asset's useful life is divided into the total cost less the estimated salvage value. The resulting annual depreciation expense is charged against income before figuring income taxes (contrast with "accelerated cost recovery"; also see "income forecast method").

strategic planning — The design of and activities relating to the critical components involved in the manner of operating a business (see "financial management").

street date — The date on which videocassette or DVD copies of a movie are made available for rental or purchase at the retail video stores (see "video/DVD revenue reporting").

strike — The dismantling of a movie set after shooting has been completed. Also, a work stoppage by union members to enforce compliance with demands made on the employer. And, to create a print from a negative (see "de facto strike" and "no strike, no lockout clause").

strip board — (see "story board").

strong package — A proposed film for which many of the elements have been developed and/or committed and the film's elements appear to be very commercial or of a high quality, including commitments from well-known actors and creative talent (see "elements" and "packaging").

student film agreement — A Screen Actors Guild agreement that permits SAG actors to defer 100 percent of their salaries if they perform in student films for students enrolled in film school. Such films must be shot entirely in the U.S. (see "low budget agreement," "modified low budget agreement," "Screen Actors Guild," "short film agreement" and "ultra-low budget agreement").

studio — Technically speaking, the term studio refers to the organization which owns and provides (for film production company use) the physical locations and other facilities including sound stages, sets, prop departments, offices, commissaries, etc. for development, pre-production, production and post-production of feature films. There are in fact studios that only provide such facilities and related services. On the other hand, some of the vertically integrated major studio/distributors also function as production companies and have studio facilities, and over the years, have been commonly referred to as "major studios" or "studios," thus the term has come to include the major studio/distributors and other film production companies that prefer to be called studios (see "lot," "major studio/distributors," "set" and "studio lots").

studio accounting practices — Various methods of accounting for motion picture revenues that have long been alleged to be unfair. Such methods include the practice of charging unauthorized and excessive expenses to a given film being produced at the studio; the rolling break-even that keeps rolling just beyond net profits; and unfair overhead charges imposed by the studio on net profit participants. In other words, the studio has the books and records, it interprets the production/distribution agreement, it computes the profit and it decides how much should be paid. Industry insiders have long maintained that there is a certain amount of inadvertent and some intentional abusive or unconscionable accounting practices regularly occurring at the studios (see "creative accounting," "improperly claimed expenses," "overreported travel" and "unconscionable").

studio approvals — The negotiated items over which a major studio/distributor has the right to approve or disapprove in the context of a feature film distribution agreement. As a general rule, the more money a producer tries to get from a studio, the more approvals a studio is likely to impose. Such approvals typically relate to the screenplay, budget, producer, director, lead performers, start date, running time, MPAA ratings, locations and production schedule (see "negative pickup" and "production-financing distribution agreement").

studio financing — The funding of the production costs of a film by a major studio/distributor. As with any form of film finance, studio financing offers some advantages along with some disadvantages. Also, certain small films or low budget films are generally not considered suitable for studio financing regardless of the advantages or disadvantages. Projects generally accepted for studio financing must have a fairly broad commercial appeal (see "financing," "in-house product," "investor financing," "lender financing" and "production-financing/distribution agreement").

studio guaranteed loan — A bank loan for the production of a motion picture that has been guaranteed by a major studio/distributor (see "negative pickup").

studio lots — The physical locations and other facilities including sound stages, sets, prop departments, offices, commissaries, etc. that are available to be used by in-house or independent production companies or producers for development, pre-production, production and post-production of films (see "major" and "studio/distributors").

studio overhead — (see "overhead," "overhead costs" and "production overhead").

studio producer — A feature film producer who works as an employee of a studio on in-house productions (see "associate producer," "creative producer," "executive producer," "independent producer," "in-house product," "line producer," "producer" and "Producers Guild of America").

studio production — A motion picture produced as an in-house production at a major studio/distributor (i.e., the studio has acquired the rights to the screenplay either from its inception or at an early stage in its development and has financed the production of the film; contrast with "production-financing/distribution agreement," "negative pickup" and "acquisition").

studio rental — The payments made by a production company to a studio for the use of studio facilities in the production of a motion picture (see "stage agreement").

studio security agreement — A written contract between a studio/distributor financier of a motion picture's development and production costs and the film's producer that provides, as consideration for the monetary advances made by the studio/distributor for the development of the project, that the studio/distributor has a security interest in the production company's script and the underlying literary property (see "collateral" and "security agreement").

stunt — The dangerous leaps and falls from tall buildings, car or boat chases and crashes, fast and trick horseback riding, fights, etc. performed during the production of a motion picture (see "stunt coordinator" and "stunt person").

stunt coordinator — The film production person responsible to a film's director for safely and effectively planning and executing all stunts required for a film production (see "stunt").

stunt person — The performer who actually performs the stunts in place of the film's principal actors (also called "stand-in"; see "stunt").

STV — (see "subscription television").

style — In music, a distinctive or characteristic mode of presentation, construction or execution (see "lyrics" and "music").

subchapter s corporation — (see "S Corp").

sub-distributor — In theatrical releases, distributors who handle a specific, limited geographic territory for a film (i.e., territorial distributors who have contracted to represent an independent distribution company). Sub-distributors sometimes sub-contract with the main distributor who co-ordinates the distribution plans and marketing for all the sub-distributors of a film. Since sub-distributors handle a limited territory or "exchange," they generally have an excellent working knowledge of their markets. However, they are paid a commission for booking a film and this system of sub-distribution often makes it difficult to audit the independent distributors. The use of sub-distributors also creates the possibility of double distribution fees (see "audit," "distributor," "double distribution fees," "film exchanges," "franchised sub-distributor," "supervision fee" and "sub-distribution").

sub-distributor fees — The compensation paid out of a film's revenue stream to sub-contractors who distribute the film in a limited geographical area. Major studio/distributors do not generally use the services of sub-distributors. Independent distributors, on the other hand, do typically use the services of sub-distributors and sometimes the sub-distributor for an independent distributor is a major studio/distributor. Sub-distributor fees may be computed in a variety of ways, depending upon the contractual provisions negotiated by the producer and the actual distributor as such provisions are expressed in the distribution agreement. Such fees may be included in the distributor's fee or be paid in addition to the distributor's fee, or may be computed based on some projected level of gross receipts (see "absorption arrangement," "cap," "double distribution fees," "override," "pass through arrangement" and "sub-distributor").

sub-distribution — The distribution of a film in limited markets or territories through the facilities of a distributor that has been sub-contracted by the film's primary distributor (see "double distribution fee," "override," "pass-through," "sub-distributor" and "supervision fee").

sub-head — A secondary headline in a motion picture advertisement utilized to stimulate additional reader interest and/or communicate more of the film's thematic appeal (see "headline").

subjective terms — Words or expressions used in contracts that are subject to or likely to be interpreted differently by different individuals, as opposed to more objective terms whose meaning may be more readily agreed upon. Subjective terms should be clearly defined or eliminated in the negotiation of such contracts (e.g., usual and customary practices in the industry; see "creative accounting," "ordinary course of business" and "takeover").

sub-key — A geographical area with a population of approximately 25,000 to 50,000, denoted by the geographical area's historical ability to produce film rental income for distributors; a sub-key's theater or theaters break a film after the near-by keys have exhibited that film (see "key," "major key" and "ordinary key").

submission letter — A written communication accompanying a screenplay that is being submitted to a production company or studio in search of development or production funding (see "submission release").

submission release — A written agreement that producers and/or production companies sometimes require to be signed by screenwriters or others submitting literary material to the producer/production company for consideration as the basis for producing a motion picture. Typically, in such submission releases the screenwriter is asked to give up his or her rights to make certain claims against the producer/production company. Some of the submission releases drafted and used by the major studio/distributors and other production companies in the industry today are ridiculously one-sided (see "contracts of adhesion," "non-disclosure agreement," "overreaching," "release," "unconscionable contract," "unsolicited material").

subordinated — Junior in claim on assets to other debt (i.e., repayable only after other debts with a higher claim have been satisfied). A bank, for example, may agree to subordinate its interest in the repayment of a movie production loan to a principal talent's right to deferred compensation (see "asset," "debt" and "lender financing").

subordination — To give one claim or debt a lower priority in relation to another claim or debt (see "subordinated").

sub-plot — A subordinated or secondary story-line in a motion picture or screenplay (see "favorable portrayal," "plot" and "unfavorable portrayal").

sub-run — (same as "subsequent run").

sub-run markets — (see "sub-run theater").

sub-run theater — A theater that primarily exhibits films on such film's subsequent runs and/or exhibits exploitation films (see "subsequent run").

sub-S-corporation — (see "S corp").

subsequent run — Any continuous exhibition of a motion picture in a designated geographic area for a specified period of time after the film's first run (see "sub-run theater").

subscriber — An investor in a limited partnership or manager-managed LLC; also a person who has agreed to take and pay for the original unissued shares of a corporation or other securities (see "subscription application and agreement").

subscription application agreement — A document included as part of the separate packet accompanying a limited partnership, manager-managed LLC or corporate stock offering memorandum that each person desiring to become a unit holder must complete, execute, acknowledge and deliver to the representative of the securities issuer, before being accepted as a unit or share holder. This document serves as both the subscriber (investor/purchaser) application to purchase the security and his/her/its agreement with the issuer (see "security" or "securities").

subscription documents — (see "subscription application and agreement" and "subscription materials").

subscription materials — In a securities offering, the documents included in a separate packet accompanying the securities disclosure document (sometimes re-printed as an exhibit and bound up in the memorandum, as a sample). For private offerings, the subscription materials generally include a purchaser questionnaire, purchaser representative questionnaire, subscription application, and corporate resolution. The subscription materials for a private offering may be fifteen pages in length, whereas the subscription application for a public offering is generally only one or two pages (also called "subscription documents"; see "limited partnership," "manager-managed LLC" and "securities").

subscription price — The price at which existing shareholders of a corporation are entitled to purchase common shares in a rights offering or at which subscription warrants are exercisable (see "subscription right").

subscription right — Privilege granted existing shareholders of a corporation to subscribe to shares of a new issue of common stock before it is offered to the public (see "rights offering").

subscription television — A pay-television program service that for a fee transmits scrambled television signals from a television station to television sets in a limited geographical area and only those sets that have a device capable of decoding the scrambled signal are able to view the programming. The television signal utilized may be UHF or VHF (see "cable television" and "pay-per-view").

subscription warrant — A type of security, usually issued together with a bond or preferred stock, that entitles the holder to buy a proportionate amount of common stock at a specified price, usually higher than the market price at the time of issuance, for a period of years or in perpetuity (also called "warrant").

subsidiaries — Companies of which more than 50 percent of the voting shares are owned by another corporation, called the parent corporation (see "affiliate" and "parent corporation").

subsidiary corporation — A corporation in which another corporation owns at least a majority of the shares and thus has control (see "holding company" and "parent corporation").

subsidies — (see "film subsidies," "foreign subsidies," "grants" and "government subsidies").

substantial performance — The performance of all the essential terms of a contract so that the purpose of the contract is accomplished. Unimportant omissions and technical defects may occur in the performance of the contract (see "contract" and "material").

substitution clause or agreement — A provision in a movie distribution agreement in which the distributor agrees to allow the producer to substitute another distributor under certain circumstances, including the payment of a substitution fee and the reimbursement of the distributor's expenses to date. Such provisions are more likely to appear in distribution agreements with small distributors and are included so as to protect the producer who may produce a movie that is desired by a much stronger distributor who can provide a wider release and more distributor support. Usually, such provision will require that the original distributor's expenses be reimbursed, that a substitution fee be paid and sometimes a percentage participation is retained. To some extent, the substitution clause, serves a purpose similar to the turnaround provision in a studio deal (see "reversion provision and agreement," "substitution fee" and "turnaround provision and agreement").

substitution fee — A sum charged by a distributor for the producer's privilege of substituting another distributor pursuant to a substitution clause in a film distribution agreement (see "substitution clause or agreement").

subtitle — A written presentation of the translation from one language to another of the movie characters' dialogue that appears on the lower part of the screen (see "dialogue replacement").

suburban venue — A theater located in an outlying part of a city (see "major markets").

successful film — A subjective term that generally refers to the financial success of a motion picture and at least implies that the film's distributor made a profit on the film. A film may be financially successful for a distributor but not for the producer (aside from the producer's fee paid out of the film's budget) or other net profit participants, including investors or other financiers, who must look to their possible participation in net profits for their return on investment (see "blockbuster," "bomb," "hit" and "sleeper").

successor — One who assumes the place of another and fulfills his, her or its role or continues in the position. A corporate successor is a corporation that takes on the burdens and assumes the rights of a predecessor corporation by merger, acquisition or other valid legal succession (also see "assigns," "personal representative" and "remedy" or "remedies").

sue us — A phrase that is descriptive of the attitude and "business as usual" tactic of some film studio/distributors and other distributors in their dealings with producers and other net profit participants, and that is used when the producer inquires about his or her share of net profits following the distribution of a film. Such distributors take the position that any net profits due the producer will not be voluntarily paid to the producer, thus the producer must audit, make demand and ultimately sue in order to be paid. Even then the distributor will generally settle out of court for less than was originally owed. In many instances, the producer (or other profit participant) will choose not to sue for fear of being blacklisted among Hollywood distributors. So what's to keep a distributor from

using this tactic? Nothing at the moment. Among other things, an association of independent feature film producers must be created to monitor such unfair business tactics, make its members more aware of the practices and contractual provisions that improve the producer's position, publicly expose the consistent use of such tactics on the part of any distributor and/or pursue legislative, regulatory and other remedies to help level the playing field in the film industry (see "blacklist," "creative accounting," "leverage," "lobbyists," "overreaching" and "stonewall defense").

suit — Any proceeding in a court of justice through which an individual pursues a remedy afforded by the law (see "action" and "remedy" or "remedies").

suitability questionnaires — Questionnaires used by issuers and broker/dealers in securities offerings to elicit information from prospective investors so that such issuers and/or broker/dealers can determine whether such prospective investors meet the investor suitability standards established for such securities offering (see "investor suitability standards").

suitability rules — (see "investor suitability standards").

sum certain — Any amount that is fixed, settled, stated or exact (see "debt" and "lender financing").

summary of the offering — A synopsis of the disclosures in a securities offering, typically set out in a three or page presentation at the beginning of the disclosure document. Pursuant to SEC interpretations of Regulation D, a summary of the offering may be circulated to prospective investors prior to the more complete offering memorandum (see "program highlights" and "Regulation D").

summer season — The most important season for the theatrical exhibition of feature films. The Christmas holidays are the second most desirable release time. Most independent distributors will avoid these two most important release periods because the major studio/distributors usually tie up all of the best play dates at the most desirable theaters during these periods (see "anti-competitive business practices," "antitrust laws" and "prime release dates").

Sundance Film Festival — Annual film festival held in Park City, Utah late in January and often promoted as the foremost platform for American independent cinema (see "film festivals").

Sundance Institute — A film organization founded partly through the efforts of Robert Redford, with offices in Los Angeles and facilities in Utah, and supported by contributions from industry entities. The institute has a script development program, in which an experienced screenwriter or story editor will work with a producer on polishing the producer's script, and a production assistance program through which funds are available for completion guarantees, short-term pre-production loans and co-producer services. Sundance also sponsors an annual producer's conference at its Utah facility (see "independent producer").

supered titles (superimposed titles) — Titles that appear over stationary or moving backgrounds (see "super-imposing").

super-imposing — The act of preparing movie titles so that they appear over stationary or moving backgrounds (see "supered titles").

supervising editor — The person engaged in any or all of the defined duties of a film's editor in addition to being responsible for the work of any other editor or editors working on a given production (see "editor").

supervising sound editor — The person responsible for overseeing the editors who work on all audio material other than music (see "sound editor").

supervision — With respect to securities law compliance, an important function of SEC/NASD broker/dealer firms relating to their registered representatives (i.e., sales executives). Individual registered representatives are not permitted to engage in private securities transactions (i.e., not reviewed and approved in advance by the supervising broker/dealer firm; see "NASD," "private securities transaction" and "SEC").

supervision fee — The difference between the distribution fees charged by a primary distributor and a sub-distributor that the primary distributor retains as its distribution fee for the market or territories handled by the sub-distributor (see "double distribution fees," "override," "pass-through," "sub-distributor" and "sub-distribution").

supplementary collateral — Security for a loan that is supplementary to primary collateral (i.e., an additional pledge of asset collateral, such as raw land, home equity, automobiles, stocks, bonds, coin collections, interests in other films or literary properties). Some banks may accept the producer's share of gross receipts as supplementary collateral to foreign and cable pre-sales if the distribution contract guarantees a sufficient number of prints, ads and quality theaters (see "collateral" and "negative pickup").

supplementary markets — Certain media for the exploitation of a motion picture, sometimes defined in a feature film distribution agreement as pay, cable and subscription television, as well as audio-visual cassettes/DVDs, discs and similar devices for transmission of audio and visual images, whether now known or hereafter devised (see "ancillary markets" and "secondary ancillary rights").

supply and demand — (see "law of supply and demand").

support — When used as a verb, to maintain or provide backing for. In the film industry, the term is commonly used to describe the prints and ads commitment made by the film's distributor (i.e., a reference to the level of support the distributor is providing for a given film; see "prints and ads commitment").

support advertising — The promotional activities designed to increase the awareness and desire in a potential audience group to see a given movie (see "advertising" and "support").

supporting player — A secondary leading actor or actress in a film (see "actor" and "bit player").

support materials — The items developed by a film distributor with the film's producer that are used to promote the film prior to and during its release. Such materials may include a press kit, cast photos, production stills, biographical information on the principals, favorable reviews or feature articles about the film, a one-sheet or poster, print ads, theater lobby displays and the trailer (see "press kit" and "trailer").

surety — An individual or business that undertakes to pay money or perform other acts in the event that the involved principal fails to do so. The surety is directly and immediately liable for the debt or performance. A film completion bond is a form of surety (see "completion bond," "completion guarantor" and "guaranty").

surety bond — A bond issued by one party, the surety, guaranteeing that he, she or it will perform certain acts promised by another (the principal) or pay a stipulated sum, up to the bond limit, in lieu of performance, should the principal fail to perform. Surety bonds are issued to film producers seeking to assure lenders that their films will be completed on time and under budget (see "completion bond" and "completion guarantor").

sweetener — A feature added to a securities offering to make it more attractive to prospective purchasers; also an inducement to a brokerage firm to enter into an underwriting arrangement with an issuer (see "equity kicker").

symphony — An orchestral composition that today usually contains four movements and is played by an orchestra (see "symphony orchestra").

symphony orchestra — A large orchestra of winds, strings and percussion that plays symphonic works (see "orchestra").

sync or synch — (see "synchronism" and "in synch").

synchronism — The relation between picture and sound on film with respect either to the physical location on the film or to the time at which corresponding picture and sound are seen and heard (i.e., picture and sound are in sync or out of sync; see "composite" and "in synch").

synchronization — The timing of the picture and sound on a feature film so that they coincide properly (see "looping").

synchronization license — The right expressed in a written agreement to use musical compositions as part of the soundtrack of a motion picture or television film in synchronization with visual images (see "sychronization").

synchronization rights — The legal power and authority to use musical compositions as part of the soundtrack of a motion picture or television film (see "synchronization").

synchronous sound — Sound in a motion picture that directly corresponds to the proper image on the film (see "asynchronous sound").

sync pulse — A timing device; a sixty-second pulse used to keep the sound and image on motion picture film in sync (see "SMPTE time code").

syndicate — The investment bankers who together underwrite and distribute an offering of securities (see "purchase group" and "selling group").

syndicate manager — (see "managing underwriter").

syndicated films — Motion pictures that are licensed for use by individual television stations

or cable systems for exhibition in their own local markets. Films are usually packaged by their distributors as a group for television syndication. There are some two hundred plus television syndication markets in the U.S. The syndication of films may create an allocation issue with respect to how the fee paid for syndication rights is allocated among the various films in the syndication package. Generally, a rather arbitrary syndication formula is imposed on the producers of the various films in the package by the distributor and the application of this formula does not vary from market to market. Producers may want to negotiate for an approval right over any such syndication formula used by a distributor on that producer's film when and if it is included in a syndicated package (see "allocation," "package" and "syndication").

syndicated television — (see "film package," "syndication" and "television syndication").

syndication — In the film and television industry, the process whereby previously exhibited or recorded material is reused by or licensed to a collection of buyers such as independent television stations, usually on a regional basis. In film finance, the selling of interests in film limited partnerships or manager-managed LLCs, usually formed to finance a single or a multiple slate of films (see "film package," "joint venture," "limited liability company" and "limited partnership").

syndication agreement — A contract between a film's producer or distributor for the licensing of motion pictures (generally a group of movies) to non-network, or independent, free television stations for broadcast to the general public (see "syndicated films").

syndication expenses — In the context of a film limited partnership or manager-managed LLC offering, expenses paid or incurred in connection with the issuing and marketing of interests in the LP or LLC, including brokerage fees and selling commissions, if any, state notice ("blue sky") filing fees, legal fees of the issuer for attorney preparation of the securities disclosure document and consultations relating to the requirements of the applicable federal and state securities laws, accounting fees, if any, for preparation of financial projections to be included in the offering materials and printing/binding costs of such offering materials. Unlike other expenses (and pursuant to the older deductibility rules), syndication expenses may not be deducted currently or amortized over a period of time, as in the case of partnership organizational expenses unless the investors make a Section 181 election (see "offering expenses," "organizational expenses," "partnership expenses," "selling expenses" and "start-up costs").

syndication revenue — Income generated through the packaging and selling of motion picture rights to independent television stations (see "syndication").

syndication version — A copy of a film that is suitable for exploitation on independent free television (see "other versions" and "U.S. theatrical cut").

synopsis — A short narrative or preliminary version of a motion picture script or a summary of a completed film (see "one-line description," "basic story outline," "outline" and "treatment").

systematic risk — That part of a security's risk that is common to all securities of the same general class and thus cannot be eliminated by diversification (also called "market risk").

synthetic music — Electronic music (see "programmed music").

tag line — The audio and/or video information provided at the conclusion of a radio or television spot announcement advertising a movie that tells the audience in what theaters the movie is or will be showing (see "body copy").

take — A single, continuous exposure of film made by a motion picture camera. A director may require several takes of a given shot (see "cover shot," "shot" and "scene").

take it or leave it — A position often taken by the more powerful party in the negotiation of an agreement when the weaker party seeks to change language favored by the more powerful party who takes the position that the agreement is acceptable the way it is and if the other party does not like it, he, she or it should just walk away from the deal (i.e., no further negotiation of that provision or the entire agreement will occur). Such a position is an element in determining whether an agreement is considered an adhesion contract. Film distributors who are often the stronger party in contract negotiations commonly use this as a negotiating tactic (see "adhesion contract" and "fully negotiated agreement").

takeover — The assumption of control over the production of a motion picture by a financier (i.e., studio) or a representative of a lender (i.e.,

completion guarantor). A production-financing/distribution agreement will typically set out the studio's takeover rights. For example, if, based on the information available, including, but not limited to, the weekly reports furnished by the production company, the distributor reasonably believes that the estimated cost of production of the picture will exceed the contingency, the studio may enter into negotiations with the production company in an effort to come up with a plan designed to reduce the projected negative costs, but if not successful the studio may take over primary responsibility for the continued production of the picture. With respect to a completion guarantor takeover the completion bond company may assert its contractual rights to assume responsibility for completing the film if the producer defaults in some way (e.g., goes over-budget or does not complete the film on time). Generally, the event that triggers the takeover rights of the completion guarantor is the subjective judgment of its on-site representative that the film is going over budget (see "completion bond," "reduction plan" and "subjective terms").

takeover rights — The power and authority of the completion bond company to assume responsibility for completing a motion picture in accordance with the terms of the completion guarantee (see "completion bond" and "takeover").

talent — As opposed to the crew on a film, any person or animal working as an on-camera performer. Some definitions of this term include off-camera performers and are so broad as to include all of those involved in the artistic aspects of filmmaking (i.e., writers, actors, directors, etc.) as opposed to the people involved on the business side of motion pictures (see "above-the-line," "actor," "actress," "director" and "screenwriter").

talent participations — Financial interests of writers, directors and/or actors who negotiate a percentage of a film's earnings at some specific level of the film's revenue stream. Such participations are commonly expressed as points, which generally refers to a percentage of the film's net profits, although technically "points" may be defined in relation to a number of different types of gross, such as distributor's gross, gross receipts, adjusted gross or film rentals. Net points may also be defined at different levels of return, such as the producer's net or partnership net for films financed by means of a limited partnership (see "adjusted gross," "gross," "net points," "net profits" and "percentage participation" or "points").

talent participation deals — (see "talent participations").

tangible asset — Assets having physical existence, plus others, like accounts receivable, that accountants have determined to be tangible (contrast with "intangible assets").

tape — A thin strip of plastic film coated with iron oxide or more sophisticated coating that is used in reproducing sound by means of the magnetic arrangement of sound patterns on the tape and in recording and playing back audio and video materials (see "video tape").

target audience — (same as "primary audience"; see "projected audience").

target market — A specific audience segment a producer and/or distributor seeks to reach with a film and its advertising and promotion campaign (e.g., teenagers; see "primary audience" and "target marketing").

target marketing — A marketing technique used in film marketing that is designed to be implemented after a movie has been analyzed and its various target markets have been identified. As part of the analysis, the distributor or marketing entity must answer the following questions: (1) is each target group of sufficient size, (2) will a reasonable percentage of the group be likely to respond to the marketing campaign, (3) are advertising vehicles available to reach each such group and (4) will their projected attendance level at the theater where the motion picture is to be exhibited be sufficient to generate enough revenue to justify the expense of that particular marketing campaign (see "marketing," "primary audience" and "target audience").

tariff — Tax on imported and exported goods; a customs duty (see "custom duties" and "tax").

tax — A rate or sum of money assessed on a person or property for the support of various levels of government. Certain taxes and associated costs are paid by a film distributor as a category of distribution expenses and this category as defined in the typical film distribution deal is rather broad. Included are taxes and governmental fees of any nature and however characterized, including costs of contesting, interest and penalties thereon (other than the distributor's or any sub-distributor's corporate income taxes), imposed directly or indirectly on the picture of any part thereof (including without limitation, the employer's share of payroll taxes with respect to deferred or contingent compensation) or on the gross receipts or the license, distribution or exhibition of the picture or collection, conversion or remittance of monies connected therewith (see "foreign tax credits," "income tax" and "tax opinion").

taxable income — The amount of income (after all allowable deductions and adjustments to income have been made) subject to tax; the amount applied to the rate of income tax in order to determine the income tax payable (see "income tax").

taxable year — The period during which the income tax liability of an individual or entity is incurred, or, in the case of certain non-taxable entities, such as limited partnerships or manager-managed LLCs, the period for which tax information is provided (see "K-1").

tax advantages — (see "tax benefits").

tax aspects — (same as "federal tax discussion").

tax basis — The original cost of an asset, less accumulated depreciation, that goes into the calculation of a gain or loss for tax purposes (see "basis" and "income tax").

tax benefits — Various useful or profitable tax provisions made available by governments in order to encourage certain types of investments. Such provisions may come in the form of immediate deductions of certain costs, the rapid

recovery of others, tax credits, deferrals or preferences. Tax benefits can only enhance the economic viability of an investment. They cannot provide economic substance to a transaction that otherwise lacks such viability. With passage of the Tax Reform Act of 1986, the U.S. government eliminated the investment tax credit which had been successfully utilized by film limited partnerships (and other types of investments) as an extra incentive for investors and also limited the use of limited partnership deductions by virtue of the passive loss rules. However, the fact that the limited partnership and manager-managed LLC are not taxable entities themselves is still a significant tax advantage in favor of these investment vehicles as compared to the regular "C" corporation and some portion of the production costs of the film will still be available to investors in the entity as deductible expenses (also called "tax advantages" and "tax incentives"; see "depreciation," "income forecast method," "ordinary expense," "necessary expense," "Section 181 of the IRS Code," "selling point" and "tax deduction").

tax consequences — The effects an investment in a security may have on an individual investor's federal income tax; a major section of disclosure in a direct participation program securities disclosure document (e.g., film limited partnership or manager-managed LLC offerings) that discusses many of the material tax issues relating to the offering. Such discussions may be required by the specific disclosure requirements associated with the exemption being relied upon. Such discussions can only be prepared by accountants and/or attorneys (see "tax aspects" and "tax opinion").

tax credit — A direct, dollar-for-dollar reduction in a taxpayer's tax liability. The Tax Reform Act of 1986 repealed many tax credits, including the investment tax credit (contrast with "tax deduction"; see "foreign tax credit" and "investment tax credit").

tax deduction — A tax provision that permits taxpayers in a jurisdiction to deduct specified expenditures from their taxable income and/or reduce their taxes by a percentage applicable to such taxpayer's tax bracket (contrast with "tax credit"). Also, in the context of a film distribution agreement, an amount that the distributor is allowed to deduct from monies paid to the producer and that are required to pay tax liabilities to various governmental entities based on the exploitation of the film (also called "withholdings"; see "foreign tax shelter").

tax deferrals — The postponement of tax payments from the current year to a later year. Many countries have substituted tax deferrals for tax shelters and have adopted the U.S. "at-risk" provisions (see "at risk" and "tax shelters").

tax discussion — (see "tax aspects" and "tax opinion").

tax-driven movie financing — Motion picture investments that are significantly influenced by prospective tax benefits for the investors (see "foreign tax shelter" and "tax benefits").

tax evasion — The fraudulent and wilful underpayment or non-payment of taxes (see "foreign tax credit" and "income tax").

tax incentives — (see "tax benefits").

tax matters partner — With respect to limited partnerships and manager-managed LLCs, the designated partner who, as required by the Tax Equity and Fiscal Responsibility Act of 1982, is to serve as the primary liaison between the partnership and the IRS with regard to partnership tax matters and proceedings before the IRS (see "limited liability company" and "limited partnership").

tax opinion — The information and beliefs provided by a practitioner (attorney or accountant) concerning the federal tax aspects of a tax shelter or other securities offering either appearing or referred to in the investment offering materials, or used or referred to in connection with sales promotion efforts, and directed to persons other than the client (i.e., promoter/issuer) who engaged the practitioner to give the advice. The term includes the tax aspects or tax risks portion of the offering materials prepared by or at the direction of a practitioner, whether or not a separate opinion letter is issued or whether or not the practitioner's name is referred to in the offering materials or in connection with the sales promotion efforts. In addition, a financial forecast or projection prepared by a practitioner is a tax shelter opinion if it is predicated on assumptions regarding federal tax aspects of the investment, and it meets the other requirements above (see "limited liability company," "limited partnership," "material tax issue," "tax aspects" and "tax shelter").

tax payer — The person who is determined to bear the tax liability for a given transaction (see "income tax").

tax shelter — A transaction through which a taxpayer reduces his, her or its tax liability by engaging in activities that provide tax deductions or tax credits to apply against his or her tax liability (i.e., method used by investors to legally avoid or reduce tax liabilities). Also an investment that has as a significant and intended feature for federal income purposes either (1) deductions in excess of income from the investment being available in any year to reduce income from other sources in that year, or (2) credits in excess of the tax attributable to the income from the investment being available in any year to offset taxes on income from other sources in that year. For tax shelter registration purposes, the IRS defines a tax shelter as any investment that meets the following two requirements (1) the investment is one with respect to which a person could reasonably infer from representations made or to be made in connection with the offering for sale of an interest in the investment that the tax shelter ratio may be greater than 2 to 1 for any investor at the close of any of the first five years ending after the date on which the investment is offered for sale; and (2) the investment is one that is required to be registered under a Federal or state law regulating securities, or that is sold pursuant to an exemption from registration requiring the filing of a notice with a Federal or state agency regulating the offering or sale of securities, or that is a substantial investment (contrast with "abusive tax shelter"; see "material tax issue," "tax aspects," "tax credit," "tax deduction," "tax opinion" and "tax shelter registration").

tax shelter registration — The IRS requirement that certain investment programs meeting the very broad definition of a tax shelter provided by the IRS must register the program with the IRS or certain penalties may be imposed on several of the parties involved (see "tax shelter").

teamsters — The union concerned with pickup and/or delivery or hauling of any description, including all vehicles on, to or from location work and studios, buses, limousines, motorcycles, picture cars, Hi-Lo's, camera cars,

Cherry pickers, Cinemobiles, trailers (loaded and unloaded), combination type vehicles of any description, and all other types of vehicles in or upon which cargo or personnel of any description is carried or which are to be photographed, whether such vehicles are rented, leased, owned or in any way made available or used by a film production company (see "captain" and "union").

teasers — Film trailers prepared for theatrical presentation in advance of the regular theatrical trailer. Such trailers typically have running times of only one minute or slightly more (see "trailers").

technical analysis — Another form of financial analysis used to forecast the future stock prices of corporations. Technical analysis relies on price and volume movements of stocks and does not concern itself with financial statistics (see "fundamental analysis").

technical personnel — Film production employees or advisors who have specialized knowledge, experience and/or training (see "production staff").

technological developments — Improvements relating to a specialized mechanical or scientific method of achieving a practical purpose (e.g., projecting a motion picture image on a screen or improving the sound systems associated with motion pictures; see "laser disc" and "new delivery technologies").

telecast — To broadcast by television (see "television").

Telefilm Canada — A Canadian feature film fund with an annual budget designed to promote the production and theatrical distribution of high-quality dramatic films with a high level of Canadian content (see "feature film fund").

telemarketers — People who work on the phones calling prospective investors or customers trying to sell various investment opportunities, goods or services by phone (see "boiler room" and "National Do Not Call Registry").

television — The broadcasting industry that utilizes an electronic system for transmitting transient images of fixed or moving objects together with sound over a wire or through space by apparatus that converts light and sound into electrical waves and reconverts them into visible light rays and audible sound (see "cable television" and "radio").

television ads — Film advertising prepared for and carried on television; similar to trailers, only shorter — usually thirty seconds. Release prints for television spots have traditionally been distributed in a 16mm format as opposed to 35mm (see "advertising").

television and film inter-relationship — The manner and effect of the common interests of the film and television industries. The television and film industries are significantly inter-related. They share a talent pool of producers, actors, directors and others and many motion pictures are exploited on television. During the past several decades, the financial highs and lows of the film business have been evened out by the production of a relatively safe and predictable television product. Today, however, the television business is less stable and this development in turn places added financial pressure and uncertainty on the motion picture business (see "financial management" and "strategic planning").

television cover shot — (see "coverage" or "cover shot").

television derivative distribution rights — The legal power and authority granted to a feature film distributor in a distribution agreement to exploit television programming derived from a feature film in the television marketplace, including television specials, movies-of-the-week, pilots, multi-part series or television series (see "derivative distribution rights" and "theatrical derivative distribution rights").

television network — (see "network").

television pre-sale — A contractual arrangement negotiated and consummated before a feature film is produced in which a television network commits to purchase or license the rights to show the feature film on television. Although no actual cash is paid by the network, such contracts or the network's letter of commitment may be "bankable" if supported by a completion bond. This arrangement is similar to a studio negative pick-up deal although no longer very common. It is more common today for the negative pickup deal to include television rights either for the domestic, international or worldwide markets (see "fractionalizing," "negative pick-up" and "split rights basis").

television program — A performance broadcast on television or carried through cable television (see "television series").

television remakes and sequels — A heading sometimes used in feature film distribution agreements wherein certain rights of the distributor relating to television distribution rights for programming derived from the motion picture are set out (see "theatrical remakes and sequels" and "television derivative distribution rights").

television sales — (see "TV sales").

television series — A weekly or daily program on television, usually one half hour or one hour in length (see "pilot").

television spots — (see "commercials").

television syndication — (see "syndication").

temporary restraining order — A court order granted without notice or hearing, demanding the preservation of the status quo until a hearing can be had to determine the propriety of injunctive relief, temporary or permanent (see "equitable remedy" and "injunction").

tentative budget — The preliminary statement of the projected costs of producing a motion picture. Obviously, a budget may change dramatically depending upon which actors or actresses become attached and since it is not always possible to get commitments from the lead performers (the ones ultimately selected) in advance of financing, reasonable estimates must be made (see "budget" and "packaging").

tentative shooting schedule — The initial and temporary (at least until further modifications are required) list of when each shot and scene called for by a feature film screenplay is to be shot, including a detailed list of all of the people and things needed to conduct such shoots (see "shooting schedule").

tentpole film — A major studio/distributor release, usually an in-house or p-f/d financed feature, with significant stars and a high production budget that is expected to perform as a blockbuster and financially help the studio subsidize its other less successful releases for the year (see "blockbuster strategy" and "tentpole strategy").

tentpole strategy — A method for marketing mediocre studio films with the same studio's anticipated blockbusters so that the studios will have leverage over the exhibitors and be able to influence the exhibitor's decision to exhibit the less desirable studio releases. Tentpole films are used as leverage by the distributor's bookers who informally negotiate with theater chains to include exhibition of some of the other studio's less desirable films as part of the deal, thus making the use of the tentpole film and the marketing strategy associated with it. In this sense, the so-called tentpole film and its use is an evolved, less formal and more difficult to prove form of the illegal studio business practice of block booking (see "block booking," "blockbuster mentality" and "tying arrangement").

term — In contracts generally, the period of time during which the conditions of the contract will be carried out. In film distribution, the period of time expressed in years that a distributor has to distribute a picture (i.e., a limited number of years or in perpetuity). If limited, the term is typically a minimum of five years but seldom more than fifteen. In a limited partnership or manager-managed LLC context, "term" also refers to the number of years the entity will operate and exist (see "distribution term").

term deal — (see "overall deal").

term loan — Intermediate to long-term (typically, two to ten years) secured credit granted to a company by a commercial bank, insurance company or commercial finance company usually to finance capital equipment or provide working capital. The loan is amortized over a fixed period, sometimes ending with a balloon payment. Borrowers under term loan agreements are normally required to meet minimum working capital and debt to net worth tests, to limit dividends and to maintain continuity of management (see "debt," "interest" and "lender financing").

term of art — Words or phrases that have a particular meaning within a given area of study or business activity. Such terms may have no meaning or a different meaning outside the context in which such terms are used in a given industry (see "contractually defined terms").

terms — In contract law generally, the provisions stated or offered for acceptance which determine the essential nature and scope of the agreement. With respect to a distributor/exhibitor agreement for example, the terms are the conditions under which the distributor agrees to allow the exhibitor to show its product in a given theater, and whereby the exhibitor agrees to show the product. Such terms typically include the basis on which film rentals will be paid (as a percentage of weekly gross box-office receipts or flat fee), playing time (number of weeks), choice of theater, dollar participation in cooperative advertising expenditures and clearance over other theaters (see "clearance" and "contract").

territorial distributors — Feature film distribution companies that handle film distribution for U.S. films in foreign countries (see "foreign distribution" and "foreign sales representatives").

territorial pre-sales — (see "pre-sales").

territorial sales — The licensing of motion pictures in foreign markets (see "outright sale").

territory — A geographical area belonging to or under the jurisdiction of a governmental authority. The term is most commonly used in the film business to describe foreign countries as film markets (see "foreign market").

test marketing — The pre-releasing of a film in one or more small, representative markets before committing to an advertising campaign. The effectiveness of the initial marketing plan can thus be evaluated and modified, if necessary, prior to the subsequent release (see "preview" and "sneak preview").

test marketing budget — The projected expenses set out by category that are anticipated to be incurred in conducting a pre-release exhibition of a movie for the purpose of gauging an audience's reaction to the film (see "test marketing").

test the waters — An SEC concept associated with Regulation A offerings in which an issuer can use general solicitation and advertising prior to filing an offering statement with the SEC, giving an issuer the advantage of determining whether there is enough market interest in its securities before incurring the full range of legal, accounting, and other costs associated with filing an offering statement. The issuer, however, may not solicit or accept money until the SEC staff completes its review of the filed offering statement and the issuer delivers the prescribed offering materials to prospective investors (see "Regulation A").

text — The original written or printed words and form of a literary work or the main body of printed or written matter on a page or in an advertisement (see "book" and "novel").

theater — Any establishment in which motion pictures are exhibited regularly to the public for a charge (i.e., the commercial viewing center for the presentation of a motion picture to the public). Theaters are owned and operated by exhibitors and may be part of exhibition chains (see "exhibitor" and "theater chains").

theater-by-theater basis — The prescribed manner in which theatrical distributors were supposed to license their film product to exhibitors in the U.S. theatrical marketplace, pursuant to the Paramount consent decrees (i.e., without discrimination in favor of affiliated theaters; see "Paramount Consent Decree of 1948," "TriStar Case" and "vertical integration").

theater chain values — The amount that may be paid in an arm's length transaction by a willing buyer to a willing seller for a theatrical exhibition circuit (see "theater chains").

theater chains — An affiliated group of theaters operating under common ownership. Examples include American Multi-Cinema, General Cinema and Cineplex Odeon (also called "theater circuits"; see "exhibitor" and "major exhibition chains").

theater holdings — The assets of a corporate conglomerate relating to motion picture exhibition. The Paramount consent decrees required the vertically integrated major studio/distributors of the time and other motion picture companies to divest themselves of their theater holdings ("antitrust laws,"

"major studio/distributors," "original Paramount defendants" and "vertical integration").

theater stocks — Corporate shares in the publicly held exhibition chains (see "major exhibition chains" and "publicly held").

theatrical — Of or relating to motion picture theaters where full-length feature films are exhibited to the public for a charge. It is extremely important that this word be used as a modifier of the word "release" in a film distribution deal since without the word "theatrical" the film distributor may be free to merely license the motion picture to video companies and cable television without its being exhibited at theaters (see "non-theatrical").

theatrical admissions — A statistical measurement of the number of people who buy movie tickets at the box office during any given period (see "box office gross" and "domestic theatrical admissions").

theatrical agents — Independent contractors who negotiate contracts and solicit employment for their clients (see "agent").

theatrical and television film basic agreement — (see "WGA agreement").

theatrical derivative distribution rights — The term used in some feature film distribution agreements to refer to the legal power and authority to exploit a subsequently produced motion picture based on a preceding film (i.e., remakes and sequels; see "prequel," "remake" and "sequel").

theatrical distribution — The exploitation of motion pictures by means of exhibition in motion picture cinemas, in contrast to the exploitation of motion pictures in other media (see "ancillary rights").

theatrical distribution contract — The agreement between a distributor and producer pursuant to which the distributor commits to provide a theatrical release for a motion picture or pictures (see "production-financing/distribution agreement," "negative pickup distribution agreement" and "acquisition distribution agreement").

theatrical exposure — The release and exhibition of a motion picture in theaters. Such exposure (i.e., promotion to and viewing by a significant number of moviegoers) is considered an important element in determining the value of the movie in ancillary markets (see "ancillary markets").

theatrical film rental — (see "film rental").

theatrical market — The exhibition of movies in theaters as opposed to other markets or media such as cable and videocassettes or DVDs (see "allied rights," "ancillary markets" and "non-theatrical").

theatrical motion picture acquisition/ distribution agreement — (see "acquisition/ distribution agreement").

theatrical release — The exhibition of a feature film in theaters as opposed to licensing to home video/DVD, pay-cable, syndication, network and other ancillary markets. The theatrical release has traditionally been the only area of film distribution where it is possible to generate a negative cash flow (i.e., where releasing costs might exceed income produced by a given film in that market; see "allied rights," "ancillary rights" and "non-theatrical").

theatrical release commitment — A contractual promise by a feature film distributor relating to the distribution of a film in the theatrical marketplace (see "release commitment").

theatrical releasing costs — The expenses associated with distributing a film for theatrical exhibition, primarily prints and advertising, although the list of distribution expenses include many other items (see "distribution expenses").

theatrical remakes and sequels — A common heading in a feature film distribution agreement that sets out the terms and circumstances under which the film distributor will exploit any films to be produced in the future that are based on the previous version (see "prequel," "remakes" and "sequels").

theatrical self-distribution — (see "four-wall" and "self-distribution").

theatrical teamsters — (see "teamsters").

theft — (same as "larceny"; see "Mafia," "organized crime," "racketeering," "RICO" and "white collar crime").

theft of ideas — The taking of another's concept for a movie unlawfully with the intention of depriving the owner of its use. Copyright does not protect ideas, it only protects the manner in which those ideas are expressed. Nevertheless, ideas, can be protected in the context of certain legally recognized relationships. A claim for theft of ideas may be pursued as an implied-in-fact contract under certain situations (see citation for Glen Kulik article "The Idea Submission Case: When Is An Idea Protected Under California Law?" in this book's "Selected Bibliography").

The Hollywood Reporter — A daily (except weekends) entertainment industry trade publication (published in Hollywood) reporting on developments in the motion picture, television, stage, home video and cable segments of the industry (see "trades" and "*Variety*").

theme — The subject (i.e., the idea or concept that forms the basis of a screenplay or feature film). In music, the theme is the musical motto that serves as the basis of the composition or movement. In motion picture advertising, the theme is the promotional campaign's central concept, that is used in ads and/or commercials. Ad themes seek to distinguish the film advertised from others competing for the movie-going audience (see "concept" and "idea").

theme song — The title song for a motion picture (see "music").

there are no rules — (see "rules").

third decade council — A film industry membership organization whose membership is made up of the younger working members of the industry and that serves as a support group for the American Film Institute (now in its third decade). With the AFI, the Third Decade Council sponsors an annual conference that is structured as an informal, off-the-record series of discussions with established members of the entertainment community (see "American Film Institute" and "industry groups").

third parties — Persons who are not directly involved as decision makers to a transaction or agreement (see "contract").

third-party beneficiary — Persons who are recognized as having enforceable rights created in them by a contract to which they are not parties and for which they give no consideration (see "contract" and "parties").

third-party escrow — An escrow account set up and maintained by an entity not a party to the investment transaction, usually a bank or escrow company (see "escrow").

third-party participation — A percentage interest in a specified level of a movie's revenue stream held by a person or entity who was not a party to the contract granting the interest (e.g., a director with a profit participation set forth in the feature film distribution agreement that is a contract between the distributor and the film's producer, would be a third-party profit participant). Third-party participations may occur at gross or net levels, although, feature film distributors routinely provide in their distribution agreements that third-party participations are to be paid out of net profits or the producer's share of net profits (see "floor," "percentage participation" and "points").

thirty-three act ('33 ACT) — The federal Securities Act of 1933, as amended. The federal legislation that regulates the sale of securities in the U.S. Federal securities law generally does not pre-empt state securities law, thus both federal and states securities laws and regulations must be complied with in any securities offering (see "dual regulation" and "NSMIA").

thirty-five millimeter (35MM) — The standard gauge of film and equipment used in professional motion picture making and commercials. Sometimes 35mm is replaced by wider-gauge film (65 or 70mm), by 16mm, which is then sometimes blown up to 35mm or digital video. Thirty-five millimeter film is 35 millimeters wide, has 16 frames per foot, and 4 perforations per frame (see "film").

threat — A declaration of an intention or determination to inflict punishment, loss or pain on another, or to injure another by some wrongful act (see "extortion," "racketeering" and "RICO").

three-party agreement — A written contract between a loan-out company and a feature film production company through which the loan-out company makes available for employment the services of the individual artist/performer who owns the loan-out company (see "borrowing agreement," "lending agreement" and "straight employment agreement").

three-run break — A film's break being available for no more than three theaters within the break's geographical area (see "two-run break" and "four-run break").

three sets of books — A reference to the alleged practice that distributors maintain several different versions of their business records, one for their own records, one for the producer and net profit participant group and another for the IRS (see "creative accounting," "net profit participant association" and "unethical business practices").

ticket pre-sales — The advance sales of blocks of motion picture theater tickets to groups that have an interest in seeing a particular type of movie produced and exhibited. Ticket pre-sales can sometimes play a role in financing the production costs of certain movies (e.g., by means of ticket pre-sales to religious groups; see "pre-sale financing").

ticket revenue — (same as "box office gross"; see "concession sales" and "house nut").

tie-in — (same as "tying arrangement").

tie-ins — Promotional campaigns for commercial products that are coordinated and otherwise related in some way to the release of a motion picture (e.g., the sale of cups with pictures of characters from a motion picture on sale at outlets of a fast-food chain; contrast with "product placement"; see "promotional tie-ins").

tier releasing — (same as "first run zoning").

time is of the essence — A term used in contracts that fixes time of performance as a vital term of the contract, the breach of which may operate as a discharge of the entire contract (see "contract").

time value of money — (see "present value").

title — With respect to ownership, a shorthand term used to denote the facts which, if proved, will enable a plaintiff to recover possession or a defendant to retain possession of property. Having title to something means having the right to possess, use and exploit it. In another sense and in relation to film, any written material that appears on a film and is not a part of an original scene. Also the registered name of the screenplay or teleplay. The person in whose name it is registered, or to whom it is transferred by sale, lease or power of attorney, is said to "have title" to the script (see "credit titles," "creeper titles" and "title opinion").

title clearance report — (see "title report and opinion").

title report — A report consisting of a listing of all prior uses of a particular title in the literary, dramatic, motion picture, radio and television fields (see "title report," "opinion" and "working title").

title report and opinion — A report prepared by entertainment attorneys that advises a producer as to whether a proposed film title has been used before, whether the use of a particular title is likely to cause confusion among the public and whether a court injunction preventing the use of such title may be successfully pursued (see "title report" and "title search").

title search — A search made through the records maintained in public record offices to determine the state of a title, including all liens, encumbrances, mortgages, future interests, etc., affecting the property; the means by which a chain of title is ascertained (see "title" and "chain of title").

title search report — (same as "title report").

title song — A song written for a movie that includes the title in its lyrics or is somewhat descriptive of what the movie is about (see "music").

title treatment — A distinctive logo of a film's title used consistently in an advertising campaign (i.e., the graphic design of a film's title). Movie title treatments should be captivating and consistent with the film's theme. Techniques used to accomplish this include choice of typeface, hand lettering and/or visual imagery (see "main and end titles").

tombstone ad — A formal advertisement usually in the financial press announcing the commencement of an offering of securities, and listing the underwriting manager and members of the syndicate. The term derives from the fact that such advertisements usually consist of all copy and no illustrations, and thus look like a tombstone. A tombstone ad is merely a public announcement concerning such transactions and does not constitute either an offer to sell or to buy the securities (see "private offering," "public offering" and "securities").

top billing — The first and/or most prominent credits on the screen (i.e., the credits placed in the most advantageous position in relation to the main title of the film). Top billing is a negotiable item in star contracts, but also may be negotiated for some producers, directors, writers, cinematographers and composers (see "credits").

topical hook — A movie concept or theme that is likely to catch the attention of the movie's target audience and that can be easily promoted (see "hook").

top sheet — The first page of a detailed motion picture budget that provides a summary of the budget (see "budget" and "tentative budget").

tort — The French word for "wrong"; a private or civil wrong or injury resulting from a breach of a legal duty that exists by virtue of society's expectations regarding interpersonal conduct, rather than by contract or other private relationship (e.g., defamation, libel and invasion of privacy; see "clearance," "errors and omissions insurance," "privacy, right of," "public figure," "droit moral," "editing rights," "moral rights," "negligence" and "unfair competition").

total capitalization — The capital structure of a company, including long-term debt and all forms of equity (see "capital," "debt" and "equity").

total return — Return on investment, taking into account capital appreciation, dividends or interest and individual tax considerations adjusted for present value and expressed on an annual basis (see "rate of return").

total revenue — A general reference to all of the income generated by the exploitation of a motion picture in all markets and media or in specified markets and media (see "film rental" and "gross receipts").

track — The physical area on a magnetic tape or optical film stock that stores audio information ("sound tracks").

track record — The prior performance of an individual or a film (i.e., the history of an individual or company involved in the production or distribution of films, for example, of a director for a film that a bank is considering for a loan; see "choosing a distributor," "lending standards" and "past performance").

tracks — The relatively fixed constellations of theaters that play a given distributor's product, the existence of which confirm that feature films are rarely, if ever, sold theater by theater, without discrimination, solely on the merits (see "antitrust laws," "block booking" and "Paramount Consent Decree of 1948").

track system — An arrangement under which most of a distributor's films are customarily exhibited at a certain exhibitor's theaters; additionally "track system" and "track" means a group of theaters within a major key, that may be operated by different exhibitors, chosen by a distributor (through negotiations with the exhibitors) to play a film simultaneously (see "tracks").

trade advertising — Movie advertisements that are carried in the trade publications and thus are directed to distributors or exhibitors as opposed to a movie's potential general audience (see "advertising" and "trades").

trade association — An organization created for the purpose of promoting and protecting the common interests of a given industry or segment of an industry (contrast with "guild"; see "association projects," "industry groups," "MPAA" and "professional association").

trade association and guild fees — Membership fees paid by members of professional and trade associations and unions (see "dues and assessments" and "trade association dues and fees").

trade association dues and fees — Money paid by members of trade associations to the organization to support its services. Also, a category of distributor expenses that are deducted from gross receipts (sometimes off-the-top) and paid as the distributor company's allocable portion of the dues and assessments of the trade association or associations to which the distributor belongs (e.g., the MPAA and AMPTP or similarly constituted or substitute organizations throughout the world). This category of distributor expense may include legal fees to such association's outside counsel (not its in-house counsel) relating to antitrust matters, which means the major distributors are deducting from gross receipts (i.e., reducing the amount of funds that other participants may share in, to pay for activities that help to continue or improve their position of market dominance). Thus, most independent producers who have to wait until a film's revenue stream reaches net profits (since most producers are relegated to a net profit's position), are contributing to the payment of the distributor association's costs incurred in conjunction with fighting antitrust claims or taking positions on issues most of which would be opposed by the independent producer whose funds are being used. That being the case, it would seem only fair that if an association of independent feature film producers were formed, then each film produced by a member production company and distributed by an MPAA distributor would contribute a portion of its gross receipts to the independent producer's association as association dues at the same time that the MPAA and other distributor trade organization dues were being deducted and paid. In addition, independently produced films that were distributed by IFTA member distributors would also contribute an allocable portion to the support of such an organization. In any case, a producer may be able to negotiate a flat-dollar cap on the amount of gross receipts that may be deducted for association dues (see "AMPTP," "association projects," "blind bidding," "industry groups," "gross receipts," "lobbying," "MPAA," "off-the-top," "piracy" and "TriStar Case").

trade association related services — (see "association projects").

trade dues — (see "trade association dues and fees").

trademark — Any word, name, symbol or device used by a manufacturer or merchant to identify his, her or its goods and to distinguish them from goods made or sold by others. The basis for trademark law lies in the tort of unfair competition, under which a seller using a mark similar to one already in use could be liable for the buyer's likely confusion between two products or services due to the seller's efforts considered as a whole (see "logo," "patent," "service mark," "trade name" and "unfair competition").

trademark report — A report covering a search of the trademark records of the U.S. Patent and Trademark Office provided for persons who wish to use a particular mark for a product or service (see "trademark").

trade name — A word, name, symbol, device or any combination thereof used by a person to identify that person's business, vocation or occupation. Unlike the trademark or service mark, a trade name does not have to be registered, although the first user of a trade name can still sue subsequent users for trade name infringement under common law principles and the unlawful use of a trade name may be enjoined (see "service mark" and "trademark").

trade practices — (same as "business practices").

trade publications — (see "trades").

trades — The daily, weekly or monthly newspapers and magazines that specialize in reporting news and information relating to the entertainment industry. The term typically refers to *The Hollywood Reporter* and *Variety*, but may also be used to describe *American Cinematographer*, *Boxoffice, The Film Journal, Millimeter, Movie/TV Marketing, Screen International* and the weekly *SMPTE Journal* (see "press release").

trade screening — The showing of a motion picture by a distributor that is open to any exhibitor interested in considering the motion picture for exhibition (see "anti-blind bidding statutes" and "blind bidding").

trade screening requirement — An implicit element of anti-blind bidding legislation providing that distributors must allow exhibitors the opportunity to view an upcoming film before contractually committing to exhibit the film. A trade screening requirement would seem to help the exhibitors make more accurate predictions about the performance of a particular film in the exhibitor's theaters, at least more accurate than those judgments based on the very small amount of information now provided by certain distributors in states that do not have the trade screening requirement (see "anti-blind bidding statutes" and "blind bidding").

trade secret — Any process, pattern, formula or machine used in someone's business during the manufacture or production of a product that may give the user the opportunity to obtain an advantage over his, her or its competitors. When trade secrets are acquired and used without the rightful owner's authorization, the owner may be able to seek money damages, and in some instances a court ordered injunction to stop and/or prevent the unauthorized use of the trade secret. In order to recover in court, the owner of the trade secret must establish that the idea or item was held in the strictest of confidence, and that it was obtained by the other party through fraud or other unfair means. Once a trade secret is discovered either by analysis of the product or by any other proper method, it is then permissible for the discoverer to use it for his, her or its own advantage (see "antitrust laws," "covenant not to compete" and "non-disclosure provisions").

trade usage — Specialized meanings given to certain terms due to their general acceptance in a trade or industry and the reasonable reliance of the persons involved in that trade or industry on those meanings. Trade usage also refers to business practices that are generally accepted and relied on in many transactions in a specific trade

or industry (see "business practices," "customary terms" and "term of art").

trade sneak — A sneak preview, usually scheduled by a film's distributor several months prior to a film's release and designed to secure distribution for the film in given markets. Exhibitors are invited to view the movie at a trade sneak along with the public and after viewing the motion picture and making a judgment regarding the audience's reaction, the exhibitors are asked to bid on the film. All expenditures incurred in the conduct of a trade sneak would generally be considered distribution costs by the distributor (see "director's cut," "sneak preview," "sneak preview advertising" and "word-of-mouth sneak").

trade union — (see "guild" and "union").

traffic in — To carry on commercial activity relating to a given commodity (e.g., feature films, videocassettes, DVDs or pornography; see "exploit").

trailer — A short promotional film exhibited in theaters (usually beginning two to three weeks prior to the release of the subject film) as a preview of coming attractions. A trailer usually runs less than three minutes (see "green band trailer," "pre-feature entertainment," "red band trailer," "teasers" and "trailer tags").

trailer crossplug — A teaser trailer shown by an exhibitor to movie patrons in one theater that advertises a movie showing in another theater, in the same complex or otherwise (see "teasers" and "trailer").

trailer revenues — Income allocated by an exhibitor and paid to the distributor for the exhibition of a trailer. A distributor may incur substantial expense in preparing trailers and advertising accessories. If such expenses are charged against the distributor's proceeds as expenses of distribution then any amounts of revenues derived from trailers and advertising accessories should be included in gross receipts to the distributor for purposes of calculating profit participations. Such payments may be made by exhibitors in certain territories. Legal requirements in many countries provide that a short or trailer be included with any film sent into such country, thus allocation issues arise with respect to what portion of a film's rentals should be allocated to the costs associated with producing the shorts or trailers. If the distributor wants to keep its revenues from trailers and accessories, it should not be able to deduct costs associated with the preparation of such items as distribution expenses (see "allocations" and "trailer").

trailer tags — A distinctive or identifying word or phrase, such as "for general audiences," assigned by the MPAA Ratings Board, that provides the rating designation for a film. Such tags are required to be included on all movie trailers for MPAA-rated films (see "ratings" and "trailers").

transaction — Generally, the doing or performance of some matter of business between two or more persons. In accounting, an event or condition recognized by an entry in the books of account. In securities, the execution of an order to buy or sell a security. For tax purposes, any sale, exchange, or other disposition; any lease or rental; and any furnishing of services (see "sham transaction").

transaction-related — Something associated with an exchange of goods, services or funds. In securities law transactions involving the sale of a security, state securities laws commonly prohibit the payment of transaction-related remuneration to persons not licensed as securities broker/dealers (see "commissions" and "finder").

transaction exemption — (same as "exempt transaction").

transcription — In music, an arrangement of a piece for some voice or instrument, or combination thereof, other than that for which it was originally intended (see "music").

transfer agent — One acting for the benefit of another with mutual consent, in this instance, usually a commercial bank acting for the benefit of a corporate business, to maintain records of the corporation's stock and bond owners, to cancel and issue certificates, and to resolve problems arising from lost, destroyed or stolen stock certificates. A corporation may also serve as its own transfer agent (see "corporate stock").

transfer of copyright ownership — An assignment, mortgage, grant of exclusive license, transfer by will or intestate succession, or any other change in the ownership of any or all of the exclusive rights in the copyrights associated with a property whether or not it is limited in time or place of effect, but not including a nonexclusive license. A transfer of exclusive rights, other than by operation of law, is not valid unless an instrument of conveyance (for example, contract, bond, deed), or a note or memorandum of the transfer, is in writing and signed by the owner of the rights conveyed or the owner's duly authorized agent. The U.S. Copyright Office does not make transfers of copyright ownership, but rather records a document of transfer after it has been executed by the parties (see "copyright assignment").

transnational cartelization — The combining of independent commercial enterprises beyond national boundaries in an effort to limit competition (see "cartel").

transportation costs — The expenses associated with moving people, animals or equipment from one point to another. Transportation costs may be a significant cost of producing a motion picture on location (see "budget," "budget categories," "living expenses" and "rising production costs").

treasury stock — Corporate stock reacquired by the issuing company and available for retirement or resale (i.e., it is issued but not outstanding; see "corporate stock").

treatment — An intermediate stage between the movie script concept and the shooting script (i.e., an essay style description of the story and characters). There is no specific length, but a treatment may be as long as twenty-five to thirty pages. It tells the story of the motion picture in sequence, showing in more or less detail the form the final film will take, with specific examples of the dialogue, setting, camera angles, etc. It is more than a bare statement of an idea or concept and it can be copyrighted and may meet WGA requirements for registration. Copyright registration, however, only covers the creative expression in the treatment itself, it does not give any protection for the general ideas revealed in the treatment, and is not a substitute for registration of the finished script or motion picture. The WGA defines treatment as an adaptation of a story, book, play or other literary, dramatic or dramatic-musical material for motion picture purposes in a form suitable for use as the basis of a screenplay (see "one line description," "basic story outline," "outline" and "synopsis").

trend — A prevailing tendency or inclination (i.e, a general movement or swing in current preferences. In the financing of independent films, a number of factors may contribute to what appear to be trends: changing economic and tax considerations, the over-eagerness for the trade press to identify and report on such trends (whether real or not), the prevailing lack of knowledge and expertise in the area of film finance among independent producers and the self-serving promotion of such trends by those who may have expertise in a limited area of film finance. Some trade reporters write stories about perceived or false trends based on inadequate research (i.e., citing just two or three examples in support of the so-called trend; see "financing," "scam" and "trades").

trims — Unused portions of film cut from a scene (see "cutouts" and "editor").

Tristar Case — A series of court hearings relating to the application of the Paramount consent decree to the motion picture distributor TriStar. In 1980, Loews' Theaters petitioned the judge who had been supervising the implementation of the Paramount consent decrees for slightly more than three decades for relief that would allow Loew's to enter the motion picture distribution business in addition to its activities as an exhibitor. The motion was granted subject to several conditions including (1) Loew's could not exhibit any films it distributed or any films in which it had a financial interest and (2) as a distributor, Loews's had to abide by the same conduct restrictions imposed by the original Paramount decree. After TriStar acquired Loews's in 1986 those two entities applied to the court for interim relief (1) to allow the exhibition of TriStar films in Loews theaters during the important Christmas holiday season and (2) for removal of the trade practice injunctions prohibiting TriStar from conducting business as a distributor with any other exhibitors except Loews. This relief was also granted, but on an interim basis. In 1987 TriStar and Loews went back to the court and asked for permanent relief from the Paramount consent decree and from the 1980 order. At that point the U.S. Justice Department offered its vigorous support for the TriStar application (based on its 1984 merger guidelines for vertical mergers) and again the TriStar/Loews motion was granted (see "conduct restrictions," "merger guidelines," "Paramount Consent Decree of 1948," "relief" and "vertical merger").

true availability — A condition whereby a film becomes available to an exhibitor either for a first run immediately upon that film's national break or for a subsequent run immediately upon the film's prior run's conclusion (see "availability").

trust — A combination of business firms or corporations formed by a legal agreement, particularly a combination that reduces or threatens to reduce competition (see "antitrust laws," "cartel," "monopoly," "oligopoly" and "transnational cartelization").

trust me — A request made to someone who may be doubting a statement or proposed course of action indicating that the doubting person can rely on the party offering the statement or proposal. During the course of negotiating an important contract, such as a feature film distribution agreement, there should be no need to accept any oral representations of this sort so long as language may be drafted to cover the subject contingency. Also, in less formal business relations (i.e., non-contractual) trust should be reserved for emergencies (i.e., those situations in which the parties are not be able to

communicate; see "entire agreement clause" and "sue us").

trustee — One who holds legal title to property "in trust" for the benefit of another person, and who is required to carry out specific duties with regard to the property or who has been given power affecting the disposition of property for another's benefit. The term is also sometimes used to describe anyone who acts as a guardian or fiduciary in a relationship to another (e.g., a partner to co-partner, a general partner to limited partners or an LLC manager to the LLC's members; see "fiduciary").

TV ads — (see "commercials").

TV print — A composite color-film print that has been balanced for xenon projection (i.e., for television; see "other versions" and "xenon projection").

TV sales — In film distribution, the licensing of films for exhibition on network and for syndication, cable, pay TV, video-cassette, video-disc and other television technologies (see "cable television," "free television" and "syndication").

TV special — (see "television special").

turnaround — A screenplay development situation in which the original studio/purchaser of a property has declined to go forward with the project beyond a certain point, has provided a turnaround notice to the original producer/seller and the project is available to be picked up by another studio or production company for a fee. The project is in turnaround (see "step deal," "turnaround provision or agreement" and "venture capital").

turnaround agreement or clause — (same as "turnaround provision or agreement").

turnaround hell — The circumstances in which a producer is not able to reacquire the rights to produce a screenplay from a studio/production company and the screenplay thus gathers dust at the studio/production company in some repository of incomplete projects (see "turnaround provision").

turnaround notice — A written notification provided by a purchaser of a literary property upon which a motion picture is to be based that such purchaser will not proceed with further development of the screenplay or production of the motion picture and that the author or owner may want to exercise its rights to reacquire the property or interest another production company in acquiring the property (see "turnaround").

turnaround provision or agreement — A clause commonly found in literary purchase agreements or production-financing/distribution agreements with studios or distributors and in studio development deals (or a separate agreement) that provides the right to a producer or screenwriter to submit a film project to another production company or studio if the original developing production company at which the project was being acquired or developed elects not to proceed with the production of the film. For example, the language may state that the film project will be turned back to the producer for twelve months if the studio does not begin production within six months after the one hundred and twenty-day development period. If there is a turnaround, it does not depend upon the occurrence of a specific event as does the reversion in an option agreement (i.e., the failure to make an option payment in a timely manner), rather, it is a right that may be exercised by the owner, at its election, to reacquire the property after notice by the purchaser/studio of its decision not to proceed with production. Such right is often contingent upon the original developing production company's development expenses to date being repaid and sometimes the original development company may retain an interest in the film's earnings (see "reversion provision or agreement" and "substitution clause or agreement").

turn-around time — The minimum and specific number of hours that must be provided to a union member in accordance with union contracts before that union member may be required to return to work. Also, the amount of time it takes to provide a product or service (e.g., a securities attorney to produce the first draft of a disclosure document for a film limited partnership or manager-managed LLC offering once the producer has provided sufficient information for the draft to be prepared (see "securities" and "union").

twenty percent rule — An informal guideline allegedly used by many of the major studio owned or controlled video/DVD wholesaler/manufacturers when dividing up the monies received from home video (and laser video disc) retail sales and rentals. Pursuant to such rule, an arbitrary share of 20 percent of the total of video company wholesale revenues is designated as a royalty to be paid to the distributor. The twenty percent rule is based on an early estimate of what video profits would be and may have no relationship to the actual current numbers. Initially, the marketing and manufacturing costs associated with the new video technology was significant, thus the initial 20 percent royalty payment to film distributors may have made sense. Now however, both the marketing and manufacturing costs relating to videocassettes and DVDs have dropped drastically (per unit) and the 20 percent royalty is significantly out of line. Some in the industry have alleged that by uniformly applying this twenty percent rule, the studios are conspiring to deny profit participants in movies and television shows their fair share from the sale of videocassettes and DVDs. Other industry observers suggest that arm's length home video deals can be negotiated in the current market place either on a royalty or distribution fee basis (see "conscious parallelism," "distribution fee basis," "royalty basis," "video/DVD revenue reporting" and "video companies").

two-run break — A film's break being available for no more than two theaters within the break's geographical area (see "three-run break" and "four-run break").

two-tiered sequential pricing structures — The traditional policy with regard to setting the retail price for a motion picture on videocassette or DVD (i.e., the initial release is priced somewhat higher — in the sixty to ninety dollar range) with the result that most initial purchases are made for video rental purposes. A later secondary sale at a much lower price (in the fifteen to thirty dollar range) encourages more consumer

purchasers of the videos at that time (see "re-release," "sell-through market" and "video/DVD revenue reporting").

tying arrangement — The sale of one product on the condition that the purchaser also buy another product, or agree to not buy the other product from anyone else. A tying arrangement is a per se violation of the Sherman Antitrust Act, in that it allows the seller to exploit his, her or its control over the tying product to force the buyer into the purchase of a tied product that the buyer either did not want at all or might have preferred to purchase elsewhere on different terms. If a seller does not possess sufficient market power to cause an actual adverse effect on competition, a court will not find a tying arrangement and therefore the per se rule will not apply. Film industry tying arrangements may occur when distributors offer films to exhibitors and talent agents offer talent packages to production companies (see "antitrust laws," "block booking" and "packaging").

typecast — The selecting of actors or actresses for film roles because they have played similar parts before or because they are very much like the characters to be played (see "actor").

U.K. version — A copy of a motion picture produced outside the United Kingdom but specifically edited in a manner that is suitable for exhibition in the U.K. (see "other versions" and "U.S. theatrical cut").

ULOE — Acronym for uniform limited offering exemption (see "Uniform Limited Offering Exemption").

ultra-low budget — A subjective term, the meaning of which may change from year to year, but that currently refers to feature films that are produced for less than a million dollars; others may choose to set the budget level for an ultra-low budget film at a different levels, for example SAG considers a $200,000 budget to be ultra-low budget. Others have gone as low as $150,000 (see "big-budget films," "low-budget films" and "medium budget films").

ultra-low budget film — A Screen Actors Guild designation for a film with a budget of less than $200,000 (see "ultra-low budget agreement").

ultra-low budget agreement — A Screen Actors Guild Agreement that permits the use of both professional and non-professional performers on films with budgets of less than $200,000 for $100 a day with no step-up fees, no premiums and no consecutive employment (except on overnight locations); see "low budget agreement," "modified low budget agreement," "Screen Actors Guild," "short film agreement" and "student film agreement").

ultra vires activities — Actions of a corporation or its officers and directors that are not authorized by its charter and that may therefore lead to shareholder or third-party lawsuits and personal liability of the corporation's officers and/or directors (see "articles of incorporation," "charter" and "piercing the corporate veil").

unauthorized distribution — The sale, rental or other exploitation of a film without a grant of distribution rights; an activity that the distributor may seek to prevent and in the process incur costs that are typically defined as deductible distribution expenses. Distributor association dues, fees, assessments or other levies are typically made to cover the costs of such activities conducted on behalf of its distributor members. Individual distributors may also incur such costs, but as with any distribution expense, such costs must be carefully reviewed, confirmed and adjudged reasonable to prevent over-stated expenses. The producer may want to ask the distributor if it anticipates any such costs beyond industry assessments for such activities (see "distribution expenses").

unauthorized cross-collateralization — A feature film distributor's unauthorized offsetting of the profits of a movie against the same movie's profits in another market, or against the profits of another movie produced by the same production company or against the profits of another movie produced by a different production company. A cross-collateralization provision may authorize one but not the other (see "allocation," "creative accounting," "cross-collateralization," "cross-collateralization of markets," "cross-collateralization of slates," "de facto cross-collateralization," "discretionary cross-collateralization," "overage" and "unrecouped expenses").

uncollectible indebtedness — Debts owed to a debtor or creditor that are determined to be impossible or impractical to collect (e.g., debts owed by a sub-distributor, exhibitors or licensees to a film's distributor, that the distributor has determined to be uncollectible). Independent producers must be wary of unscrupulous distributors who may fraudulently claim that such debts cannot be collected when in fact they have been or will be in the future (see "bad debt").

unconscionable — Not guided or controlled by conscience; shockingly unfair or unjust; unscrupulous; unreasonably detrimental and one-sided. Many of the provisions in the distribution contracts of the major studio/distributors have been held by courts to be unconscionable (see "adhesion contract," "Buchwald Case" and "unconscionable contract").

unconscionable contract — A contract that is so unfair or unreasonably detrimental to the interests of a contracting party as to render the contract legally unenforceable. The basic test is whether, in the light of the general commercial background and the commercial needs of the particular trade or case, the clauses involved are so one-sided as to be unfair or intolerable under the circumstances existing at the time of the making of the contract. This term refers to a bargain so one-sided as to amount to an "absence of meaningful choice" on the part of one of the parties together with contract terms that are unreasonably favorable to the other party. Ordinarily, one who signs an agreement without full knowledge or understanding of its terms might be held to assume the risk that he or she has entered into a one-sided bargain. But when a party of little bargaining power and hence little real choice, signs a commercially unreasonable contract with little or no knowledge or understanding of its terms, it is hardly likely that his or her consent was ever given to all the terms. In such a case the usual rule that the terms of an agreement are not to be questioned may be abandoned and a court may consider whether the terms of the contract are so unfair that enforcement should be withheld (see "Buchwald Case," "contract of adhesion," "overreaching" and "submission release").

unconscionable provision — A single paragraph, article or section of a contract dealing with one subject or issue that is shockingly unfair or unjust (see "adhesion contract" and "unconscionable").

uncontrolled distribution — Securities terminology for an offering of securities by selling stockholders (as opposed to the issuer of the securities) on a random basis through any number of broker/dealers who are willing to assist such persons or an offering by such persons without the use of a broker (see "controlled distribution" and "distribution").

uncrossed — Not cross-collateralized (see "cross-collateralization," "cross-collateralization of slates" and "de facto cross collateralization").

underage — The amount an exhibitor falls short in meeting a film rental commitment to a distributor on a given film. Exhibitors sometimes use excess film rental earned in one circuit theater to fulfill a rental commitment defaulted by another. This practice effectively cross-collateralizes the financial results of several unrelated films (see "cross-collateralization" and "overage").

underbudgeting errors — Mistakes in estimating the production costs of a movie (i.e., not enough money is allocated for certain budget items; see "budget").

undercapitalization — The failure to provide sufficient cash capital to give a corporation or other business a reasonable chance of survival. Undercapitalization is one of several operational defects that may cause the loss of a corporation's separate identity from its owners (see "piercing the corporate veil").

underlying material — (see "underlying property").

underlying property — The literary or other work upon which rights to produce and distribute a motion picture are based. Such works may include a book, play, treatment, synopsis, outline or original screenplay (see "literary materials" or "literary works" and "property").

underlying rights — The legal privilege, power and authority upon which the licenses to produce and distribute a motion picture are based. Such rights refer to the ownership of the script and/or the literary property on which the script is based (see "clearance" and "underlying property").

underlying rights agreements — The contracts between a writer or producer and the author, owner or publisher of a literary or other work upon which rights to produce and distribute a motion picture are based (see "clearance" and "underlying property").

underreported rentals — The false and understated totals relating to the revenues earned by a given film as prepared and reported by the film's distributor to the film's producer and other net profit participants. This is less likely to occur if the distribution fee is a percentage of the distributor's gross receipts, but if the distributor fee is based on some form of adjusted gross (i.e., not calculated until after certain deductions are made from gross receipts it would make more sense for an unscrupulous distributor; see "audit," "creative accounting" and "skimming").

underwrite — To ensure the sale of stocks, bonds or other securities by agreeing to buy, before a certain date, the entire issue if they are not sold to the public, or any part of the issue remaining after the sale. Underwriting is one method used by corporations to raise capital. A conventional underwriting is handled by an investment banker who agrees to buy the issue from the seller and who forms a syndicate to provide the necessary capital and distribution network. The syndicate then sells the issue to investors and the proceeds of that sale, less an underwriting fee, are paid to the client company (see "primary distribution," "securities" and "underwriter").

underwriter — An investment banker who, singly or as a member of an underwriting group or syndicate, agrees with an issuer or other person on whose behalf a securities distribution is to be made (a) to purchase securities for distribution to investors or (b) to distribute securities to investors for or on behalf of such issuer or other person or (c) to manage or supervise a distribution of securities for or on behalf of such issuer or other person, hoping in the process to make a profit on the underwriting spread. Also, defined as any person, group or firm that assumes a risk in relation to the offer or sales of securities in return for a fee, usually called a premium or commission (see "issuer sales," "selling group" and "underwrite").

underwriter risk — The risk taken by an investment banker that a new issue of securities purchased outright will not be bought by the public and/or that the market price will drop during the offering period (see "risk").

underwriter's questionnaire — A questionnaire circulated by the underwriting manager to all prospective members of the underwriting syndicate to obtain information to be used in a securities offering, including the names and addresses of the underwriters, any relationships with the issuer and stock ownership (see "due diligence").

underwriting agreement — Agreement between a corporation issuing new securities to be offered to the public and the managing underwriter as agent for the underwriting group. The agreement sets out the underwriter's commitment to purchase the securities, the public offering price, the underwriting spread (including all discounts and commissions), the net proceeds to the issuer and the settlement date (see "managing broker/dealer agreement").

underwriting group — A temporary association of investment bankers, organized by the originating investment bank in a new issue of securities (see "purchase group" and "selling broker/dealers").

underwriting spread — The difference between the amount paid to an issuer of securities in a primary distribution and the public offering price (see "firm commitment" and "selling concession").

unearned income (revenue) — In accounting, income received but not yet earned, such as advances from customers. For income tax purposes, income from sources other than wages, salaries, tips, and other employee compensation (e.g., dividends, interest and rent; see "income").

unearned interest — Interest that has already been collected on a loan by a financial institution, but that cannot yet be counted as part of earnings because the principal of the loan has not been outstanding long enough (also called "discount"; see "interest").

unencumbered assets — Property that is free and clear of all liens (i.e., creditor claims; see "asset," "debt" and "liquid asset").

unethical — Not in conformance with accepted or prescribed professional standards of conduct (see "conflicts of interest," "ethical malaise," "ethics," "proclivity for wrongful conduct" and "professional code of responsibility").

unethical business practices — Procedures and activities engaged in by commercial enterprises that are not in conformance with accepted standards (see "antitrust laws," "anti-competitive business practices," "blind bidding," "close bidding," "creative accounting," "five "o'clock look," "franchise agreements," "predatory practices," "price fixing," "product splitting" and "reciprocal preferences").

unfair competition — A tort (private or civil wrong or injury resulting from a breach of a legal duty that exits by virtue of society's expectations regarding interpersonal conduct rather than by contract or other private relationship) consisting of representations or conduct that deceives the public into believing that the business name, reputation or good will of one person is that of another; unfair, untrue or misleading advertising that is likely to lead the public into believing that certain goods are associated with another entity; imitation of a competitor's product, package or trademark in circumstances where the consumer might be misled (see "ethical malaise," "fair competition," "predatory practices," "proclivity for wrongful conduct," "reciprocal preferences," "tort," "trademark" and "unethical business practices").

unfair negotiating tactics — Inequitable, unethical or unjust bargaining methods (see "anti-competitive business practices" and "negotiation").

unfavorable portrayal — (same as "negative portrayal").

uniform limited offering exemption (ULOE) — A model statute promulgated by the North American Securities Administrators Association that most states have adopted in some form or another to provide a state transactional exemption from the securities registration requirement that is somewhat compatible with one or more of the federal Regulation D exemptions (see "Regulation D," "limited offering exemption," "NASAA" and "NSMIA").

uniform limited partnership act — A model statute promulgated by the North American Securities Administrators Association that most states have adopted in some form or another to govern the creation and activities of limited partnerships in their respective states (see "limited partnership" and "NASAA").

unintegrated exhibition and distribution capacity — In the context of the U.S. Justice Department, merger guidelines a phrase that refers to the number of motion picture distribution and exhibition companies that are not vertically integrated. The stated policy suggests that if there are a substantial number of such firms at either or both of the distribution and exhibition levels of the motion picture business, the fact that another firm (TriStar in this case) had become vertically integrated does not necessarily mean that competition in distribution or exhibition would be unreasonably restrained (see "business practices," "conduct restrictions," "market power," "merger guidelines," "restraint of trade," "TriStar Case," "vertical integration" and "vertical merger").

union — An association of workers whose main purpose is to bargain on behalf of such workers with employers about the terms and conditions of employment (see "guild" and "teamsters").

union labor — Film crew made up of union members. Typically union film crews are more expensive than non-union crews but presumably more experienced and capable (see "artificial pickup" and "union").

union list — A list prepared by a union or guild and made available to its members that provides the names of film production companies that have become signatories to the union or guild's contract and have agreed to abide by the union's fair-practice standards. The list may also include the names of production companies that are not signatories to the union contract or whose labor practices are deemed to be unfair by the union. The phrase union list may also refer to a listing of union members who are active members of the union and are thus available for employment on a union job (see "union").

union and guild flight accident insurance — Insurance that provides aircraft accidental death insurance to all performers and production crew members, according to the union or guild contract requirements (see "insurance").

unissued stock — Shares of a corporation's stock authorized in its charter to be issued, but not yet issued (see "corporate stock" and "issuer").

unit — A commonly used term in limited partnership and manager managed LLC offerings to describe a ratable interest in the limited partnership or manager managed LLC of a unit holder or purchaser (i.e., the measure of participation in the ownership of the entity — a partnership or LLC interest). Often the minimum purchase is limited to one (1) unit, or in the discretion of the general partner or manager, fractional units may be offered (see "limited liability company," "limited partnership" and "majority-in-interest").

unit production manger — The producer's executive assigned to a motion picture production and responsible for coordinating and supervising all administrative, financial and technical details of the production, and overseeing the activities of the entire crew on a given film or production unit. The unit production manager coordinates, facilitates and oversees the preparation of the production unit, all off-set logistics, day-to-day production decisions, locations, budget schedules and personnel (see "line producer," "production manager" and "production unit").

unit holder or unit purchaser — A term commonly used in limited partnerships and manager managed LLCs to identify the investors in such entities (i.e., those who purchase one or more units, or an approved purchase of a fraction of a unit, and has thereby obtained a pro rata share in the financial results of the entity's business activity; see "limited partner" and "member").

United States Copyright Office — The federal administrative agency responsible for implementing the copyright laws (see "copyright").

unit publicist — The publicist assigned to a film during pre-production and production for the purpose of generating publicity (see "publicist").

universe — A term often used in film distribution agreements to indicate that the distributor has the right to distribute the film in all markets (i.e., throughout the world or everywhere; see "distribution territories").

unlisted security — An over-the-counter security that is not listed on a stock exchange (see "securities" and "stock exchange").

unpaid dividend — Dividend that has been declared by the board of directors of a corporation but has not reached its payment date (see "corporate stock").

unqualified audit — (see "complete audit").

unrecouped expenses — The expenses incurred in the production or distribution of a film that have not been recouped in distributing the film. Distributors may use a variety of business practices to offset such losses with profits on other films or in other markets (see "allocation" and "cross-collateralization").

unreturned capital contribution — In the context of limited partnership and manager-managed LLC offerings, a term used to mean any investor's capital contribution minus the cash which has been distributed to that investor pursuant to the partnership or LLC operating agreement. Not all such entities use this terminology (see "capital").

unsecured debt — An obligation not backed by the pledge of specific collateral (see "collateral" and "debt").

unsolicited material — Literary works submitted to producers or production companies that were not requested (see "submission release").

up front — In a film context, before a production begins. The phrase may refer to a commitment to pay compensation to an executive producer, producer, director, etc. prior to the commencement of principal photography. In the context of a limited partnership or manager-managed LLC, the phrase may refer to the expenses to be incurred by the general partner or manager in organizing and selling the entity's units or interests and may include some legal, accounting, printing, binding, art and marketing costs including broker/dealer due diligence fees, if any (see "front-end load" and "offering expenses").

up front distribution money — Funds provided by a distributor to the producer of a film prior to the production of the film (see "producer's advance").

up front expenditures — In the context of a limited partnership or manager-managed LLC, the expenses of organizing and selling the entity's interests (see "organizational costs," "start-up costs" and "syndication expenses").

up front financing — A significant financial contribution by a film's distributor to the production cost of the movie. Sometimes up-front financing is required by a lending bank of the distributor so that the distributor has a financial stake in the picture and the distributor will therefore be motivated to open the film in the better theaters and to provide adequate expenditures for prints and ads (see "financing" and "rent-a-major").

up front salary — Monies paid to film talent before the production begins or during production, as opposed to back end participations (see "back end participations" and "contingent compensation").

ups and downs — In a business context, the rise and fall of the fortunes of various segments of an industry. In the motion picture business, the fortunes of individuals and entities can rise and fall with amazing swiftness. With such incredible compensation being paid to the top performers in each area of the motion picture business (i.e., studio executives, actors/actresses, directors, agents, entertainment attorneys, etc.), it is easy for the industry to attract more than enough top talent in all of these fields. On the other hand, if for any reason (justifiable or not), such persons suddenly become out of favor with the sources of such inflated compensation, the fall can be sudden and devastating. This phenomenon further amplifies the power of the individuals and entities at the top of the pecking order in the movie industry, skews the economic principle of supply and demand and creates artificial barriers to entry for organizations that cannot pay the inflated costs (see "'A' title," "barriers to entry," "Hollywood insiders," "law of supply and demand," "leverage," "pied piper," "polarization" and "rising production costs").

upside potential — The possible upward price movement an investor may enjoy in a particular investment or the prospective profits of an investor. Also, a speculative reference to the amount of money a motion picture may make. Since investing in independent films is considered so risky, it may not be attractive to investors to place any kind of ceiling on the upside potential of their investment (see "downside exposure").

Universal Serial Bus (USB) Device — A component used with personal computers and video games to allow several peripherals to be connected by using a single standardized interface socket and to improve plug-and-play capabilities by allowing devices to be connected and disconnected without rebooting the computer.

(USB) Device — [see Universal Serial Bus (USB) Device]

U.S. box office gross — The total amount of money paid by movie-goers for admission tickets to see a motion picture at theaters in the United States. The MPPA publishes statistical information relating to the U.S. box office gross for its member movies each year (see "box office gross" and "MPAA").

U.S. dollar denominated letters of credit — Written guarantees issued by a foreign bank that state that on delivery of the film, the bank will pay a specific amount in U.S. dollars (see "letters of credit").

use of proceeds — A major required section in the disclosure document for a securities offering that sets out the principal purposes for which the net proceeds of the offering are intended to be used and the approximate amount intended to be used for each such purpose. Also, if less than all the securities to be offered may be sold and more than one use is listed for the proceeds, the order of priority of such purposes must be indicated. The estimated use of proceeds for a film production offering is somewhat similar in level of detail to a budget topsheet, but with offering expenses including syndication and organizational expenses set out separately from the film budget since these are not film budget items. In addition, such line items as "marketing to distributors" and "entity maintenance" may also be set out separately (sometimes called "estimated use of proceeds"; see "disclosure document," "entity maintenance," "marketing to distributors" and "mini-maxi offering").

U.S. free television version — A copy of a motion picture that has been edited so that it is suitable for exhibition on the broadcast television networks in the United States (see "other versions" and "U.S. theatrical cut").

U.S. Justice Department — The federal agency responsible for, among other things, enforcing criminal provisions of the U.S. antitrust laws (see "Federal Trade Commission," "merger guidelines," "Paramount Consent Decree of 1948" and "TriStar Case").

U.S. network broadcast — Television programming telecast by one of the television networks based in the U.S. (see "network" and "network broadcast").

U.S. theatrical — The feature film market in theaters located within the United States or in areas under U.S. control (see "domestic theatrical market").

U.S. theatrical admissions — The number of movie-goers who purchase tickets to see motion pictures at U.S. theaters. NATO publishes admission numbers each year (see "theatrical admissions").

U.S. theatrical cut — Generally, the first version of a motion picture released for exhibition in the domestic theatrical marketplace (i.e., that version of a film that is shown in U.S. theaters; see "cutting rights," "final cut," "other versions" and "U.S. free television version").

usurious contract — A contract that imposes interest on a debt at a rate in excess of that permitted by law (see "loan sharking," "RICO" and "usury").

usury — An unconscionable or exorbitant rate of interest; an excessive and illegal requirement of compensation for forbearance on a debt (interest). State legislatures in each state determine the maximum allowable rates of interest that may be demanded in any financial transaction, however, usury laws generally do not apply to corporate borrowers. Individual independent producers whose films are being financed by a studio which charges interest on the production monies provided may want to consider whether usury laws apply to the transaction (see "creative accounting," "loan sharking" and "usurious contract").

value — The monetary worth of a thing; marketable price; estimated or assessed worth (see "asset value" and "fair market value").

vanity screening — A preview of a completed motion picture sponsored by the producers or actors of the film as opposed to a distributor (i.e., the film does not yet have a distributor). A vanity screening may, in some circumstances, be considered a form of self-distribution (see "four-walling" and "self distribution").

Variety — An entertainment oriented newspaper published weekly in New York for international distribution and daily in Los Angeles. *Variety* is owned by Cahners, a division of the British publishing company Reed International (see "Daily Variety" and "trades").

VCR — (see "videocassette recorder").

venture capital — A source of financing for start-up companies or others embarking on new or turnaround ventures that entail some investment risk but offer the potential for above average future profits. Sources of venture capital include wealthy individual investors; subsidiaries of banks and other corporations organized as small business investment companies (SBICs); groups of investment banks and other financing sources

who pool investments in venture capital funds or venture capital limited partnerships. The Small Business Administration promotes venture capital programs through the licensing and financing of SBICs. Venture capital financing supplements other personal or external funds that an entrepreneur is able to tap, or takes the place of loans or other funds that conventional financial institutions are unable or unwilling to risk. Some venture capital sources invest only at certain stages of entrepreneurship, such as the start-up or seed money stage, the first round or second round phases that follow or the mezzanine level immediately preceding an initial public offering. In return for taking an investment risk, venture capitalists are usually rewarded with some combination of profits, preferred stock, royalties on sales and/or capital appreciation of common shares (see "business plan," "development funds," "entrepreneur," "IPO," "plan of business," "preliminary/development funding," "risk capital," "second round," "seed money" and "turnaround").

venture capital financing — The funding of the production and/or distribution costs of a motion picture with infusions of cash from venture capital firms. Such companies usually invest in "going" concerns as opposed to a "one-shot" movie project and more typically in the high-tech arena. Venture capital funds will rarely invest in a single independent film (see "venture capital").

venture capital limited partnership — An investment vehicle organized by a brokerage firm or entrepreneurial company to raise capital for start-up companies or those in the early processes of developing products and services. The partnership will usually take units or interests in the company in return for capital supplied. Limited partners receive income from profits the company may earn. If the company is successful and goes public, limited partners' profits could be realized from the sale of formerly private securities to the public (see "limited partnership" and "venture capital").

vertical integration — The unified ownership of several different levels of production and distribution in the same industry (e.g., a film industry in which the same owner is allowed to own or control a studio facility, development entities, production companies, a distribution entity, exhibitor chains or any two of the above that deal directly with each other, is vertically integrated). Following the issuance of the U.S. Justice Department merger guidelines and the TriStar Case, questions relating to whether film industry companies are vertically integrated at the distributor/exhibitor levels, and if so, whether such integration makes it more difficult for other companies to compete at those levels of the industry without being vertically integrated have been pivotal to the analysis regarding the anti-competitive effects of vertical mergers in that industry (see "anti-competitive business practices," "arm's length," "antitrust laws," "blind bidding," "distributor," "exhibitor," "formula deal," "global integration," "major exhibition chains," "merger guidelines,"

"number of screens," "Paramount Consent Decree of 1948," "producer," "studio," "transnational cartelization," "TriStar Case" and "vertical merger").

vertical merger — The combining of the ownership of two companies at different levels in a given industry (e.g., the combining of a feature film distribution company with an exhibitor; see "merger guidelines").

vertical price fixing — A combination or conspiracy formed for the purpose and with the effect of raising, depressing, fixing, pegging or stabilizing the price of a product engaged in by members of different levels of an industry (e.g., in the film industry, at the production, distribution and/or exhibition levels; see "horizontal price fixing" and "price fixing").

video — An electronic image-making system recorded on magnetic tape. The medium is primarily used for television, commercials and music videos although some movie producers are beginning to experiment with the medium for feature length presentations (see "HDTV").

videocassette — A magnetic tape that is housed in a light tight magazine and used to record and play back video images (see "digital video disc," "video" and "videocassette recorder").

video/DVD affiliate — In the context of the motion picture industry, a company that is engaged in the wholesale distribution or retail sales of feature film home videos whose stock is partly owned (i.e., less than a majority of voting shares) by a feature film distribution company or both of such companies are subsidiaries of a third company (see "video/DVD subsidiary").

videocassette jacket — The carton, covering or other packaging used to protect and market videocassette reproductions (see "jacket").

video/DVD subsidiary — In the context of the motion picture industry, a company that is engaged in the wholesale distribution or retail sales of feature film home videos whose voting corporate shares or more than 50 percent owned by a feature film distribution company or a common parent corporation (see "arm's length," "conflicts of interest," "predatory practices," "twenty percent rule," "reciprocal preferences," "unethical business practices," "video/DVD affiliate" and "video/DVD revenue reporting").

video/DVD license agreement — (see "video rights agreement").

videocassette recorder (VCR) — Any videotape device that both records and/or plays back a magnetic tape. The video tape formats include one-half an inch, three quarters of an inch, and one inch. These formats may be for both professional and/or home use, but the one inch format is typically used for professional video recording and replaces the standard two inch tapes used originally for television broadcasting. Also, the one inch system does not operate with self-contained cassettes but with reel to reel recording tape (i.e., the tape moves from feed roll to take-up roll; see "videocassettes").

video/DVD revenue reporting — In recent years, the video market (including DVDs) has been the fastest growing revenue source for films, thus, some of the major studios have created wholly-owned subsidiaries or joint ventures to distribute videocassettes and DVDs and these entities typically only pay 20 percent of wholesale receipts as a royalty fee to the parent distributor. In other words, unlike other areas of motion picture revenue reporting, home video is handled on a royalty basis (more like the record industry) rather than remitting the distributor's share of the wholesale revenues on a distribution fee basis. The system then switches back to the distribution fee basis at the distributor level, since the parent distributor, in turn, charges a distribution fee (usually about 30 percent) leaving only a very small percentage remaining for profit participants. By allowing a studio/distributor to take a fee on a related company transaction (i.e., two bites at the apple), this structure and these calculations permit the distributor to keep a disproportionate share of video/DVD revenues. In situations where the distributor is participating in the wholesale revenues of the video company, producers must address this issue in negotiations relating to the distribution agreement and seek to substitute a reasonable distribution fee for the typical 20 percent royalty at the wholesale level so that the distributor will include a higher percentage of the wholesale revenues in its gross receipts. This, in turn, may allow the profit participants to participate in a larger net profit pool. In addition, the producer should seek to reduce the distribution fees being taken by the distributor in recognition of the fact that the distributor is also sharing in the wholesale revenues of its wholly-owned or subsidiary video company (see "arm's length," "home video royalty," "predatory practices," "royalties," "royalty basis," "twenty percent rule" and "unethical business practices").

video companies — Entertainment industry businesses that operate at the wholesale level and market videocassettes or DVDs to retail outlets who in turn sell or rent to the general public (see "video/DVD revenue reporting").

video corridor — The revenue stream generated by the sale of feature film videocassettes and DVDs through a film distributor to a video wholesaler as distinct from the revenues generated by the exploitation of the same film in other media. Sometimes additional or separate percentage participations may be granted to certain individuals or entities in this video revenue corridor (see "outside the pot" and "participant").

videodisc — A disk or "record" on which digitized video images and audio signals are stored to be electronically reassembled for playback. In the U.S., originally, a needle-in-groove system, similar to the old phonograph system was utilized, but subsequently a laser video system, is being used. This system is played by a light beam with no pickup device actually touching the disk. The Japanese videodisc system utilizes a magnetic field with a "needle" floating over it but not actually touching the disk (see "compact disc" and "laser disc").

video format — The number of lines a television picture utilizes in reproducing an image. There are three basic video-broadcasting formats in the world: the U.S. and Japan use a 525 line format (the NTSC format) while the Russian and French system (the SECAM system) and the system used throughout the rest of Europe and Australia (the PAL system) both use over 600-line images (see "HDTV").

video rights agreement — The contract between a film's distributor or copyright owner and a video company that sets forth the terms pursuant to which a film may be distributed in the home video market (see "first sale doctrine" and "release commitment").

video tape — A magnetic tape on which visual images are electronically recorded. Such tapes typically have a side track for synchronized sound (see "tape").

video tape recorder (VTR) — An electronic device that permits the user to record visual images on magnetic tape (see "videotape").

video tape recording — The act of creating a visual record on magnetic tape using a video tape recorder (see "video tape recorder" and "videotape").

viewing restrictions — Limitations placed on screenings of leased or purchased educational or informational films (e.g., no paid admissions, no subcontracting for live, theatrical or television screenings and/or no direct optical projection for paying or nonpaying audiences; see "unauthorized distribution").

visual effects — Special effects or techniques used to obtain a certain look for a feature film. Such effects may include sets being designed for light absorbency, pushed-stop filming, customized lab work, special lighting and creative utilization of standard camera filters, speeds and lenses (see "optical effects").

voice over — A performer engaged to give off-camera voicing who is not involved in an on-camera performance (see "dialogue replacement").

voidable — A contract that can be annulled by either party after it is signed because of the existence of fraud, incompetence, another illegality or a right of rescission (see "rescission").

volume discounts/rebates — A reduction in price or the return of a portion of the price for a product sold in larger than usual numbers. In the film industry, feature film distributors sometimes receive discounts or rebates from the exhibitor retailers with whom they place their films, because of the large number of films the distributor supplies to the exhibitor. If such transactions are not contemplated by the terms of the film distribution agreement, the distributor may and usually does choose not to credit a given film's gross receipts for an allocable portion of such discounts or rebates, thus none of the participants who are supposed to be participating in all forms of valuable remuneration generated by the exploitation of their specific film will receive any benefit from such discounts or rebates. The distributors argue that they should be the sole benefactors of such discounts or rebates since such benefits are awarded because of the volume of business directed to an exhibitor by the distributor. Participants counter that the distributors would not have any volume were it not for the films produced by the participants. This is another issue that should be discussed during the negotiations of the film distribution agreement (see "adhesion contract," "unethical business practices," "predatory practices," "reciprocal preferences" and "settlement transactions").

voodoo accounting — A slang reference to movie studio accounting practices that are believed by many in the film industry to be quite unfair (see "creative accounting" and "studio accounting practices").

voting security — Any security presently entitling the owner or holder thereof to vote for the election of directors of a company (see "corporate stock" and "securities").

voting stock — Shares in a corporation that entitle the shareholder to voting and proxy rights (see "proxy").

voucher — A documentary record of a business transaction; a written affidavit or authorization (see "corporate stock").

VTR — (see "video tape recorder").

waiting period — The period between the date the registration statement in a public securities offering is initially filed with the SEC and the date it is declared effective. This so-called cooling-off period may be extended if more time is needed to make corrections or add information to the registration statement and prospectus (see "acceleration," "effective date," "prospectus," "public offering," "red herring" and "registration statement").

waiver — An intentional and voluntary giving up, relinquishment or surrender of some known right. In general, a waiver may either result from an express agreement or be inferred from circumstances (see "conflict waiver," "nudity waiver," "release" and "waiver of moral rights").

waiver of droit moral — (see "waiver of moral rights").

waiver of moral rights — The intentional and voluntary giving up, relinquishment, or surrender of the rights known as droit moral (French for moral right). Moral rights refer to the right of an author or artist (such as a film producer or director) to object to any deformation, mutilation or other alteration of his or her work. Although the term is widely recognized in civil law countries, it is not mentioned in the U.S. Copyright Act. Nevertheless, a right analogous to a moral right has been recognized in this country in several situations in which the integrity and reputation of an artistic creator was protected by the courts. The express grounds on which common law protection has been given include libel, unfair competition, copyright and the right of privacy. The right of droit moral gives the author of a work certain power to prevent changes, notwithstanding the provisions of his or her contract (e.g., a director may be able to prevent cutting and editing of his or her picture — except for editing for television and censorship). Producers should be aware that film distribution agreements often contain such a waiver and unless the producer is satisfied with the provisions of the distribution agreement with respect to the distributor's editing rights, the producer should consider deleting any attempted waiver of droit moral rights (see "creative control," "editing rights," "final cut" and "moral rights").

walk-on— A small non-speaking part in a film (see "bit player").

Wall Street — The popular name for the financial district at the lower end of Manhattan in New York City where the New York and American Stock Exchanges and numerous brokerage firms are headquartered. A reference to Wall Street interest in an industry, such as the film industry, alludes to whether or not such brokerage firms want to direct investor client funds into various film industry investment vehicles. Securities broker/dealer firms have traditionally not been very interested in raising funds for low budget independent films (see "corporate stock," "financing," "investor financing" and "securities").

wardrobe — Any clothes (personal, purchased or rented) worn before the camera and during rehearsals or used in connection with a film's production (see "costumer and wardrobe supervisor").

warranties — (see "warranty").

warranties and representations — A common heading in a contract (see "representations" and "warranty").

warranty — An assurance by one party to a contract of the existence of a fact upon which the other party may rely, intended precisely to relieve the promisee of any duty to ascertain the fact, and amounting to a promise to indemnify the promisee for any loss if the fact warranted proves untrue. Such warranties are either made overtly (i.e., express warranties, or by implication — implied warranties). In a film distribution agreement producer warranties and representations are likely to be made regarding the quality of the picture (i.e, it will be fully edited, titled, synchronized with sound and of a quality, both artistic and technical, for general theatrical release), as well as for numerous other matters relating to content, ownership, the discharge of the producer's obligations, no infringements, no advertising matter, no impairment of rights granted, valid copyright and MPAA rating. On the other hand, film distributors seldom provide many warranties

relating to their side of the bargain, if any (see "covenant of good faith and fair dealing" and "representation").

warranty of quiet enjoyment — A warranty given by the producer (i.e., the producer warrants that the distribution has the right to the unimpaired use and enjoyment of the film property) if it does not know of any actual, or potential, adverse claims which might be made against the distribution of the picture. If the distributor wants this warranty and representation included in the distribution agreement, the producer should seek language limiting the warranty to matters known as of the date the agreement was signed (see "warranty").

water craft liability insurance — Insurance providing coverage when water craft (such as boats, etc.) are used in connection with a production. Such policies are generally written on a case by case basis (see "insurance").

watered stock — In corporate law, shares of stock that have been issued by the corporation for less than full lawful consideration; also stock representing ownership of overvalued assets, a condition of overcapitalized corporations, whose total worth is less than the invested capital (see "corporate stock").

wealthy partner financing — The funding of the production and/or distribution costs of a motion picture with an active partner who provides most if not all of the monies needed. Generally speaking, if such partner is not a "silent" partner (i.e., is active in the management of the project), such fundings will not be considered securities. In other words, if the financial arrangement is structured and actually operates as a general partnership, joint venture, investor financing agreement or member-managed LLC, as opposed to a corporate stock offering, limited partnership offering or manager-managed LLC, the securities laws will generally not apply. On the other hand, film producers must be careful that this active investor does not want to interfere with the filmmaker's vision for the project (see "business plan," "investor financing agreement," "joint venture," "member-managed LLC" and "securities").

weekly house allowance — (see "house nut").

weekly house expense — (see "house nut").

weekly reporting papers — Production and financial reports filed with a motion picture studio/financier by the production company (see "production reports").

weekly *Variety* — (see "Variety").

we're different — An assertion that one party is not the same as another. Often distributors will make oral representations early in discussions with producers that their distribution organization is not typical of other feature film distributors (i.e., suggesting indirectly that they do not conduct their activities in a manner substantially characterized as described in this book). The proof of such self-serving descriptions, should lie in the language of the distribution agreement, the actual conduct of the distributor over a period of time and in a consistent pattern of behavior that avoids much of the above described business practices (see "sue us" and "trust me").

WGA agreement — The Writer's Guild of America Theatrical and Television Film Basic Agreement which, among other things, sets out minimum credit and compensation requirements to be observed by motion picture production companies that are signatories to the agreement in their hiring of screenwriter members of the WGA. The WGA agreement minimums are also commonly used as guides for non-WGA member writer agreements (see "compensation schedules" and "Writer's Guild of America").

WGA basic agreement — (see "WGA agreement").

WGA registration — The filing of a treatment or screenplay with the Writer's Guild of America for purposes of establishing evidence that the author reduced that specific expression of a proposed motion picture to a tangible form as of a certain date (see "copyright registration" and "submission release").

well known talent — Motion pictures actors, actresses or directors who are familiar to general movie-going audiences (see "highest leverage position").

when interest charges stop — (see "interest").

when the money's paid — A reference to one of the most critical concepts relating to film finance and the recoupment of invested funds which focuses on that point in a motion picture's revenue stream at which funds are deducted for purposes of compensating a specified party. For example, the term "gross receipts" is typically defined as an earlier stage in the revenue stream than "net profits," thus, "gross receipts" is a larger pool of money than "net profits" and a percentage participation in gross receipts is a substantially larger interest than the same percentage interest in net profits. The same is true of the terms "net profits" and "producer's share." Typically, the "producer's share" is defined as a later stage in the film's revenue stream, thus it is a smaller pool of money (if any) and percentage participant's in the "producer's share" would be getting a smaller amount of funds than a participant in the "net profits" pool with the same percentage. This concept also becomes an important factor in the decision relating to how to finance a film, since, for example, the bank providing a production money loan pursuant to negative pickup deal will insist on being paid its loan proceeds, interest and fees by the distributor when the film is delivered, whereas traditionally the investors in a limited partnership or manager-managed LLC have had to wait until the revenue stream reaches net profits (if ever) before even recouping their investment (see "adjusted gross," "accountable gross," "box office gross," "breakeven," "gross receipts," "house nut," "net profits," "outside the pot," "producer's share," "reciprocal preferences," "revenue corridor" and "revenue stream").

white collar crime — A phrase connoting a variety of frauds, schemes, corruptions and commercial offenses committed by business persons, con artists and public officials; a broad range of non-violent offenses that have cheating and dishonesty as their central element (see "crime," "fraud," "Mafia," "organized crime," "racketeering," "RICO," "rules," "theft" and "scam").

wholesale receipts — The monies received for the sale of a product from the retail sellers of such product by a business operating as a middle-level distributor of the product (see "video/DVD subsidiary" and "video/DVD revenue reporting").

wholesale selling price — The amount of money given or set as consideration for the sale of a

product in quantity and for resale (see "conscious parallelism," "distribution fee basis," "predatory practices," "royalty basis," "twenty percent rule," "unethical business practices" and "video/DVD revenue reporting").

wide release — In the context of domestic theatrical exhibition for a motion picture, an extensive exhibition pattern including multiple bookings in most of the theatrical markets. In a period of ever increasing movie screens this phrase will inevitably involve larger numbers of prints and screens. A domestic theatrical opening on at least five hundred screens throughout the country is considered a wide release by many in the industry. On the higher end of the scale wide releases may involve three thousand or more screens (see "general release," "limited engagement," "mini-multiple," "national release," "prints," "regional release pattern," "release pattern" and "specialized distribution").

wide screen aspect ratio — An aspect ratio of 2.35 x 1 (see "aspect ratio").

wild lines — Short words or phrases that are recorded wild (i.e., off camera when the recording of the sync recording is questionable; see "wild picture").

wild picture — Film shot without sound (see "wild recording").

wild recording — A sound recording not made synchronously with the filmed picture. Sound effects, random voices, narration and music are generally recorded in this manner; also referred to as non-synchronous sound (see "in synch").

wild sound effects — Recordings of sound effects not made synchronously with a filmed picture. Common examples include footsteps, dog barks, shattering glass, body hits, tire squeals and gunshots (see "wild recording").

winding up — The process of liquidating a corporation or partnership; the process of collecting the assets, paying the expenses involved, satisfying the creditors' claims and distributing whatever is left, the net assets, usually in cash but possibly in kind to the entity's owners in order of preference (see "dissolution" and "liquidation").

window — Generally, a limited time during which an opportunity should be seized or it may be lost. In film, the period of time in which a film is available in a given medium. Some windows may be open-ended, such as theatrical and home video, or limited, such as pay television or syndication. For U.S. made films, domestic theatrical distribution is typically the first window (see "direct to video release," "made for video" and "release sequence").

winner-take-all — An extreme economic principle that whoever wins in any business competition has the right to take all of the benefits of that win, with no obligation or responsibility for the loser. The economic system that has evolved in the Hollywood-based U.S. film industry over the past one hundred years seems to closely approach this model, although "winner-take-most" may be a more accurate description of the Hollywood-based U.S. film industry. If we have learned anything from history, it is that human systems need limits (see "it's only money").

withholding — Another form of over-budget penalty sometimes imposed by a studio that is financing the production of a film, in which the studio will withhold a significant amount of the producer's fee until delivery of the film's answer print. If the picture is delivered within budget the producer receives his or her complete fee, but if the film has gone over budget, the producer has to wait until net profits to receive the balance as a deferment (see "double add-back," "over-budget penalty" and "penalty-free cushion").

withholdings — The portion of wages earned that an employer, such as a motion picture production company, deducts, usually for income tax purposes, from each salary payment made to an employee. The amount deducted is then forwarded to the government to be credited against the total tax owed by the employee at the end of the taxable year. U.S. production companies involved in international co-productions must be careful to withhold for the foreign partner so as to avoid the joint and several liability that may apply to such withholdings in certain circumstances (see "international co-productions and agreements" and "tax deductions").

withholding taxes — (see "withholdings").

without recourse — A loan in which only the property used as collateral for the underlying debt may be reached to satisfy a judgment (i.e., as opposed to the party or parties signing the note; see "recourse").

word-of-mouth — The opinions of moviegoers regarding a specific motion picture as expressed to potential moviegoers who have not yet seen the subject film. Word of mouth may be favorable or unfavorable and is considered a very significant factor in the success of a film beyond its opening period (see "legs" and "sneak preview").

word-of-mouth sneak — A motion picture sneak preview designed to initiate word-of-mouth publicity for the film. Generally, a word-of-mouth sneak is scheduled approximately two weeks before the film's release. A cooperative local or national advertising campaign may be launched in support of such a sneak (see "director's cut," "preview," "sneak preview," "sneak preview advertising" and "trade sneak").

worker's compensation insurance — An insurance coverage required to be carried by state law that applies to all temporary or permanent cast or production crew members. The coverage provides medical, disability or death benefits to any cast or crew member who becomes injured in the course of his or her employment (see "insurance").

working capital — Funds invested in a company's cash, accounts receivable, inventory and other current assets. Working capital finances the cash conversion cycle of a business (i.e., the time required to convert raw materials into finished goods, finished goods into sales and accounts receivable into cash; same as "net current assets").

working control — Effective control of a corporation by a shareholder or shareholders with less than 51 percent voting interest. Working control by a minority shareholder, or by two or more minority shareholders acting together, is possible when share ownership of a firm is otherwise widely dispersed (see "minority interest").

working title — The tentative name given to a film until a final name has been chosen and cleared (see "release title" and "title report").

work made for hire — A copyright law concept that describes a literary work written by an employee (e.g., a writer hired by an employer to write a screenplay). The author and copyright owner of a work made for hire is the employer, not the employee. The U.S. Copyright Office Form TX, that is used to register textual works and Form PA, used to register motion pictures, asks whether the contribution to the work was a "work made for hire" (see "commissioned work," "copyright" and "writer for hire").

work print — The film print that the editor assembles from the dailies and that will undergo any number of editings before finally reaching a version that is determined to be the final cut to which the negatives will be conformed. Also, a lab print from a developed original, that is used by the editor to first synch up to sound and then to put into a first assembly. More generally, the visual material used for film editing [see "work print (picture)"].

work print (picture) — A positive print that usually consists of, among other things, intercut daily prints, film library prints, prints of dissolves, montages and titles. A picture work print constantly maintains synchronism with the corresponding sound work print (same as "locked picture"; see "work print").

work print (sound) — A term (no longer in common use) that refers to a sound print that usually contains all of the sound tracks (including sound effects, original sound and dubbed sound), but commonly does not include the final musical score, which in many situations is added to the finished film (see "editor's worktrack").

world-wide pickup — The acquisition of rights to distribute a motion picture throughout the world (see "acquisition distribution agreement," "domestic pickup" and "negative pickup").

world-wide rights — The right to exploit a film in all markets and throughout the world or universe (see "distribution territories").

world-wide theatrical — The distribution of a motion picture in theaters throughout the world (see "theatrical distribution").

wrap — An end to a given segment of filming relating to a motion picture. A "wrap" may refer to the end of a particular day's shooting, to the completion of a particular film assignment or location shoot or to the end of principal photography on a film (see "second unit").

wrinkle — A novel feature that may attract a buyer for a new product or security (see "selling point").

write-downs — (see "write-off").

write-off — Charging an asset amount to expense or loss. The effect of a write-off is to reduce or eliminate the value of the asset and reduce profits. The term also refers to the practice of taking a tax deduction in the current year (same as "write-downs").

writer — A person who is engaged by a film production company to write literary material, including making changes or revisions (see "screenplay"").

writer agreement — (same as "writer employment agreement").

writer employment agreement — (same as "writing services agreement").

writer for hire — A screenwriter who writes for an employer and gives up all elements of ownership to the resulting screenplay. In copyright terminology, the phrase is "work-made-for-hire" (see "copyright" and "work made for hire").

writer's certificate — (see "certificate of authorship").

writer's developmental deal — A financial arrangement for a production company or studio to fund the expenses of developing a motion picture screenplay wherein such funds are paid to a screenwriter as opposed to a producer or director (see "development," "director's development deal" and "producer's development deal").

Writer's Guild of America (WGA) — The film industry union for screen writers (see "WGA agreement").

writing services agreement — The basic contract for the hiring of a screenwriter, usually by a producer or production company, setting forth the terms and conditions under which the screenwriter may write a screenplay or provide other specific services in connection with a particular literary work (e.g., writing a synopsis, treatment, outline, polish, revision, etc.), or render continuing services relating to more than one motion picture project (also called "writer employment agreement"; see "WGA agreement").

written by — The screen credit awarded to the writer or writers who developed the story and wrote the screenplay (see "screenplay by" and as "write-downs").

written releases — (see "release").

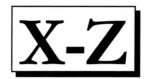

X-Z

xenon projection — A film being shown on the screen through the use of a xenon projector (see "xenon projector").

xenon projector — A motion picture theater projector that is replacing the arc projector in theaters. The xenon projector uses a bulb instead of a glowing element, and the bulb allows a longer period of use for the projector before the bulb has to be changed. It also does not require a full ventilation system to carry off the extreme heat generated by an arc projector (see "film" and "screen").

X-rating (X-rated) — An MPAA rating discontinued in the 1990 but which indicated that a motion picture had been reviewed by the MPAA's Classification and Rating Administration, and that no one under the age of seventeen was to be admitted to see the film (i.e., that the film's material was considered to be patently adult). In some states, an "X" rating meant that the material was for adults only — twenty and over. Often an "X" rating showed that the film dealt with explicit sex, but such a rating may have in the alternative indicated the film contained graphic violence or language that could be offensive to some moviegoers. Some newspapers refused to carry ads for "X-rated" movies. The "X" rating was effectively replaced by the "NC-17" rating (see "MPAA," "NC-17" and "ratings").

year end adjustments — Changes in the accounting statements on a motion picture made at the end of a given year. The authority to make such adjustments is commonly provided for in the film distribution agreement in relation to the net profits computation. Such adjustments are ostensibly made to make corrections and/or to report items overlooked (see "selling subject to review" and "settlement transaction").

yield — The return on an investor's capital investment; the current return on a stock expressed as a percentage of the price (see "return on invested capital"). In lending, the total money earned on a loan (i.e., the annual percentage rate of interest multiplied by the term of the loan; (see "debt," "interest" and "rate of return").

yield spread — The difference in yield among various issues of securities (see "rate of return" and "securities").

zone — Market areas in each city where a movie is shown at only one theater. Movie theater operators and the movie studios that provide them films divide each city into these market areas. In theory a movie only plays one theater in any one zone (see "competitive theater area" and "first run zoning")

504

BIBLIOGRAPHY

BOOKS

Andersen, Arthur & Co., *Tax Shelters: The Basics*, Harper & Row, Publishers, 1983.

Anger, Kenneth, *Hollywood Babylon*, Dell Publishing, 1981.

Anger, Kenneth, *Hollywood Babylon II*, Penguin Books, 1984.

Bach, Steven, *Final Cut: Dreams and Disaster in the Making of Heaven's Gate*, William Morrow & Co., 1985.

Ballio, T. ed., *The American Film Industry*, 2nd rev. ed. Madison: University of Wisconsin Press, 1985.

Bart, Peter, *Fade Out: The Calamitous Final Days of MGM*, Anchor Books, 1991.

Baumgarten, Paul A., Farber, Donald C. and Fleischer, Mark, *Producing, Financing and Distributing Film: A Comprehensive Legal and Business Guide*, 2nd edition, Limelight Editions, 1992.

Bayer, William, *Breaking Through, Selling Out, Dropping Dead and Other Notes on Filmmaking*, First Limelight Edition, 1989.

Biederman, Berry, Pierson, Silfen and Glasser, *Law and Business of the Entertainment Industries*, Auburn House, 1987.

Billboard Publications, Inc., *Producer's Masterguide*, 1989, 1990 & 1991.

Billboard Publications, *Hollywood Reporter Blu-Book*, 1990.

Blum, Richard A., *Television Writing (From Concept to Contract)*, Focal Press, 1984.

Brady, Frank, *Citizen Welles: A Biography of Orson Welles*, Anchor Books, 1989.

Brownstein, Ronald, *The Power and the Glitter: The Hollywood-Washington Connection*, Vintage Books, 1992.

Cameron-Wilson, James & Speed, F. Maurice, *Film Review 1994*, St. Martin's Press, 1993.

Cohen, Sarah Blacher, *From Hester Street to Hollywood*, Indiana University Press, 1983.

Collier, Peter & Horowitz, David, *The Kennedys: An American Drama*, Warner Books, 1984.

Commerce Clearing House, Inc., *Blue Sky Law Reporter*, 1984.

Cones, John W. *Hollywood Wars: How Hollywood Insiders Gained and Maintain Illegitimate Control Over the Film Industry*, Marquette Books, 2006.

Cones, John W., *The Feature Film Distribution Deal: A Critical Analysis of the Single Most Important Film Industry Agreement*, Southern Illinois University Press, 1996.

Cones, John W., *A Study in Motion Picture Propaganda: Hollywood's Preferred Movie Messages*, (self-published, 1996).

Cones, John W., *Who Really Controls Hollywood*, (self-published), 1996.

Cones, John W., *Forty-Three Ways to Finance Your Feature Film*, Southern Illinois University Press, 1995.

Cones, John W., *Patterns of Bias in Motion Picture Content*, (self-published, 1995).

Cones, John W., *Motion Picture Biographies*, (self-published, 1995).

Cones, John W., *Film Industry Contracts*, (self-published) 1993.

Cones, John W., A Dictionary of Film Finance and Distribution: A Guide for Independent Producers, Marquette Books, LLC, 2007.

Corman, Roger & Jerome, Jim, *How I Made a Hundred Movies in Hollywood and Never Lost a Dime*, Dell Publishing, 1990.

Curran, Trisha, *Financing Your Film*, Praeger Publishers, 1985.

Custen, George F., *Bio/Pics: How Hollywood Constructed Public History*, Rutgers University Press, 1992.

Delson, Donn and Jacob, Stuart, *Delson's Dictionary of Motion Picture Marketing Terms*, Bradson Press, Inc., 1980.

Dinnerstein, Leonard, *Anti-Semitism In America*, Oxford University Press, 1994.

Downes, John and Goodman Jordan Elliot, *Dictionary of Finance and Investment Terms*, 2nd Ed, Barron's Educational Series, Inc., 1987.

Duncliffe, William J., *The Life and Times of Joseph P. Kennedy*, New York, 1965.

Ebert, Roger, *Roger Ebert's Video Companion*, 1994 Edition, Andrews and McMeel, 1993.

Eberts, Jake and Lott, Terry, *My Indecision Is Final*, Atlantic Monthly Press, 1990.

Eisenberg, Dennis et al., *Meyer Lansky: Mogul of the Mob*, New York, 1979.

Ephron, Henry, *We Thought We Could Do Anything*, W.W. Norton & Co., 1977.

Erens, Patricia, *The Jew in American Cinema*, Indiana University Press, 1984.

Evans, Robert, *The Kid Stays in the Picture*, Hyperion, 1994.

Farber, Stephen and Green, Marc, *Hollywood Dynasties*, Putnam Publishing, 1984.

Farber, Stephen and Green, Marc, *Outrageous Conduct*, Morrow, 1988.

Farber, Donald C., *Entertainment Industry Contracts; Negotiating and Drafting Guide*, Matthew Bender, 1990.

Field, Syd, Screenplay: *The Foundations of Screenwriting*, Dell Publishing Co., Inc., 1985.

Fox, Stuart, *Jewish Films in the United States*, G.K. Hall & Co., 1976.

Fraser, George MacDonald, *The Hollywood History of the World*, Viking Penguin, Inc., 1989.

Frederickson, Jim & Stewart, Steve, *Film Annual: 1992*, Companion Publications, 1992.

Fried, Albert, *The Rise and Fall of the Jewish Gangster in America*, Revised Edition, Columbia University Press, 1993.

Friedman, Lester, *The Jewish Image in American Film*, Citadel Press, 1987.

Gabler, Neal, *An Empire of Their Own: How the Jews Invented Hollywood*, Anchor Books, 1988.

Gilroy, Frank, D., *I Wake Up Screening: Everything You Need to Know About Making Independent Films Including a Thousand Reasons Not To*, Southern Illinois University Press, 1993.

Goldberg, Fred, *Motion Picture Marketing and Distribution: Getting Movies into a Theatre Near You*, Focal Press, 1991.

Goldman, William, *Adventures in the Screen Trade*, Warner Books, 1983.

Gomery, Douglas, *Movie History: A Survey*, Wadsworth Publishing Company, 1991.

Gomery, Douglas, *The Hollywood Studio System*, MacMillan, 1986; New York: St. Martin's Press, 1986.

Goodell, Gregory, *Independent Feature Film Production*, St. Martin's Press, 1982.

Goodman, Ezra, *The Fifty Year Decline and Fall of Hollywood*, Simon & Schuster, 1961.

Gribetz, Judah, Greenstein, Edward L. and Stein, Rigina, *The Timetables of Jewish History*, Simon & Schuster, 1993.

Hearst, William Randolph, Jr.. & Casserly, Jack, *The Hearsts: Father and Son*, Roberts Rinehart Publishers, 1991.

Herrman, Dorothy, *S.J. Perelman, A Life*, Simon & Schuster, 1986.

Higham, Charles, *Howard Hughes: The Secret Life*, Berkley Books, 1993.

Hill, Geoffrey, *Illuminating Shadows: The Mythic Power of Film*, Shambhala, 1992

Holsinger, Ralph L., *Media Law*, McGraw-Hill, Inc., (2nd edition), 1991.

Houghton, Buck, *What a Producer Does: The Art of Moviemaking (Not the Business)*, Silman-James Press, 1991.

Hurst, Walter E., Minus, Johnny and Hale, William Storm, *Film-TV Law*, 3rd Ed, Seven Arts Press, Inc., 1976.

Johnson, Paul, *A History of the Jews*, Harper & Row, 1987.

Katz, Ephraim, *The Film Encyclopedia*, Harper Collins, 1994.

Kennedy, Joseph P., ed. *The Story of the Films*, W. W. Shaw Company, 1927; reprint, Jerome S. Ozer, 1971.

Kent, Nicolas, *Naked Hollywood: Money and Power in The Movies Today*, St. Martin's Press, 1991.

Kim, Erwin, *Franklin J. Schaffner*, Scarecrow Press, 1985.

Kindem, Gorham, *The American Movie Industry: The Business of Motion Pictures*, Southern Illinois University Press, 1982.

King, Morgan D., *California Corporate Practice Guide*, 2nd Ed, Lawpress Corporation, 1989.

Kipps, Charles, *Out of Focus*, Century Hutchinson, 1989.

Koppes, Clayton R. and Black, Gregory D., *Hollywood Goes to War: How Politics, Profits and Propaganda Shaped World War II Movies*, University of California Press, 1987.

Kosberg, Robert, *How to Sell Your Idea to Hollywood*, HarperCollins, 1991.

Kotkin, Joel, *Tribes: How Race, Religion and Identity Determine Success in the New Global Economy*, Random House, 1993.

Lasky, Betty, *RKO: The Biggest Little Major of Them All*, Roundtable Publishing, 1989.

Lasky, Jesse, Jr., *Whatever Happened to Hollywood?*, Funk & Wagnalls, 1975.

LeRoy, Mervyn and Kelmer, Dick, *Mervyn LeRoy: Take One*, Hawthorn Books, 1974.

Levy, Emanuel, *George Cukor: Master of Elegance*, William Morris, 1994.

Linson, Art, *A Pound of Flesh: Perilous Tales of How to Produce Movies in Hollywood*, Grove Press, 1993.

Litwak, Mark, *Dealmaking in the Film & Television Industry: From Negotiations to Final Contracts*, Silman-James Press, 1994.

Litwak, Mark, *Reel Power: The Struggle for Influence and Success in the New Hollywood*, William Morrow and Company, Inc., 1986.

Lucaire, Ed, *The Celebrity Almanac*, Prentice Hall, 1991.

Lyman, Darryl, *Great Jews on Stage and Screen*, Jonathan David Publishers, 1987.

Maltin, Leonard, *Leonard Maltin's Movie Encyclopedia*, Penguin Group, 1994.

Martin, Mick and Porter, Marsha, *Video Movie Guide: 1989*, First Ballantine Books, 1988.

McClintick, David, *Indecent Exposure*, Dell Publishing, Company, 1983.

Medved, Michael, *Hollywood vs. America: Popular Culture and the War on Traditional Values*, Harper Collins, 1992.

Medved, Harry & Medved, Michael, *The Hollywood Hall of Shame: The Most Expensive Flops in Movie History*, Angus & Robertson Publishers, 1984.

Moldea, Dan E., *Dark Victory (Ronald Reagan, MCA, and the Mob)*, Penguin Books, 1987.

Monder, Eric, *George Sidney: A Bio-Bibliography*, Greenwood Press, 1994.

Murphy, Art, *Art Murphy's Box Office Register*, 1990.

National Association of Securities Dealers, *NASD Manuel*, September 1990.

National Association of Theatre Owners, *Encyclopedia of Exhibition*, 1990.

Navasky, Victor S., *Naming Names*, Penguin Books, 1980.

O'Donnell, Pierce and McDougal, Dennis, *Fatal Subtraction: How Hollywood Really Does Business*, Doubleday, 1992.

Palmer, James & Riley, Michael, *The Films of Joseph Losey*, Cambridge University Press, 1993.

Parrish, James Robert, *The Hollywood Celebrity Death Book*, Pioneer Books, 1993.

Penney, Edmund, *Dictionary of Media Terms*, G.P. Putnam's Sons, 1984.

Phillips, Julia, *You'll Never Eat Lunch in this Town Again*, Julia Phillips, Penguin Books, 1991.

Powdermaker, Hortense., *Hollywood: the Dream Factory; an Anthropologist Looks at the Movie-Makers*, Reprint of 1950 ed. New York: Ayer, 1979.

Prifti, William M., *Securities: Public and Private Offerings.* (Rev Ed), Callaghan & Company, 1980.

Prindle, David F., *Risky Business: The Political Economy of Hollywood*, Westview Press, 1993.

Rappleye, Charles and Becker, Ed, *All American Mafioso: The Johnny Rosselli Story*, Doubleday, 1991.

Ratner, David L., *Securities Regulation*, 3rd Ed, West Publishing Company, 1989.

Rawlence, Christopher, *The Missing Reel*, Atheneum, 1990.

Research Institute of America, Inc., *Federal Tax Coordinator 2d*, 1990.

Reynolds, Christopher, *Hollywood Power Stats: 1994*, Cineview Publishing, November, 1993.

Rollyson, Carl, *Lillian Hellman: Her Legend and Her Legacy*, St. Martin's Press, 1988.

Rosen, David and Hamilton, Peter, *Off-Hollywood: The Making & Marketing of American Specialty Films*, The Sundance Institute and the Independent Feature Project, 1986.

Rosenberg, David, *The Movie That Changed My Life*, Viking Penguin, 1991.

Rosenfield, Paul, *The Club Rules: Power, Money, Sex, and Fear: How It Works in Hollywood*, Warner Books, 1992.

Russo, Vito, *The Celluloid Closet: Homosexuality in the Movies*, rev. ed., Harper & Row, 1987.

Sachar, Howard M., *A History of the Jews in America*, Vintage Books, 1993.

Scheuer, Steven H., *Movies on TV and Videocassette*, Bantam, 1987.

Schwartz, Nancy Lynn, *The Hollywood Writers' Wars*, McGraw-Hill, 1982.

Shapiro, Michael, *The Jewish 100: A Ranking of the Most Influential Jews of All Time*, Citadel Press, 1994.

Siegel, Eric S., Schultz, Loren A., Ford, Brian R. and Carney, David C., *Ernst & Young Business Plan Guide*, John Wiley & Sons, 1987.

Silfen, Martin E. (chairman), Counseling Clients in the Entertainment Industry (seminar book), Practicing Law Institute, 1989.

Simensky, Melvin and Selz, Thomas, *Entertainment Law*, 1984.

Sinclair, Andrew, *Spiegel: The Man Behind the Pictures*, Little, Brown & Co., 1987.

Sinetar, Marsha, *Reel Power: Spiritual Growth Though Film*, Triumph Books, 1993

Singleton, Ralph S., *Filmmaker's Dictionary*, Lone Eagle Publishing Co., 1990.

Sklar, Robert. *Movie-Made America: A Cultural History of American Movies*, Random House, 1975.

Sperling, Cass Warner and Millner, Cork, *Hollywood Be Thy Name: The Warner Brothers Story*, Prima Publishing, 1994.

Squire, Jason E., *The Movie Business Book*, (2nd edition), Simon & Schuster, 1992.

Stanger, Robert A., *Tax Shelters: The Bottom Line*, Robert A. Stanger & Company, Publisher, 1982.

Steel, Dawn, *They Can Kill You...But They Can't Eat You: Lessons From the Front*, Pocket Books, 1993.

Tartikoff, Brandon and Leerhsen, Charles, *The Last Great Ride*, Random House, 1992.

Trager, James, *The People's Chronology*, Henry Holt & Co., 1992.

Van Doren, Charles, *Webster's American Biographies*, Merriam-Webster, 1984.

Vidal, Gore, *Who Makes the Movies?*, (a collection of essays), "Pink Triangle and Yellow Star," published by William Heinemann, Ltd., London, 1982.

Vogel, Harold L., *Entertainment Industry Economics: A Guide for Financial Analysis*, Cambridge University Press, 1986 & 1990.

Von Sternberg, Josef, *Fun in a Chinese Laundry*, Mercury House, 1965.

Wakeman, John, *World Film Directors* (Volumes One & Two, 1890-1985), 1987.

Walker, John, *Halliwell's Film Guide*, Harper Collins, 1991 & 1994.

Wallis, Hal and Higham, Charles, *Starmaker, The Autobiography of Hal Wallis*, MacMillan, 1980.

Warshawski, Morrie, *Distributing Independent Films & Video*, The Media Project (Portland) & Foundation for Independent Video and Filmmakers (New York), 1989.

Waxman, Virginia Wright & Bisplinghoff, Gunther, *Robert Altman: A Guide to Reference & Reason*, G.K. Hall & Co., 1984.

Wigoder, Dr. Geoffrey, *The New Standard Jewish Encyclopedia*, 7th Edition, Facts on File, 1992.

Writers Guild of America Theatrical and Television Basic Agreement, 1995.

Yule, Andrew, Picture Shows: *The Life and Films of Peter Bogdanovich*, Limelight Editions, 1992.

ARTICLES, FILMS, MEDIA REPORTS AND PAPERS

Abode, P.J., "Pick-Ups, Pre-Sales and Co-Ventures," *Montage* (IFP/West publication), Winter 1991/1992.

Achbar, Mark and Wintonick, Peter, *Manufacturing Consent: Noam Chomsky and the Media*, (a documentary film), 1992.

Auf der Maur, Rolf, *Enforcement of Antitrust Law and the Motion Picture Industry,* student paper presented to UCLA Extension class "The Feature Film Distribution Deal" (instructor: John W. Cones), 1991.

Barsky, Hertz, Ros, and Vinnick, *Legal Aspects of Film Financing,* April, 1990.

Berry, Jennifer, *Female Studio Executives,* (a research paper for "Film Finance and Distribution," UCLA Producer's Program, Fall, 1994.]

Bertz, Michael A., "Pattern of Racketeering Activity-A Jury Issue," *Beverly Hills Bar Journal,* Vo. 26, No. 1, Winter, 1992.

Bertz, Michael A., "Pursuing a Business Fraud RICO Claim," *California Western Law Review,* Vol. 21, No. 2, 1985.

Bibicoff, Hillary, "Net Profit Participations in the Motion Picture Industry," *Loyola Entertainment Law Journal,* Vol. 11, 1991.

Bowser, Kathryn, "Opportunities Knock (Co-Production Possibilities with Japan and Britain)," *The Independent,* November, 1991.

Brett, Barry J., and Friedman, Michael D., "A Fresh Look At The Paramount Decrees," *The Entertainment and Sports Lawyer,* Volume 9, Number 3, Fall 1991.

Brooks, David, "A Fantasy at the Speed of Sound," *Insight,* May 26, 1986.

Cash William, "Too Many Hoorays for Hollywood," *The Spectator,* October, 1992.

Chrystie, Stephen, Gould, David and Spoto, Lou, "Insolvency and the Production and Distribution of Entertainment Products," *The Entertainment and Sports Lawyer,* Vol. 6, No. 4, Spring 1988.

Cohen, Roger, "Steve Ross Defends His Paychecks," *The New York Times Magazine,* March 22, 1992.

Cohodas, Nadine, "Reagan Seeks Relaxation of Antitrust Laws," *Congressional Quarterly,* February 1, 1986, 190.

Colton, Edward E., "How to Negotiate Contracts, Deals in the Movie Industry," Edward E. Colton, *New York Law Journal,* September 23, 1988.

Colton, Edward E., "What to Include in Pacts Between Author & Film Co.," *New York Law Journal,* October 7, 1988.

Colton, Edward E., "Defining Net Profits, Shares for a Motion Picture Deal," *New York Law Journal,* September 30, 1988.

Cones, John W., "Feature Film Limited Partnerships: A Practical Guide Focusing on Securities and Marketing for Independent Producers and Their Attorneys," *Loyola of Los Angeles Entertainment Law Journal,* 1992.

Cones, John W., "Three Hundred Thirty-Seven Reported Business Practices of the Major Studio/Distributors," (self-published compilation, 1991).

Cones, John W., "Maximizing Producers' Negative Pick-Up Profits," *Entertainment Law & Finance,* Vol. VIII, No. 3, June, 1992.

Continuing Education of the Bar, California, *Tax Literacy for the Business Lawyer,* (seminar handout, September 1991).

Corliss, Richard, "The Magistrate of Morals," Richard Corliss, *Time,* October 12, 1992.

Fleming, Karl, "Who Is Ted Ashley?" *New York,* June 24, 1974.

The Hollywood Reporter, "Antitrust Suit By Theater to Proceed," January 14, 1992, 6.

"JFK and Costello," *New York Times,* July 27, 1973.

Custolito, Karen and Parisi, Paula, "Power Surge: Women in Entertainment," *The Hollywood Reporter,* December 6, 1994.

Dekom, Peter J., "The Net Effect: Making Net Profit Mean Something," *American Premiere,* May-June, 1992.

Dellaverson, John J., "The Director's Right of Final Cut: How Final Is Final?," *The Entertainment and Sports Lawyer,* Vol. 7, No. 1, Summer/Fall 1988.

Denby, David, "Can the Movies be Saved?," *New York,* July 21, 1986.

Disner, Eliot G., "Is There Antitrust After 'Syufy'?: Recent Ninth Court Cases Create Barriers to Enforcement," *California Lawyer,* March 1991, 63.

Eshman, Jill Mazirow, "Bank Financing of a Motion Picture Production," *Loyola of Los Angeles Entertainment Law Journal,* 1992.

Farrell, L.M., "Financial Guidelines for Investing in Motion Picture Limited Partnerships," *Loyola of Los Angeles Entertainment Law Journal,* 1992.

Faulkner, Robert R. and Anderson, Andy B., "Short-Term Projects and Emergent Careers: Evidence from Hollywood," *American Journal of Sociology*, Volume 92, Number 4, January 1987.

Feller, Richard L., "Unreported Decisions and Other Developments (RICO and Entertainment Litigation)," *The Entertainment and Sports Lawyer*, Vol. 3, No. 2, Fall 1984.

Freshman, Elena R., "Commissions to Non-Broker/Dealers Under California Law," *Beverly Hills Bar Journal*, Volume 22, Number 2.

Gaydos, Steven, "Piercing Indictment, Steven Gaydos," *Los Angeles Reader*, December, 1992.

Glasser, Theodore L., "Competition and Diversity Among Radio Formats: Legal and Structural Issues," *Journal of Broadcasting*, Vol. 28:2, Spring 1984.

Goldman Sachs, "Movie Industry Update: 1991," *(Investment Research Report)*, 1991.

Gomery, Douglas, Failed Opportunities: "The Integration of the U.S. Motion Picture and Television Industries," *Quarterly Review of Film Studies*, Volume 9, Number 3, Summer 1984.

Goodell, Jeffrey, "Hollywood's Hard Times," *Premiere*, January, 1992.

Granger, Rod and Toumarkine, Doris, "The Un-Stoppables," *Spy*, November, 1988.

Greenspan, David, "Miramax Films Corp. V. Motion Picture Ass'n of Amer., Inc. The Ratings Systems Survives, for Now," *The Entertainment and Sports Lawyer*, Vol. 9, No. 2, Summer 1991.

Greenwald, John, "The Man With the Iron Grasp," *Time*, September 27, 1993.

Gregory, Keith M., "Blind Bidding: A Need For Change," *Beverly Hills Bar Journal*, Winter 1982-1983.

Hammond, Robert A. and Melamed, Douglas A., "Antitrust in the Entertainment Industry: Reviewing the Classic Texts in The Image Factory," *Gannet Center Journal*, Summer 1989.

Hanson, Wes, "Restraint, Responsibility & the Entertainment Media," Wes Hanson, *Ethics Magazine,* Josephson Institute, 1993.

Harris, Kathryn, "Movie Companies, TV Networks and Publishers Have Been Forced to Audition the Same Act: Cost Cutting," *Forbes*, January 6, 1992.

Honeycutt, Kirk, "Film Producer Mark Rosenberg Dies at Age 44," *The Hollywood Reporter*, November 9, 1992.

Independent Feature Project/West, "Feature Development: From Concept to Production," (seminar), November, 1991.

Jacobson, Marc, "Film Directors Agreements," *The Entertainment & Sports Lawyer*, Vol. 8, No. 1, Spring 1990.

Jacobson, Marc, "Structuring Film Development Deals," *Entertainment Law & Finance*, September, 1990.

Kagan, Paul, and Associates, *Motion Picture Investor* (newsletter), June and December issues, 1990.

Kagan, Paul, and Associates, *Motion Picture Finance*, (seminar), November, 1991.

Kasindorf, Martin, "Cant' Pay? Won't Pay!," *Empire*, June 1990.

Kopelson, Arnold, "One Producer's Inside View of Foreign and Domestic Pre-Sales in the Independent Financing of Motion Pictures," *Loyola of Los Angeles Entertainment Law Journal*, 1992.

Kulik, Glen L., "The Idea Submission Case: When Is An Idea Protected Under California Law?," *Beverly Hills Bar Association Journal*, Winter/Spring, 1998.

Layne, Barry and Tourmarkine, Doris, "Court Vacates Consent Decree Against Loews," *The Hollywood Reporter*, February 20, 1992, 3.

Lazarus, Paul N, III, "Ensuring a Fair Cut of a Hit Film's Profits," *Entertainment Law & Finance*, Leader Publications, November, 1989.

Leedy, David J., "Projecting Profits from a Motion Picture" (excerpts from an unpublished work), presented Fall 1991, for UCLA Extension class: "Contractual Aspects of Producing, Financing and Distributing Film."

Levine, Michael and Zitzerman, David B., "Foreign Productions and Foreign Financing: The Canadian Perspective," *The Entertainment and Sports Lawyer*, Vol. 5, No. 4, Spring 1987.

Litwak, Mark, "Lessons In Self Defense: Distribution Contracts and Arbitration Clauses," Mark Litwak, *The Independent*, 1993.

Logan, Michael, "He'll Never Eat Lunch In This Town Again!," *Los Angeles Magazine*, September 1992.

Los Angeles Times, "Film Studios Threaten Retaliation Against States Banning Blind Bids," June 1, 1981.

Marcus, Adam J., "Buchwald v. Paramount Pictures Corp. and the Future of Net Profit," *Cardoza Arts & Entertainment Law Journal*, Vol. 9, 1991.

Mathews, Jack, "Rules of the Game," *American Film*, March, 1990.

McCoy, Charles W. "Tim," Jr., "The Paramount Cases: Golden Anniversary in a Rapidly Changing Marketplace," *Antitrust*, Summer 1988, 32.

McDougal, Dennis, "A Blockbuster Deficit," Dennis McDougal, *Los Angeles Times*, March 21, 1991.

Medved, Michael, "Researching the Truth About Hollywood's Impact: Consensus and Denial," *Ethics Magazine*, Josephson Institute, 1993.

Moore, Schuyler M., "Entertainment Financing for the '90s: Super Pre-Sales," *Stroock & Stroock & Lavan Corporate Entertainment Newsletter*, Vol. 1, Q1 1992.

Morris, Chris, "Roger Corman: The Schlemiel as Outlaw," in Todd McCarthy and Charles Flynn, eds., *King of the Bs*, New York: Dutton, 1975.

Nochimson, David and Brachman, Leon, "Contingent Compensation for Theatrical Motion Pictures," *The Entertainment and Sports Lawyer*, Vol. 5, No. 1, Summer 1986.

O'Donnell, Pierce, "Killing the Golden Goose: Hollywood's Death Wish," *Beverly Hills Bar Journal*, Summer, 1992.

Olswang, Simon M., "The Last Emperor and Co-Producing in China: The Impossible Made Easy, and the Easy Made Impossible," *The Entertainment and Sports Lawyer*, Vol. 6, No. 2, Fall 1987.

Phillips, Mark, C., "Role of Completion Bonding Companies in Independent Productions," *Loyola of Los Angeles Entertainment Law Journal*, 1992.

Phillips, Gerald F., "Block Booking: Perhaps Forgotten, Perhaps Misunderstood, But Still Illegal," *The Entertainment and Sports Lawyer*, Vol. 6, No. 1, Summer 1987.

Phillips, Gerald F., "The Recent Acquisition of Theater Circuits by Major Distributors," *The Entertainment and Sports Lawyer*, Vol. 5, No. 3, Winter 1987, 1.

Powers, Stephen P., Rothman, David J., and Rothman, Stanley, "Hollywood Movies, Society, and Political Criticism," *The World & I,* April 1991.

Pristin, Terry, "Hollywood's Family Ways," *Los Angeles Times* Calendar Section, January 31, 1993.

Richardson, John H., "Hollywood's Actress-Hookers: When Glamour Turns Grim," John H. Richardson, *Premiere*, 1992.

Robb, David, "Police Net is Arrested by Boxoffice Drop," *The Hollywood Reporter*, September 8, 1992.

Robb, David, "Net Profits: One Man's View from Both Sides," *The Hollywood Reporter*, August, 31, 1992.

Robb, David, "Net Profits, No Myth, But Hard to Get Hands On," *The Hollywood Reporter*, August 17, 1992.

Robb, David, "Net Profits: Breaking Even is Hard to Do," *The Hollywood Reporter*, September, 14, 1992.

Robb, David, "Net Profits, 'Endangered' by Big Budgets," *The Hollywood Reporter*, August 24, 1992.

Rodman, Howard, "Unequal Access, Unequal Pay: Hollywood's Gentleman's Agreement," *Montage*, October 1989.

Royal, David, "Making Millions and Going Broke, How Production Companies Make Fortunes and Bankrupt Themselves," *American Premiere*, November/December 1991.

Sarna, Jonathan, D., "The Jewish Way of Crime," *Commentary*, August, 1984.

Schiff, Gunther, H., "The Profit Participation Conundrum: A Glossary of Common Terms and Suggestions for Negotiation," Gunther H. Schiff, *Beverly Hills Bar Journal*, Summer, 1992.

Screen, "Vertical Integration, Horizontal Regulation: The Growth of Rupert Murdoch's Media Empire," Volume 28, Number 4 (May-August, 1986).

Sills, Steven D., and Axelrod, Ivan L., "Profit Participation In The Motion Picture Industry," *Los Angeles Lawyer*, April, 1989.

Simensky, Melvin, "Determining Damages for Breach of Entertainment Agreements," *The Entertainment and Sports Lawyer*, Vol. 8, No. 1, Spring 1990.

Simon, John, "Film: Charlatans Rampant," *National Review*, February 1, 1993.

Sinclair, Nigel, "U.S./Foreign Film Funding (Co-Production Tips)," *Entertainment Law & Finance*, March, 1991.

Sinclair, Nigel, "Long-Term Contracts for Independent Producers," *Entertainment Law & Finance*, November, 1986.

Sinclair, Nigel, "How to Draft Multi-Picture Deals," *Entertainment Law & Finance*, January, 1987.

Sinclair and Gerse, "Representing Independent Motion Picture Producers," *Los Angeles Lawyer*, May, 1988.

Sobel, Lionel, S., "Protecting Your Ideas in Hollywood," *Writer's Friendly Legal Guide*, Writer's Digest Books, 1989.

Sobel, Lionel S., "Financing the Production of Theatrical Motion Pictures," *Entertainment Law Reporter*, May, 1984.

Sperry, Paul, "Do Politics Drive Hollywood? Or do Markets Determine What Studios Make?," Paul Sperry, *Investor's Business Daily*, March 19, 1993

Stauth, Cameron, "Masters of the Deal," *American Film*, May, 1991.

Tagliabue, Paul J., "Antitrust Developments in Sports and Entertainment Law," *Antitrust Law Journal*, 1987.

UCLA Entertainment Law Symposium, Never Enough: The "A" Deal, Business, Legal and Ethical Realities, (Sixteenth Annual), February, 1992.

Weissman, Eric, "Hollywood's Ethical Malaise," *Variety.com*, October 12, 2004.

Whitney, Simon N., "Antitrust Policies and the Motion Picture Industry" (article appearing in Gorham Kindem's book: *The American Movie Industry: The Business of Motion Pictures*, Southern Illinois University Press, 1982.

Wilson, Kurt E., "How Contracts Escalate into Torts," *California Lawyer*, January, 1992.

Wolf, Brian J., "The Prohibitions Against Studio Ownership of Theaters: Are They An Anachronism?," *Loyola of Los Angeles Entertainment Law Journal*, Vol. 13, 413.

Zitzerman, David B. and Levine, Michael A., "Producing a Film in Canada: The Legal and Regulatory Framework," *The Entertainment and Sports Lawyer*, Vol. 8, No. 4, Winter 1991.

About the Author

John W. Cones is a securities/entertainment attorney based in Los Angeles. He is licensed to practice law in California and Texas. He manages a private practice, advising independent feature film, video, television and theatrical producer clients regarding federal and state securities law compliance obligations.

Mr. Cones is author of 10 other books and numerous articles on the legal and political aspects of filmmaking. His journal article "Feature Film Limited Partnerships" appeared in the January 1992 symposium issue on independent productions published by the Loyola of *Los Angeles Entertainment Law Journal*.

He has lectured extensively in Los Angeles, Las Vegas, Dallas, Houston and San Francisco on "Investor Financing of Entertainment Projects" for the American Film Institute, the University of Southern California Cinema-Television Alumni Association, Loyola Marymount Continuing Education Division, Cinetex '90, UCLA Extension and others. He has also lectured for UCLA Extension on "The Film Distribution Deal" and served as a Course Coordinator/ Instructor for the UCLA Extension course "Contractual Aspects of Financing, Producing and Distributing Film."

He is a member of the California and Texas state bar associations.

Mr. Cones is a 1967 graduate of the University of Texas at Austin with a Bachelor of Science degree in Communications and a 1974 graduate of the UT Austin School of Law with a Doctor of Jurisprudence degree.

Prior to 1975, Mr. Cones was a radio-television news reporter at KTBC (Channel 7) television in Austin, where he also worked occasionally as a television news anchor and as a sports or weather anchor. Mr. Cones worked at KTBC full-time while attending law school at UT Austin. He had also performed on-the-air news reporting duties previously at KRIS-TV Corpus Christi and KITE radio in San Antonio.

In 1975, and immediately following graduation from law school, he served as legislative counsel to the Texas House of Representatives. In that position he drafted, edited and reviewed state legislation and counseled legislator-sponsors with respect to state constitutional requirements..

From 1976 through 1981, Mr. Cones worked as a lobbyist/association executive and in-house counsel for professional associations headquartered in Austin and Chicago. In those positions, along with his more general association management responsibilities, he prepared and delivered congressional testimony, drafted legislation and wrote and edited books, magazines, magazine articles, newsletters, speeches and press releases.

His article "What Lobbyists Really Do" has been reprinted in four state association publications in three states. As an association executive he was also involved in long term planning, board meetings, conventions, seminars, staff supervision and association membership activities.

Mr. Cones practiced law in Houston from 1981 through 1986. During that time, he supervised state securities compliance aspects of Regulation D (private placement) limited partnership and corporate offerings (including movie production/distribution, oil and gas, real estate, equipment leasing, night clubs, restaurants, cattle breeding/feeding, thorough-bred breeding and medical technology). In 1987, Mr. Cones moved his law practice to California in 1987 specifically to work with independent producers. He has helped more than 150 clients prepare disclosure documents and comply with federal/state laws.

Other Books by the Same Author

Film Industry Contracts — A collection of 100 sample film industry agreements relating to acquisition, development, packaging, employment, lender financing, investor financing, production, distribution, exhibition, merchandising and licensing.

43 Ways to Finance Your Feature Film — A comprehensive overview of film finance with a discussion of advantages and disadvantages of forty-three different ways to finance feature films and other entertainment projects.

The Feature Film Distribution Deal — A provision by provision critical analysis of the single most important film industry agreement. The book also provides samples of five different film distribution agreements in its appendix.

Hollywood Wars: How Insiders Gained and Maintain Illegitimate Control Over the Film Industry — A comprehensive analysis and discussion of hundreds of the specific business practices used during the nearly 100-year span of control of the Hollywood-based U.S. film industry by the so-called Hollywoodcontrol group (or traditional Hollywood management).

Motion Pictures — *A Complete Guide to the Industry* — A comprehensive overview of the core of the film industry along with the affiliated cottage industries. The book also explores the economics of the industry, film industry jobs and organizations and provides a candid assessment of the industry's problems and issues.

Patterns of Bias in Motion Picture Content — An analysis of the various populations in the diverse U.S. society that have been consistently portrayed in Hollywood films in a negative or stereotypical manner.

Who Really Controls Hollywood — A more thorough re-examination of the question raised earlier by Neal Gabler, Michael Medved, Joel Kotkin and others about who really controls the Hollywood-based film industry and is therefore primarily responsible for the decisions made with respect to which movies are produced and released, who gets to work on those movies and the actual content of such films.

Motion Picture Biographies: Hollywood's Spin on Historical Figures — A study of the specific genre of biopics, designed to determine what patterns of bias exist in such films.

Motion Picture Industry Reform — A discussion of various techniques, strategies and methods that may be useful in bringing about the long-term reform of the U.S. motion picture industry, which is considered by the author to be one of the most significant media for the communication of ideas yet devised by human beings.

Inquiries should be addressed to:

John W. Cones, Attorney
794 Via Colinas
Westlake Village, California 91362
jwc6774@roadrunner.com